IN CELEBRATION OF
TEXAS

Picture Research by
Robert F. O'Connor and Laura K. Reneau

Partners in Progress by
Richard Dillard, Darlene Garrett, Anne Morris,
Mark Seal, Bill Sloan, Donald Walker, Ann Quin Wilson, and
George Wood

Produced in cooperation with
the East Texas Historical Association and
the Harris County Heritage Society

Windsor Publications, Inc.
Northridge, California

IN CELEBRATION OF
TEXAS

An Illustrated History by Archie P. McDonald

Windsor Publications, Inc.—History Book Division

Publisher: John M. Phillips
Editorial Director: Teri Davis Greenberg
Design Director: Alexander E. D'Anca

Staff for *In Celebration of Texas*

Senior Editor: Susan L. Wells
Editors: Marilyn Horn, Lissa Sanders
Director, Corporate Biographies: Karen Story
Assistant Director, Corporate Biographies: Phyllis Gray
Editor, Corporate Biographies: Judith Hunter
Sales Representatives, Corporate Biographies: Walter Black, Angie Carder, Mary
    Carter, Curtis Courtney, Nita Hawley, Jo Mohr, Barbara Whitaker
Editorial Assistants: Kathy M. Brown, Laura Cordova, Marcie Goldstein,
    Pat Pittman, Sharon Volz
Layout Artist: S.L. Wells
Corporate Biography Layout: Mari Catherine Preimesberger

Library of Congress Cataloging-in-Publication Data

McDonald, Archie P.
    In celebration of Texas.

    Bibliography: p. 478
    Includes index.
    1. Texas—History. 2. Texas—History—Pictorial
works. 3. Texas—Description and travel—Views.
I. Title.
F386.M34   1986   976.4   86-5651
ISBN 0-89781-165-8

Page Six: *Blue Bonnets, the state
flower, carpet the fields along
Texas highways every spring.
Courtesy, Texas Highway Department*

CONTENTS

To all Texans,
Past, Present, and Future
—and Especially to Judy

INTRODUCTION

Texas is land. Before any humans came to draw their needs from the land, before they installed their political, economic, and cultural institutions, before they agreed among themselves on laws and boundaries and ownership, the land survived geological and environmental changes of sweeping proportions. Some came quickly, some were, literally, glacial in pace. The signs of all ages are yet to be found—some in pools of energy thousands of feet below the surface of the earth, some rising above the plains where wind and water have worn away softer layers. All the elements, fire, water, and wind, have left their mark.

Then, Texas became people. First came the Paleo-Americans. Mysterious in their coming and going, these early folk hunted much and bothered the land little. Afterwards the American Indians, a Mongolian group, came. They also hunted, but a few farmed and some remained in one place longer than the hunters. Still, their mark upon the land remained slight. The Spanish, and even less so the French, left only the remnants of forts and missions to mark their passage. Early Mexican immigrants were few and disturbed the land little. But the Anglo-Celts, and those who came with them and after them—the Germans, Poles, Czechs, Italians, and scores of others—disturbed it much. They claimed it and thought they had tamed it. Some farmed, some ranched, some cut trees for sale to others, some punched holes in the land in search of mineral wealth. After they arrived in Texas in the nineteenth century their kind multiplied many times over during the following 150 years, and the volume of their numbers changed and altered the land immensely. Great cities developed and industry was born and grew to great size.

In time these people looked at their past, at what they had done to and with the land, and most called their story a success. So they decided to celebrate their achievement. They chose the 150th anniversary of their founding as an independent people as a fitting occasion. The Texas Sesquicentennial in 1986 covers a wide range of activities, some gaudy, some fleeting, and, perhaps, some of lasting quality. All characterize the ways Texans celebrate their state and themselves. This book may help them to remember although Texas has become people, it always will remain what it was in the beginning—land.

The author is grateful to the East Texas Historical Association and the Harris County Heritage Society for their joint sponsorship of this book. Specifically I wish to acknowledge HCHS director Bill Griggs, and Bob Bowman, president of the East Texas Historical Association at the time that organization agreed to support the writer in this endeavor. Both are fine gentlemen. Bob Bowman, a believer in things good for Texas and a writer of Texas himself, is recognized for his support and gratefully thanked for his friendship.

President William R. Johnson of Stephen F. Austin State University, and Edwin W. Gaston, James V. Reese, and William J. Brophy, all of the same institution, are generous administrators and friends who permitted me time and support, and are tolerant of a historian who wants to write as well as teach.

Karen Gehring deserves a halo for turning rambling words in an illegible scrawl into a typed manuscript. And Texas deserves the most thanks of all for just being itself, something to think about, and marvel at, and finally, something of wonder to write about.

As Texas moved further away from its frontier beginnings, parades and community celebrations became more important as ways of maintaining ties to the past. Here, townspeople enjoy the Merchants Centennial Parade in Nacogdoches, Texas, in 1936. Courtesy, Barker Texas History Center

The Land and the People

Land comes before anything else in Texas. Long before the first humans arrived, in a time when rivers only flowed toward the Gulf of Mexico without serving as political boundaries or arteries of commerce, before the heavens thundered with the sonic sounds of aluminum birds, before teeming cities sprang from the soil, growing from their own regeneration, before people converted the open spaces to enclosures and claimed exclusive ownership and use of certain parts of the earth, before attitudes and morals and ethics and prejudice, Texas was just land.

And this Texan land changes every day. Wind and water daily alter its face. Tides rearrange its 370-mile coastline, and sometimes, during hurricane season, dramatically. To the west the wind is seemingly constant, and the lighter soils rise to the sky in sunsets of splendor; in winter the winds

The Rio Grande, the fifth longest river in North America, flows 1,800 miles before reaching the Gulf of Mexico. From the Colorado Rockies, it travels through New Mexico, Journada del Muerto, and then through Big Bend National Park, as seen here. Photo by George O. Miller, courtesy, TexaStock

turn to chill, and freezing water seeps into the cracks of stones and breaks them into smaller pieces, time and again, until giant rocks crumble into soil. Nature builds, rearranges, destroys, and builds again. Now the earth's forces raise the land, pushing the sea back; erosion carves down the land and the sea returns, adding a new layer of animal and vegetable deposits to fossilize and sometimes to transform itself into a black liquid called oil, much valued by contemporary Texans.

Two hundred fifty million years ago, in a time of the earth's life known as the Pennsylvania Age, there was no Texas and no Texans. Mountains stretched northeasterly from the area later known as the Big Bend on the Rio Grande toward the Red River country and beyond. A shallow but active sea covered the earth to the north, while to the south, in the area later known as the Gulf of Mexico, a dry plain dominated. Animals strange to modern peoples, reptiles, amphibians, and vegetation unseen by any human, abounded. The earth heaved, uplifting the land to the north and draining the Permian Sea onto the now lower dry land, and it became an ocean. The wind wore away the mountains and sediment settled over the plant and animal life, sealing it forever. Fresh soils washed down to cover the sediments, and new life emerged. Nearly 100 million years ago, in a Cretaceous Age, waters covered the land to the east and west of the dry land middle ground. Dinosaurs and other creatures, vegetarian and carnivorous, appeared, and swamps teemed with animal and plant life. And then again the earth heaved, capturing the residue of this life in pockets where pressure and time formed it into fuel for the future.

Once more mountains were lifted up. Texas assumed its present form, with a southeasterly slope and a drainage that carries the rains and snows of the more northerly sections down creeks and rivers to the Gulf of Mexico. The basic features of Texas, Southern Forest land, Central Prairies, and mountains (also the basic features of North America) at last were formed.

The earth cooled, warmed, cooled again, and

This 1707 engraving portrays animals of the New World, including birds, deer, and various members of the cat family. Courtesy, University of Texas

the western area dried until some of it became a desert, still fertile but without life-giving water. The eastern portions retained moisture and thus could support human life in greater numbers. Within this framework regions developed. A Coastal Plain extends along the rim of the Gulf, moving inland for various distances sometimes as much as 200 miles. Its sandy soils change from marshes to savannahs to timberland within a few miles, and its salt grasses fed cattle when the Europeans brought them there. Salt domes captured pools of oil for later exploitation, and some of it can even support row-crop agriculture.

In East Texas, generally the area between the Sabine and Trinity rivers, the soils are sandy or

red until they become black in the northwestern section. Pine forests flourish, with hardwood growing along the streams, and thickets dominate in the lower regions. This section receives Texas' major rainfall, up to fifty-five inches annually, and it supports abundant plant and animal life. Parts of East Texas produce orchids, bays, chiquapin, and such fauna exotics as armadillos, reptiles, and countless ticks. Dense pine, and, farther west, oak, in this section gave rise to Texas' first major industry, lumbering. It supplied timber for every phase of the state's industrial development from railroads to modern skyscrapers. Cotton ruled in the central portions of East Texas until the middle of this century, but now wood processing—plywood and paper—has replaced cotton as the region's main product, with cattle, chickens, peas, watermelons, and other crops sharing in the economy.

North and west of the Coastal Plain and East Texas lies the Central Prairies. The Colorado River forms its western boundary and this region extends to the Red River in the north. The Central Prairies are interrupted by the Eastern Cross Timbers, near Dallas, and by the Cross Timbers west of Fort Worth. These outcroppings have some trees—oak and mesquite—but mostly the rolling, open country supports grain, cotton, livestock farming, and oil wells in the area around Wichita Falls.

The celebrated Hill Country claims Austin as its external extremity and features young mountains as its terrain, or at least one might think so, until viewing the real thing in the Basin and Mountain Country to the west. Mountain cedar and juniper grow easily there and short grasses support sheep, goats, and some cattle.

The semitropical Rio Grande Plain to the south is Texas' food market. It rivals California's Imperial Valley and the central plains of Florida in citrus and vegetable production, and is a haven for "snowbirds," or Northerners who come south to escape severe winters. Its heavy Latin influence is strong in the Rio Grande Valley's towns and farms. The King Ranch, just to the north, is the state's largest.

Just north of the Valley, the Edwards Plateau spans the lower central area of Texas. San Antonio and San Angelo are its principal service cities, although neither is actually on the Plateau. This section leads the state and the nation in the production of wool and mohair, despite the fact that much of its productivity has been lost to dryness and erosion.

The Basin and Mountain Country, or Trans-Pecos, resembles New Mexico and Mexico, its neighbors to the west and south. This is true mountain and desert country, fit only for livestock and people who can stand the dryness and the sun. El Paso, and its border twin, Ciudad Juárez, wrap around the Franklin Mountains and share the Rio Grande in international tranquility. Here Texas' highest mountain, Guadalupe Peak, rises to 8,749 feet. The Cap Rock Escarpment separates the semiarid High Plains from its lower portions. The true High Plains, high near Amarillo and south near Lubbock, were named *Llano Estacado* (Staked Plain) by the Spanish; now it is the row-

Facing Page: The First Furrow, *a Charles M. Russell painting, depicts a pioneer farmer making the first furrow while an Indian approaches. Courtesy, Snook Trading Post, Billings, Montana*

Above: *Between 1540 and 1542, Francisco Vásquez de Coronado searched the Southwest for the rumored golden cities of El Dorado. Coronado and his party are depicted in this Frederick Remington painting. Courtesy, Institute of Texan Cultures*

Right: *This watercolor by M. Emanuel depicts Estéban, Cabeza de Vaca, Dorantes, and Castillo as they enter an Indian village in Texas around 1528. Courtesy, Institute of Texan Cultures*

crop headquarters of the state. It was grazing country until the miracle of the underground rain, sucked to the surface by windmills, quickened the fertility of its volcanic loess soils into high productivity. Now maize, corn, cotton, and other crops grow abundantly. Feedlots abound, each seemingly crammed with thousands of cattle, located there to take advantage of the grain crops.

The diversity of Texas climate is proverbial, which is only fitting for a state constituting one-twelfth of our country's land mass. Extreme cold and snow is plentiful in the Panhandle, and the growing season there is less than 200 days annually. The season increases along horizontal lines, as one views the map of the state, but precipitation grade lines are vertical, and decrease toward the west. The intersections of the lines help determine the kind of lifestyle, economics, and culture that can exist. The environment always dominates. Technology, such as windmills, can alleviate this a bit, but in the end nature cannot be permanently changed.

Texas may have a number of different ecologies, but the sun is a constant factor throughout the state. It bathes the land in its warming rays, giving life to lands with sufficient moisture to take advantage of it. It also gives Texas the nation's summer, and often winter, high temperatures. The sun browns, weathers, gives outdoor Texans reddish-brown skin, and stores its energy for a growing season in citrus and forever in petroleum.

To this land called Texas the people came. The first were the Paleo-Americans, a Caucasoid group who moved southward as far as the Central Plains as early as 15,000 years ago, perhaps earlier. Archaeologists differ on their arrival date because they have so few artifacts with which to work. They generally agree that the Paleo-Americans lived mostly in the plains areas oriented to the Clovis and Folsum cultures, named for discoveries of fluted spear points at sites in New Mexico. These points are often located in conjunction with fossilized vertebrate of large animals that are now extinct. Since many are found at such sites, socializing action on the hunt is fairly certain. Spear

points and human bones have been discovered at sites near Abilene, Plainview, Midland, and Lubbock. In the east, on the Trinity River near Malakoff, three head-shaped sculptures have been attributed to these people. "Midland Minnie," human bones of a female, are the earliest skeletal remains yet discovered.

The Paleo-Americans evidently migrated with some social organization and cultural maturity. They stood erect, and used weapons of stone or bone of their own manufacture with skill sufficient to bring down large prey. They used fire ceremonially and functually, and wore skin garments. And then they vanished. Their departure is as mysteri-

This Indian cord-marked pot is a relic of Native American artistry, preserved for modern Texans as a reminder of the state's history. Courtesy, Panhandle-Plains Historical Museum

War parties grew more common as Europeans encroached heedlessly upon Indian territory. This early twentieth century depiction is sadly ironic—war parties were essentially extinct by then. Courtesy, Texas State Library Archives

ous as their arrival, and centuries later, little evidence of Paleo-American culture remains.

The American Indians are of Mongolian stock, and they also migrated to the Southwest several thousand years ago. Only about a million or so occupied the land north of Mexico, and they had so acclimated to the environment and divided into small bands that by the time of European discovery they hardly recognized other Indians as their own kind.

Regardless of tribe or clan, they usually referred to themselves as "the people" to distinguish themselves from other natural phenomena. Separate groups lost the skill to communicate orally with others when they dropped words, changed meanings, or adopted words to fit new situations and things. They did, however, generally retain the ability to communicate by hand signals. These Indians are divided by lifestyle into three groups. The Forest Dwellers, the most prosperous because they lived on lands that provided the most food,

the Plains Indians, a wandering group that lived on animals and wore their skins, and the Inter-Mountain Seed Gatherers, the poorest of Indians who lived on whatever they could get. These groups reflect their environment more than any previous cultural achievements.

All three groups lived in Texas, but none achieved civilizations as high as that of the Mound Builders to the east and the Aztecs to the south. Some mounds have been discovered in East Texas, especially at Nacogdoches and Alto. Although boundaries were vague, territories were staked out by the various tribes in Texas.

In the east, the Caddo, who belonged to a larger confederacy, dominated. The wing that occupied Louisiana and Arkansas was known as the Caddo, and the Hasinai Caddo occupied the Angelina and Neches River areas in Texas. Tribal or clan names are similar. Nacogdoche, Naconiche, and Natchtoche peoples lived in villages that stretched along creeks and rivers. They lived in structures made of stakes, twigs, mud, and plant life. These ingredients were layered to a pointed dome at the top. The Caddoes were weavers of reeds, which they used as baskets, rugs, and bedding, among other things, and they gathered the plentiful produce of the forests and streams, including animals, fish, and plants. By the time of the arrival of the Europeans they had also come to harvest their own crops, an important step in civilization. And

they were traders. They provided the Comanches
with forest foods and wood products, especially
bois d'arc wood for bows, in return for flint. And
they were emotional, by some accounts. Unlike
the stoic Indians of popular legend who never
show emotion or pain, the Caddoes were said to
weep to show joy or grief.

South of the Caddo country the Attakapa, hunters and fish gatherers, lived. Known by the clan
names of Deadose, Orcoquisac, and Bidais, they
roamed the coastal plain and the lightly timbered
country. Farther south and west of the Attakapa,
and for a great distance down the coast, the Kar-
ankawa lived. They, too, roamed the forest's edge,
the marsh lands, and even the seacoast for what
food they could find. They annointed their bodies
with a foul-smelling concoction of animal grease
to ward off the heavy mosquito population of their
homeland, and they are thought to have practiced
ritualistic cannibalism, as did many Texas Indians,
as late as the arrival of the Europeans in the sixteenth century.

The real Indian farmers lived in South Texas.
Although a fairly bellicose group, the Tonkawa
husbanded crops in addition to hunting. South of
them lived the Coahuiltecans, the diggers and
grubbers and perhaps the poorest of Texas Indians. Their lands yielded little food, and required
great effort to do so. Spiders, ants, and other offenses to the modern Texan's palate were their
fare, when they could find them. When the Spaniards arrived with their missions, the Coahuiltecans proved the most cooperative, largely because
the Spanish promised to feed them physically as
well as spiritually.

The group the whites labeled the "Apache" Indians lived in the far west, mostly in New Mexico
and Arizona, and they arrived there somewhat
later than the others, so they had to fight for territory. To Europeans they seemed always to be
fighting, and they dominated their area until the
Comanches mastered horsemanship, thanks to the
Spanish, and descended from their mountain
homes to become known as the lords of the
plains. Apaches, whether Western Apaches, Chira-

cahuas, Mescaleros, Lipans, or Jicarillas, established their authority as great hunters and fighters, although most of them also engaged in some farming. But they learned to respect the Comanches, who became the fiercest of all Texas Indians in defending their hunting grounds. The Comanches never accommodated to the Spanish, whom they met in Texas in the early 1700s, and they remained a formidable obstacle even to American settlement until the end of the nineteenth century.

Although their environment and the resulting lifestyles differed, Texas Indians shared much in common. They constitute what has been called a "cultural sink" between the richer cultures to the east, south, and west, but it may be unfair to judge cultures so. They reflected the diversity of their kind and of their time and place. Unlike the Paleo-Americans, who retained a cultural unity because of their limited territory and few numbers, the American Indians occupied the entire hemisphere, although often separated from each other by great distances. Most understood effective, if primitive and artful, functional ways to make tools from bone, wood, stone, and reed. They developed skillful use of the spear, the atlatl, and later of the bow and arrow. Many had domesticated dogs they used for hunting and sometimes for carrying objects. Most Texas Indians practiced some form of agriculture by the time of the European arrival. In fact, Indian husbandrymen developed about half of the world's edible crops, including corn, potatoes, beans, squash, pumpkins, and peanuts, and some grew tobacco and cotton as well. They did so without the use of horses as draft animals or for transportation and, when they did obtain horses from the Spanish, they became expert in using them for hunting and fishing.

The beginnings of Indian life in Texas is, to some degree, speculative, but the end of their time of dominance can be more positively known. The Europeans, whether Spanish or Anglo-Celt, did not regard the Indians as owners of the lands they used, so they took what they wanted, when they wanted it, if they were able. The Spanish did at-

tempt to use the Indians as slaves, and some of them cared enough for the Indians' souls to try to Christianize them, and the French tried to trade with them for furs. But the English and their descendants only wanted to remove the Indians. Together, they crushed cultures thousands of years in the making. And the Spanish came first to have their way.

McConico Battise poses contemplatively with symbols from his ethnic heritage. Courtesy, Mrs. E.S. Shill

THE LORDS OF THE PLAINS

Calling themselves *Nermernuh,* or "The True Human Beings," the Comanche were known to the Utes as Koh-mahts, or "Those Against Us." Many others regarded the Comanche in the same way, including early Spanish explorers, missionaries, settlers, and especially Anglo-American frontiersmen. Once the Comanche descended from their mountain homes and obtained the horse culture of the Spanish they became the most powerful and determined of all North American Indians to resist the advance of immigrants into their lands. They became, in fact, the Lords of the Plains.

With the assistance of their Kiowa allies the Comanche became expert cavalrymen who combined their skills as horsemen with an obsession to defend their territory. They were the first Indians in the north to stop the Spanish, and they helped block the French attempt to penetrate the Southwest. The Comanche continued to harass the Mexican border area long after Mexico was independent of Spain and had ceased attempts to convert or control the Indians. The Comanche also delayed and occasionally even pushed back the advance of Anglo-American settlement in Texas for sixty years.

The Lords of the Plains came to their power late. Before the eighteenth century they were hunters and gatherers who lived in the Yellowstone country to the Colorado Rockies, existing but not really prospering in a land not coveted by more powerful tribes. They were transformed by unintended gifts from the European invaders: horses and firearms. The North American Indians who learned to ride and use firearms were better able to resist the Spanish and Americans who wanted their lands. None excelled the Comanche in their proficiency. Where other Indians learned to ride, the Comanche learned to live on his horse. With horses they could

not only escape from attempts made to subdue them, they could also retaliate. Descending from their mountain homes, they moved out onto the plains, pushing the Pawnee, Wichita, Waco, and even the Apache out of their way. Now able to follow the buffalo freely, the Comanche hunting grounds encompassed an area from present central Kansas to South-Central Texas and from Oklahoma to eastern New Mexico.

After destroying the San Saba Mission in 1758 the Comanche held the Spanish army in check and often raided Mexico. At first they left Stephen Austin's Anglo-American colonists alone because being so far south they were not perceived as a threat. But as the Anglos pushed westward into Comanche country, conflict became inevitable.

Although Anglo-Comanche warfare continued until the 1870s, the most remembered Comanche raid on an Anglo settlement occurred at Fort Parker in 1836. Silas and Lucy Parker had migrated to Texas in 1833 from Illinois. They came to the colony begun by Parker's brother James in present Grimes County. The next year the Parker brothers built Fort Parker on the Navasota River. On May 19, 1836, several hundred Comanche warriors approached the fort under a flag of truce to demand a cow. They killed Benjamin Parker when he refused to surrender the cow and stormed into the fort. Silas Parker was killed attempting to rescue his niece and her son. Lucy Parker and her two younger children escaped, but the Indians carried off the two older children, Cynthia Ann and John. In all five men and two women were killed.

Cynthia Ann and John Parker were raised by the Comanche. For three years their uncle, James Parker, tried to rescue them. In 1845 the Texas Legislature appropriated $300 for their ransom but the money was not

used because they could not be located.

John Parker grew to manhood among the Indians. He married a Mexican girl he met on a raiding party in her country. After the Indians abandoned Parker when he developed smallpox, the girl traveled to Texas with him and nursed him back to health. He returned with his wife to Mexico and became a rancher. During the American Civil War Parker served in a Mexican company of the Confederate army in Texas, and afterwards lived with his family in Mexico until 1915.

Five years after Cynthia Ann's capture she was seen by Lem Williams on the Canadian River. Williams tried unsuccessfully to buy her from the family with whom she lived. In 1843 a trading party again found her on the Canadian River. By then she had become the wife of Peta Nacona, a Comanche chief, and had borne two sons, Pecos and Quanah Parker. She told the traders that she was happily married and had no desire to return to her relatives. She was seen again in 1858 at the Battle of Antelope Hills and was captured at a battle on the Peace River in 1860. By then she had a daughter, Prairie Flower. At thirty-four years of age only her blue eyes and fairer skin distinguished her from the Indians. She was taken to Fort Cooper to await the arrival of her uncle, Isaac Parker. She could not reconcile to her new environment. Many Anglos resented her acceptance of the Indian way of life, especially her marriage to Peta Nacona. Cynthia Ann died in 1864 at her brother's home in Anderson County.

During the American Civil War Comanche raids pushed Anglo settlement eastward approximately 100 miles. With so many Texans fighting in the Confederate army, the remaining Texans had a difficult time defending frontier outposts from raids.

Albert Pike negotiated a treaty with the Comanche for peace in return for an agency, but only a brief truce resulted. James Norris' Frontier Regiment of 1,000 men continued to patrol the frontier as best they could, but the Comanche easily evaded the patrols. By the end of the war J.E. McCord had assumed command of the regiment and he developed a somewhat more successful program of irregularly scheduled patrols. In the war's aftermath Comanche raids intensified, and by July 1867 more than 160 whites had been killed by raiders. A more vigorous program by the United States Army, in addition to the elimination of the buffalo, forced them to accept the life of reservation Indians.

The fiercest of the Texas Indians were the Comanche, shown here in this nineteenth century photograph. From Thrall, Pictorial History of Texas, *Thompson & Co., 1879*

The Search for Gold

The Spanish were, in many ways, uniquely qualified to begin European settlement of the Americas. Courageous, audacious, and above all convinced of the righteousness of their religion and culture, they quickly made their mark on the Caribbean and the lands that rimmed the Gulf of Mexico, as well as Central and South America. By 1519 Hernando Cortez had taken the Yucatan and conquered the Aztecs in Central Mexico, and soon Almagro and Pizarro did the same with the Incas in northern South America. Firearms, trained dogs, horses, and an intense rapacity made the Spanish conquistadores—most of whom came from the harsh and poverty-ridden Estremadura region of Spain—more than a match for the Indians, who outnumbered them greatly but lacked leadership and the technological means to resist. Many of the new lands the Spanish explored in those early years contained

This 1707 engraving portrays Indians bringing gold ore to a seated European while soldiers look on. Lured by stories of incredible treasure, Europeans were, for the most part, disappointed in their searches. Courtesy, Institute of Texan Cultures

gold and silver in quantities beyond the dreams of avarice. So for 200 years they sought more. They were willing to go anywhere to find these metals, including Texas.

The first European to see Texas, Alonzo Alvarez de Piñeda, came on just such a mission in 1519. Commissioned by the governor of Jamaica to explore the coast from Florida to Tampico, Piñeda commanded four vessels during his search of the coast. When he reached Cortez's outposts in Mexico, his vessels were driven off and he moved back north to the mouth of the Rio Grande, which he called the Río de Las Palmas, where he remained for six weeks. His men explored the area while Piñeda mapped it and dreamed of returning with reinforcements to plant a colony in the land he called Amichel, the earliest European name for Texas. Piñeda later reported the natives hospitable and full of tales, which he evidently believed, of giants and pygmies on the land.

Diego de Camargo commanded a second expedition to the area a year later. His three ships brought soldiers and craftsmen to build the colony Piñeda had intended. At first the Indians seemed friendly, but then they became hostile and killed several of Camargo's men, forcing his withdrawal to Vera Cruz. Three years later the Jamaican governor, Francisco Garay, followed with a fleet of sixteen ships and 700 soldiers to locate Camargo and to strengthen the claim against Cortez. He explored the Rio Grande and the coastline, and decided to abandon Amichel to the Indians. He moved on to Cortez's plantation where he was imprisoned, and also where he met Pánfilo Narváez, whom he told about the Rio Grande country. Narváez returned to Spain, and, in 1525, received a commission to plant a colony north of Cortez's, to be called Panuco-Victoria Garayana. His command included the entire Gulf Coast from Florida to the Rio Grande.

Narváez returned to Cuba in 1528 to organize his venture. He moved northward to Florida, where he divided his command. The vessels sailed along the coast while he led a group into the interior to battle mosquitoes, swamps, and hostile In-

dians, then moved to the rendezvous point to meet his ships. But no ships were there. Finally Narváez's men built rafts and tried to float along the coast to Mexico. Near Galveston, called Mulhado then, a hurricane drove their rafts ashore. Nearly eighty men had made it thus far, but only fifteen survived the year, and in the end, only four made it back to a Spanish community. These four included the company's treasurer, Alvar Núñez Cabeza de Vaca, Captain Alonso del Castillo Maldonado, Andrés Dorantes de Carranza, and Carranza's Moorish slave, Estevánico.

The amazing story of Cabeza de Vaca began in November 1558 when he and the men with him found Indians friendly enough to engage in trade. Cabeza de Vaca performed some kind of healing on one of the Indians, reportedly removing an arrow from the Indian's chest, and after that the natives treated Cabeza de Vaca and the others with kindness and allowed them to roam about

their camps. They would not let them go, however, evidently thinking that they had a sure source of healing in Cabeza de Vaca's ability to perform "miracles." The Spaniards kept moving, first northwestward, then south, probably crossing their own tracks several times, until they ran into a Spanish patrol in Northern Mexico who first thought they were Indians and then believed them crazy because of their tattered dress and odd behavior. Cabeza de Vaca convinced the soldiers that he was Spanish and the soldiers took him and his group to Mexico City. He eventually returned to Spain, but not before he told the viceroy stories about rumors of golden cities he had heard in the lands to the north. His almost unbelievable six-year adventure is related in his narrative, *La Relación,* and gave the authorities greatly expanded information on the lands he had traversed.

The Spanish dispatched Marcos de Niza, a

Above: *Alvar Núñez Cabeza de Vaca and his three companions, Alonso Maldonado, Andrés Dorantes, and Estevánico, are depicted passing through the Big Bend Country in 1536. Courtesy, Mrs. Cleofas Calleros, Institute of Texan Cultures*

Left: *This drawing shows Cabeza de Vaca and his companions restoring health to the Indians they met in the Texas region. From Castañeda,* Our Catholic Heritage in Texas, 1519-1936, *Von Boeckmann-Jones Co., 1936*

This was supposedly the first
American play, written by a
Captain Farfan, staged on the
banks of the Rio Grande near
Socerro, Texas, April 30, 1598.
This is an artist's conception of
the event, by José Cisneros.
Courtesy, Mrs. Cleofas Calleros,
Institute of Texas Cultures

priest burning with zeal to carry the message of
Christianity to the Indians, to check on Cabeza
de Vaca's tales of the "Seven Cities of Cíbola."
Estevánico, the Moorish slave, went along as
guide, but little came of it. Then a more auspi-
cious investigation, led by the young governor of
New Galicia, Francisco Vásquez de Coronado, was
mounted, with de Niza as guide. This *entrata* was
composed of several hundred soldiers, priests, Indians, and women to function as cooks and servants. For two years Coronado searched in vain
for the golden cities; de Niza returned in disgrace
and soon died. But Coronado's band moved on
through New Mexico. His men ranged as far west

as the Grand Canyon, and after wintering at the
pueblo of Tiguex on the upper Rio Grande between present-day Albuquerque and Bernalillo, he
moved eastward past the Palo Duro Canyon,
where the red soils and layered crystals reminded
the Spanish of the swirling skirts of dancers. He
moved due north through Oklahoma and into
Kansas, perhaps as far north as Nebraska, searching
for Quivira and cities made of gold. He found
only prairie, which he observed might be good for
cattle grazing because buffalo used it thus, but
without gold the land did not interest him—nor
did it much interest his superiors, who subjected
him to an official investigation for his pains.

Other Spaniards approached from the east.
Hernando de Soto landed in Florida in 1539 and
began a long exploration across Alabama, Mississippi, Arkansas, Oklahoma, and down into Texas
as far as the Trinity River. De Soto died there,
and his successor, Luís de Moscoso, took his body
back to the Mississippi for burial. Like Coronado,
they found no gold, only emptiness. They did pass
oil seepages, a kind of gold their technology could
not yet appreciate, and they made significant ob-
servations about Indian life and natural history,
but without the gold they gratefully quit the
country.

Then Juan de Oñate came again from the west
in 1601. He had traveled as far as Santa Fe in
1598, establishing a permanent settlement there
with missions, silver mines, and other outposts
stretching back to Central Mexico. Then he headed
east across the Texas Panhandle, bringing friendly
Indians to aid him with hostile ones, bringing settlers, and above all, looking still for gold. He
found none, of course, and soon the settlers he
left behind returned to centers of Spanish civilization. But the livestock that had strayed or were
abandoned remained to found herds of cattle and
horses.

The next Spanish activity in Texas had higher
motives than the search for gold. Jumano Indians
arrived at a mission in Albuquerque in 1629, tell-
ing a strange and wonderful story. They had been
commanded to go there, they said, by a "Lady in

Blue" who appeared in their village and instructed them in Christianity. She had sent them to the mission for baptism. Father Juan de Salas received permission to return to their village to baptize the others. He and Father Diego León did so, and they found other Indians who had seen the Lady in Blue, but unfortunately the padres did not see her. They informed their Father Superior, Alonso de Benavides, of the miracle, and when he returned to Spain, Benavides heard of Sister María Jesús de Ágreda, a young nun who experienced the miracle of transportation. In trances she visited places with strange, painted peoples, but she did not know where they were. Convinced that the nun had visited the Jumanos, Benavides sent word to continue the contacts with the Indians. In 1632 the Albuquerque padres visited the village a second time to convert and to baptize. And when the Spanish came to East Texas they learned that the Lady in Blue had preceded them there as well.

Several other *entratas* followed the Jumanos routes. Hernán Martín and Diego del Castillo traveled as far south eastward as the Nueces River, and Diego de Guadalajara came to explore the country the Spanish would call Tejas in 1654. In 1675 Father Juan Larios visited the Edwards Plateau, and in 1683 Juan Domínguez de Mendoza led an expedition with Father Nicolás López to establish a mission there, thinking the chances of success were good since the Mission Corpus Christi de Isleta had been established in the El Paso country two years earlier. Again the Jumanos provided the spark. They requested Spanish help in dealing with the Apaches. The Mendoza-López party established their mission in the San Saba River country, but the Apaches drove them away. All these ventures, whether secular or church-oriented, found no gold, and official Spain again lost interest in the lands to the north until Frenchmen appeared on the Gulf Coast to challenge them for empire.

The French explored much of the Atlantic coast of North America as early as the sixteenth century, but their first permanent settlement came at Quebec in 1608. Moving along a crescent-like

arch, they explored the interior below the St. Lawrence River, the Great Lakes, and the Mississippi River Valley. Quebec, Montreal, Detroit, St. Louis, and finally New Orleans marked their trail. Father Jacques Marquette and Louis Joliet were among the earliest to explore the Mississippi area, and in 1682 René Robert Cavelier, Sieur de La Salle, planted the *fleur-de-lis* on the lower country and claimed it all in the name of his sovereign, Louis XIV. Thus the French became neighbors of the Spanish in the interior of North America, both of them directly in the path of English expansion. Showdowns between all of the empires thus became inevitable.

This engraving of Juan Ponce de Leon searching for the Fountain of Youth in the sixteenth century appeared in Henry Brownell's Pioneer Heroes of the New World *in 1856. Courtesy, Institute of Texan Cultures*

THE LINK BETWEEN CHURCH AND STATE

Religion played a prominent role in the conquest and settlement of the New World. Given the pervasive role of Christianity in contemporary European life, it could hardly have been otherwise. But there were differences of opinion among the Spanish about the specific role of religion in their colonial system. For example, some Spaniards believed that American Indians did not have souls. Therefore, they reasoned, harsh treatment could be employed to break the Indians' resistance to Spanish authority and thus they could be used as slaves. Others, notably Bartholomew de las Casas, believed that the Indians already had souls and that enslaving them was sinful.

There were always religious zealots who yearned to present the good news of Jesus Christ to the Indians; they became the link between the church and state in the mission-presidial system. The state used the activities of the missionaries to supplement the function of the *presidio,* or the military, in holding and extending Spanish dominion. Perhaps many state officials also agreed with the missionaries that the souls of the Indians should be saved.

The missions, as agencies of the state and church, had two primary functions: to convert the Indians and to extend and civilize the frontier of the Spanish empire. The missionaries taught Christian doctrine to the Indians but they also demanded submissiveness to the state. In this way the Spanish government hoped to counteract invasion of their lands by keeping the Indians from falling under the influence of distant Indian tribes or other European powers. By adopting the mission way of life, the Indians would also be accepting Spanish government and society and meanwhile develop agricultural and industrial methods appropriate to the area of the mission. When the area was thus "reduced," the mission would be turned over to the secular clergy and the lands divided among the mission Indians and Spanish settlers in the area. Since the missions had trained the Indians to be docile and not resist the Spanish settlers, all were expected to live in harmony.

Missionaries were prohibited from engaging in trade or commerce and were required to make a periodic accounting of all the mission's property. They performed Christian sacraments for the Indians and recorded all births, baptisms, marriages, and deaths.

The missions were usually quadrangle-shaped with a protective surrounding wall. Within the quadrangle the daily drama of mission life was played. The mission church, dominating the interior of the quadrangle, was the center of activity. Nearby was the *convento,* or missionaries' house, workshops of craftsmen such as carpenters and blacksmiths, the granary, looms, kilns, quarters for soldiers assigned to the mission, and housing for the Indians. The latter usually was located in the quadrangle walls. Within the mission an Indian pueblo, or small town, existed under the supervision of the missionaries, although the Indians selected their own leaders. Beyond the quadrangle's protective walls lay the fields where crops were grown, and beyond them were pastures and grazing lands for the livestock.

The daily routine of the mission began at dawn when the neophytes attended mass. They had breakfast and then worked about four hours in the mission's shops or fields. Here they learned many European agricultural and mechanical practices. They also learned fine arts such as singing, dancing, and playing musical instruments, as well as the Spanish language. In the afternoon they ate another meal, took a *siesta* to escape the afternoon heat, and then worked for several more hours. At sunset they attended mass and classes in Christian doctrine. In the early evening they had amusements and entertainments of their own making. The children played and the adults visited or sometimes engaged in games.

According to Spanish policy, assimilating the Indians into Spanish culture would take approximately ten years. The more primitive culture of Texas Indians, however, always required longer than that and even then the attempt was not usually completely successful.

The oldest missions in present Texas were established in the region of El Paso, not then regarded as part of Texas. The first mission established in the northeastern provinces was San Francisco de los Tejas; its function differed from previous policy as it was a warning signpost to the French following La Salle's penetration into Spanish territory in 1684. This mission was shut down after three years when no other French arrived in the territory. However, when St. Denis again presented a French threat in 1714, the Spanish founded six more missions in the northeast, including one in present Louisiana. Eventually nearly thirty missions operated in various parts of Texas; most tribes had a least one mission specifically designed to serve them.

The missions in Texas, with the exception of those located in the San Antonio area, were less successful than their predecessors in Mexico. The missionaries baptized fewer Indians, and had difficulty convincing Indians to become permanent residents of the missions and to accept European ways. In 1772 all the East Texas missions were pulled back to San Antonio or closed completely.

José Cisneros drew this conception of the Mission San Francisco de los Zumas, which was
established around the present
site of Fabens, Texas, by Franciscan fathers. Courtesy, Mrs.
Cleofas Calleros, Institute of
Texan Cultures

French explorer René Robert Cavelier, Sieur de La Salle, claimed land, including what is today Texas, for France. Courtesy, Institute of Texan Cultures

The French troubled the Spanish first. La Salle obtained permission to return to America to plant a colony along the Gulf Coast, presumably in the area of the Mississippi River. Instead, he sailed 400 miles farther west, perhaps by accident but probably by design, to push French interests westward. His voyage proved ill-fated. He had quarrelled at sea with the ships' captains and with those who would become colonists with him. They made landfall in the Matagorda Bay area and pushed inland a few miles out of sight from passing Spanish vessels to found Fort St. Louis. Their

palisaded fortress became an unhappy home. Mosquitoes, unfriendly Karankawas, a shortage of food, and above all, their internal dissention, undercut any hope of success. La Salle searched the area, locating the Brazos River and other delights, but he could find no riches, no friendly Indians, and no relief for the near-starvation of his men. To ease the colonists' problems, La Salle proposed to leave the bulk of the company there and to strike off for known French settlements along the upper Mississippi. The few men he took along mutinied somewhere in Central or East Texas and murdered him. Some of the men scattered in the wilderness to hide their crime, but others continued to Illinois, where they joined Henri de Tonti, who led an unsuccessful relief expedition to Texas.

The Spanish became alarmed when news of the French presence in Texas reached them. Alonso de León, governor of Coahuila, launched eleven expeditions, some by land and some by sea, to search for the French fortress. In April of 1689 he located the ruins of the fort and learned that the Karankawas had done his work for him. From a few survivors, mostly captives or Frenchmen who had gone insane in the wilderness, he learned that those in command had invited the Indians inside the fort to show their friendship and the Karankawas simply turned on their hosts, killing as many as possible, and then burned the fort.

Even though the French threat seemed eased, de León determined to place a visible signpost of Spanish claims in the way of the French. In 1690 he returned to Texas with Franciscan Father Damián Massanet to found a Spanish mission among the Caddo Indians. San Francisco de los Tejas was situated near the Neches River. Later a second mission, Santisimo Nombre de María, was located nearby. Only three days were required to erect the log structures. At first the Indians showed interest in the bright vestments and the ritual of the priests, but they had little interest in Christianity, and soon the priests quarrelled with the soldiers left to protect them, and the Indians grew tired of feeding the Spanish and of their efforts to put them to work. So they simply dis-

This engraving titled The Murther of Mons. de La Salle *depicts the French explorer being attacked by an ambusher. La Salle's men mutinied in Central or East Texas and murdered him in 1687. Courtesy, Institute of Texan Cultures*

appeared. Within three years the mission was withdrawn. This first mission in Texas proper—Isleta was not then in Texas or even thought to be within Texas until 1849—performed the function that de León had intended. The mission alerted the French to the fact that the Spanish meant to retain the territory, and also gives San Antonio the honor of being the first Texas town established by Europeans. With that accomplished, the Spanish were content to leave Texas alone until the next French threat. The most successful thing about the mission was the adoption of part of its name, San Francisco de los Tejas, for the area. Among names then applied to Texas by the Spanish was Neuvo Reyno de la Montaña de Santander y Santillana, but increasingly the name of Tejas, or Texas, gained currency.

Spanish methods of dealing with the Texas Indians failed. Their techniques of exploitation and administration had been developed among the more civilized Indians of Mexico, where it seemed to work. They divided their conquered lands into *encomiendas,* and they awarded its use to those who had conquered it. These *encomienderos* received four-fifths of the land's produce (the government got the rest) and the use of its resident Indians as laborers. They did have to instruct the Indians in the catechism, but their authority over them was supreme. Before long the troubled consciences of the Spanish priests caused the substitution of Africans as laborers in many parts of the empire, but the Spanish continued to use mission Indians to tranquilize, or "reduce," the land to productivity. This failed in Texas because the Indians there lacked sufficient cultural maturity to accommodate to the system, and because Spanish administration was less efficient. Even so, the church and the state cooperated fully in claiming and retaining the land, the former to save the souls of the Indians and the latter to retain political authority. The bond of the cross and the sword marked the remainder of Spanish activity in Texas.

The next French threat came from the zeal of a priest to move back to Texas. In 1700 a Father Hidalgo wrote an unauthorized letter to the French governor of the territory of Louisiana, Cadillac, proposing a joint venture to Christianize the Indians of Texas. Cadillac knew that Hidalgo lacked permission for the proposal, but he viewed it as an opportunity to move into the area for trade purposes. He dispatched Canadian-born Louis Juchereau de St. Denis to explore the region. In 1714 St. Denis moved up the Mississippi and Red rivers, established a cache of trade goods at Natchitoches, Louisiana, then set off across Texas. He made it all the way to the Rio Grande without seeing a Spaniard, which naturally troubled the Spanish. He was placed in a kind of house arrest by presidio (garrison) commander Diego Ramón, but he was treated more like a guest, and was even given permission to court Manuela Sánchez, Ramón's granddaughter, whom St. Denis later married. He had to travel to Mexico City to obtain his freedom, but he also came away with a kind of partnership with the Spanish, who agreed to accompany St. Denis back to East Texas to found missions and to open the Indian trade.

With Domingo Ramón, brother of Diego, and his new bride, St. Denis helped the Spanish found six missions in Texas. They rebuilt San Francisco de los Tejas, leaving Father Hidalgo in charge. They then moved eastward to found Nuestra Señora de la Purisima Concepción at a Caddo village in the eastern portion of present Nacogdoches County, Nuestra Señora de Guadalupe at the present city of Nacogdoches, and San José de los Nazonis at a Nazoni village near present Cushing. Moving eastward toward the French outposts, including St. Denis' cache, they established Nuestra Señora de los Dolores among the Aís Indians near present San Augustine and San Miguel de Linarea among the Adáes near present Robiline, Louisiana. Ramón also established a presidio at Nuestra Señora de los Dolores de los Tejas on the Neches River to guard all the missions. A Franciscan padre, Antonio Jesús de Margíl, the greatest of all the mission founders, had charge of ecclesiastical functions. Until his death in 1744, St. Denis continued to trade with the Indians, enriching himself in the process and earning designation as a chevalier by order of the French king. His real contribution lay in hastening Spanish activity in Texas.

The new missions required close attention. Martín de Alarcon, new governor of Coahuila, and Father Antonio de San Buenaventura Olivares, came to Texas in 1718 to establish a supply center and more missions between the Rio Grande and East Texas. Together they founded the mission San Antonio de Valero, naming it for a marqués who sponsored their efforts, and they named the river they found there the San Antonio because they reached that point on St. Anthony's Day. By 1721 a presidio, San Antonio de Bejar, joined the missions. Of all Texas missions, those in San Antonio proved the most successful because of the milder climate, a shorter supply line, and because

they had brought submissive mission Indians with them as an example to the others. By 1726 more than 200 Spaniards lived in the region, marking the beginnings of a real settlement.

Then the French stirred again. In 1719 a French patrol raided the mission at Los Adaés to plunder the Spanish outpost. A flock of chickens caused such a clamor that a Spanish padre escaped and reported the French invasion. This quixotic episode is sometimes called the "Chicken War." The Spanish viceroy responded quickly by appointing the Marqués de San Miguel de Aguayo to lead a force to East Texas to reestablish Spanish authority. Aguayo arrived at San Antonio in March 1720 and found that most of the East Texas priests had returned there to found the Mission

Mission Concepción was originally founded in 1716 by the Ramón Expedition. Courtesy, Texas State Archives

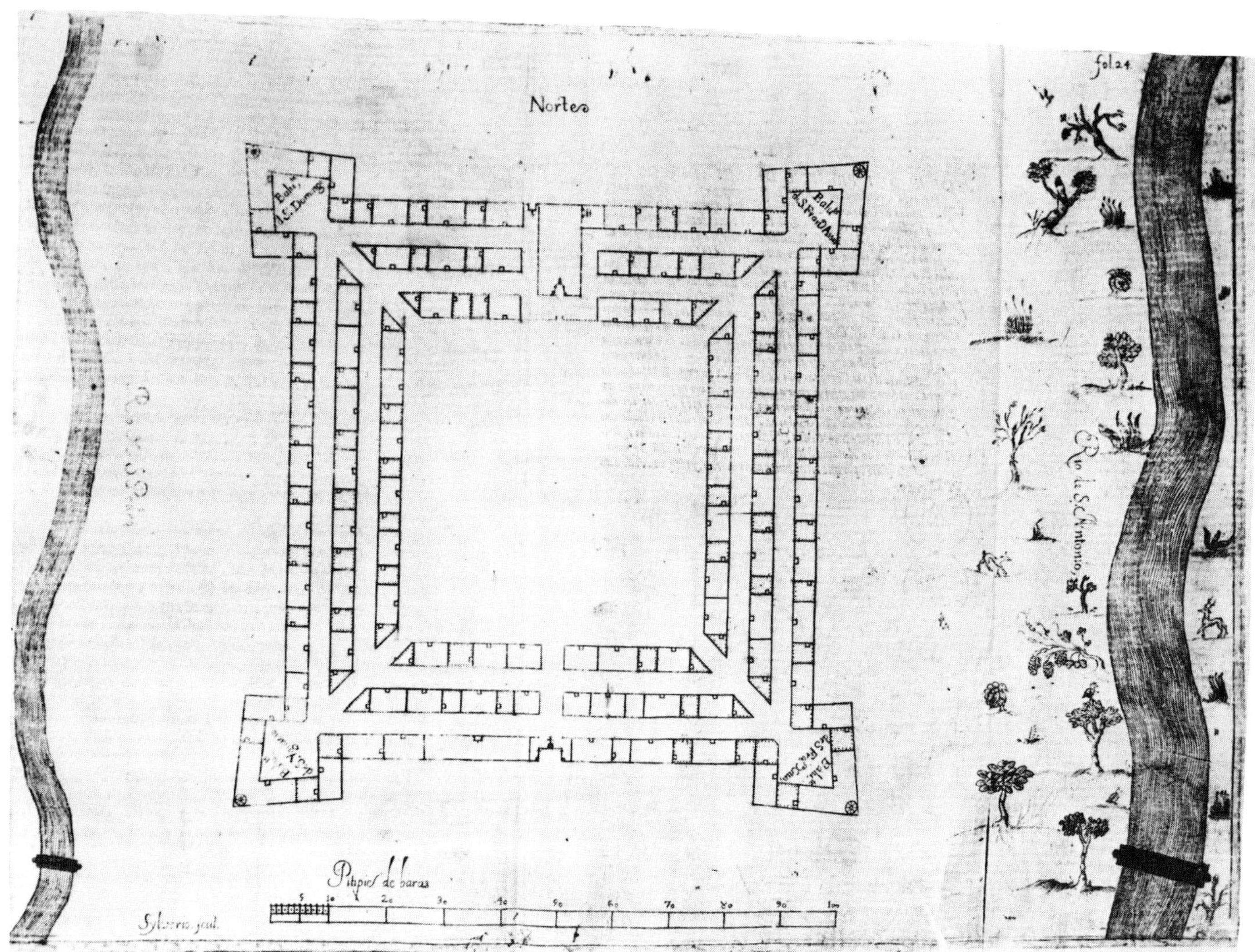

This is the plan of the presidio of San Antonio de Bexar in the province of Texas, located between the San Pedro and San Antonio rivers. The flora and fauna of the vicinity are included in this Spanish map. Courtesy, Institute of Texan Cultures

San José y San Miguel de Aguayo in his honor. He moved to secure La Bahía del Espiritu Santo, as the Spanish called the site of Fort St. Louis, then he pushed on to East Texas, which he found abandoned by the French as well. He relocated the San Francisco mission on the Neches, and left new priests and supplies at the other sites as well. At Los Adaés he constructed the Presidio Nuestra Señora del Pilar as a more formidable signal to the French. He returned to La Bahía to found another presidio, La Bahía de Loreto, and the mission Nuestra Señora del Espiritu Santo de Zuniga, and both became commonly known as La Bahía.

Aguayo reestablished a functioning mission-presidio system but he reported that more civilian personnel should be located there to give the Spanish a firmer grip on Texas. As a result, more than 100 families were recruited from the Canary

Islands to move to the San Antonio region. Only fifty-six persons actually came, but they also brought the first legally recognized civilian government to Texas, called the Villa San Fernando de Bejar.

Things remained quiet for a time following the Aguayo expedition. The Spanish had rimmed Texas with missions and presidios along the coast and in the eastern parts, and along the western rim they had the New Mexican missions. But the interior lay vacant still, and there was not much settlement between Central Mexico and Texas. To change this, José de Escandón received a commission in 1746 to locate a settlement line along the Rio Grande on large riparian grants. In 1747 he entered Nuevo Santander as governor with 2,500 settlers, 750 soldiers, priests, and plenty of supplies. He established twenty-three towns along the river, including Laredo and Dolores, and developed the pattern that was followed in the area thereafter. The grantee was known as a *patron,* and this person controlled the land and its people in authority second only to that of the governor. His people provided labor, his priests supplied religious services, and they all built towns. The *patron*'s house became the seat of government, and eventually became a city hall; the church lay to one side, and the *patron*'s granaries and storehouses filled in the other side of a plaza. Around this nexus a town proper grew. Later settlers' houses and businesses assembled behind the primary plaza as the town grew, and among these people a rich cattle culture known as *charro* emerged.

Then, to fill in the heartland, more missions followed. The San Gabriel site received a mission founded by Father Mariano Francisco de los Dolores y Viana for the Tonkawas, and later he founded San Francisco Xavier de Horcasitas a short distance away. San Ildefonso and Nuestra Señora de la Candelaria followed. In 1755 all three missions were moved to the head of the San Marcos River near present New Braunfels.

The Apaches received the next missions. A New Mexican mine owner, Pedro Romero de Terreros,

offered to help finance a mission to pacify the Apaches and thus keep down trouble for his mine. His relative, Father Alonzo Giraldo de Terreros, was placed in charge. In 1766 Father Terreros led other priests, Christian Indians, and soldiers commanded by Colonel Diego Ortíz de Parilla to found the Mission San Saba de la Santa Cruz on the San Saba River. Parilla established the presidio San Luis de las Amarillas two miles distant at Terreros' insistence. At first the Apaches appeared hospitable, then they just disappeared. The Spanish quickly learned why. The Apaches had led them to found a mission in Comanche country, and the Comanches did not want it there. They

This drawing by José Cisneros depicts a priest celebrating mass for Indians in about 1629. Courtesy, Mrs. Cleofas Calleros, Institute of Texan Cultures

attacked the mission, then moved on to the presidio. Parilla escaped to report the loss, then led an expedition back. He mistakenly attacked a Taovayas village, but he was overwhelmed by these Indians as well, partially because they had assistance from French traders.

One last mission effort for the Apaches followed. The Spanish founded San Lorenzo de la Santa Cruz and Nuestra Señora de la Candelaria del Cañon in 1762 on the upper Nueces River. The Apaches came to neither of them.

Meanwhile, the Spanish reorganized their missions. In 1749 the La Bahía mission was moved from the Guadalupe River to the lower San Antonio River, and the resulting community became known as Goliad. Another mission, Nuestra Señora del Rosario, was erected four miles from La Bahía to serve the Karankawas. The East Texas missions were all relocated in the San Antonio area, and by the end of the century, all had become secular parish churches.

These changes resulted from a shift in basic policy. As a result of the European clash known as the Seven Years' War (the French and Indian War in the New World) and the Peace of Paris that concluded the conflict in 1763, the victorious Spanish and English divided France's North American empire. Now Spanish lands extended to the Mississippi River, and their new neighbor, the English, seemed a long way off and less threatening. They even allowed a few of the English, or Americans, to migrate to their lands if they would become Spanish citizens and Catholics, and in other moves known in American history as the Spanish Conspiracy they tried to create a new buffer out of territory *east* of the big river.

The Spanish also adopted a new policy for Texas. In the late 1760s the Marqués de Rubí inspected Spanish holdings from Texas to Baja in California, and recommended policy changes to King Charles III that became effective in 1772 with the publication of the *New Regulation of the Presidios.* De Rubí found only weakness north of Mexico. The mission-presidio system had failed to "reduce" the land to economic productivity, and

everywhere the missions seemed more in danger from the Indians than anything else. He recommended that the missions on the periphery of Texas be closed and relocated in San Antonio, which would be developed as a center of political, economic, and military strength. Instead of a hub of Spanish activity in Texas, the city would become the frontier line. War should be made on the Apaches and Comanches, he further suggested, and all Spanish settlers in East Texas should be compelled to move to San Antonio. Athanase de Mézières, a Frenchman in Spanish pay, became

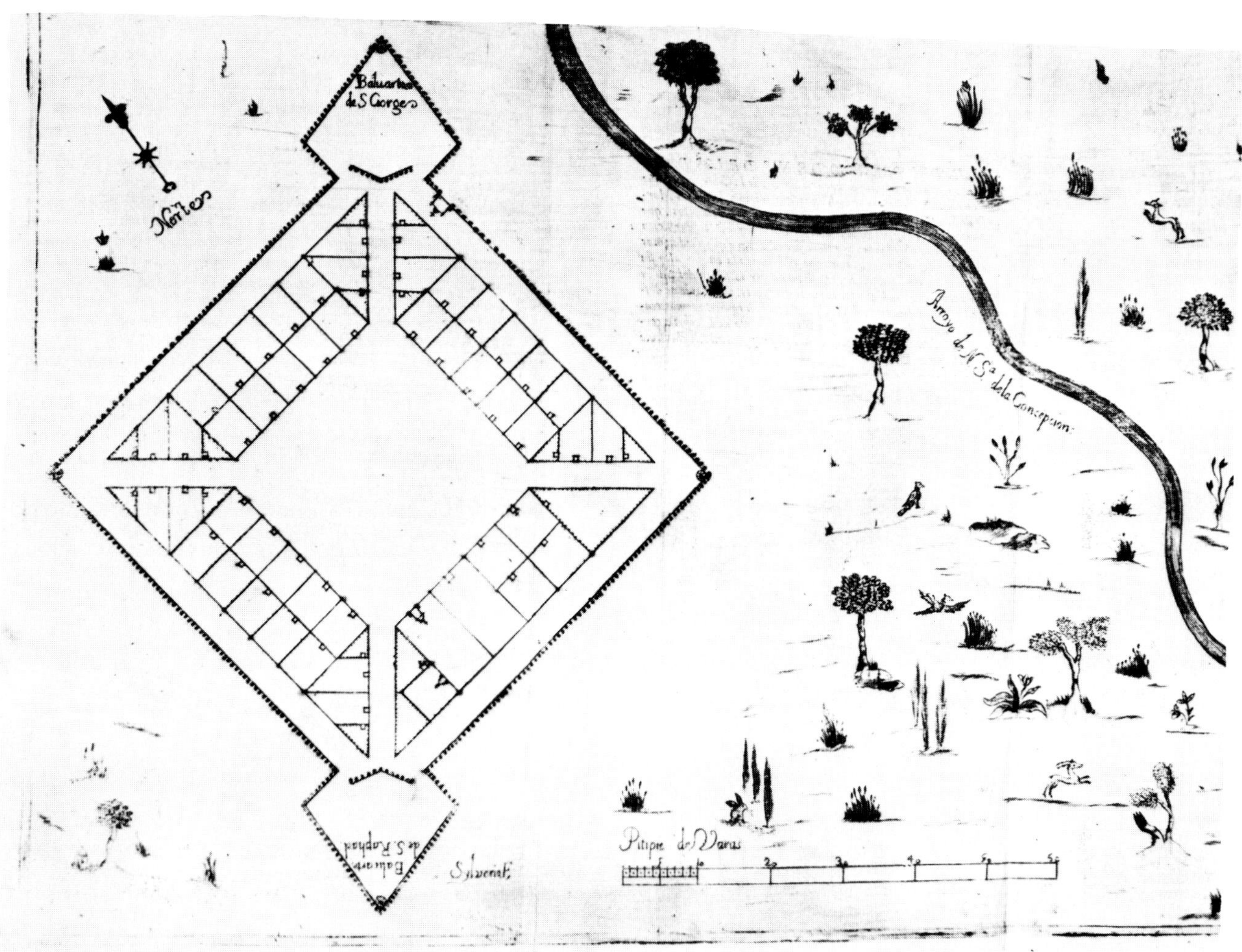

Above: *This is the 1722 plan of the presidio of Nuestra Señora de los Delores located four miles from the Angelina River in Nacogdoches County. Courtesy, Institute of Texan Cultures*

Facing page: *This José Cisneros drawing depicts Spaniards and their Indian converts worshipping together as the priest leads them in song. Courtesy, Mrs. Cleofas Calleros, Institute of Texan Cultures*

the principal Indian "pacifier" and trader for the Spanish, and Teodoro de Croix drew the assignment to make war in the west. Both were fairly successful, at least in establishing an uneasy peace.

Juan María Vincente, the Baron de Ripperda and new governor of Texas, had to enforce the edict of removal on the East Texas settlers. His soldiers forced the unhappy East Texans to move, punctuating their orders by burning buildings and trampling crops so they would not return. Some escaped into the wilderness until the soldiers left, then quietly moved back to their homes. The others trekked to San Antonio, grumbling all the way. Antonio Gil Ybarbo, a rancher from the Lobinillo Creek area, emerged as their leader.

As soon as Ybarbo arrived in San Antonio he

asked Ripperda for permission to return to East Texas. The governor allowed Ybarbo to petition higher authority, Viceroy Bucareli, in Mexico City, and within a few months they received permission to return part of the way to their former homes, but with a condition: they could move no closer than 100 leagues of Natchitoches. In August of 1774 Ybarbo led his group back to the Trinity River crossing of the San Antonio Road, or *El Camino Real,* where they established a community they named Bucareli in honor of the viceroy who had permitted them to leave San Antonio. Floods and Comanche raids made this only a temporary home. After four years of torment Ybarbo again led his group eastward, this time stopping at the old mission site in Nacogdoches. This was probably the only Spanish structure standing in all of East Texas. Ybarbo laid out a townsite and called it Nacogdoches. He reported his actions, and surprisingly he received confirmation from the San Antonio authorities that they would accept his action. In October he was commissioned captain of militia and lieutenant governor of the pueblo of Nacogdoches, with full accountability to the authorities. This was the first official founding of a Spanish town in East Texas.

Ybarbo proved a successful leader. He wrote a code of conduct for Nacogdoches residents with punishments ranging from death to years of service on Spanish galleys to corporal chastisement for scores of offenses. He built the Stone House for trading and business purposes, and since he was the government, it became government headquarters as well. Subsequently known as the Stone Fort, it stood on the northeast corner of the town plaza until razed in 1902. Within a few years Ybarbo was banished from Nacogdoches because of alleged, and probably actual, smuggling activities. But his town remained, and despite numerous setbacks, flourishes today.

Escandón and Ybarbo found the correct way to deal with the Texas wilderness. Spanish attempts to control Texas through missions and presidios failed everywhere except San Antonio, and there they required constant attention. All their efforts were really negative, intended only to stop someone else from possessing the land. And they were always corporate. Escandón and Ybarbo came with individuals and allowed each settler the freedom to work his own way in the environment, for his own well being, so long as he remained true to the church and to the state. In the end, that way worked best. These latter invaders came to the land itself, and they came to stay.

The Spanish experience in Texas has been termed "a successful failure." It succeeded in that Spain left a permanent mark in language, religion, architecture, and in the cattle industry. More significant Hispanic influences came later, remained on the Rio Grande for a time, then swept over the state in the present century. But the Spanish failed to retain its New World empire, including Texas, failed to permanently impact the Indian population, failed to keep the lands from other European penetration even while they controlled it, and in the end they lost the land itself.

The 1774 withdrawal proved a setting sun for the Spanish in Texas. Beyond San Antonio, only the individual achievements of men such as Ybarbo remained. Occasional patrols wandered the land to police Indian uprisings or stop Anglo filibusters, but Spain's time in Texas was over. Already a new wave of invaders, the Anglo-Celts, were starting to cast inquiring glances at the land.

This Frederick Remington drawing, First of the Race, *shows a conquistadore on horseback, trailed by a young foal. Courtesy, Institute of Texan Cultures*

Filibusters, Empresarios, and Colonists

The Spanish, soldiers and priests and a few would-be settlers, invested nearly two centuries in exploring and planting and occupying the lands that were theirs, including Texas, before the first Anglo-Celts, now known as Americans, made much effort to see or to have the land themselves. But once they saw it, they would have to possess it.

While the Spanish carved their New World empire out of gold and silver, the English passed their first 200 years in America in a very different fashion. The English might have envied the Spanish insistence upon religious, economic, and political homogeneity, but they could never achieve such a goal in their colonies because it escaped them in their homeland as well. But therein lay their ultimate strength in both places. While the Spanish, and to a lesser degree the French, counted heavily upon the produce of

This painting depicts an 1812-1821 filibustering expedition into Texas. Courtesy, Institute of Texan Cultures

their colonies and failed to develop sufficient strength in Europe, the English grew constantly stronger everywhere.

But this did not insure a permanent connection between the mother country and the colonies. The diversity, independent-mindedness, and self-confidence born of wealth from the land's bounty from Carolina to Massachusetts forged a new people whose boundless energy propelled them ever westward. Soon they were pushing west directly across the path of the French, who occupied the St. Lawrence Valley, the Great Lakes, and the Ohio and Mississippi valleys in an arc across mid-America. A clash between England and France, never the best of friends in Europe, was inevitable.

In the New World, in the 1750s, control of the Ohio country was at issue; British and French colonists fought each other for two years before the mother countries were fully involved. Known in American history as the French and Indian War, in England as the Great War for Empire, and elsewhere as the Seven Years' War, this contest proved mortal for French imperial interests in North America. A negotiated peace, the 1763 Peace of Paris, awarded Great Britain all French territory west of its colonies as far as the Mississippi River. And because the Spanish sided with the British, they received French lands eastward from Texas to the great river.

Now the Spanish had a new worry. As long as French territory separated them from the English, they had concerned themselves little with Anglo expansion, except in Florida. Now they had a new neighbor, with a large alien population along their eastern border, and although a great, vacant distance separated them from the English, many Spaniards knew that the years would erase the miles rapidly. So they tried what is known in American history as the Spanish Conspiracies. One ploy was to arouse the Indians to slow down American settlement or perhaps to lure some Americans to establish a buffer state east of the river; another, begun by Don Francisco Bouligny, commander of Upper Louisiana (Missouri) in 1776, admitted some Americans to Spanish territory to

This engraving portrays the terror white settlers felt at Indian existence in the new land. Titled Our Indian Troubles, *it first appeared in* Frank Leslie's Illustrated Newspaper *on May 20, 1882.*

live among the existing French population upon their agreement to become Spanish vassals and Roman Catholic.

Generous land settlements lured some Americans across the river, among them a lead miner named Moses Austin, who observed there the implementation of the first American empresarial grant made by the Spanish. They permitted Colonel William Morgan of New Jersey to introduce Americans to settle a new community at New Madrid on the Mississippi River in the hopes that these and other settlers to follow would form a barrier against American *political* acquisition of the territory. Governor Bernardo de Gálvez, Boul-

igny's superior, agreed because he had been ordered to convert the area into an economically
productive unit of the empire.

Gálvez might as well have agreed, because the
Anglos were coming anyway. First hunters and
trappers crossed the river without caring that it
served as a political boundary; then Loyalists and
finally American revolutionaries filtered into the
Amite River country, and others pushed across the
border to seek the land that lured them or to gain
distance from whatever drove them from the east.
Gálvez's successor, Estéban Rodríguez Míro, accelerated the policy, and Spanish agents in the infant
United States even recruited settlers for Missouri,
pinning their hopes on stopping America with
Americans.

Morgan's group did not entirely please the
Spanish. He allowed the settlers to elect him as
their leader, while the Spanish assumed that he
would command as they did, arbitrarily. But

Morgan's scheme worked well, because it was in
the familiar pattern of individual settlement so
successful everywhere in the English colonies and
also successful in isolation in Texas as in the
Escandón and Ybarbo settlements. Before long,
enough Americans came to Spanish lands west of
the river to cause concern, partly because they so
outnumbered the Spanish and partly because
many of them behaved as if they and not the
Spanish ought to be the superior population.

By 1819 the Spanish succeeded in establishing
a new and firm boundary to the west, which excluded this first borderland population, but the
motivation was not entirely their own. In the first
place, in 1797 Napoleon Bonaparte forced the
Spanish to return the lands taken from France in
1763, and then six years later he sold this same
territory to the United States. No one knew the
western boundary of these exchanges, so the
Americans sought to push their claims as far westward as possible while the Spanish always maintained that the boundary should be farther east,
somewhere in Louisiana.

In this time of contesting wills, a new element
appeared: the filibuster. The type is as old as Sir
Francis Drake, who sailed as a privateer but whose
sailings also benefited his sovereign. In this vein,
such men as Philip Nolan, Augustus Magee, and
James Long, among countless others, sought personal gain and even empire in the troubled land

*Moses Austin answered the call
of the Texas frontier, moving his
family onto Spanish territory after he was granted empresarial
rights by Spain in 1821. From
Cirker,* Dictionary of American
Portraits, *Dover, 1967*

that lay between the Americans and the Spanish, or, eventually, the Mexicans, and neither side could ever be certain about how much official sanction such men had received from the United States government. Even if they had none, the mere fact that they were Americans advanced the interest of the United States. General James Wilkinson, commander of American forces along the Mississippi River and probably a double agent, played a significant role in the careers of the early filibusters, adding to the appearance of government sanctions.

Philip Nolan often visited with Wilkinson after returning from mustang raids into Spanish Texas. He would lead a group of men into the mustang country, round up horses, then break them enough to trail them to Louisiana where they would be sold. He also mapped, catalogued information, and aroused the Spanish into believing that he served as an American spy in addition to profiteering in wild horses. At first Nolan operated with the permission of the French governor, the Baron de Carondelet, but he continued well after the second French exit from the territory, and Juan Bautista de Elguezabál, the Spanish governor of Texas, determined that he must be stopped.

A Spanish patrol led by a Lieutenant Musquíz encountered Nolan and his men on the Central Texas plains, and in a fight that followed Nolan was killed and his men were captured. They were taken first to the Stone House in Nacogdoches, then moved to Mexico where it was decided that they should be decimated. As only nine still survived, a single captive, Ephraim Blackburn, suffered execution for them all and the rest were cast into prison. Peter Ellis Bean, who succeeded Nolan in command of the Americans, proved a true survivor. When a revolt led by a General Morelos developed, Bean convinced his captors that he could assist them in supressing the revolt. Once out of prison, he joined Morelos, then convinced that gentleman that he should be sent to New Orleans for supplies. Morelos consented, and Bean did send the supplies, but he did not accompany them. Later, Bean returned to Texas and entered

the royal, and afterwards the republican, military service.

Wilkinson, still serving as a double agent, next stirred the pot by dispatching United States troops under Zebulon Pike to explore the Arkansas River country. Pike also doubtless had orders to penetrate Spanish lands as far as possible, for when he reached Colorado, Pike turned southward toward Santa Fe where his men surrendered to royal forces. Since Pike's command, unlike Nolan's, wore uniforms, they could be accepted as merely lost, relieving the Spanish of the necessity of regarding them as pirates and having to execute them to save face. Pike's men surrendered their arms, then enjoyed a circuitous march through Mexico and Texas on their way back to United States territory.

The stories Pike's men told of their wanderings changed history in several ways. For one thing, Pike confirmed what many Americans already suspected and some knew: the Spanish empire's strength, at least in the northern parts, was more cosmetic than real. Their numbers few, their wealth depleted, and their resources sparse, their society shown with a glow that could easily be snuffed out. Otherwise Pike reported that most of the country in the Great American Desert, as he termed the area, was barely habitable anyway. This report helped turn westward migration patterns northward.

Another curious incident, which many would not even call a true filibustering expedition, developed on the border. Aaron Burr, former vice president under Thomas Jefferson who had won a duel with Alexander Hamilton, spent much time along the Ohio and Mississippi rivers storing supplies and recruiting men. Wilkinson, who was first Burr's friend but who later accused him of treason, monitored and perhaps participated in these activities. Then Wilkinson turned on Burr, claiming that he was planning to take a part of the United States as his personal empire. Burr was declared innocent at a trial in Virginia by a narrow interpretation of treason by Chief Justice John Marshall, and much later he claimed that his

Filibuster Philip Nolan is depicted here as Spanish troops approach his fort. Courtesy, Institute of Texan Cultures

scheme more resembled the consequences of what later developed in Texas under the leadership of Stephen F. Austin and Sam Houston in settlement and independence of *Spanish* lands under his control. Nevertheless, his image in American history has remained that of an unscrupulous, if not traitorous, schemer.

These border activities alarmed the Spanish. General Simón Herrera met with Wilkinson in 1807 to work out a Neutral Ground agreement, which called for both commanders to refrain from sending patrols into a specified area between the Sabine River and the Arroyo Hondo, thus pre-

TEXAS COLONIAL LIFE

Life in colonial Texas was said to have been hell on women and horses. In actuality, life in colonial Texas after 1824 was similar to that in the United States because the people living in San Felipe and other frontier communities had recreated the towns and villages they had come from. And the frontiersmen who hated crowded neighborhoods lived in isolated homesteads as they had done before.

By the late 1820s sailing vessels made regular visits to Texas from New Orleans, bringing needed supplies to the Brazos River communities and to Galveston Bay in exchange for agricultural and forest products. Money was more scarce in Texas than it had been in the United States. Settlers, dependent on an insufficient supply of gold and silver coins from around the world, developed a barter economy. Certain items had a standard value. For example, a cow and a calf equalled ten dollars.

While many frontiersmen continued to live, often by preference, in rough log cabins, more affluent colonists planked their homes with wooden boards when sawmills such as those on the Brazos River and Buffalo Bayou in the late 1820s made such materials available. Glass windows, paint, and nicely finished interiors were seen in Texas frontier homes increasingly after 1830.

Poor families walked or rode horseback, but those who could afford a Dearborn spring wagon provided more comfortable transportation for their wives and children. A magnificent coach arrived in San Felipe in 1829 when General Mier y Terán brought his scientific exploratory expedition to Texas. Ferries operated at busy river crossings and charged fees set by the *ayuntamiento* in San Felipe.

Although tree stumps still rotted in some village streets, causing some visitors to assume incorrectly that there was no plan of development, most villages were laid out in an orderly fashion. Streets ran with cardinal compass points just as Mexican law required. Each block in San Felipe was divided into six regular lots measuring 120 feet by 180 feet. Ten-acre suburban garden plots were available to the wealthy if they wanted more privacy from the activity of the town square.

Stores in the villages carried imported staples such as flour, sugar, pickled meat, tea, coffee, kitchen ware, farming tools, medicine, and sewing materials. In addition merchants also sold locally produced items such as eggs, butter, fruits, nuts, and corn that had been brought in for barter. In 1828 a butcher at San Felipe offered portions of beef at four cents per pound. Special orders placed with local merchants for goods from the United States usually arrived in about one month, depending on when vessels sailed from New Orleans.

Most villages had professional services. Lawyers were everywhere, often of the "cornstalk" variety, meaning that they lacked training, licenses or both. At least three doctors practiced medicine in San Felipe, and they, like physicians in other villages, made house calls to treat both white families and slaves.

Schools were irregular and often short-termed, which was not unusual in the United States at that time. Most children attended at least elementary classes. One merchant maintained a lending library with books by such popular writers of the day as Sir Walter Scott.

Entertainment in colonial Texas included visiting, barbecues, and dances. The standard United States celebrations such as the Fourth of July were observed; a special gala was also held in San Felipe in March 1826 in honor of the adoption of the Mexican Constitution. Merchants provided a feast and Brown Austin, Stephen F. Austin's brother, fired a twenty-three gun salute from the town's cannon in honor of the states and territories of the Republic while a red, white, and green national flag flew overhead. A visiting circus and fireworks display from New Orleans attracted a large crowd in San Felipe on another occasion.

The role of women was much the same in Texas as in the United States. Drudgery prevailed for those without slave help in the house and garden. Frontier women spun thread and wove their own cloth before fashioning garments for their families; sometimes they made clothing from buckskin. Women in the villages bought cloth and occasionally ordered ready-made wearing apparel from New Orleans. Several women in San Felipe were dressmakers on a semi-professional basis; a few sold surplus foodstuffs or took in boarders to supplement the family income. Those without slaves sometimes employed a laundress from the lower classes, including native Mexican women. A number of women rode horseback for pleasure and for visiting, presumably using sidesaddles. Most frontier women were skilled with a gun. Rural women milked cows, fed hogs and chickens, raised turkeys and geese, and planted vegetable gardens. Contrary to some travel accounts, most Texans had a variety of seasonal foods. Critical visitors who complained about having only coffee, cornbread, and pork probably visited destitute homes where the weather, many visitors, or insects had demolished the food stores.

Even after Texas was no longer a colony of Mexico, it continued to be an economic colony of the United States. The major events of the revolution were disruptive temporarily, but day-to-day activities connected with making a living on the frontier resumed their normal pace.

Apache Indians are depicted attacking a wagon train. Indians were one of the more colorful rigors facing pioneers pushing into the new territory. Courtesy, Barker Texas History Center

venting clashes between them. This was only a military agreement, but it almost assumed a political status in establishing a boundary. And from this agreement, more disagreement emerged.

Neither Herrera nor Wilkinson could have prevented lawless individuals from drifting into the unpatrolled, sparsely populated territory. Many did so, and soon caused trouble for both sides. Since Wilkinson's resources and troops were closer, Herrera allowed him to move troops into the territory occasionally to police this lawless element. Lieutenant Augustus Magee performed these duties well, but good performance failed to keep him from being passed over twice for a promotion he felt he deserved. Through an agent named William Shaler, Magee fell in with Bernardo Gutiérrez de Lara, a Spanish republican refugee from the revolt led by Father Miguel Hidalgo in 1810—the first of a succession of republican uprisings that ultimately freed Mexico from Spain's grasp. For now, however, Gutiérrez had taken refuge in Louisiana and awaited an opportunity to return to continue the cause of Mexican republicanism.

Gutiérrez and Magee created a "Republican Army of the North" in 1812, at least partially recruited from Magee's former opponents in the Neutral Ground. They promised forty dollars a month and generous land grants to their followers under a new constitutional government, which would be established once they controlled the territory. Magee crossed the Sabine River with his adventurers in August 1812, and chased a few Spanish soldiers from Nacogdoches. Flying his green flag above the Stone House, Magee proclaimed Texas independent from Mexico and accepted more recruits from the community and from others who drifted in. Then, he and Gutiérrez pressed on to La Bahía, where they chased José Antonio Saucedo and his troops from their garrison. There the invaders remained, sustained by Saucedo's supplies, until he returned later and besieged them. Magee died during this delay, by his own hand according to Gutiérrez, who now revealed a constitution for his republic that provided more benefits for its Mexican population than for

the Americans.

Samuel Kemper briefly replaced Magee, but when he saw the direction of the movement under Gutiérrez, he and others who might be termed a little more honorable abandoned the invasion and returned to New Orleans. First Rueben Ross and then Henry Perry assumed command of a force that chased Saucedo back to San Antonio and beyond. Even Gutiérrez suffered disposal as commander of the civilian wing of the pretender government when José Alvarez de Toledo arrived and forced Gutiérrez to relinquish control of the force. The Gutiérrez-Magee expedition now became the Toledo-Perry expedition, with a totally different character and mission. To oppose these invaders the Spanish first sent men commanded by General Ignacio Elizondo, and they suffered defeat by Perry's men at Alazan Creek. Then came General Joaquín de Arredondo, who met and defeated Perry at the Medina River on August 18, 1813, almost exactly a year after the expedition had entered Texas. Most of the Americans were killed. A few survivors were taken into San Antonio where they were corralled along with local citizens who had cooperated with them. All were executed the next day.

Perhaps the most significant outcome of the affair resulted from the fact that Lieutenant Antonio López de Santa Anna, who served under Arredondo, learned from his general how to deal with *piratas*. A great purge of all who had cooperated with the expedition at La Bahía, Nacogdoches, and elsewhere followed, and the first attempt at taking Texas from Spain (or Mexico) died a bloody death. Others waited their chance, and some just moved into Texas without any intention of making it independent. The true pirate Jean Lafitte operated out of Galveston in 1817-1819, for example, and as long as he left their ships alone the Spanish government made no move to dislodge him.

An event in 1817 in Florida, as unlikely as it may seem, caused the next problem for the Texas borderland. In that year militia General Andrew Jackson of Tennessee, the hero of the Battle of

Antonio López de Santa Anna played a vivid and turbulent role in Texas history. Courtesy, Barker Texas History Center

New Orleans, pursued raiding Indians into Spanish Florida, "conquering" Pensacola, and provoking an international incident. The result was the admission by the Spanish that they could not control the Indians. They agreed to cede Florida and the remainder of their holdings along the coast of the Gulf of Mexico to the Sabine River to the United States. This was due to the skill and tenacity of John Quincy Adams, who negotiated with Spain for a boundary that gave the United States a huge chunk of the lower midwest and the northwest as well as Florida. The Adams-Onís Treaty, which effected this agreement, did many things, and one of them was the exposure of Spain's weakness. But the most dramatic immediate result was furor over the fact that Texas was excluded from the new acquisition. We now know that Adams could have gotten Texas if he had

pushed Spanish minister Onís harder, but he received no support from President James Monroe, nor even Andrew Jackson, for that endeavor. He did, however, get all the blame when Americans realized how inconvenient it was to settle Texas under foreign rule.

The most immediate response came from the Southerners in the United States. Protest meetings in several Deep South cities in 1819 demonstrated their determination to move west and to carry their institutions, including slavery, along as part of their cultural baggage. A protest meeting at Natchez authorized Dr. James Long to lead an expedition into Texas. Such an invasion (actually a filibuster) would not only violate the rights of Spain and international law, but also breeched the treaty of Long's own country. Nevertheless, Long assembled about eighty men and crossed the Sabine River in June 1819. He paused in Nacogdoches and soon recruits swelled his ranks to more than 300 men. One of his new helpers was none other than Bernardo Gutiérrez de Lara, still looking for a soldier to help him win his republic. Long established his headquarters at the Stone House, as had Magee, and here he proclaimed Texas independent from Spain. And like Magee, he found the proclamation far easier to draft than to realize.

Long knew that he would need more assistance than the few men he had assembled, so he traveled overland to Galveston to try to persuade Jean Lafitte to join him. Lafitte refused; his island haven remained undisturbed as long as he left the Spanish alone, and he refused to forfeit the status quo in the unlikely event that Long would succeed. Rebuffed, Long retreated to Nacogdoches and then to Natchez, but he was not finished. At New Orleans he received financial support from several expansionist Southerners, and with Don Felix Trespalaciso, a Mexican republican in exile, Long organized his "patriot" army for an invasion of Texas. And this time he was to be accompanied by his bride, Jane Herbert Williamson, a relation of James Williamson. Her strength and role in Texas history would equal that of her husband.

The Longs and their support force traveled by boat to Point Bolivar on Galveston Bay. Here Long established a headquarters in a small palisade and left Jane, her children, and her black servant, Kiamatia (or Kian), and a few men while he moved on to Goliad with the remainder of his force. At first his command chased the Spanish troops from Goliad, but they returned to reclaim their position and to capture Long. The invaders were mostly slain, but the Spanish spared Long and sent him to Mexico City. In the final fighting between the victorious Mexican revolutionists under Augustín Iturbide and the Spanish royalists, Long's case seemed forgotten. Then the small reserve at Point Bolivar heard that Long had been killed, and all the men there determined to return to the United States. Jane refused to accompany them. Believing that her husband had been murdered, she remained in Texas throughout the severe winter of 1821-1822, alone save for Kiamatia and her infant daughter, Mary James, probably the first Anglo baby born in Texas. They survived on seafood and their own determination, occasionally chasing away curious and potentially hostile Indians by firing a cannon left behind by the men. Then, in the spring, Jane Long traveled to Mexico City to attempt to have her husband's "murderers" punished. She failed. She returned to Point Bolivar, then returned to New Orleans and Natchez, and finally, years later, came back to Texas to live in Richmond until her death in 1880. Long became known as the Mother of Texas, and if that title is valid, then Kiamatia should be known as the black Mother of Texas, for her courage equaled that of Jane Long.

The failure of Long's expedition preceded the lawful admission of Americans to Texas under the authorization of the new Republic of Mexico and its constituent state of Coahuila y Texas, and thus it may be said to have ended the age of the filibuster, at least in Texas. The filibuster's day was brief, but it had been meaningful and may be regarded as a natural aspect of American westward expansion. After all, about the only difference in the nature and personality of the filibusters and

the Texas immigrants of the next two decades lay in the decriminalization of their common act, not the act itself. Both came in search of land and the land's rewards; the former was rejected by the existing government and the latter was accepted, at least for a while, by its successor. By their exploits the filibusters advertised the availability of Texas to Americans who had yet to think of it or about it as the next place for United States expansion or their peculiar institutions. Many, including Moses Austin, thought of it until it became an obsession.

Moses Austin, a follower of the mineral frontier, had been among the earliest of the Americans who accepted the opportunity offered by the Spanish Conspiracies to move onto Spanish lands west of the Mississippi River. He helped open up the lead-mining areas of north-central Missouri, and he established the community of Potosi as his headquarters. Austin moved his family, including his son Stephen Fuller Austin and his daughter Emily, to Spanish territory. Stephen Austin returned to Lexington, Kentucky, for schooling at Transylvania University, then returned to Missouri to aid his father in various business enterprises, including the mine, a mercantile establishment, and later in banking. Stephen Austin was born in 1793, and doubtless took little notice of the political events that made his new home the property of the French and then the United States after 1803. In his youth he probably aspired to no more than the logical succession to his father's business, never thinking that he would live to plant colonies and become known as the Father of Texas.

Moses Austin's businesses suffered when the War of 1812 hindered trade in furs and other products along the Mississippi River line, and during the business slump following the war. He participated in the establishment of the Bank of St. Louis in the hope that a strong financial base would help the region survive, but the Panic of 1819 forced the bank to close and made Austin a poor man. Stephen Austin, meanwhile, served in the Missouri Territorial Legislature, became an officer in the militia, and generally gave the appear-

After the death of his father, Moses, Stephen F. Austin was lured by the new lands and opportunities available in Texas. Austin carried his father's dream through to reality. From Cirker, Dictionary of American Portraits, *Dover, 1967*

ance of a young man on the rise until the family fortunes turned for the worse. He then explored Arkansas as a place for the family to make a new start, and while there was appointed a territorial judge although he was not a lawyer and probably never held court. He traveled on to New Orleans where he began to read for the law in the office of Joseph Hawkins, probably in preparation for his judicial office in Arkansas. But then Moses Austin changed his family's lives again.

Remembering the career of William Morgan, the New Madrid empresario, Moses Austin decided to take up the promise the Spanish had made on the forfeiture of the Louisiana Territory to the French in 1797 that any vassal who wished to do so could move to other Spanish lands. He secured his son's consent to help with the venture, a pledge possibly given only half-heartedly to humor the older man. Austin traveled to San Antonio and petitioned Governor Antonio de Martinez for recognition of the pledge and permission to settle families on the Spanish lands of Texas. He planned to obtain fees for his services and thus gain a new start. Martinez refused; his orders were to keep all Americans, even former Spanish vassals, as far as he knew, out of his jurisdiction. After leaving the governor's palace, Austin crossed the plaza and encountered an old friend, the Baron de Bastrop, who remembered him. Together they returned for another audience with the governor, and Bastrop verified Austin's identity and vouched for his conduct and good name. Martinez agreed to submit the request to higher authority, and he was doubtless surprised when Moses Austin's request was granted.

The Spanish had reasons for doing so. Beset with revolutionaries in Mexico proper, they could spare but few soldiers to control the filibusters and Indians in Texas, and some still hoped that Texas could be developed into a profitable enterprise and a buffer against the United States. This had seemed to work in Missouri until the French interfered. Perhaps it could work here. Or perhaps they did not care anymore. In any event, Austin received permission to settle the families, but unfortunately he did not live to fulfill his last dream.

Soon after returning as far as Natchitoches, Moses Austin died of pneumonia. Now Stephen F. Austin was captured by the dream. There is little evidence that he gave much thought to Texas until his father's death; thereafter it captured his attention for the remainder of his life.

Austin visited San Antonio as soon as practical to verify his father's claim, but before he could secure it—it would have mattered little if he had—the royalists lost to the Mexican republicans. Austin persevered. He traveled to the state capital and then to Mexico City to request confirmation from Iturbide, the new leader of Mexico. His petition was granted, and even confirmed by the national congress, making Austin's grant the only American empresarial enterprise authorized by the national government before the government itself was replaced by the federalist constitution of 1824, which was influenced to some degree by Austin, who gave some advice to its framers.

This constitution gave the state governments control over most matters of immigration and land policy and the legislature of Coahuila enacted a colonization law for Texas in 1825. Long before this, however, Austin already had begun to settle Americans in Texas. Under the first grant of recognition by the national government he explored Texas, and having the first choice, selected his territory wisely. He claimed a large block of Central Texas from the coast to a distance of several hundred miles that was divided approximately into three equal parts by the Colorado and Brazos rivers. This area was less timbered than the land to the east, and less arid than that to the south or west. It could easily support the corn, cane, or cotton that its likely inhabitants knew how to grow.

The first of the actual settlers, totalling 300 families, arrived aboard a coastal vessel, the *Lively*, before Austin had secured even the first acknowl-

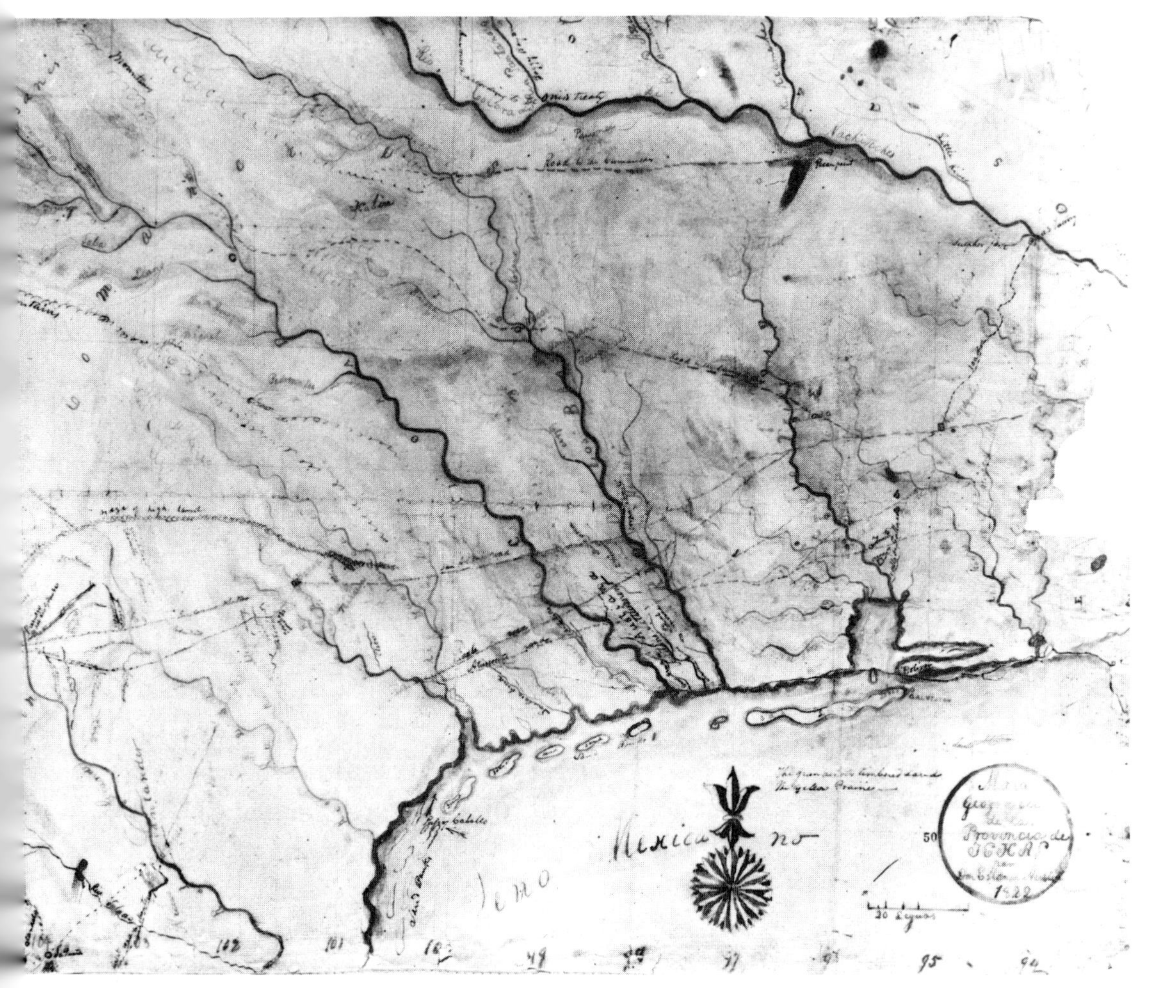

"Mapa geografico de la Provincia de Texas," by Stephen Fuller Austin, depicts the territory of Tejas, or Texas, in 1822. Courtesy, Texas State Archives

edgment of his father's claim. The settler generally agreed to be the first to receive a claim under Austin's sponsorship was Andrew Robinson. Robinson, along with all the rest, had to renounce his citizenship and accept Mexican citizenship; he had to be or become Roman Catholic and raise his children as Catholics; and he had to prove his good character with evidence from his former residence. Assuming that these things were done, colonists could locate their land with Austin's assistance and petition the government agent for the actual transfer.

Austin established his headquarters near the Brazos River at San Felipe de Austin, and there he and the Baron de Bastrop, the government's land alienation agent, gave away one *labor* (177 acres) to farmers and one *sitio* (4,428 acres) to stock raisers. With such terms it is not surprising that most settlers decided that they were stockmen. Additional lands were available for each member of the household including slaves, which went to the head of the household. Austin hoped to obtain fees for his services, but he received little money. What he did receive came from Bastrop, who was entitled to charge a fee of 12.5 cents per acre for his services. Bastrop gave some of his revenue to Austin. Austin did receive significant amounts of lands, upwards of 48,000 acres, but where land was given away free by the government this represented little more than potential wealth. Nevertheless, as long as he lived Austin remained the primary leader of the Texas colonists; even those who owed him money expected him to represent them to the Mexican governments, national and state, and to many, he *was* the local government.

Under the terms of the national constitution and the state colonization law, the settlers were granted a seven-year exemption from taxes, and they were permitted some local government. Recognized communities such as San Felipe were entitled to an *ayuntamiento,* or local council, and might also have an *alcalde,* a combination of administrator and jurist. But the empresario retained much power over his grant area, and it was to this person that the government mostly looked for accountability.

Austin was soon joined by others who were also granted empresarial rights. Perhaps the most significant empresario after Austin was Green Dewitt of Missouri, who received a grant in 1825 to locate 400 families along the Guadalupe River some distance from the coast. Below Dewitt's grant, Juan de León held similar rights in the lower river area. Dewitt laid out the town of Gonzales and his colony did well until Indians frightened many of the settlers, who moved south to de León's grant. Later, following James Kerr, some of them returned to Gonzales and the colony was sustained.

In extreme northeast Texas, so far in that direction that for years many regarded it as part of Arkansas, Arthur G. Wavell and Ben Milam received a grant to colonize 500 families, and in central East Texas, Haden Edwards, the son of a former United States senator from Kentucky who had befriended and helped finance Austin's lobbying activities at Saltillo and Mexico City on behalf of colonization, received a sizeable grant in the Nacogdoches area. His difficulties there, known as the Fredonia Rebellion, forced forfeiture of his empresarial authority in 1827 and his lands were regranted to David G. Burnet, Joseph Vehlein, and Lorenzo de Zavala in separate grants. These three contracted with the Galveston Bay and Texas Land Company to advertise in the United States for settlers.

Another empresario, Sterling Robertson, represented the Nashville Company in Texas. Robertson quarrelled with Austin over his grant. Austin and his secretary, Samuel May Williams, convinced the government that Robertson had not fulfilled his obligations to settle families on the land and Austin received the rights to do so, along with other grants. Robertson traveled to Saltillo to present his case, and he did so successfully, although actual control of the grant remained under litigation for years and continued for generations to breed enmity among descendants and supporters. Robertson even blamed Austin for an attempt on his life while on a journey to Saltillo

Lorenzo de Zavala was a colonist and leader in the move to consolidate early Texas. Courtesy, Barker Texas History Center

to present his case.

In South Texas James Power and James Hewettson received a grant to settle immigrants directly from Europe, as did John McMullen and James McLoin, whose "Irish Colony" was situated south of San Antonio. Because of previous settlement patterns, no empresarial grants were given in the San Antonio area. Some twenty-five grants were made before the Law of April 6, 1830, closed the initial phase of Anglo colonization in Texas under Mexican authority. By that date, Texas had a population of perhaps 20,000 plus their slaves; even so, they outnumbered Spaniards and Mexicans by a five-to-one majority.

Life in the Anglo colonies can only be called harsh. Motives for migration *from* the United States varied with the individual, but included economic, legal, or perhaps marital difficulties; motives for coming *to* Texas generally involved land, a new start, or some other aspect of renewed opportunity. The colonists migrated in various ways, reflecting their circumstances. Some walked, and thus were limited in their resources to what they could carry on their backs; others walked beside wagons laden with furniture, seeds, and provisions, reluctant to displace such valuables with their own weight. Some came by boat, others by horseback. Most were subsistence-level in their wealth; yet some were as wealthy as Jared Groce, who moved his plantation, slaves, and his family in a train of more than fifty wagons. Once in Texas, all faced problems of obtaining a land title, and the probability of difficulties with Indians and the environment. Land was obtained through the empresario and the government agent for the price of a change of citizenship and perhaps of religion; but many became squatters, at least until they were discovered, then they went through the prescribed process, usually on credit. Food brought along soon disappeared to appease appetites raised by the labor of clearing land, plowing, and building shelter.

As in most wilderness settings, food in the form of nuts, berries, wild greens, fish, and various animals was available to those with the industry and the skill to obtain them. Once farms and gardens were established, food was more abundant but still seasonal. Even in the long Texas growing season, broad-leaf vegetables will not grow the year around. So methods of preserving, mostly drying or coating with honey, insulated the settlers from starvation during the winter. Their health was necessarily affected by this uneven diet; vitamin and mineral deficiency was common. So were bad teeth. Mortality from accidents, snake bites, childbirth, and other circumstances remained high because of poor medical services—sometimes increasing when those services were provided by the unskilled. Often the ill were better off under the care and remedies that had been learned from the experience of previous frontiersman and practiced as a folk art.

The colonists needed shelter. Sometimes they began their life in Texas by sleeping under their wagon, if they had one; if not, then they slept with no cover at all until a hut of some kind could be constructed. Most built a log cabin as soon as possible. This form of shelter reflected their American origin, for it had been the basic housing unit of the Eastern frontier. It provided for all family functions within a single room and perhaps a loft. The fireplace provided heat for the household and for cooking, as well as illumination, and the fuel was available to the industrious in abundance. Candles, which were more expensive, or burning pine knots, supplemented the need for light as well. Some furnishings survived the journey to Texas, but others were provided by the settler from materials at hand. All such homemade furnishings could be called functional rather than of any particular style. Tables and chairs could be made from logs, forks or spoons could be carved from cane or wood, and gourds could be fashioned into dippers or other drinking vessels.

The colonists also provided themselves with clothing from available materials. Those who could afford to do so might import their clothing or the cloth from which to make them, but others relied on deer skins for leather garments from shoes to hats and possibly trousers and blouses.

The religious life of the colonists did not approach the government's demand for uniform Catholicism, although there were, of course, some Roman Catholics among the Americans. Most immigrants accepted the spurious conversion process as a necessity, then went on believing or non-

believing as they chose. Some even skirted most of the formalities by becoming "Muldoon Catholics," a euphemism for an insincere conversion named for a Father Michael Muldoon, who winked at many such conversions. Muldoon allegedly did so because of alcoholism, but perhaps he accepted the situation for what it was: a political gesture.

Many Anglos belonged to evangelical Protestant churches. Methodists operated societies in East Texas as early as 1831, following the preachings of an itinerant minister named William Stephenson. By 1832 Samuel Doak McMahon operated a Methodist Sunday school near his home, and the still-extant McMahon's Chapel in Sabine County

testifies to the faith he brought. Baptists were also soon operating, after Joseph E. Bays and Thomas J. Pilgrim arrived to preach their faith's version of the Gospel, and the Presbyterians were not far behind. Schools were still absent, as were banks, and most other institutional services, but worship of many varieties remained available for those early Texans who felt the need for them.

The filibusters opened avenues of interest and immigration for the colonists who followed them to Texas, and by 1830 many regarded Texas as their home. But the decade ahead posed many problems, and their permanent residence in Texas was still in doubt.

IV

Establishing Texas Independence

Hispanic and Anglo-American influences produced a volatile chemistry in

Texas. Their incompatibility and mutual misunderstanding may have been

rooted in the very fabric of their nations' souls, but in time it was clear that

there were many practical conflicts of interest, too.

The Anglos who came to Texas during the 1820s answering the call of

the empresarios knew they were abandoning certain legal protections, and

they generally were willing—at least in principle—to accept new rules about

religion and citizenship for cheap land and fresh starts. But ultimately they

insisted on bringing their "rights" along, too, even if their host government

did not understand.

Mexicans, in the heady period of the founding of their republic, wished

no harm or hardship for their people or their guests in Texas, but they were

This drawing depicts the Polish charge at the Battle of San Jacinto in 1836, the decisive altercation in the Texan push for independence. From Miles, History of South America and Mexico With a Complete View of Texas, H.H. Huntington, Jr., 1838

more inclined to centralism than the Americans in Texas were, meaning that provisions made by the government in Mexico were binding on *everyone.* The Americans rarely noted, and more rarely understood, Mexican political debate, including federalism-versus-centralism during the 1820s. It was enough for them that they had entered Texas under the provisions of the federalist constitution of 1824, which gave much power, including authority over land alienation, to the states. For the Americans, then, the state government of Coahuila y Texas, headquartered in Saltillo, *was* the government, and they expected things to stay that way. This was the kind of government many of them had wanted in the United States, the kind Thomas Jefferson had believed in, the kind that John C. Calhoun would soon champion in the nullification struggle of the early 1830s. So the Americans made sincere efforts to become good Mexican citizens. Stephen F. Austin made the most sincere ef-

fort of all, even signing his name *Estéban.*

Some, of course, could not make the change rapidly enough. These regarded their host nation as lazy. The Spanish, and then the Mexicans, had held Texas for nearly 300 years and still it lay undeveloped. They felt superior to the Mexicans because of their own greater gains in a shorter period of time. They could not have imagined that the Mexicans might regard them as interlopers on their land. For their part, many in Mexico thought of the arrival of the Americans as a calamity for their new nation. Nearly every effort made by the immigrants to gain more freedom of choice was seen as a plot conceived in the United States to take Texas from them. Unfortunately for both sides, few besides Austin tried to hold them together, and several incidents during the 1820s and 1830s combined to complete the rift. The Fredonia Rebellion at Nacogdoches in eastern Texas is a prime example.

Juan Veramendi was mayor of San Antonio between 1824 and 1830 and governor of the state of Coahuila y Texas. This drawing is by Thom Ricks. Courtesy, Institute of Texan Cultures

Haden Edwards, son of a former United States senator from Kentucky, arrived in Mexico at about the same time as did Austin. The two collaborated, largely using Edwards' money, and eventually both obtained extensive empresarial grants in Texas after the state legislature enacted the Colonization Law of 1825. They had helped to draft the law and had even influenced the Constitution of 1824, which turned such matters over to the state. And both were familiar with the requirement that preexisting land grants from the Spanish period that fell within their areas must be honored. Austin's lands had few, if any, such grants, but Edwards received a large area of eastern Texas along the Neches, Angelina, and Sabine rivers where previous grants were probably the most numerous above the Rio Grande and beyond San Antonio.

When Edwards arrived in Nacogdoches to begin operations he really did not know how to go about determining which land was his and which belonged to previous grantees. Unlike the Americans, with their tradition of courthouse registration, many early Spaniards had only held their original grants until they were lost by fire, careless-ness, or neglect. They knew which lands were theirs but they lacked a way to prove it. Edwards knew only that lands that did not belong to others belonged to him, so he posted a notice at the Stone House in Nacogdoches requiring all claimants to come forward with proof of ownership or forfeit their holdings. The unhappy settlers, some of whom were Anglos, protested to the officials in San Antonio. Then more trouble occurred when Edwards supported his son-in-law, Chichester Chaplin, in an election for a new *alcalde* (mayor). The older settlers supported Samuel Norris, and when Edwards proclaimed Chaplin the winner, they again protested to the officials. This time they got results. The governor at San Antonio reversed the election results and ordered Chaplin and Edwards to turn over the office to Norris.

In the spring of 1826 Edwards returned to the United States to recruit settlers. In his absence his brother Benjamin had charge of the colony's affairs. Benjamin Edwards wrote bitter letters to Austin complaining of mistreatment at the hands of the Mexican officials, and Austin cautioned him not to send such letters to the authorities themselves. Austin gave sound advice, but his motive was also self-serving: he did not want other Anglos in Texas to offend the government and thus jeopardize his own colony.

Edwards did not heed Austin's advice, however, and he again posted a notice requiring the older settlers to come forward with proof or lose their land. This time the settlers' complaint to Governor Victor Blanco produced an order that the Edwards grant would be forfeited because of the sarcastic and disrespectful tone of their correspondence and the unlikelihood that the colony's problems could be solved so long as the Edwards brothers were associated with it. Instead of obeying Blanco's orders, Edwards arranged with the Cherokee leaders, John Hunter and Richard Fields, and the newer settlers to proclaim their land independent from Mexico. Flying a red and white flag symbolizing the Anglo-Cherokee alliance, with "Liberty, Justice, and Independence" emblazoned on it along with the signatures of some of its supporters, the Fredonia Rebellion headquartered briefly in the Stone House in Nacogdoches. Haden Edwards returned to lead this new republic, however briefly. The Mexican government dispatched Lieutenant Colonel Matéo Ahumada with 110 infantrymen and twenty dragoons to put down the rebellion. When they reached Austin's colony he joined them with some of his militia. Before they reached Nacogdoches, in December 1826, the rebellion had already collapsed. Edwards' few supporters vanished in the face of advancing Mexican troops, and the Edwards brothers fled to Louisiana. The Cherokee executed Fields and Hunter to purge their own involvement, and Ahumada could report his mission was

accomplished by January 1827.

In spite of this anticlimactic conclusion to still another attempt to declare Texas free, the rebellion was a disturbing incident. Mexican officials were alarmed by the potential for additional trouble from the growing American population, despite the efforts of the Americans under Austin to help put down the rebellion and to demonstrate their loyalty. They also continued to worry about the intentions of the United States toward their territory. And a diplomatic blunder by President John Quincy Adams and his minister Joel Poinsett fed their suspicions.

In 1824 Adams defeated three candidates, including Andrew Jackson of Tennessee, a hero in the West, to become President of the United States. Adams was not popular in the West because of his Eastern background and his failure to win Texas and the Southwest in the 1819 treaty negotiations. To gain reelection, Adams courted Western voters with an assertion that the Adams-Onís line should have been the Brazos River instead of the Sabine River. It was merely a confusion resulting from inexact maps, he claimed.

Adams sent Poinsett to Mexico with an offer to purchase Texas. Adams' sincerity was suspect. He may only have wanted to court Western votes with a show of interest, but Poinsett undertook his mission in earnest. Unfortunately, he blundered from the start. Because he was the first American minister to Mexico, he was widely entertained and often asked to speak. At one gathering he announced the purpose of his mission before the Mexican government had made its decision, apparently in an effort to force them into agreement. Whatever his intention, the government resented his action.

Then Poinsett meddled further in Mexican affairs by organizing a York Rite Masonic body to compete with the Mexicans' version of Masonry, the Scottish Rite, which had been founded earlier. It was not substance but the political differences between the two forms of Masonry that were at issue. Scottish Rite Masonry, because of the secret nature of the organization, had provided a haven for free thinkers and a safe meeting ground for conservatives and Mexican nationalists opposed to federalism. York Rite Masonry had migrated to America with the English colonists, and many early Texas settlers belonged to it; hence, it was associated with them. Poinsett's lodges gave those Mexicans who opposed the conservatives a meeting place as well. He hoped to generate sentiment favoring the sale of part of Texas, but his action only earned him the opposition of stronger Mexican voices and he had to return to the United States without accomplishing his mission. Worse, he helped arouse further opposition to admitting Anglos to Texas.

The Fredonia Rebellion and the Poinsett mission alarmed such anti-Anglo leaders as Manuel Mier y Terán, José María Tornel, and Lucas Alamán, who launched an investigation of conditions in Texas to confirm their fears and prejudices. The investigation revealed that Anglos outnumbered Mexicans by a ten-to-one margin, and that the Mexican population was losing social, economic, and political control. These leaders determined to stop this trend. Alamán persuaded President Vincente Guerrero to proclaim an official end to slavery in Mexico in 1829. Since Texas alone had slaves, this was obviously intended to control the Anglos there. A year later the nationalists secured passage of the Law of April 6, 1830, to quell the crisis in Texas that they imagined to be more acute than it really was. This law closed Texas to further Anglo immigration and restored such matters to national, rather than state, control; it also stopped the importation of slaves and called for

Roundtop House in Victoria, Texas, was built by Placido Benavides in the shape of a fort for protection against Indian raids in about 1830. Courtesy, Institute of Texan Cultures

sending more Mexicans, including convicts, to Texas; it provided for the collection of customs; and it encouraged direct European immigration in Texas to weaken Anglo solidarity.

The Anglos in Texas resented these measures. After meeting good citizenship requirements for admission to Texas, now they were to have convict neighbors; they feared that closure of immigration and slave importation would end their growth and leave them permanently weakened; they resented the customs collection, even though their seven-year exemption had nearly expired; and they resented the insult to their parent nationality. Each side misunderstood the other. So far the vast majority of the Anglos had kept their promise to become Mexican citizens and they resented restrictions and impositions they felt were unwarranted. The troubled Mexican leaders, on the other hand, were trying to prevent a revolt by the Americans that they believed was already under way, at least in Texans' hearts. They only hastened the revolt by their action.

Americans did not understand the rapid changes in Mexican government then taking place. In the early 1830s President Vincente Guerrero suffered defeat by Gomez Pedraza in his bid for reelection, but Guerrero refused to relinquish his office. Anastacio Bustamante expelled Guerrero by force and Pedraza temporarily filled the office he had won by election, but he did so on the basis of military strength. Then Bustamante and Antonio López de Santa Anna fought for supremacy, a struggle eventually won by the latter, and as the Americans watched these contests from Texas they scarcely understood the stakes. Politics in early America were rough-and-tumble, but so far election results had been accepted with whatever grace the losers could muster. They came to know the meaning of military government soon enough.

While Bustamante and Santa Anna fought for supremacy, nationalist forces under the Eastern Province commander, General Manuel Mier y Terán, occupied Texas. Terán placed Colonel José de las Piedras with 350 soldiers at Nacogdoches, Juan (John) Davis Bradburn commanded 150

more at Anahuac, and Colonel Domingo de Ugartechea had 100 or so men at Velasco.

This military "occupation" first met opposition at Anahuac. Perhaps the Americans expected favoritism from Bradburn because he was an American, and perhaps he felt he had to prove himself to higher authorities. The difficulty grew from the same issues dividing all of Mexico: federalism vs. centralism. As a centralist authority, Bradburn sought to enforce the Law of April 6, 1830, in all aspects, while the Americans, supported by state officials, wanted to continue the concept of federalism still guaranteed in the Constitution of 1824. Shortly after Bradburn established his post at Anahuac he ordered all ships calling at ports in Texas to obtain clearance papers from his headquarters and to settle tax accounts with the customs office at Galveston, run by George Fisher, a Serbian exile and now a Mexican government official. Most captains ignored the order if they could do so and they were irritated if they could not. Their irritation was rooted more in resentment of the tax and in inconvenience than in sincere political opposition, but the result was the same.

Then Bradburn confronted the Coahuilan officials directly. Governor José María Letonia reopened land settlement procedures in Texas in empresarial grants already awarded prior to April 6, 1830, and Francisco Madero, his general land commissioner, began to issue land titles. Some of these grants were located in the area of the new settlement of Liberty that he commissioned in a restricted zone too near the coast. Bradburn ordered Madero to cease operations and when that officer refused, he and his surveyor, José María Carbajal, were arrested, and Bradburn annulled Madero's charter for Liberty. Angry Americans who had been counting on Madero for their land now found fault with everything Bradburn did. They even accused him of confiscating their slaves and supplies.

They opposed his every action, especially the arrest of several of their number. The arrests began in the summer of 1832 when a resident of Louisiana, William T. Logan, arrived in Anahuac in pur-

This is the original proclamation by Antonio López de Santa Anna, calling for solidarity against Anglo insurrection. Courtesy, Institute of Texan Cultures

suit of runaway slaves. Bradburn refused to release the slaves because Logan did not have legal evidence of ownership. Logan left to obtain the evidence after hiring William B. Travis as his lawyer, but before he left he assured Bradburn that he would return with sufficient help to obtain his property with or without Bradburn's consent. This unsettled Bradburn and he became easy prey for a harrassing prank Travis played upon him. Late one night Travis handed a sentry a note that claimed Logan had returned with a large force. After reading the note Bradburn turned out his garrison for a futile search for Logan. Embarrassed, and realizing he had been tricked, Bradburn ordered Travis' arrest.

When the soldiers arrived for Travis, they had to arrest his partner, Patrick Jack, because of his strenuous protest. Jack's brother, William, hastened to San Felipe for help, and finding Austin absent, he had little trouble in rounding up a force to go to Anahuac to free the captives. The would-be rescuers captured a Mexican patrol and offered a hostage trade, but Bradburn tricked them into releasing their men first, then refused to release Travis and Jack. The Americans withdrew to a campsite on Turtle Bayou where they pledged their continued support to the federalist constitution and their opposition to Bradburn and the centralists in the Turtle Bayou Resolutions.

John Austin was dispatched to Brazoria to obtain a cannon for an assault on Bradburn's position. Further violence was prevented by the arrival of Piedras from Nacogdoches. Although he sided with Bradburn in his heart, prudence told him to act otherwise. He removed Bradburn from command and ordered Travis and Jack released to civilian authorities, who later set them free.

When Piedras returned to Nacogdoches he determined to avoid such trouble for himself by ordering all the men in his district to bring their guns to Nacogdoches for surrender. They brought them to town, but not to turn them in. The men of the Ayish Bayou country arrived on the eastern edge of town at the home of Adolphus Sterne in late July. Sterne led them via Lanana Creek to a position north and west of the Stone House where the Mexican soldiers lived, and of Piedras' headquarters at the Cartel several hundred yards away. The Americans attacked late in the evening of July 30, 1832. Piedras and his men escaped during the night, but they were caught the next day at the Angelina River and another fight occurred. Piedras surrendered, and his command was escorted to San Antonio.

The final disturbance of 1832 occurred when John Austin brought the cannon intended for use

José Antonio Mexia was Santa Anna's lieutenant in the north of Mexico in 1832. From Frost, Pictorial History of Mexico and the Mexican War, *Harrold and Murray, 1848*

at Anahuac past Ugartechea's position at Velasco. Several men on both sides were killed, and Ugartechea was forced to leave for Matamoros. The result of these actions was the removal of all Mexican forces from Texas by the end of the summer of 1832.

Mexican politics provided the next stimulus for activity in Texas. Santa Anna, a true centralist, was then posing as a states' righter in his quest for absolute power. His lieutenant in the north, José Antonio Mexia, ceased a campaign against the centralist leader José Mariana Guerra long enough to come to Texas to investigate the disturbances of 1832. Stephen Austin greeted Mexia warmly, and the Mexican leader received a welcoming party in his honor at Brazoria. A true states' righter, Mexia accepted their pledges of loyalty to the de-

centralized form of government they thought Santa Anna desired. So he accepted the Americans at their word and returned to the fight in Mexico.

Mexia, like most Texans, was misled by Santa Anna. At the time Santa Anna seemed to be their principal hope. A national hero after the 1829 invasion at Tampico, the last attempt on the part of the Spanish to reclaim Mexico, he always appeared one jump ahead of trends in Mexican politics. He could pose as a states' righter, a nationalist, a liberal, a conservative, or whatever would advance him toward his ultimate goal: absolute power in Mexico. At the moment it suited his purpose to support the states' rights position against the centralist Bustamante, and since this suited the Texans just fine, they found it easy to pledge support to Santa Anna, to Mexia, or anyone else. But things would change.

In 1833 Santa Anna was elected Mexico's president, with Valantin Gómez Farías, a genuine reformer, as vice president. Santa Anna took temporary leave of his office, allowing Farías to attempt sweeping reforms of Mexico's trinity of conservatism; the army, the church, and the land-owning system. Santa Anna knew that too much change would be resisted, so he allowed Farías to attempt a social revolution and at the proper moment he would return and lead what amounted to a counterrevolution against his own government. But this time, he would consolidate all power unto himself.

Without knowing Santa Anna's plans, the Texans helped provide an opportunity to implement them. Feeling uneasy after the disturbances earlier in 1832, and desiring some change in their relationship with the state and national governments, on August 22 the *ayuntamiento* of San Felipe sent out a call to the districts to elect delegates to a convention. Fifty-seven delegates came and elected Austin to preside. They pledged their loyalty to the government and to its federalist constitution, and they asked for repeal of the Law of April 6, 1830. They also petitioned for further exemption from taxes, reopening land grants to immigrants, providing for schools and postal services, and jury trials in Texas, and most importantly, for separation from Coahuila as a state of the Mexican republic in their own right.

When the political chief at San Antonio received their petition, he sternly returned it with the reminder that they lacked authority to hold such a meeting. To him their convention may have represented only a lack of respect for their status, but to some Mexican leaders the Texans' action resembled the *grito,* or first cry, of a now-familiar pattern of revolution. To the Texans their petition was an orderly, reasonable request, conducted in a manner keeping with their Anglo heritage. So they tried again the following year, and in the meantime they formed a Central Committee of Safety and Correspondence to keep the districts informed of developments. The Committee issued a call for a new convention in January 1833 and again it met at San Felipe, but this time Austin did not preside. Instead the delegates selected the more militant William H. Wharton as their president, and they renewed their petition of the previous year for easing immigration restrictions, suspension of the customs, and separation from Coahuila. This time they also added a proposed constitution so the Mexican authorities would understand their peaceful intentions. They asked Austin to deliver the petition, and he was their best choice. Of all Texans, he clearly had the best diplomatic skills for the job. To the Americans, they were merely following the pattern to statehood they had learned in the United States. Whenever the people of a territory felt themselves ready for statehood, they wrote a constitution and petitioned the American Congress. But to many Mexicans the addition of the proposed constitution to the petition resembled the *pronunciamento,* or second stage, of a Latin revolution.

Austin's arrival in Mexico City on July 18 found Farías still in charge of Mexican affairs. Farías had his hands full with the hostile reaction to his liberal reforms, and he had little time for Austin. Their earlier meetings were brief and inconclusive, despite Austin's success in enlisting the aid of such liberal reformers as Lorenzo de Zavala. Finally Austin's patience wore thin, and in candor he told Farías that Mexico might as well grant Texas separate statehood since they were already operating that way.

This illustration depicts the militia uniforms authorized in 1834 by the state of Coahuila y Texas. Courtesy, Barker Texas History Center

Farías took Austin's statement as a threat. In a pique after the meeting, Austin wrote to the *ayuntamiento* at San Antonio that it should begin to implement the plan of separate statehood, apparently in the belief that this would somehow convince Farías. Instead they sent Austin's letter to authorities in Mexico City.

As Austin prepared to leave for Texas, Santa Anna returned to his capital and reclaimed power. He met with Austin and the two seemed to come to a friendly agreement. Santa Anna agreed to the restoration of Anglo immigration and even accepted the request for jury trials. But he claimed that the Texans did not have sufficient population for separate statehood. At last Austin heard an argument he could accept, because the United States also had a minimum population requirement. Santa Anna also told Austin that soon he planned to send more soldiers to help with Indian defense. Evidently Austin missed the point of this pledge because of Santa Anna's conciliatory manner. He left Mexico City in early December and reached Saltillo on January 3, 1834. He stopped by the state offices to pay a courtesy call and found himself under arrest. The soldiers brought Austin back to Mexico City, where he was held at the Prison of the Inquisition without being brought to trial.

When the Texans learned of Austin's arrest they were stunned, but quiet, fearing that protest might cause him harm. Things became so inactive, in fact, that within a few months Austin began to feel as if they had forgotten him. When Peter Grayson and Spencer Jack learned this, they hastened to Mexico City with funds and petitions ready to bribe or beg Austin out of jail. They succeeded in gaining his release on Christmas Day, 1835, but he had to remain in Mexico City. Austin finally received permission to return to Texas during the following summer under the provisions of general amnesty. Without ever being charged with a specific crime, he had spent eighteen months under arrest.

During much of this time things seemed to improve in Texas. The lifting of immigration barriers encouraged those already in Texas, and the creation of new administrative departments headquartered at Nacogdoches, San Felipe, and San Antonio, coupled with recognition of English as an official language, provided a liberalizing image to the circumstances. Religious regularity seemed more relaxed, judicial procedures were revised, and Texas even received three seats in the twelve-member state congress. Most Texans remained uninvolved anyway, busy with chores or isolated in the wilderness, and some were even hostile to complainers or malcontents whom they feared would disturb the tranquility.

The Texans managed to remain aloof from an argument over the location of the state capital. Saltillo, the traditional capital, was challenged by states' righters who wanted to move the capital while the central government advocated leaving it where it was. General Martín Perfecto de Cós, Santa Anna's brother-in-law and military commander in the northern provinces, arrested Governor Augustín Viesca and replaced him with Rafael Eca y Músquiz. Músquiz then established his headquarters at Saltillo.

Generally, Texans did not care where the capital was located. They wanted a separate capital anyway, one located nearer to their own settlements. But they did not resent the arbitrary use of power to determine the issue. Then, in 1835, the issue of centralism came home to them. Captain Antonio Tenorio arrived in Anahuac and renewed the collection of customs, and again, as in 1832, clashes occurred. One involved local merchants Andrew Briscoe and Dewitt C. Harris, who were arrested after they refused to allow the search of a box containing rocks for ballast on a ship. It was foolish not to cooperate, and of course Tenorio had to force the issue. Unfortunately, someone walked up on the scene and alarmed the Mexican soldiers, who began firing. When Cós learned of this incident he ordered Tenorio to hold firm and to be prepared to use sufficient force to do his duty. And he promised reinforcements. The courier bearing Cós' message reached San Felipe, where a body of men captured him and read his dispatches. They learned of Viesca's arrest and the

DECLARATION
OF THE PEOPLE OF TEXAS,
In General Convention assembled.

Whereas, General Antonio Lopez de Santa Ana, and other military chieftains, have, by force of arms, overthrown the Federal Institutions of Mexico, and dissolved the social compact which existed between Texas and the other members of the Mexican Confederacy; now the good People of Texas, availing themselves of their natural rights,

SOLEMNLY DECLARE,

1st. That they have taken up arms in defence of their *rights* and *liberties,* which are threatened by the encroachments of *military despots,* and in defence of the republican principles of the Federal Constitution of Mexico, of 1824.

2d. That Texas is no longer morally or civilly bound by the Compact of Union; yet, stimulated by the generosity and sympathy common to a free people, they offer their support and assistance to such of the members of the Mexican Confederacy, as will take up arms against military despotism.

3d. That they do not acknowledge that the present authorities of the *nominal* Mexican Republic have the right to govern within the limits of Texas.

4th. That they will not cease to carry on war against the said authorities, whilst their troops are within the limits of Texas.

5th. That they hold it to be their right, during the disorganization of the Federal System, and the reign of despotism, to withdraw from the Union, to establish an independant government, or to adopt such measures as they may deem best calculated to protect their rights and liberties; but that they will continue faithful to the Mexican government, so long as that nation is governed by the Constitution and laws that were formed for the government of the Political Association.

6th. That Texas is responsible for the expenses of her armies, now in the field.

7th. That the public faith of Texas is pledged for the payment of any debts contracted by her agents.

8th. That she will reward by donations in land, all who volunteer their services in her present struggle, and receive them as citizens.

THESE DECLARATIONS we solemnly avow to the world, and call God to witness their truth and sincerity, and invoke defeat and disgrace upon our heads, should we prove guilty of duplicity.

B. T. ARCHER, *President.*

Municipality of Austin.
THOMAS BARNETT,
WYLY MARTIN,
RANDALL JONES,
WM. MENIFEE,
JESSE BURNAM.

Municipality of Matagorda.
R. R. ROYALL,
CHARLES WILSON.

Municipality of Washington.
ASA MITCHELL,
PHILIP COE,
ELIJAH COLLARD,
JESSE GRIMES,
A. HOXIE.

Municipality of Mina.
J. S. LESTER,
D. C. BARRETT,
R. M. WILLIAMSON.

Municipality of Columbia.
HENRY SMITH,
EDWIN WALLER,
J. S. D. BYROM,
JOHN A. WHARTON,
W. D. C. HALL.

Municipality of Harrisburgh.
LORENZO LE ZAVALA,
WM. P. HARRIS,
C. C. DYER,
MERIWETHER W. SMITH,
JOHN W. MOORE,
D. B. MACOMB.

November 7, 1835.

Municipality of Gonzales.
J. D. CLEMENS,
BENJAMIN FUQUA,
JAMES HODGES,
WILLIAM ARRINGTON,
WILLIAM S. FISHER,
G. W. DAVIS.

Municipality of Viesca.
S. T. ALLEN,
A. G. PERRY,
J. G. W. PIERSON,
ALEXANDER THOMPSON,
J. W. PARKER.

Municipality of Nacogdoches.
SAMUEL HOUSTON,
DANIEL PARKER,
JAMES W. ROBERTSON,
WILLIAM WHITAKER.

Municipality of Bevil.
JOHN BEVIL,
S. H. EVERETT,
WYATT HANKS.

Municipality of San Augustin.
A. HOUSTON,
WM. N. SIGLER,
A. E. C. JOHNSON,
A. HORTON,
MARTIN PALMER,
HENRY AUGUSTIN,
A. G. KELLOGG.

Municipality of Liberty.
J. B. WOODS,
A. B. HARDIN,
HENRY MILLARD,
C. WEST.

P. B. DEXTER, *Secretary.*

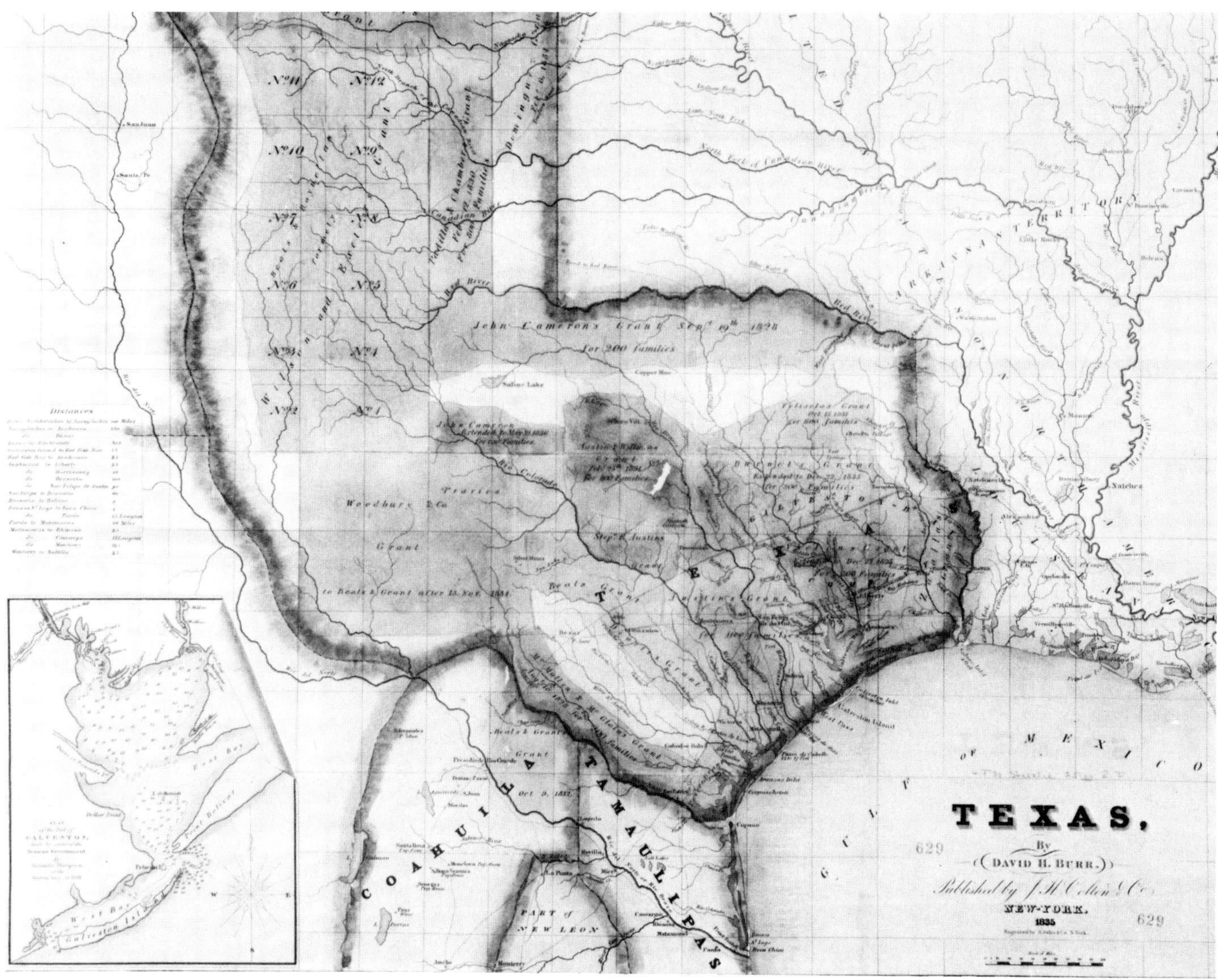

This map of 1834 Texas was drawn by David H. Burr. The shaded area marking Texas from neighboring Mexico and "Arkansas Territory," delineates the land grants in effect at that time. With so much territory at stake, it is no wonder that both sides of the Texas Revolution fought so hard. Courtesy, Texas State Archives

promise of more soldiers coming to Texas. As the news spread through the Anglo population, small groups began to meet to plot resistance. One, led by J.B. Miller, political chief of the Brazos department, determined to send William B. Travis and twenty-five men to Anahuac to drive Tenorio away.

Travis' group left from Anahuac by barge while he called on David G. Burnet at Harrisburg to inform him of their mission. The group announced their arrival at Anahuac while still aboard their barge by firing their weapons. Anahuac's citizens came down to the landing to learn the cause, and most of them were astonished and offended when they saw Travis. They knew no good would come to their town from his return. Travis demanded an immediate surrender from Tenorio, who naturally refused. But most of Tenorio's men left their encampment in the unfinished Fort Anahuac for the safety of nearby woods. Later that evening Travis convinced Tenorio to surrender. The next day he sent his captives under guard to Brazoria. When the group arrived in time for a Fourth of July party, the guards were disappointed when the Mexican soldiers were received as honored guests while they were snubbed. Most people in Texas reacted this way to the incident, fearing that Travis' action would only bring down the wrath of the Mexican military upon them. Those espousing this sentiment, called the Peace Party, condemned Travis to the point that he took out newspaper advertisements asking the people to withhold judgment until they had heard his explanation.

In one sense the people were correct in assuming that this second action at Anahuac would produce a harsh reaction. Their apologies to Cós fetched only his demand for the surrender of Travis and the other "outlaws" for military trial. He also demanded that they produce Lorenzo de Zavala, who had come to Texas after Santa Anna reassumed power in Mexico. The Texans might condemn Travis, even apologize for him, but they would not surrender him. Their committees of correspondence exchanged rumors of Cós' threat to bring iron hobbles for every troublesome Texan and rumors of invasions. And then, finally, Stephen F. Austin came home. Holding war or peace in his grasp, he told a meeting of the Committee of Public Safety at San Felipe that "war is our only resource."

Still undecided, but with the scales tipping in the direction of armed resistance, the Committee of Public Safety decided to issue a call for a "Consultation" of all Texans or their delegates to determine a course of action. Calls for this meeting actually began at Bastrop (Mina), but soon every community was doing the same. After a meeting at Columbia, the date of October 15 and a meeting site at San Felipe was agreed upon. Before that meeting occurred, an armed clash at Gonzales had already determined the outcome.

It began over a six-pound cannon left by empre-sario Green Dewitt. Colonel Ugartechea, military commander at San Antonio, dispatched a patrol to Gonzales to confiscate the cannon. Andrew Ponton, *alcalde* of Gonzales, refused the soldiers' request because they lacked written orders. Meanwhile, others buried the cannon to prevent its discovery. News of the incident spread while the patrol returned to San Antonio for direct, written orders. More than 160 Americans hastened to Gonzales. They elected Colonel John Moore as their leader and dug up the cannon and prepared it to defend itself. Lieutenant Francisco Castañeda and 100 Mexican soldiers brought back Ugartechea's emphatic written order for the surrender of the cannon. They arrived at the Guadalupe River on September 29, but found no boats on their side of the river in which to cross, and armed Americans on the other side of the river. Then, four days later, Moore's men crossed the river themselves. They had their cannon loaded and they displayed a crude flag with a picture of a cannon drawn upon it with the words "COME AND TAKE IT" painted upon the flag. The Americans fired at the Mexican position, and the latter returned to San Antonio because their orders had not authorized the use of force. Captain George M. Collinsworth, on his way to help at Gonzales, learned that Cós, who had recently arrived in Texas to assume personal command, had vacated Goliad to move to San Antonio. Collinsworth altered his route to capture Goliad.

More men gathered at Gonzales after the crisis had passed, but they had nothing to do. It required but a suggestion to start them for San Antonio and a confrontation with Cós. Austin arrived at Gonzales on October 12, and although he lacked military training or experience, he agreed to become their "general" for an assault on San Antonio.

Cós' soldiers met the advance at Mission Concepción with an attack upon men commanded by James Bowie and James W. Fannin. After that action the Mexican troops retreated into town and the Americans partially surrounded the city in an attempt to lay siege to it. Actually, they did not

THE FATHER OF TEXAS

Some regard Stephen Fuller Austin as the greatest proprietor in North American history. With due respect to William Penn and Lord Calvert, it is difficult to overemphasize the significance of Austin in the founding of the Anglo community in Texas.

Austin was born on November 3, 1793, in Virginia where his father, Moses Austin, owned a lead mining business. A native of Connecticut and a business veteran in Philadelphia, Moses Austin moved to western Virginia after the development of lead mining fields in the area. Later he moved his family beyond the United States frontier to Missouri while it was part of Spanish territory. He founded the community of Potosi, in present-day Washington County, and again entered the lead mining business. As he prospered he also added a mercantile establishment to his holdings; eventually he helped found the Bank of St. Louis. Stephen Austin received his education in Connecticut and also at the Transylvania University in Kentucky. When he returned to Missouri in 1810, seven years after the transfer of the Louisiana Territory to the United States, Austin worked in his father's mercantile store and eventually assumed full responsibility for the family's lead mining interests. He became adjutant in the local militia and won election to the territorial legislature where he strongly supported economic development.

During the Panic of 1819 the Bank of St. Louis failed. This loss, combined with other financial reversals, depleted the Austin family's fortune. The family had to start over again, as they had in the raw territory years before. Austin moved to Arkansas where he was appointed a federal judge, then journeyed on to New Orleans to read law.

Meanwhile, Moses Austin traveled to San Antonio. In Missouri the Spanish had permitted a man named William Morgan to encourage American settlement west of the Mississippi River. He was called an empresario, and his settlers were given generous land grants in return for becoming Spanish citizens and Roman Catholics. Moses Austin wanted to become an empresario in Texas as a way of regaining his prosperity. After encountering opposition at first, he eventually received permission from the Spanish government to bring settlers into Texas, but died before he could implement his plan.

Because it was his father's final dream, Austin traveled to San Antonio to confirm the government's permission to colonize Texas. Governor Antonio María Martinez confirmed Austin's inheritance of his father's grant. He was permitted to give each settler 640 acres with an additional 320 acres for his wife and each child. Austin was responsible for the colonists' conduct; Martinez urged him to admit only persons of industry and good repute. Austin returned to Louisiana to advertise for settlers, and the first group arrived in Texas in December 1821.

Unfortunately, Austin's title to the land was voided when the first Mexican government replaced the Spanish regime. They owed him nothing and were suspicious of his dealings with the Spanish. Austin traveled to Mexico City to deal personally with the new republican regime and with two additional governments before he finally received permission from the congress in 1823 to introduce legal Anglo settlement in Texas. Later such matters were transferred to the state government of Coahuila y Texas, and Austin thereafter had to deal with that government.

The new arrangement was in Austin's favor. He was authorized to award a league and a *labor* of land (4,605 acres) to each settler in return for a fee of 12.5 cents per acre. He could settle as many as 300 families on his grant, which was located in South-Central Texas between and on either side of the Colorado and Brazos rivers. Later Austin obtained additional grants under the colonization law of 1825.

The law also permitted additional empresarios to obtain grants, and ultimately as many as thirty men received permission to introduce settlers into Texas. But Austin remained the foremost leader of all Anglos in Texas. He earnestly worked to Mexicanize himself, and acted as the fulcrum of a lever between the Mexican officials and the Anglo settlers in Texas. He tried to promote understanding and acceptance between the two groups. He had excellent political skills and understood the various groups he came into contact with, whether they were Mexican, Anglos, or nationals of other countries. Although not ideological, he was sincere. He did not want to take Texas away from Mexico. Until the political events of the 1830s forced him to choose between Mexican and Anglo interests, he steadfastly worked to convince the colonists to become good Mexican citizens.

In the early phases of the Texas Revolution, Austin advised caution and compliance with Mexican law. He presided over an 1832 convention that attempted to capitalize on the nationalist-states' rights dispute to achieve separate statehood within the Mexican republic. He carried a similar request from a convention in 1833, but after quarrelling with Acting President Valentín Gomez-Farías, Austin was arrested and detained in a Mexican prison for eighteen months.

During this period Austin despaired that the Texans had forgotten him. They had not: for most of Austin's imprisonment those who advocated resistance to Mexico were held in check by others who feared for his safety. When he was released in the summer of 1835 on a general amnesty, never having been charged or tried for any crime, Austin returned to Texas a genuine revolutionary. He announced at Brazoria that "War is our only resource," and later accepted a military command that laid siege to San Antonio in the fall of that year.

When a Consultation of Texans asked Austin to go to the United States to raise men and money for the revolution he answered the call. Branch T. Archer, William Wharton, and Austin worked during the remainder of the revolution to arouse support in the United States. They were successful among private citizens but not with the government.

Following the successful revolution Austin returned to Texas and in 1835 ran for president of the new Republic of Texas. He was defeated by military hero Sam Houston, but accepted appointment as Houston's secretary of state. He served only about a year. He died from pneumonia on December 27, 1836, at the age of forty-three.

The role Austin played in Texas is inestimable. His diplomacy made his father's dream of a colony in Texas come true. For his contributions he is appropriately remembered as the Father of Texas.

Stephen F. Austin is known as the Father of Texas. Courtesy, Barker Texas History Center

James Bowie, the legendary craftsman of the deadly Bowie knife, died defending the Alamo on March 6, 1836. Courtesy, Barker Texas History Center

know what to do. Austin remained with the army, as did many other elected delegates, even after the Consultation began. He finally left in late November at the Consultation's request to become a representative to the United States to ask for aid. Before he left, however, the Grass Fight, a raid on a foraging expedition the Americans mistook for a paymaster's train, occurred.

Additional men joined the army before San Antonio, but many also drifted away to return to their farms. Gradually the nature of the army began to change. Many of the newcomers were recent arrivals, ready for action. Edward Burleson replaced Austin in command, but he seemed indecisive. Worried about the departure of of so many dependable pioneer Texans and the hot-headed nature of their replacements, he decided to go into winter quarters. Before the men could leave, however, a captured Mexican courier revealed that the Mexicans were near surrender. This was far from the truth, but it encouraged the Texans to answer Ben Milam's challenge, "Who will go into San Antonio with Old Ben Milam?" He assaulted the city with 300 men on December 5 while Burleson held the remainder of the Texan force in reserve. Milam was killed during the five-day, house-to-house battle, and Francis W. Johnson succeeded him in command. On December 9 Cós surrendered all weapons and supplies, agreeing to leave and never return to Texas.

While these events occurred, other Texans attempted to create political structure for their movement. Even before the Consultation met, the Committee of Public Safety at San Felipe commissioned a Permanent Council with R.R. Royal of Matagorda as president. Although it only lasted three weeks, the Permanent Council raised volunteers and supplies, commissioned privateers, tried to establish a postal system, and sent Thomas McKinney to the United States to recruit supplies, money, and men.

The Permanent Council passed from existence when the Consultation finally met on November 3 at San Felipe. Fifty-five delegates representing twelve communities named Branch T. Archer as president. The most significant debate revolved around the issue of independence, with many favoring it immediately and just as many wanting to work for separate statehood and reform within the Mexican union. The latter position prevailed, at least temporarily. They did agree to fight against the current central government and to meet again the following March 1 to reassess their position. The Consultation also asked Archer, Wharton, and Austin to seek financial aid and volunteers in the United States, and they authorized an army and asked Sam Houston to serve as its commander. Henry Smith and James Robinson were named governor and lieutenant governor to administer the Consultation's affairs with an appointed Council until the full body met again. The arrangement never worked, but it survived. Smith quarreled with his council and Robinson and became ineffective. And even Houston's early leadership was blocked. A scheme to take Matamoros best illustrates this governmental paralysis.

Soon after the Texans' victory at San Antonio, Dr. James Grant arrived there to convince the Texans to march on Matamoros to oppose Mexican forces there. He wanted them to help regain his confiscated lands, but he promised the men the booty of Matamoros for their help. Johnson at first refused, then became swept up in the scheme. The Council authorized the campaign if Colonel James Fannin would lead troops he commanded at Goliad in the action. At one time even James Bowie was proposed as a leader. Houston opposed the scheme completely. He wanted all Texan troops under his command, and he opposed any expedition into Mexico that might bring more soldiers north. Johnson and Grant took nearly all the supplies in San Antonio and traveled as far as San Patricio before they stalled. With all these commanders refusing to accept his leadership, Houston left for East Texas where he, Adolphus Sterne, and William Goynes negotiated a treaty of peace with the Cherokee Indians. This at least kept the Indians neutral during the remaining months of the revolution.

These events in Texas convinced Santa Anna

that the time had come to assert his authority there. He had already surprised other resistance to his centralist control, and now he could turn his attention to Texas. The attack at San Antonio and the Matamoros expedition spurred him into action. He dispatched General José Urrea with 1,500 cavalrymen to Matamoros to hold that city, then move into Texas to capture Refugio and Goliad. Then, on February 16, 1836, he accompanied General Joaquín Ramirez y Sesma's command of approximately 6,000 men as they crossed the Rio Grande bound for San Antonio to redeem the national insult of Cós' surrender there. He promised the nation that he would rid Mexico of all Americans.

The few Texans left in San Antonio, about thirty men under the command of Colonel James C. Neill, obviously were not prepared to face such an army. Even when James Bowie arrived on January 17 with 100 volunteers, or later in the month when William B. Travis showed up with about thirty regulars, the Texans were grossly outnumbered and under-supplied. Shortly after Travis arrived on January 30, he found himself in command at San Antonio when Neill left on personal leave, and he was soon embroiled in a command dispute with Bowie. Bowie's volunteers voted to continue to follow him, not Travis. In the end the two worked out a joint command arrangement, which lasted until Bowie became incapacitated with a serious illness.

With the help of engineer Green B. Jamison, Travis' men readied their fortress as best they could. They repaired the walls of the old mission San Antonio de Velaro, known as the Alamo, built palisades and cannon emplacements, and got supplies within the walls. Travis sent dispatches to Fannin and Johnson asking them to come to San Antonio to join him. And he waited. Only David Crockett and a few volunteers from the United States arrived.

Dr. John Sutherland and John W. Smith first saw Santa Anna's advance when he arrived on February 23. Travis gathered all his men within

Left: *Gregorio Esparza and his young son Enrique are depicted by Thom Ricks at a cannon during the Battle of the Alamo. The Esparza family sought refuge at the Alamo upon hearing of Santa Anna's approach. Courtesy, Institute of Texan Cultures*

Facing page: *This 1925 view of the Alamo shows the barren plains surrounding the fort, and exposes its great vulnerability. Courtesy, Barker Texas History Center*

the Alamo's protection, including some Mexicans, or Tejanos, and sent couriers to Gonzales to request help and to spread the word. He also sent another request to Fannin. On the following day Travis' letter to "all Americans in the world" left the Alamo. In the most enduring literature of the Texas Revolution, Travis promised to fight until death. His plea immediately brought the help of the entire adult male population of Gonzales, thirty-five men; eventually it brought so many men from the United States that the Americans would have won had the battle taken place a few days later.

The Gonzales company raised the number of the Alamo's defenders to approximately 185. They endured a twelve-day siege, cannon bombardments, musical serenades to disturb their rest—especially the dreaded *duegello,* the bugle call signifying that no prisoners would be taken—and on March 6 Santa Anna finally attacked. Wave after wave of assault troops used scaling ladders to get over the Alamo's walls. Furious hand-to-hand fighting

eventually killed all of the Americans except Suzanna Dickinson (wife of artillerist Almeron Dickinson), her daughter, Travis' slave, Joe, and seven other men, including David Crockett, who surrendered when continued fighting would have been futile. The seven men were then executed. Travis died early in the assault, a bullet through his head. Bowie died in his sickbed.

Santa Anna had the bodies of the Texans burned and sent Suzanna Dickinson with her daughter down the road to Gonzales to spread the word of his victory. Meanwhile, Fannin was captured at Goliad by General Urrea, after first making an attempt to go to the relief of the Alamo. When Urrea arrived Fannin and his men were caught in the open, so he surrendered. Fannin and most of his men were executed. From now on the Texans had their battle cry: "Remember the Alamo! Remember Goliad!"

The quarreling between Smith and the Council ceased with the reconvening of the Consultation of March 1 at Washington-on-the-Brazos. The

Left: *This portrait of David Crockett was said by Crockett himself to be the only "correct likeness" of him. Crockett was executed by Santa Anna after the fall of the Alamo. Courtesy, Barker Texas History Center*

Facing page: *The Texas Declaration of Independence stated the motives and rules for the drive for freedom from Mexico. Courtesy, Texas State Archives*

next day that body declared Texas independent, and within two weeks it wrote a constitution for the new republic. David G. Burnet was named interim president with Lorenzo de Zavala to serve as vice president, and Sam Houston again was named commander-in-chief of the army. Houston left for Gonzales on March 11. He found 374 men there, as usual arriving after the crisis and lacking leadership. This he provided. He dispatched Erastus "Deaf" Smith down the San Antonio road to gather information, and Smith encountered Suzanna Dickinson. He brought her and the grim news of the Alamo's fall back to Gonzales.

Houston decided to burn Gonzales and retreat to the Colorado River to make a stand. Arriving at Burnham's Ferry just ahead of Santa Anna's scouts, he learned of Fannin's fate at Goliad. He decided to move on eastward to the Brazos River. This frightened the civilians, who also had learned of the defeat at San Antonio and at Goliad, into a wild scramble for safety known as the Runaway Scrape. Burnet reflected their anxiety in letters to Houston demanding that he stop and fight.

Houston trained his men at the Groce plantation on the Brazos River for almost two weeks, then prepared to move on eastward. Santa Anna dispatched Urrea in the same direction along the

Texas Declaration of Independence

SURVIVORS OF THE ALAMO

"Thermoplyae had her messenger of defeat; the Alamo had none." This romantic claim ignores Moses Rose, a Napoleonic veteran who decided not to remain within the Alamo's walls and await the final assault of Santa Anna's attackers. Rose was the original teller of the tale that William B. Travis drew a line in the dirt with his sabre and invited all who would fight to the death to cross over. Only Rose, according to his own story, did not cross over; instead he climbed over the wall under the cover of night and made his way to the Zuber farm.

Torn by thorns and exhausted, Rose was nursed back to health while at the farm. He told the family the "inside" story of the Alamo and of the famous sabre-drawn line. The Zuber's son Frederick, when he returned from the San Jacinto campaign, heard Rose's account and wrote a story about it for publication in the 1857 *Texas Almanac.* Most historians claim that there is no real evidence to prove Rose's story, which is a conglomeration of hearsay and second-hand evidence.

But even without Rose the Alamo would have had a messenger. She was Suzanna Dickenson, wife of Captain Almaron Dickenson, artillery commander in the Alamo. A native of Tennessee, Suzanna was only fourteen years old when Almaron Dickenson, originally from Pennsylvania, settled near her home. Within a year they were married, although Dickenson had intended to wed someone else and Suzanna was supposed to be the bridesmaid in the wedding.

After he and Suzanna eloped, they migrated to Texas in 1835. They settled at Gonzales after obtaining a headright in Green Dewitt's colony. Dickenson was a blacksmith, but soon became a soldier in the army of the revolution. He joined the volunteers in San Antonio and brought his wife and young daughter Angelina there to live with the family of Ramón Musquíz, a merchant who opposed Santa Anna. Suzanna was only eighteen years old when the showdown at the Alamo occurred.

When the Mexican army arrived Travis ordered all available men into the Alamo compound. Dickenson hurried to the Musquíz hacienda, put his wife and daughter on his horse, and brought them to the Alamo as well.

The siege of the Alamo lasted from February 23 until the early morning of March 6, 1836. Suzanna cooked and nursed the ill and wounded while the men prepared for the major attack. The final assault, when it came, was a living nightmare.

In the midst of smoke and flying bullets, sixteen-year-old Balba Fuqua from Gonzales ran to Suzanna, trying to tell her something; she could not understand him because his jaw was shattered. Later, Dickenson ran to her, exclaiming, "Great God, Sue, the Mexicans are inside the walls!" He kissed her good-bye and said, "If they spare you, save our child." She never saw him alive again. Near the end of the action Jacob Walker, a gunner in her husband's crew, ran into the room where she was hiding. Four enemy soldiers ran in after him, shot him, then lifted his body on their bayonets.

Suzanna fled the room with her baby to find her husband. She found his body and was wounded in her leg. After being treated in the Musquíz hacienda she had a brief audience with Santa Anna. Five days later Suzanna was given a horse and told to carry the news of the Alamo as warning of what awaited the rest of Texas. Accompanied by Travis' slave Ben, Suzanna and Angelina started down the Gonzales road. Before they reached the small town they met Sam Houston's scout, Erastus "Deaf" Smith, who brought her and her grim tale to the widows of Gonzales and to the 374 men who had assembled there. Every household in the small town had lost a relative in the tragedy.

Suzanna Dickenson's life after the Alamo did not get any brighter. Eighteen years old, a widow, and lacking education—she could neither read nor write—she moved to Houston where she met Pamela Mann, operator of the Mansion House. Suzanna lived in the Mansion House where Mann allegedly introduced her to the profession of prostitution. In late November 1837 Suzanna married John Williams, a cruel drunk; they were divorced in March 1838 after he beat her, causing her to have a miscarriage.

In December 1838 she married Francis P. Herring, a Houston water carrier, who died in September 1843. Again destitute, Suzanna returned to prostitution. She rented a boardinghouse in Houston and operated it herself even after marrying a man named Peter Bellows. She eventually began to attend church and tried to change her way of life. Despite the minister's efforts in her behalf the hostility of other church members drove her away. In June 1857 Bellows divorced her, accusing her of "sleeping with strange men."

After this divorce Suzanna moved to New Orleans where she married John W. Hannag. Hannag later ran a photography shop in Austin and Suzanna again began regular attendance at church. She also gave frequent testimony before the Board of Land Commissioners so they could award land to the families of the Alamo's defenders.

Suzanna Wilkinson Dickenson Williams Herring Bellows Hannag died in Austin October 7, 1883, and was buried in Oakwood Cemetery. Though she died nearly fifty years after the battle was fought, Suzanna— as her life of hardship testifies—was a victim of the Alamo.

THE TEJANOS' DILEMMA

Mexicans in Texas, also known as Tejanos, faced a difficult decision in 1836. Should they support the Texas insurgents, with whom they agreed in their opposition to a strong central government and in their commitment to Texas' economic development? Or should they remain loyal to their ethnic base and oppose the Anglos in their independence movement? Unable to feel completely comfortable in either camp, they ultimately lost status in both. Juan Neponuceno Seguin, a principal Tejano leader, personifies this dilemma.

Seguin was born in San Antonio on October 28, 1806. His influential family had grown even more wealthy from the new economic opportunities following the arrival of the Anglos in Texas. Like his father, Seguin established friendships among the Americans. He became political chief of San Antonio and in 1834 provided strong leadership for Texas during the dispute over whether to locate the Coahuila y Texas state capital at Monclova or Saltillo. He was accused of holding "the first strictly revolutionary meeting in Texas" to set up a provisional government pending the outcome of the dispute. General Martín Perfecto de Cós, Mexican military commander of the northern provinces, including Texas, reprimanded Seguin for this action. But Seguin continued to oppose the centralizing efforts of the government under Antonio López de Santa Anna. By the time Cós arrived in San Antonio in late 1835 Seguin had raised Tejano volunteers to fight against the Mexican army.

Seguin's men joined Stephen F. Austin's troops in Gonzales, which had gathered in October to defend a cannon that the Mexicans had ordered seized, then moved on to lay siege on San Antonio. Seguin fought alongside James Bowie in a skirmish at the Concepción mission, headed foraging expeditions, and convinced men in Cós' army to desert and join with the Texans. Following the Battle of San Antonio in early December he served with William B. Travis in an effort to obtain as many horses from the Mexican army as possible.

In January 1836 Seguin was commissioned a captain in the Texas cavalry and reported for duty in San Antonio. He was not with the Alamo's defenders during Santa Anna's final assault in March because he had been sent as a courier to bring reinforcements. After the fall of the Alamo Seguin joined Houston's forces at Gonzales, and when they retreated he was placed in charge of the rear guard to make certain that no family was left behind. Seguin was with Moseley Baker when he disrupted Santa Anna's crossing of the Brazos River, then he rejoined Houston before the Battle at San Jacinto on April 21, 1836.

Following the successful battle Seguin received a promotion to lieutenant colonel and was ordered to take over the military government of San Antonio, where his presence presumably would reassure the Mexican population. The following year General Felix Huston instructed Seguin to destroy San Antonio because he did not believe it could be defended from Mexican raids, but Seguin refused. Though President Sam Houston agreed with him, Seguin's refusal to follow Huston's orders made him enemies among the Anglo commanders of the Texas forces who became increasingly anti-Mexican in the aftermath of the revolution.

Seguin received a discharge from the army in May 1838 to assume a seat in the Texas Congress. He worked for improved understanding between Tejanos and the Anglo Texans, and urged that laws be printed in Spanish as well as English. He participated in a raid on the Comanche Indians led by John C. Hays during a recess of Congress. His popularity was such that the town of Walnut Springs changed its name to Seguin.

In 1840 Seguin was elected mayor of San Antonio. The election of a Tejano to such an important post alarmed many in the Anglo community who also believed rumors that Seguin had relayed information to the Mexicans that resulted in the defeat of the Texan's Santa Fe Expedition. Nevertheless, Seguin was reelected in 1842. Criticism of Seguin was renewed when Rafael Vásquez led a raid on San Antonio and many believed that Seguin had aided him in the venture. When opposition would not subside Seguin resigned as mayor in April 1842 and moved to Mexico. In September Santa Anna forced him to accompany General Adrian Woll's raid on San Antonio as a Mexican soldier, an action that confirmed the belief of many that Seguin had been disloyal to Texas all along.

In April 1848 Seguin wrote to Houston that he wanted to return to Texas no matter what the consequences. Exactly when he did return is uncertain, but church records in San Antonio indicate his presence at the baptism of his daughter on November 22, 1849. In 1852 Seguin was elected justice of the peace of Bexar County, and in 1855 he served on a committee to draft the Democratic Party's platform for Bexar County. Later in the year he moved to Floresville, and in 1862 he returned to Monterrey to offer his services to the revolutionary army of Benito Juárez. He remained in Mexico until 1871, when he returned to Floresville.

For years thereafter Seguin alternated between residences in Texas and Mexico. Considered a traitor and a patriot by Mexico and Texas at different times, Seguin died in Nuevo Laredo on August 27, 1890.

Right: *C.B. Normann painted this portrait of James Walker Fannin. Courtesy, Texas State Archives*

Below: *This painting by Colonel Andrew J. Houston portrays the fateful march of Fannin's men to their deaths at Goliad in 1836. Courtesy, Texas State Archives*

Above: *This drawing by Norman Price depicts the terrible March 27, 1836, massacre of Fannin and his men at Goliad by Mexican troops during the height of the Texas Revolution. Courtesy, Barker Texas History Center*

Right: *M. Waters conceptualized the Goliad massacre in this 1975 work. Courtesy, Institute of Texan Cultures*

Frederick Lemsky, a Czechoslavakian fifer, played this song, "Will You Come to the Bower?" at the Battle of San Jacinto. Courtesy, Barker Texas History Center

coast and followed with Sesma's command on the path Houston had taken. Urrea was to capture Burnet at Columbia, if possible, while Santa Anna tried to overtake Houston. When Santa Anna reached the Brazos he found the crossing guarded by only a few men under Mosely Baker, who had

refused to retreat any farther. He chased them away with little difficulty. Convinced that Houston was on his way to the United States, Santa Anna turned south to try to capture Burnet himself after the Texas president fled to Harrisburg. To do so he moved ahead of Sesma's main body with only 500 men. Learning this, Houston started southeast himself, and he picked up the "Twin Sisters," cannons that had arrived as gifts from the people of Cincinnati. Since Houston did not disclose his plans, even to his officers, resentment grew in the ranks. In a letter to Henry Raguet written on April 18, Houston told his friend that he intended to fight, but he told no one in the army. For all they knew they were headed for Lynch's Ferry on the San Jacinto River on the road that led to Louisiana. When the army reached a fork in the road, the ferry and safety in Louisiana in one direction and Harrisburg and Santa Anna in the other, the lead split the fork because no one issued orders. Some have speculated that Houston allowed the men to make the decision, knowing they would fight, so they would fight all the harder. Others accused him of cowardice then and during the battle, and claimed that he was indeed headed for Louisiana. The march line decided the issue anyway. Some of the men started south toward Harrisburg, and the rest followed.

Santa Anna barely missed capturing Burnet at Harrisburg, and as he turned back north he faced Houston's men. With their backs against Buffalo Bayou and the San Jacinto River to their left, the Texans looked across a rolling plain at 500 Mexican soldiers on the afternoon of April 20, and a skirmish resulted. All night long reinforcements under Cós raised the number of Mexican soldiers on the field until they outnumbered the Texans. All morning on the twenty-first Houston's men anxiously awaited orders. In late afternoon, while many of the Mexican troops rested from their sleepless night, Houston formed a battle line. He led about 700 men nearly the entire distance between the two camps before the Mexicans knew they were coming. Marching to the cadence of a fife and drum playing "Will You Come to the

Bower I Have Shaded for You?" the Texans crossed the field with accelerating speed. The "Twin Sisters" opened a hole in the Mexican line and the Texans poured through, taking the sleeping soldiers completely by surprise.

The battle lasted but eighteen minutes, but the killing lasted much longer into the night. More than 600 Mexicans were killed and another 700 were wounded. The Texans miraculously lost only two men immediately; thirty more were wounded and seven died from their injuries. Santa Anna fled from his tent in the midst of the battle, attempting to rejoin his main force. He was captured the next morning and brought before Sam Houston, who had been wounded in the leg during the battle. Many wanted to kill Santa Anna, but Houston insisted that he be kept alive. Houston had to leave negotiations with Santa Anna to Burnet and go to New Orleans for treatment of his wound, but before he left he had Santa Anna write General Vincente Filisola, his second in command, to hold the Mexican Army at the Brazos River. Surprisingly, Filisola obeyed these orders; with more than 5,000 men at his command

he easily could have defeated the Texans.

Burnet negotiated with Santa Anna until May 14, when they signed the Treaty of Velasco. By its provisions Santa Anna recognized the independence of Texas and promised to work for a commercial treaty between the two countries. In a secret passage he also recognized the Rio Grande as the border between Texas and Mexico. This was unusual because it had never been so regarded before. Burnet agreed to send Santa Anna to Vera Cruz. Both men promised more than they could deliver. Mexico naturally and justifiably rejected all of Santa Anna's concessions, and when Burnet tried to release his captive, the Texas army refused to permit it. Nonetheless, the Texans regarded the Mexican concessions as binding, and behaved as if they were.

With independence secured, the Texans thought, and their Republic established, and the possibility of joining the United States open to them, many Texans returned to everyday pursuits such as planting spring crops. They could not have imagined the problems that lay before them as the Lone Star rose over their new Republic.

This drawing portrays General Santa Anna's appearance before Sam Houston after the Mexican defeat at San Jacinto. The wounded Houston refused to allow the Mexican general's execution and instead exacted concessions from him that helped ensure the Texans' independence. Courtesy, Barker Texas History Center

The Republic

Each of the fifty states of the American Union is unique, each has its

sources of pride and distinction. Texas' greatest source is rooted in its expe-

rience as an independent republic. Begun during the military activities of

the revolution, its existence in jeopardy even after the cessation of hostili-

ties between Mexico and Texas, a recollection of the Lone Star Republic

still is a source of pride and something of a thrill for all who honor their

Texas heritage.

The draft of the Texas Declaration of Independence that George Chil-

dress compiled in the late winter of 1836 closely resembled the document

written earlier by Thomas Jefferson for the United States; so, too, did the

Texans' constitution resemble that of their homeland, especially their

Southern homeland. The constitution provided for legislative, executive,

The Reading of the Texas Declaration of Independence *by Fanny V. and Charles B. Normann hangs in the San Jacinto Museum of History. The painting depicts a realistic rendering of the momentous occasion. Courtesy, Joe Fultz*

This portrait of George Childress, author of the Texas Declaration of Independence, was painted on ivory. Courtesy, Barker Texas History Center

and judiciary branches of government, and its first section set out qualifications for those who would fill its offices and prescribed the functions and powers of their positions. Like the United States Constitution, it provided for a president and a vice president, but the first president would serve only two years. This undoubtedly reflected the delegates' negative reaction to the Consultation's governor, Henry Smith. They wanted to be rid of

their chief executive should his performance prove similar. Subsequent presidents served three-year terms, and no president could immediately succeed himself, although he could serve as many non-consecutive terms as the electorate would allow. The legislative branch, or congress, was bicameral, and the judiciary would be headed by a supreme court.

Other articles defined the congress' powers, including the authority to collect taxes, coin money, declare war, regulate commerce, establish a postal service, establish and maintain an army and navy or militia, and to make "all laws deemed necessary and proper" to achieve its defined goals. The constitution also provided for an *ad interim* government to govern Texas until elections were held to select executive and legislative officers. Curiously, the document prevented "Ministers of the gospel . . . or priests of any denomination" from service in any legislative or executive position in a reaction to the required state-church affiliation in the colonial era.

David Gouverneur Burnet received the convention's approval as interim president, and Lorenzo de Zavala became vice president. Samuel Price Carson was named secretary of state, Thomas Jefferson Rusk became secretary of war, Bailey Hardeman became treasury secretary, Robert Potter was named secretary of the navy, David Thomas was named attorney general, and John Rice Jones became postmaster general. Only Potter and Jones served until the permanent government took over, while six men attempted to fill the position of secretary of war with little success. The undisciplined army lacked confidence in them or preferred someone else.

Burnet's administration had to deal with major problems. Several thousand Mexican troops still campaigned in Texas when he assumed office, and others were near the border in Mexico. After he moved his office to Harrisburg to avoid capture by Santa Anna, he had to move again, this time to Galveston, when the Mexican commander pursued him. Even after Santa Anna's defeat, thousands of his soldiers remained in Texas. They eventually obeyed his orders to return to Mexico, but so long as they were in Texas they presented a major danger to the infant republic.

Once the Mexican forces, now led by General Vincente Filisola, recrossed the Rio Grande, Burnet proceeded to establish a regular government and took over the task of negotiating the Treaty of Velasco with Santa Anna when Houston was taken to New Orleans for medical treatment. After Santa Anna signed the treaty, Burnet agreed to release him unharmed with an escort to Vera Cruz. Both sides violated their pledges, or at least failed to fulfill them, but for the Texans, Santa Anna's concessions crystalized their attitude about their independence and their border. Mexico rejected these concessions because they were made under duress, and they were well within their rights under international law to do so. And it would be

Navarro County settlers fought Kickapoo Indians October 8, 1838, in what is known as the Battle Creek Fight. Courtesy, Institute of Texan Cultures

some time before Santa Anna again saw Mexico. The treaty at least demonstrated Burnet's interest in getting his government into operation.

Burnet's problems foreshadowed those of the Republic itself. Problems of sufficient revenue, hostile Indians, immigration, land alienation, and foreign recognition remained essentially unsolved for years, although he and the three presidents of the Republic tried heroically to do so. The fact that he operated without a congress or courts or an established administrative structure compounded Burnet's difficulties. But he did his best before turning the reins of government over to his successor later that year.

The first thing Burnet had to do was to find a suitable capital site. He moved from Galveston to the San Jacinto battlefield, then to Velasco, and eventually to Columbia.

Texas was in financial ruin. The Runaway Scrape, a fearful flight of civilians in advance of Santa Anna's invasion, had left much of the people's material wealth abandoned or lost. Some had been cached, but much had been thrown beside the roads or left at river crossings. Spring crops went unplanted and livestock untended. When residents returned they often found that their property had been stolen. Some Mexican or United States money remained but it was hoarded, and other mediums of exchange hardly exceeded barter. And there were not many Texans yet. Only 30,000 or so Americans, and about 22,000 Mexicans, Indians, and slaves populated the Republic. But more were on the way.

The agents of the various revolutionary movements, plus the news of the revolution itself and the promise of land in return for service against Mexico, drew thousands of potential Texas citizens. So many came so quickly that Burnet did not know what to do with them, especially those entering military service. Anxious for action against the Mexicans but without battles to fight, these undisciplined men refused to accept the established military leadership and cast about for things to do. Some of them even prevented Burnet from releasing Santa Anna. In early June he had the Mexican leader placed aboard the *Invincible,* bound for Vera Cruz. Rebellious soldiers boarded the ship and prevented it from sailing. And, in further defiance, the army refused to follow orders from Secretary of War Thomas J. Rusk or Mirabeau B. Lamar, who replaced Rusk.

Realizing that Texas could not long withstand such strains, Burnet issued a proclamation on July 23, 1836, calling for general elections on the first Monday in September. This anticipated the timetable of the convention by three months, but Burnet wanted an elected president to assume responsibility. This election would select all constitutional officers, ratify the constitution, and address a resolution on annexation by the United States.

At first no one came forward as a candidate for president. After much persuasion, Stephen F. Austin, now returned from his mission to the United States, agreed to run. Henry Smith soon announced, and friends of Rusk and Branch T. Archer tried to persuade both of them to enter the race. Rusk argued that the constitution's age requirement disqualified him, and Archer also refused. Just eleven days before the election, Sam Houston announced that he would serve if elected, and 5,119 voters, mostly remembering his military leadership more kindly after the victory at San Ja-

cinto, cast their ballots for him. Austin received but 587 votes while Smith polled 743. Mirabeau B. Lamar, also a hero of San Jacinto, won the vice presidency. The constitution was ratified overwhelmingly and nearly 3,000 voters also endorsed annexation by the United States.

Houston associated as many of the revolutionary leaders as possible with his government. Austin became secretary of state, Smith assumed the treasury post, Rusk accepted the war department, James Pinckney Henderson was appointed attorney general, S. Rhoads Fisher became secretary of the navy, and Robert Barr served as postmaster general.

Houston replaced Burnet at Columbia and convened the first Congress there. The House of Representatives selected Ira Ingram as its speaker, while Lamar presided over the Senate. Congress then named James Collinsworth as Chief Justice of the Supreme Court, and Houston and Congress made additional appointments to fill out the list of those who would administer the government's affairs.

The new president inherited the old problems of

Sam Houston became the first president of the new Republic of Texas. He faced the tremendous task of building a new republic. From Cirker, Dictionary of American Portraits, *Dover, 1967*

the Burnet government. Mexico still regarded Texas as a part of its country, having formally denounced the Treaty of Velasco and Santa Anna's recognition of independence. Therefore a state of war, or at least revolution, still existed, and there was danger of a new invasion. Although the point would appear moot, the two sides still disputed the Rio Grande as a boundary. The Treasury had no funds at all. Smith even complained to Houston that he lacked stationery to write to creditors to beg time before paying debts. The people's need for money as a medium of exchange for goods and services was great, made even worse by the needs of Runaway Scrape refugees for credit to rebuild and the needs of the new immigrants to build their first residences in Texas. Perhaps most pressing was the need to do something about the expanding military that threatened attacks on Mexico, thus bringing the problem full circle. Houston knew that another Mexican invasion, properly led, could mean the end of his government.

Houston tried to deal with these problems but most survived his administration. First, he imposed a policy of rigid economy, especially hoping to avoid spending more borrowed money on any military activity against Mexico or the Indians. He tried to persuade Congress to ratify the Cherokee treaty that he had negotiated late in 1835 to prevent a second front for the Texans, but Congress refused to agree since the immediate danger had passed. And his administration, and Texas, lost a great deal on December 27, 1836, when Stephen F. Austin died at the age of forty-three. Working in a cold, drafty office in the capitol in Columbia, Austin developed pneumonia and died within a short time.

Houston's term ended in 1838, and ineligible to succeed himself, he first hoped to prevail upon Thomas J. Rusk to become a candidate. Content to remain with his law practice in Nacogdoches, Rusk declined. Houston then asked Peter Grayson to run. Grayson accepted, then took his own life while on a trip to Tennessee. Casting about for a replacement, Houston persuaded James Collins-

worth to become his candidate, but he too died before the election when he jumped from a ship at Galveston while intoxicated. Mirabeau B. Lamar would probably have won the race anyway, but the failure of the Houston forces to field a creditable candidate insured his victory. Even Lamar had worried about a Rusk candidacy because the popular East Texan lived where the most Texas voters were. When Rusk declined to run, Lamar knew that victory was his.

Mirabeau B. Lamar, the son of a Georgia planter, had arrived in Texas just in time to participate in the Battle of San Jacinto. He had come to Texas in 1835 with Fannin to do historical research, and decided to stay. He began the San Jacinto campaign as a private and ended as Houston's cavalry commander, distinguishing himself in battle. Burnet had tried to make Lamar commander of the army after Houston left, but the soldiers refused to follow him. With experience in education, newspaper publishing, politics, and merchandising, he was just the kind of person needed to develop the young Republic, and he quickly became Houston's principal rival. He served the first term as vice president, and when he won election to the highest office in the Republic's second administration, he prepared a lengthy challenge for Texans in his inaugural address, which promised to lead them boldly in new directions. Houston's impromptu remarks, which preceded Lamar's speech on the inaugural program, lasted for nearly three hours. Embarrassed and angered, Lamar merely handed his speech to an aide and stalked away. Houston continued to plague Lamar as a member of Congress representing the San Augustine district throughout his three-year term.

Lamar's administration differed from Houston's almost totally. Instead of parsimony, he intended to spend. Instead of stepping lightly around Mexico's feelings, he intended to force recognition, even at the expense of a renewed fight. Instead of pacifying Indians with treaties, he intended to push them back on all fronts so whites could settle their lands. Although his program cost many

Facing page: *Mirabeau B. Lamar served as vice president and then president of the Republic of Texas. From Cirker,* Dictionary of American Portraits, *Dover, 1967*

Below: *The early Republic faced everything from debts to hostile Indians, especially the fierce Comanche. Courtesy, Institute of Texan Cultures*

dollars Texas did not have, he dreamed of solving the Republic's problems with boldness. Thus the image the world seems to have of Texans, a brash, bold, bragging image, comes mostly from Lamar rather than from Houston.

Their physical differences and personal history would not indicate this. Former governor of Tennessee, protegé to Andrew Jackson, fighter against the British, Indians, and Mexicans, robust despite several wounds, and large of frame, Houston would seem to be the leader who would fix his image upon early Texans. Lamar, on the other hand, suffered numerous health problems, some so severe he had to take leaves of absence to obtain medical treatment. A relative intellectual, a dreamer, and a poet, Lamar actually was the leader who had the grandest ambitions for Texas. He dreamed of Mexico's recognition of Texas independence more than annexation to the United States; he wanted to establish economic health and expand Texas' border all the way to the Pacific, rather than be absorbed by another nation, even the

United States; and he wanted to place the Republic on its own sound educational and cultural footing. His term, like Houston's, ended without many of these things being close to achievement. Yet he is regarded as a highly effective orator, a good poet, and the father of Texas public education.

Houston returned for a second term after the election of 1841. Since Lamar could not succeed himself there was no contest, although David Burnet did seek the office. Edward Burleson, despite being an old friend of Houston's, won the vice presidency as an independent. The Republic's third administration brought back austerity and a renewed effort to court the United States for annexation. Lamar's administration expended or obligated more than 2.5 million dollars, while Houston held expenditures to about $500,000 during his second term. He did this by shifting expenses to local agencies, making many services voluntary, and leaving a good deal undone. He took a 50 percent pay cut and recommended the same for Congress and other officials; he abandoned the policy of policing or removing Indians, except in response to specific raids; he reduced the size of the army and the navy; and he worked hard to get Texas into the American Union so a larger government could absorb these problems. As a result the situation in Texas did not grow appreciably worse, and by the end of Houston's second term, the United States had moved closer to annexation.

Houston passed the administration of Texas' affairs to Dr. Anson Jones following the election of 1844. Jones had served in Houston's administration as secretary of state and was thought of as a supporter of Old Sam. He resented this, but he did not denounce Houston publicly. And when annexation was achieved during his administration, he styled himself as the "Architect of Annexation," despite the fact that Houston had been working for that achievement for a decade.

The story of the efforts of these three very different men, Houston, Lamar, and Jones, to solve Texas' many problems is complicated. The Con-

sultation accumulated debts so rapidly its officials hardly had time to worry about them. Pressed with active military campaigns and the threat of Indian problems, they did what they had to do. Even the Burnet government, lacking revenue, operated on credit and the anticipation that its successor would somehow produce the revenue to pay its debts. Most Texans assumed that their vast lands would be the ultimate solution, but they gave so much of it away as payment for military service that little could be sold. The Congress of the Republic did attempt to impose taxes of various kinds, but their expenditures exceeded revenues because some would not pay, others could not, and evasion was easy.

Houston's solution in both of his terms of office hardly exceeded the idea of keeping expenses to a minimum and waiting for the United States to assume the Republic's debts. Even so, daily expenses required some revenue, and as anti-expansion and anti-slave forces in the United States Congress delayed the annexation of Texas,

the need for revenue grew more pressing. So
Congress authorized the administration to issue
$650,000 in promissory notes that were payable
in twelve months and drew 10 percent interest.
Called "Star Money" because of the star printed
on their faces, these notes circulated well during
Houston's administration and their value remained near par. Subsequent issues did not circu-
late as well, and when they were accepted at all it
was usually at a reduced value, sometimes as low
as sixty-five cents on the dollar. Currency issued
during Lamar's time, called "Redbacks" because
of the ink color on the reverse side, depreciated to
as low as twelve cents on the dollar. Diarist Adolphus Sterne lamented the fate of this "Texas
Money" in his journal, representing most Texans
who preferred to trade in United States or even
Mexican coinage, or in kind. This depreciation
also lowered the confidence of most Texans in
their government and troubled foreign nations
considering diplomatic recognition.

Nearly $800,000 in notes outstanding greeted
Lamar, who issued an additional $3,552,800 dur-
ing his three-year term. No precious metals backed
these issues and the policy of giving land away
prevented the Republic's principal asset and best
potential source of income from being of assistance, so these notes floated on public confidence
alone. The Lamar administration's receipts,
$1,083,661, hardly balanced expenditures, which
reached $4,855,313, so Lamar passed on a com-
bined debt from the first two administrations of
more than six million dollars. And he passed these
debts back to the man he had succeeded, Sam
Houston. Houston immediately imposed austerity
again. He cut government services, had Congress
repeal all currency laws—repudiating whatever value such money might have had—and asked for
the issuance of "exchequer bills," which would be
legal tender and would be accepted at par value
for taxes. This was a ploy to stabilize the value of
the bills, but they quickly lost value except for the
payment of taxes. Texans used them at face value
to satisfy their tax obligations but hoarded their
precious metals or other money for necessities.

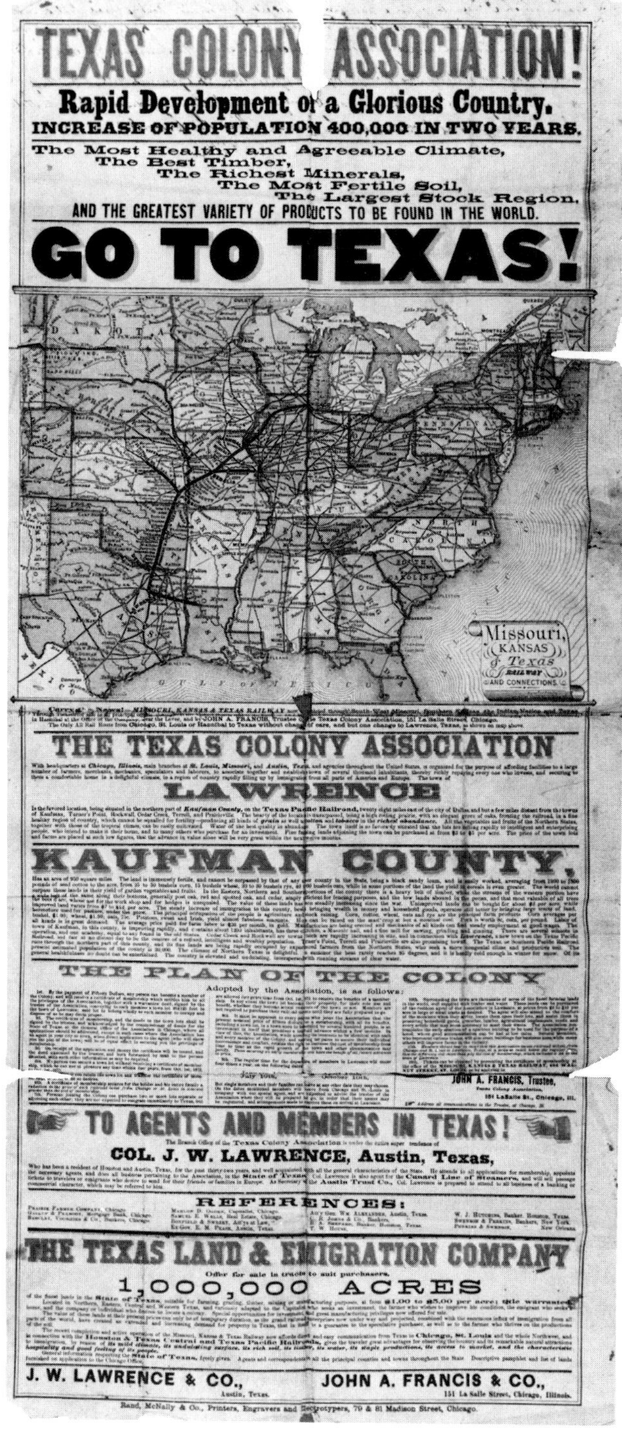

The Republic did receive some money from customs, and in the form of gifts from private individuals—especially from the United States—but
such largesse usually came only during times of
military crisis, such as threats of a new invasion by
Mexico or the military raids of 1842. Lamar tried
to bolster the Texas economy by borrowing five
million dollars, and he was not particular where it
came from. He sent James Hamilton to borrow
from the Second Bank of the United States, then
operating under a state charter in Pennsylvania,
and to financial houses in England and on the
Continent. Hamilton obtained $500,000 from the

American bank but his efforts were unsuccessful in Europe. He was near success in obtaining a loan from the French when they received a negative report from their minister to Texas, Alphonse Dubois de Saligny, following a disagreement he had with the Texas government on private matters. His report killed chances of a loan from France. Without these funds Lamar's idea for a Texas national bank, modeled after the institution sponsored by Alexander Hamilton that had been instrumental in the founding of the United States, was not needed.

Anson Jones' ideas were similar to those of Houston when it came to finance. He tried to spend as little as possible. He succeeded during his brief tenure as president and was able to turn over the Republic's fiscal problems to the United States before his term expired. Texas did retain authority over its public lands by the terms of the annexation agreement, as well as the obligation to satisfy its public debt, but wiser use of these lands was possible as a state of the American Union than as an independent nation.

Facing page: *This 1836 "Go to Texas" ad was posted in New Orleans in hopes of populating the young Republic. Courtesy, Texas State Archives*

Below: *Titled* A Texas Hail Storm—the Frightened Mules Halted, *this newspaper illustration acknowledged another problem facing Texan settlers—the unpredictable elements. Courtesy, Texas State Archives*

Its public lands, by this time some 150 million acres, constituted the greatest resource of the Republic of Texas. The attitudes of both Houston and Lamar were similar in the matter of land disposition, and both could be called liberal. Their congresses agreed, and both executive and legislative branches reflected the universal opinion in Texas that land should be given away. The constitutional fathers endorsed this concept by awarding white heads of households residing in Texas on March 2, 1836, the day independence was declared, a "first class headright" of a square league and a *labor* of land, amounting to 4,605 acres. Single men seventeen years of age and older received one-third of a league, or 1,476 acres. Settlers already in possession of some land could claim the difference between their holdings and the headright. For either group this was simply a reward for being in Texas on Independence Day. And they were not required to reside on the land. Later congresses established a "second class headright" of 1,280 acres for heads of households and 640 acres for unmarried men who arrived after March 2, 1836, and prior to October 1, 1837; a "third class headright" for those arriving between October 1, 1837, and January 1, 1840, and a "fourth class headright" for those arriving between January 1840 and January 1842. Bounty grants of 320 acres were awarded for each three months of military service, up to a total of twelve months or two sections. By these measures Texans claimed 36,876,492 acres of the public lands as a reward for service in military and civilian capacities in the revolution or to the Republic.

The constitution also required the creation of a general land office, and in 1837 the Congress established this agency to record land titles and direct the surveying of public lands into sections. The general land office used the American system of sections rather than the league unit as used by the Spanish and Mexican governments. This office also administered the large blocks of land that Congress intended to award to new *empresarios* as well as those set aside for such uses as the support of education. A board of land commissioners met in each county to rule on claims, assist in the awarding of land, and supervise surveying. The central office issued the titles, or patents, to the land. Members of the central office conveyed the property in ritualistic ceremonies harkening to the middle ages. They literally "put" the new owner in possession of his land in front of witnesses, adjoining owners, and other officials, and the claimant then fixed stakes or made other evidence that he was in fact in possession of the land. After that it was his to sell, trade, or will to heirs.

The Texas Congress attempted to return to the empresarial system in 1841, partially as a way to phase out the headright program. The government hoped to contact agents to sponsor groups of immigrants much as Stephen F. Austin and others had done in the 1820s. W.S. Peters and Associates, also known as the Texas Emigration and Land Company, the German Emigration Company, Charles G. Mercer, Henri Castro, and others were awarded ten sections of land for each 100 families they brought to Texas. The Peters company received 16,000 acres in the Red River country. They also received compensation for surveying and other services associated with the transfer of the property. When a proposed grant to the Franco-Tenienne Company, which wanted to locate French immigrants in Texas, reached Congress, it was blocked despite Houston's efforts for passage. A majority in Congress opposed it partially on the grounds of nativism. However, Mercer and Castro received grants on land along the Nueces and Rio Grande rivers, and both settled non-United States immigrants on their grants. The German company sponsored a large number of Germanic immigrants, although they mostly came after Texas joined the American Union. Dissatisfaction led to the abandoning of the contract system in 1844.

Lamar's administration also advocated legislation to protect Texas landowners from credit foreclosure. Many Texans had left former homes because of debt, either to escape foreclosure or after it had occurred. In 1839 Congress passed the first Texas Homestead Law, although it was partially based on previous legislation enacted by the

This land grant certificate was issued by the Republic of Texas for service in the army. This recipient was honorably discharged because of a disability and received 1,280 acres. Courtesy, General Land Office

Coahuila y Texas legislature. The 1839 law protected up to fifty acres on a farm or a town house and lot and the tools of trade from foreclosure for nonpayment of debt. This guaranteed Texans the chance to make a living, and it also encouraged immigration. Although later changes reflected newer needs, some form of this protection has remained in Texas statutes until the present.

Even when a new Texan obtained his land and had it partially protected from debt, he often had to worry about Indian troubles. The English and their American descendants had more difficulty co-existing with the Indians than did other Europeans. The French, Spanish, and Dutch established trade with the Indians more easily, they tried to provide religious missions to them, and the Latin peoples often intermarried with the Indians. Undoubtedly, success varied—some tribes tolerated the Europeans more easily than others. The English, for many reasons, usually tried to push the Indians aside to acquire their lands. As inheritors of this mentality, Texans, outside of the few who agreed with Houston, followed the same practice. And by the time the Americans reached Texas, many of the Indians who survived Spanish rule had acquired horses, guns, and other means of resistance along with two centuries of experience with Europeans. They—particularly the fierce

and highly skilled Comanches—did not give up easily. During the revolution Houston had "neutralized" many Texas Indians by friendship or treaty, thus keeping an estimated 15,000 potential allies of Mexico out of the fight. His work was mostly among the relatively passive Cherokees in East Texas who had come there after being removed from Georgia and other Eastern states by the westward expansion of the whites, not the Comanches in Central and West Texas. Now the whites in East Texas, by far the most populous area of the Republic, worried about such a large number of Indians, and many coveted their land. So when Houston presented the treaty he had negotiated with the Cherokees to Congress, a treaty that promised them title to their land in return for their neutrality, it failed to gain ratification. The danger from Mexico had apparently passed and now Congress saw little need to worry about the Cherokees. The Indians were shocked, but they continued to hope that Houston would eventually bring the Congress to agreement. Then Vincente Cordova, former *alcalde* of Nacogdoches, led a revolt against the Texas government in East Texas. His followers, about 600 Mexicans, half-breeds, and a few unhappy Indians, all looked like Indians to the East Texans. General Thomas J. Rusk directed the militia in suppressing the Cordova Re-

Left: *Plagued by unpredictable weather, angry Indians, ill health, and often short supplies, Texan settlers pressed on and braved still another of the wilderness' surprises—wild horses. Courtesy, Texas State Archives*

Facing page: *This 1874 engraving from* Harper's Weekly *typifies the terrain and lodging of the settlers heeding the extended invitation to come to Texas. Courtesy, Institute of Texan Cultures*

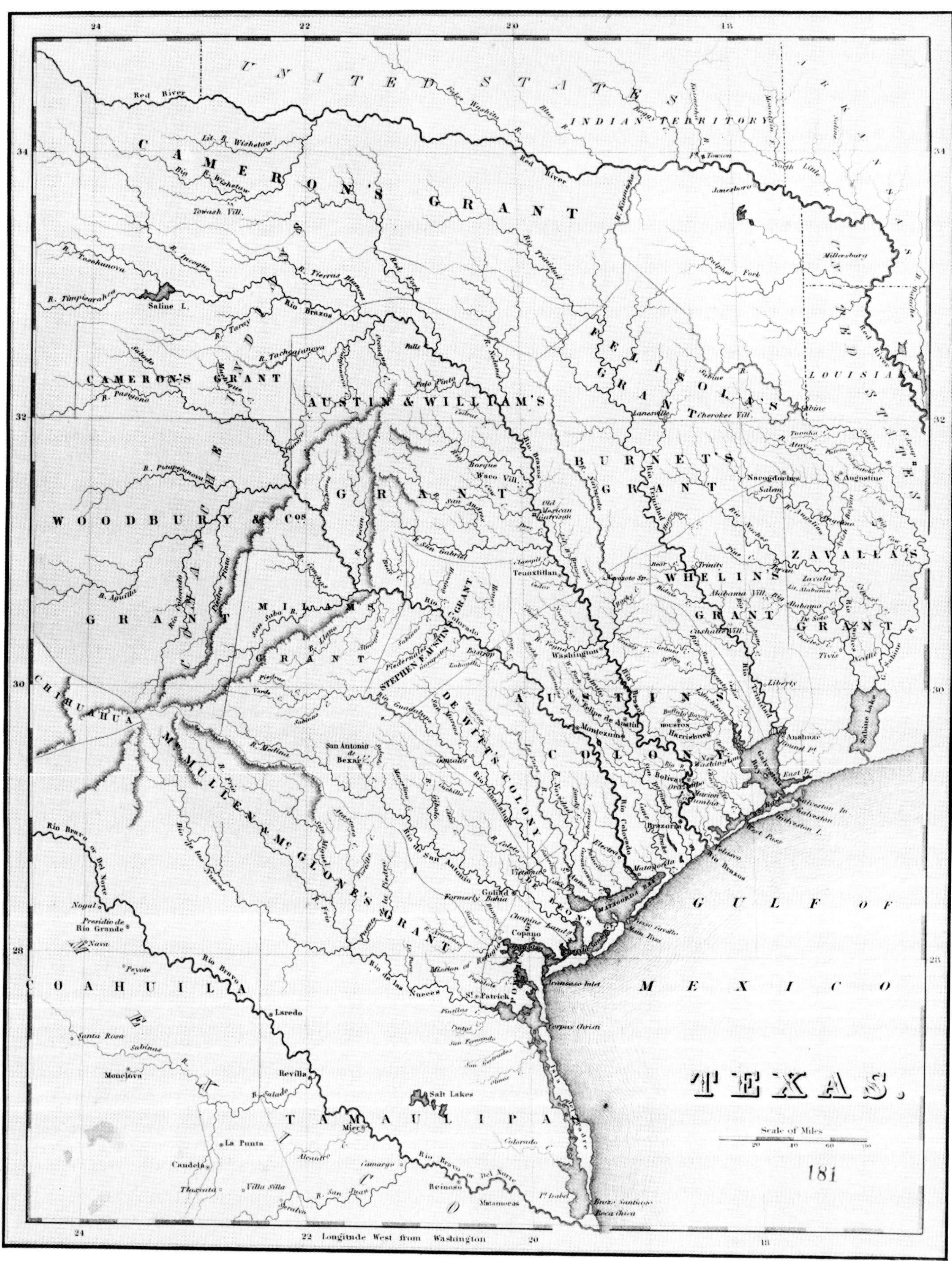

UNITED STATES
INDIAN TERRITORY
LOUISIANA
ARKANSAS
CAMERON'S GRANT
AUSTIN & WILLIAM'S GRANT
CAMERON'S GRANT
WOODBURY & Cos. GRANT
MILAM'S GRANT
STEPHEN F. AUSTIN'S GRANT
DE WITT'S COLONY
McMULLEN & McGLONE'S GRANT
BURNET'S GRANT
WHELIN'S GRANT
ZAVALLA'S GRANT
FELISOLA'S GRANT
AUSTIN'S COLONY
CHIHUAHUA
COAHUILA
TAMAULIPAS
GULF OF MEXICO
TEXAS.
Red River
Rio Brazos
San Antonio de Bexar
Galveston I.
Nacogdoches
S. Augustine
Laredo
Revilla
Matamoras
Corpus Christi
Copano
Goliad
Washington
Scale of Miles
20   40   60   80
181
Longitude West from Washington

bellion, and the following year General Kelsey Douglass led a force at the Battle of the Neches on July 16, 1839, which resulted in the defeat of the Cherokees under Chief Philip Bowles. The eighty-three-year-old Bowles, with whom Houston had negotiated the peace treaty during the revolution, was killed and most of the other Cherokees fled northward to modern Oklahoma. Lamar favored this action, as he did expeditions against the Indians elsewhere, despite the fact that they sometimes represented brazen attempts to obtain Indian land. It remained his belief that the Indians interfered with the development of the Texas empire he envisioned, and most whites agreed.

A good example of Lamar's policy can be seen in the Council House fight at San Antonio on March 19, 1840. Southern Comanche chiefs requested a conference to trade hostages and arrange for peace. When the Indians arrived they brought only a fifteen-year-old girl named Matilda Lockhart, although they admitted that other Indians held an additional fifteen to twenty hos-

Facing page: *This map shows the boundaries of the Republic of Texas in 1838. Courtesy, Barker Texas History Center*

Right: *Illustrations such as this helped convey the isolation and danger of living on the frontier. From Braun,* Jugenblatter, *Stuttgart, 1861*

tages. They insisted that each exchange must be bargained separately. The commissioners, Hugh McLeod and William G. Cooke, and militia commander William S. Fisher, became outraged, especially after seeing that the girl had been mutilated by burning off part of her nose. They called in armed men and announced that the Indians present were themselves hostages until all white captives were produced. The room exploded into a fight. Seven whites and nearly all the Indians present were killed. A few escaped and warned the Indian camp. They retreated, but plotted revenge. Five months later more than 600 Comanches traveled around San Antonio and raided Linnville and Victoria in South Texas while many of the whites were away on an expedition against raiding Mexicans. This also convinced them that Mexican agents had helped plan the Indian raid. They retaliated with a raid against the Indians at Plum Creek led by Felix Huston, and militia under Colonel John H. Moore defeated several Indian villages on the upper Colorado River.

Concern over Indian raids and the periodic invasions in the 1840s by Mexican troops produced a demand that Texas Rangers should be employed by the government to protect civilians. The Rangers had begun during the colonial period when Stephen F. Austin had employed men to "range" over the countryside to protect his settlers. Financial difficulties prevented the government from using the army for this task after independence, so the Rangers were considered an excellent alternative. They patrolled the Rio Grande border and the frontier line on a periodic basis, and their no-holds-barred tactics produced results quickly despite their few numbers. Brave, resourceful, and rarely concerned with methods so long as they produced results, the Rangers earned fame that endures to the present. They introduced the revolver, or six-shooter, to Texas Indian fighting and law enforcement when they obtained a shipment of Samuel Colt's new weapon intended for use by the Texas navy. Captain Samuel Walker recommended modifications that made the weapon even more efficient. Able to shoot six times without reloading, the revolver enabled the Texas Rangers to be successful despite their small numbers.

The military might have been employed to fight the Indians, but a regular army had proven too much of a burden for the young Republic. There always seemed to be too few or too many soldiers in the early years. Getting enough men to oppose Santa Anna proved a problem not because they were unwilling, but because there were so few in Texas at the time. Adolphus Sterne and Thomas McKinney recruited in New Orleans, and Stephen F. Austin, Branch T. Archer, and William Wharton went even farther east to encourage Americans to come to Texas to fight. All were successful, and quite a few immigrants arrived in time to fight in the battle of San Jacinto. But after the surrender of Santa Anna and the retreat of his army across the Rio Grande, there remained little for the expanding Texas army to do. Still they came, some as individuals, some in organized companies, and by the end of 1836 more than 2,000 men, twice the number Houston commanded at San Jacinto,

This drawing depicts Texas Rangers preparing for a scout. Known for sometimes unorthodox methods in their efforts to control often chaotic situations, their bravery and resourcefulness have become a deeply rooted part of the Texas myth. Courtesy, Texas State Archives

had enlisted. These men were uncontrolled, especially with Houston in New Orleans for medical treatment. Some entertained the idea of invading Mexico, posing the threat of renewed hostilities.

Burnet tried to appoint Rusk as their commander, but they rejected his leadership; Lamar next accepted Burnet's invitation to command, but the army produced their own leader, Felix Huston. When Sam Houston became president he did not want the unruly Huston to command the army so he asked Albert Sidney Johnston to accept the position. When Johnston tried to assume command he was challenged to a duel by Huston, who hoped to establish his authority with his pistol. And he succeeded. Under other circumstances Johnston might have simply ordered Huston's arrest, but he knew the Texans would not obey such an order. So he accepted Huston's challenge and suffered a wound in the leg. Fearing that the army would then follow Huston to Mexico, and realizing that maintaining such a force was a significant drain on Texas' financial resources, the president furloughed about 600 men. They could still claim their land grants but they were no longer an army and he did not even have to give them severance pay.

When Lamar became president he wanted to enlarge the army so he could implement his plans for expansion. He needed troops to patrol the Rio Grande and to claim the lands east of the river in present New Mexico for Texas, as provided in the Treaty of Velasco. Eventually he hoped to expand Texas' borders all the way to the Pacific Ocean, but in June 1841, he was willing to accept these lands in New Mexico. Lamar dreamed of bringing Santa Fe under Texas authority. With its long-standing trade center and connections to both the United States and Mexico, it would be an excellent plum for his administration. Lamar's Santa Fe Expedition became one of his greatest failures—but it is also an excellent example of his dreams for expansion.

Feeling that he had assurances from the citizens of Santa Fe that they would accept the authority of Texas, Lamar asked Congress to authorize an expedition to New Mexico to proclaim it a part of Texas. Both houses of the Texas Congress endorsed the expedition, although not in the same language, so its legality was questionable. Nonetheless, Lamar started his commissioners, with Hugh McLeod leading 270 militiamen, businessmen, and others, including New Orleans newspaperman George Wilkins Kendall, westward to Santa Fe to establish business connections and Texas authority. Kendall later wrote of their incredible journey. Expecting to travel about 600 miles, they more than doubled that distance when they lost their way. The environment would have been hard enough, but they also faced hostile Indians. And when they finally reached Santa Fe they found even that place inhospitable when they were rejected by the town's population and found a Mexican militia there. They were forced to surrender and were marched to a prison in Mexico where they were held until released in 1844.

Soldiers were needed in 1842 when Mexican troops invaded Texas in two significant raids. In March of that year General Rafael Vásquez and 500 men raided San Antonio. Their arrival produced another Runaway Scrape, although less significant than the flight of 1836. Vásquez claimed Mexican sovereignty over the region he had raided, including San Antonio, but he fled within two days when Houston called out the militia. The Texans pursued the raiders and a skirmish occurred at the Nueces River, but Vásquez escaped across the Rio Grande.

Then, on September 11, Mexican troops under General Adrian Woll again raided San Antonio. He did not tarry long, but he took hostages when he fled back to Mexico before the militia under Alexander Somervell. When the Texans reached the Rio Grande, Somervell ordered them to stop as Houston wanted them to do. However, the Texans were in no mood to break off the chase, so they elected William S. Fisher to lead them across the river to lay siege to the Mexican community of Mier. While they waited for tribute from the Mexicans, reinforcements arrived in the city and captured nearly 300 Texans after a battle. Many escaped but most were recaptured, and eventually 176 Texans were taken to Castle Perote for imprisonment. They were all sentenced to death, but when the prison commander refused to execute the order, it was commuted to decimation—one in ten would die. Seventeen black beans were placed with 159 white beans, and the men drew them by lot to determine who would die. The remainder were held at the prison until September 16, 1844, when they were released because of pressure from European and United States diplomats.

In 1843 another expedition under the command of Colonel Jacob Snively tried to establish some Texas influence in New Mexico. Snively's men tried to capture a wagon train traveling the Santa Fe Trail from St. Louis, Missouri. They first defeated a body of some 500 Mexican troops who also wanted to attack the train, but when the caravan arrived it was protected by United States troops who captured the Texans. Snively's men were forced to march home without their muskets and without many supplies. They suffered terribly from the desert conditions—and also from embarrassment.

The Texas navy fared even worse than the New Mexican campaigns of the army. The navy had controlled the Gulf Coast during the revolution with only four vessels, owing some of their success to the weakness of the Mexicans in this area. But within a year all of the original vessels were out of commission. The *Liberty* was sold for debt, the Mexicans captured the *Independence,* and the *Invincible* and the *Brutus* were wrecked. Congress funded the purchase of seven additional vessels. The *Zavala* was steam-powered, while the *Austin,* the *San Jacinto,* the *San Antonio,* the *San Bernard,* the *Wharton,* and the *Archer* moved under sail. The largest, the *Austin,* was a 600-ton vessel. Houston's first administration did not have the use of most of these vessels, but Lamar had plans for them when he became president. He named Edwin W. Moore as commander of the fleet and directed Moore to guard the Texas Coast. Sometimes the navy even attacked Mexican ships, and Moore used the navy to assist Yucatan rebels attempting to overthrow the government by preventing Mexican ships from landing troops and supplies in the region to suppress the rebellion. Sometimes the Texas ships were used offensively in the Yucatan revolt. Houston disliked this because he feared it would provoke renewed Mexican military activity in Texas. When he again became president he sent a commissioner to order Moore to desist before he interfered with Houston's own attempts to negotiate a peace settlement. Moore received these orders in New Orleans, but he disobeyed them. He convinced Houston's agent to allow him to sail again to the Yucatan on the grounds that his was the surest way to bring the Mexicans to terms. Learning of this disobedience, Houston invited the navies of the world to take the Texas ships as prizes because their commander had become no more than a pirate. Moore returned to Texas and demanded a court-martial to clear his name, but Houston ignored him and ordered the navy disbanded.

One of the Texans' grievances against Mexico before independence was the failure of the government to provide for a system of education in Texas. The few schools in colonial Texas were private subscription schools, and most education was achieved by apprenticeship or self-study. Parents taught their children what they knew of reading

This drawing by Norman Price depicts a Texas Navy recruit on board the Austin *at anchor in Matagorda Bay. Despite initial high hopes, the navy suffered physical losses and poor management and was eventually disbanded by an angry Sam Houston. Courtesy, Barker Texas History Center*

and writing, how to make a living or become a homemaker, and such "book learning" as most of them acquired. Most immigrants from the United States possessed literacy skills, but they feared that their children would mature uneducated unless schools were established. So the Texas Constitution writers included a provision allowing for a public education system, but no Texas Congress found the money to create one. Lamar tried to persuade them to do so, earning him the title of the Father of Texas Education. Congress did designate a large portion of the public lands as an endowment for education. Beginning in 1839, Congress awarded three leagues of land to each county to support an academy, but they gave away so much land to settlers that the counties had difficulty selling or leasing their school land to obtain funds for education. Congress also provided for higher education by reserving fifty leagues of land to help fund two universities. This land was mostly located in West Texas, and from time to time additional lands were designated by the state legislature for the support of education. The discovery of oil on some of this land in the twentieth century made The University of Texas, founded in 1883, one of the most highly endowed institutions in the nation, and Texas A&M University, which began in 1876 and shares this largesse, one of the best-funded land grant institutions in the United States. But this developed well after the Republic ceased to exist. While it lasted education still lagged behind its potential. A few academies such as Marcus A. Montrose's San Augustine Academy or the Nacogdoches University, hardly more than elementary or secondary institutions, provided what formal education Texans enjoyed.

The unsettled nature of the Republic is also illustrated by differences over the location of its capital. Houston assumed the presidency at Columbia, where Burnet had presided over the *ad interim* government. In 1837 he accepted the invitation of entrepreneurs A.C. and J.K. Allen to move the capital to a new community they wished to develop near Harrisburg on Buffalo Bayou. Some thought he did so because the Allens named the city in his honor. The government pledged to remain in Houston for three years to assist the promoters, who agreed to provide a capitol. At the end of that time the capitol remained incomplete and it did not please many of the representatives. As early as 1838 Congress wanted to move, but Houston vetoed that on the basis of

Left: *This street scene of Austin and the capitol building depicts the struggling young town. Courtesy, Texas State Archives*

Facing page: *Angelina Belle Eberley fires off the cannon during the Archives War in Austin in 1842. From Baker,* A Texas Scrapbook, *A.S. Barnes and Company, 1875*

the government's pledge to the Allen brothers. Some wanted to move the capital further west so it would remain nearer the center of the expanding population. Others wanted to move it even further east to keep it safe from Mexican soldiers and Indians.

When Lamar became president he chaffed at having to serve in a capital named for his rival. He persuaded the Congress to create a commission to relocate the capital at a site north of the San Antonio Road and between the Trinity and Colorado rivers. Lamar himself allegedly selected a site along the Colorado River near the village of Waterloo while on a buffalo hunt. He reportedly proclaimed a rise a mile or so from the river as an appropriate home for an empire. Congress designated that site, now named Austin in honor of the founder of Texas, as its new seat of government, and Lamar moved there as quickly as possible. He ignored criticism, which was quite accurate, that he had placed the government beyond the frontier line and therefore in jeopardy of Indian raids. When Houston again became president he refused to serve in Austin, and following the Mexican raids of 1842 he ordered all other gov-

ernment agencies to join him in Houston. The citizens of Austin, following the leadership of Angelina Eberly, manager of Bullock's Hotel, prevented the removal of the Republic's archives. This quixotic "Archive War" testified to the unsettled nature of the Republic's affairs.

Annexation to the United States also concerned Texans for the entire time between their declaration of independence until the time annexation was finally achieved. They had even voted to seek annexation on the same day their government was ratified and its officers were elected. Houston's relations with other foreign countries, as well as Lamar's, concerned this issue although each had different ends in mind. Burnet had designated James W. Collingsworth and Peter W. Grayson as agents in Washington to feel out the federal government on this issue. Daniel Webster and John C. Calhoun favored the annexation of Texas, but anti-slavery men such as John Quincy Adams opposed it, bearing the admittance of another "slaveocracy" to the Union. President Andrew Jackson had to appear neutral because of relations with Mexico, but he sent Henry M. Morfit to investigate and report to him on Texas' readiness for

Above: *Anson Jones was the last president of the Republic of Texas. Courtesy, Institute of Texan Cultures*

Facing page: *This drawing shows the first capitol of the Republic of Texas in Austin in 1839. Courtesy, Barker Texas History Center*

annexation. Morfit observed the election results in 1836, realized the problems of the growing debt, and decided that Mexico would make further efforts to regain Texas. He was impressed with the vast lands of Texas, and although he recommended caution to Jackson, he did suggest that Texas would be valuable to the United States. Jackson responded by refusing to put the issue of annexation to Congress at that time. So William Wharton was sent to Washington to persuade the United States Congress that annexation was in that country's best interest. Wharton hoped that Jackson's caution could be overcome if Congress would act first. Soon the Senate passed a resolution favoring at least diplomatic recognition, and the entire Congress appropriated funds to support a diplomatic mission to Texas. Jackson then appointed Alcee Louis La Branche of Louisiana as *chargé d'affaires* to Texas on March 3, 1836, giving Texas its first recognition by a foreign government.

Houston sent James Pinckney Henderson to seek recognition in Europe. Henderson secured a trading convention in England, and in France, which was then irritated with Mexico over its "Pastry War" involving claims by a French baking firm against Mexico, he found things even friendlier. The French moved closer to recognition when Houston withdrew Texas' request for annexation from Washington in embarrassment that it had gone so long unanswered.

Lamar next sent James Hamilton to Europe to seek loans and recognition. He was more successful only with the latter. England did extend recognition and offered to mediate the continuing dispute between Mexico and Texas. Full relations were established with England by 1842, and with the Netherlands and Belgium shortly afterwards. The French sent Alphonse Dubois de Saligny to Texas to represent them, and he soon quarrelled with nearly everyone in Austin, especially with hotel keeper John Bullock. Their dispute focused on an incident caused by Bullock's pigs eating corn that de Saligny had purchased for his horses. He had his servants shoot the pigs, and following the "Pig War" he left Texas. His negative report

ended Hamilton's hopes to secure loans from France.

Efforts to deal with Mexico proved equally difficult. Houston tried to keep things quiet, but Lamar hardly seemed to care. Lamar's Santa Fe Expedition and Moore's activities on behalf of the Yucatan rebels hardly could be termed conciliatory. He did send Bernard E. Bee to try to treat with the Mexican government for renewed recognition of Texas independence, but Bee would not even be received. James Treat and James Webb suffered the same experience. Houston's second administration faced the raids of Vásquez and Woll and such mistakes as the Mier expedition, so the sides moved further apart.

The renewed interest in annexation developed, and Britain and France began to pressure Mexico to make concessions to Texas in the hope of keeping it independent. Neither country wanted to see the United States strengthened by the addition of the vast Texas territory. Many American officials were concerned that an independent Texas would block their own expansion, and they were especially concerned with the prospect of British and French influence over Texas. With such sentiment on the rise, Houston sent James Reilly and Isaac Van Zandt to explore the matter with President John Tyler. Tyler was interested, but problems with Mexico and concern over the opposition of abolitionists caused him to delay taking the matter to Congress. Then suddenly he changed his mind and suggested that talks be renewed. James Pinckney Henderson joined Van Zandt in Washington and together they negotiated a treaty of annexation with Secretary of State John C. Calhoun, which called for Texas to join the Union as a territory and to surrender its public lands and also its debts to the United States. Before the Texans could respond the United States Senate rejected the treaty on June 8, 1844, by a vote of 35 to 16.

Their hopes dashed again, the Texans elected Anson Jones as their fourth president, expecting to remain the Republic of Texas. But the treaty rejection had raised the issue of annexation, and troubles with Great Britain over the Oregon Territory, as the primary issues in the presidential election of 1844. Martin Van Buren and Henry Clay failed to understand this and evaded the issue. But the Democrats and their candidate, James Knox Polk, grasped the fact that westward expansion and "manifest destiny," an expression coined in this rambunctious period by editor John L. O'Sullivan, were the issues of the hour. They boldly embraced the annexation of Texas and a strong position in Oregon and carried the election easily. Now Tyler moved quickly. Even before Polk assumed office he had the issue of the annexation of Texas presented to the Congress as a joint resolution. Neither house required a two-thirds majority, as the Senate had required for a treaty, and the resolution passed 118 to 101 in the House and 27 to 25 in the Senate. Texas would enter the Union as a full state and retain its lands and its debt, the only state in the Union to do so.

Now the British and the French brought heavy pressure to bear on the Mexicans to recognize the Texans in the hope that this would keep them independent. They did not want the United States to expand its size or its power on the continent. And they persuaded Jones to give them a ninety-day delay to work on the Mexican government. Their efforts were successful, and Jones presented both the Mexican and the United States offers to the Texas Congress and to the people of Texas. They favored the United States when the issue was voted upon, and on December 29, 1845, Polk signed the formal papers recognizing Texas as the twenty-eighth state of the American Union.

On February 19, 1846, President Jones proclaimed that "the Republic of Texas is no more." The first Texas governor, James Pinckney Henderson, took the oath of office, and led Texas in its new role as a state.

The Republic of Texas lasted just a few months less than a decade, but its legacy has loomed large for subsequent Texans. Somewhat like the Camelot of myth, its memory gives modern Texas a recollection of an independence—even imperialist dreams—not shared by any other of the United States.

Titled The Republic of Texas is No More, *this Norman Price drawing illustrates the ceremony heralding the annexation of Texas to the United States on February 19, 1846. Courtesy, Barker Texas History Center*

VI
The First Attempt at Statehood

Texans trace their origins from all over the world. From the Paleo-Americans and Indians and on to the Spanish, French, and Anglo-Celtic influences, all Texans came from somewhere else. By the time Texas became a state of the American Union in 1845, the first four of these groups no longer influenced Texas directly, except the Indians. The Spanish-become-Mexican influence lingered, of course, but mostly in South Texas, and more in numbers than in power. The Anglo-Celtic influence, or more simply now the American influence, predominated. Indians, Mexicans, a few Spanish and French perhaps, and a scattering of other nationalities were present but outnumbered. Only rarely did they exert political or economic power. This new man, this American who ran things, tumbled across the landscape of North America, dropping some of his cultural baggage when the environment

Gathering Corn *depicts early farm life in Texas. Note the black man working alongside the white men. Blacks played an important role in the taming of the Texan wilderness. From* Harper's Weekly, *October 14, 1865*

José Antonio Navarro, a Texan of Mexican birth, was a signer of the Texas State Constitution. Courtesy, Navarro Elementary School

the lure of adventure, the promise of land, and for some a desire to escape conditions wherever they had come from brought them by the thousands in the 1840s and 1850s. When the Republic began in 1836, barely 50,000 people of all colors and nationalities inhabited it. Ten years later, when Texas became a state, the population had increased to more than 120,000, including 40,000 slaves. By 1850 at least 300,000 lived in Texas—more than 60,000 of them slaves—and even that number doubled by the time the state seceded from the American Union and joined the new Confederacy. They mostly came from the southern part of the United States, but a significant number came from Europe, especially from Germany. Like everyone who came to Texas before them, they came for land. Such growth usually comes from prosperity and peace, but instead these were years of political and military turmoil with Mexico and Indians, and years of disagreement and tension between Texas and New Mexico and Texas and the central government itself. And they were not years of prosperity, at least not for the majority. In 1860 Texas still struggled with what can best be termed a colonial culture and economy.

A new constitution written in 1845 established the twenty-eighth state. The convention that wrote the document elected Thomas Jefferson Rusk to preside over it, and other delegates included J. Pinckney Henderson, a cabinet member and diplomat under Houston, Isaac Van Zandt, a Texas congressman and agent to the United States. Other well-known representatives included R.E.B. Baylor, N.H. Darnell, Abner S. Lipscomb, Hiram G. Runnels, and José Antonio Navarro, the sole native-born Texan. The Southern American influence was evident. Eighteen delegates had migrated from Tennessee, eight came from Virginia, seven from Georgia, six from Kentucky, and five from North Carolina. Several had previous positions in the government of the Republic and in their former state legislatures or as judges. Runnels had been a governor.

The constitution they wrote reflected their heritage as Americans as well as Texans. They copied

would not accept it, and learning new ways that worked. Religion, law, learning—everything changed to accommodate the practical demands of living in a new land. By the time his kind reached Texas, full grown, the time and the place and the background came together to create a new image, a new self-image, and a new name—Texan.

Texans remained few in number until after their revolution and independence from Mexico. But the Republic's homestead provision and prohibition against ministers of the gospel from service in the legislature; the organized government reflected the national example with an executive-legislative-judicial separation of powers, and their offices were similar to those of other states of the Union. They specifically established the institution of African slavery. There were also some differences: the state legislature met only every two years, not yearly as had the Texas Congress; the governor served only a two-year term and could serve no more than four years out of six. Representatives to the lower house of the legislature also served two-year terms, but senators served for six years. A two-thirds vote in both houses could charter businesses, except banks, which could not be chartered at all. The state government could not exceed $100,000 in public indebtedness, and married women received protection for their property rights.

Possibly the provision against clergymen is the least explicable and that against banks the most unwise. An anticlerical impulse traced its prejudice to the Declaration of Independence, which denounced a one-church society, and probably private indebtedness to banks and other financial sources in the United States had caused many of the framers to be in Texas in the first place. The one thing Texas needed most in 1845 was credit, yet they denied themselves the most obvious source of it.

Anson Jones still presided over Texas when the constitution was ratified and elections held to select officers for the new state government. Henderson and J.B. Miller ran for governor with Henderson victorious, and Albert C. Horton won the lieutenant governor's post against N.H. Darnell. Houston and Thomas Jefferson Rusk received the legislature's approval to become Texas' first two United States senators. Rusk won the long term in the alteration scheme, and these two men represented their state in the Senate until Rusk's death in 1857 and Houston quit to become governor in 1859. They established lines of succession that are still maintained today. The constitution permitted

Henderson to appoint most of the non-legislative offices, including the justices of the state's supreme court. John Hemphill received appointment as the first chief justice of the court.

As soon as the United States accepted Texas into the Union, tensions arose between both state and nation and their neighbor to the south. The Mexican government had never officially recognized the independence of Texas, although it had behaved as if it had for most of the tenure of the Republic, even acceding to European diplomatic urging by offering in 1845 to grant recognition in return for Texas' continued independence. Mexico could accept that but not the admission of Texas to the American Union, for it had been American interference and encouragement that had incited the revolution in the first place. Except for two raids on San Antonio and periodic border troubles, Mexico had come to a *de facto* acceptance of an independent Texas. Now they renewed threats of war against the United States over annexation. And when the union was completed, Juan Almonte, Mexico's minister at Washington City, requested his credentials and returned to Mexico. Santa Anna, briefly again president of Mexico, fanned the flames of nationalism at this insult to his country.

As far as President James K. Polk and other American expansionists were concerned, Texas had ceased to be involved either as a purpose or a goal for a war with Mexico. They hardly needed to fight the Mexicans to hold Texas; it was already securely within the Union. What they really coveted was all the territory between Texas and the Pacific Ocean, especially California. Of course, Polk did not admit this publicly. But after settling the issue of the annexation of Texas and the question of joint occupation of Oregon with Great Britain, this territory alone remained to fill out the map of the United States. Polk at first tried to buy the territory. John Slidell, a Louisianian experienced in diplomacy, went to Mexico as Polk's agent to deliver his offer to purchase all Mexican lands west of Texas. José Herrera, who replaced Santa Anna as president, refused even to talk to

Slidell or have any other official give recognition of his mission. Polk and many other Americans chose to regard this as an insult to the United States, and soon demands for war could be heard both north and south of the Rio Grande.

Both sides now felt offended, although Mexico, in the midst of crippling domestic turmoil and with half of its territory at stake, may have had more reason to be belligerent.

When the spark that started the war came, both the United States and Mexico could claim that they had been invaded by the other. This resulted from a dispute over the territory between the Nueces River and the Rio Grande. Texans had regarded the Rio Grande as their boundary only since the Treaty of Velasco in 1836, but they were determined to hold that line and they had been annexed with the understanding that it was their true southern and western border all the way to its headwaters in the San Juan Mountains in what is now southwestern Colorado. It had never been regarded as a boundary prior to 1836. The Nueces, on the other hand, had been the traditional boundary between the Anglo colony in Texas and the Mexican states of Coahuila and Tamaulipas, and it was so recognized by statute while the Texas settlements were still a colony. Mexico, never under the legal obligation to honor the Treaty of Velasco, still regarded the Sabine River as their true boundary with the United States, citing the properly-executed Adams-Onís Treaty of 1819 by which the United States had renounced "forever" any claims beyond the Sabine.

The Polk administration was determined to enforce the Texans' interpretation of their boundaries and surely knew how unprepared Mexico was to go to war with the United States. Polk ordered General Zachary Taylor's command to occupy a line along the Nueces River as soon as the United States Congress voted to admit Texas to the Union. Taylor set up headquarters at Corpus Christi in July 1845. Shortly afterwards General Mariano Arista moved troops north to the Rio Grande. The territory between the Nueces and the Rio Grande remained unoccupied by either force

Above: *James Knox Polk spurred the United States into the war against Mexico in 1846-1848. From Cirker,* Dictionary of American Portraits, *Dover, 1967*

Facing page: *Zachary Taylor commanded the United States Army in the Mexican War, and was instrumental in winning the decisive Battle of Buena Vista. From Cirker,* Dictionary of American Portraits, *Dover, 1967*

until John Slidell reported his cold reception in Mexico. Then Polk ordered Taylor to occupy the land south of the Nueces, and Major Jacob Brown moved southward to a position near the mouth of the Rio Grande opposite the Mexico community of Matamoros in April 1846. His bivouac, and later a fort, began the American town of Brownsville. Patrols from both armies roamed the disputed territory until April 24, when sixty of Taylor's cavalry encountered a large force of Mexican soldiers. Following a clash, Arista attacked Brown's camp and Taylor immediately brought 2,300 men to the river line with supplies for a campaign. Now both sides communicated to their governments that a fight on their own soil had occurred and that it had been started by the other side. Polk pushed a declaration of war through the American Congress, and the outraged Mexicans declared war as well.

Taylor launched an overland invasion of Mexico, winning easily at Palo Alto and Resaca de la Palma, then prepared to march on Monterrey. He

continued his southward push past Monterrey, but there his orders and his supplies brought him to a halt. Winfield Scott, the army's highest-ranking commander, coveted the role of conqueror of Mexico. He refused to provide Taylor with sufficient men and supplies to continue the invasion. Instead Scott established a forward base at Port Isabel on the Texas coast and then personally led the first amphibious invasion in United States military history, landing at Vera Cruz. From there he moved inland to capture Mexico City. Santa Anna, leading the remains of the Mexican army, moved north for a battle with Taylor's men. Taylor's victory over Santa Anna at Buena Vista on February 22, 1847, effectively ended the war in the Rio Grande area.

Texans participated in the Mexican War in various ways, and always with gusto. They hosted the Taylor and Scott encampments and fought in their campaigns in volunteer units. Their principal mark—some would call it a black mark—came from the activities of the Ranger companies that fought with both Taylor and Scott. *Los Diablos Tejanos,* as the Mexicans called them, killed their foes with zeal and they did not always try to distinguish a hostile Mexican soldier from a harmless civilian. Taylor commanded them more firmly than did Scott, who often worried about their excesses, but both utilized their battle skills when they were needed. Ben McCullock, Samuel H. Walker, and John S. "Rip" Ford led their hard-fighting Rangers in battle, perhaps remembering the atrocities at the Alamo and Goliad a little too vividly. Even the Texas governor, James Pinckney Henderson, joined in the fighting, taking leave of office to lead a volunteer unit into Mexico.

The victories of Taylor and Scott in Mexico brought an end to the war, and, after tedious negotiations by Nicholas Trist, both nations agreed to a settlement in the Treaty of Guadalupe Hidalgo, signed on February 2, 1848. Mexico agreed to the Rio Grande as its Texas-United States border, and also agreed to surrender additional lands from their northern provinces totalling some 1.2 million square miles. These eventually became the Ameri-

This portrait of Texan hero Ben McCulloch is from John Frost's Pictorial History of Mexico. *Courtesy, Institute of Texan Cultures*

can states of California, Arizona, New Mexico, Nevada, Wyoming, Utah, and Colorado. In return the United States paid the Mexicans fifteen million dollars and assumed claims of United States citizens against them.

Because of the way the war was started and the huge land acquisition resulting from it, one effect of the war was to deepen Mexican resentment and suspicion of the victor. Not all Americans have been proud of this event in history and even in the modern period this can produce flared tempers. In the early 1960s Robert F. Kennedy addressed a press conference in Indonesia, and in answering questions about American imperialism,

referred to the Mexican War as a "dark episode" in United States history. Governor Price Daniel retaliated with an angry telegram, and letters of protest from many Texans found their way to Kennedy's office in Washington. Texans of the 1840s were proud and pleased. The war confirmed their territorial claims and, at least in their minds, their separation from Mexico.

A different kind of border problem lay to the west. Modern Texans are accustomed to seeing the outline of their state displayed on maps with the Rio Grande winding around the Big Bend and on to El Paso, then the boundary cuts sharply back to the east before moving north along the 103rd meridian. Still claiming the Rio Grande as their western border, Texans assumed that this border extended to what was later identified as about one-half of New Mexico. Since their point had been proven with Old Mexico to the south, they were encouraged that their claims toward New Mexico could be established as well. But matters did not turn out that way. Except for the area around Santa Fe, most of the land lay vacant. This ancient city of Indian pueblos and Spanish churchmen, soldiers, and merchants constituted a tempting addition to Texas if it could get the New Mexicans and the United States to go along with the idea. Actually, the New Mexicans had little in common with the Texans and even less inclination to develop in that way since they had ties to Mexico and even to the United States up the Santa Fe Trail to Missouri. They had refused Lamar's efforts to bring them into Texas, and now the United States Army was ready to help them remain outside of Texas.

During the Mexican War General Stephen Kearny occupied Santa Fe and controlled the area. Soon after the hostilities ceased Governor Henderson sent Judge Spruce M. Baird to Santa Fe to assume civilian control, thus effecting Texas' claim to the entire territory. Baird found Colonel John M. Washington in command after Kearny moved to California. Washington rejected Baird's claims. He was encouraged by local residents as well as political influences who wanted to control Texas' size and power. Washington told Baird that he could not relinquish command over Santa Fe without orders from higher authorities. President Polk, who agreed with the Texans, had given such an order already and Washington knew it, but that officer still refused Baird's request for the transfer of authority.

The matter remained at an impasse until after the next gubernatorial election, which saw George Thomas Wood replace Henderson. Wood called the legislature to special deliberations and swore he would defend this Texas soil as strongly as past Texans had defended other lands. The legislature created four counties, Worth, Buckel, Santa Fe, and El Paso, in the disputed area, and Robert S. Neighbors, a former Ranger and Indian agent, drew the assignment of organizing local governments in each county. He succeeded at El Paso but the three more northerly areas refused to acknowledge allegiance to Texas. Then, in 1849, Zachary Taylor became President of the United States. Even before his inauguration Taylor met with representatives from California and New Mexico who desired admission to the Union as full states. He consented to work for the admission of California and pledged his support for the formal organization of New Mexico Territory, which then included lands later known as Arizona as well. And it included the three counties that did not want to become a part of Texas. This settled the matter, at least as far as New Mexico was concerned, and under Millard Fillmore, who became President following Taylor's death in 1850, it became permanent by the enactment of the Compromise of 1850.

This last major legislative attempt to compromise the tensions of the Union over slavery admitted California as a free state, organized New Mexico and Utah territories, banned the slave trade but not slavery itself within the District of Columbia, and put in force a harsher fugitive slave law that made federal law enforcement available to assist with the return of runaway slaves. Curiously, it also addressed the Texas-New Mexico border dispute. By provisions of the act sponsored by James

A. Pearce, Texans agreed to cede all land north and west of the 103rd meridian and the parallel of 36° 30' to New Mexico or to the United States in return for ten million dollars from the national government. Because debts that had accumulated since the Revolution still begged to be paid, it was considered an acceptable arrangement by Texans, who voted two to one in favor of the legislation. Thus Texans surrendered claim to lands that became parts of New Mexico, Colorado, Wyoming, and Oklahoma, and received some money, though by no means all they needed, to pay their debts.

Personalities continued to dominate Texas politics during the early years of statehood, but party politics began a slow development in response to national trends. Henderson served as the state's first governor, except when on leave to lead volunteers in the Mexican War. During his absence Lieutenant Governor Horton ran the state's affairs. George T. Wood, a Trinity River planter, replaced Henderson when the latter did not run for reelection. Texans failed to support fellow slaveowner Taylor in the Presidential election of 1848 despite the fact that he was popular during the war. Instead they voted for Lewis Cass out of loyalty to the Democratic Party. Peter Hansborough Bell defeated Wood in his bid for a second term in 1848, and assumed office in time to accept the Compromise of 1850 for Texas. Elisha M. Pease, who had come to Texas in 1835 from New England, won the governorship in 1853 and again in 1855. Pease tried to stimulate business expansion, especially with rail construction and river improvement subsidies. He also lobbied the national government for a vigorous Indian policy that would allow Texans to expand to the west. He was always a nationalist despite the fact that his adopted state thought of itself as decidedly Southern and edged toward secession. The Whig and Know Nothing parties expanded in Texas during his years also. The American Party, better known as Know Nothing because of its secret nature and the stock answer of its members when asked about their party, stood for nativism and opposition to foreign immigration and Roman Catholicism.

Many Texans found these tenets agreeable because of their attitude toward Mexico and its citizens. The Know Nothings reportedly claimed R.E.B. Baylor and Lieutenant Governor D.C. Dickson as well as other prominent Texans in their party.

Sam Houston's career was full of great triumphs and bitter disappointments; it is surprising how he was sometimes treated in his adopted state. He returned to state politics in 1857 to run against Hardin R. Runnels for governor but lost. He had been too long out of local politics, too isolated in Washington, and his state had moved too close to the standard Southern positions on national affairs. Houston was always a nationalist, and now he found the new immigrants from the South, the states' righters and fire-eating sons of John C. Calhoun who spoke of nullification and secession, to be strangers. Runnels defeated Houston in a campaign that boiled with character assassination. Houston was often booed and insulted when he tried to speak. By the end of the campaign he had reminded Texans often enough of his suffering and serving in Texas to at least get their attention, and when he ran again in 1859 he was successful in defeating Runnels, who ran then for a second term. Since the state had moved even closer to secession during that two-year period, Houston's victory was primarily a personal one, as he was politically out of step with the majority in the state.

Houston's problem with the newer immigrants testified to the changing nature of Texas society. These new arrivals who swelled Texas' population were almost all Southerners, and although they came to escape the same problems or fulfill the same dreams as did the colonists and the Republic's citizens, they were much more wedded to states' rights and slavery and they saw the Union as a far less sacred and secure principle than did their predecessors.

Texas differed from other Southern states because of its frontier line. Texans still had to worry about hostile Indians, as did their fellow frontiersmen to the north in Kansas and Nebraska, but those immigrants inherited a different attitude about slavery and the Union from New England

backgrounds. At least 90 percent of the Texans came from the South, and perhaps because of their frontier status, they were often more vehement in their expression of support for Southern attitudes and principles. Surprisingly few of them came from Louisiana or Arkansas, Texas' immediate neighbors. More came from Tennessee and Alabama than from any other states. These fiercely independent and often clannish folk passed up the Eastern settlements to start homes and farms on the frontier line, and they established a corn culture there as well. Georgians and Mississippians filtered into the pine country and red-dirt areas so familiar to them and took over farms already in cultivation to grow cotton. Some Louisianians migrated to the Brazos country where they grew sugar cane. Missourians moved even beyond the Alabamians to the rolling plains. Although none came in groups sponsored by their native states, they did tend to settle together for support, much as later Irish or Polish immigrants clustered together in cities for the familiarity of language and lifestyle. They recreated the kind of culture they knew about in their new home. But again the en-

vironment changed them and they had to learn what would work in their new home.

They had to learn about some new neighbors, too. Foreign immigration, mostly from Germany, increased during the statehood period. A few Irish and German immigrants had come to Texas during the colonial period but most were absorbed into the predominant Anglo-Celtic culture. When Texans spoke of "foreigners" before the late 1840s they mostly meant Mexicans. But by 1860 there were 43,422 foreign-born residents in Texas, and only 12,000 of them were Mexican. The vast majority of the Mexican population still lived in greatest numbers in the area south of San Antonio where most worked the farms and ranches of others. Few spoke English or took much account of Anglo doings that did not affect them directly. They took little part in economic or political affairs even in areas they dominated numerically. Few voted and none held public office. The Germans were most numerous among the remaining 30,000 foreign-born in Texas. Poles and Czechs also came, but most Anglo-Celtic Texans generally thought of them as German. A few French mi-

grated to operate a socialist utopian village called La Reunion in the area that became Dallas, but their experiment lasted only briefly before many returned to France.

Henri Castor brought a group of French- and German-speaking immigrants to Medina County where he established Castroville. They mostly came from the Upper Rhine country and called themselves Alsatians, Swabians, and Werteembergers; some were Swiss. Nearly 2,000 of them established a bit of the Old World on the new frontier.

The most significant German settlements came in the area north and west of San Antonio. These *Einwanderers,* as they called themselves, came seeking new opportunities and homes but wanted to recreate their fatherland in this new place. To assist them, Prussian nobles founded the Society for the Protection of German Immigrants in Texas, or *Adelsverein,* in 1842. Its purpose was to assist the *Einwanderers* in their journey, acquire land in Texas, build homes, plant crops, provide markets for their produce, and to remain German while doing so.

This engraving details an altercation between white settlers and Indians. Courtesy, Barker Texas History Center

THE HEARTY SETTLEMENT ON THE COMAL

German colonists arriving in Texas for the first time in the 1840s probably had a similar reaction to that of a twentieth-century German woman visiting West Texas for the first time. As the airplane made its approach into El Paso, she saw the desolate, arid country, and commented, "This must be how the world looked in the beginning." If this was not exactly the earliest German colonists' impression, many of them still must have felt that they had come to the end of the earth.

In the 1840s many people in the German provinces decided to immigrate to Texas. Some came for economic reasons, some for political reasons, and some for adventure. In 1842 the *Adelsverein,* a society organized to assist their countrymen in emigration, sent representatives to investigate the territory and prepare the way for the settlers. The most significant of the investigators, Prince Carl of Solms-Braunfels, reached Galveston in the summer of 1843 and immediately began preparation to receive a major wave of immigrants the following winter. He bought land on Matagorda Bay as a seasoning station for the new arrivals where they could be outfitted for the overland journey to new homes. He also purchased land for a permanent settlement on the Guadalupe River near its descent from the Balcones Escarpment.

In December 1844 three ships carrying German immigrants reached Galveston. They traveled southwestward along the coast to Carlshafen (Carl's Harbor), Prince Carl's haven for them. The site was later known as Indianola and became a major port of entry on the Texas coast before being destroyed by a hurricane. A warehouse of supplies awaited them but there were no living accommodations. They camped temporarily on the beach.

After remaining at Carlshafen only a short time, the German settlers loaded wagons and ox carts for the journey to Prince Carl's planned settlement. They arrived at a site on the Comal River on Good Friday, 1845, and immediately began to erect a town. They named it New Braunfels in honor of the prince and his ancestral estate on the Lahn River. New Braunfels quickly took on an Old World look. The men worked communally to erect houses, a fort, a church, and to break the land for their farms.

A second wave of immigrants arrived on the coast a year later, but this time the results were less happy. The *Adelsverein's* funds were depleted and less provision for the immigrants' arrival had been made. The political climate in their new home was troubled by hostilities between the United States and its southern neighbor, Mexico, capping a controversy between Americans and Mexicans dating at least to the revolution in the 1830s. When they arrived on the Texas coast they found that the teamsters who had been employed to haul their belongings to the settlement had been drafted to haul war materials for the army to embarkation points on the lower coast. Abandoned on the hostile coast in winter, nearly 1,000 people died from exposure; additional casualties succumbed when they attempted to move inland for shelter. The daughter of Louis Cachand Ervendbert, pastor of the New Braunfels church, recorded her parents' troubled journey to their new home. Most of the people suffered from scurvy or some kind of fever; frequent rains caused the roads to become quagmires and the ox carts mired in the bottomless mud; and when they finally drew near enough to see their new home across the Guadalupe River, the water was so high that they could not cross for days. Additional deaths resulted while they waited for the waters to subside.

Provisions were still scarce after the arrival of the second wave of immigrants into New Braunfels. Fish were available from the river but beef, pork, and other meat were in short supply. Ammunition was scarce so even hunting failed to supply their need for meat. Before their farms produced dairy products and vegetables, they had to be warned not to eat cactus. Theirs was a completely dependent situation: everything they could not produce had to be hauled to them at great expense and effort.

Gradually the immigrants overcame these early hardships and New Braunfels grew into a small town with some urban services. The Germans were hardworking, skilled craftsmen; their industry began to show in their productive farms and neat houses. Minor nobles and prominent intellectuals also arrived. A paleontologist-geologist, Dr. Ferdinand Roemer, who was sent by the Berlin Academy, arrived in 1846. Encouraged by the potential of the town, he predicted that New Braunfels would grow to 12,000 people and become entirely successful. Others were not so impressed. Ida Kapp said in 1850 that the town "presented a pitiable impression with its little slab houses along the dirt streets which during rains became bottomless. There are . . . three bakers, other artisans, and many stores." Kapp found the transition to the Texas frontier unpleasant, but did admit that she envied the young people's opportunity for advancement in the town. Frederick Law Olmstead visited New Braunfels in 1857 and praised it for its fine food, which he attributed to cleanliness and hard work.

Eventually the German immigrants and their descendants occupied most of the heartland of Central Texas. Their language and lifestyle remain prominent today, a sign of the first German colonists' determination to survive in the Texas frontier.

THE FLAGS OF TEXAS

Texas' famous amusement park, "Six Flags Over Texas," takes its name from the six nations that at one time or another claimed sovereignty over Texas. Some parts of the state had even more flags flown over them because of the early declarations of independence by the filibusters, but these governments never established control over the territory they claimed and were not recognized by other nations.

The first flag was that of imperial Spain. That nation's red and gold standard represented claims over Texas from the time of Columbus' arrival in the New World in 1492 until the Republic of Mexico established its independence in 1821. The second and somewhat more tentative claim was that of France. The House of Bourbon's *fleur-de-lis* arrived with René Robert Cavelier, Sieur de La Salle, at Matagorda Bay in 1685 and was represented again by the arrival in 1714 of the French trader Juchereau de St. Denis. The French claim expired in 1763 when that nation surrendered its lands west of the Mississippi River without a definite border to Spain by the Peace of Paris at the end of the Seven Years' War. It was renewed briefly when Napoleon Bonaparte reclaimed these lands from the Spanish around 1800, then surrendered again when he sold the Louisiana Territory to the United States in 1803.

Most of what was later known as Texas became Mexican territory after the Republic of Mexico was established in 1821. There are several versions of the Mexican flag, but the most well-known is composed of three vertical bars of red, white, and green. In the center is pictured an eagle perched on a cactus holding a serpent in its mouth.

When the Texans established their independence from Mexico a new flag was obviously required. In the fall of 1835 some Texans fought under a white banner with a picture of a cannon and the words "Come and Take It" painted on it; individual units, especially those from the United States, had their own flags at the Alamo, Goliad, and San Jacinto.

Meanwhile the Consultation sent Stephen F. Austin, Branch T. Archer, and William Wharton to the United States to obtain men and money for resistance against the Mexican government. These commissioners believed that Texas soon would declare independence and they developed a flag for the anticipated new republic. Austin thought the flag should be a square Union Jack to identify Texas with North America; stripes to identify it with the United States; red, white, and green in honor of Mexico; and a single star to represent Texas itself. The others insisted that blue be used instead of green, and Austin finally agreed. They also wanted the sun portrayed instead of a star, a picture of George Washington on it, and the phrase "Lux Libertas" replaced with "In His Example There is Safety." This flag was never adopted, although Austin sent a description of it to his cousin, and wrote that a friend had painted the flag, "sun, Washington, and all," on white silk.

In 1836 the Consultation designed a new flag for the Republic once independence was declared. Also never adopted or flown, it had a blue field with a white star of five points with the letters T, E, X, A, and S on the tip of each point.

The first official flag of the Republic was David G. Burnet's flag, adopted on December 10, 1836. It consisted of a large golden star displayed against an azure background. In 1838 a committee submitted a recommendation for a new flag to Congress. Congress agreed to it, as did President Mirabeau B. Lamar, and the official flag evolved into its present form: a blue vertical stripe with a white star of five points in the center, and two horizontal stripes of white and red.

When Texas was annexed by the United States it adopted the Stars and Stripes, on which Texas was represented as the twenty-eighth star. The Lone Star flag of the Republic of Texas then became the official state flag.

Texas joined its sister Southern states in the Confederate States of America in 1861 and thus received a new flag. The first Confederate flag, called the Stars and Bars, was similar to the Stars and Stripes of the United States and led to confusion during the early battles of the Civil War. For practical purposes, a Confederate battle flag was designed. It consisted of a St. Andrew's Cross of blue extending diagonally from corner to corner, edged in white and studded with white, five-point stars representing the Confederate states plus Missouri and Kentucky. In May 1863 the Confederate congress adopted a second official flag that was white with a red field in the left corner with two blue bars studded with white stars. Finally, the Confederate congress changed the flag again in March 1865 by placing a red bar across the right-hand margin.

At the end of the war the Stars and Stripes returned, and the Lone Star flag continued to be the official flag of Texas in the restored Union. In 1933 the Texas legislature adopted a salute to the Texas flag:

Honor to the Texas flag
I pledge allegiance to thee.
Texas, one and indivisible.

Prince Carl of Solms-Braunfels took the lead in these enterprises. He bought land previously awarded to the empressarios Henry Francis Fisher and Burchard Miller. This land lay some distance from the coast and was still in danger of Indian raids. He tried to buy safer property and twice was cheated by swindlers. Finally he purchased property north of San Antonio that he intended to use as a bridge to the land beyond. His people could settle there and then assist others who came later to occupy the original site. Settling on the limestone rocky soils of Central Texas, and using Indianola as their coastal base, thousands of *Einwanderers* migrated to a life of real hardship. Finally, a new leader, Otfried Hans, Freiherr von Meuseback, who soon became simply John O. Meuseback, arrived in Texas and helped the German immigrants find ways to adapt to their new home rather than fight the environment by insisting upon retaining too many of their Old World ways. Meuseback led settlers west from New Braunfels. He made treaties with the Comanches that he insisted the Germans keep, and he founded more communities, including Sisterdale, Boerne, Comfort, and Fredericksburg, probably the best-known of the German communities in later decades. The Germans adapted their farming techniques to the Texas conditions, some ranched, and some ended up in towns as professionals, but they retained their language, religion, folkways, and foodstuffs—especially beer and sausage—and eventually became a powerful force in the cultural life of Texas.

Like the Germans, other Texans remained essentially rural during their first attempt at statehood. Galveston remained the largest town with a population of 4,000 until San Antonio assumed that role with 8,000 in 1860. Austin, Houston, New Braunfels, and Marshall could be called towns. All afforded only dirt streets. Few had anything but one-story buildings, and when the Menger Hotel in San Antonio opened in 1859 it was the tallest building in the state besides the three-story capitol in Austin. Texas towns offered some trade goods, mostly imported from other American states, and professional services in the law, medicine, religious ministry, and newspapers. Only two factories, a hat manufacturer in Houston and a textile plant in Henderson county, constituted Texas' total commercial industry.

Texans still lived in one-room cabins made of logs or stone, depending on which material was most abundant, and they farmed or ranched or trapped or worked for someone who did. Gradually the two-cabin dwelling, or dog-run house, became common, and it might be sided with sawed boards when the owner could afford it. Often the logs remained unchinked, however. Frederick Law Olmsted complained of spending the night in one farmer's home where he gazed at the stars through the cracks between the logs.

Most settlers had enough to eat if they were skillful at hunting and fishing, and salt, sugar, flour, or beans could be purchased if they had sufficient funds. Lacking methods of preserving foods, their vegetable consumption remained limited to growing seasons. Milk cows did not abound, even amid a growing cattle industry. Meat, sweet potatoes, or corn prepared in various ways, including whiskey, constituted a regular diet for many. They made as much as possible of what they consumed from available resources because store-bought items were expensive and not always available. Citizens of the state lived much as had those of the Republic or even the colonial period.

Most Texans did not own slaves, but nearly all of them believed in slavery. Most could not have imagined what to do with the 182,000 blacks in

The German influence in Texas has been reflected in the many fests brought from Europe. Here, Houston celebrates a folkesfest parade with flower-covered wagons in 1870. Courtesy, Houston Public Library

T.W.HOUSE
CLOTHING.
A.SESSUMS
BOOTS & SHOES
Texas Volksblatt.
P. Gabels
Im Wein ist Wahrheit, Wahrheit...
Der bleibt ein...

Texas in 1860 had they not been slaves. Farmers and planters who owned slaves usually used them to grow cotton. They thought slavery the most suitable labor pool for this kind of work; year-round availability for planting, chopping, and picking was thus insured. Although Texans owned only about 6 percent of the slaves in America, and slaves were a small minority even in Texas, investment in slave property exceeded even that of real estate and slave owners ruled the politics, economy, and culture of the state.

Negro slavery arrived in Texas with the earliest Spaniards. Slaves became a significant portion of the laboring class during the Spanish, Anglo colonial, and republican eras, and even after statehood these were considered essential by the white majority to keep the agricultural economy going.

When Texas declared its independence in 1836 an estimated 5,000 slaves lived in Texas; by 1860 more than 180,000, a third of the total population, lived there. There were only 21,781 slaveholders, and nearly 60 percent of them—12,781—owned fewer than six slaves. An estimated 20 per-

cent owned from six to nine slaves, and perhaps 15 percent owned ten to twenty. The remaining half were owned by fewer than 10 percent of the slaveholders.

Because large plantations were scarce, most of the slaves lived with few of their own kind on isolated rural farms. Mostly employed as field hands, some also worked as blacksmiths, masons, carpenters, or at other skilled positions. They usually worked for their owners but occasionally they might be hired out to others. They lived in quarters on their master's farms, sometimes in the same house; and their general fare was not much worse than that of the family or individual who owned them. But they were not free, they were not eligible for formal education, and the privileges and responsibilities of citizenship were denied. Like their masters, who did not know it, they were trapped in an unmanageable and uneconomic labor system that cost both parties far more than it was worth.

Transportation in Texas remained poor. Walking or riding horseback still got most Texans from

place to place, unless they hauled supplies or produce in wagons. Few Texas rivers were really navigable more than a short distance from the Gulf of
Mexico, and then usually only during spring or fall
floods. Otherwise rafts or snags prevented all but
the smaller boats from plying the inland waters.
Railroad construction did not begin in Texas until
the 1850s, and in 1860 only 400 miles of track
existed and these did not connect major towns.
Stagecoaches crossed northern Texas along routes
to the far West, but the service was irregular,
sometimes dangerous, and usually tedious and uncomfortable.

Texans made their work their principal source
of entertainment. Horse racing, usually matched
races, elevated a pride in work into a source of
amusement. Dancing and feasting among the Germans offered diversion in celebration of folk or religious holidays, denied by the Puritan influence
among the Anglo-Celts. Barbecues, politics, militia muster, court days, and church meetings also
provided entertainment. Touring companies made

occasional appearances in Texas towns. Newspapers, especially the *Telegraph* in Houston and the
Galveston News, were devoured no matter how
old they might be. The Masonic Lodge was an important part of life for many Texas males, and
temperance societies and patriotic celebrations
such as the Fourth of July or Texas Independence
Day offered some relief from the isolation of rural
life.

Towards the end of the 1850s, politics attracted
the attention of many Texans. Houston's return to
local political wars, the arrival of Southern fire-
eaters such as Louis T. Wigfall, and a growing
concern about the abolitionists and antislavery advocates in the North excited their concern. After
struggling so hard for ten years, however sporadi-
cally, to gain admission to the American Union, it
would seem unlikely that after only fifteen years of
statehood Texans would be listening to advocates
of secession. But more and more they did so, as
the wedges of separation on the national political
scene split the nation in two.

VII

The Confederate and Reconstructed State

The events and tensions of the 1850s took their toll in Texas as well as other

slave states in the American Union. Texans' ideological migration to South-

ern nationalism began long before most of them even became Texans; com-

ing from Southern states, most were in agreement with the states' rights

arguments expressed in the Kentucky and Virginia resolutions of 1798 and

the nullification arguments of John C. Calhoun that emerged in the early

1830s. They came to resist Northern domination in economic matters and

resented their dependence upon that section, and an evangelical strain pro-

duced a growing nationalism that led them to protect their own cultural in-

stitutions in a newer union.

The Presidential campaign and election of 1860 finally brought matters

to a head, and when it did Texans found themselves firmly on the Southern side. The state's delegates to the Democratic convention in Charleston, South Carolina, including Guy M. Bryan, R.B. Hubbard, Francis R. Lubbock, Tom Ochiltree, and Hardin Runnells, agreed with other Deep South delegates that their party's platform had to contain a positive statement about slavery instead of following Stephen A. Douglas' desires for an endorsement of popular sovereignty. They would follow William L. Yancy and others out of the convention should it fail to adopt the Alabama Platform on slavery. The Dred Scott decision of 1857, which confirmed the right of slave owners to travel or live in the territories, ought to have comforted them, but continued agitation from abolitionists and fears of the election of a Black Republican in 1860 drove them, in vain, to demand this reassurance from their own party.

When the Deep South delegates failed to have their way at the convention, they walked out. The convention adjourned without nominating a candidate, but decided to meet later in Baltimore to do so. There they nominated Stephen A. Douglas. Other Democrats met at Richmond and nominated John Cabell Breckenridge of Kentucky, a man Texans and most other Deep South residents tended to endorse because of his commitment to retaining slavery. The Republican nominee, Abraham Lincoln of Illinois, turned out to be something less than a strong abolitionist, but Texans feared that his election would open the door for the abolitionists and many vowed to work for secession in the event of his election.

Such threats called forth the compromisers. The Constitutional Union Party hoped to block an electoral majority so the House of Representatives could elect a moderate president, one somewhere between the extremes of Lincoln and Breckenridge. Sam Houston coveted the nomination of this party and many outside Texas wanted him, but John Bell of Tennessee defeated Houston by eleven votes on the first ballot at their convention. Texans supported Breckenridge in the November election, by a margin of three to one. He received 47,548 votes, Bell received 15,463, while Douglas polled only 410 votes. Lincoln was not even on the ballot in Texas.

Lincoln's election was all the threat the Deep South, and Texas, needed. Separationists in South Carolina began the process when a secession convention met on December 17 and concluded its act of separation three days later. Then Georgia, followed by Florida, Alabama, Mississippi, and Louisiana, voted by the end of January to leave the Union and agreed to send delegates to a convention at Montgomery, Alabama, to consider forming a Southern government. Texas was expected to become the seventh state in this new government.

Governor Houston worked to avoid that result. As best he could he ignored demands for elections for a secession convention until separationist leaders went around him and requested district judges call for the election of delegates in each district on January 8, 1861, to attend a convention in Austin on January 28. On December 17 Houston issued a call for a special session of the legislature for January 21, hoping to either prevent or block the special election, but to his disappointment many of the legislators were elected as delegates to the convention and they refused to interfere with the process already begun.

When the secession delegates met in Austin they selected Oran M. Roberts as their president, then voted 152 to six to separate Texas from the American Union should a popular election endorse such action. They disavowed the legislative action of 1845 accepting admission as one of the United States, and submitted the resolution for the approval of the voters in an election called for February 23. Their separation vote, held on February 1, was conducted in an atmosphere of tension. A few Unionists, principally J.W. Throckmorton, cast their negative votes orally to a chorus of protests from other delegates and visitors. Throckmorton's bold response, "Mr. President, when the rabble hiss well may patriots tremble," was a courageous affirmation that Houston did not stand completely alone.

The resolution received full attention from Texans and the debate often became bitter. The

Wigfall's Texas Brigade posed at Seven Pines, Virginia, in 1861. They later became known as Hood's Texas Brigade, after their first commander in the Confederate Army, John Bell Hood of Kentucky. Courtesy, Colonel H.B. Simpson, Confederate Research Center, Hill County Junior College

Southern Intelligencer and the *Bastrop Advertiser* opposed secession while the *Galveston News* and the *Texas Republican* championed it. Debates, discussions, and vehement arguments punctuated the deliberation, but the outcome essentially reflected the vote for President: 46,129 endorsed secession, while about one-third of those voting, 14,697, opposed it. Ten counties in Central Texas, some in North Texas, and, inexplicably, Angelina County in East Texas, generally a mirror of the Old South, voted against secession, while the rest of the state favored separation.

Buttressed by this overwhelming vote, the convention met in Austin on March 2, not accidently placed on Texas Independence Day, and three days later voted for the separation of Texas from the American Union and also for affiliation with the Confederate States of America then being organized at the Montgomery convention. Already Texas had unofficial delegates in Montgomery, and their status changed formally as soon as the vote was taken in Austin. Then, on March 16, the convention summoned all elected officials to take an oath of loyalty to the new government of Texas and its new affiliation with the Confederacy. Most officials did so with little hesitation, but not Houston. He sat up the previous night, agonizing over what to do. Then, when his name was called first, owing to his office, he refused to enter the chamber to take the oath. Finally, after Houston was summoned three times, Lieutenant Governor Edward Clark agreed to take the oath and temporarily succeeded Houston until new elections produced a permanent successor. Houston quietly disposed of an offer from President Lincoln that he use federal troops stationed in Texas to hold his office. He claimed that he had fought for Texas and would not fight against her, but his desire to avoid real bloodshed was a more important reason.

These troops, commanded by Georgian General David Twiggs, constituted a significant portion of the federal army. They were in Texas because of its need for frontier defense, but now their pres-

Albert Sidney Johnston, Texas' most prominent officer, commanded the Western Theater of the Confederate Army. He died at the Battle of Shiloh in April 1862. Courtesy, Institute of Texan Cultures

ence alarmed many Texans who demanded their immediate surrender. Twiggs tried to honor both loyalties. He attempted to resign so he could remain loyal to his oath, yet he wanted the troops and their supplies to pass to the Texans. Before his replacement arrived the Texans grew impatient and, following Ben McCulloch, rode to United States Army headquarters in San Antonio and captured the federal soldiers without a fight. Thus Twiggs allowed approximately 10 percent of the Union's army to be captured. They were exchanged before real fighting began.

Texas hastened to organize itself as a Confederate state. The secessionists controlled the state so the contest for such offices as governor became one of personality rather than party loyalty. Clark attempted to remain in office but lost to Francis R. Lubbock by only 124 votes, and John M. Crockett of Dallas became lieutenant governor. The first Confederate administration supported the central government with zeal, then Lubbock left office after only one term to become an advisor of Confederate President Jefferson Davis in Richmond, Virginia. He was replaced by Pendleton Murrah of Harrison County in 1863. The Confederate postmaster, John Henry Reagan, was Texas' highest-ranking civilian in the Confederate government and was one of only two cabinet members who held their post for the entire war. He was captured with Davis after they left Richmond in April 1865, still attempting to serve his president. Texas' senators included W.S. Oldham and Louis T. Wigfall.

Lubbock left the domestic policies of the Houston-Clark administration as unchanged as possible except where wartime exigencies required a different tack. His support of the central administration's war policy remained unreserved and wholehearted, and he worked hard to organize and prepare his state for the conflict. He organized home guards to replace the federal military in Indian defense, enlisted others to join the regular Confederate army, and worked with the legislature to ready the state for the demands of the war itself. Along with the comptroller and treasurer,

Lubbock constituted the Military Board, a cooperating agency charged with broad powers to establish priorities for military and domestic preparedness. The board took charge of federal bonds and other resources within the state and attempted to negotiate them to obtain needed supplies; because many of the state's workers, from planters to day laborers, were in the military, they suspended debtor laws; they attempted to obtain revenue for the suppprt of military personnel on active duty; and they administered Confederate treasury warrants, when available, for state needs.

When Lubbock reported for duty with the Confederate government he left a functioning, if troubled, state government to Murrah. Lubbock had had to double taxes, a severe measure to many because so many taxes had been remanded during the 1850s. But the wartime demand for revenue increased constantly, and more and more families became dependent upon the government or private charity. The state purchased cotton cards so the people could card, spin, and weave their own cloth, and part of local tax revenues were allowed to remain at home to provide for the destitute, especially widows and orphans. Local commissioners' court records in every county testify to this growing need. Murrah's devotion to the Confederacy never wavered despite the declining economy of his state. At the end of the war, when Texas and the rest of the Confederacy collapsed, he escaped to Mexico, still a confirmed Confederate. A few other Confederates, including some from other states, also fled to Mexico, but most eventually returned to their homes.

As usual, Texans rose to the challenge of a fight, even though Texas itself was not an important theater in the war. At the beginning of the war the state was organized into military districts under the command of Earl Van Dorn, who was soon replaced by General Paul Octave Hebert of Louisiana. The Texans never liked Hebert and they quarreled with him frequently, especially over the conscription law.

The Texans resented the law, many feeling that anyone worth having in the army would join vol-

This photograph of nine of the survivors of the Tom Green Rifles was taken in Austin in 1866. The Tom Green Rifles group was one of the many Texan troops fighting for the Confederate cause. Courtesy, Texas State Archives

untarily, and others resented being forced to serve. The 1860 Census indicated that there were approximately 90,000 men between the ages of eighteen and forty-five in Texas, and between 60,000 to 70,000 of them served, including more than 20,000 who volunteered during the first year of the conflict. The familiar pattern of American military volunteerism prevailed in Texas. A planter or wealthy merchant would organize and finance a unit and usually would serve as its commander. Later, when conscription was implemented, additional men were assigned to these units. The first draft called men between eighteen and thirty-five years of age, but demands of the war caused this to be broadened to seventeen to forty-five years of age. Hebert was replaced by General John Bankhead of Virginia late in 1862, and that officer remained in command until the end of the war.

General Albert Sidney Johnston, the state's most prominent soldier at the beginning of the war—and perhaps the South's best-known soldier in 1861—commanded the Western Theater of the Confederate army until he was killed at the Battle of Shiloh in April 1862. Texas provided many other general officers but only Felix Huston Robertson was a native-born Texan.

Texas also provided military supplies and much-needed troops to the Confederate cause. The thirty-two companies Lubbock raised in 1862 were officially called the Texas Brigade, but are most often called Hood's Texas Brigade after their first commander, General John Bell Hood of Kentucky. The brigade later contained units from Arkansas and North Carolina but it was always called a Texas brigade and served primarily under Robert E. Lee in the Army of Northern Virginia. Lee called them all "my Texans" and usually deployed them where the fighting would be the fiercest. Only 700 of the more than 4,000 who served in the unit survived the war. Terry's Texas Rangers, commanded by General B.F. Terry, fought valiantly in the Western Theater. Lawrence Sullivan Ross' brigade also fought in the Western Theater and in the Trans-Mississippi Department after it was created in 1863. The creation of this department proved necessary after federal troops and gunboats succeeded in gaining complete control of the Mississippi River in 1863, virtually isolating Texas, Arkansas, and much of Louisiana from the rest of the Confederacy. Command of the department went to General Edmund Kirby Smith of Virginia.

Only a few engagements and no major battles were fought in Texas, but significant action occurred along its borders. In May 1861 a Confederate force under W.C. Young attacked forts Arbuckle, Cobb, and Washita in Oklahoma be-

yond the Red River. In August of that year John R. Baylor invaded southern New Mexico and claimed the territory as far west as Tucson. Baylor became the governor of the Confederate Territory of Arizona, at least in name. General H.H. Sibley and General Tom Green won an impressive victory at Valverde on February 2, 1862, then lost to federal troops under General Edward R. Canby at Glorietta in northern New Mexico. Canby's victory effectively reclaimed all of New Mexico and Arizona from Confederate control.

Along the coast a Union blockade gradually tightened its grip after July 1861, and by October Union forces occupied Galveston. General John Baulshead Magruder reclaimed the island city and port on January 1, 1863, with a combined assault of troops from Virginia Point and others on flat-bottomed riverboats with decks lined with cotton bales for protection. The Confederates retained possession of Galveston until the end of the war.

The most significant battle in Texas was fought at Sabine Pass, on the upper coast, in September 1863. Sabine Pass, an inlet from the Gulf of Mexico to a saltwater lake that received the waters of the Sabine and Neches rivers, commanded access to interior rail lines connecting to Houston and Louisiana. Both rivers were navigable for some distance inland. As early as September 1862, federal ships forced the Confederates to abandon the pass; but it was quickly reclaimed and an artillery battery under the command of Lieutenant Dick Dowling occupied the terrain and aimed their guns in such a way as to control access in the main channel. They prepared a rough compound called Fort Griffin. A year later General Nathaniel Prentiss Banks tried to send seventeen ships and 4,000 men through the pass to move up the rivers to the rail lines. As they came under Dowling's guns, the lead ships were disabled, blocking the channel, and the remainder of the federal troops had to return to New Orleans. President Davis, desperate for relief after recent losses at Gettysburg and Vicksburg, hailed the battle as the most significant of the war. He obviously overstated the case, but the federal defeat, just as it seemed as if

TEXAS RANGERS.

ATTENTION!

DO NOT WAIT TO BE DRAFTED.

The undersigned having been authorized by his Excellency, the Governor, to raise a company of Rangers, under the provisions of an act entitled "An act to provide for the protection of the frontier of Texas," and appr ved Dec. 21, 1861, has been granted the privilege to receive men from any portion of he State, with a view to select the very best materia the country affords, that efficient service may be rendered.

The act requires each man to furnish his own horse, arms and accoutrements, and I need not say that I wish th m to be of the best kind obtainable—double-barreled shot guns, light rifles and six-shooters, if possible.

The pay offered by the State Government is very liberal and equal to the most favored troops in the service—equal to the pay of any troops of the same class in the Confederate Army.

All persons desirous of availing themselves of this last opportunity of serving their State, are invited to rendezvous at Concrete, De Witt co., on the Guadalupe r.ver, on the last day of ebruary, 1862, for the purpose of enrollment and organization the following day, fro u which time they will be provided for by the Government. **JOHN J. DIX.**

McMullen Co., Feb. 11, 1862.

With so many men fighting for the Confederacy away from home, Governor Francis Lubbock organized Texas Ranger companies to fight against Indians on the frontier. This recruiting poster for Rangers appeared in McMullen County in 1862. Courtesy, Barker Texas History Center

the war had turned permanently in their favor, did contribute to lengthening the conflict.

Banks did better elsewhere on the coast. His forces controlled every port below Galveston, including Corpus Christi, Aransas Pass, and Indianola. But he did not do as well in the interior. In 1864 he again used naval vessels to carry troops up the Mississippi and Red rivers with the intent of joining General Frederick Steele, who would come southwest from Little Rock, to capture

North Texas. Van Dorn succeeded in stopping Steele, and General Richard Taylor, son of Zachary Taylor, attacked Banks at Mansfield, Louisiana. Learning of the campaign, East Texas civilians, many unarmed, hurried to Mansfield to join Taylor. Banks' advance was stopped and he fell back to Pleasant Hill, where Taylor again attacked him, this time with little success. But Banks continued to withdraw, giving Taylor a strategic victory anyway. And in the final action of the war, John S. Ford's command fought Union troops, many of them black, near Brownsville at Palmito Ranch in May 1865. Ford knew that the war had ended but committed his troops to battle anyway.

Texans also had to fight Indians. The only Confederate state with a frontier line, this problem became theirs when the hopes that the Davis government would assume the job abandoned by Twiggs' captured soldiers were dashed. The Confederate government had too many Union soldiers to worry about to send troops to Texas for Indian defense. Lubbock tried to handle the Indian problem with militia under the command of James M. Norris. Norris' scheme of regular patrols in the Indian country failed because of the predictability of the patrols. J.E. McCord replaced Norris and had better luck with irregular patrols, but he lost some of his effectiveness when many of his men left for regular service with the army elsewhere. Later J.W. Throckmorton organized troops who, like himself, would fight Indians but not federal troops. The most celebrated and bizarre Indian fight occurred at Adobe Walls, north of Amarillo, where Union and Confederate soldiers fought together against Comanches, and the least successful resulted from the ill-advised attack by 370 state troops upon more than 1,400 Kickapoo Indians. The Indians won that battle.

Texans may not have suffered in the same way as did Virginians and Tennesseans, but there were still many problems within the state. Some did not like the Confederacy from the start. Houston remained relatively quiet, and prior to his death in 1863 he had even come to support Confederate military activity, mostly because of friends and relatives in the service. Some others simply left; financier S.W. Swenson emigrated from the state, taking with him his valuable leadership in fiscal matters. E.J. Davis symbolized bolder Unionists who left and then returned in command of Union troops. The Germans, who largely disapproved of slavery anyway, tended to support Union nationalism. Some tried to escape to Mexico rather than serve in the state or Confederate forces. Dissent also developed in North Texas, which became a gathering place for deserters from both sides, and a Peace Party developed there. It was partially to reach these people that Banks tried to come up the Red River in 1864. Loyal Confederates in the area became alarmed and hanged forty Peace Party advocates at Gainesville and other places.

One of the principal problems was the need to keep the South's cotton flowing to Mexico for export. A conference of Western state representatives held in Marshall in 1863 produced a plan to keep this trade going. They called upon the government to take charge of the trade, purchase half of each planter's cotton, exempt the remainder from impressment, and generally provide the incentive to maintain production. Murrah came up with a "state plan" which provided for the state to take over the trade, return half of what arrived in Mexico to the owner, and secure the remainder with state bonds. Cotton growers disliked this plan because it left all control in the hands of the

The Civil War reached Galveston Bay in 1863. This sketch depicts the United States gunboat Westfield *being destroyed. Courtesy, Institute of Texan Cultures*

state, and their fears were not eased when the Confederate Congress preempted the state by taking over the trade itself to insure the flow of goods and the opportunity to obtain supplies in Mexico.

Cotton production declined anyway as the war raged on and more men joined the military forces. Women, children, and draft exempters attempted to continue the work with lessening success. Inflation, the shortage of consumer goods, and other problems burdened their efforts. Salt became scarce and the people turned to substitutes for such things as coffee. They parched rye, okra, or acorns and ground them to brew a coffee-colored beverage, they used corncob ashes for soda, and they wore homespun clothing. Murrah was inaugurated in such a suit, partly because so many others wore them. Lack of newsprint forced many newspapers out of business, and the shortage of other paper interfered with business. Often letters would be answered on the same page by turning it ninety degrees and writing across the original lines.

Little industry was located in Texas at the beginning of the war, but soon arms factories were established at Austin and Tyler. Ironworks were begun in East Texas, and the state penitentiary at Huntsville became a leading producer of cloth in Texas. The state also became a refuge for white noncombatants and slaves shipped to Texas to escape capture or prevent them from running away. Both migrations brought additional problems to Texas. Kate Stone, a refugee from the Vicksburg campaign, fled from her family's plantation, Brokenburn, in Louisiana, to Tyler, Texas, which she called the "dark corner of the Confederacy." She criticized the backwardness of Texas in her diary and longed for the civilized life of the Eastern regions. She may be forgiven her unhappiness with Texas because of the reason for her migration, but actually Texas functioned fairly well under wartime conditions, at least until the latter stages when shortages became acute.

The Civil War ended at different times for Texans. Those serving in Virginia in Hood's Brigade were surrendered by General Robert E. Lee on April 9, 1865; Terry's Texas Rangers were surrendered at Bentonville, North Carolina, on April 19; and the Department of the Trans-Mississippi was surrendered on June 2. Most Texans, black and white alike, mark June 19, 1865, as the real end of the war. On that day General Gordon Granger, representative of theater commander General Philip H. Sheridan, arrived in Galveston to proclaim the war at an end in Texas and all wartime proclamations, including the Emancipation Proclamation, in effect. Whites generally resented the event, and most blacks rejoiced, if they learned of it; in subsequent years it became "Juneteenth," their special holiday of freedom, a kind of Fourth of July all their own. The celebration diminished during the push for civil rights in the 1960s and 1970s but showed signs of resurrection in the 1980s.

There are several definitions of Reconstruction. If that term refers simply to the readmission of Texas to the Union, Reconstruction ended in

1870; if it refers to the restoration and diversification of Texas' economy, it was not accomplished until after the turn of the century, and then not completely; and if it refers to the social accommodation of black and whites, it is yet incomplete.

Five plans of Reconstruction emerged from Northern politicians and at least four interpretations of the circumstance of the Union came from both sides. Southerners were content to assume that their loss meant that they had not left the Union; Lincoln said they were merely out of their proper relationship to the Union and needed to be adjusted as one might set a broken arm; Thaddeus Stevens led one group of Radicals who argued that the South was merely a conquered province under the control of Congress; and Charles Sumner led another group who believed that the Southern states had committed suicide and their remains were also under the control of Congress.

Lincoln began the Reconstruction process with his "Ten Percent" plan in 1863 as an act of the war itself; he wanted to show the South how easy

Facing page: *This painting is titled* Battle of Palmito Ranch, *and depicts that important Civil War battle. Courtesy, Texas Southmost College Library*

Right: *North and South engaged in furious battle on the Gulf Coast just outside Galveston, in this 1863* Harper's Weekly *Civil War chronicle. Courtesy, Institute of Texan Cultures*

it would be to stop fighting and rejoin the Union. He said that if 10 percent of the voters in 1860 would take an oath of future loyalty to the Union they could elect delegates to a convention to write a new constitution that accepted wartime proclamations. He selected Andrew Jackson Hamilton to organize such a movement in Texas, but Hamilton got no closer than New Orleans until the end of the war.

Refusing to accept Lincoln's plan, the Radicals in Congress responded in 1864 with their own plan in the Wade-Davis Bill. Instead of ten percent of the voters in 1860 it required 50 percent to take an "iron-clad" oath of past as well as future loyalty. No state could qualify and the Radicals did not want any to do so; they wished to prolong the process until they could control it completely. Following the death of Lincoln, new President Andrew Johnson came forward with a third plan. It specified no percentage of the voters of 1860 to take an oath of future loyalty but implied that the more who did the better it would be. They could then elect the delegates, accept the required proclamations, and apply for readmission to the Union. Texas and the other former Confederate states attempted to implement this plan but all eventually were rejected by the Radicals.

The fourth plan was embodied in the Fourteenth Amendment. It defined citizenship for all whites and blacks, denied citizenship to high Confederate officials, and guaranteed freedmen "due process" and "equal protection" under state laws. When Tennessee alone accepted the amendment, it was readmitted. The other Southern states were subjected to much harsher treatment under the fifth and final plan enacted in the Reconstruction Acts of 1867. Now the Radicals insisted on full and complete black suffrage in the South and treated the "former states" as conquered provinces. They were arranged into five military districts—Texas shared Military District Five with Arkansas and Louisiana—and were completely under the control of the Army for administration, voter registration, and rewriting the state constitutions.

The ordeal of Texas under this process did not really begin until the third, or the Johnson, plan. Returning veterans and weary civilians alike mostly welcomed the end of the war. Society had nearly disintegrated, money was worthless, land values uncertain, crops mostly neglected. Mobs attacked Confederate supply warehouses and a mob looted the state treasury with the idea that the funds and supplies had been for their use anyway. The looters only netted $5,000, far less than the reported $300,000 that was supposed to be there. Many slave owners neglected to tell their former chattels that slavery had ended. Indeed, as late as 1868 some were discovered who were ignorant of the fact that they were legally free.

Nearly 50,000 federal troops occupied Texas after the war. Texas was bigger and its population more separated than other states, and its frontier required soldiers to deal with the Indians; but many troops were also stationed along the border as a diplomatic tool to force the French to abandon the influence they had established over Mexico during the war. Some of them, such as General George A. Custer, who headquartered in Austin at the Deaf and Dumb Asylum, were accepted and even liked; others were disliked and resisted, particularly if they lingered too long.

Andrew Jackson Hamilton reached Austin on August 9, 1865, two years after his appointment, to begin the process of Reconstruction in Texas. Unionists James Bell became secretary of state and William Alexander became attorney general. Hamilton appointed officers to implement Johnson's plan. He called an election for January 8, 1866, to elect delegates to a constitutional convention which he scheduled to begin on February 7. The convention would be required to abolish slavery, secure the status of blacks, renounce secession, and repudiate state and Confederate debt.

The election sent mostly ex-Confederates to the convention, but there were a few Unionists and also a conservative element that just wanted an end to the trouble. J.W. Throckmorton, a representative of all three elements, became president of the convention. They side-stepped the secession

Continued Indian resistance forced the United States Army to reestablish a line of abandoned frontier forts in West Texas in 1868. Soldiers reoccupied older posts and established new ones, including Fort Davis. Courtesy, Institute of Texan Cultures

issue by assuming that the Confederate loss provided *de facto* evidence that secession had not succeeded. However, this did not assert, as Hamilton wanted, that secession was illegal. They also did not ratify the Thirteenth Amendment outlawing slavery on the grounds that it was already in effect and did not require their agreement. They attempted to provide for the security of freedmen but enacted a Black Code, which the Radicals considered little better than slavery. Blacks were denied equal access to the courts, could not vote or hold office, and suffered other restrictions. The convention cancelled all state debt but approved other state actions that had no direct bearing on the war. These and other provisions were submitted as amendments to the constitution of 1845, which had been amended previously in 1861 to make Texas a Confederate state. The people approved these changes in an election on June 25. They also elected Throckmorton governor and G.W. Jones lieutenant governor. Throckmorton presided over Texas even after the Reconstruction Acts officially abolished the state. Johnson had recognized the Throckmorton government on August 20, 1866.

Texans gave little evidence of remorse for its Confederate experience. The legislature elected David G. Burnet and Oran M. Roberts—the latter had presided at the secession convention—as their senators. Along with the members of the House of Representatives they delivered the new constitution to the Congress. The Radical majority refused to seat any of them, effectively rejecting the constitution and the readmission of Texas to the Union, because of the failure to provide adequately for blacks and for refusing to ratify the Thirteenth and Fourteenth amendments. John H. Reagan, home from imprisonment in the North, had urged the Texans to ratify the amendments and do anything else necessary to get Reconstruction over with as soon as possible, but they refused and now were forced to undergo additional years of Radical rule.

The Radicals could justify their actions. The new constitution and the legislative appointments failed to show any remorse, and blacks would still be in a second-class relationship to the dominant whites. For a variety of reasons, including the desire to solidify their position with black voters in the South and a genuine concern for the blacks, the Radicals undertook the remaking of Southern society. They used the Freedman's Bureau, directed in Texas by E.M. Gregory, to assist blacks in labor contract negotiation, teach literacy in Bureau schools, and distribute direct relief when necessary. The act creating the Bureau was the first significant welfare legislation in United States

history. Whites generally opposed the Bureau, although some of them accepted its food and supplies, because they resented its role in recruiting black voters. Sometimes the local Bureau agent doubled as a representative of the Loyal Union League, a Radical political agency, among the blacks.

Despite the Congressional acts of 1867, Throckmorton continued to preside as governor with the tolerance of the military. General Sheridan commanded Military District Five until succeeded by generals W.S. Hancock and Edward R. Canby, and General Charles Griffin commanded the subprovince of Texas until relieved by General J.H. Reynolds. Griffin replaced Throckmorton with former governor E.M. Pease following a disagreement over pardoning blacks in the state penitentiary. Throckmorton refused to do so because they were criminals, and Griffin assumed, perhaps rightly in some cases, that they were in jail because they were black. Pease's government and Griffin's soldiers registered 53,633 whites and 49,479 blacks for the vote, although many whites protested that they were not registered because of Confederate activities and sympathies. This was, however, within the authority of the registrars. From February 10 through 14 voters selected dele-

Facing page: *Edmund J. Davis, a controversial political figure during Reconstruction, served as a Republican governor of Texas from 1870 until 1874, when he was finally forced out of office. Courtesy, Institute of Texan Cultures*

Below: *After the Civil War, the Freedmen's Bureau became the agency for black social reform and for policing black-white relations. Courtesy, Institute of Texan Cultures*

gates to a new constitutional convention. Many whites stayed away because the Reconstruction Acts required a majority of those registered to participate in order to have a valid election, but the ploy did not work.

The convention of ninety-four delegates, ten of them black, gathered in Austin in June 1868 and argued for weeks over the issue of *ab initio,* or the legal status of acts by the Confederate state government not related to the war. At issue was the validity of such matters as marriages, bond disposition, and licensing. E.J. Davis led the Radicals who wanted all acts since secession voided, while Hamilton's so-called Moderates wished to uphold all acts not directly related to the war. The convention also acted as a legislature and chartered railroads, investigated lawlessness, and handled

JUNETEENTH

Music, laughter, and the sounds of a celebration resounded throughout rural Texas each June 19 for nearly 100 years following the American Civil War. On that day in 1865 Union General Gordon Granger arrived in Galveston to announce that the wartime proclamations of President Abraham Lincoln, including the Emancipation Proclamation, were in effect in Texas. Issuing it in preliminary form September 1862, Lincoln had proclaimed that all slaves owned by persons in rebellion against the United States on January 1, 1863, would thereafter be considered free. He did not define their new status—that was worked out in the Fourteenth Amendment passed in 1868—and his proclamation did not immediately free many slaves when it went into effect. This was because slaves owned by masters who were not in rebellion were exempted, and those who were still in rebellion had the Confederate army to defend them. It did, however, commit the United States to the end of slavery.

Once the Confederate military forces surrendered to the Union army, occupation forces arrived in the former Confederate states to begin Reconstruction. A part of that process was the enforcement of the wartime proclamations. General Granger's General Order Number 3, issued on June 19, 1865, ordered the 21,878 slave owners in Texas to release 182,566 slaves from bondage. His order also affected a similar number of slaves who had been sent to Texas during the war to prevent them from running away or protect them from harm. All were free at last.

Thereafter the day of liberation was known in both the black and white communities as "Juneteenth." Blacks in the North usually celebrate the date of the Emancipation Proclamation while blacks in the South usually celebrate the date that emancipation became effective in their respective states. This differed from state to state, and Texas' Juneteenth celebration is the latest on the calendar.

While emancipation did not mean citizenship, blacks entered a new relationship with society and government. This era of optimism was reflected in every aspect of black life. Not only could blacks register to vote, some held elective offices in the Radical Republican government. Such significant gains called for celebration.

Juneteenth parties varied from community to community, but the celebration usually included a parade, commemoration service, a picnic, games, and a party and dance that sometimes continued throughout the night. Black churches served as the primary organizers, but schools, Masonic lodges, and sometimes businesses, fraternities, and sororities also helped organize the party.

The parade began the day's activities. It wound its way through the heart of town and concluded at a church, school, or other public meeting place. Large crowds of black and white spectators of all ages gathered to hear music and speeches that reminded both races of the significance of emancipation. Prayers of thanksgiving were followed by jubilee songs such as "Free at Last" and "In That Great Gettin' Up Mornin'," celebrating the joy of freedom, and patriotic songs that affirmed the loyalty of the black community. Then a preacher would deliver a sermon or a leading citizen would orate on the life of Abraham Lincoln, "the Great Emancipator." In later years, the speaker might advocate a community project. It was customary to read Granger's declaration of freedom and a highlight of the commemoration was the testimony of former slaves about their lives before and after emancipation.

Later the crowd gathered at a local park for a picnic and events such as baseball, horse racing, stunt riding, and rodeos. Food preparation and sharing was a principal attraction for most celebrants. Local merchants, politicians, and patrons of both races donated pork or beef; while the men barbecued it, women made fried chicken, potato salad, sweet potato pie, peach cobbler, and homemade ice cream. Soda pop, alcoholic beverages, and "glassade," a blend of shaved ice, sugar, and fruit syrup, added liquid refreshment to the menu. The meat was shared by everyone but usually families prepared and shared the other food together. After dinner the celebrants danced to the music of whatever instruments were available.

Juneteenth was an important occasion in every Texas community that had a population of former slaves. Harris County had established their annual celebration of freedom as early as 1872. Under the leadership of the Reverend Jack Yates of the Antioch Baptist Church, the black community in Houston raised $1,000 to purchase a ten-acre site for their party. They named it Emancipation Park, and constructed a baseball field, dining pavilions, and a bandstand. It provided a place for family reunions, especially during Juneteenth Celebrations.

Juneteenth was celebrated with the support and cooperation of white employers and patrons until well into the twentieth century. Many gave their black employees the day off; some even donated food and helped organize the event. It was celebrated less during the 1950s, 1960s, and 1970s: many blacks no longer wanted to be reminded of slavery and many whites withdrew support of the celebration due to civil rights activism. Fortunately, Juneteenth celebrations reappeared in the 1980s to remind all Texans of the joy of freedom.

During Reconstruction, blacks could vote for the first time in former Confederate states. Courtesy, Institute of Texan Cultures

other matters not directly related to constitution making.

By late summer the convention adjourned until after elections scheduled for the fall, each side hoping for support from the electorate. They also had to levy a special tax to support the extra session. The victory of Republican Ulysses S. Grant over the Democratic nominee, Horatio Seymour, strengthened the Moderates. When the convention met in January 1869, E.J. Davis tried to separate Texas into a state of West Texas and East

Texas in the hope that he could control at least one of them. Hamilton blocked him and also won on the issue of *ab initio* and on requiring only an oath of future loyalty for former Confederates. The convention adjourned again on February 8, 1869, without finishing the constitution. They turned their records and resolutions over to Reynolds, who appointed a committee to draft the document. In spite of this questionable procedure the constitution thus created was perhaps the best of the state's foundational documents. It centralized authority, confirmed white and black male suffrage, gave the governor a four-year term and significant appointive and administrative power, abolished needless local offices, and provided for public education better than any previous constitution by guaranteeing at least one quarter of state revenue for this function.

Davis worked to convince President Grant and the Congress to reject the constitution. When he failed in this effort he determined to·run the government himself, and despite previous defeats by Hamilton, he won the governorship in an election held on November 2, 1869. Reynolds certified 39,910 votes for Davis and 39,002 for Hamilton, then destroyed the ballots. Hamilton felt as if he had been cheated out of the election and he probably was correct, but both sides were guilty of fraud. The new constitution was ratified by a vote of 74,466 to 4,928, and Pease resigned so Davis could assume office even before the appointed date.

Davis called the legislature into session on February 8, 1870, to ratify the Thirteenth and Fourteenth amendments. They also selected Morgan Hamilton and J.W. Flanagan as senators. President Grant signed legislation formally readmitting Texas to the American Union on March 30, 1870, and at least political, if not economic or social, Reconstruction had ended in Texas.

The Thirteenth Legislature met in three sessions during 1870 and 1871 and Davis dominated their activities. His legislative agenda, termed the "Obnoxious Acts" by Moderate Republicans and Democrats, included the creation of a state police force and a state militia entirely under Davis' authority, authorized him to employ a state printer—creating an "official" newspaper—and enabled him to fill vacancies in any public office, including nearly 8,000 positions. He could also postpone state elections to bring them into alignment with federal elections, giving current officeholders, nearly all of them Republicans, an extra year in office. Speaker of the House Ira Evans opposed this program so strongly that Davis' supporters removed him from office.

An examination of Davis' actions reveals that there was some justification for these laws and also that he was not guilty of wholesale abuse of his powers. The militia was needed for Indian defense, and the police could be justified by widespread lawlessness in Texas in the aftermath of the war. The Special Police, especially those commanded by Captain L.H. McNelly, did genuine law enforcement work. Davis' appointments placed many good men in office, and he did permit local elections in the fall of 1871. Nevertheless Davis was despised by the Democrats. They protested his use of martial law in Limestone and Freestone counties to stop a feared rebellion which did not materialize after the killing of a black policeman, and in Hill and Walker counties where troops were needed to maintain order. They criticized Davis for granting bonds as railroad subsidies, which he did because the constitution forbade land grants for this purpose. He had opposed the legislative authorization of these bonds, thought necessary to help rebuild and expand transportation services, but he received the blame from the Democrats because of the expense. Regardless of the politics involved, the International Railroad Company, the Southern Pacific, and the Southern Transcontinental Railway received 8 percent bonds and used them to begin construction.

In September 1871 delegates at a gathering in Austin protested the extravagance of the Republic administration. Democrats won all four seats in the United States House of Representatives, their Presidential candidate, Horace Greeley, won the state from Grant, and the Democrats won control of the legislature in the 1872 elections.

The Fourteenth Legislature stripped Davis of as much power as possible. They repealed the police act, narrowed his authority to declare martial law, and restricted his appointive powers. They decentalized the school system and provided for an election of state officers on the first Tuesday of December in 1873. This act changed the constitutional requirement of a four-day election to a single day.

The Redeemer-Democrats selected Richard

Coke and Richard Hubbard, both former Confederate officers, as their candidates for governor and lieutenant governor to oppose Davis. Coke drew 85,549 votes to Davis' 42,663, but Davis refused to relinquish the office. He sought confirmation from the courts because the legislature had changed the four-day election to a single day in defiance of the constitution, and the Supreme Court, manned by his appointees, found in his favor because of the punctuation in the constitutional clause, earning it the name the "Semi-Colon" court.

With Davis holding forth in his office on the main floor of the capitol, Austin became an armed camp that required only a spark to start a riot. When Grant refused to send troops to assist Davis, Coke's men took possession of the second floor of the capitol and late in the evening of January 13, 1874, inaugurated their man as governor. Davis yielded when even his own militia abandoned him.

Coke replaced the "Semi-Colon" judges and appointed Oran M. Roberts as the new chief justice. The legislature voided railroad bonds and substituted land grants authorized by a constitutional amendment in 1873, and cut expenses in half. They tried the amendment process again to change the Constitution written in the Radical era but this failed even in the legislature, so they called for the election of delegates to a convention to meet in August 1875. Ninety delegates, including six blacks and nine other Republicans, mostly farmers, met to rewrite the state's constitution for the third time in nine years. The Patrons of Husbandry, or the Grange, was the most significant force at the convention, although lawyers were also well represented. The work was a deliberate reaction to the Davis administration. They sought to remove as much power as possible from the governor, award only what power they must to the legislature, and then tried to keep that body from meeting as much as possible. They began by lowering their own per diem, and that of the legislature, from eight dollars per day to five dollars per day, reduced the salary of the governor and other

officials, and permitted the legislature to meet only every other year or by special call. The comptroller, treasurer, land commissioner, attorney general, and all court justices were to be elected, not appointed. The governor could declare martial law only within narrow limits but he retained the item veto and was to "faithfully execute" all laws within the limits of the constitution.

The convention agreed to subsidize railroads with land grants and reauthorized a homestead program for western land settlement. Rejected were the poll tax for voter registration and a measure to allow the vote to women. They eliminated many state jobs to save money, which seems to have been their overriding concern in all matters. They undid the best work of the constitution of 1868 by eliminating the office of state school superintendent, abolishing compulsory attendance, creating segregated schools, and failing to make a provision for local funding of education. They did, however, continue the land endowment for the future development of higher education.

This constitution, still in use in Texas today, was adopted by voters by a margin of 136,606 to 56,652 on February 15, 1876. Reflecting the mood of 1876, it is restrictive in modern times. Many routine legislative matters in other states must be handled by constitutional amendments in Texas. By the mid-1980s more than 400 amendments had been proposed with only 62 percent of them winning acceptance. Efforts to replace the constitution in 1919 and 1975 were rejected, however, because the proposed revisions were judged even worse than the constitution.

At last in the Union for good, Texas was once again under the control of conservatives. The era of secession, Civil War, and Reconstruction had changed much, especially for black Texans. For the moment farmers reigned supreme, but industrial development was about to move to the forefront and after the turn of the century would provide the dominant force in state affairs. Texans, thinking that things had returned to normal, could not have imagined the many changes awaiting them.

Black soldiers at the San Antonio Garrison amuse themselves by feeding a bear in this sketch. Courtesy, Institute of Texan Cultures

VIII

The Western Impulse

Nationalism and reform are two persistent themes of United States and Texas history, and the westerning impulse is involved in both. The nation's westward migration, its expansion toward new horizons in pursuit of the setting sun, gave Americans a sense of destiny fulfilled every time a tree crashed to make way for a road or a new town, every time a sod hut appeared as evidence of civilization in the middle of nowhere, every time a cattle drive ended at a railhead to provide food and energy for laborers elsewhere in the United States. And the problems of Westerners affected not just that section's residents but also those who lived in more settled Eastern areas, so the need for reform is a part of the story of the final settlement of the West.

Many hardships accompanied this westering, and among the greatest

This drawing by Frenzeny and Tavernier titled The Texas Cattle Trade *appeared in* Harper's Weekly *May 28, 1874. Courtesy, Institute of Texan Cultures*

was the conflict between Indians and Anglos. The conflict lasted until the turn of the century, but the outcome was a foregone conclusion. The Indians, who had used the land in Central and West Texas for a millenium as nomads following the buffalo, had only a few years left of this way of life when "Texas" became an entity. Repeating the pattern established in the East, the whites moved West, pushing the Indians aside to reservations or shallow graves. The Indians—those who had survived the devastating epidemics the whites in Texas had brought—resisted as best their limited resources permitted, sent a few whites to their graves, and ended up on reservations as shadows of their former selves. Thus the drama of America's past played again on the plains of Texas, and in the inevitable climax, the whites won, established their farms and ranches, and dominated the land with new, and renewed, customs.

The United States government had helped protect white Texans from the Indians during the first period of statehood and many expected it to do so again after Texas was restored to the Union. But they were disappointed, at least for awhile. During Reconstruction federal soldiers registered voters, kept the peace, enforced wartime proclamations, and patrolled the Rio Grande as an arm of American diplomacy to keep an eye on the French in Mexico, but few fought Indians. And perhaps some of them did not care much if they protected former Confederates anyway. The memory of the forced surrender of David Twiggs' command in 1861 and wartime hardships of their own had hardened them.

As time passed and Indian resistance to the white advance increased, these obstacles disappeared. (The French did leave Mexico and their puppet Maximillian, whom they had installed as emperor of a now-bankrupt Mexico while the Americans were preoccupied with their Civil War. It had become obvious that the United States would fight them to enforce the Monroe Doctrine, as would Mexican nationalists under Benito Juárez.) After the agony of voter registration, the uncertainty of the Throckmorton and Pease era,

and other aspects of military involvement with Reconstruction had passed, more troops were available for use against the Indians. As Indian raids, especially by Comanches and Kiowas, increased, the Army more and more assisted the Special Force, the Rangers, and private individuals to remove the Indians from Texas almost completely. Raiding Indians killed seventy-eight people in 1865, and 162 more during 1866 and 1867. The settlement line in Texas had already been slowed during the Civil War because of Indian activity and because so many men were in the military service out of state. After the war the line actually moved eastward in places. Denton and Wise counties experienced a great deal of hostile activity from the Indians during this period, and Gainesville and Waco, formerly well settled areas, became mere outposts on the frontier.

Governors Throckmorton, Pease, and Davis represented greatly dissimilar positions on most political issues, but all three worked to defend white Texans on the frontier. And the federal government also made the defense of settlers a priority item again. They pushed for a peace settlement with the Southern Plains tribes, including the Comanches, Kiowas, Cheyennes, Arapahos, and smaller groups, and their efforts resulted in the 1867 Treaty of Medicine Lodge Creek. By this agreement the Indians received a three-million-acre reservation in Indian Territory (Oklahoma) in return for guarantees of federal annuities and the promise that federal forces would prevent whites from invading or using reservation lands.

Despite this agreement, the full impact of which was probably not understood by the Indians, renegade bands continued to raid in Texas. Comancheros, or traders from New Mexico who gave the Indians whiskey, weapons, and ammunition for stolen horses, cattle, and other goods, added to the incentive for raids. One desperate rancher, John Hittson, raided the Comancheros' "stronghold" in New Mexico in an effort to put a stop to his losses. But it was a bigger job than any individual could achieve, and in 1868 the United States Army garrisoned a line of forts on the fron-

After the Civil War, many Southwestern United States Army forts were staffed with "buffalo soldiers," black troops under the command of white officers. This Frederick Remington drawing appeared in Harper's Weekly *August 21, 1886. Courtesy, Institute of Texan Cultures*

tier. Some of them, such as forts Concho and Griffin, were new installations, and some were reactivated. Black recruits mainly staffed these outposts, but white officers commanded them. The Indians referred to these black soldiers in blue uniforms as "Buffalo Soldiers." They performed well, but their small numbers and the wide separation of the posts prevented them from becoming as effective as they might have been.

In 1869 President Ulysses S. Grant directed the Army to enlist Quaker agents to work among the Indians. This "Quaker Peace Policy" was based on the "hitherto untried policy . . . of endeavoring to conquer by kindness," and that these peaceful, benevolent people could deal with the Indians of the American Southwest as effectively as they had the Indians in Pennsylvania a century or so earlier. But many factors made this impossible. The Comanches and Kiowas in Texas enjoyed the use of more powerful means of resistance to the white advance, including horses and firearms, and they became expert in the use of both. They also were more primitive, comparatively speaking, than the Pennsylvania Indians, and less accustomed to getting along with others.

Lawrie Tatum, who headed the Quaker peace

effort in Texas, worked diligently but he had to admit failure. Even Tatum recognized that the military would have to be employed. A more aggressive policy resulted. The Army increased their patrols and, after 1874, the resurrected Texas Rangers joined them in policing the Indians. But the principal cause of the final reduction of the Indians resulted from activities of the buffalo hunters, a consequence welcomed but probably unintended by the hunters themselves. By eliminating the buffalo herds they deprived the Plains Indians of their primary food supply and forced them to become dependent on agents and reservations. Be-

fore that happened, however, much hardship was experienced by Indians and whites alike.

The Quaker Peace Policy was abandoned in 1871 as a direct result of the Salt Creek Massacre. This incident occurred near the present town of Graham in Young County in April during a visit to Texas by generals William Tecumseh Sherman and Randolph B. Marcy. A Kiowa and Comanche raid led by the Kiowa war chief Satanta fell upon a military wagon train that trailed the caravan of Sherman and Marcy by only a few miles. The generals reached Fort Richardson safely, but both realized that the raid could just as easily have been

156

upon their convoy. This realization forced Sherman into action. He committed the military to an active policy of policing the Indians and traveled personally to the reservation near Fort Sill to arrest Satanta and return him to Texas for trial. Convicted and sentenced to the Texas penitentiary at Huntsville, Satanta regained his freedom when he received a pardon in 1873 from Governor E.J. Davis. Davis' action so angered Sherman that he reportedly wrote to the governor that he hoped Davis would be the first victim of Satanta when he resumed his death raids.

Fortunately Davis did not suffer this fate but Satanta did resume his raids, and Colonel Ranald S. MacKenzie, commander of the Fourth Cavalry, determined to end such activities for good. MacKenzie drew this assignment because he was regarded as one of the rising stars of the military. He had served under Grant during the Civil War and came to Texas in 1868 to command the Fourth Cavalry. He quickly established himself as the most aggressive of the military officers there. He led expeditions against the Indians in 1871 and 1872, attacking, fighting, and pushing the Comanches away from the settlements. He reduced the frequency of Indian raids by these attacks of his own and saved the lives and property of many whites. MacKenzie moved to the Mexican border in 1873 to continue his campaigns against Kickapoo and Lipan Apaches in the Eagle Pass area. He pushed these Indians into Mexico and all but eliminated their raids north of the border for a time.

In 1874, then, MacKenzie became the principal leader in a great roundup of the Plains Indians in Texas at what proved to be the last major campaign in the state. He devised a pincer movement with several units converging on the principal Comanche tribes on the High Plains. Colonel Nelson A. Miles' command came south from Kansas, Colonel William Price's men would come east from New Mexico, Colonel John Davidson's unit headed west from Fort Sill, and Colonel George Buel's men came west from Fort Griffin to rendezvous with MacKenzie. The Army committed more than

3,000 men to surround the Indians and force them to move to the Oklahoma reservations. MacKenzie found a major concentration of Comanches in Palo Duro Canyon. His men descended into the canyon and from high places shot or stampeded more than 1,400 horses, preventing the Comanches from escaping and denying them a means of continued resistance. The Comanches had no alternative but to head for their reservation; most of them never left the reservation after this, since the whites had virtually eliminated the buffalo from the Great Plains.

Before the arrival of Europeans the humpshouldered animals they came to call the buffalo, after the French term *bouefs,* roamed much of the present United States. The advance of the Anglo-Americans pushed the buffalo westward, but in the mid-nineteenth century the animals still dominated the Great Plains in mighty herds that roamed this inland isolation. The Indians' use of them provided a natural harvesting process. They killed only as many buffalo as they needed for survival, keeping the herds more or less in balance with the available grazing resources. And the Indians used the entire animal. They ate its meat,

used its hide for clothing and shelter, and even employed its bones for tools or ornaments. Their life was nomadic; they followed the herds season in and season out, each complementing the life cycle of the other.

Coronado sighted the buffalo herds as early as 1540 and reported that the abundance of these cattle-like creatures indicated that the land could be used for grazing cattle as well. Some whites had taken buffalo for meat or hides in the early days of their westward migration, but it was not until they reached the plains that a real industry in buffalo harvesting developed. This really began when the transcontinental railroad construction crews reached out to span the country with their steel rails. Far from supply areas, they hired hunters such as William F. "Buffalo Bill" Cody to provide meat for the hungry crews. Cody allegedly killed more than 4,000 buffalo personally and led a crew that harvested even more.

When tanners determined that the heavy buffalo hide could be worked as well as that of cattle, a rich industry developed for that purpose alone. If beef or other meat was available, hunters slaughtered the buffalo for its hide. They moved on to the plains armed with .50 Sharps rifles and relentlessly followed the herds. They would seek to place themselves downwind of a herd where they could establish a "stand;" from there they would shoot the animals undetected until sometimes their rifle barrels would overheat. Usually the buffalo would not run away, even as others were shot in their midst, if they did not smell or sense the presence of the hunters. Then the skinners moved in, removed the hide from the carcass, and allowed the remains to rot unless they cut out the tongue or extracted a tender steak to eat. The hides were stretched, dried, and the rotting sinew scraped away. Then they could be stacked and eventually hauled to market. This process produced a peculiar odor that disclosed the occupation of the hunters to any with whom they came into contact.

Later, after the flesh had rotted from the skeletons of the buffalo, other entrepreneurs gathered the bones for grinding into a calcium fertilizer.

Bob and Jim Cator were among the first to arrive in the Panhandle region of Texas to hunt buffalo, doing so as early as 1872. J. Wright and John Mooar, George Causey, Joe S. McComb, Billy Dixon, and Bat Masterson, among many others, soon followed. They headquartered at Adobe Walls, the site of the 1864 Civil War battle, where A.C. Myers and James Hanrahan began stores and a saloon. Plains Indians attempted to prevent this rapid depletion of their livelihood with raids on isolated hunters and outposts, and on June 27, 1874, a band of 700 or more raided Adobe Walls. The hunters held out until the Indians abandoned their efforts, partially because reinforcements were on the way to the community. Billy Dixon reportedly shot an Indian off his horse at a distance of one mile with his buffalo gun, which must have been a discouragement to the attackers. Such raids called forth MacKenzie's roundup of the Comanches and their eventual removal to the reser-

vation in Oklahoma. By 1880 buffalo had all but disappeared from the Plains, helping to seal the Indians' fate and opening the country to cattle raising.

The Texas cattle industry—indeed, the American cattle industry as practiced in the West— began in the Spanish colonial period. Adapting European techniques to the New World environment, as in the *charro* culture along the Rio Grande, cattle raising eventually spread across Central and West Texas and on across the plains as far north as the lower Canadian provinces. The reign of the Texas cattle barons peaked between 1860 and 1890, but Spanish priests had herded cattle to support their missions and the industry remains a Texas trademark today.

The distinguishing characteristic of the Texas or Western cattle industry was the way the cattle were worked, especially in the large herds which streamed northward to railheads in the aftermath of the Civil War. The cowboy, a romantic figure always on horseback, personifies this industry. Actually, many cattle had been and still are raised in

the East, but there they are worked on foot and within enclosures. In the West, at least until the latter part of the nineteenth century, they were worked from horseback on an open range. In the East the numbers were great but the perspective seemed diminished; in the West the majesty of the Big Sky seemed to be matched by the big herds, and fences came much later.

Coronado and Oñate brought the first cattle to Texas. They were descendants of the first animals unloaded from Spanish ships by Cortez at Vera Cruz as early as the 1520s as food and seed of an industry for the Spanish colonists. Priests brought them along for the same purpose when they established missions. They intended to teach the Indians ranching skills along with the catechism. Then, along the Rio Grande, José Escandón located *patrons* on large riparian grants where a *charro*

culture developed after the 1740s. Some missions ran truly large herds; Espíritu Santo claimed a herd of 15,000 cattle and Rosario reportedly had more than 10,000 head. Some strayed, others were lost or abandoned, and, in the way of nature, they found each other and procreated, producing a hybrid called the longhorn, a scrawny-looking critter with great endurance and a will to survive that transcended even its harsh Texas environment. Anglos arriving in Texas found thousands of these cattle roaming free, apparently belonging to no one, although some doubtless belonged to Mexican ranchers. The Anglos harvested what they wanted and claimed the rest, if they could get away with it. They ate the meat, used the hides for saddles and chair bottoms and other leather goods, hollowed the horns to make dry containers for their gun powder, and made hunting horns.

Since they received more land from the Spanish if they swore they were livestock raisers rather than farmers, many claimed to be ranchers, but few really regarded themselves as such. They did little to husband the livestock or improve the breed; theirs remained essentially an extractive industry until the Civil War.

The cradle of the Texas cattle industry, observed Walter Prescott Webb, rocked in a diamond-shaped area formed by the Nueces River, the Rio Grande, and the Gulf of Mexico. Its warm climate and low vegetation proved ideal for cattle, whose numbers seemed to increase geometrically. By 1836 hundreds of thousands of cattle roamed Texas, and 1860 estimates claimed that cattle outnumbered people in Texas by six to one. The importance of the business in the minds of Texans is reflected in the fact that Texas adopted a branding law in 1848.

Marketing the Texas cattle proved difficult. The Spanish settlers had made a few drives to New Orleans in spite of their government's prohibition of trade with French or English or American agents. Early Anglo settlers also made such drives. James Taylor White, often regarded as Texas' first real cattle baron, drove cattle from his spread in present Liberty County to Louisiana. During the period of the Republic and early statehood, others staged drives to Louisiana, Arkansas, and Missouri, and if they could persuade riverboat captains to take on such cargo, shipped them to Northern markets. During the 1850s these drives virtually stopped for several reasons. For one thing domestic cattle along the route of the drives often developed a bovine disease called "Texas Fever" which did not seem to affect the trail herds. No one knew then that the disease was caused by a parasitic tick to which the trail herds were host, and because of long years of accumulated immunity the Texas cattle were affected but little by the disease. It was not until later that the source of the problem was learned, or that it could be controlled by dipping the cattle prior to the drive. The second reason for stopping the drives was human. Arkansas, especially, harbored unscrupulous raiders who stampeded the herds to pick up strays or robbed the drovers and ranchers on their way home from selling their cattle. So for a few years the Texas cattle industry became essentially a hide and tallow trade. Herds were driven to the coast, slaughtered, skinned, and the meat rendered for tallow which was shipped to New Orleans or other markets. The crews ate a small amount of the beef but most of it was dumped into the Gulf of Mexico. Then the Civil War brought the industry to a halt. Most of the cowboys and drovers became soldiers, and the few who remained in the state could not get the cattle across the Mississippi after 1863 to the rest of the Confederacy because the Union commanded the river.

With little harvesting and the natural process of reproduction continuing, the number of cattle in Texas increased dramatically between 1861 and 1865—to an estimated five million head. But their monetary value diminished. Few people had money to buy them, or needed to do so; they could round up all they could eat with little difficulty. But there was a great demand for beef in the Northeast, where cattle, thanks to the war, were now scarce and where many farmers had

turned to industry. Increasing numbers of European immigrants also had enlarged the market. Some Texans quickly realized that they could "figure up a fortune" if they could get the cattle to market. In the fall of 1865 a few cattlemen rounded up a herd for a drive to Sedalia, Missouri, without paying attention to brands, where they sold them for as much as forty dollars per head— ten times their value in Texas. Some drives went on north to Iowa. Now many saw the potential of the drive. Ignoring resentment from farmers who feared the "Texas Fever," raiders, fences, and Indians if they crossed part of Oklahoma to Fort Smith, the cattlemen started trailing north, often over unfenced and unpatrolled federal lands.

Joseph G. McCoy took the idea of the long drive a step further when he convinced Kansas Pacific Railroad executives to build a line into western Kansas to make the settlement of Abilene the first real cowtown. It had vast holding pens beside the tracks, boardinghouses, saloons, brothels, and anything else a thirsty, hungry, or adventurous drover might want at trail's end. He sent riders

down a trail Jesse Chisolm had blazed in 1865 through the Indian territory to tell the Texans to head due north to the railhead at Abilene. This route, the Chisholm Trail of legend, skirted the settlement line and left them only the environment and the Indians to worry about. More than 35,000 head arrived that year, more than twice that many came the following year, and by 1869 at least 350,000 head came to Abilene.

Other trails developed to the west as the settlement line progressed in that same direction, enabling the drives to stay clear of some conflict with settlers for a while. The Dodge City, or Western Trail, began at San Antonio and ran north through Kerrville, Albany, and Vernon, forded the Red River at Doan's Crossing, then ran north to Dodge City and the Santa Fe Railroad connection; some drives went up this trail as far as Ogallala, Nebraska, where the Union Pacific Railroad awaited them. In 1866 Charles Goodnight and Oliver Loving developed a trail from the Middle Concho River to Fort Sumner, New Mexico, then

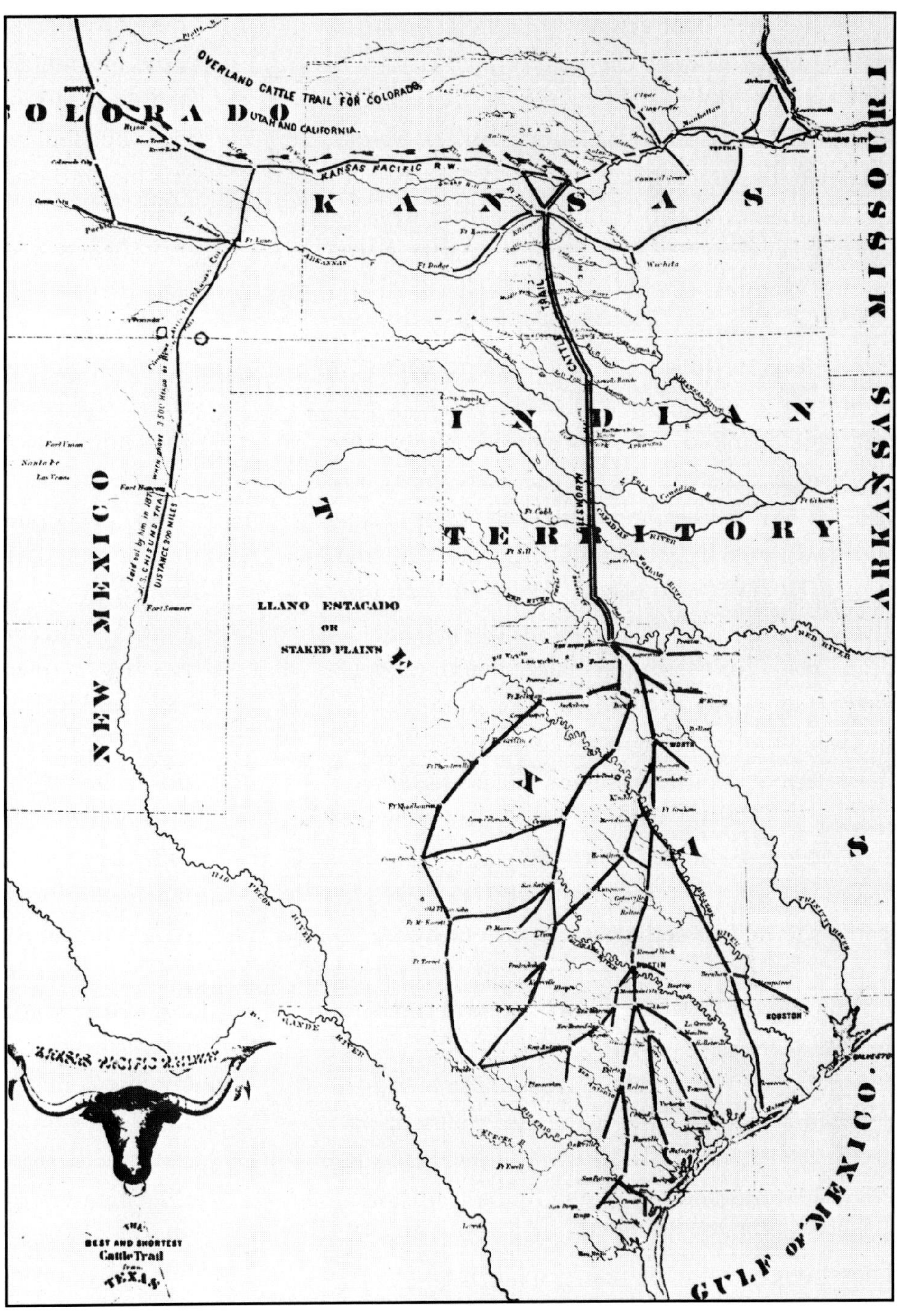

cut north through Raton Pass into Colorado. Because the settlement line moved west at about the same pace as the development of trails, the problems of fences and quarantines accompanied them. So the National Cattlemen's Association called upon the United States Congress to establish a trail under federal jurisdiction so the cattle could move along unfettered by local or state restriction. This was an unusual proposal from an organization so rooted in states' rights and localism, and the Congress did consider it but failed to take action.

A roundup began the process of organizing a trail drive. In the days immediately following the Civil War, this might be done with little regard to actual ownership of stock, but soon property rights, at least of branded animals, were carefully observed. The ranchers at first branded their own cattle, then trailed them north. But soon most moved to a system by which they rounded up their stock and then contracted with a professional trailing outfit to drive the herd to market for a dollar a head. John T. Lytle, Charles Schreiner, and John Henry Stephens, among others, were available for such service.

The number of cattle on a given drive was usually smaller than fictional accounts, particularly motion pictures, would lead us to believe. About 2,000 head constituted a good-sized drive, given the dangers of the trail. The outfit operated along clear lines of command and responsibility. The trail boss operated with maximum authority. He was usually assisted by a ramrod, or foreman, who relieved him for sleeping, bookkeeping, or dealing with townsmen or other problems such as quarantines. The cook, who usually traveled a half-day ahead of the herd to have a meal of beef and beans ready for the drovers, also sometimes doubled as an amateur physician. He had the responsibility of pointing his wagon tongue toward the North Star on clear nights in case there was any question about their direction. The cook usually had the assistance of a swamper, or helper.

Drovers woke and breakfasted before dawn, selected the first of perhaps three or four horses from their "string" in the *remuda* that they would ride during the day, and began to move the herd. A good day's drive would cover about ten miles, depending on the terrain. A scout rode ahead to determine trail conditions, the availability of water, settler or Indian hostility, or other problems. Point men rode on either side of the lead stock to keep the herd moving in the proper direction. These were usually the most experienced and expert drovers whose skills would be tested during a stampede: in that event they would turn the herd and make the stock mill in a circle until calm. Flankers rode at intervals along the sides of the herd to keep the cattle bunched. Usually cattle will follow their leaders blindly, so once the herd was in motion there was little need to prod them, but occasionally one or more would break away and the flankers would chase them back into line. Inexperienced cowboys or those requiring discipline rode drag, or to the rear of the herd, in the

dust or mud. Their job was simply to keep the herd moving along the 1,000 or so miles to the railhead. Monotony was the drover's greatest problem, but foul weather or a stampede could turn his life into one of adventure and danger in an instant.

Ranchers whose stock arrived at the railhead early in the season earned the highest prices, but as the prices dropped in the fall many began to winter their cattle on the Kansas or Nebraska prairies and then sell them after they fattened out on the spring grass. Even though the growing season was shorter to the north, the grasses were richer. Thus Texas ranchers spread the Cattle Kingdom to the north. Most of the cattle were "dropped" (born) in Texas, allowed to mature into yearlings, trailed north for a season or two of fattening on ranches or spreads owned by secondary cattlemen, then sold to the commission agents of packing companies. The Texas longhorns' unique constitution suited them perfectly for such husbanding, but soon the demand for better grades of beef—especially the Hereford—severe Northern winters, fences, overproduction, and market changes slowed the demand for the rugged animal.

Great spreads, or ranches, developed in Texas during the Cattle Kingdom years. H.L. Kinney established a trading post and ranch in the Rio Grande country during the 1840s, and Richard King and Mifflin Kenedy, riverboat operators who came to the Rio Grande in the 1840s, acquired the Santa Gertrudis grant in 1852 and built it into one of the major ranches of the state and nation. They divided their holdings in 1868. Kenedy acquired other land for a ranch in what became Kenedy County; King's operation, centered in

Frank Collinson typifies the Texan cowboy as he sits astride his trusted horse, ready for work. Courtesy, Panhandle-Plains Historical Museum

THE KING RANCH

In the 1950s Edna Ferber's novel, *Giant,* the story of the Reata ranch, became a major motion picture. Many Texans assumed the story was based on the King Ranch located in southern Texas below Corpus Christi. Whether it was or not, a line from the movie's theme, "Just like a sleeping giant, sprawling in the sun . . ." captures the essence of the King Ranch. Most Texas ranchers did not think that the film portrayed them accurately, but for moviegoers everywhere it presented the cattle barons as most people believed they were.

Richard King founded the ranch that still bears his name in 1852. Born in New York City on June 10, 1825, he was apprenticed to a jeweler as soon as he could work. He so disliked that trade that in 1835 he stowed away on a ship and ended up in Mobile, Alabama. He served on an Army steamboat during the Seminole War in Florida where he met Miflin Kenedy. In the Mexican-American War (1846-1848) they became partners in a steamboat business that carried men and supplies to Mexico for General Zachary Taylor. After the war they remained in southern Texas to operate a steamboat business along the coast and on the Rio Grande.

King bought the Santa Gertrudis land grant in 1852 for $300. Eight years later he sold a half interest in the spread to his friend Kenedy, and during the American Civil War they made a small fortune exporting cotton to European buyers by way of Mexico. Using their profits to enlarge their land holdings, they operated the ranch together until they dissolved their partnership in 1868. Kenedy later operated his own ranch in what became Kenedy County, and King retained the original Santa Gertrudis grant, which would later become the headquarters of an international operation. He adopted the distinctive "Running W" brand that remains the logo of a worldwide business.

King married Henrietta M. Chamberlain in December 1854 and they became the parents of five children. King died of stomach cancer at the Menger Hotel in San Antonio on April 14, 1885, and was buried in Kingsville, the town named for him. Henrietta King asked Robert Justice Kleberg, her husband's trusted attorney, to become the manager of King Ranch; he later also became her son-in-law. Henrietta King retained ownership of the ranch until her death in 1925, when the ranch became a private corporation wholly owned by her five immediate heirs. It is still owned by her more than sixty descendants.

Kleberg proved an excellent manager and developer of the King Ranch during his forty-seven year tenure. When he assumed control of the ranch it contained only 600,000 acres; upon his retirement in 1933 he managed more than 1.2 million acres. His most significant contribution were his efforts in tick eradication. Upon his retirement, his son, Robert Kleberg, Jr., became manager.

The King Ranch raised longhorn cattle in its early years. Thousands of these cattle were of a hybrid breed developed in the Rio Grande region; they were branded and became the foundation of the herd. Later, Brahman and Hereford cattle were imported for selective breeding, and the result was the Santa Gertrudis cattle now marketed worldwide by the King Ranch. The ranch also participated in the development of the quarter horse, and received the American Quarter Horse Association's first certificate of registration for its stallion, Wimpy, a horse that won the Southwestern Exposition and Live Stock Show's Grand Championship. They also were involved in thoroughbred racing, and their horse, Assault, won the Triple Crown in 1946. Other big money winners from the ranch included High Gun and Rejected. Both horses won at least $500,000 in purses during the 1950s.

In 1933 the King Ranch entered the oil business. After eight years of negotiation with Humble Oil and Refining Company they leased the mineral rights to their holdings between Corpus Christi and the Rio Grande. Drilling did not really get under way until after World War II. The discovery of the Gorregas Field in 1945 led to other significant discoveries and eventually there were more than 2,700 oil and gas wells and a refinery in Kingsville. To add another potential industry to its empire, in 1967 the King Ranch bought more than 50,000 acres of timberland in San Jacinto, Liberty, Montgomery, and Harris counties.

From the beginning there was a firm bond between the ranch's management and employees. In the early years the sheer vastness of southern Texas and the necessity to defend the ranch borders, especially along the Rio Grande, reinforced the feeling of unity. The cowboys, known as *Kinenos,* or the King's Men, sprang from a tradition of faithfulness to the *patron,* or the ranch owner or manager. The *Kinenos* still like to say that they work with, and not just for, the management. Some of their families have been on the land as long as the King and Kleberg families. The Quintanilla, Cavazos, Flores, Garcia, Garza, and Trevino families have been a part of the ranch for generations. In fact, Spanish has always been the official "working language" of the ranch.

Today the King Ranch covers 825,000 acres in the Santa Gertrudis, Laureles, Encino, and Narias divisions of Texas, along a 100-mile stretch of land from Corpus Christi to Raymondville—an area as large as the state of Rhode Island. The land contains 60,000 or more cattle and at least 350 windmills. The ranch also operates eight million acres scat-

This Frederick Remington drawing personifies the tough Texas
cowboy. Courtesy, Institute of
Texan Cultures

tered throughout Argentina, Brazil, Venezuela, Morocco, Spain, and Australia.

The modern King Ranch is vastly different from that of the day of Richard King, but three elements still tie the present to the past. The managers still headquarter on the land King initially bought in 1852, they still have a strong relationship with the *Kinenos,* and Spanish is still the working language of the ranch.

Kingsville, benefited from the assistance of his son-in-law, Richard Kleberg, who helped continue the ranch's development. The buffalo hunters J. Wright and John Mooar, Jim Cator, and Abel H. "Shanghai" Pierce founded large spreads in the Panhandle. Charles Goodnight, perhaps the most influential nineteenth-century Texas cattleman, established the JA Ranch on the capital of his Irish partner, John Adair, in the 100-mile-long Palo Duro Canyon after the Comanches were forced out. He used the canyon walls for fences and could ride line with only a few cowhands at the canyon's lower end.

Joe Browning's buffalo hunting headquarters and homestead became the center of the largest ranching operation in North America when A.M. Britton and H.H. Campbell bought Browning's holdings and founded the Matador Cattle Company. They sold the ranch to Scottish investors in 1882 and thereafter it became part of a string of spreads ranging from Texas to Canada that continued in operation until 1952. Perhaps the largest ranch wholly in Texas was the XIT, also located in the Panhandle. The XIT spread across the three million acres awarded to the Capitol Syndicate that financed the construction of the new state government building in Austin. The state could not afford to pay its construction bill in money, so they gave the land, at a rate of one dollar per acre, to the company while selling other lands for as little as fifty cents per acre. Facing that kind of competition, the syndicate determined to go into the ranching business until rising land prices made it possible to sell at a profit. Six thousand miles of fence separated their holdings from the rest of Texas, and included lands that eventually became ten separate counties, resulting in the legend that the XIT brand was intended to mean "ten in Texas." The outfit bought supplies in boxcar lots and was the major economic enterprise of its region until the land was sold off to other ranchers, farmers, and tradesmen.

By about 1890 the end of the open-range method of raising cattle and the long drives to the north was at hand. Soon railroads were constructed

to Texas, obviating the necessity for the drives, and farmers and ranchers closed off the trails with barbed wire to keep other's livestock from using their grass or water. State policy also encouraged Western land settlement, and the wire and the windmill made it possible to husband larger numbers of cattle within enclosures. These devices also made row crop agriculture more possible as well as practical.

The 1876 Texas constitution reauthorized land grants as an encouragement for railroad construction, and naturally the rail executives encouraged settlement along their tracks so they could have a market to serve. This pattern had been established by the federal government elsewhere in the United

These cowboys were photographed on a trail drive from Hudspeth Ranch headquarters in Val Verde County, to Altuda Ranch, near Alpine in Brewster County, which took place from November 29 to December 20, 1926. The ranch's owner, Congressman Claude B. Hudspeth, is the second on the right. Courtesy, Claudia Abbey Ball, Institute of Texan Cultures

States where the right-of-way crossed essentially unsettled land. In Texas it followed a slightly different pattern. The lines had to be constructed in the more settled eastern part of the state and often the subsidy land had to be located in the less settled west where it was available. The legislature authorized sixteen sections of land in a checkerboard fashion for each mile of track. The rail companies had to pay for surveying, which cost approximately fifty cents per acre—and in effect paid for the surveying of the state-owned, interconnecting sections—but found they could sell little land at a profit because the state lands went for the same fifty cents per acre. The companies were given only eight years to sell the land, but many evaded this requirement by creating dummy corporations and selling the land to them. Some sold at a loss to bona fide settlers but most were able to retain control of the land through subsidiaries until the legislature again stopped the land grants in 1883.

The state still pushed sales of its western lands as a source of revenue, and in 1894 the legislature passed the Four Section Settler Act that enabled a settler to purchase up to four sections at fifty cents per acre. The state also leased grazing rights on the reserved school lands at rates beneficial to the cattlemen. The ranchers did not like the policy at first because they were accustomed to using the land for nothing; then they determined to turn it

Above: *J.F. Glidden was instrumental in the creation of barbed wire. Barbed wire made it possible to enclose ranches and farms, thus ending the open ranges and cattle drives in Texas. From Cirker,* Dictionary of American Portraits, *Dover, 1967*

Facing page: *Passengers navigate a perilous crossing on the Red River in this 1874* Harper's Weekly *sketch. Courtesy, Institute of Texan Cultures*

to their benefit by purchasing land for their headquarters and other developments and then use the political processes to keep the grazing rates as low as possible. Often cowboys would front for their employers and obtain land, then sell their rights to the boss at a low rate to retain their jobs.

The cattlemen, contrary to popular fiction, used

barbed wire more frequently than did farmers. They fenced out settlers from waterholes and the best grazing land, or fenced them in to deny access to market. Still, the farmers came. Some purchased land from the XIT, which was anxious to sell, other spreads, the railroads, or the state. They had to learn to plow deeper in the arid country of West Texas to obtain moisture, to conserve light showers and even the dew with mulches or by keeping the crust of the earth loose in row middles. The development of the windmill, which could suck the "underground rain" to the surface, transformed the fertile loess soils of the Caprock into Texas' center of row crop agriculture by the mid-twentieth century. Farmers also used barbed wire to protect their crops from wandering livestock. In a treeless land it became their only practical fencing material. At first they used smooth wire, but this did not control wandering cattle. Then in the late 1870s an Illinois farmer, J.F. Glidden, patented a wire with a short piece of wire twisted around a smooth strand at intervals with each end barbed. Isaac L. Ellwood produced the wire and H.B. Sanborn and John W. "Bet-A-Million" Gates marketed it in Texas. It was an ideal solution. Occasionally severe disputes arose when farmers or ranchers fenced each other from access to water or grass or market. Wire cutters were carried in many saddlebags or knapsacks and an estimated twenty million dollars in damage resulted before new laws against cutting the fences were enforced by the Rangers. Another law required a gate at three-mile intervals and still another provision prohibited fencing out a property owner from access to his land.

Another conflict often exaggerated by fiction was that between cattlemen and sheepherders. Sheep arrived in Texas as early as did cattle and G.W. Kendall established a large sheep ranch as early as 1857 in Kendall County, but sheepherding did not become a major business until the end of the nineteenth century. By 1879 an estimated 1,223,000 head of sheep grazed in Texas. Ten years later there were an estimated six million head. Sheep raising declined thereafter until 1930,

then increased to eleven million by the 1950s. Angora goats also arrived in Texas in 1849, and presently more than four million goats produce 97 percent of the nation's mohair.

Some cattlemen even grew sheep for the meat or wool, but there was a conflict between those who herded one animal or the other exclusively. These arguments concerned the use of the land, not ingrained prejudice, as presented by fiction. Often it is believed that cattle and sheep will not graze on the same land or drink from the same water sources. This is easily disproved by penning them together and watching the natural result. The animals do not know the difference, but cattlemen look at how much closer the sheep crop the grass and translate the loss in beef. Usually cattlemen, sheepherders, and farmers lived amicably together. The farmers were valued as sources of extra labor, vegetables, and eggs, and the cattlemen often sold beef to the farmers.

By 1900 the Cattle Kingdom had all but vanished, but the cattle industry, using wire, windmills, and other technological wonders as well as improved methods of animal husbandry, continued. Farmers and sheepherders shared the land with them. Texas was, at last, more or less settled. Its counties were organized and its major centers of population were at least founded. From the Sabine to the Pecos, the Red to the Rio Grande or the Gulf of Mexico, Texas appeared at last tamed and on the road to recovery from the psychological and financial setbacks of the Civil War and Reconstruction. None could have imagined the growth to come in the next century.

THE TEXAS RANGERS

The Texas Rangers, the state's legendary law enforcement agency, began in Anglo colonial days when Stephen F. Austin hired ten men to "range" over the countryside to protect the colonists. There is no record of their specific activity, but presumably they mostly fought Indians. In 1835 the Consultation authorized the Rangers to protect the western frontier. They continued during the period of the Republic when the army disbursed, fought as military units during the Mexican-American War in the mid-1840s, and later faded away during the American Civil War. Immediately following Reconstruction the Rangers were reorganized. Some defended the frontier against Indians, some chased outlaws, and most did both.

The Rangers differ from local peace officers because their jurisdiction is statewide, and from the army because they are not subject to military law and regulations. Although they do have a military organization, they have never worn uniforms. Their primary function has been to intervene in situations that go beyond the ability or jurisdiction of local officers.

Because of the Rangers' reputation in the nineteenth century and the courts' tolerant attitude, many Texans believed that Rangers could kill without being prosecuted. Many Mexican-Americans still resent the Rangers' function as strikebreakers in the Rio Grande Valley farm workers' strikes in the 1960s and 1970s.

In the 1930s the Rangers fell into bad days. During the Depression the legislature reduced the Rangers' budget and their number from seventy-five to about forty officers. The Rangers were considered outdated; their procedures and equipment had not kept pace with science and technology. Criminals had fast automobiles that allowed them great mobility and quick escapes. Rangers provided their own cars and each Ranger company only received fifty dollars per month for vehicle repairs and operation. Each Ranger had one carbine provided by the state while gangsters could use any kind of weapon, including submachine guns.

Things became more bleak in 1932. In that year the Rangers tried to improve their chances with the legislature by openly backing the election of Governor Ross Sterling. When Miriam Ferguson won the re-election she fired all Rangers on active duty and appointed a new force of thirty-two Rangers who were loyal to the Fergusons. Most of them were inexperienced and incompetent. She also used a Special Ranger appointment as a political payoff, and eventually named 2,344 men to this status. The *Austin American* editorialized that "about all the requirements a person needed . . . to be a Special Ranger was to be a human being" and, they should have added, a Ferguson supporter.

The results of these changes were decidedly negative. Criminals came to Texas from all over the country to take advantage of the situation, and of course Texas grew many of its own. George "Machine Gun" Kelly, Raymond Hamilton, and the notorious Bonnie Parker and Clyde Barrow were among the criminals who operated in Texas in the 1930s.

Parker was born at Rowena, Texas, on October 1, 1910. Her family moved to Dallas after the death of her father in 1914. She later married Roy Thornton, and when he was sent to the penitentiary she met Clyde Barrow, who was also in jail. Barrow was born on March 24, 1909, in Telesco, Texas. His first arrest in 1922 was for stealing an automobile, and after several other arrests he was sentenced to fourteen years in the penitentiary following a burglary in Waco. After receiving parole he immediately joined Parker. They became the most wanted outlaws in Texas after January 1934 when they killed a prison guard near Huntsville while helping four convicts escape.

In April Bonnie and Clyde murdered two highway patrolmen near Grapeville who stopped to investigate their parked car. Eventually they were accused of killing fifteen people. Lee Simmons, superintendent of the Texas Prison System, hired former Ranger Frank Hamer as a patrolman and assigned him to track down Bonnie and Clyde. Hamer accepted the assignment on February 10, 1934. He studied the outlaws' lives and the patterns of their crimes, and observed that they operated in a circle from Dallas to Joplin, Missouri, to northern Louisiana. He recruited another former Ranger, B.M. "Manny" Gault, and Bob Lacorn and Ten Hinton, deputies in the Dallas sheriff's department, and planned to intercept Bonnie and Clyde as they made their "circle." He contacted Henderson Jordan, sheriff of Bienville Parish, Louisiana, who also assigned a deputy to the case.

The six law enforcement officers planned to ambush Bonnie and Clyde at their "post office," a place along a lonely road approximately eight miles from Gibsland, near Plain Dealing, Louisiana, where they received mail from associates. At 9:20 a.m. on May 23, 1934, Bonnie and Clyde approached, and as their car drew to a stop, the officers filled the car with bullets, killing both occupants. Hamer's assignment had required 102 days to complete. His terse report to Simmons reflects the Rangers' tradition of efficiency. He wrote: "I done the job."

This 1861 Harper's Weekly *engraving captures an early Texas Ranger. Courtesy, Institute of Texan Cultures*

IX
Industrial Expansion and the Reform Movement

Texas recovered slowly from the economic setback of the Civil War and Reconstruction, but the development of the cattle industry and the advance of the frontier line, bringing new lands in West Texas into production by pioneer farmers, partly helped sustain the recovery. These were important influences that captured the imagination of Texans as well as the rest of the world, and urbanization, social and economic reform, and rapid industrial development, at least in some areas, changed the state dramatically by the end of the nineteenth century. The expansion of railroads, the shift to cash crops such as cotton rather than subsistence crops in agriculture—resulting in an increase in farm tenancy—and the demands of blacks, labor, and farmers for a fairer share of the benefits of the expanding economy characterized the final decades of the century. And James Stephen Hogg, crusading

attorney general and progressive governor of Texas, came to personify the spirit of reform in the state.

An accelerated railroad construction program led other industries in the economic development of Texas, and the need for cross ties and lumber for boxcars and depots brought prosperity to the sawmilling industry as well. Then the railroads could haul lumber to more distant and profitable markets in the symbiotic relationship characteristic of a maturing economy. The rails, or at least some kind of adequate transportation, were necessary for the development and sustained growth of Texas as an industrial society. None of the state's rivers could be turned into true arteries of trade, as in the case of the Mississippi or the Ohio, and the

great size of Texas required a transportation net spanning broad areas where there were no rivers anyway.

During the decade of the 1850s, the major argument about internal improvements concerned whether the state should subsidize rails or river improvements. Since there were fewer than 500 miles of track in Texas on the eve of the Civil War, it might appear that river improvement advocates won the argument; but this was not the case, for little was achieved in that area as well. Most of Texas' prewar rail construction networked into Houston but did not connect the Bayou City with other major population centers. Texas lagged behind even other Southern states in rail construction, as well as all of the North, where railroads had begun as early as the 1830s.

The state legislature had attempted to stimulate construction in 1852 by agreeing to award eight sections of land, increased to sixteen sections two years later, for each mile of track constructed. The Henderson and Burkville Railroad received the first charter, but even with this encouragement little was achieved. Other priorities caused by the war mostly halted rail construction, but in the postwar period Texans witnessed a boom in rail construction and by 1900 their state's 10,000 miles of track led the nation.

The boom began immediately after the war with all Reconstruction governments in Texas favoring development in the area. The Radical constitution of 1869 substituted bonds to subsidize construction rather than granting land. Four years later the constitution was changed to permit a return to the land subsidies, and then the Redeemer constitu-

tion of 1876 continued this method until 1882. Within thirty years the state granted at least thirty million acres to numerous construction projects, but the railroad companies failed to realize as much as they anticipated because of conditions attached to the grants, including the necessity to accept the lands where the state had it available— which was not always where the tracks were laid— and the requirement that the companies pay for the surveying of the land and agree to sell it within eight years. In addition, they had to provide their own right-of-way. Since it cost them approximately fifty cents per acre for surveying their grants, and the state sold its own lands for that amount, it was not possible for the rail companies to sell at a profit, at least for a while. Some of them evaded the intent of the transfer law by selling their grants to a subsidiary, hoping for a rise in land prices in the future. Actually, they

Facing page: These officers of the United States Second Cavalry pose in 1898, flanked by flags, tents, and tall trees. Courtesy, San Antonio Conservation Society

Right: These railroad officers are busy at work in this interior view of the office of the San Antonio and Aransas Pass Railroad. Courtesy, San Antonio Conservation Society

were usually anxious to sell the land to develop markets or to regain construction costs.

The railroads also received assistance from many communities as an inducement to have the lines built to their area, and sometimes the companies deliberately routed their path away from some cities if such assistance was not forthcoming. It was a great boost for a city to have rail service, so many of them were willing to contribute money or land for depots, right-of-ways, roundhouses, and even outright bonuses. Often the rail lines would have their taxes remanded for a period of time as an added inducement. Dallas is a good example of a small community that measurably benefited from its rail connections. Located far inland, with only a faint but persistent hope that one day the Trinity River could be opened as an artery of transportation, the railroad made it possible for Dallas to become not only one of the three major urban areas in Texas but also one of the nation's leading manufacturing and marketing centers.

Jefferson, in East Texas, is an example of what could happen when rail connections were either absent or not supported. The persistent legend is that Jefferson died when Jay Gould condemned it to have grass grow in its streets because its leaders refused to provide subsidies. In fact, Jefferson had a rail connection long before Jay Gould visited Texas and before the destruction of the raft on the Red River which backed up waters in various bayous and creeks and made the city Texas' second leading port of entry. But townspeople did fail to capitalize on their early advantage and Gould's Texas and Pacific Railroad was built sixteen miles to the south of Jefferson through the city of Marshall, which then grew as Jefferson declined after the removal of the river obstructions. Sweetwater, Abilene, and scores of other cities along the Texas and Pacific's route in West Texas were creatures of the railroad construction itself. Eventually Texas was crisscrossed with many major lines, including the Texas & Pacific, the Missouri, Kansas, & Texas (KATY), the Fort Worth & Denver, the International & Great Northern, the Missouri Pacif-

ic, the Santa Fe, and the Southern Pacific.

The Texas & Pacific began in 1870 when Grenville Dodge, having achieved fame as the construction engineer for the Union Pacific, the nation's first transcontinental line, came to Shreveport, Louisiana, to head this new project. He intended to build a line from East Texas to San Diego, California. Actual construction began in 1873 and the rails reached Fort Worth by 1875, but there Dodge stalled, so Jay Gould took over control of the line in Texas to gain a portion of this rapidly expanding market. His company began laying track again in 1880. Collis P. Huntington's Southern Pacific moved eastward across the southern portions of Arizona and New Mexico, intending to enter Texas at El Paso and continue across the state to New Orleans. Gould's crews raced toward El Paso to tie up as much of the Texas market as possible. The lines reached each other near Sierra Blanca, approximately eighty miles east of El Paso, in 1882. Gould and Huntington agreed to joint use of the lines into the city. Huntington finally realized the original goal when he constructed a southern route through Laredo, merged with or purchased more than thirty other lines, and extended the Southern Pacific from Southern California to New Orleans.

The principal period of railroad expansion really began in 1876 with the reappearance of a stable government and a definite policy of encouragement of rail construction; it peaked in 1882 when the state withdrew its offer of land subsidy for rail construction. Approximately 5,000 miles of track, or about half of the state's total, was laid during this period. In 1877 more miles of track were laid in Texas than in any other state, and in 1878 the pace increased to the point where Texas rail construction equalled that of the nation as a whole.

The railroads revolutionized all aspects of the Texas economy and society. Prior to the availability of rail transportation, industry in Texas remained small and decentralized. It was essentially extractive and domestic, and in most respects had remained unchanged since the colonial period, especially in lumber milling and the processing of

Right: *A water cart winds its way slowly through 1900 Laredo. Courtesy, Yolanda Parker*

Left: *San Agustin Church in Laredo rises majestically from the dusty border town in this photo taken between 1875 and 1880. Courtesy, Yolanda Parker*

agricultural produce. Usually the farmer or producer did what processing was done on his own
crops, consumed what he could, and marketed the
remainder to secondary consumers at the nearest
town. A few sawmills and gristmills operated, but
they had to move to new locations frequently to
be near the source of their materials because they
lacked a convenient or cost-effective way to transport the materials to permanent locations. The
availability of the railroads made possible the concentration of major processing and manufacturing
institutions by bringing the resources to the mill
or factory and taking its produce to distribution
centers and markets.

In 1870 the total value of all products manufactured in Texas remained just less than twelve million dollars, only about 25 percent of the total
value of agricultural products. Only one percent of
the state's population, or 8,000 workers, labored
in slightly fewer than 2,500 shops. Since the colonial period, Galveston had dominated manufacturing in Texas, and this dominance continued into
the last quarter of the century with an annual
gross production value of $1.2 million. Milling was
the state's leading processing operation. In 1870
there were 533 gristmills in operation. By 1900
the number of mills had dropped to 289 but the
volume and value of the processed grains more
than doubled. The number of shops in Texas engaged in some form of manufacturing reached
5,200 and more than 36,000 Texans earned their
daily bread by working in them. By 1900 the total
value of manufactured products reached seventy
million dollars annually, and lumbering had re-

placed flour milling as the state's primary industry. Cottonseed oil extraction became a close competitor and after 1900 assumed second place after lumber.

The growth of the Texas lumber industry illustrates the new scale of business after the coming of the railroads. Essentially an extractive industry for all of the nineteenth century, the lumber industry in East Texas preceded legal Anglo immigration to the area. As early as 1816 a sawmill was located at San Augustine and a mill operated in Nacogdoches as early as the 1820s. These mills served the descendants of Spanish settlers and newly arrived Anglos even before Stephen F. Austin and other empresarios received permission from the Mexican government to introduce legal settlement. The early lumbermen did nothing to husband the growth of the timber. They merely cut what was available in abundance and then moved on to new stands when an area played out. For the most part they went after pine, ignoring the hardwood stands along the streambeds until a few enterprising barrel makers moved in to harvest the white oak for their own purposes. When the demand for wood products for use by the railroads developed, lumbering became the state's leading industry and remained so until the great oil discoveries in East Texas after the turn of the century.

The lumber industry centered its activities between the Sabine River and the Trinity River, or where the Southern Forest met the prairies of Central Texas. The most significant lumbering area was north of Orange and Beaumont, a 68,000-square-mile region with an estimated 300 billion board feet. There lumber barons such as John Henry Kirby, H.J. Lutcher, and G.B. Moore operated massive harvesting and milling operations until the virgin timber all but disappeared. Many lumbermen moved to the West, particularly Oregon, Washington, and Idaho, by the 1920s in quest of new forests to cut, but some stayed in East Texas, replanted pine stands, and remained to harvest the results. Timber harvesting and wood processing remains one of the leading industries of the region, and it is worth noting that the Kirby Lumber Company was the state's first million-dollar corporation.

At the apex of the early timber boom more than 600 mills operated in Texas. They ranged from jackleg operations, which moved regularly to new stands, to the Kirby Lumber Company, which operated its own tram lines to bring the logs to mills located at Beaumont, Kirbyville, or Silsbee.

Facing page: The Galveston, Harrisburg, and San Antonio Railroad advertised its sunset route to San Antonio in this 1877 ad. Courtesy, Barker Texas History Center

Right: This 1890s photo of the Peter Tatsch home in Fredericksburg stands as a stolid example of Hill Country homesteading. Courtesy, Barker Texas History Center

THE LUMBER BARONS

In the last third of the nineteenth century a major lumber industry developed in East Texas. A 68,000-square-mile area north of Beaumont and Orange contained an estimated 300 billion board feet of pine lumber; by 1900 lumber replaced milling as the state's number one industry. It also enjoyed a symbiotic relationship with the railroad industry, another leading industry in Texas. Millions of cross ties were required to support rails, and once they were in place the rails became avenues of export for millions of board feet of lumber.

More than 600 sawmills in East Texas converted pine and hardwood into lumber and other wood products. They were mostly located in company towns where laborers worked for minimum wages and were paid in script redeemable only at the company store, rented housing from the lumber company, and sometimes even worshiped in company-owned churches. The masters of this industry were sometimes called "lumber barons" because of their business practices; others thought of them as entrepreneurs. The early Texas lumber magnates are best exemplified by John Henry Kirby, Joseph Hubert Kurth, and Ernest Lynn Kurth.

Kirby was born near Peachtree Village in Tyler County in 1860. He obtained some education at Southwestern University until lack of funds forced him to leave school. Returning to Tyler County, he became an office clerk for Samuel Bronson Cooper, a leading attorney in Woodville. Because of Cooper's influence, Kirby was appointed calendar clerk of the Texas Senate, 1882-1884. In 1883 he married Lelia Stewart of Woodville.

Kirby studied law with Cooper and was admitted to the bar in 1885. The following year he represented a group of eastern landowners in a title case. They were so impressed with Kirby that when they formed the Texas and Louisiana Land and Lumber Associa-

tion and the Texas Pine Land Association they made Kirby manager. As head of two of the largest timber companies in Texas, Kirby moved to Houston in 1890 and joined the firm of Hobby and Lanier. To log his extensive holdings more efficiently Kirby began construction of the Gulf, Beaumont, and Kansas City Railroad in 1893. It operated between the Neches and Sabine rivers on land he controlled.

During the economic reverses of the 1890s Kirby continued to buy land and extend the railroad. He built his first sawmill at Silsbee in 1896 and expanded his markets. In 1901 Kirby Lumber Company received a separate charter and entered the manufacturing and exporting aspects of the lumber trade. At one time the company had twelve mills, five logging camps, and five logging fronts in operations that employed at least 16,000 workers.

Although remembered principally as a lumberman, Kirby was a competent lawyer, banker, and businessman. He was also president of the Southwestern Oil Company. A civic-minded Texan, Kirby was elected to the Texas House of Representatives, was a member of the War Industries Board, lumber director of the United States Shipping Board's Emergency Fleet Corporation during World War I, and a consultant on President Warren G. Harding's Conference on Unemployment. Dedicated to his industry as well as to his country, Kirby was the first president of the Southern Pine Association and of the National Lumber Manufacturer's Association. Kirby died on November 9, 1940, the patriarch of Texas' first million-dollar corporation.

Joseph Hubert Kurth was born July 3, 1857, in Bonn, Germany. He attended a university there and immigrated to the United States after being arrested in a student riot. He arrived at Galveston in 1878. With-

out money or skills and speaking little English, he could only find work in a Galveston sawmill. After many years of laboring in several sawmills in southeastern Texas, he bought a small mill in Polk County alongside the Houston, East & West Texas Railway. The place was later called Kurth's Station. Kurth married Hattie Glenn of Hartley in 1882, and six children were born to them.

Kurth purchased a sawmill two miles west of Lufkin at Keltys in 1888. Two years later, in partnership with S.W. Henderson and Eli and Sam Wiener, Kurth formed the Angelina County Lumber Company. The company became one of the lumber giants, and by 1912 it was a multi-million-dollar operation. The company owned more than 150,000 acres of excellent pine-producing land. Kurth's other holdings and developments included the Lufkin National Bank, Lufkin Foundry, Angelina and Neches River Railroad, and several sawmills. In 1924 Kurth was a Republican candidate for lieutenant governor of Texas. He died on June 16, 1930, leaving his legacy to his son.

Ernest Lynn Kurth was born July 25, 1885, at Kurth Station in Polk County. He attended school in Angelina County and also Southwestern University, from which he was graduated in 1905. He joined his father's business and became general manager of the Angelina County Lumber Company. When Joseph Kurth died Ernest Kurth became vice president and then president of the family enterprise. He expanded and modernized the operations. Kurth's most significant contribution was a company to produce newsprint from southern yellow pine. With the assistance of chemist Charles Herty and several East Texas businessmen, Kurth founded the Southland Paper Mill in 1936. When Southland began production in 1940 it opened a new era

for the use of southern pine.

Kurth was president and board chairman of Southland. He held similar offices in the Angelina County Lumber Company, Lufkin National Bank, Lufkin Foundry, East Texas Theatres, KTRE television, Angelina and Neches Railroad Company, Southern Pine Association, and Lufkin Chamber of Commerce. He was also vice president of the National Lumberman's Manufacturers Association and president of the board of directors of Lufkin Memorial Hospital, which he helped to found. Ernest Kurth died on October 26, 1960.

Modern Texas industry was founded and developed by such individuals as John Henry Kirby, Joseph Hubert Kurth, and Ernest Lynn Kurth. Today the wood products industry employs thousands of Texans; the industry is also the prime tax revenue source for many East Texas local governments. The contributions of such men are difficult to estimate, but it's clear to see that Texas would be very different without them.

In many ways timber barons such as John Henry Kirby operated in the same paternalistic way as the cattle barons. They bought or leased vast amounts of land where lumberjacks and mill workers lived in company towns and were paid in company scrip which was redeemable only at company stores and was discounted when converted into legal tender. The workers often even worshipped in churches owned by the company. For the company the object was to hold the workers by any means. Labor unions would call such tactics exploitation, but the lumber companies did provide employment for many who might otherwise have had none, or have been condemned to the dreary existence of the sharecropper. In the twentieth century legislation required mill operators to pay their employees in legal tender rather than scrip, but work in the woods and mills remained dangerous and difficult.

Another major industry, the processing of cottonseed to extract the oil and the grinding of the pulp to make cottonseed cake, resulted from the Texas farmers' conversion to cotton as their primary cash crop. By the end of the century at least half of the planted acreage in Texas produced cotton. Cotton had been grown in Texas in abundance before the Civil War, but its production escalated following the war because of the expanding national and international market for cotton products. "King Cotton" continued to be just that until almost World War II, and is still a major crop in West Texas in the area around Lub-

bock. The gin removed the tenacious seed from the fiber and for decades the small, hard seeds produced in an abundance exceeding the needs for replanting were dumped in huge piles beside the gins to rot. When it was learned that a rich, light oil could be squeezed from the seed, and that the remaining pulp could be ground into an excellent nitrogen fertilizer or feed supplement for livestock, a fourteen million dollar annual business in cottonseed processing emerged by 1900. Experimentation at Texas A&M continues to find new uses for the cottonseed, once considered merely a waste product.

Cotton played a major part in the changing agricultural picture of Texas following the Civil War. One of the noticeable changes was the shift of the farming center from East Texas to the blacklands of Central Texas and, by century's end, moving on to the South Plains following the development of dry-land farming techniques and the discovery through technology of ways to make irrigation feasible. Most farmers grew some vegetables for their own tables, but when it came to growing something to sell they usually planted cotton. And as their need for money increased, cotton often displaced even corn, long considered the primary crop of the American farmer.

The farmer was caught in a terrible spiral of having to produce more each year just to stay even, but the price dropped with the production of more cotton and the costs of production, especially for credit, constantly escalated, even in years

when the weather or other factors reduced production. In 1870 Texas farmers produced a cotton crop valued at ten million dollars; by 1900 this increased to $100 million. The number of bales increased from 35,000 to 2.5 million in the same period, yet Texas farmers individually received less money because the price dropped from thirty-five cents per pound to five cents per pound in the same period, and farm income dropped from eighty-eight million dollars to sixty-eight million dollars.

This spiral reduced most Texans engaged in agriculture to the status of sharecropper, share tenant, or at least to being dependent upon the crop-lien system. This was a sharp reversal from the pre–Civil War circumstance when almost all Texas farmers were freeholders of their own land. Since the colonial period, friendly governments had made land available to settlers at generous rates, and although most Texans could be called poor by modern standards, they were land-poor as well. Losses suffered during the Civil War and Reconstruction, the exhaustion of the public domain by the 1880s, and general hard times during the period of recovery forced many to sell their land to pay their debts or taxes or forfeit it if they could not sell it. Many were then hired by the new owners to farm land they formerly owned, or moved to new land they farmed on a sharecrop basis.

Under the sharecrop system the farmer usually had only his labor to invest. The owner put up the land, shelter, equipment, seeds, and credit for the farmer to draw against for his necessities until the crop was harvested. The farmer usually received a quarter of the crop for his labor, but since he had to pay for his draw at the local store, usually also operated by the landowner, he often found that his debts equaled or exceeded what he received for his year's labor. This bound the sharecropper, white or black, to the land, almost as effectively as slavery. The share tenant fared a little better. He usually provided his own equipment, seeds, and credit, and rented the land and shelter from the owner. His percentage of the yield was usually a little better, perhaps one-half, but it also often fell short of enabling him to purchase his own land.

Above: *This woman is shown spinning cotton outside her frontier home in this 1880s photo. Courtesy, Texas State Archives*

Facing page: *This photo of an El Campo cotton platform appeared in the* El Campo Leader-News *in 1905. Courtesy, Institute of Texan Cultures*

Under the crop-lien system the farmer borrowed against the anticipated crop from the local banker or storekeeper and paid off the debt when the crop was harvested. He might even own his own land, and he provided his own shelter, equipment, and seeds. But if the crop failed, which happens periodically to all farmers, he had to borrow even more at high interest rates to try again the following year.

With the decks stacked against them, most farmers fell further into debt each year regardless of how hard they worked. They blamed landowners, storekeepers, banks, insurance companies, railroads, the monetary system—anything or anyone could become a scapegoat for the economic hardships they faced. Many joined the Greenback Party in the 1870s because it advocated expansion of the monetary system by retaining and then increasing the amount of paper money in circulation. Later they supported the Populist Party's program, including the unlimited coinage of silver, especially when this issue received endorsement from the Democratic Party. It seemed obvious to them that they stood a better chance of having money if there was more of it around; actually, they were no more likely to gain increased purchasing power this way. The distribution of wealth and economic control would have remained in the same hands regardless of the monetary system unless other changes occurred. And Populist-leaning Texans still voted Democratic because of the role the Democratic Party had played in Redemption and in regaining local control in race relations, but they enthusiastically supported the Farmer's Alliance, joined the Farm Bureau or even the Grange in some areas, and dreamed and worked for ways to keep a greater share of the wealth they produced.

Laborers also began to voice concerns over their share of the wealth. As the mills and factories increased, so did the concentration of labor to operate them. Inevitably these laborers wanted to organize to present more effectively their requests for better working conditions and higher wages. Texas did not have labor unions prior to the latter part of the nineteenth century. Previous to that time a few benevolent associations and societies existed among tradesmen, such as the Screwmen's Benevolent Association organized in Galveston in 1866 for the benefit of longshoremen. In 1879, the remarkable black leader, Norris Wright Cuney, organized a similar association for black longshoremen. Houston, Galveston, and Austin had units of the International Typographical Union by the 1870s, and many Texans joined the nationwide Knights of Labor, led by Terence V. Powderly in the 1870s. The Knights of Labor lacked the fundamental power necessary for a viable labor union,

Facing page: *The new state capitol building, which was constructed of native pink granite, required skilled stone cutters from Scotland. It was completed in 1888. Courtesy, Texas State Archives*

Below: *San Antonian Julia Wood poses in the late 1870s in the finery of the era. Courtesy, Martha Staley Martin*

however. They refused to strike to achieve their goals, preferring instead to work for legislation or the use of persuasion to achieve labor's goals. Without the threat of a strike, however, they usually proved ineffective. Another weakness was their method of organization. They admitted virtually everyone to their union, even those who did not work as laborers, and the memberships were individualized, rather than the laddered effect of later unions where individuals belonged to locals, locals were affiliated with state organizations, and these were bonded to international organizations of workers in a common skill or trade. The United Mine Workers organized a few locals in 1884 among coal miners in Erath and Palo Pinto counties.

Texas experienced some strikes in the 1880s. The dock workers struck in Galveston, there were rail strikes against the Gould lines, and stonemasons struck in Austin during the construction of the state capitol over the issue of foreign laborers. The most bizarre strike of the period occurred on several ranches in West Texas when approximately 300 cowboys left their jobs in a demand for higher pay. Their effort was spontaneous and non-union; also unsuccessful. They scabbed on each other

and soon all were back at work at new jobs that paid exactly the same wages as they had earned before. During the decade strikes cost Texas employers an estimated 700 working days by more than 8,000 employees.

In this era of protest and demand for reform, the most pervasive issue turned out to be liquor. Texans, like most frontiersmen, had easy access to alcohol from the beginning, but even in the antebellum period temperance societies sprang up in their state. Usually the Friends of Temperance, a juvenile counterpart called the Bands of Hope, or the Women's Christian Temperance Union, tried to persuade Texans to stop drinking or to drink less. In 1886 the reformers tried to pass a constitutional amendment prohibiting the manufacture or distribution of alcoholic beverages. They failed in the effort, but they elevated Prohibition to the highest status among political issues in the state until after the turn of the century.

Texans were sharply divided over the issue of Prohibition. Such powerful publications as *The Texas Christian Advocate* and the *Texas Baptist Herald,* and popular figures such as John H. Reagan, Senator Samuel Bell Maxey, and David Culbertson spoke for the "pros," and James

Left: *This photo of an unidentified saloon was probably taken in Brady, Texas, in 1910. Courtesy, Wayne Spiller, Institute of Texan Cultures*

Facing page: *Women's temperance groups, seeking to change drinking habits and laws in the late nineteenth century, provoked scenes such as this outside saloons. Courtesy, Institute of Texan Cultures*

Stephen Hogg, George Clark, and Roger Mills spoke for the "antis," or those who opposed Prohibition. More than 222,000 voted to keep liquor and only 120,000 voted to prohibit it, but the issue did not die until 1915, when Governor James Ferguson vowed to veto any legislation dealing with liquor. Three years later, of course, the nation adopted the Eighteenth Amendment instituting Prohibition. Even today "wet-dry" elections under the state's local option laws produces heated debate, warnings of dire social consequences, and the greatest election participation.

Reform became the most prominent feature of post-Redemptive politics in Texas. The Redeemers reformed the state as much as they could but their successors wanted to reform Texas even more in their own way. Governor Richard Coke began with a determined effort to curtail the high expenditures of the Edmund J. Davis administration. Coke was forced to do this, he claimed, because he inherited a significant debt, a treasury with no more than $40,000, estimated expenses of $1.2 million per annum, and only $500,000 in projec-

ted revenue. He renegotiated some state bonds to obtain more favorable interest rates, funded some of the outstanding debt with new bonds at low interest rates, and offered land grants in lieu of money to some of the state's creditors. And the constitution of 1876 reduced the level of state government activity to hold the expenditures to a minimum. Coke sponsored some business taxes but reforms in collection methods resulted in a loss of revenue from railroads and telegraph companies. A few occupational taxes, such as one on fortune tellers, were passed, but these were considered regulatory rather than revenue-producing. A poll tax of one dollar on every adult male proved impossible to collect.

Coke resigned during his second term to replace Morgan Hamilton in the United States Senate, and his successor, Lieutenant Governor Richard B. Hubbard, continued Coke's parsimonious policies. Hubbard tried for a term of his own in the election of 1878 but a deadlock at the nominating convention between the governor, former governor J.W. Throckmorton, and William Lang produced a compromise candidate, Supreme Court Justice Oran M. Roberts.

Roberts won the race and also election to a second term two years later. He became the most significant governor of Texas between E.M. Pease in the 1850s and Governor James Stephen Hogg in the 1890s. He was also the most fiscally conservative governor of Texas in the nineteenth century. Roberts forced bond holders to renegotiate with the state for lower interest rates, reduced pensions to Confederate veterans, and forced a reduction in state expenditures for education to exceed no more than one-sixth of the total budget by vetoing the school appropriation bill twice.

Roberts reorganized tax collection methods to produce a higher yield and introduced such new taxes as the "bell punch" tax on liquor sales and the "drummer" tax on traveling salesmen. The bell punch tax was laughed out of existence. When a sale of liquor was made, the vendor was supposed to punch a hole in the tax paper with a

metal shaft which then rang a bell, indicating that the tax had been paid. Later, collectors tabulated the tax due the state by counting the holes in the tax paper. The device proved so easy to rig in the vendor's favor that the scheme was abandoned. The drummer tax, which was aimed at tax companies doing business in Texas without real property on the tax rolls, probably was counterproductive because it discouraged services to Texans. It also violated the commerce clause of the United States Constitution which reserves the regulation of interstate commerce to the national government.

Roberts accelerated the alienation of the public domain to settlers in West Texas as a means of bringing the land into production and as a way to get it on the tax rolls. The Four Section Settler Act and the Fifty Cent Law made state land available at rates below railroad lands, and also exhausted the public domain, except for school lands, by 1880. Land Commissioner W.C. Walsh vainly tried to stop this policy because it led to

A leading reform figure at the end of the nineteenth century, United States Congressman John H. Reagan introduced legislation creating the Interstate Commerce Commission. He later served as the first chairman of the Texas Railroad Commission, which was created in 1891. Courtesy, Texas State Archives

rampant speculation.

John Ireland defeated a coalition of the Republican and Greenback parties to become governor in 1882. They nominated George W. Jones, but Ireland won and later secured a second term as well in the election of 1884. Ireland opposed Roberts' policies on the public domain and he persuaded the legislature to change the land laws to reflect the principal of graduation, or setting the value of land on the basis of proximity to market, transportation facilities, fertility, and other factors, rather than valuing all land the same. He also secured the passage of legislation calling for the sale of public land by auction, which tended to increase the price through competitive bidding. But

in other areas Ireland continued Roberts' policies of austerity and worked for reform in the prison system and for more support for higher education. The University of Texas was founded during his administration.

The election of 1886 produced a showdown on the issue of Prohibition. Lawrence Sullivan Ross, a Confederate brigadier general in the Civil War, led the Democratic ticket as his party's nominee for governor and he proved immensely popular. But a younger candidate for the office of attorney general, James Stephen Hogg, provided the real thunder and lightning for the next several years in Texas politics. Both men were elected and then awarded second terms two years later. Hogg's two terms as attorney general, followed by two terms as Texas' chief executive, coincided with a major thrust for reform in both the state and the nation. During this period Congressman John Henry Reagan of Texas introduced legislation that created the Interstate Commerce Act and co-sponsored another measure better known as the Sherman Anti-Trust Act. At home the Texas Legislature also passed antitrust legislation that became effective just in time to help regulate the vastly expanded petroleum industry shortly after the turn of the century. They also prohibited price-fixing and other restraints of trade by monopolies.

Hogg led the reform movement in Texas, and he began to make his presence known while still attorney general. He issued a circular letter in February 1887 to local prosecutors offering to assist them in the prosecution of insurance fraud. Quite a few accepted his offer and filed suits against insurance companies, resulting in many of the poorly financed companies going out of business, or at least out of Texas. L.L. Foster, state insurance commissioner and a Hogg supporter, maintained that Hogg's program saved Texas premium payers more than one million dollars. Hogg was not always successful. He lost the state's defense of the drummer tax in the United States Supreme Court, and his feud with Judge Frank Willis cost him support among ranchers. This feud developed when Hogg prosecuted violaters of the lease laws at Willis' court in what was termed the "Grass Lease Cases." Hogg accused Willis of being biased in favor of the ranchers, and he was probably correct. A legislative investigation of Willis failed to turn up incriminating evidence and proved to be inconclusive, but the incident resulted in a loss of support for Hogg among cattlemen.

In his second term as attorney general, Hogg shifted his regulatory efforts to the railroads. He attempted to force them to provide full service to consumers, even when it proved unprofitable, because he insisted that the railroads had been built with subsidies from the state and the local communities, and they were entitled to full service, especially when the railroads showed profits from their other investments. Hogg went to court to make the railroads restore abandoned lines, to extend other services, and to maintain grades and rolling stock in good repair. These things he accomplished with existing regulatory laws. What he really wanted was a full state agency, a Railroad Commission, charged with the exclusive regulation of the railroads in all aspects of their business. The companies fought back through the Texas Traffic Association, which they also used as a method of fixing prices. Hogg prosecuted the TTA under the state's antitrust act and won, but the companies moved out of state and reorganized as the International Traffic Association, thus escaping his jurisdiction. Hogg also quarreled with Jay Gould over the issue of receiverships. The railroads sometimes declared bankruptcy within Texas to avoid paying debts there. Hogg wanted state-appointed receivers to administer their affairs to insure that Texas creditors would be paid, and Gould and the companies wanted federal receivers to handle such affairs because they would be more friendly to business interests.

When Hogg ran for governor in 1890, the principal issue was the Railroad Commission. The Farmer's Alliance supported him fully because farmers believed that the railroads, on which they were dependent, were their worst enemies. But the railroads, cattlemen, the insurance industry, and other business interests opposed him bitterly. In

this case Hogg benefited from the makeup of his enemies; with the possible exception of cattlemen, all of these groups were mistrusted by the voters. He won easily and the amendment to the state constitution authorizing the Railroad Commission carried handily. His opponents tried to prevent the legislature from implementing the amendment, but the act establishing the commission passed on April 3, 1891. John Henry Reagan came home from Washington to accept Hogg's nomination as chair of the powerful regulatory agency, partly with an eye to succeeding Hogg as governor. L.L. Foster and William P. McLean joined Reagan on the commission. Reagan proved an excellent choice as chair. He had served Texas in many capacities, including four years as Postmaster of the Confederacy and many years in the Congress, and was

Social and political reformer Norris Wright Cuney was the leader of the black faction of the Republican Party in the latter part of the nineteenth century. Courtesy, Institute of Texan Cultures

JAMES STEPHEN HOGG

James Stephen Hogg is the benchmark governor of Texas. Every governor since his administration is compared to him. Reformer, crusader, and champion of the underdog, Hogg was also the first native-born governor of Texas.

Hogg was born on March 24, 1851, near Rusk. His father was a lawyer and planter who became a brigadier general and died in service of the Confederacy in 1862. Hogg's mother died a year later, leaving three boys and two girls. The family estate was gradually sold to pay the children's living expenses while they were being educated. The boys wanted to become lawyers as their father had been. Prior to the Civil War the Hogg children attended the McNight School; after the war Hogg attended a school near Tuscaloosa, Alabama. He returned to Texas to study with Peyton Irving and to work as a typesetter for the Rusk newspaper, a job that helped improve his spelling and vocabulary.

As a young man, Hogg sometimes aided the sheriff of Cherokee County in the performance of his duties. Hogg's assistance to the sheriff made him many outlaw enemies—he was subsequently shot in the back. After recovering Hogg moved to Tyler County where he again worked for a newspaper. He operated his own papers in Quitman and Longview in the early 1870s, and crusaded against subsidies to railroads, Reconstruction lawlessness, and government corruption. Early in his career he married Sallie Stinson and reared four children.

Hogg was elected justice of the peace at Quitman in 1873. While in office he continued to study law and was admitted to the bar in 1875. Hogg ran for the state legislature in 1876 but was defeated by John S. Griffith in the only political race he ever lost. In 1878 he won election as the Wood County attorney, and from 1880 to 1884 served as district attorney for the Seventh District where he established a reputation as an aggressive prosecutor.

Hogg had also become a good campaigner. In the Presidential election of 1884 he persuaded voters to cast their ballots for Grover Cleveland and captured Smith County for the Democrats for the first time since the end of the Civil War. After this many urged him to run for Congress, but he declined, preferring to remain in his private law practice.

In 1886, however, he agreed to run for state attorney general. Hogg's friends, who were well established in the Democratic Party, and his own achievements made his nomination and election easy. Hogg became the most aggressive attorney general in the state's history. He encouraged legislation to protect reserved public school lands, and supported all Texas district attorneys who brought charges against fraudulent insurance companies. The state insurance commission estimated that the resulting suits saved Texas premium payers more than one million dollars.

Hogg next went after the railroads, the most powerful business interest and political lobby in Texas at that time. He forced some lines to improve their service and equipment and others to restore service they had abandoned. Hogg's position was that nearly every mile of railroad track in Texas had been constructed with public funds and the railroads therefore were obligated to provide service. He succeeded in breaking up the Texas Traffic Association, a pool of the powerful railroads in Texas that fixed rates and controlled labor; they later reorganized on an interstate basis to avoid state regulation. Hogg helped write the Texas anti-trust law, the second in the nation. Believing that state regulation of the railroads was still too limited, he advocated the creation of a Railroad Commission to oversee operation on a daily basis.

The creation of the Railroad Commission was Hogg's principal platform in his first campaign for governor in 1890, and was among the first things he, as governor, asked the legislature to address. His legislative package, known as the "Hogg Laws," included: creation of the Railroad Commission; a stock and bond law to curtail fraud; a law forcing land corporations to sell their holdings within a reasonable time period; an Alien Land Law to stop the awarding of public land to out-of-state corporations so it would be available for Texans, and a law restricting the amount of indebtedness counties and municipalities could undertake. With the passage of the package, Hogg appointed Congressman John H. Reagan as chairman of the powerful Railroad Commission.

Hogg ushered Texas into the Progressive Era a step before the national reforming movement began. He encouraged industrial development in Texas by persuading northern and eastern capitalists to locate businesses in the state; promoted the development of public schools and higher education institutions; and encouraged development of a division of the state archives to promote historical document preservation.

When Hogg completed his second term as governor in 1894 he was encouraged to run for the United States Senate. Instead he returned to his private law practice in Houston. The low pay he received while in public office had put him in debt, but his circumstances soon changed. Eventually Hogg became one of Texas' wealthiest men. His prosperity began when his private practice provided him with capital which he used to invest in oil fields. Following the discovery of vast oil reserves near Beaumont in 1901, Hogg amassed a significant fortune.

Business success did not diminish his interest in politics, however. Although he never again ran for office himself, he campaigned vigorously for Democratic candidates.

A railroad reformer until the end, Hogg was injured in a railroad accident from which he never recovered. His last public speech was at a banquet for President Theodore Roosevelt in Dallas on April 5, 1905. He was scheduled to speak at the State Fair later that year but illness prevented his appearance. He died on March 3, 1906, and was buried in Austin.

James Stephen Hogg championed the reform movement during his two terms as governor between 1890 and 1894. Courtesy, Institute of Texan Cultures

trusted by nearly everyone except the railroads he helped to regulate. He weathered the court battles over the commission's legal status and when he retired in 1903 he left a functioning, effective agency. Later, when charged with regulating the state's petroleum industry as well as common carriers, the commission sometimes functioned less ably as a true regulator in the public trust.

Hogg had to work hard in his race for a second term in 1892. The Populist Party nominated Thomas L. Nugent and drew away some of his reform and agrarian support, and the conservative Democrats opposed his nomination bitterly. The state nominating convention met at Houston in a trolleycar roundhouse, the only structure in town sufficiently large enough to house them. Known as the Car Barn Democrats, they nominated Hogg. Another group known as the Turner Hall Democrats met there to nominate George Clark. With a divided Democratic Party and with the Populists competing for reform votes, the Republicans had their best chance for victory since Redemption. But they lost their opportunity through a division within their own ranks over party control. Ostensibly the argument involved race; Norris Wright Cuney had earned a place of leadership in the party by long service and the ability to deliver needed black votes, but a group known as Lily White Re-

publicans opposed his leadership. To compound the divisions, the Prohibitionists nominated Albert C. Prendergast, who campaigned against the "anti" Hogg. In the long run all these divisions meant little as Hogg went on to victory in November. He interpreted his reelection as a mandate to continue his reform. His second term produced a body of legislation known as the Hogg Laws, including the Perpetuities and Corporation Law, which forced certain businesses to divest their real estate holdings within fifteen years, the Stock and Bond Law, which gave the Railroad Commission authority over stock and bond transactions of railroads to curb watered stock abuses, and the Alien Land Act, which required out-of-state landowners to sell their real estate in Texas within six years.

Hogg had promised Reagan his support in the

Fredericksburg, Texas, celebrated its Germanic roots with a Saengerfest parade down the main street in the late 1880s. Courtesy, Kilman Studio, Fredericksburg

gubernatorial race in 1894, but a new force in Texas and national politics, Edward M. House of Austin and Galveston, decided otherwise. House's family had amassed a fortune in the cotton trade and he retired from business at an early age to pursue his interests in politics. Never coveting elected office himself, House groomed the next four governors of Texas and through his influence saw that they were nominated by the Democratic Party and elected before he moved on to national politics and became a powerful force in the administration of Woodrow Wilson.

In 1894 House decided that Charles M. Culberson, not Reagan, would be governor, and he prevailed over even Hogg's efforts in the latter's behalf. Culberson faced Jerome C. Kearby, the Populist candidate, as well as nominees from the Republican and Prohibitionist parties, but with House's assistance he won the race and a second term in 1896 as well. Generally, Culberson left Hogg's reform program in place and defended it in the courts. His attorney general, M.M. Crane, successfully prosecuted the Waters-Pierce Oil Company, a subsidiary of Standard Oil, for violation of the state antitrust act. Waters-Pierce returned to Texas after a reorganization effort and hired Texas U.S. Senator Joseph Weldon Bailey as its legal advisor. The state once again prosecuted and proved that the company was still controlled by Standard Oil. But Culberson and Crane lost a dispute in the federal courts with Oklahoma over which fork of the Red River was the true border between the two states and Texas lost Greer County to its northern neighbor.

The last quarter of the nineteenth century witnessed dramatic changes in the demography of Texas. From 1870 to 1900 the state's population increased from 818,570 to 3,048,710, and Texas moved up from nineteenth to sixth in the nation in population. About as many of the new Texans were native-born as migrated from other states or other nations, and most native-born immigrants came from other Southern states. The urban population increased from 6.7 percent to 17.1 percent of the total, leaving Texas still a predomi-

nantly rural state. Blacks increased in number but dropped in their percentage of the total population because of the significant increase in the number of whites. The ratio of foreign-born to native-born residents remained approximately the same over the three decades, with persons born in Mexico predominant in their numbers, but they still numbered less than the total of European-born Texans. The percentage of Mexican-born remained steady until the revolutionary period in Mexico in the first two decades of the twentieth century, when many Mexicans attempted to escape the ravages of war there.

The continued rural nature of Texas can be seen from an examination of the population of cities and counties. The five largest counties in population in 1870 were Washington, Harris, Rusk, Fayette, and Caldwell, and the five largest cities were Galveston, San Antonio, Houston, Brownsville, and Jefferson. By 1900 the five largest counties included Dallas, Bexar, Harris, Travis, and Tarrant and the largest cities were San Antonio, Houston, Dallas, Galveston, and Fort Worth. The 1900 county-city list is a much closer match.

Higher education made significant gains in the period from 1870 to 1900. Texas accepted the national government's offer under the Morrill Land Grant Act to establish the Texas Agricultural and Mechanical College in 1876. Six faculty members and forty students were present for the opening matriculation. Within a century, Texas A&M grew to more than 30,000 students and its ROTC program trained more officers who served during World War II than did the United States Military Academy at West Point. Since Texas A&M dropped its compulsory officer training program and admitted women students, its role as a preparatory school for a military career has declined.

Texas A&M exclusively served white males for most of its first century, so Prairie View A&M was established in 1885 to serve black students. It was soon converted to a normal school for the preparation of black teachers. Sam Houston Normal School, now a university, opened in Huntsville in 1879 and served as the model for additional

teacher preparation schools authorized by the legislature in 1917. Mirabeau Lamar's dream of a University of Texas became reality when that institution opened its doors in 1883 with thirteen faculty members and 221 students, with its main campus located in Austin and a medical branch situated in Galveston. The University of Texas at Austin grew to approximately 45,000 students by 1980 with branches located in Tyler, Dallas, Arlington, El Paso, Permian Basin (Midland-Odessa), and four medical branches.

Texas Christian University, located in Fort Worth since 1910, began as Add-Ran College in Thorpe Spring in 1873. It was named for benefactors Addison and Randolph Clark. The Disciples of Christ sanctioned the school and moved it to Waco for a while before permanently locating it in Fort Worth. The Baptist General Convention of Texas had operated Baylor University since 1846, and it has been located at Waco since 1886. The Baptists also established Howard Payne University at Brownwood in 1889, and Hardin, now Hardin-Simmons University, at Abilene in 1891. The Roman Catholic church operated St. Mary's in San Antonio for men and Incarnate Word and Our Lady of the Lake for women. The Methodists established Southwestern University at Georgetown in 1873 and Texas Wesleyan University in Fort Worth in 1891. Trinity University, first located at Tehuacana and later in San Antonio, served

Facing page: San Antonio's Menger Hotel stands in this 1877 photo in all its early splendor. Courtesy, Pioneer Flour Mills

Right: Tryon Hall, the main building of Baylor University, stands in Independence, Texas, where the university was first located in 1846. Courtesy, Evelyn Streng Collection, Institute of Texan Cultures

Below: This photograph features such important Texans as Bill McDonald and Quanah Parker. Theodore Roosevelt is just "one of the guys" on this 1906 wolf hunting expedition in West Texas. Courtesy, Panhandle-Plains Historical Museum

Facing page: *These children play croquet in the front yard of a Victoria, Texas, home in 1898. Grander homes simply added more gingerbread detail and an extra story, but shared tin roofs with the more modest ranch-style homes. Courtesy, Estate of Roger Fleming, Woodsboro*

Above: *This early 1900s photo of the Welder residence in Victoria, Texas, is evidence of the stately and often grandiose homes built in the Lone Star State. Courtesy, Institute of Texan Cultures*

Right: *This family poses for a turn-of-the-century photo at the Sheppard plantation in Brenham, Texas. Courtesy, Institute of Texan Cultures*

Presbyterian students, as did Austin College, which began in Huntsville but later relocated in Sherman.

Elisabet Ney dominated Texas' cultural affairs at the end of the century. Ney, the wife of Dr. Edmond Montgomery, moved to Texas with her husband in 1870. They lived at Liendo Plantation on the property established by colonist Jared Groce. Ney was already an internationally known sculptor and enjoyed the liberation her European background and reputation permitted. She delighted in shocking her neighbors by riding horseback astride, swearing, and smoking in public. Her best known works in Texas are the statues of Stephen F. Austin, Sam Houston, and Albert Sydney John-ston displayed in the state capitol. Her *Lady Macbeth* is in the National Gallery in Washington, and *Sursum* is displayed in the Chicago Art Institute.

Texas' most important painters of this period included H.A. McArdle and William H. Huddle. McArdle's *Battle of San Jacinto* and *Dawn of the Alamo* hang in the Senate chamber in the capitol, and Huddle's *Surrender of Santa Anna* hangs elsewhere in the building. William Sidney Porter (O. Henry) lived and wrote in Texas at this time. He migrated to Texas from North Carolina in 1882, worked at several jobs, and served a prison term in Huntsville. These experiences provided him with the resources for some of his better-

known short stories. And Mrs. Percy Pennybaker's history of Texas, written in the 1870s, remained the standard school text into the next century. It perpetuated many of the myths of early Texas so dear to modern professional Texans.

Art, culture, and politics combined in the building of the state capitol still in use in Texas. The Constitution of 1876 authorized the use of three million acres of the public domain to finance a new capitol but work was not begun until a fire destroyed the existing capitol in 1881. Then the legislature created a Capitol Board to arrange for the disposition of the land and added 50,000 acres to cover architectural costs. The contractor, Matthaes Schell of Illinois, accepted the land as payment for the building. He sought financing from other Illinois businessmen, especially Charles B. and John V. Farwell, A.C. Babcock, and Abner Taylor. Taylor, who eventually saw the venture through to completion, endured many problems. He wanted to use limestone but the board rejected this proposal because the limestone discolored when exposed to the weather, so he agreed to use granite. This required skilled stonemasons unavailable in Texas so he imported them from Scotland and the Texas laborers went out on strike. Taylor solved that problem by hiring scab laborers. He wanted to construct the roof of slate instead of the copper called for in the specifications, but Attorney General Hogg forced him to follow the

original plan. When the building was dedicated on May 16, 1888, in a heavy rainstorm, the copper contracted from the temperature change and the roof leaked. The builders, organized as the Capitol Syndicate, had to obtain additional funds from European backers, who then received the three million acres as security. Construction costs in dollars just about equalled the number of acres they received, so they paid an average of one dollar per acre for land otherwise valued at fifty cents. Instead of dumping the land at a loss, they formed the XIT and became ranchers until land values rose, permitting them to regain their losses.

The building remains in use and is a cherished monument to Texans. Only slightly smaller than the national capitol in Washington, its pink granite dominated the Austin scene until modern highrises began to compete for the sky. It houses the governor's office, both houses of the state legislature, and the business offices of the legislators. Texans and visitors from all over the world stalk its halls between legislative sessions and during them pack its corridors with lobbyists, both professional and amateur. The Texas Capitol Building, completed near the end of one century, symbolizes the passage of the state into the next. The Progressive governors and legislators waiting to take their places in its public rooms used this building as a forum to change Texas forever.

Above: *These 1910 visitors to the San Jacinto battlefield monument were no doubt reminded of the importance of the famous Texas Revolution battle. Courtesy, Institute of Texan Cultures*

Right: *Mrs. Peter Hooge and her children visit the Mission Espada bastion in 1907. Courtesy, Mary Persyn*

ELISABET NEY

A new development in Texas culture began in 1892 when the German sculptor Elisabet Ney opened a studio on the outskirts of Austin. At the time only a few professional artists worked in Texas, but when Ney died fifteen years later many prominent sculptors and painters were calling Texas their home. During this Texan "renaissance" several cities opened museums, and both public and private exhibitions displayed the work created by native artists of the Lone Star State.

Ney may not have been the main cause of this expanded artistic activity, but her work paralleled its development and her career reflected the problems faced by all artists in Texas at that time. She was also a unique and interesting individual who lived a fascinating life.

Like other artists in early Texas, including Richard Petri, Hermann Lungkwitz, and Theodore Gentilz, Ney was not a native of the state. Born on January 26, 1833, in Munster, Westphalia, she came from the family of a stone carver and determined at an early age that she wanted to become a sculptor. She left home at the age of nineteen to enroll in the Munich Academy of Art, the first woman to do so. She moved to Berlin two years later to study with Christian Daniel Rauch, an acclaimed sculptor of the time. From him Ney learned the neoclassic style that marked her later work.

Ney wanted to become a sculptor so that she could "meet the great persons of the world." Her wish was fulfilled. She sculpted pieces of the leading European intellectual, artistic, and political leaders of her age, including Joseph Grimm, the publisher of fairy tales; Giuseppe Garibaldi, the leader of the Italian revolution; Otto von Bismarck, the leader of German unification; and King Ludwig II of Bavaria.

Ney left Europe in 1870 for rea-

sons she never disclosed. There is speculation that she may have been involved in a maneuver during Bismarck's unification movement that forced her to flee; others think she had become infatuated with utopian thought and wanted to try an idealized life in the New World. She lived first in Georgia, but moved with her husband, Dr. Edmund Montgomery, to Liendo Plantation near Hempstead in 1873. Her first ten years in Texas were devoted to rearing her son and helping to run Liendo. She often shocked rural Texans by smoking cigarettes in public, riding horseback astride, and wearing trousers.

Ney resumed her work in the 1880s, but found few clients. Texas was not a booming market for artists and the few commissions she received were not artistically demanding. Indeed, she felt that stone masons could have done the work she was asked to do. Her first meaningful commission came when a women's group asked her to sculpt statues of Sam Houston and Stephen F. Austin for display in the Texas Building at the 1893 Columbian Exposition in Chicago. This opportunity began a prolific career. Ney moved her studio to Austin where she produced statues of other Texas leaders, including former governors Lawrence Sullivan Ross and Francis Lubbock, former Congressman John H. Reagan, and Governor Joseph Sayers.

Ney continued to work with women's organizations such as the Daughters of the Republic of Texas until her statues were displayed in the Texas capitol building and in the United States capitol. The United Daughters of the Confederacy helped her obtain a commission from the state legislature to produce a sculpture of General Albert Sidney Johnston that is displayed at his grave site in the Texas State Cemetery in Austin. Ney tried unsuccessfully to

establish an art department at The University of Texas and she was unable to obtain commissions for major public monuments, but her studio in Austin became a haven for Texan artists and patrons.

Ney continued to live her life as she pleased. She used her maiden name sixty years before the 1960s women's movement made this fashionable and acceptable, and she usually wore her artist's attire wherever she went. Those not among her circle of friends and admirers enjoyed gossiping about her. This sometimes troubled her. She wrote that she felt as if she had drifted among "bushmen." Still, she liked Austin and Texas and believed both could be centers of artistic activity. She claimed to be devoid of patriotism, but asserted that Texas had a charm available nowhere else in the world.

Ney died on June 29, 1907, and was buried at Liendo Plantation. Ella Dancy Dibrell of Seguin purchased her studio in Austin and established the Elisabet Ney Museum there. With many of Ney's supporters Dibrell founded the Fine Arts Association to maintain the museum and to encourage the development of the fine arts in Texas. Both establishments remain active in the arts, and through them the talent and spirit of Elisabet Ney endure.

Sculptor Elisabet Ney moved to Texas in 1873. Her statues of important Texas figures, such as Austin, Houston, and Johnston, grace the state capitol building. Courtesy, Ney Museum

LODGE No 561
AF AM
AND
J.F.KELLAM HARDWARE
GARAGE
Firestone
TIRES TUBES
CITY GARAGE
REPAIRING - GASOLINE

The Progressive Thrust into the Twentieth Century

America's thrust for reform, like nationalism, the other principal theme of our history, found a home in Texas in the first decades of the twentieth century, a time of rapid and sometimes bewildering change. The roots of progressivism, one feature of this era, may be seen throughout the history of the nation, and especially in the rise and fall of the Greenback and Populist parties and agitation for Prohibition.

Progressivism has several definitions and connotations, each depending on the viewpoint of the interpreter. Generally it is the belief that human beings and their governmental, social, and economic institutions can be improved—indeed, need to be improved—through the exercise of political power, especially legislation. In Texas, in the early twentieth century, "progressives" wanted to have a hand in reshaping laws on issues as diverse

Johnson City hosted a Prohibition Parade down the main street in 1916. Courtesy, United States Department of the Interior

205

as Prohibition, minority rights, improved labor conditions, prison conditions, voting rights, business practices, and even that modern object of reform efforts, taxes. Some who called themselves "progressives" favored reforms we no longer associate with Progressivism: issues relating to public and private morals, nativism, and religious strictures.

James Stephen Hogg is the preeminent elected leader of Progressivism in Texas, but Edward M. House became his equal, and perhaps the master of Progressivism in the state. Hogg supported John Henry Reagan as his successor in the governor's office, but House decided instead to elect Charles Culberson, and he successfully engineered the victory of his candidates for the next several elections. Joseph D. Sayers, S.W.T. Lanham, Thomas Mitchell Campbell, and Oscar Branch Colquitt, Texas' governors between 1899 and 1915, held office as much because of House's support as they did from their own efforts or their progressive attitudes. These were years of the progressive harvest in Texas, with Campbell perhaps the most progressive of all. Yet all called themselves conservatives. And by 1912 House had lost interest in state affairs and moved to the national arena to work for the election of Woodrow Wilson as President.

The day of the old-school Bourbon Democrats, Southern businessmen who courted Northern capitalists, had passed in Texas, but their spirit lingered on in the career of Mississippi-born Joseph Weldon Bailey, who styled himself as the "Last Democrat" and gave his name to the last-ditch opposition to Progressivism. "Baileyism" came to mean any conservative opposition to regulating and reforming done in the name of Progressivism. Bailey's profession was the law, and he

These first Jewish immigrants to Galveston wait tentatively for their futures in the Lone Star State in 1907. Courtesy, Archives of Temple B'nai Israel

maintained a corporate practice while serving in the United States House of Representatives and in the Senate. Throughout a nearly three-decade tenure in the Congress he also served as counsel to Henry Clay Pierce, chief of the Waters-Pierce Oil Company, during its antitrust difficulties with the state. It was Bailey who advised Pierce to reorganize the company on an interstate basis to mask its continued affiliation with Standard Oil. A second case involving the company arose in 1906 when Waters-Pierce was found guilty a second time of violating the antitrust law and fined $1.8 million. Hearings also disclosed that Bailey, despite his office, had continued to act as a silent counselor and had received fees of $100,000 for his service. In the face of the apparent conflict of interest represented by his action, Bailey freely admitted receiving the money but asserted that it was payment for his legal services. A legislative committee looked into the matter and found Bailey not culpable of any legal transgression. Further, he led the Texas delegation to the National Democratic Convention in 1908. For more than a decade Bailey polarized state politics, and along with the issue of Prohibition was perhaps the most significantly divisive element in Texas politics.

The defeat of the Prohibition amendment by a wide margin in 1887 had not dimmed the hopes of the ardent "pros." They continued their work of educating the public about the evils of drink, pushed for wet-dry elections at the local level, and looked forward to the day when they could again challenge the entire state with another constitutional amendment. By 1919 they had succeeded in voting 167 counties completely dry and sixty-one partially dry, leaving only twenty-one counties with alcoholic beverages available throughout their jurisdiction. Despite the slant of these figures, however, most Texans lived in the more urban counties where Prohibition had not been successful. Still, the Texas Local Option Association, organized in Dallas in 1903, and the Anti-Saloon League, organized in 1907, continued to advocate a statewide Prohibition amendment.

The Texas Brewers Association and the Retail

A Fort Sam Houston soldier poses solemnly beside a gargantuan pile of baked dough in 1905. Courtesy, Pioneer Flour Mills

Liquor Dealers Association, as well as interested individuals, opposed the efforts of the Prohibitionists for the survival of their business interests or their personal choice. But the Prohibitionists caught the crest of the progressive reform. In 1902 they joined with others to push through a poll tax requirement for voting, hoping to limit pro-wet votes. In 1910 they succeeded in getting another Prohibition amendment on a future ballot with the support of the Democratic organization, which somewhat inexplicably also nominated Colquitt, a wet, for governor.

The election, held the following year on July 22, again turned down Prohibition by a small margin. Far from being discouraged, the drys worked even harder despite Governor James Ferguson's threat to veto any liquor laws they might pass in the legislature. The Prohibitionists charged in 1915 that the Brewers Association had violated state election laws, but Ferguson's position kept them from using the issue effectively.

The First World War gave Prohibitionists the edge they needed. Texans were willing to limit alcoholic beverage production to save grain for servicemen and America's European allies and to protect the morals of soldiers. The legislature eliminated the legal sale of liquor within ten miles of a military base during the war, and at the national level Texas Senator Morris Sheppard introduced the Eighteenth Amendment to the Constitution that prohibited the sale or distribution of most alcoholic beverages. Texas ratified the amendment by a vote of 188,982 to 130,907. The Volstead Act (Eighteenth Amendment) implemented Prohibition for the entire nation within a year. An estimated 2,500 saloons closed in Texas, but illegal stills and bootlegging quickly replaced legal sales and led to widespread violation of the law. Governor Pat Neff used the Texas Rangers to combat what he termed a "crime wave" in the early 1920s, and called on the legislature for even tougher liquor laws. In response the legislature defined the possession of one quart of liquor as *prima facie* evidence of guilt in 1923. Despite the crackdown on stills and arrests of violators, determined Texans continued to drink liquor anyway.

The Eighteenth Amendment was not Texas' only essay into national progressive politics. Tiring of his role in Texas, E.M. House moved to the national scene in 1912 when he learned about Woodrow Wilson, the progressive governor of New Jersey, who was campaigning for the Democratic nomination for President. House moved to New York, met Wilson, and the two became good friends. At the Democratic convention House pulled the Texas delegates behind Wilson for forty ballots, earning them the name of the "immortal

forty" in his contest with Missouri Congressman Champ Clark for the nomination. And House continued to support Wilson in the November election against President William Howard Taft and former President Theodore Roosevelt. All three candidates were progressives, but Wilson was a Democrat, a Southerner by birth, and, by now, a close friend of House. During the campaign House brought Texas Ranger Captain Bill Mac-Donald to New Jersey to serve as Wilson's bodyguard—Presidential candidates were not then protected by the Secret Service.

After his election to the Presidency, Wilson repaid the Texans handsomely. He appointed Texans Albert Sidney Burleson as his postmaster general and David Franklin Houston to the post of secretary of agriculture. House did not receive an official appointment; indeed, he did not want one. Even at the national level he preferred the role he had established for himself in Texas, that of unofficial but powerful advisor to those who held executive office. He became Wilson's closest friend and advisor—his alter ego, as Wilson expressed it—and for a time even resided in the White House after Wilson's first wife died in 1913. Especially as an envoy to European policy makers, House represented Wilson in the early phases of the Great War in Europe.

Women played a strong role in the progressive movement in Texas, working especially for the benefit of children and their own political rights. Many began by working for Prohibition in such organizations as the Women's Christian Temperance Union (WCTU), but, lacking the right to vote, all they could do was try to persuade men to vote the state dry. Petitions for woman suffrage had not succeeded at the constitutional conventions in 1869 and 1876 or in subsequent legislative sessions. "Suffragettes" organized the Texas Equal Rights Association in 1893, but it proved ineffective because of internal quarreling over national affiliation with other women's rights groups. Then, beginning in 1913, an annual convention of the Texas Woman Suffrage Association passed resolutions calling for the vote for women, and local groups, including some all-male organizations, began to join in their demand. And there was opposition, even among women. One such woman was Mrs. James Wells of Brownsville, who led a group opposed to extending full citizenship rights to women because of the "evils which would result."

Efforts to extend the vote to women failed in the legislature in 1915 and 1917, but the special session that ratified the Prohibition amendment passed measures enabling women to vote in party primaries and the following year Governor William Hobby secured passage of an amendment enabling women to vote in general elections as well. Even before this action became effective, the Nineteenth Amendment to the United States Constitution, granting the suffrage to all qualified women in the nation, was ratified in time for women to vote in the election of 1920. Texas led the South in ratifying the amendment and was the ninth state in the nation to do so. This did not give women full citizenship, however. They did not serve on juries in Texas until 1954 and equal property rights and credit policies remain somewhat clouded.

A natural disaster provided Texas and the nation with a major progressive reform in urban government. In early September of 1900 a hurricane swept across Galveston Island. Heavy waves chased bathers from the beaches on September 7, and by dawn the next day winds of 120 miles an hour lashed at the island. The tide swept across the entire island, reaching an estimated fourteen feet in depth. Galveston was flooded by at least five feet of water for hours. The city of 38,000 people saw more than 6,000 of their friends and relatives die in the storm, and every building suffered damage. Many buildings were simply no longer to be

The cry for women's suffrage led to an amendment to the Texas Constitution in 1918 allowing women to vote in the primaries. The Nineteenth Amendment to the United States Constitution was ratified in Texas the following year. Courtesy, Herzik Studio, Institute of Texan Cultures

found. The storm swept on across Texas. Farmers 300 miles inland claimed that chickens roosted at four o'clock in the afternoon, so black did the sky become in the storm's advance.

The storm simply suspended all governmental and other functions in Galveston for several days. Then the Galvestonians pulled themselves togeth-er. They organized relief programs and attempted to dispose of the large number of corpses by dumping them at sea as a health precaution. When the tide floated many of the bodies back to the beaches they were burned in pyres. Galveston organized itself on an *ad hoc* basis into a commis-sion form of government with each commissioner responsible for one primary city function. One su-pervised the police, another the fire fighters, an-other sanitation, and others additional functions vital to the cleanup. The system worked so well that the legislature chartered the first official city commission for Galveston the following year and within a decade hundreds of other cities in Texas and throughout the nation adopted the city com-mission method. Houston did so in 1905, and in 1913 Amarillo adjusted the system by placing dai-ly administrative matters in the hands of a city manager, a professional administrator who served

under elected officials. The city manager concept also gained wide acceptance and is in place in nearly every city in Texas today, although elected officials play stronger roles in some cities. The leg-islature approved a measure in 1912 that enabled cities of 5,000 or more to incorporate by drawing up their own charters. The process then no longer required legislative approval.

The legislature also passed reform measures in the state's political processes, in labor and busi-ness regulations, in taxing procedures, and in the administration of prisons. Since the rise of politi-cal parties in Texas, the process of selecting candi-dates for elected offices from the local level to governor and senator had remained a prerogative of delegates to conventions. Often, however, a small clique controlled the conventions and se-lected the candidates. A preliminary election code revision passed the legislature in 1903, and a fur-ther reform measure passed in 1905, known as the Terrell Election Law after its sponsor, Alexander Watkins Terrell, established the party primary as the nomination process. It permitted anyone who wanted to seek an office to run in a public elec-tion and the winners received delegate support on an instructed basis at the convention. Then, in

1918, a further modification provided for a second primary, or runoff election, when no candidate received a majority of the votes cast in the initial primary. However, in 1923 the legislature also allowed the parties, by now principally the Democratic Party, to restrict blacks from the primary elections on the grounds that such elections were private rather than public enterprises. In 1944 the Supreme Court overruled this practice in the case of *Smith v. Allright* on the grounds that the primary constituted the actual election. This systematic exclusion of any group from participation effectively disenfranchised them.

Abuse in the employment of children in Texas received the attention of progressives. Long before the federal Keating-Owens Act, Texans moved to regulate child labor and prohibit abuse as early as 1903. The legislature banned the employment of children less than twelve years of age in industrial plants and younger than sixteen in mines, distilleries, and breweries, and raised the minimum ages to fifteen and seventeen years respectively in 1911. Adult workers got some reforms, too. As a safety measure, legislation limited the number of consecutive hours trainmen could work without rest, required protection for streetcar motormen from the weather, and prohibited an employer from forcing employees to patronize the company's products or from paying them in scrip or tokens redeemable only at company stores. Maximum working hours for telegraphers were also limited to eight hours per day.

Business practices also received legislative attention. The Robertson Insurance Law of 1907 required insurance companies doing business in the state to invest a minimum of 75 percent of their receipts from premiums paid by Texans in Texas real estate or other securities and to deposit their reserves in Texas banks. The intent was to block the flow of capital from the state to be certain that monies would be available to settle claims by Texans. Insurance executives protested that investment in Texas was uncertain and twenty-one companies withdrew from the state, probably because they were under-capitalized and unable to do business under the new regulations.

The legislature created a Departmentof Agriculture and a Department of Insurance and Banking to investigate and report on practices in their areas within the state. In 1911 the legislature established a guaranty system for bank deposits similar to the Federal Deposit Insurance Corporation created at the national level during the 1930s. This measure was repealed, however, when conservative bankers argued that it made them all responsible for the mistakes of less cautious bankers, in effect making all of them liable for the bad investments of a few.

These firemen posed on a pontoon on San Pedro Lake in San Antonio in this turn-of-the-century photo. Courtesy, San Antonio Light *Collection*

This 1910 public hanging in Wharton became a focus of attention as townspeople gathered to observe. Courtesy, Wharton County Historical Museum

Tax revision was attempted but yielded little success. The legislature tried to impose a more accurate rendition of property values in 1905 and attempted to bring personal property and corporations under the tax system in 1907, but both efforts were unproductive. Attempts to reform the prison system were more successful. The system consisted of the main unit at Huntsville, the historic center of the state's penal efforts, iron smelting plants at Huntsville and Rusk, two juvenile institutions, and several farms. Convicts were often leased to local governments for road work and other duties and even to private lessors, mostly for agricultural work. Fees from these contractors provided significant supplementary revenue for the prison system, but charges of prisoner abuse, a persistent and inherent danger of the leasing system, were constant. Once in the hands of the lessor, corporal punishment, food, shelter, and general conditions of life for inmates were determined by someone whose chief interest was the greatest production for the smallest expenditure. When an investigating committee confirmed these conditions, the legislature passed the Prison Reform Act of 1910. It abolished the leasing system, provided for the classification and segregation of prisoners, did away with the wearing of black and white striped uniforms, and provided for a small wage for the prisoners' work.

The loss of revenue that resulted from doing away with the leasing system eliminated the profits formerly reported by prison officials and made them completely dependent upon the legislature for support. It also established a cycle of upgrad-

ing Texas prisons to national leadership, followed by years of neglect during which the state's prisons fell behind other states in the nation before the legislature was spurred into action again. The cycle continues today. Most legislators in Texas favor strong punishment for crime, but they usually provide the penal system with at least minimal support, and in recent years with recreational and educational programs. Personal abuse by some guards and deliberate affronts to authority by some prisoners keep prison life in turmoil in Texas as well as in other states. In the 1980s Texas prisoners sued the state in the federal courts because of crowded conditions and abuse by guards and trusties. The state was placed under court order to relieve and redress these conditions. Later individual acts of violence against prisoners by fellow inmates underscored the need for more attention to prison problems.

The administration of Governor James E. ("Farmer Jim") Ferguson, which began in 1915,

These prisoners paused for a photographer at the Marble Falls quarry in 1880. Courtesy, Texas State Library

213

Right: *Corpus Christi offered a stately beachfront hotel and bathing and boating piers for luxury loving tourists in 1906. Courtesy, Institute of Texan Cultures*

Below: *Early twentieth century Texan homes often combined gingerbread trim and tin roofs. The John Hildebrand San Antonio residence displays this typical residential architecture in 1907. Courtesy, Margaret Hildebrand and Amelia H. Knoll*

Above: *Fashion was no stranger to Texas women around the turn of the century. Here, Mary Lee Thompson poses in Austin in 1907. Courtesy, Beatrice M. Richards*

Left: *Somber faces greet the photographer of this 1887 photo of Rose Lambert and her daughter, Jamie, who are in mourning for Rose's husband James W. Lambert. Courtesy, Estate of Jamie L. Hynes*

witnessed continued efforts by progressives. The colorful Ferguson entered the governor's race in 1914 without having served in any elected capacity before. A native of Bell County, Ferguson had worked as an itinerant laborer, studied law, wandered the land in search of himself, and finally settled at Temple where he became a prominent banker and businessman. He apparently held the Populist-Progressive philosophy that everyone could be governor if he appealed to enough people. Established political leaders regarded the upstart Ferguson with disdain until he proved he could attract votes. By then it was too late to stop him and "Fergusonism" was unleashed upon the state. The name of Ferguson was on a Texas ballot nearly every two years for more than two decades.

Jim Ferguson sensed that Texans were weary of the forty-year-old Prohibition issue. Although known as an anti-Prohibitionist, he stated that he would veto any liquor or Prohibition legislation, thus establishing an apparent posture of neutrality while in effect taking a strong stand for the pres-

ent status of local option.

Instead of worrying about the liquor vote, pro or con, he went after the pocketbook interests of the farmers. In the current atmosphere, in which tenancy had become the way of life for two-thirds of Texas agrarians, Ferguson understood their resentment and campaigned hard for their votes. Of his 155 campaign speeches, only ten were made in an incorporated town or city, and he promised the croppers a law to fix the share due the laborers so they could count on receiving a fair reward for their efforts. He defeated prohibition candidate Thomas H. Ball in the primary and faced only slight opposition in the general election. And he made good on his pledge to the farmers. The first session of the legislature after he assumed office passed the Farmer Tenant Law, fixing shares at one-quarter for cotton and one-third for other crops. The courts later ruled the law unconstitutional.

Ferguson pushed ahead for more reform. He secured the passage of the Rural High School Law that enabled rural high schools to combine

This wagonner stopped his mules in Brownsville to smile for the photographer in 1907. Courtesy, Texas Southmost College Library

their resources to provide better facilities and instruction than they could afford individually; compulsory attendance laws were passed; and he advocated the availability of free textbooks for the state's scholastics. In 1917 the legislature established the Texas Highway Department at his request, although the Texas Good Roads Association had advocated the department since before the turn of the century.

Ferguson completed his first term in 1916 on good terms with his farmer constituency but amid difficulties in Austin where his enemies collected. They charged him with using state funds for such personal expenses as groceries and rumors of other malfeasance abounded. Ferguson won reelection, but his second term had just begun when he became embroiled in a dispute with University of Texas President Robert E. Vinson. It began as a disagreement that ultimately reached the level of a major confrontation. Some University of Texas faculty members were critical of Ferguson's administration and he asked Vinson to keep them quiet or to fire them. Vinson resented the governor's interference with his administration of the university and the threat to academic freedom it implied; he refused to bow to Ferguson's wishes. The governor responded by vetoing the legislative appropriation for the university. This action angered the university's powerful board of regents and alumni, who offered to underwrite the university's budget from private resources if necessary and vowed to rid the state of Ferguson. Their denunciations of Ferguson resulted in a Travis County grand jury investigation, and, on July 21, 1917, the indictment of Ferguson on nine counts for misuse of state funds.

Two days later the speaker of the state House of Representatives summoned the legislature into special session "for the purpose of considering the impeachment of the governor," although he lacked the constiutional power to do so. Ferguson claimed that only he could legally call a special session and hoped the issue would pass. He tried to help that process along by announcing his candidacy for a third term. But the clamor would not die, and just three days before the special session was to convene Ferguson sanctioned the gathering "just to make it legal," and opened the session to consider reappropriating funds for the university. The legislature quickly passed the appropriation bill and moved on to their more pressing concern, the accusations against Governor Ferguson.

The hearings and resulting trial revealed much damaging information about Ferguson and his practices, including disclosures of unsecured bank loans used to cover additional loans at other banks, a $156,000 unpaid loan from liquor interests, the depositing of state monies in banks controlled by Ferguson, and threats of improper influence over other state officeholders. The legislature convicted Ferguson on ten of the twenty-one articles of impeachment, ordered the forfeiture of his office, and denied him the opportunity ever to serve again in a state office.

Ferguson is the only Texas governor to be removed from office. Actually, he resigned the day before the verdict was disclosed, as his daughter stated, to "tie a knot in the end of his rope." Ferguson hoped to claim that the verdict's prohibition against future service would not apply since he was not in office when it was rendered. Although he later ran for President and United States senator, both federal offices, he did not return to political power until the mid-1920s when his wife, Miriam A. Ferguson, ran as his surrogate. Even so he remained a powerful force in Texas politics for two decades, and his personal newspaper, the *Ferguson Forum,* exerted influence beyond its readership because of its publisher.

When Ferguson resigned, Lieutenant Governor William P. Hobby assumed the governor's office. A newspaperman from Beaumont and Houston, Hobby had never intended to move beyond the lieutenant governorship. Now governor by the force of events, he also won reelection during World War I to a full term in 1918.

Domestic Progressivism had to share center stage with international affairs in Texas, as it did in the nation at large. The state's most immediate concern focused on its border with Mexico, especially after the global conflict began in 1914 in Europe. The United States attempted to remain aloof from European affairs, but trouble along the Rio Grande border with Mexico could not be ignored by either national or state officials. Border tensions were never completely absent since Texas separated from Mexico in 1836, but there were periods of less intensity. After 1906, however, the border remained in a constant state of turmoil as efforts to overthrow the longtime Mexican dictator Porfirio Díaz fermented in the area. Flores Magon, Gilberto Guerrero, Francisco I. Madero, Bernardo Reyes, Victoriano Huerta, and Venustiano Carranza, among others, launched revolutions from exile in the United States, usually from a Texas base. Then, after Madero succeeded in winning control, they quarreled with each other. The initial fighting in each movement occurred along the Texas-Mexican border, and naturally such activity in Juárez would concern and perhaps involve United States residents in El Paso, or in sister cities along the border all the way to Brownsville. From Fort Bliss to Fort Brown United States military garrisons were expanded to prevent the fighting—which claimed fully one million Mexican lives in this decade—from spreading north of the river.

Texans became particularly troubled when the British released an intercepted secret communication from German Foreign Minister Arthur Zimmerman to the Mexican government. The Zimmerman Note anticipated the day when Ger-

Right: *During the Mexican Revolution, Pancho Villa raided border towns, hoping to lure the United States into the conflict.*

Facing page: *Illegal activities between Mexico and the United States date back to the nineteenth century. This* Harper's Weekly *sketch in 1886 depicts smugglers crossing the Rio Grande. Courtesy, Institute of Texan Cultures*

man submarine warfare against neutrals continuing to supply the British and French, including those of the United States, would widen the war. Should the United States enter the war against Germany, Zimmerman invited the Mexicans to participate on their side and, should they prove victorious, promised to return all territory acquired from Mexico by the United States, including Texas. Texans were outraged at this proposal, making them more willing to fight against the Germans.

The activities of Francisco (Pancho) Villa provided additional resentment against Mexico. Following the long struggle for leadership in Mexico, Madero succeeded in replacing Díaz, only to be overthrown and murdered by Huerta, and then Carranza launched a movement against even this new regime. President Wilson had recognized the Madero government and was shocked by his murder. Wilson refused to recognize the "butcher" Huerta or support Carranza's efforts against him, but Carranza succeeded without United States support. Tension between the countries remained high, and the United States Navy patrolled the Mexico coast in a policy of "watchful waiting."

An incident involving off-duty Navy personnel at Tampico resulted in an invasion of Vera Cruz in which both American and Mexican casualties resulted, greatly escalating the tension between the governments.

Pancho Villa became a factor in the difficulty at this point. Like the other Mexican leaders, he dreamed of ruling his native land. Realizing that he could not defeat Carranza alone, he schemed to have the United States do it for him. Hoping to lure American troops into Mexico to do just that, he stopped a train en route to Mexico City and murdered all Americans on board. Prior to the incident at Vera Cruz, this incident might have provoked Wilson into action, but now he was more cautious. So Villa raided Columbus, New Mexico, in March 1916, and this invasion of United States territory compelled Wilson to respond. He authorized an expeditionary force commanded by General John J. Pershing to pursue Villa into Mexico.

Carranza at first welcomed the Americans, hoping to rid himself of a dangerous enemy, but when Villa lured Pershing's force deep into Mexico, always staying just far enough ahead of his enemy to escape capture, Carranza had to oppose this intrusion or lose the support of the Mexican people. A second war with Mexico might have erupted had it not been for the bad news coming from Europe.

England and France had kept secret as long as possible just how close they were to defeat, hoping that German submarine activities would provoke the United States sufficiently to enter the war. Finally the Allies had to admit their weakness and, coupled with a growing feeling in America against the Germans (and Wilson's pro-British sentiments), Wilson reluctantly asked Congress for a declaration of war on April 6, 1917. Edward M. House played an important role in this decision. He traveled to Europe several times after war began in 1914, seeking to mediate the differences between the hostile powers, but eventually he came to side with the British-French alliance. For the next nineteen months most Texans and other Americans enthusiastically joined the crusade.

In addition to House, other Texans prominent in the war effort included John Nance Garner, chairman of the House of Representatives Ways and Means Committee who visited the White House weekly, ostensibly to see Joseph Tumulty, Wilson's secretary, but actually to visit the President to coordinate administrative-legislative efforts. Senator Tom Connally served on the Foreign Affairs Committee, and the young Sam Rayburn, in the early part of a remarkable congressional career, sponsored the War Risk Insurance Act to provide servicemen with a $10,000 life insurance policy.

At home Texans joined other Americans in patriotic efforts. Because of the Zimmerman Note military installations along the border were enlarged in case Mexican or German activities developed there. Actually, there was never much chance that this would happen. And Texas became a training center for troops bound for Europe. Camp MacArthur at Waco, Camp Logan at Houston, Camp Bowie at Fort Worth, and Camp Travis at San Antonio became the temporary home and training ground for thousands, and Fort

John Joseph Pershing was sent in pursuit of Mexican outlaw Pancho Villa deep into Mexico in 1916. From Cirker, Dictionary of American Portraits, *Dover, 1967*

Sam Houston became the headquarters for all military operations in Texas. Coastal defense was coordinated out of Fort Crockett on Galveston Island. More than 400,000 Texans registered for the draft on June 5, 1917—Registration Day—and before the war ended 989,571 men had registered. Approximately 200,000 Texans served in the military during the war, and 5,147 of them died as a result of their service, about half from battle casualties and about half from disease, especially the influenza epidemic that broke out in 1918. America was still substantially a rural nation and many who entered the service had lived their lives in sufficient isolation to prevent them from suffering much communicable disease. Now bunched in military installations, epidemics swept through the ranks with as much devastation as German bullets.

The legislature created the State Council of Defense to coordinate state affairs during the war. Similar in form to the Military Board of Civil War days, it oversaw the enlargement of the National Guard and the Texas Rangers, looked after property of servicemen against forced sale for debt, remitted poll taxes for those in the military, and encouraged patriotism in the public schools. Texans made personal sacrifices on the home front. In response to the request of Food and Fuel Administrator Herbert C. Hoover, they did without meat on Fridays and grains on other days to share these things with servicemen and the allies; many bought Liberty Bonds and savings stamps; and they did without liquor.

Sometimes excessive fervor led a few to persecute German-Americans, and the German Department at The University of Texas found itself out of business when Governor Hobby vetoed their appropriation.

Among the more interesting wartime developments in Texas was the activity of the Aeronautical Division of the Signal Corps, the beginning of the air power in the armed forces. The first U.S. Army pilot, Benjamin D. Foulois, arrived in San Antonio in 1910 to practice with the division's only airplane. Foulois could fly the plane well enough, but he had to survive several crash landings before mastering the crucial art of bringing the aircraft down safely. He flew the first military mission in 1911, a flight from Laredo to Eagle Pass, which set the world's distance record for powered flight to that time. New pilots and aircraft arrived in San Antonio that year. The division temporarily moved to Georgia but returned to a more or less permanent home in San Antonio in 1913 when the corps established the San Antonio Aviation Center there because of the good flying weather in South-Central Texas.

Foulois flew missions for Pershing during the American advance into Mexico, then moved to Europe to fly against German aviators. The American Aviation Section in Europe consisted of thirty-five pilots and few aircraft but they proved their worth in combat and soon both were increased. The development of American air power was reflected in Texas. Kelly Field, named in honor of George E.M. Kelly, who died in a crash while training in 1911, was established in San Antonio, and later Randolph Field, the "West Point of the Air," began operations in 1928. All American pilots were trained there until the beginning of World War II, and during that conflict pilots, navigators, and other crewmen for a greatly expanded Army Air Corps, the forerunner of the modern Air Force, trained there as well.

At the conclusion of the First World War E.M.

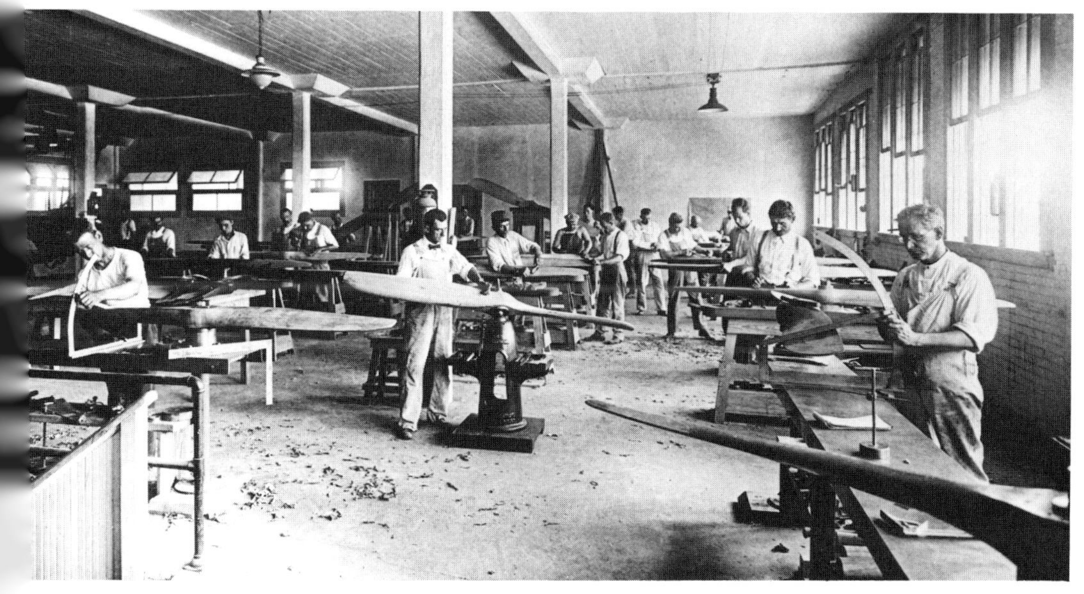

During World War I, the military effort escalated Texas industry. Workers at Steves Sash and Door Company manufactured airplane propellers in San Antonio around 1918. Courtesy, Marshal Steves, Institute of Texan Cultures

Above: *Even the smallest Texas towns staged Armistice Day celebrations in 1918. Here, townspeople in Riviera line up with American flags for a march through town. Courtesy, John E. Connor Museum*

Right: *The First National Bank car flutters festively as it parades past the First National Bank in Eagle Lake in 1918. Courtesy, First National Bank*

Left: *Members of the 369th Infantry Regiment, who served under the French Army in World War I, return to New York on February 12, 1919. Courtesy, KLRN-TV*

Below: *The first world war drew recruits from throughout the United States. These soldiers parade in Fort Worth in 1918— happy to be home again. Courtesy, Marion T. Dillon*

Anita McLean poses with her students in a rural two-room school in Castell in about 1915. Courtesy, Anita McLean, Institute of Texan Cultures

House had a major impact on United States policy. Wilson's plan for peace, the Fourteen Points, had been formulated in discussions among Wilson, House, and other advisors, and many think that the concept of the League of Nations was House's idea. House was a part of the team Wilson took with him to Europe in 1919 to negotiate at Versailles, and after the signing of the treaty he remained in Europe. Relations between the two good friends became strained following Wilson's marriage to Edith Bolling Galt, a Washington socialite, and thereafter House was never as influential.

Texas industry received a major stimulus from wartime demands. Manufactured goods doubled in value, accompanied by significant increases in manufacturing, building materials, and in processing of agricultural products, especially cottonseed oil and meal. Coastal shipbuilders received government contracts, and of course the oil industry worked hard to meet wartime demands for petroleum products. Labor cooperated under the influence of the War Labor Board for the duration of the war out of patriotism and in consideration of job secu-

rity. But at war's end the nation, as well as Texas, experienced a season of labor-management strife. In 1920 longshoremen struck at Galveston for higher wages and to gain the concession of a closed shop. Some violence accompanied their efforts, and the legislature responded with the Open Port Law, eventually extended to cover railroads as well as ships, making it a felony to interfere with anyone working in the transportation field.

Other changes occurred during the postwar period, as they do following all wars. In politics, William P. Hobby continued to preside over the state until succeeded by Pat Morris Neff, a Waco attorney. Neff defeated Joe Bailey and three other candidates and became the first governor of Texas who had earned a college degree. Later he served as president of Baylor University. During Neff's administration the progressive thrust continued despite the stresses of the war and social readjustment. Education illustrates this well. The value of Texas school property increased from nine million dollars in 1900 to more than seventy-two million dollars by 1920, students in Texas schools in-

Above: *These parade floats are really floats in this 1920s New Braunfels water parade. Courtesy, Mrs. Robert Murray*

Left: *San Antonio men and boys line up for a 1919 Labor Day parade minus the women who, for the most part, were not yet part of the labor force. Courtesy, Rudolph San Miguel*

creased during the same period from 708,125 to 1,233,860, and the ranks of teachers expanded from 15,019 to 31,880. State financial aid per student increased from $4.50 to $14.50, yet Texas remained thirty-ninth in the nation in per capita expenditure.

Secondary education fared less well than did elementary education because of the need in many families for children to work on farms or in industry at a relatively early age or because some felt that elementary school was as much education as should or could be supported at public expense. The University of Texas took the lead in advocating mandatory attendance in secondary schools and used its admissions policy as a kind of unofficial accreditation of schools. The Interscholastic League, founded at the university, coordinated athletic and academic competition to regulate those activities and to popularize high schools. Ferguson's rural consolidation law had reduced the number of country schools but the quality of facilities and instruction was improved, and the availability of free textbooks made education more accessible to all. Higher education also received its share of attention. The legislature authorized additional "normal" (teacher preparation) schools in 1917. War interfered with the founding of these schools for a time, but by the mid-1920s East Texas, Southwest Texas, North Texas, West Texas, Sul Ross, and Stephen F. Austin State Teachers colleges (all now ranked as universities) began training teachers in the various regions of the state. Texas Woman's University, Texas College of Mines (The University of Texas at El Paso), Texas A&I University, and Texas Tech College (later University) began operation. William Marsh Rice Institute (now University) was founded in Houston in 1912; three years later Southern Methodist University in Dallas opened its doors.

Progressivism, for good or ill, continued in the political arena. For example, the Seventeenth Amendment to the United States Constitution allowed Texans and other Americans to elect their senators directly, rather than having them selected by the legislature. Meanwhile a rejuvenated Ku

Above: *Texas has been affected by many ethnic groups, but none have been as influential as the Mexican culture. Here, a Mexican food vendor and his daughter pose in the border town of Laredo in 1915. Courtesy, St. Mary's University*

Facing page: *Surrounded by lawmen and onlookers, J.W. Hall and Thomas Eagan are seen here under arrest after robbing the Fredonia post office in 1914. Courtesy, Wayne Spiller*

Klux Klan became a powerful force in the politics of many states, including Texas, and was a significant issue even in the Presidential election of 1924. Reorganized in Georgia in the postwar period, the Klan took its name and secret organizational techniques from the group that had used white-sheeted anonymity to enforce political regularity during Reconstruction. The Klan was anti-Negro by definition, but now it had little to do to keep blacks under control because state law did so quite effectively. So in the 1920s it became a nativist, anti-Semitic, anti-Roman Catholic organization that tried to enforce its definition of morality on others. W.J. Simmons, the Imperial Wizard of the Klan, brought the movement to Texas in 1920. They used threats, beatings, secrecy, tar and feathers, and even castration to control moral offenders, wife beaters, or violators of "one hundred percent Americanism." These activities often went unpunished because law enforcement officers looked the other way; some were even members of the Klan. Senator Earle B. Mayfield of Tyler was thought by many to be a Klan member because the organization supported him strongly. Burning crosses and the singing of "The Old Rugged Cross" punctuated many Texas evenings with pride for members and supporters and fear for others.

Governor Neff ignored the Klan for a time because he viewed a massive crime wave in Texas as a greater danger. This was partly due to Prohibition violators, but more violent criminal activity exemplified by the activities of Clyde Barrow and Bonnie Parker was also a major problem. With others, these two famous outlaws robbed banks and roamed the countryside until tracked down and killed by Texas Rangers and other police officials in Louisiana. For many the Klan seemed a way to restore society to older, more settled ways. And when a Texan, a Dallas dentist named Hiram W. Evans, became Imperial Wizard, many feared that the Klan would take over the state. But Mayfield's election in 1922, with obvious Klan support, produced a reaction. Both Oscar Underwood of Georgia and William Gibbs MacAdoo, Wilson's son-in-law, came to Texas in 1924 to begin their campaign for the Democratic Presidential nomination. They did so in Texas to denounce the power of the Klan.

Miriam A. Ferguson, called "Ma" by combining her initials, announced her intention to run for governor as an opponent of the Klan. Obviously

running because her husband Jim Ferguson could not, she never denied her role. She began her political career with the statement that she did not know much about politics but "I do know that my Redeemer liveth!" She pledged that "a vote for me is a vote for Pa," Ferguson's new nickname, and claimed that Texas would have "two governors for the price of one." Despite Jim Ferguson's impeachment and losses in the races in 1920 and 1922, Miriam Ferguson ran second in the first primary and then defeated Felix D. Robertson in the runoff despite his strong support from the Klan. Unwilling to see another Ferguson in office, the Republicans ran their strongest race in some time with University of Texas professor George C. Butte, but "Ma" Ferguson won the general election by a four-to-three margin.

True to Miriam Ferguson's campaign pledge, her husband became the real power in the administration. Jim Ferguson had an office in the capitol and attended all meetings where the governor had to be present, sometimes without Miriam. He dispensed more than 2,000 pardons to penitentiary inmates—up from 100 or so under Neff—claiming it would save the state money; others charged that he accepted bribes to do so. He awarded textbook and highway contracts, according to Texas Contractor Association executive L.W. Kemp, on the same basis. When confronted with Kemp's charges, Ferguson pledged to make Kemp the goat of the scandal if the charges were released, as they later were in a publication titled *The Goat Bleats.* Ferguson fought back in the pages of the *Ferguson Forum* but the accusations resulted in Miriam Ferguson's loss to Attorney General Dan Moody in 1926. She later claimed that she had never trusted Moody because his eyes were too close together, but he proved a true progressive.

Under Moody's administration the Highway Department was reorganized, providing for more public participation in the awarding of road contracts, and a State Board of Education was created. Moody was reelected in 1928, the year the Democrats held their national nominating convention in Houston. Although a victim of polio, Franklin Delano Roosevelt struggled to the podium to place the name of Alfred E. Smith of New York in nomination. Smith, a Yankee, a Catholic, and a "wet" on the Prohibition issue, became the first Democrat to lose Texas since Reconstruction. Texas voters, as well as others in the nation, favored the Republican candidate Herbert C. Hoover, the Great Engineer, over the abrasive Smith.

The greatest event in the Texas economy in the early twentieth century came from the phenomenal growth of the oil industry. Oil had been dis-

covered in Texas as early as 1866 when Lynn T. Barrett drilled the first well west of the Mississippi River near Oil Springs in Nacogdoches County. Lacking a market and with insufficient production to develop one, this discovery amounted to little, as did other minor strikes in Brown County in 1878 and in Bexar County in 1886. Then, in 1894, drillers attempting to find adequate water resources for the development of Corsicana in Navarro County located a significant pool of oil instead. Joseph S. Cullinan came south from Pennsylvania to develop the field, build the first refinery in Texas, and create a market for oil—as a dust-settling agent for roads and as a fuel for railroad locomotives.

The largest single oil strike occurred near Beaumont in Jefferson County on January 10, 1901, when Anthony Lucas brought in the Spindletop gusher on a site where Patillo Higgins had been predicting that oil would be discovered for years. The oil gushed 100 feet into the air and formed a lake around the wooden derrick before the well

Facing page: Wearing hats to help protect their heads from a searing Texan sun, workers harvest vegetables from a field in Weslaco in 1927. Courtesy, Harlingen Public Library

Right: Miriam A. "Ma" Ferguson was elected governor of Texas in 1924 as a stand-in for her husband, Jim, on a platform of "Two Governors for the Price of One." Although scandals contributed to her defeat in 1926, she won another term in 1932 during the Depression. Courtesy, Library of The Daughters of the Republic of Texas

could be capped nine days later. Soon a person could walk from drilling rig to drilling rig, so close were the wells located. Beaumont became an instant boom town. Hotels rented rooms by the hour, food prices doubled, and excursion trips ran daily from Houston and New Orleans. Tourists bought oil for one dollar per bottle from enterprising youths while the price declined to a few cents per barrel at the wellhead. The Spindletop field produced fifty million barrels in the first ten years. Deeper drilling produced a second major boom during the 1920s, and the field is still in production.

Guffey Oil Company, soon changed to the Gulf Oil Company, established a refinery south of the field near Port Arthur and ran pipelines to the

Above: *The Spindletop gusher in 1901 spawned the oil industry that changed the Texas economy. Courtesy, Barker Texas History Center*

Left: *John W. Galey was a major drilling contractor at Spindletop. Courtesy, Spindletop Museum*

Valeria Kornegay poses with her daughter in front of an oil derrick in the early 1920s. Courtesy, Helen K. Barfield

BLACK GOLD

When the Lucas Gusher, also known as Spindletop, blew in on January 10, 1901, the course of history for Texas, the United States, and the world was changed forever. Since then oil and Texas have become synonymous.

The forces and elements that formed oil lay beneath the earth's surface long before discovery of Spindletop. The first recorded use of petroleum in Texas was in 1543 when Hernando De Soto's men caulked their boats with the thick black substance they found seeping from the earth. Indians used the exuding oil and tar for medicinal purposes, as did the early Spanish settlers in East Texas.

Early oil explorers include Jack Graham, who dug a pit in Angelina County in 1859 to encourage seepage, and Lynn Taliaferro Barret of Melrose, who drilled the state's first bona fide oil well in 1866. Barret only drilled 106 feet with an auger powered by a steam engine before striking oil, and his well yielded only ten barrels per day. Barret's attempts to discover oil had begun years before, even before the first oil well in the United States was drilled in Pennsylvania, but poor financing and the war interrupted his efforts.

Barret capped his hard-earned well and traveled to Pennsylvania for financing and equipment to explore further. John F. Carl brought equipment for a second attempt, but gave up after drilling only eighty feet. Some, including Dick Dowling, drilled near seepages with few results, while others, such as Martin Meichinger, found oil without even looking for it. Attempting to drill a water well near Brownwood, Meichinger hit a small oil pool that he bottled and sold for medicine. Some early drillers also hit gas pockets that occasionally ignited. Because of these dangers water well drillers often filled the holes when they discovered oil or gas.

Water well diggers at Corsicana made news when they hit oil at about 1,000 feet. Determined to find water, they continued to drill another 1,000 feet until they found it, while the oil continued to flow up around the casing.

There was only a light demand for oil in Texas, but farsighted entrepreneurs knew a market could be developed for such an abundant commodity. J.M. Guffey and John Galey came to Corsicana to drill five wells. Their first well was a small pool; their second, a dry hole; but their third produced more than twenty barrels a day, enough to encourage them. Other drillers moved in, and by 1897 more than fifty wells had been drilled in or near Corsicana.

Joseph S. Cullinan arrived and revolutionized the business. His company, later known as the Magnolia Petroleum Company, constructed the first commercial oil refinery in Texas. He persuaded the Cotton Belt Railroad to convert from coal to oil as an energy source for their locomotives, and other rail lines followed. By 1900 the Corsicana field was producing nearly one million barrels per year. The success of the Corsicana field proved that Texas had abundant oil reserves, and this stimulated well drilling elsewhere in the state.

Pattillo Higgins was convinced that oil existed abundantly in the Beaumont area. While on Sunday school picnics on a small rise south of town he entertained children by sticking his cane into the ground and setting fire to the escaping gas. Mineral water also seeped from springs in the side of the hill. A geology student, Higgins felt sure that oil lay beneath the hill. In 1892 he and some friends formed the Gladys City Oil, Gas, and Manufacturing Company, named for Gladys Bingham, a member of Higgins' Sunday school class. Higgins predicted that oil would be discovered at 1,000 feet. The contracted drillers attempted only two wells, neither of which reached below 500 feet. Others despaired when a state geologist visited Beaumont and told them that there was no oil in the area. For several years thereafter Higgins was regarded as a crank.

Realizing that he could not obtain local support, Higgins ran an advertisement in an engineering journal. He received a reply from Anthony Lucas, who joined Higgins in Beaumont. Born in Austria as Antonio Luchiach, he graduated from the Austrian Naval Academy before coming to the United States to become a mining engineer. Lucas replied to Higgins' ad because he knew that oil and sulphur often were found together. From Higgins' description of the salt dome south of Beaumont, he hoped to find the lucky combination beneath the dome's surface.

Lucas started to drill in July 1899. He abandoned the effort because his equipment was too light but not before he found a small amount of oil. With his samples he tried to interest major oil companies but had no luck until Galey and Guffey of the Corsicana fields agreed to back another well.

Lucas hired Curt, Al, and Jim Hammil to drill the well. It was spudded in on October 26, 1900. On January 9, 1901, they had trouble penetrating a rock formation. They pulled out the stem to mount a new bit and had begun to lower it again the next morning when mud began to spurt high into the derrick. The Hamills ran just in time to escape six tons of drill stem bursting up through the floor and breaking into sections. As they approached the demolished derrick the earth began to tremble and roar. Mud, gas, and finally heavy crude oil spurted 200 feet into the air, less than twenty feet from where Higgins predicted oil would be found.

Townspeople flocked to Gladys Hill to see the gusher, and soon even excursion trains came from as far as New Orleans to behold the sight. A lake of oil surrounded the small hill before the well was capped. A fire began, but was extinguished before any great damage was done. The capping itself proved difficult. Mule power moved a heavy valve over the flow, the valve's mounting was nailed to the legs of the derrick, and then the valve was closed. After nine days of flow, the valve and derrick were surrounded by oil.

Beaumont became a boom town. Its small population doubled and doubled again for days. Men rented sleeping spaces and bought leases for exorbitant prices. Land not considered a bargain at twenty dollars an acre was now worth thousands. Multitudes came to see the Lucas Gusher, also called Spindletop after a tall cypress tree in the vicinity which looked like an inverted spindletop.

The Spindletop discovery changed the oil industry permanently. Capable of producing 3.5 million barrels a year in the early period, it temporarily glutted the oil market; but the abundant product also stimulated new uses. Refineries were built to convert the fluid, pipelines were laid to transport it, and oil field equipment was re-engineered to accommodate stronger flowing and deeper wells.

Spindletop's discovery coincided with the early production of internal combustion automobile engines. Today, the world runs on oil. The revolution could have started practically anywhere, but it happened in Beaumont, Texas, right where Pattillo Higgins said it would.

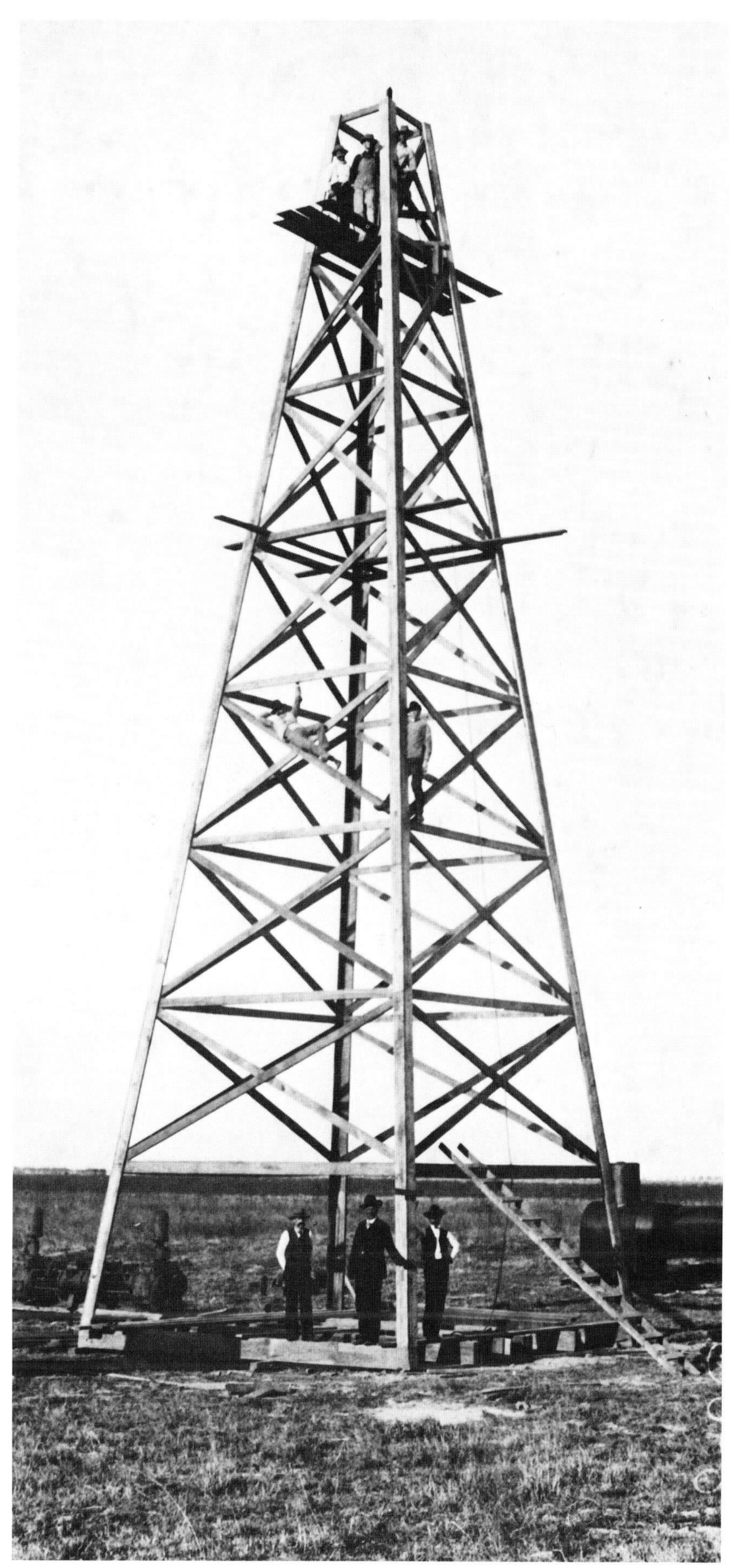

field. Then the Texas Fuel Company, Texaco, founded by Cullinan, James S. Hogg, and J.W. Gates, also operated at Port Arthur. Both are still the largest refineries in their respective companies. At Beaumont, Magnolia Oil, Mobil, also established a refinery.

The oil boom spread to other parts of the state. Major discoveries were made at Sour Lake in 1902, at Burkburnett and Batson in 1903, at Humble in 1905, at Petrolia and Powell in 1906, at Goose Creek in 1908, at Electra in 1911, and at Mexia in 1912. Probably the most celebrated boom was at Rangor, largely because a 1940 Hollywood movie starring Clark Gable and Spencer Tracy titled *Boom Town* was centered there.

The oil boom provided spinoffs for related industries. In Beaumont Howard Hughes, Sr.,

Right: *Colonel M.L. Crimmins and Mary Astor visit San Antonio in 1926 amidst much public fanfare. Courtesy, San Antonio* Light *Collection, Institute of Texan Cultures*

Facing page, top: *Joseph Valentine adjusts a motion picture camera under a plane in preparation for an aerial shoot. Experimentation with cameras became crucial with adventure films like* Wings, *where so much action occurred in the air. Courtesy, San Antonio* Light *Collection, Institute of Texan Cultures*

Facing page, bottom: *San Antonian Milred Overton poses with a new radio in 1926. Courtesy, San Antonio* Light *Collection, Institute of Texan Cultures*

bought the rights to a rotary drilling bit from a local bicycle repairman and made a fortune selling drilling bits and other equipment; Kirby and other lumber interests geared up new mills to provide timber for wooden drilling derricks, and the pipeline industry was born to carry oil from wells to refineries and on to holding tanks and ships. The oil boom represented a major new taxing source for Texas, although the state used it only reluctantly. Texas is one of the few states with a major depletable resource without an adequate extraction tax. But in property values alone the oil fields and refineries enriched local schools and government greatly.

Apart from the obvious creation of new wealth, the discovery of oil had another profound effect upon Texans. Suddenly a major force in the nation's industrial picture, Texans found new economic and political power open to them. Other than Sam Houston, John Henry Reagan, and Edward M. House, few Texans had exerted major influences at the national level. This changed completely.

The boom-or-bust attitude of the oil wildcatters seemed to characterize the state's attitude about itself and the attitude of others toward Texas. Some would call that attitude pride, others thought of it, and think of it, as arrogance. From the apparent prosperity of the 1920s it was easy to overlook the depression in agricultural circles, the fact that laborers' wages did not keep pace with prices, or that stock prices were wildly out of sync with actual value. The Great Depression of the 1930s and a world again at war brought new realities to Texans and other Americans in the decades ahead.

The Great Depression and Global War, Texas Style

The Wall Street Crash in October 1929 marks the official beginning of the Great Depression for many Americans. Actually, much of the Western world had experienced periods of economic hardship since the end of the First World War, and even before. In America farmers had remained in a depressed economic state since the loss of the expanded markets produced by the war. Many Texas farmers and laborers later humorously claimed that they never knew any difference because they had been in a depression all their lives. Perhaps this was so for some, but things could and did get worse for the majority.

President Herbert Hoover's administration began in March 1929, with the apparent prosperity of the nation that had marked the Republican ascendancy of Warren G. Harding and Calvin Coolidge still in place. The

A newly married Mr. and Mrs. Theron parade through an arch of shovels at a Civil Works Administration camp in San Antonio during the Depression. Courtesy, San Antonio Light Collection, Institute of Texan Cultures

upper levels of the American economic and social strata lived in contemporary luxury, profits and economic growth made many euphoric, and stock prices seemed to climb higher each day. Then calamity struck. On "Black Thursday," October 29, 1929, more than sixteen million shares of stock changed hands on Wall Street, mostly for less value at each transaction. For the majority of Americans prosperity ended and a decade-long depression, the worst in the nation's history, began.

Some businesses closed immediately throughout the nation, followed by the failure of financial institutions that had extended them credit; then manufacturers laid off workers and often closed down because retailers could no longer sell their products. Farmers found it difficult or impossible to sell their products to processors or even individual consumers because, without jobs, they lacked the money to purchase them or because they produced so much that prices declined even below production costs. Farmlands, homes, businesses, indeed, all classes of property, were forfeited to mortgagers who had too much on their hands al-

ready and no customers to relieve them of the burden. Tenancy, already at 70 percent, increased.

By 1930 the economic wheels of the nation and of Texas slowed to a crawl, then nearly stopped completely. Texas lacked heavy industrial development so it escaped that part of the Great Depression for the first year. Before long, however, 5.5 percent of Texas' white population were not only unemployed, they were on relief, and 8.8 percent of the blacks shared their fate in segregated bread lines. Countless others survived by the generosity of friends or relatives. Soon armies of hobos tramped the Texas highways or had to ride the rails as unpaid passengers on freight trains to look for work wherever it was rumored to be. Many lived on handouts provided by charitable organizations, solicited from individuals in their businesses or residences, or just lived by their wits. The edges of railroad yards became gathering places for wanderers who lived in cardboard huts or packing case shelters they called "Hoovervilles" with reproachful humor. Hoover's picture and statements that prosperity was "just around the corner" appeared in newspapers that covered the homeless on the bare ground or on park benches, and were termed "Hoover blankets." Depending on the section of the state, armadillos, jack rabbits, or other small game obtained for a makeshift stew became "Hoover hogs."

Hoover's policies in only eight months in office had not caused the Depression—he inherited long-standing economic policies thought sound by nearly everyone—yet he received all the blame. Texans also blamed Governor Ross Sterling, who won the governorship from Miriam Ferguson in 1930. Governor Sterling, a founder of the Humble Oil Company and a wealthy contractor, echoed Hoover's claim that direct relief from government was wrong. Both believed that the best way to improve the economy would be to aid business, thus keeping people employed. Sterling advocated a state bond issue to improve highways at the same time Hoover's Reconstruction Finance Corporation was founded by the Democratic Congress to

aid business at the national level. Neither asked their legislative branches for relief for individuals.

Sterling's agricultural program was based on principles similar to those later employed by President Roosevelt in his Agricultural Adjustment Administration. Governor Sterling called upon Southern farmers to limit their production of cotton to relieve a market surplus of the crop, hoping this would result in raised prices. This program was difficult to explain to farmers experienced for six decades in the concept that one earned more by producing more. Cotton sold for six cents per pound in 1931, but the five million bales Texas farmers produced that year cost them money. The legislature followed Sterling's leadership in passing the Cotton Acreage Control Law that limited cotton acreage to 30 percent of a farmer's total land holdings. Sterling tried to convince other cotton-producing states to do the same, and some did pass acreage control laws but would not implement them until at least 75 percent of all cotton

Facing page: Frightened by the deepening Depression, hundreds of depositers flocked to this San Antonio bank to withdraw their funds. Courtesy, San Antonio Light *Collection, Institute of Texan Cultures*

Right: Soup kitchens helped those down-on-their-luck all over the nation during the Depression. J.E. Gray is shown here getting a coffee refill at a San Antonio dispensary in 1933. Courtesy, San Antonio Light *Collection, Institute of Texan Cultures*

Above: *Sam Houston peers steadily from the pages of a Texas history book, opened for a 1930s look by Winona Binghurst. Courtesy, San Antonio Light Collection, Institute of Texan Cultures*

Right: *San Antonian Mary Louise Elan poses in 1930 before a period radio. Courtesy, San Antonio Light Collection, Institute of Texan Cultures*

Facing page: *Hard times did not always mean an end to fashion as Mrs. John H. Calhoun and Mrs. Edward Tewes prove in this 1932 photograph in San Antonio. Courtesy, San Antonio Light Collection, Institute of Texan Cultures*

Two San Antonio boys laze away the afternoon by Woodlawn Lake in about 1935, the problems of the Depression far away. Courtesy, San Antonio Light Collection, Institute of Texan Cultures

states passed corresponding legislation. So only Texas enforced the cotton acreage control law, much to the dissatisfaction of the state's farmers.

Within three years the Agricultural Adjustment Act attempted the same thing at the national level until the program was declared unconstitutional by the Supreme Court. By then it was gone from Texas as well because the Court of Civil Appeals declared the Cotton Acreage Control Law in violation of the state constitution in March 1932. With or without the law, cotton prices remained

depressed, more and more farmers lost their land or tenants lost their positions, and both groups congregated in shanties near cities and towns, hoping to find work.

Even nature appeared to be against the farmers. In addition to the economic reversal they suffered, dust bowl conditions made their lives even more miserable. Decades of deep plowing, drought, and high winds carried precious topsoil away until only sand remained. Splendid orange-red sunsets were a thing of beauty until the admirer realized that the glorious colors were produced by the soils carried to the heavens by the winds. More than farms were gone with the wind. The lives of the farmers changed forever.

East Texans lucky enough to live in the vicinity of Kilgore received some relief from the Depression after the discovery of oil near there on October 30, 1930. Columbus M. "Dad" Joiner brought in a wildcat well known as the Daisy Bradford No. 3 and changed East Texas forever. Within a few months Joiner drilled additional wells, confirming a field forty miles in length and from four to eight miles in breadth. At first the discovery was ignored by the major oil companies who judged Joiner's well an isolated strike. So the independent oil producers mostly developed the field, making many of them instant millionaires. Later they sold their product to the major refineries. As soon as word of the discovery spread, thousands rushed to Kilgore in search of riches, or, perhaps in the case of many, just in search of a job. Kilgore increased in population by 5,000 people within a few days and more than 1,000 wells were drilled within six months. Production reached 100 million barrels the first year and increased to 200 million barrels by 1933, eclipsing the total production of the remainder of the state.

The independent producers who controlled the production in the absence of the major companies were enriched, and those employed to develop the East Texas field found jobs, but it was not developed on an orderly basis and overproduction soon brought the price of oil tumbling down to ten cents per barrel. This jeopardized the value and stability of all oil investments in the state, and the major producers fought back. They had Governor Sterling request that the independents in East Texas voluntarily cut back production.

His plea fell on deaf ears. The independents were making money and had no intention of stopping. Some vowed they would defend their wells with weapons if necessary but they would not turn the valve and reduce production. Sterling ordered Texas National Guard Commander Jacob F. Walters and his troops to East Texas. Since Sterling was a founder of Humble Oil and Walters served as an attorney for the Texas Company, East Texans suspected that these men were merely using state power to protect the major oil companies at their expense.

Walters shut down the East Texas field for a time, then it reopened under the control of the

Broadway goes Texan as owner Tom Arapulos poses in front of his Manhattan Cafe in Houston. Courtesy, George Petheriotes Family

Railroad Commission chaired by Ernest Thompson. The Commission issued a production schedule with a "daily allowable" of 225 barrels per well, later dropped to a maximum production of only 100 barrels per day. Prices did rise, but not as high as hoped. The independents could not resist the temptation to produce "hot oil" in excess of the daily allowable as long as they could find buyers, often at higher prices. Sometimes employees did this on their own, in effect stealing the oil for their own profit. Landowners were unhappy because they could never be certain that their royalties reflected true production levels. Hot oil production probably exceeded legal production before the situation was stabilized by state legislation requiring refineries to account for all purchases of

crude oil. Violence often erupted in the oil patch, and Thompson was forced to ask the Texas Rangers to restore order when the Supreme Court ruled Sterling's use of the National Guard for that purpose unconstitutional.

Hot oil stimulated the development of refining in East Texas. More than ninety "skimming units" and "cracking units" were established near the oil fields to produce what was termed "cheap gas" or "East Texas gas," generally thought by many to be of lower quality and at a lower price than that produced by the major companies. Gradually the majors bought out many independent producers, acquiring their wells, refineries, and retail outlets, and eventually achieved control of at least 80 percent of the East Texas oil business from the oil field to the consumer.

Texans who lacked oil wells or employment from the discovery of mineral wealth generally looked to political leaders for the solution to their problems. Texas voters turned against Sterling in 1932, preferring instead the same Miriam Ferguson they had rejected in 1926 and 1930. And they warmly embraced New York Governor Franklin Delano Roosevelt, the Democratic nominee for President. Hoover's and Sterling's ways had not solved the problems of the Depression and they were willing to trade old leaders for anyone with a different idea of how to help them. Speaker of the House of Representatives, Texas Congressman John Nance Garner, joined the Democratic ticket as vice presidential nominee after making an unsuccessful bid for the top spot.

Garner enjoyed great popularity in Texas and great political power in Washington, and he proved a major asset to Roosevelt in the campaign and in the New Deal that followed. Garner seemed content with being vice president, at least during the first term, but he grew unhappy with Roosevelt over plans to reorganize the federal judiciary in 1936-1937, and fell out with him completely about the third-term issue in 1940. In the beginning, however, he helped push the New Deal through Congress where he had as much influence in the House as he did in the Senate over which he presided. Together they passed the Emergency Banking Act, the Agricultural Adjustment Act, the National Recovery Act, and scores of other laws creating agencies for relief, regulation, and recovery. Later the Supreme Court declared both the Agricultural Adjustment Act and the National Recovery Act unconstitutional but Roosevelt found other means to set recovery wheels in motion.

The Hoover Administration's Reconstruction Finance Corporation was taken over by Roosevelt, who appointed Jesse Jones of Houston as its administrative chief. Jones later became federal loan administrator in charge of all federal lending agencies, and after 1941 he also served as secretary of commerce. By holding all these offices Jones became second only to Roosevelt in the power structure of the New Deal. Other Texans whose careers were affected by New Deal programs were Lyndon Baines Johnson, administrator of the National Youth Administration (NYA) in Texas and his associate, John Bowden Connally.

As prosperity returned for a few, businessmen increasingly opposed these intrusions by government into the private sector, but most Americans and Texans supported Roosevelt through four elections until his death in April 1945. Many regarded him as a savior, others thought him the

Facing page: *Workers pause to contemplate progress at a 1933 Works Progress Administration public work project site in San Antonio. Courtesy, San Antonio* Light *Collection, Institute of Texan Cultures*

Right: *Domingo Cortinas boxes vegetables at this San Antonio Relief Commissary in 1933. Courtesy, San Antonio* Light *Collection, Institute of Texan Cultures*

devil. The arrogant, upward slant of his cigarette holder alternately inspired or irritated, but his "fireside chats" on the radio, expressions of concern, and positive efforts to help them made many Texans lifelong Democrats.

In Texas Miriam Ferguson's second administration proved less controversial than her earlier term, and she and Jim Ferguson generally supported the New Deal. They took advantage of Texas Independence Day, March 2, to declare all Texas banks closed days in advance of Roosevelt's "bank holiday," hoping to save financial institutions in the state until the New Deal could take effect. Jim Ferguson began the enabling proclamation with the customary "by the authority vested in me," speaking for Miriam Ferguson of course, then said, "Oh hell, by the authority by me assumed . . ." The Fergusons' liberal pardoning policy returned as a way to save state expenditures. Such economy was necessary because the state's revenues had de-

clined sharply during the Depression. Miriam Ferguson requested that the legislature pass a state sales tax to compensate for this loss of revenue, but the legislators refused. They also shelved the report of the Woodruff-Graves Commission, appointed by Governor Sterling, that recommended the state streamline its agency structure downward from 129 departments to twenty. The legislature claimed this would be too expensive to accomplish under the depressed circumstances. They did pass a special twenty million dollar relief fund, legalized prize fighting, redistricted Congressional jurisdictions, approved the production of beer with an alcohol content of 3.2 percent, and ratified the Twenty-First Amendment repealing Prohibition and statewide Prohibition as well, returning the state to the prewar local-option system. Some counties remained dry while others quickly voted to allow the sale of alcoholic beverages. Ultimately the local options included a completely dry jurisdiction, one which permitted package sales for off-premises consumption, beer and wine only, or liquor-by-the-drink. Some counties even divided themselves on precinct lines to determine such issues.

James V. Allred successfully defeated six other candidates, including his principal competitor, Tom Hunter, for the governor's office in 1934. Allred won reelection to a second term in 1936, and he is often judged Texas' best governor between James Stephen Hogg and Allan Shivers or John B. Connally. His was a truly progressive administration. Allred's tenure as attorney general convinced him that changes in government were in order. He advocated a public regulatory commission forty years before one was created, and he campaigned for a pardons board to recommend clemency cases to his office to help erase the stigma of the Fergusons' pardoning policy. He also pushed for a modern police system for the state.

Governor Allred also advocated a tax on crude oil but he failed to secure one because of opposition from producers and from labor after management convinced workers that taxes on oil would somehow translate into lost jobs. He did succeed in efforts to improve the state policing system. Under the Ferguson administration the Texas Rangers had been politicized through an appointing policy that rewarded supporters rather than placing trained and experienced law enforcement officers on duty. Allred persuaded the legislature to combine the Rangers and the Highway Patrol to form a new agency, the Department of Public Safety. The number of Rangers was greatly reduced but they retained their unique identity and shed the image of political tampering. The new agency, commonly known as DPS, evolved into an efficient law enforcement department.

Allred's administration also established a statewide old-age-assistance program through a constitutional amendment and subsequent legislative action. Hard times persisted in Texas throughout his administration, and in 1938 more than 300,000 of the state's people still were on direct relief from state or federal agencies. Although

Above: *Adella Roberts solicits Christmas funds for the Salvation Army on a San Antonio corner in 1935. Courtesy, San Antonio* Light *Collection, Institute of Texan Cultures*

Right: *Oil transformed many Texans' lives as gushers popped up quite literally in backyards. C. Erben is shown tending his own backyard oil well in San Antonio in 1929. Courtesy, San Antonio* Light *Collection, Institute of Texan Cultures*

Facing page: *San Antonian B.H. Klock is shown astride a prize porker in 1938. Courtesy, San Antonio* Light *Collection, Institute of Texan Cultures*

Right: *Eager viewers lean from roof tops and line the parade route in anticipation of a 1931 Battle of Flowers extravaganza in San Antonio. Courtesy, San Antonio* Light *Collection, Institute of Texan Cultures*

Right: *Mexican Matachine dancers pose in 1935 with a picture of the Virgin. Note the Aztec and Spanish dancers around the Virgin, a demonstration of the religious and secular elements comprising contemporary Mexico. Courtesy, San Antonio Light Collection, Institute of Texan Cultures*

Above: *Longhorns were aptly named, as demonstrated by Texan Tom Youngblood, who is balancing a mounted pair in 1938. Courtesy, San Antonio Light Collection, Institute of Texan Cultures*

Left: *Battle of Flowers Parade participants wait for the procession to begin in a 1934 extravaganza in San Antonio. Courtesy, San Antonio Light Collection, Institute of Texan Cultures*

249

Governor James V. Allred chats in a flag-draped parade car with General Frank Parker in this 1936 photo. Courtesy, San Antonio Light *Collection, Institute of Texan Cultures*

his tenure as governor had achieved success in securing reforms that would prove meaningful for the state in the future, it was undramatic. In 1938 the people were ready to turn to a kind of folk hero to lead them.

W. Lee O'Daniel, a native of Ohio, moved to Texas in 1925 to take a job as sales manager for the manufacturer of Hillbilly Flour in Fort Worth. To boost sales he appeared as master of ceremonies and occasionally as a performer on a daily radio broadcast that reached the entire state through local radio station affiliates. The show featured a three-piece Western band named The Light Crust Doughboys who sang religious as well as secular music in the hillbilly or country style. O'Daniel was introduced on each show with the line, "Pass the Biscuits, Pappy," and "Pappy" became a familiar name to thousands of Texans who tuned in to hear his homilies, poems, and homespun philosophy mixed with flour commercials.

The Doughboys began to make personal appearance tours around the state in the interest of sales. O'Daniel was aware of their great popularity but he hardly translated that perception into a po-

litical ambition until a listener mailed in a card suggesting that he run for governor. Reading cards and letters from listeners was a regular part of the show's format, so O'Daniel broadcast the request and asked his radio audience for advice. He was inundated with more than 55,000 requests that he run for the office.

If O'Daniel was not surprised by the response, surely the reaction caught the state's political regulars off guard. Probably it should not have done so. Louisiana had elected a colorful man of the people, Huey Long, as public service commissioner, governor, and senator on much the same kind of charismatic appeal, and soon would elect hillbilly singer Jimmie Davis governor of their state.

O'Daniel decided to accept the advice of his listeners. Announcing that he would run on a platform of the Ten Commandments and the Golden Rule, he continued to tour with the Light Crust Doughboys. They gave free performances, still advertised flour, and passed flour barrels for campaign contributions at public gatherings and shows. Opponents laughed at O'Daniel's method of raising campaign funds, missing the point com-

pletely. Every hard-scrabble farmer who invested even a dime in reality was pledging a vote in the election. Perhaps O'Daniel had entered the race as a publicity ploy to sell flour, but he carried the primary without a runoff and won 95 percent of the vote in the general election in November.

Like Ferguson, O'Daniel shared a lack of experience in office and, ultimately, a loss of much of the good will that had placed him there. Both administrations suffered from legislative confrontations. Always flamboyant, O'Daniel advocated a "transaction tax," a euphemism for the sales tax, but instead the legislature remained with the traditional sources of revenue. The tax on tobacco and natural resources was increased, and they levied a new tax on gasoline, the telephone, and other utility companies, and selected business receipts, especially in insurance. O'Daniel won election to a second term but soon afterwards won a special election to succeed Senator Morris Sheppard.

Above: State liquor agents George Cox and C.W. Berry empty an illegal still in San Antonio in 1938. Stills such as this one were found all over the state during the Depression. Courtesy, San Antonio Light *Collection, Institute of Texan Cultures*

Right: Boxers Jimmy Perrin and Chick Sanchez battle it out before an enthusiastic San Antonio crowd in 1939. Courtesy, San Antonio Light *Collection, Institute of Texan Cultures*

Left: *Chinese pilot Yaching Lee smiles for photographers in San Antonio in 1939, on a brief stopover in Texas. Courtesy, San Antonio* Light *Collection, Institute of Texan Cultures*

Below: *The 1938 pecan shellers strike necessitated strikers working together in order to achieve the gains needed. These women work in assembly-line efficiency to make tortillas for the strikers. Courtesy, San Antonio* Light *Collection, Institute of Texan Cultures*

Above: *Amelia Earhart was photographed chatting with autograph seekers at a 1933 stopover in San Antonio. Courtesy, San Antonio* Light *Collection, Institute of Texan Cultures*

Above left: *Achieving beauty could be a sobering experience in 1938. Here, Catherine Moto waits patiently for a permanent wave to take effect. Courtesy, San Antonio* Light *Collection, Institute of Texan Cultures*

Left: *Amelia Earhart may be the most famous of early feminine fliers, but she was not the only female aviator. Mrs. C.E. Shankla posed in 1938 with her mail bags in preparation for an airmail flight. Courtesy, San Antonio* Light *Collection, Institute of Texan Cultures*

Above: *A Communist Party member explains literature on display at the San Antonio City Auditorium, a presentation that sparked a riot in 1939. Courtesy, San Antonio* Light *Collection, Institute of Texan Cultures*

Left: *Firemen train a powerful stream of water on rioting political adversaries in an attempt to regain control of a massive fight between Communist Party members and anti-Communist citizens. Courtesy, San Antonio* Light *Collection, Institute of Texan Cultures*

Left: *An unknown woman climbs through an open window during the Auditorium Riot in San Antonio in 1939. The dispute arose over a meeting of the Communist Party at City Auditorium—a meeting that many San Antonians of the time resented. Courtesy, San Antonio* Light *Collection, Institute of Texan Cultures*

Right: *Secure in their beliefs, rioters storm a Communist meeting at City Auditorium in San Antonio in 1939. Courtesy, San Antonio* Light *Collection, Institute of Texan Cultures*

O'Daniel's departure from state affairs to serve in the Senate came as a welcome relief for the legislature and political regulars.

Lieutenant Governor Coke R. Stevenson served out the time remaining in O'Daniel's term and won reelection in 1942 and 1944. His tenure coincided with the years of global war and returning prosperity to Texas, and he governed with a quiet and conservative dignity that he thought earned him the privilege of also following O'Daniel to the Senate. Such was not the case, and Stevenson's bid for a Senate seat in 1948 against Lyndon Baines Johnson ended his career in bitterness. Meanwhile, he could at least brag that he had served as governor when the state once more enjoyed some prosperity, even if marred with the realities of war.

Texans and other Americans failed to understand the Nazi menace in Europe or that of the militarists' rise to power in Japan in the late 1930s. Most supported the Neutrality Acts passed by Congress in an attempt to keep the nation aloof from the struggle for power going on in Europe and in the Orient, especially after war actually began in 1939. In a spirit reminiscent of 1916, Americans mistakenly thought that the massive oceans would insulate the nation from harm if they would only mind their own business. But the world had shrunk through expanded air and sea power, and so we soon realized that the United States would have to aid Britain, the last resort against the Germans. Roosevelt did all he could under the restrictions of the neutrality legislation, lending ships and war materiel when he was prohibited from selling them in return for leases on Atlantic naval bases.

December 7, 1941, changed everything. Roosevelt announced the surprise attack to a startled nation that afternoon, regretting to inform them, he said, that "very many American lives" had been lost at Pearl Harbor. Roosevelt summoned Congressional leaders to the White House for consultation, among them Senator Tom Connally of Texas, a prominent member of the Senate Foreign Relations Committee. The next day Connally introduced a resolution calling for a declaration of war against Japan. Shortly afterwards the Germans and the Italians honored their Axis powers treaty with Japan by declaring war on the United States, and the nation was soon at war on two fronts.

All branches of the armed services used Texas facilities as major training bases. The Third Army, stationed from Florida to Arizona, headquartered in San Antonio. Later the Fourth Army also headquartered there as it prepared soldiers for service in Europe. Thirteen additional Army training bases operated elsewhere in Texas. The Army Air Corps trained at forty different bases in Texas, including Brooks Field, Kelley Field, Lackland Field, and Randolph Field, all in San Antonio, and naval air stations were also located in the state, especially in the vicinity of Corpus Christi and at Grand Prairie. Lubbock, Wichita Falls, San Angelo, San Marcos, and Midland had major facilities for flight training for pilots, navigators, and other crewmen in both fighter planes and bombers. In all some 200,000 aviators received their flight training at Texas bases, including 45,000 pilots in addition to navigators, bombardiers, and gunners. Approximately 1.25 million service personnel received their military training in the state.

Texans responded to the need for personnel to win the war. As usual a greater percentage of the military forces came from Texas than from any other state. Approximately 750,000 Texans, including 12,000 women, served in the Army, Navy, Marine Corps, Air Corps, or Coast Guard. Perhaps 8,000 Texas women volunteered for the Women's Army Corps (WACs), and more than 4,000 enlisted in the Women Accepted for Volunteer Emergency Services (WAVES), the auxiliary services of the Navy, or in women's units of the Marines and the Coast Guard. All of the women and a significant number of the men volunteered and the remainder were drafted. Unfortunately, Texans also had high casualty rates. Approximately 15,764 Texans died in combat or from wounds while serving in the Army and an additional 7,258 died while serving in the Navy, Marines, or Coast Guard. A much larger number

Corporal D.T. O'Connor stands at relaxed attention behind an airport beacon at Kelly Air Force Base in 1938. As flying became more of an everyday activity and less of a novelty, more instruments were required to run air fields safely and efficiently. Courtesy, San Antonio Light Collection, Institute of Texan Cultures

Texan United States Air Force
cadets lounge together for an in-
formal photo in 1942. Courtesy,
Alice E. Sackett

suffered non-fatal but often crippling wounds.

Thirty-six Texans received the Congressional Medal of Honor, and ten more earned the Navy's Medal of Honor. Audie Murphy of Farmersville became the most decorated American soldier and the most decorated soldier of any army in World War II. He tried to enlist several times before being accepted, because the induction officials judged his slight frame and immature appearance unsuitable for service. Once in action, however, he proved that he had unlimited courage. Murphy's autobiography, *To Hell and Back,* is an excellent account of his service to his state and country. He became a movie actor after the war, specializing in Western films, and, in 1971, at the age of forty-seven, he died in an airplane crash in Virginia while on a business trip. Murphy is buried in Arlington National Cemetery. The Navy's most decorated sailor, Samuel D. Dealey, of Dallas, was also a Texan. Dealey was killed in action. One outstanding hero of the attack on Pearl Harbor was Doris Miller, a black steward aboard one of the ships. Miller, although untrained, manned an anti-aircraft gun and downed one of the Japanese planes. For years his action went unrecognized largely because of his race.

Texans produced 135 general officers in the Army, including Dwight David Eisenhower, who was born in Denison, then moved with his family to Kansas at an early age. Twelve Texans achieved the rank of admiral in the Navy, including Chester Nimitz of Fredericksburg, the Pacific Fleet Commander. Colonel Oueta Culp Hobby, Governor William P. Hobby's second wife, headed the Women's Army Corps.

Most Texans joined units throughout the services and fought in every theater of the war, but some units were composed mainly of Texans. One such unit, the Thirty-Sixth Division that fought at Salerno, Italy, were the first American troops on the Continent, and remained together for 400 days of fighting across Italy, France, Austria, and Germany itself. The Lone Star flag of Texas accompanied Old Glory, and the Thirty-Sixth was often called the "Texas Army." The Ninetieth Division, the 130th Division, the First Cavalry Division, and the 112th Cavalry Division also had a large percentage of Texans.

At home the war put nearly every Texan to work who did not serve in the military. Shipyards along the coast, especially at Orange, Beaumont, Port Arthur, and Houston, and aircraft assembly plants at Fort Worth, Garland, and Grand Prairie, provided nearly instant jobs for people out of work only months before. Many worked in around-the-

Admiral Chester Nimitz of Fredericksburg was the Pacific Fleet Commander during World War II. Courtesy, Admiral Nimitz Museum

clock shifts, and some were women or other minorities who would not have been employed under even peacetime prosperity. Now, committed to victory, any Texan who could work could find it. But it was not without tension. Hurried marriages and long separations placed unbearable strain on relationships, and racial incidents flared in a number of places, especially in Beaumont where a major race riot occurred in 1943. Residents of smaller communities and farmers migrated to the cities to take defense jobs, while some were frozen in essential positions. Wages, prices, and rents were placed under a ceiling and local agencies and the national Office of Price Administration worked to enforce the controls.

Along with other Americans, Texans drew ration books at their post office and used the stamps in them to purchase gasoline, sugar, coffee, shoes, and other rationed items, and "red points," or small plastic tokens, to purchase meat. Cigarettes were almost self-rationing by their short supply since the tobacco industry sent most of its production to servicemen. Long lines outside a grocery store often indicated that the establishment had received its weekly allotment of Camels, Chesterfields, or Lucky Strikes.

Synthetic rubber plants opened in the petrochemical centers along the Gulf Coast as a solution to the loss of natural rubber supplies in the Far East. Munitions plants were established in many Texas cities. For example, IDECO in Beaumont built bomb casings and the Lone Star Armament Works near Texarkana assembled other war materiel. A steel mill opened in Daingerfield and a smelter produced tin at Texas City. The petroleum industry and the paper and pulp business went to maximum production for the war effort. School children purchased savings stamps, converted to Victory Bonds when sufficiently accumulated, and workers bought bonds through payroll deductions to help finance the war and make an investment for the future. This also helped curb inflation and the black market because it took ready cash out of the hands of workers who were earning higher wages than they could have imagined only a few years before. Women used a dye substance to paint their legs, hoping that when dry it would resemble the stockings they could no longer purchase because silk was used to make parachutes. Texas children played "soldier" in emulation of the real-life activities of absent relatives.

Women and children were a major part of the war effort. Women worked in defense plants and learned to be welders and electricians and still kept their homes. Children collected "tin foil"

from cigarette packages, scrap paper, and metal for reuse. Vacant lots and backyards blossomed with "victory gardens," and many homes displayed little flags in their windows with stars in them to represent family members in the service. A black border around the flag meant that the soldier or sailor would not come home, and a black-bordered telegram from the military became a dreaded communication.

The flood of people into the cities sometimes did not produce a harmonious mixture. Country folk of all races congregated in the larger towns. Blacks from the country, Cajun French from nearby Louisiana, and Mexicans in South Texas all entered new relationships. Some benefited from opportunities now opened to them.

Coke Stevenson served as governor throughout the war years and his popularity increased. W. Lee O'Daniel won reelection to the Senate despite strong candidacies by the "Gold Dust Twins," O'Daniel's name for former governors Dan Moody and James Allred. A group called the Texas Regulars strongly opposed a fourth term for Franklin Roosevelt in 1944, but a majority of Texans helped him win the unprecedented victory. The Regulars later became the core of a conservative Democratic movement that ultimately prevailed in the state and led it into the win column for Republican candidates Eisenhower, Nixon, and Reagan in future elections.

Depression and war dramatically and permanently changed the Texas scene in many ways. By 1950 the state's population reached 7,711,194 and

Facing page, bottom: *Japanese Texans take a break for a friendly chat outside their San Benito house in 1936. Courtesy, George R. Kitamura*

Left: *An unknown guard patrols forbidding barbed wire surrounding a Japanese Internment Camp outside Chrystal City in the 1940s. Courtesy, Mona Baskin*

Above: *Life continued in the internment camps during World War II. Here, elementary school graduates line up for a class picture in Chrystal City in 1945. Courtesy, R.C. Tate*

Facing page, top: *The Chrystal City Japanese Internment Camp high school graduates sit solemnly for their class picture in 1945. Courtesy R.C. Tate*

Facing page, bottom: *The staff of the Chrystal City Japanese Internment Camp pose for this photo in the 1940s. Courtesy, Margaret N. Williams*

Above: *Texan war hero Audie Murphy receives a medal for courage in battle from French General Charles De Gaulle. Courtesy, United States Department of the Army*

Facing page: *Audie Murphy from Farmersville was the most decorated United States soldier in the second world war. Courtesy, United States Department of the Army*

Texas became the fifth largest in population among the forty-eight states. This represented a dramatic increase from 3,048,710 in 1900. The growth trend progressed steadily at approximately 20 percent per decade, but there were fluctuations. For example, while both whites and blacks increased, whites did so at a rate higher than blacks and much more so than other non-whites such as Chinese, Japanese, and Indians. Blacks also remained more rural before the war, although they moved in massive numbers to the cities and to Northern states during and after the end of the conflict.

The foreign-born population increased during the first half of the century. Mexicans dominated this group with approximately 70 percent, and Germans, Czechs, Anglos, Russians, Austrians, Poles, and a variety of other nationalities shared the remaining 30 percent. Many of the Mexicans who had migrated to Texas during the years of revolution at the turn of the century returned to Mexico during the Depression because they could not find work. The 1930 Census listed Mexicans as non-whites, indicating an increase in segregation and discrimination for them. Many returned during the war when employment again became possible. Prejudice against them continued, and as late as the 1950s many businesses in Texas had "Only Anglos Need Apply" signs over their employment windows.

Facing page: *Texas has attracted people from all countries. Here, George Petheriotes poses with his employees at his Elite Cafe in Houston. Courtesy, George Petheriotes Family*

Below: *Texas has always been a home to various religious groups. Here, a congregation poses in front of a Baptist church on a Sunday in 1943. Courtesy, Alex Bachman*

Texas became increasingly urbanized during the first half of the century. In 1900 83 percent of the population lived in rural areas, and the largest cities were San Antonio, Houston, Dallas, Galveston, Fort Worth, Austin, Waco, El Paso, Laredo, and Denison, respectively. By 1950 only 40 percent of the population remained in rural areas, and the largest cities were Houston, Dallas, San Antonio, Fort Worth, Austin, El Paso, Corpus Christi, Beaumont, Waco, and Amarillo.

The Texas industrial picture also changed dramatically during these years. Petroleum refining, lumber, and food processing were the principal businesses in 1930. Livestock processing increased as a result of the location of meat packing plants at Fort Worth by both Armour and Swift, only two of the nearly seventy plants operating in the state. Pecan shelling, cultivation and shipping of citrus and truck crops in the Rio Grande Valley, and the manufacturing of food products increased.

Right: *Retired Panhandle cowboys gathered for this reunion portrait after an Amarillo barbeque in 1945. Courtesy, Amarillo Chamber of Commerce*

Below: *Fort Worth remains well known for its stockyards. Cattle trade provided a basis for Fort Worth's early economy, and processing greatly increased after World War II. Courtesy, Texas Highway Department*

Facing page: *After the war, the cultivation and shipping of citrus crops increased greatly. Courtesy, Texas Highway Department*

The end of Prohibition brought back the brewing industry, especially in San Antonio (Pearl, Lone Star) and Galveston (Southern Select). New industries were born of the demands of war. In East Texas the production of pulp and paper products had a dramatic effect on the timber industry, especially when Time, Inc., became a major purchaser. The "Big Inch" pipeline constructed during the war was only one of many that carried Texas-produced natural gas to Northern homes and factories. Heavy industry continued to grow as such firms as IDECO in Beaumont converted from making bomb casings to building oil drilling derricks, and the Le Tourneau Company in Longview became a major producer of earth-moving equipment. The aircraft industry suffered a great deal at the end of the war, dropping from 80,000 to 5,000 employees, and the shipbuilding industry on the coast suffered a similar decline. But many of these workers found employment in the expanding petrochemical industry to produce nylon, orlon, dacron, tetraethyl, and such plastics as styrene and polyethylene. By 1950 the Texas coastal industry produced 80 percent of the nation's petro-chemical products. Other Texans worked in plants that produced aluminum, antimony, tin, and steel.

World War II brought real prosperity to Texas. The New Deal had helped Texans endure the worst economic depression in history, but the war gave them jobs and a renewed sense of achievement. It also made Texas into a major industrial state, changed living patterns and lifestyles, and made the state a major force in the postwar world. As vast as the changes seemed to Texans at the time, the technological changes that awaited them made earlier achievements seem as small as the earth must appear from the moon. And when the first Americans traveled to the moon they began their journey in Texas.

Facing page: *There may have been a Depression, but at Pearl Brewery, work went on as usual in 1933. After the war the brewing industry returned in full force to Texas. Courtesy, San Antonio* Light *Collection, Institute of Texan Cultures*

Below: *Although shipbuilding suffered a decline with the end of World War II, today the Houston shipyards present a picture of bustling commercial activity. Courtesy, Texas Highway Department*

MAKING *THE ALAMO* WITH JOHN WAYNE

John Wayne personified the Western movie hero for most Americans. His career began in the 1920s in silent films, but his first major movie, *The Big Trail,* made in 1930, was a Western. It was not a commercial success, so for most of the 1930s he became a stock player in the "B" Westerns that were often shot in as few as four days. Wayne's big break came in 1938 when John Ford cast him as the Ringo Kid in the classic *Stagecoach.* From then until his death in 1979 Wayne was a top box-office draw. His films were admittedly predictable: Wayne played Wayne, a hero who exemplified traditional American values.

The screen persona and the real John Wayne were not very different. Wayne loved America and especially the American West. He believed in patriotism, in courage, and in the American way. Many of his films, even if mostly made in Utah's Monument Valley, were set in Texas. He loved the story of Texas, especially the saga of the Alamo. To him the staunch defense of the small isolated fortress against a multitude of Mexican soldiers captured the spirit that had made America great. He also admired the Mexican soldiers who, although led by a tyrant, also exhibited courage in fighting for what they believed was right.

The story of the Alamo provides plenty of action for a Western movie. And Wayne felt that this story had to be told, his way, on film. It had been filmed before as early as 1914 by D.W. Griffith, a pioneer of the film industry. Several others had treated the subject one way or another, usually as part of a larger story. Wayne wanted to tell it his way because he thought all Americans needed to learn that "freedom isn't free." To attract an audience, he knew it would have to be an epic film.

Late in the 1930s Wayne began to work on the project. He asked Herbert Yates, executive at Republic Studios, where most of his "B" Westerns were filmed, for support. Yates led him to believe that support would be forthcoming, but it never was. Wayne did not give up hope. After forming his own production company, Batjac, he continued the dream. In 1953 he traveled to Peru to scout locations because making the film would be cheaper there, but again there was no studio support. Even his friend Howard Hughes, with whom he made *Jet Pilot* and *The Conqueror,* failed to provide the necessary funds. Finally Warner Brothers offered to put six million dollars into the project, but Wayne would have to come up with the rest of the money. Some funds were obtained from Texas investors who wanted to see the Alamo story on film, especially if it was made by Wayne. He had not originally intended to act in the film, preferring instead to direct it, but some of the necessary funds could only be obtained if he starred in the movie. Finally, when everything Wayne could beg or borrow was invested in the film, the wheels began to turn.

Wayne determined to make the movie as close to the actual site as possible. His old friend James Edward Grant researched the Texas archives and wrote the screenplay. Meanwhile, an art director supervised the construction of a set on the ranch of Happy Shahan near Bracketville. The set was a complete town—including a church and cantina—to represent San Antonio and the Alamo.

Producer-Director Wayne cast himself in the role of David Crockett, the Tennessee frontiersman-congressman who came to Texas just in time to die in the Alamo. He cast Lawrence Harvey as Colonel William B. Travis, the garrison's commander, Richard Widmark as Jim Bowie, the knife-fighting leader of the volunteers, and Richard Boone as General Sam Houston. His son Patrick Wayne played Jim Bonham, and his four-year-old daughter, Aissa, played Captain Almaron Dickenson's child, Angelina.

Frank Leyva recruited an army of 4,000 extras to portray Santa Anna's troops. Frank Beetson designed twelve different uniforms for the makeshift army, and a retired Marine Corps sergeant trained and drilled the extras to charge with real bayonets. Fifty gunsmiths kept their rifles in firing order; it cost $1,500 in ammunition every time they fired a volley.

The size of the cast, crew, and livestock posed major logistical problems in feeding and housing. With a population of 1,858, Bracketville could be only so much help. Living quarters, complete with showers and air-conditioning, were provided near the set. Rolly Harper served 4,000 box lunches and 800 hot meals daily. Walk-in freezers were installed near huge mess tents to store frozen food. Cooks and waiters provided 4,000 steaks, 14,000 pounds of roast beef, 1,400 pounds of ham, and 4,800 pounds of sausage and bacon upon demand. Food costs for the eighty-one-day filming ran to more than $250,000.

The film cost nearly twelve million dollars, more than 40 percent over budget. Additional money had been raised from United Artists, but Wayne provided the bulk of the funds for the overruns by mortgaging his own investments. He claimed, "I'm not worried in the least bit. It's real American history, the kind of movie we need today more than ever. It'll make money for years to come." Although he was correct, he was forced to sell his interests and realized little of the multi-million-dollar profits that the film eventually earned.

Wayne was also cheated of much

John Wayne (center), playing the role of David Crockett, directs Richard Widmark as Jim Bowie (left) and Lawrence Harvey as William B. Travis (right) during the filming of The Alamo *in Bracketville. Courtesy, United Artists Corporation*

of the credit for making *The Alamo.* Some charged that "ghost" directors actually had made the film. It was released during the political battles of Richard Nixon and John F. Kennedy, and the critics seemed biased against the director for his well-known conservative views. *The Alamo* won eleven Oscar nominations, but did not win an award.

Hurt by the critical reaction, Wayne still did not regret making the film. Eventually his work was rewarded by the public. After an initial release that was less than spectacular, the people began to come to the theaters to see it and millions more worldwide saw *The Alamo* after it was released on television in 1971. It remains a classic film.

Right: *Movies about Texas or those filmed in Texas have always been popular. This 1926 photo shows actor "Buddy" Rogers posing by a plane he is to pilot during the filming of* Wings *at Camp Stanley.* Wings *was the first film to win an Academy Award. Courtesy, San Antonio* Light *Collection, Institute of Texan Cultures*

Left: *Actors Charles Farrell and Charles Emmett Mack pause beside a car during a 1926 visit to San Antonio to film* The Rough Riders. *Courtesy, San Antonio* Light *Collection, Institute of Texan Cultures*

Facing page: *As the Texas myth strengthened, movie makers were drawn to the state because of both its temperate climate and to create movies based on the myth. Here, Wallace Beery films a 1934 scene from* West Point of the Air *at Randolph Air Force Base. Courtesy, San Antonio* Light *Collection, Institute of Texan Cultures*

. . . . .

KMAC
KMAC

Facing page: *Will Rogers speaks to an admiring throng during a 1931 San Antonio visit. Courtesy, San Antonio* Light *Collection, Institute of Texan Cultures*

Above: *Texans have always loved movies. Al Deutsch focuses his movie camera in preparation for a shoot in 1928. Courtesy, San Antonio* Light *Collection, Institute of Texan Cultures*

Left: *Producer/director Cecil B. DeMille confers with co-workers in San Antonio in 1938. Courtesy, San Antonio* Light *Collection, Institute of Texan Cultures*

Above: *Randolph Scott takes a break during filming of* The Texans *at the La Mota Ranch in 1938. Early filmmakers were drawn to Texas partly because of the equable climate and partly because of the romantic myths surrounding the Lone Star State. Courtesy, Amanda Bell Newman and Virginia Bell Sturges*

Facing page, bottom left: *Actors break for dinner on the set of* The Texans. *Courtesy, Amanda Bell Newman and Virginia Bell Sturges*

Left: *A very young Robert Cummings poses for a publicity shot during the shooting of* The Texans. *Courtesy, Amanda Bell Newman and Virginia Bell Sturges*

Below: *Dr. R.A. Kennedy treats Joan Bennett after an accident on the set of* The Texans. *Courtesy, Amanda Bell Newman and Virginia Bell Sturges*

Right: *Mae West poses for a San Antonio photographer in one of her provocative slouches during a 1939 visit. Courtesy, San Antonio Light Collection, Institute of Texan Cultures*

Below: *Actress Mae West traveled with an entourage of trunks, crates, and her hat collection when she visited San Antonio in 1939. Courtesy, San Antonio Light Collection, Institute of Texan Cultures*

*Movie actors and producers
weren't the only ones to cause a
stir in Texas. Here, fan dancer
and striptease artist Sally Rand
decorates a San Antonio fire
engine during a 1935 visit.
Courtesy, San Antonio Light
Collection, Institute of Texan
Cultures*

XII
Toward a Modern State

For some Texans World War II ended on the beaches of Normandy or Iwo Jima, but most returned to their families following the surrender of the German and Japanese. Others left defense plants and shipyards because they were laid off or because they wanted to start new careers in other fields. Few returned to the farms and small towns. Instead they sought other employment while returning servicemen reclaimed old jobs in the larger towns. The appearance of Texas had changed forever. Once a rural state, Texas now employed most of its people in oil fields or refineries and related industries. The old Texas still remained at the crossroads, in the woods of East Texas, and in the open spaces of West Texas, but it faced changes and new relationships as Texans moved toward modern statehood in the environment of the postwar world long before its sesquicentennial year.

A 1967 view of the Texas capitol building, facing south on Congress Avenue in Austin, is a symbol of Texas' glorious past and promising future. Courtesy, Texas Highway Department

Things changed even more rapidly in the new environment than in the old. A world at war had fathered the nuclear age, jet propulsion, and a myriad of technological innovations that produced space exploration, computers, and a future shock for older Texans almost daily. New social arrangements, especially for blacks, Hispanics, and women of all races and groups also sprang from a war stimulus that then advanced from self-generated energy. The message of the World War I song, "How you gonna keep 'em down on the farm after they've seen Paris?" became even more meaningful following this second global conflict.

Change began even as the war continued. The news of the death of Franklin D. Roosevelt from a cerebral hemorrhage on April 12, 1945, numbed Texans as it did other Americans and citizens of the world. An age died with him. Hated by some but revered by many, a shocked nation mourned the passing of America's most significant President since the Civil War. The new President, Harry S Truman, a veteran of rough Missouri politics, the United States Senate, and briefly of the vice presidency, concluded the war with the assistance of Roosevelt men such as House Speaker Sam Rayburn. Rayburn served as Speaker longer than any other member of Congress, representing a rural district in Northeast Texas from 1913 until his death in 1961.

When Truman became President he knew nothing about the Manhattan Project; within months he had to make a decision that resulted in the atomic bombing of Hiroshima and Nagasaki, ending the war but leaving behind the now-familiar image of the mushroom cloud, a constant reminder for Texans as well as others of our common peril.

Little did it dampen euphoric victory celebrations, though. Returning Texas servicemen embraced their families and friends and attempted to resume their prewar occupations and relationships. Many did so successfully. Others took advantage of both national and state educational assistance programs and loans, and some were rehabilitated at veterans' medical facilities. Home folks proclaimed that it was good to have them home, to

be at peace with the world, and to look forward to renewing the Texas of old. It was not to be so. Too much had happened to the state and to its people during the experience of the war. Too soon the United States again went to war in Korea, and then Vietnam. The nation had become a superpower and could never again withdraw from the world stage. At home the issues of racism, poverty, drug addiction, environmental deterioration, and disillusionment would have to be faced. The contest for racial equality in the modern period began when a black mail carrier from Houston, Heman Sweatt, used the courts to gain admission to the law school at The University of Texas. Later decisions forced the integration of all public schools and facilities. Some resistance, including a renewal of the Ku Klux Klan, accompanied these changes. The modern era began as if the state could be restored to its former self. The governor's race in 1946 featured an old-fashioned Texas showdown between fourteen candidates for governor. The most controversial was Homer Price Rainey, a preacher and college professor who became president of The University of Texas then lost his job after a dispute with the board of regents. He sought election to the state's highest office as vindication.

The trouble began over the issue of hiring and firing of faculty and escalated into a dispute involving the administration of research funds and especially library holdings at the university. Finally the board fired Rainey in 1944 and made him an instant hero to defenders of academic freedom and freedom of conscience. He began a radio program that earned him further notice, and he entered the governor's race two years later. All of Rainey's opponents except Beauford Jester of Navarro County, a former regent of the university,

Three Texans, John Ulbig, Anthony Fenoglio, and Frank Ulbig, pose at an oil rig outside Montague in the late 1950s. For many Texans, oil is more than a money-maker—it symbolizes a way of life. Courtesy, Fill Fenoglio

In the twentieth century, Texans have figured prominently in national politics. Posing left to right with Harry Truman are three of the most influential: Lyndon B. Johnson, John Nance Garner, and Sam Rayburn. Courtesy, Sam Rayburn Library

attacked Rainey as a defender of immorality. One even read lurid passages from books reportedly from the university's library at "For Men Only" rallies. Of course Rainey responded, and by the end of the campaign he and his opponents had so smeared each other that Jester claimed that he was the only candidate who could assume office without "slime and filth" on his hands. Jester won the race and also reelection in 1948, but his second race was overshadowed by the election for senator between Lyndon B. Johnson and former governor Coke Stevenson.

Johnson had challenged W. Lee O'Daniel for the Senate in 1942 and lost by only 1,100 votes.

Johnson had counted on his association with Roosevelt to earn him votes. "He was just like a daddy to me," Johnson claimed, and it undoubtedly helped even though he failed to win. Johnson briefly served in the Navy during World War II but returned to Congress at Roosevelt's request. He entered the Senate race early in 1948. Stevenson thought his successful years as governor entitled him to the seat. O'Daniel first mounted a campaign for reelection, but soon dropped out in the face of two such powerful opponents.

The race between Johnson and Stevenson offered Texas voters a choice between the personifications of the old and new Texas. Stevenson's conservatism and his slow, deliberative nature contrasted sharply with Johnson's youth and vigor. Stevenson talked about his role in returning prosperity to Texas after the Depression, and Johnson promised a greater future. Stevenson toured the state in a Plymouth station wagon buying only five gallons of gasoline at a time so he could stop more often to remind voters that he had "made money" for them while governor. On the other hand, Johnson barnstormed in a heliocopter named the *Johnson City Windmill,* the first such use of this kind of aircraft. It enabled him to move to campaign appearances more easily and sometimes he would shout down at people without even stopping. The race appeared close on the eve of the election with perhaps an edge to Stevenson.

Johnson's greatest political asset was his wife, Claudia Taylor Johnson, better known as Lady Bird, who refused to give up. Lady Bird was from East Texas, and even when she became First Lady, 1963-1969, her speech betrayed her background. The night before the election she staged a telephone campaign, personally calling hundreds of voters. Many credit her efforts with Johnson's victory in the state's closest election ever. The first returns proved inconclusive, but the final unofficial count showed Stevenson a slight victor with 494,330 votes to Johnson's 493,968. When the official returns began to arrive in Austin during the next few days, however, Stevenson's lead disappeared and Johnson edged ahead with a total of

494,191 to 494,104 for Stevenson, a margin of only eighty-seven votes. In the official returns of one box in South Texas Johnson received a majority of 201 to 1, a reversal of the unofficial returns. Stevenson went to court to block Johnson from taking office before an investigation could verify the reversal, but Supreme Court Judge Hugo Black rejected his appeal, claiming that a party primary in a state election did not come within the court's jurisdiction. Johnson's election earned him the dubious moniker of "Landslide Lyndon." Six years later he became majority leader in the Senate, and with Speaker Sam Rayburn helped run the most powerful deliberative body in the world.

Harry Truman ran successfully against New Yorker Thomas E. Dewey for a term of his own in the Presidential race the same year that Johnson won his Senate seat. Truman's victory surprised nearly everyone, especially the conservative Democrats in Texas, soon to be led by Governor Allan Shivers.

Shivers assumed office following the death of Beauford Jester on July 11, 1949, from a heart attack while on a railroad train between Dallas and Austin. Shivers, who was born in Lufkin, raised in Woodville, and lived in Port Arthur before moving to Austin, completed Jester's term, then won election to three more two-year terms. His first legislative session proved harmonious, but thereafter his career was marked with controversy with the National Democratic leadership, especially with Harry S Truman and Governor Adlai Stevenson of Illinois, the Democratic Presidential candidate in 1952. In 1950 Ben Ramsay of San Augustine became lieutenant governor and he remained in that office throughout Shiver's tenure as governor. Many thought Ramsay wielded as much power as the governor through alliances with such leading senators as A.M. Aiken and Ottis Lock.

Shivers and Ramsay exemplified the conservative nature of state party leadership, which continued to rule Texas for three decades. They sharply contrasted with national leaders such as Truman and Stevenson, whom they considered too liberal and oriented to national rather than state's rights

Above: *Not all of the Texas Rangers' duties are exciting or dangerous. Here Rangers Purvis and Peoples run a check on cattle being driven into the state in 1949. Courtesy, Texas Department of Public Safety*

Facing page: *These Texas Ranger badges were used in 1962; owning one meant having a career that was often rough and sometimes dangerous. Courtesy, Texas Department of Public Safety*

positions. Shivers assumed leadership of the old Texas Regulars, now in opposition to Roosevelt's successor. Along with others in the nation they denounced scandals involving influence peddling in the Truman administration still filled with old New Dealers who to them typified dubious morality. They opposed Truman's attempt to integrate the military racially, knowing that integration would eventually move into the civilian sector. They also disapproved of Truman's opposition to Senator Joseph McCarthy of Wisconsin who accused the Department of State and other agencies of having Communist employees. But what they disliked most about Truman was his refusal to agree that Texas and other states with offshore oil

development should retain tax revenues from such sources.

The tidelands issue had been raised in the 1930s when Secretary of the Interior Harold L. Ickes asserted that the federal government should control mineral exploration and production along the nation's shores. There was not much drilling activity at that time, when a policy could have been established with the least amount of resistance. Roosevelt's administration failed to do so, however, and then the war intervened in such domestic matters. In 1947 the Supreme Court ruled in a California case that the offshore jurisdiction belonged to the national government rather than to the states. Thus the only hope for Texas to re-port revenue from drilling along its shores lay in electing a President and a Congress who would quit-claim the area to them. This became a major reason for Shivers to look with disfavor on Truman's choice of Adlai Stevenson to succeed him. Stevenson let it be known that he would not sign such legislation even if Congress passed it.

Shivers and the Texas conservative Democrats, even some who would later be involved in scandals themselves, then became extremely critical of what they perceived as low morals and alleged Communist infiltration among the Washington hierarchy. They denounced the "five percenters" who took rakeoffs in government contracting and accepted such well-publicized gifts as fur coats and deep freezers. Some Texans became disciples of McCarthy's "witch hunts" for Communists in government. The opportunistic and ruthless senator first claimed that there were hundreds of Communists working for the government, especially in the State Department. When pressed for proof he lowered the number but persisted in his claims until most of the nation, though still believing the possibility of truth in his accusations, lost confidence in his ability to prove it.

The Communism issue lingered in Texas for some years. Texas Congressman Martin Dies, Sr., of Lufkin, became McCarthy's equal in his quest to expose Communists in labor unions and especially in the entertainment industry. The heralded hearings of his House Un-American Activities Committee (HUAC) drew a great deal of press notice because of the names of movie actors, writers, directors, and technicians under investigation. Evidence that some of them had had Communist leanings during the 1930s surfaced, but almost anyone accused of Communist sympathy found themselves blacklisted by the conservative moguls of Hollywood who feared dropoffs in box office receipts and renewed government interference in their industry.

McCarthy, Dies, and others failed to prove a widespread Communist network in America, but they did alarm the nation to the possibility of one. And every time a witness before either of their committees claimed Fifth Amendment rights against self-incrimination, most Texans and other Americans assumed their guilt.

In Texas the legislature determined to make at least some of the state's residents take a stand. They required all state employees and even students in public colleges to sign a loyalty oath to the United States and a disclaimer that they were not or had ever been a member of an un-American organization. State employees had to sign such oaths monthly to receive their paychecks until the mid-1960s.

Such issues were paramount in Governor Shivers' decision to support the Republican nominee in 1952. He and Attorney General Price Daniel of

Liberty prepared a case claiming that the California offshore oil ruling should not apply to Texas because, unlike California and the other states, it had once been an independent republic and by its treaty with the United States had retained rights to an offshore jurisdiction for a distance of three leagues, or 10.5 miles. Congress passed quit-claim legislation recognizing this position after the courts had rejected it, but Truman refused to sign the bill. So Shivers led the Texas delegation to the nominating convention in Chicago determined to nominate a conservative Democrat who would sign the legislation as well as reestablish a high-principled, anti-Communist administration in Washington. Liberal Texas Democrats led by Maury Maverick of San Antonio opposed Shivers and secured a pledge that the "Shivercrats" would support the Democratic nominee. However, when the convention nominated Adlai Stevenson, Shivers began to look elsewhere.

Ironically, Texas Republicans also sent a split delegation to their nominating convention in 1952. Some were pledged to "Mr. Republican," Senator Robert Taft of Ohio. Others favored Denison-born General Dwight D. Eisenhower. Eisenhower, considered the more liberal of the two, won the nomination. He also won the "Shivercrats," who bolted their party when Eisenhower agreed to sign the quit-claim if elected. In return for the support conservative Democrats gave Eisenhower, the Republicans did not run candidates for the top state offices or other positions where Democrats supported Eisenhower.

Shivers faced stiff competition from liberal Democrat Ralph Yarborough in his own party's primary, but he won anyway. Price Daniel, who had wanted to run for governor and who had expected that Shivers would not seek office again, gave up and announced for the Senate to replace the retiring Tom Connally. John Ben Sheppard then became the Democratic candidate for attorney general, and all three won election while Eisenhower carried Texas, the first time a Republican had done so since 1928 and only the second time this had occurred since Reconstruction. Eisenhower kept his word to the Texans. When Rayburn and Johnson pushed the quit-claim legislation through Congress, this time introduced by Senator Price Daniel, he signed it and made Texas unique in the control of its offshore oil exploitation, at least for a while.

Shivers won election again in 1954 with Yarborough once more his opponent. For the first time he was forced into a runoff, although he carried the race by 100,000 votes.

In state affairs the Jester-Shivers administrations achieved significant gains for Texans. The Fifty-First Legislature, the concluding legislature under Jester's leadership, passed the state's first billion-dollar budget, and they reorganized state government and public policy for decades. A state board for Texas State hospitals and schools for the mentally handicapped reorganized public health care. The board administered the work of regular hospital care, mental treatment, and assistance for the handicapped. The legislature required minimal science requirements for health practitioners and required the licensing of chiropractors. For the first time in decades the prison system came under review. An investigation found Texas prisons overcrowded and inadequate, and the legislature responded with funds to modernize prisons, and institute education programs and other contemporary concepts in penology.

Perhaps the legislature's most significant efforts came in the area of education, and this work was not completed until after Shivers became governor. It began with a study in 1947 that revealed a need to reorganize the educational system completely.

Representative Claude Gilmer and Senator A.M. Aiken responded with legislation establishing minimum foundational support for teachers' salaries. The Gilmer-Aiken Law required all districts to pay a minimum salary that was partially supported with state revenues, and districts were encouraged to supplement salaries as local resources permitted. The goal was to equalize and increase teachers' salaries statewide. The program also provided for increments based on merit in

teaching performance and additional training through a certification program that encouraged teachers to return to college for additional education themselves. The law created an elected state board of education with one member from each congressional district. The board appointed a commissioner who administered the Texas Education Agency, the state's bureaucracy for supervising public education.

In Shivers' second term the legislature had to find additional resources to fund expanding state activities. They levied additional taxes on natural gas and increased taxes on all other areas covered by the Omnibus Tax act of 1941 by 10 percent across the board. They also passed the first redistricting bill in three decades to give greater representation to urban areas.

During Shivers' final term the legislature again had to raise the tax on gasoline, which was dedicated to the highway fund, and they also increased the taxes on cigarettes and alcohol. A Commission on Higher Education was created to integrate the efforts of state universities and colleges, and they passed the first regulatory legislation for the insurance industry since the Robertson Insurance Law of 1907. As a result numerous insurance companies were forced out of business because they could not stand increased state supervision.

Texas insurance companies operated under laws that were adequate fifty years earlier prior to the state's rapid growth in population and wealth. The absence of adequate scrutiny and regulation, however, created an environment in which unscrupulous businessmen could prosper at the expense of Texas consumers. For example, as late as the 1950s an insurance company could be founded on as little as $25,000 capitalization with no limit to the amount of stock they could sell. Stock sales thus became the primary income for hundreds of shady companies instead of premium payments on policies. And if the company failed, those who had purchased insurance policies or investors who had bought watered stock lost their money. In 1950 Texas had more than 1,300 insurance companies and an additional 700 chartered elsewhere

HEMAN SWEATT

Not many Texans remember Heman Sweatt, but they should. He did not lead an army, hold a high political office, or make a major oil discovery, but he helped change the course of Texas and United States history as much as the better known Texans. Heman Sweatt sued The University of Texas Law School after it denied him admission because he was black. His case eventually set in motion a major effort throughout the nation to integrate public education from elementary to post graduate schools.

Most blacks who came to Texas during the nineteenth century came as slaves. After the Mexican government outlawed slavery they were brought to Texas as indentured servants but their status had not changed. Few slaves received an education, and those who did obtained it illegally.

In the aftermath of the American Civil War, Congress created the Freedmen's Bureau, the first welfare act in American history. It fed destitute former slaves (and hungry whites, in some cases), assisted them in labor contract negotiations, and established schools. After the Redeemers regained control of Texas, Jim Crow laws, economic discriminations, and segregation became pervasive. Legal separation of the races became a way of life. Local ordinances or state laws required blacks and whites to use separate facilities in common carriers and public places, especially schools. Most communities had two school systems, and most of their resources went to the white schools. Texas was not singular in this system. It was typical of all former slave states and also became a *de facto* circumstance in many areas that had never had slavery. Even the United States Supreme Court sanctioned segregation in the *Plessy v. Ferguson* and *Cummins v. Board of Education* cases, dealing with common carriers and schools respectively,

when it ruled separate-but-equal facilities as constitutional.

In Texas and elsewhere most blacks received substandard education. Often their school terms were not as long nor did their schools have as many grades. None had the opportunity to attend college in their state except at a few denominational schools or at Prairie View A&M, and even there they did not have access to as many programs or have equal facilities or instructors. Most importantly, graduates of these institutions could not interact and form friendships with the future business, professional, and political leaders of their communities and state.

The National Association for the Advancement of Colored People became the primary agency involved with trying to change this situation. They first challenged voting rights discrimination, citing the Fifteenth Amendment, some parts of the Fourteenth Amendment, and even congressional legislation passed during Reconstruction. Because of the NAACP's efforts, the Supreme Court ruled in *Smith v. Allwright* that the Democratic Party could no longer bar blacks from their party primary in Texas.

Turning next to public education, the NAACP searched a year for a qualified black with the courage to step forward and face the very real hazards that might result from an attempt to enroll in an all-white Texas university. They located Heman Marion Sweatt, a postal carrier in Houston, who sincerely wanted to become a lawyer but who had no chance of realizing his dream under the circumstances. Sweatt attempted to enroll in The University of Texas Law School, and, as anticipated, was denied admission.

The NAACP attorneys filed suit in the state court in Austin. Judge Roy Archer heard the case, Attorney General Price Daniel and his assis-

tants Jake Jacobson and Joe Greenhill represented the law school and the university, and Thurgood Marshall, James Nabrit, and W.J. Durham represented Sweatt. Before the trial began the state hastily established a separate law school in the basement of an office building near the capitol. The state hoped that it could apply the separate-but-equal doctrine to its case. The fact that the school had no students, faculty, or real facilities made it obviously far from equal to the prestigious University of Texas Law School. Nevertheless, the state's argument carried in state court, and while the NAACP appealed the case in federal court, the state also established an entire school for blacks in Houston, again hoping its argument would be accepted should blacks attempt to enter other schools.

Sweatt refused to enroll in either school. Marshall argued that the facilities were not equal and that any type of segregation was discriminatory, an argument that the Supreme Court eventually accepted and applied in the *Brown v. Board of Education of Topeka* case that led to the desegregation of most public schools in the nation. The Sweatt case was heard before the Supreme Court in April 1950. Marshall urged the justices to consider more than the physical properties of the law schools. He pointed out that the reputation of a school and the status of its alumni play an important part in the success of its graduates. On June 5, 1950, the Supreme Court ruled that the exclusion of Sweatt was discriminatory and that qualified blacks must be admitted to graduate and professional schools.

Sweatt enrolled in The University of Texas Law School, as did several other blacks, that fall. The decision led to other cases that eventually desegregated all of the Texas and national educational systems.

Heman Marion Sweatt registers for classes at The University of Texas in 1950 following four years of legal wrangling. When the United States Supreme Court decided in Sweatt's favor, UT admitted its first blacks— but only to selected graduate programs. Courtesy, Almetris Marsh Duren Collection, Barker Texas History Center

This nineteenth century specimen of elegant living may show its age in this 1969 photograph, but the building still stands as a testament to fine Texan workmanship. Courtesy, Institute of Texan Cultures

did business here. Too many were under-capitalized and oversold on stock, yet they were not in violation of state law.

The problem came to the legislature's attention when Lieutenant Governor Ben Ramsay pointed out the large number of such businesses that declared bankruptcy each year. The legislature responded with the passage of twenty-two laws regulating the insurance industry. One law created a Board of Insurance Commissoners to oversee companies doing business in Texas; another required a minimum of $250,000 in capitalization; another created a rating system for policies sold in Texas, and still another provided for state registration and regulation of insurance agents and investigated all insurance companies doing business in the state. The Board of Insurance Commissioners denied licenses to some companies and forced others to discontinue operations. Even with this supervision, however, some companies failed even after they had been investigated. The largest was U.S. Trust and Guaranty, a constituency of the I.C.T. Corporation, a holding company that controlled seventy-two insurance and finance companies. Its chief, Ben Jack Cage, had created a fortune by manipulating stocks in the absence of laws or practices strong enough to prevent it. When news of the company's problems leaked out, an investigation revealed that it held only one-fifth of needed reserves against claims but had been allowed to continue in business because of friendly legislators who had received payments from the company. The corporation came tumbling down and Ben Jack Cage fled to Brazil with the company's assets, leaving stockholders and policy owners with worthless paper. Further investigation revealed that Insurance Commissioner Garland Smith had received expensive gifts and vacation trips from the insurance industry. This disclosure forced the legislature to investigate all state officials who might have received such gifts, unearthing the major scandal of the decade.

In 1950 the legislature established a $100 million fund to purchase land for resale to veterans at modest interest rates. This was an effort on the part of the state to join in the spirit of the federal government's G.I. Bill of Rights. Under the terms of the Veterans Land Board legislation, a veteran could purchase land for 5 percent down and pay 3 percent interest for up to forty years. The fund was administered by Land Commissioner Bascom Giles, and Governor Allan Shivers and Attorney General John Ben Sheppard served as the other two commissioners. The program benefited thousands of veterans, but dishonest promoters found a way to profit from it also. Under the rules the veteran found his land and examined it personally. The state then sent an appraiser to establish the value of the land. Once this was done the state purchased the land and resold it to the veteran. Giles directed that all large tract purchases be handled by his office directly. Then he sent selected appraisers to establish inflated prices. Sometimes the promoters even made the down payment for the veterans, who then occupied the land in ignorance that the state, and they themselves, had paid too much for it or that the promoters and some state officials were getting rich on the scheme.

Dewitt County Attorney Wiley L. Cheatham began an investigation into the land fraud when it was called to his attention. He involved the Department of Public Safety and Attorney General Sheppard, who cooperated with the investigation. Giles' role in the scheme came to light following an inadvertent admission in an interview with the *Cuero Record* editor Kenneth Tower, who later won a Pulitzer Prize for his report on the scandal. Giles was convicted on ten counts of fraud and received concurrent six-year sentences in the state penitentiary. Congressman John V. Bell, a former state senator, was convicted of receiving illegal fees from Giles, and many real estate agents were ruined by the disclosure. Shivers and Sheppard, although not charged with any crime, suffered political embarrassment because they had not paid close enough attention to their duties as Land Board commissioners. It effectively ended the elected careers of both, although they remained active in state affairs.

Price Daniel had been waiting for a chance to become governor for years, and Shivers' decision not to seek reelection in 1956 brought him home from the Senate for the race. Others in the election included former governor and senator W. Lee O'Daniel, J. Evetts Haley, J.J. Holmes, Reuben Senterfitt, and Ralph Yarborough, by now a perennial candidate for the office and the only liberal in the race. O'Daniel withdrew before the first primary. Haley was the arch-conservative in the race. Known for his antipathy to anything liberal, particularly racial integration, he was at one end of the political spectrum, Yarborough at the other, and the remaining candidates, including Daniel, fell somewhere in between. Daniel won the primary, defeated Yarborough in the runoff when all the conservatives rallied to his side, and went on to defeat Republican William R. Bryant in the November election.

Daniel had risen to prominence as the attorney general who fought the tidelands cause, as the senator who helped win the issue, and for his early war on drugs while in the Senate. At his inauguration he revealed that he had taken an oath of public office eleven times as legislator, serviceman, speaker of the House of Representatives, attorney general, and senator. He won reelection in 1958 and 1960 but was defeated when seeking a fourth term in 1962.

Daniel appointed a conservative oilman and rancher from Dallas, William A. Blakely, as his senate replacement until a special election could be held. Blakely lost the special election to Ralph Yarborough, who had finally given up hope he would ever be elected governor. He completed Daniel's term and served two of his own before losing to Lloyd Bentsen. His liberal voice achieved much in the Congress, including the Cold War G.I. Bill, and the establishment of the Padre Island National Seashore and the Big Thicket Biological Preserve.

Big Thicket Biological Preserve is seen in this Michael D. Sullivan photograph. Courtesy, TexaStock

The Governor's Mansion near the capitol in Austin sits in regal majesty on a carefully tended lawn. Courtesy, Texas Highway Department

As governor Price Daniel discovered additional malfeasance from previous administrations. For example, an investigation into lobbying practices revealed that many state officials, including legislators, had received expensive gifts from lobbyists. Meals and free transportation provided by lobbyists had become a common practice. Perhaps the most interesting revelation concerned Representative James E. Cox and Dr. Howard Harmon, president of the Texas Naturopathic Physicians. Cox received $5,000 from Harmon to kill a bill to prevent the practice of naturopathic medicine in the state. Cox denied receiving the money until Harmon produced a tape of the meeting where the money was paid. Then he tried to claim that he was merely trying to trap Harmon, but few believed him.

In the 1958 race Daniel again faced O'Daniel, but more importantly a new factor emerged in the candidacy of Henry B. Gonzalez of San Antonio. For the first time in the state's history a strong Hispanic candidate for governor was in the race. Daniel won, but Gonzalez served in the United States House of Representatives. Thereafter Hispanics assumed a far more active role in state politics. Daniel also defeated Jack Cox in 1960 as well as Republican challenger William M. Steger in a year in which each candidate claimed he was more conservative than the other.

The 1960 race is among the most interesting in Texas history. Lyndon Johnson, having become majority leader in the Senate in 1954, decided to run for President. Johnson's Senate position also came up for reelection in 1960 and he hated to surrender it without assurances that he would win the Democratic nomination and the Presidency. He solved the dilemma by running for both offices simultaneously, a course made possible by legislation passed by the Texas Legislature especially for his benefit. Johnson's scheme proved fortunate because he did not secure the Democratic nomination at the party convention in Los Angeles. Instead that honor went to Senator John F. Kennedy of Massachusetts, who outlasted Minnesota Senator Hubert H. Humphrey and Johnson in the primaries where Johnson had posed as a Westerner instead of a Southerner because of the importance of civil rights in the campaign. Johnson tried to make a stand at the convention, but a strong movement to draft Adlai Stevenson for a third attempt at the Presidency alarmed the Kennedy forces even more. Actually, they had the convention sewn up tightly and Kennedy won on the first ballot. He startled the party the next day by offering the vice presidency to Johnson, who surprised the world by accepting. Advisors in both camps advised against the political marriage of the urban Easterner with the image of a liberal, and the (some thought) crude Texan believed to be conservative. Kennedy's brother Robert particularly

did not like Johnson, and in Texas Speaker Rayburn and Governor Daniel could not understand why Johnson would surrender the majority leadership for the less powerful vice presidency. And former Vice President John Nance Garner reportedly told him, "Lyndon, the vice presidency ain't worth a pitcher of warm spit." One reason Johnson accepted was that Lady Bird wanted him to do so.

Kennedy primarily wanted Johnson to gain support in the South and West, but he also judged him the best qualified among the available candidates to become President should some unforeseen event precipitate a mid-term succession. Johnson just wanted the higher office. His campaign slogan, "All the Way with LBJ" had come to mean the second place on the ticket with no one aware just how soon he would advance to the higher office.

Kennedy and Johnson defeated Republican candidates Richard Nixon and Henry Cabot Lodge in the November election, and Johnson also won reelection to the Senate, in that race opposing the Republican candidate, John G. Tower. Tower, a political science teacher at Midwestern University, was reelected to the office three times, providing the Republican Party an anchor and helping to develop Texas as a two-party state. Since Johnson could not serve in both offices, Daniel appointed William Blakely once more to serve until a special election could be held the following year. More than seventy candidates filed in the winner-take-all special election, and the conservatives of both parties rallied behind Tower, giving him the victory. Tower won reelection in 1966, 1972, and 1978 before deciding not to run in 1984. For years he remained the only Republican officeholder from Texas of any significance, and given the generally Democratic majority in Texas, ought to have been defeatable in each election. He survived mostly because conservative Democrats gave him their support and because he had the good fortune to run when Republicans did well in the state with Presidential and gubernatorial candidates. Most Democratic candidates who opposed him, such as

Attorney General Waggoner Carr, only promised to be as conservative as Tower was and could only ask Democrats to support them because they were Democrats. Tower campaigned hard, rose high in Republican councils at the national level, and survived.

Governor Daniel sought a fourth term in 1962, and it proved one election too many for the man who had served his state successfully in so many capacities. A number of candidates, including Johnson's protegé John Bowden Connally, right-wing former General William A. Walker, East Texan Marshall Formby, and former Attorney General Will Wilson entered the Democratic primary also. Connally had recently resigned as secretary of the Navy to make the race. From Floresville, after graduating from The University of Texas, he had become a successful lawyer in Austin. Connally won the Democratic nomination and defeated Jack Cox in the November election. Cox, a former Democrat, began a trend later followed by Connally himself when he switched parties to run in the Presidential election of 1980.

Connally served three two-year terms as governor and modern conservatives of both parties frequently call him the best governor in their memory. Broad action by the legislature resulted from Connally's leadership. For example, he increased the sales tax to provide additional revenues for the state. The regressive tax had won acceptance by the legislature while Daniel was governor. It began as a 2 percent tax on most sales with exclusions for food and medicine, and Daniel allowed it to become law without his signature, apparently not wanting to be actively associated with the tax that had been advocated first by Miriam Ferguson and later by W. Lee O'Daniel. Connally increased the tax to 4 percent and local government received the option of adding an additional one percent. The revenue from the tax provided the state and cities with additional revenue, needed in Texas because the state is prohibited by its constitution from engaging in deficit spending. But liberals still disliked it because it was not based on ability to pay, which was precisely why

John B. Connally served three terms as governor of Texas between 1962 and 1968. Courtesy, Institute of Texan Cultures

conservatives favored it. They claimed it was fair because it would be paid only when purchases were made.

President Kennedy, whose administration was criticized both by conservatives and liberals on various issues, owed much of his effectiveness to two Texans; Lyndon Johnson in the Senate and as a foreign representative, and Speaker Sam Rayburn in the House.

In November of 1963 Kennedy began to prepare for the 1964 race. He was persuaded to make a trip to Texas to help heal a breach between conservatives and liberals in the party, personified by the difference between Johnson and Connally and Senator Ralph Yarborough. Appearances in San Antonio, Houston, and Fort Worth went smoothly with both Johnson and Yarborough present, although they never rode together at parades. The President spent the night of November 21 in Fort Worth, where the next morning he bantered with reporters outside his hotel about his having to wait for Mrs. Kennedy to get ready for the trip to Dallas, where he would address a gathering at the World Trade Mart. He assured them however, that the wait for her was worth it.

Just past noon Kennedy and his entourage paraded down Elm Street, then headed for the interchange near the Texas School Book Depository Building to take the Stemmons Freeway to the Trade Mart. Kennedy, Connally, their wives, and the ever-present Secret Service rode in an open car. Just past the Depository, gunfire erupted. Many had feared some kind of incident might develop in Dallas. Only a short time before United Nations Ambassador Adlai Stevenson had been struck with a sign by a well-dressed conservative protester, on another occasion both the Vice Pres-

ident and Lady Bird Johnson had been spat upon in the city. That very day anti-Kennedy ads appeared in the Dallas press.

A bullet struck Kennedy in the head, throwing his body into his wife's lap. Governor Connally also suffered a wound in the chest—according to the Warren Commission, from the same bullet that had first struck Kennedy. The President's car sped to Parkland Hospital where he was pronounced dead following unsuccessful attempts to sustain his life. Doctors later said they believed he had been brain-dead from the moment the bullet passed through his head. The assassin, Lee Harvey Oswald, fled the building to the Texas Theatre, where he killed a pursuing Dallas police officer, J.D. Tippitt. Two days later Oswald was killed by nightclub owner Jack Ruby while the nation watched on television. The Dallas Police were attempting to transfer Oswald to a more secure place when Ruby walked out of a crowd in the garage of the police station and shot him. There have been conspiracy theories aplenty since November 22, 1963, speculating on what the "whole story" of the assassination, Oswald's murder, and the ensuing investigation might be. But for most Americans, the most important thing was to see that government continued to function in an orderly manner.

Within hours Johnson was taken to Air Force One at the Dallas airport where he took the oath of office, administered by Judge Sarah Hughes, before departing for Washington with Kennedy's body aboard. The nightmare continued throughout the week. Kennedy's memorial service in the Capitol, his funeral, and results of investigations into the backgrounds of Oswald and Ruby flooded both electronic and print news media. The nation blamed Texas, and Dallas especially, for being the site of the murder. Eventually, of course, reason returned and most came to realize that the assassination could have happened anywhere. But for years Dallas was known as much for being the site where Kennedy was slain as for anything else.

President Johnson quickly secured Kennedy's domestic program from the Congress both by his

skill in dealing with that body and by invoking the dead President's memory. In the 1964 Presidential race Johnson soundly defeated the father of the modern conservative movement, Senator Barry Goldwater. Johnson received the largest percentage of votes cast in such a race in the nation's history, and "Landslide Lyndon" took on a new meaning.

In his own term Johnson declared war on poverty. In his address to Congress asking for sweeping programs to combat poverty, he remembered the poor Mexican children in Cotulla, where he had taught school after graduating from Southwest State Teachers College in San Marcos. He told congressmen that he had promised himself that if he ever had the chance to help those children he would do so. "Well," he said, "I have that chance now, *and I mean to take it.*" His program included a volunteer force similar to Kennedy's Peace Corps to work with domestic poverty, known as VISTA, a Job Corps to train youth, and a myriad of assistance and entitlement programs. There is little doubt that Johnson had the best intentions, or that his program was enormously expensive. While in place it employed, fed, or trained many of the nation's impoverished people.

The war on poverty faced opposition from the first, but Johnson's escalation of the United States' military role in Vietnam from 1963 to 1969 produced even greater opposition. In 1968 he bowed to their negative verdict following his loss in the New Hampshire primary and withdrew from the Presidential race in favor of Vice President Hubert H. Humphrey. Humphrey lost to Richard M. Nixon in the November election, although he carried Texas. Johnson returned to Texas and supervised the building of the LBJ Library on the campus of The University of Texas at Austin.

Governor Connally's program produced major changes in the state. Under his leadership the legislature created a Coordinating Board to manage the state's colleges and universities. Other agencies had oversight responsibility for welfare programs and other matters. Following the Supreme

Court's ruling that the poll tax was unconstitutional, Connally's administration devised a new method of voter registration. Generally he provided Texas with a businessman's administration, although, reflecting the changing times, more blacks were appointed to state positions than at any time since Reconstruction.

Lieutenant Governor Preston Smith, a movie exhibitor from Lubbock, waited patiently for Connally to decide to stop being governor. Despite his colorless personality and discomfort with public address, Smith courted voters with mailouts and other impersonalized techniques that easily won him the governor's office in 1968. A youthful Ben Barnes became lieutenant governor, and with Gus Mutscher as speaker, the three principal state leaders continued a business-oriented administration. Many predicted that Barnes would be the next governor. Under Smith's leadership the legislature created new medical schools, including one in Smith's home town, reduced the voting age to eighteen, and increased state assistance for vocational training. He reflected his West Texas background by working for additional water supplies for Texas, especially for his home region. Smith won reelection in 1970, defeating Republican Paul Eggers. The latter's strong showing began a trend that resulted in victory for the Republican Party only eight years later. The 1970 race witnessed the defeat of Senator Ralph Yarborough by Lloyd Bentsen, a Houston business executive. The strong showing of Eggers and the victory of Bentsen signaled a change in Texas politics.

Smith, Barnes, and Mutscher began new terms in 1971 expecting a continuation of a peaceful administration, but they were not to have it. Federal agents of the Securities and Exchange Commission accused them of participating in a scheme to

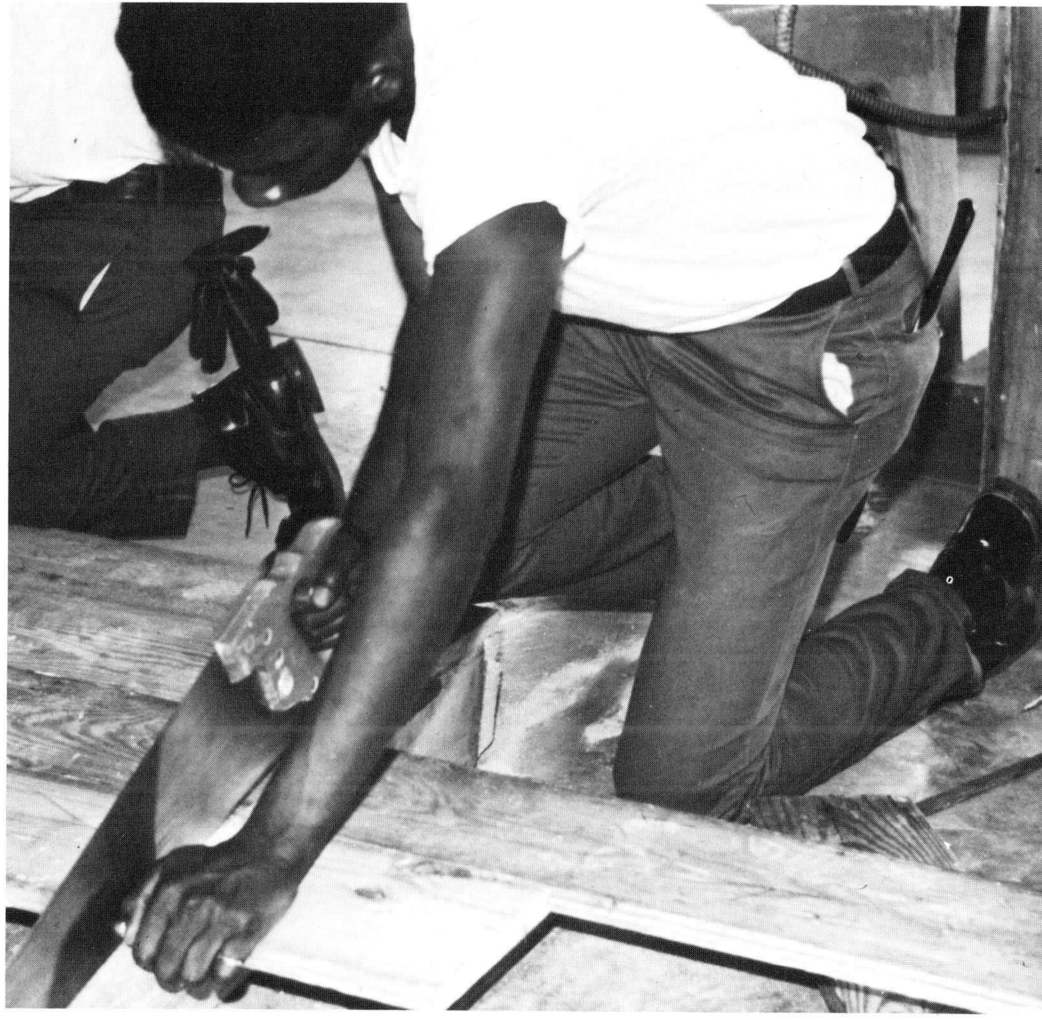

LBJ's legislative agenda included the War on Poverty, which expanded educational and job training opportunities for disadvantaged youth. Through the Job Corps program, young Texans learned trade skills, such as carpentry, at Camp Gary in Hays County in 1970. Courtesy, Institute of Texan Cultures

LYNDON BAINES JOHNSON

Lyndon Baines Johnson was born near Stonewall, Texas, on August 27, 1908. On November 22, 1963, he became the thirty-sixth President of the United States. November is not the usual time for inaugurating presidents; Johnson assumed office when President John F. Kennedy was killed by an assassin's bullet. As vice president it became Johnson's duty to assume the Presidency. In many ways he was the most experienced person who ever did.

Johnson attended school in Albert before graduating from Johnson City High School in 1924. He spent nearly a year working at various jobs in California before returning to Texas to enroll in Southwest Texas Teachers College. To support himself, he worked at the school as a janitor and later as a secretary in the president's office, and became active in campus politics. Before graduating in 1930 he interrupted his studies to teach at the Welhausen School for Mexican-Americans in Cotulla. After graduating he taught debate and public speaking at Sam Houston High School in Houston.

Johnson worked in Richard Mifflin Kleberg's campaign for a seat in Congress in 1931; following Kleberg's victory Johnson accompanied him to Washington to work as his legislative secretary. Johnson's first notice in Washington came in 1933 when he was elected speaker of the "Little Congress," an organization of congressional aides modeled after the House of Representatives. He enrolled in night school at Georgetown University in 1934 to study law, but returned to Texas in 1935 when he was named the state's National Youth Administration chief. His management of the NYA made it a model of efficiency that was envied by other states.

Following the death of Congressman James P. Buchanan, Johnson defeated eight opponents in an election on April 10, 1937, to fill his vacant post. In Congress Johnson supported President Franklin D. Roosevelt's program wholeheartedly, endearing himself to the chief executive. When Roosevelt visited Texas in 1937 Johnson was invited to ride on the President's train, and the two became good friends. Johnson liked to say afterwards, especially at election time, that "F.D.R. was just like a daddy to me."

In Congress Johnson demonstrated energy and gained power. He helped organize the Lower Colorado River Authority and helped Austin obtain a slum clearance project. In 1940 he was placed in charge of the Democratic Congressional Campaign Committee, giving him power over funds to help reelect Democratic congressmen. Then, when Senator Morris Sheppard died on April 9, 1941, Johnson ran in the special election to replace him. Governor W. Lee O'Daniel won the race by 1,311 votes.

When the Japanese attacked Pearl Harbor on December 7, 1941, Johnson became the first congressman to enlist in the armed services. He joined the Navy, and on June 9, 1942, received the Silver Star for gallantry in action in New Guinea. Soon afterwards Roosevelt ordered all members of Congress in the armed services back to Washington, and Johnson returned to his elected duties. He became chairman of a special investigating subcommittee of the Naval Affairs Committee. In 1943 Johnson and his wife, Claudia Taylor "Lady Bird" Johnson, bought Austin radio station KTBC; investments of this nature eventually made the Johnsons wealthy. Johnson also continued to be in favor with Roosevelt, and in 1945 was named a member of the House Committee on Post-War Military Policy.

In 1948 Johnson again ran for the Senate. He defeated former Governor Coke R. Stevenson by a margin of only eighty-seven votes, earning him the nickname "Landslide Lyndon." His hard work continued and in 1951, although only forty-three years old, he became majority whip in the Senate. In 1953 he became minority leader, the youngest senator ever named a floor leader, and became chairman of the Democratic Steering Committee and the Democratic Policy Committee. He remained totally loyal to his party, even when his state voted Republican in 1952, and refused to sign the "Southern Manifesto" denouncing the Supreme Court's famous *Brown* decision that ordered desegregation of public schools. He became Senate majority leader in 1955.

Johnson suffered a heart attack on July 2, 1955, but by the end of the year he was back in the Senate. In the 1956 Presidential race he was considered a possibility for his party's nomination. He supported John F. Kennedy for the vice presidential nomination that eventually went to Estes Kefauver. In 1960 Johnson and Kennedy were the final candidates at the Democratic convention in Los Angeles. When Kennedy won the nomination, he startled the party the next day by asking Johnson to accept the vice presidential nomination. Johnson startled everyone even more by accepting. Many could not imagine why he would relinquish his powerful position in the Senate for the privilege of presiding over it.

In 1961 Kennedy and Johnson were inaugurated, and until Kennedy's death Johnson strongly supported the measures of the New Frontier. Following the tragedy in Dallas he became President.

His first acts as President calmed the alarmed nation. Then, in the name of the slain president, he quickly obtained a tax cut, introduced civil rights legislation, and launched a whirlwind of his own.

Hardly any area of political life was left unchanged. His programs included the development of the Kennedy Cultural Center, the National Endowment for the Arts, the Voting Rights Act of 1964, a bill of rights for Indians, anti-age discrimination, the war on poverty, Medicare, food stamps, fair housing, the Department of Housing and Urban Development, aid for elementary education, aid to higher education, school breakfasts, student loans, flexible interest rates, truth-in-lending, aid to small businesses, the Inter-American Development Bank, the Chamizal Convention (which ended a long-standing border dispute with Mexico), food for peace, arms control agreements, protection against hazardous radiation, aircraft noise abatement, air pollution control, safety programs, truth-in-packaging, pesticide controls, wilderness areas, scenic rivers and trails, new national parks, recreation areas, national seashores, highway beautification, the transportation department, urban mass transit, library services, better training for nurses, public broadcasting, and a host of other programs.

These monumental achievements in domestic legislation comprise Johnson's legacy. But others remember his escalation of the war in Vietnam following the Bay of Tonkin incident and the resulting protests in our city streets. To encourage world peace, Johnson did not seek reelection in 1968 as a concession to the North Vietnamese so they would come to the bargaining table. Following his retirement he returned to the LBJ Ranch near Stonewall, where he died on January 22, 1973. He is buried in a grove of oak trees not far from the ranch house.

Lyndon B. Johnson posed here with his brother and sisters. Courtesy, LBJ National Historic Site

aid Houston banker Frank Sharp evade Federal Deposit Insurance Corporation regulations by passing laws favorable to banking interests. Known as the "Sharpstown scandal," it eventually discredited Smith and Barnes and Mutscher, and two aides were convicted and removed from office. Smith escaped prosecution because he had vetoed the laws Mutscher and others passed that Sharp favored, although many believed that all three officials had profited from stock information provided by Sharp.

Mutscher's downfall was also precipitated by the opposition of the "Dirty Thirty," a coalition of state representatives from every political persuasion who believed him guilty. Probably the most significant of this group was Francis "Sissy" Farenthold of Corpus Christi. She ran for governor in 1972 against Smith, Barnes, and South Texas rancher and banker Dolph Briscoe. The Sharpstown scandal neutralized Smith and Barnes, and Farenthold's liberalism gave the race to Briscoe, but signalled a growing participation in Texas politics by women. Notable was the election of Barbara Jordan, a black woman from Houston, to the Texas Senate and later to the United States House of Representatives, Kathy Whitmire as mayor of Houston, and Ann Richards as state treasurer, the only woman to hold a statewide office since Miriam Ferguson.

Briscoe served the last two-year gubernatorial

term. During his first administration the governor's tenure of office was expanded to four years, and Briscoe narrowly won election to the first such term in 1974 by defeating Houstonian Henry Grover, the Republican candidate who carried 49 percent of the vote in November. Briscoe's constant theme was to pledge "No New Taxes" regardless of the state's needs. Opponents charged that Briscoe was rarely in Austin, that under his administration higher education, highways, and other state functions suffered, and that he was the only man in Texas who made Smith seem warm and articulate.

In 1974 Speaker of the House Price Daniel, Jr., led the fight to revise the state's constitution, which had been in place since 1876. Texans generally agreed that revision was needed. But the legislature named itself as the constitutional convention instead of creating a new body of elected delegates for the purpose. This proved to be a mistake. The legislature-convention sat for five months and spent more than a million dollars on the revision effort, then refused to submit their work to the electorate. Their constitution was criticized for bias in matters such as protecting the Permanent University Fund for the exclusive use of The University of Texas and Texas A&M University, and the state's revered right-to-work law. To make matters worse, some sacred cows of others were ignored. As a result, even the parts of it submitted as eight constitutional amendments the following year went down in defeat.

In the mid-1970s the state and the nation reacted to Richard Nixon's downfall as a result of the Watergate scandal. Yet the march of the conservative Republicans to victory in Texas was not impeded by these events. Indeed, in 1978 Texans elected a former deputy secretary of defense under Nixon, William P. Clements of Dallas, as governor. Clements, the self-made millionaire president of SEDCO, an oil field equipment company, came from out of nowhere to defeat longtime Republican stalwart Ray Hutchison in the Republican primary and then surprised Democrat John Hill, who had taken the nomination

from Briscoe in the primary, in the November election. Clements spent more heavily than any previous candidate to earn name recognition and to preach that Texans were tired of liberalism in the state as well as at the national level. His election, as well as the victory of Ronald Reagan and George Bush, a transplanted New Englander who made a fortune in the oil business at Midland and Houston, in 1980 and 1984, carrying Texas both times, proved that Clements was correct.

Clements' abrasive nature, his plain-spoken and often harsh statements, and his tough stand on issues pleased many Texans who felt certain he would win a second term. He controlled a legislature mostly made up of conservative Democrats more effectively than any governor since Connally, who now announced that he would like henceforth to be known as a Republican also. Governor Clements provided Texans with a businessman's administration, jousted with Federal Judge William Wayne Justice over prison reform and schooling for alien children, and appointed mostly Republicans to state boards and commissions. His solution to Justice's order to deal with overcrowding in the state's prisons was to order tents for them. When some complained of discomfort, Clements responded that he had lived in a tent as a soldier and that they were good enough for convicts.

So many Texans seemed satisfied with Clements in 1982 that his reelection seemed inevitable. Attorney General Mark White, with whom Clements had frequently quarreled, Buddy Temple of Diboll, and Land Commissioner Bob Armstrong believed otherwise, and all three sought the Democratic nomination. White emerged the victor, then Temple and Armstrong joined forces behind him against Clements. Running with Ann Richards, Gary Moreau, and Jim Hightower—Democratic candidates for state treasurer, land commissioner, and agriculture commissioner—and Lieutenant Governor William P. Hobby, conservative, liberal and middle-of-the-road Democrats got together to reclaim the state's highest office for their party.

White assumed the governorship of a Texas which in 1983, was in the grips of a recession.

What used to be a painful and arduous task is made quick and (somewhat) easy with the help of this mechanical cotton picker. Courtesy, Anderson, Clayton and Company

Texas, along with the rest of the Sunbelt, was not, after all, recession-proof, as Clements had claimed. The state still had no comprehensive water plan, inadequate control of public utilities, and was troubled by inadequate educational and penal systems. A major fire in the senate wing of the capitol early in the legislative term got the new administration off to a rocky start.

White's team provided strong conservative leadership in the early years of the 1980s. Efforts were made to restore fiscal responsibility to the state. State Treasurer Richards saved millions of dollars by modernizing revenue collection and depositing practices, Moreau administered the state's land and increased revenues from them, and the irrepressible Hightower continued his populist ways. A special session of the legislature passed House

Left: *Cotton, long a staple product of East Texas, is still big business today. In this 1968 photo, cotton balls spill from a cotton gin. Courtesy, Anderson, Clayton and Company*

Below: *Cotton bales—a well-known "trademark" of the South—are prepared for shipping in this 1968 photo. Courtesy, Anderson, Clayton, and Company*

Facing page: *Greek dancers cultivate ethnic traditions in this Houston display. People from all over the world find their promised land in Texas. Courtesy,* Houston Post

Right: *Pieces of the world always find their way to Texas. Here, those pieces come in the guise of Japanese pastry at the Tokyo Restaurant in Houston in 1969. Courtesy,* Houston Chronicle

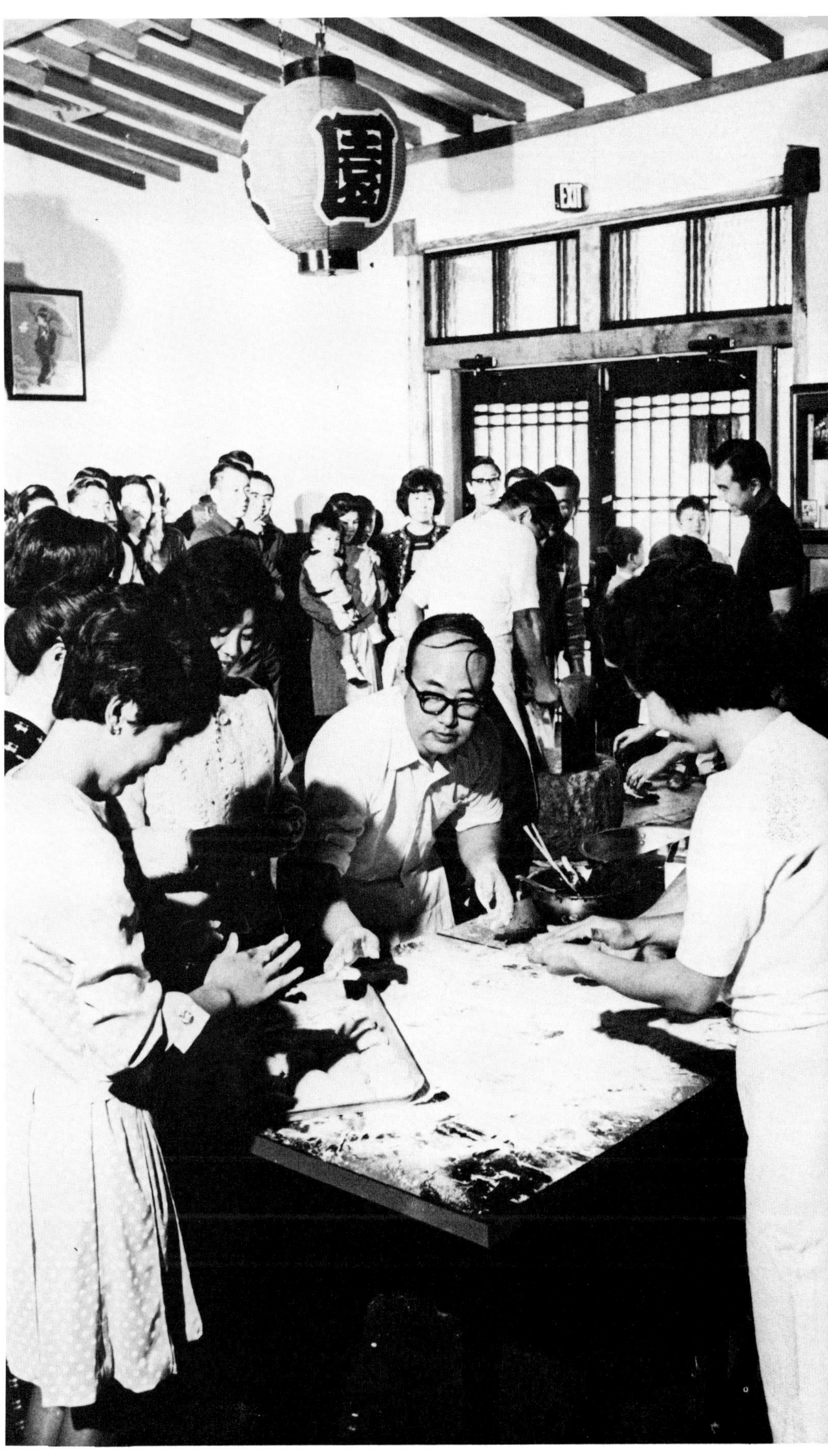

The 1974 Fourth of July celebration drew scores of Houstonians to Sam Houston Park. A statue of Houston stands dwarfed by the modern skyscrapers encircling the park. Courtesy, Texas Highway Department

TENNECO

Bill 72 in 1983 to reorganize the state's educational system after a blue-ribbon committee headed by H. Ross Perot, the state's richest man in the 1980s, with money earned in data processing, reported that it was among the worst in the nation. The legislature did away with the elected state board of education and substituted a fifteen-member appointed board. It increased pay for teachers, attempted to tighten requirements for teacher certification, and reduced the time students could be away from academic studies for extracurricular activities. The no-pass-no-play rule proved the most controversial item passed by the legislature in years, especially during the 1985 football season.

The results of their efforts will not be known for years, and the state has other problems. Violence continues to threaten the lives of penitentiary inmates, where more than 2,000 are stabbed or injured each year, public health—particularly for patients in state hospitals for the insane and the mentally retarded—is inadequate, and a loss of state revenue hampers the development of all state agencies, especially in higher education.

Texans have weathered tough times before. Fires, famines, invasions, and scandals are part of their heritage. But so is expansion, jobs, pride in the resources and achievements of their state and its citizens, and, above all, the grand myth of Texas itself.

Four hundred and fifty years ago a few thousand Indians hunted and harvested the forests, Savannahs, and uplands of Texas. On Census Day, April 1, 1980, 14,228,383 Texans represented scores of cultures, ethnic groups, religions, and races. Their number exceeded sixteen million by mid-decade. The 1980 figure exceeded the previous Census total by three million, an increase of 27 percent. The population density, 54.3 persons per square mile, was up from 24.9 persons fifty years before and from 6.1 persons a century ago.

Texas' growth was 11 percent greater than that of the nation as a whole, exceeded only by California. And its growth is nearly statewide with 210 of the 254 counties reporting increases, although the most significant growth occurred in Harris, Travis, Dallas, Bexar, and Tarrant counties. Harris county, which grew by 668,000 persons, accounted for 22 percent of the state's gain. The twenty-six urban areas contained 80 percent of all Texans in 1980, a figure that increased by 1985. Houston, Dallas, and San Antonio are among the nation's

Left: *San Antonio is one of the most beautiful of all United States cities. A unique feature is its fabulous river walk. Courtesy, Institute of Texan Cultures*

Facing page: *The San Elizario Presidio gleams white in a Texan winter sun. Courtesy, Institute of Texan Cultures*

ten largest cities, and although rural areas also reported increases, Texas is becoming more urbanized daily.

In frontier days males outnumbered females by great margins. Now there are approximately 250,000 fewer males than females in the state. And Texans are getting older. In 1900 the median age was 18.7 years; by 1980 it had jumped to 28.2 years, and the group of people sixty-five and older increased by 38 percent. Anglos comprised 66 percent of the population, followed by Hispanics at 21 percent and blacks at 12 percent. Other nonwhites comprised only one percent, but Texas ranked third in the nation in black population and second in Hispanic population.

Texas' growth in population was partially due to a favorable increase in birth-death ratio, but it was mostly due to a significant migration from frostbelt states where industrial complexes were disintegrating. Many came as individuals, but sometimes whole corporations, such as American Airlines, moved to the state. An abundance of labor, a favorable business climate underscored by a right-to-work law, and the availability of adequate if diminishing water sources, were major attractions for corporations in areas with few if any of these advantages to offer. The state's economy and identity in the twentieth century has been intertwined with the oil industry. More than 400,000 Texans work actively in the oil industry still, and most of the massive skyscrapers that seem to grow overnight in the major cities have some link to oil.

Left: *A 1974 view of the "Come and Take It" parade in Gonzales shows the pride citizens have for their Texas forefathers. Courtesy, Texas Highway Department*

Below: *Traditions and ethnic heritage survive and thrive in this 1970 Texas parade in Ennis. Although they come from many different cultures, Texans are Texans, first and foremost. Courtesy, Dallas Morning News*

Frontier days are remembered
in this 1971 parade in Ennis.
The Old West is still alive and
kicking throughout the state.
Courtesy, Ennis Chamber of
Commerce

Many Texans remain churchgoers. In 1980 nearly two million claimed to be Baptists, and with Roman Catholics, United Methodists, members of the Churches of Christ, Presbyterians, Episcopalians, Lutherans, and a host of other faiths, worshipped God in their own way. And Texas hosted the nation's leading atheist, Madilyn Murray O'Hair, a resident of Austin. The religious influence can be seen still in the absence of legalized gambling, restrictive liquor options, and blue laws that regulated the sale of forty-two classes of merchandise until September 1, 1985. Oddly, one could not buy a baby bottle on Sunday in Texas but a bottle of beer could be purchased.

Texas schools remain far below their potential, as was pointed out by the Perot Committee in 1984. Legislative efforts to upgrade them await judgment, and were instituted amid protests from school administrators and athletic coaches who found the value of their schools in the win-loss column. Perot pointed out that more than half of the state's school administrators were former coaches. As long as Texans remain content only to exceed the educational levels of Arkansas or Kentucky, states far behind the nation's third largest and richest state in resources, education cannot achieve its potential. Texas had more than 150 colleges and universities in 1980. Only The University of Texas at Austin and Texas A&M University, among state-supported institutions, and such private schools as Rice University, were among national leaders in higher education.

Today Texans are members of Rotary, Kiwanis, Lions, Optimists, Business and Professional Women, the Pilot Club, Masons, Knights of Columbus, the American Legion, and any other organization human beings can imagine. They like football from high school to the Dallas Cowboys and the Houston Oilers and Houston Gamblers, they are proud that the National Aeronautics and Space Administration, which helped develop the Mercury, Gemini, and Apollo programs, and still controls the space shuttle program, is located in their state and that the first word spoken on the moon was "Houston," they take pride in Neiman Marcus,

Texas Monthly, Gilley's, and anything else that smacks of their uniqueness. One of the best-selling bumper stickers in the state in recent years simply proclaims "NATIVE TEXAN," an attempt to embarrass those who are not. And a recent source of pride to most is the publication of James A. Michener's *Texas,* which sold out its first printing of 750,000 copies before it was officially released.

Texas: modern myths such as the successful play and movie based loosely on the closing of a bordello in La Grange, *The Best Little Whorehouse in Texas,* contrasts with the traditional myths of the Alamo, the Texas Rangers, cowboys, and oil gushers. J.R. Ewing may now be the best known "Texan" in a world that remembers the pioneer work of Stephen F. Austin and Sam Houston, if at all, in quieter ways. But J.R. is not the real Texas. It is still the land and the people who live upon it. People who shop in air-conditioned malls and drive air-conditioned cars, who like barbecues and church suppers and iced tea, who see their time as a stewardship of the land. They are aware of the people who lived on it before them and who will come after them. Some still pollute it, and some leave it, but it is always there, waiting. Regardless of what Texans do with their land, they can never completely change it. The land and what it has done to the lives of people who have invaded it and thought they owned it is the real Texas.

What is their future? Texans will continue the trend of urbanization and perhaps become more like other Americans because of the influence of the national electronic media. Eventually they will have to come to grips with their environment, especially in water resources, and learn new ways to finance public programs with the further depletion of their petroleum industry. Texans will have to learn to celebrate their diversity. Texas is not, as Governor Clements claimed, recession-proof, so more economic development is also needed. Hopefully these things can be achieved before the sun sets on the sunbelt, and that the Texas of the future will still retain the best parts of its past.

The sparkling beauty of Austin's Lake Travis provides this sailboat a dazzling scene as it heads for port. Photo by Bob Daemmrich, courtesy, TexaStock

Facing page: *The varied hats of Texas are placed within the environment of mythical Texas in this graphic by Austin artist Shannon Patterson.*

Left: *The date 1835 marks the cannon at the Gonzales Memorial for the terrible massacre that occurred there. Courtesy, Texas Highway Department*

Below: *This San Antonio sculpture immortalizes the heroes of the Alamo, who, rather than surrender to Mexican forces, died to protect their land. Courtesy, Texas Highway Department*

Left: *This portrait of Antonio López de Santa Anna depicts the aristocratic Mexican general as an accomplished equestrian. Courtesy, Barker Texas History Center*

Facing page: *This painting shows Sam Houston in his later years. Courtesy, Institute of Texan Cultures*

Below: *Titled* French Cooking, *this scene shows the ubiquitous, and in this case, unfortunate armadillo about to become supper for Texan troops during the 1836 Texas Revolution. Courtesy, Institute of Texan Cultures*

Left: *This color portrait shows James Bowie, who died at the Alamo for Texan liberation from Mexico. Courtesy, Institute of Texan Cultures*

Below: Dawn at the Alamo, *by H.A. McArdle, depicts the thirteenth day of siege at the Alamo by Santa Anna's army, March 6, 1836. Courtesy, State of Texas*

Above: *The Battle of San Jacinto was the decisive battle in Texas' fight for independence. It took H.A. McArdle more than forty years to research and paint this work, which now hangs in the state capitol in Austin, along with other historical paintings. Courtesy, State of Texas*

Left: *Titled* Samuel McCullough, Jr., Charging the Fort at Goliad, *this painting by Kermit Oliver depicts the 1835 Battle of Goliad. Courtesy, Texas Southern University Art Department*

Next page: *The Surrender of Santa Anna, by William H. Huddle, depicts the day after the Texas victory at the Battle of San Jacinto on April 26, 1836. A wounded General Sam Houston accepts the surrender of the Mexican general. Purchased by the State of Texas shortly after its completion in 1901, the painting now hangs in the capitol in Austin. Courtesy, State of Texas*

Left: *This modern-day cowboy shows off his calf-roping skills while trying to beat the clock. Rodeos are a popular crowd-pleaser in the state that is proud of its Old West traditions. Courtesy, Texas Highway Department*

Far Left: *These West Texas wranglers keep their herd of horses moving in this photograph by Skeeter Hagler, courtesy, TexaStock*

Left: *Although the cattle drive has seen many changes, beef cattle's importance to the state continues, and Texas remains the leader in the nation for producing prize-winning stock. Photo by Skeeter Hagler, courtesy, TexaStock*

Far left: *These ranch hands move longhorns to a fresher pasture. Cattle ranching remains a vital part of the economy and of the state's history and image. Photo by Mike Boroff, courtesy, TexaStock*

Above: *This dairy farm is located in Central Texas. Photo by Bob Daemmrich, courtesy, TexaStock*

Left: *Perfectly formed horns make "Texas Jack" one of the most prized Texas longhorn bulls. Photo by Mike Boroff, courtesy, TexaStock*

Facing page: *Spring in Texas means meadows carpeted in wildflowers. Photo by George O. Miller, courtesy, TexaStock*

Facing page: *Devil's Backbone is a favorite sight at Big Bend National Park, which covers 1,100 square miles along the Rio Grande. Photo by Bob Daemmrich, courtesy, TexaStock*

Left: *One characteristic of the arid regions of Big Bend National Park are the cacti that provide companionship to the desert wildflowers. Photo by Bob Daemmrich, courtesy, TexaStock*

Below: *Kayaking along the Colorado Canyon in Big Bend Texas is an exciting sport. Photo by Bob Daemmrich, courtesy, TexaStock*

Located in southeast Texas is Guadalupe Mountains National Park, with its featured landmark, El Capitan. Photo by George O. Miller, courtesy, TexaStock

*Smith Springs, located in Gua-
dalupe Mountains National
Park, displays the colors of fall.
Photo by George O. Miller,
courtesy, TexaStock*

Above: *Fishing is among the most popular pastimes along the Gulf Coast. This photo shows Port Aransas, near Corpus Christi. Photo by Ralph Barrera, courtesy, TexaStock*

Left: *Shrimp boats working off-shore provide a backdrop for this beautiful Galveston Island beach scene. Photo by George O. Miller, courtesy, TexaStock*

Facing page: *These folks are enjoying a day at Port Aransas gathering some of the beautiful shells that can be found with a little luck. Photo by Michael D. Sullivan, courtesy, TexaStock*

Facing page: *These Austinites enjoy frolicking in the water—a good way to beat the summer heat. Photo by Michael D. Sullivan, courtesy, TexaStock*

Above: *Texas is rich in opportunities for sportsmen and for those who just want to relax. These people are enjoying the colorful scenery surrounding Town Lake. Photo by Michael D. Sullivan, courtesy, TexaStock*

Left: *Lake Somerville is seemingly surrounded by bright yellow wildflowers in this George O. Miller photograph. Courtesy, TexaStock*

Facing page: *Lake Austin provides visitors with their choice of watersports. Photo by Ralph Barrera, courtesy, TexaStock*

Below: *A dark orange sky reflects on the quiet waters of Falcon Lake as these fishermen head out into the dawn. Photo by Michael D. Sullivan, courtesy, TexaStock*

A peaceful sunrise captures the capital city's skyline from the countryside. Photo by Ralph Barrera, courtesy, TexaStock

Above: *Loop 360 Bridge is shown here on a rare snowy day in Austin. Photo by Jay Godwin, courtesy, TexaStock*

Facing page: *The Tom Miller Dam divides Town Lake and Lake Austin on the Colorado River. Photo by Ralph Barrera, courtesy, TexaStock*

Left: *The Japanese Sunken Gardens serves as an exotic escape for tourists and residents of San Antonio. Photo by Michael D. Sullivan, courtesy, TexaStock*

Left: *El Paso gleams in the dusky shadows of surrounding mountains. Courtesy, Texas Highway Department*

Below: *These modern highways lead to Houston. Courtesy, Texas Highway Department*

San Antonio comes alive with lights once the sun goes down. Courtesy, Texas Highway Department

Right: *A line marker, carved in the shape of Texas, welcomes motorists on Interstate Highway 10 at the Louisiana-Texas border. Courtesy, Texas Highway Department*

Facing page: *This picture captures the vitality of the Texas crude oil industry. Texas continues to lead the nation, as it did from the turn of the century, in its production of petroleum. Photo by Michael D. Sullivan, courtesy, TexaStock*

Below: *Driving on Texas' Interstate Highway 10 can offer some very eerie and beautiful scenery. Photo by Kevin Vandivier, courtesy, TexaStock*

TEXAS

XIII

Partners in Progress

It was a seemingly limitless supply of cheap, arable land that brought the first settlers to Texas. And it was the vast agricultural bounty produced by that land that formed the basis for most of the early business development in the Lone Star State.

Almost invariably, the fastest-growing, most prosperous communities in early-day Texas were those built around the production of cotton in East Texas and cattle in West Texas. For many years after the sprawling territory became a state, these two products and the task of getting them to distant markets accounted for the bulk of Texas' commercial activity.

Not surprisingly, such gulf ports as Galveston and Houston and the river port of Jefferson grew into vital centers of commerce in the years immediately before and after the Civil War, largely because of their role as exporters

353

of Texas cotton and beef and importers of the manufactured goods needed by Texas farmers of that era.

But the arrival of the railroads in the 1870s marked the first major turning point in Texas' commercial development. As the rails stretched out through the forests and across the prairies, they bypassed some bustling towns and soon left them dozing in stagnant backwaters or dusty byways. But they also transformed many once-drowsy villages into booming cities in the pivotal forty-year period between 1870 and 1910.

During that time, for example, Dallas gained strategic importance as the junction of two major railroads and mushroomed from a hamlet of 3,000 into a city of 92,000. Meanwhile, its role as a port enhanced immeasurably by its rail connections, Houston grew from a population of 9,000 to nearly 80,000. Fort Worth exploded from a 500-person dot on the map into a city of 73,000, thanks to its role as a shipping and processing point for West Texas cattle, huge herds of which could now be moved by rail, instead of in slow, exhaustive cattle drives. And San Antonio, as a main gateway to Mexico and chief distribution center for South Texas, grew from 12,000 to 96,000.

Of even greater significance in the state's economic history, however, was the development of the Texas oil industry, born in 1901 when the fabulous Spindletop gusher blew in near Beaumont and set off the biggest oil boom the world had yet seen. A decade or more later, other major oil fields were discovered near Electra and Burkburnett in West Texas. But the most sensational discovery of all came in 1930, when the legendary "Dad" Joiner brought in the well that opened the gigantic East Texas Field and made Texas the undisputed center of the international petroleum industry.

In 1910, even with Texas cities growing at a phenomenal rate, more than three out of every four Texans still lived and worked in rural areas, deriving their livelihood either directly or indirectly from crops and livestock. But in the 1980s, more than 80 percent of all Texans reside in one

of the state's many urban areas and, more than any other single factor, this massive population shift can be attributed to the Texas oil industry. Oil has been the chief catalyst in making Houston the fourth-largest U.S. metropolis, and in creating such urban centers as Midland and Odessa—cities that did not even exist when the twentieth century began. And oil has also played a vital role in the emergence of Dallas as the nation's seventh-largest city and one of its principal financial centers.

But just as Texas began to move away from economic dependence on farming and ranching a century ago, today's Lone Star State is rapidly reaching out into new areas of business and industrial growth and into what may be termed a "post-petroleum" era of development.

Dallas/Fort Worth, for example, has established itself in the 1980s as one of the world's foremost centers for electronics, data processing, and other types of high-technology enterprises. Within the past few years the area has become widely known within the high-tech industry as "Silicon Prairie," and currently ranks as the third-largest concentration of technology-related business activity in the United States. To the south, Austin, formerly a small, quiet city revolving around the state capitol and the main campus of The University of Texas, has similarly evolved into a high-tech center and one of America's fastest-growing cities. Over the past fifteen years Austin's population has virtually doubled, to around 500,000. Even Houston, still known around the globe as "Oil City," has become headquarters for the U.S. space program and is diversifying its economic makeup to guard against the volatile "ups and downs" associated with oil.

Just as they did in its earliest settlement days, when the hardy pioneers of Stephen F. Austin's colony found their way to Texas and launched the "Americanization" of what was then Spanish territory, land and real estate continue to play an important part in the economic development of Texas. Although it is no longer free or cheap—and is in increasingly short supply in some of the state's hottest growth areas—land remains one of

Texas' chief resources, and its creative development continues to add significantly to the healthy state of the Texas economy. During the 1980s Texas cities have led the nation in every category of construction and real estate development, from office towers to apartments and condominiums.

Today Texas and Texans excel in countless areas. The state is still the world's largest producer of both cattle and cotton, but it also ranks among the top ten states in the production of no fewer than fourteen top agricultural commodities. While oil is still its best-known natural resource, and it remains the largest U.S. producer of oil and gas, Texas is also rich in many other types of minerals, including coal, limestone, sand and gravel, uranium, gypsum, and sulfur. Manufacturing is one of the fastest-growing areas of the Texas economy, with total manufacturing employment approaching 1.5 million. Texas ranks third nationally in banking and financial activity, and is becoming an increasingly major force in foreign trade, handling more cargo each year than any other state.

This economic diversity is one of Texas' basic strengths, but perhaps even more important to the state's continued economic well-being is the strong spirit of entrepreneurship that has always prevailed in Texas and remains as robust today as ever. Texas possesses a dynamic business climate, one unexcelled anywhere on earth and one that attracts business investment, business risk-takers, and aggressive, farsighted companies from around the globe.

There is still the feeling in Texas that the individual can go as far and grow as big as his or her own stamina and ability can justify. Even in the age of space exploration, instant communications, and high technology, Texans still adhere to a straightforward, uncomplicated style of doing business. Within this style and approach lies the appeal that draws tens of thousands of newcomers to Texas annually.

For 150 years business people in Texas have been pioneering, looking ahead, working hard, and striving for excellence. Today there is no indication that they plan to do less in the future. As long as this holds true, "business as usual" will continue to be business at its best all across Texas.

The organizations whose stories are detailed on the following pages have chosen to support this important literary and civic project. They illustrate the variety of ways in which individuals and their businesses have contributed to the state's growth and development. The civic involvement of Texas' businesses, institutions of learning, and local government, in cooperation with its citizens, has made the Lone Star State an excellent place to live and work.

EAST TEXAS HISTORICAL ASSOCIATION

Texas, as everyone knows, is a big state. To make geographic sense of their native land, Texans divide it into convenient chunks. They still cooperate on really important things such as electing governors, and they do have available excellent statewide historical agencies, but regional identity is important in many areas of Texas life. So it makes sense that there is a historical association or society in nearly every county and sizable city, and for most of the regions of the state.

A pioneer East Texas Historical Association debuted in 1929 but soon became a victim of the Great Depression. Then, in the early 1960s, four "godparents" got together to launch a new organization. President Ralph W. Steen of Stephen F. Austin State University, located in Nacogdoches, Texas; Dr. C.K. Chamberlain, chairman of the History Department at the university; and attorneys F.I. Tucker of Nacogdoches and F. Lee Lawrence of Tyler, Texas, invited interested lay and professional historians in East Texas to attend a meeting at the university on September 29, 1962. Steen pledged the support of the university, Chamberlain agreed to become editor of the organization's *Journal,* and Tucker and Lawrence provided the vision and energy to recruit members and launch the program of the association.

They agreed to hold an annual meeting in the fall in Nacogdoches and to meet elsewhere in East Texas in the spring. In the beginning these meetings consisted of sessions where lay and professional historians read papers on some aspect of East Texas history, a luncheon, and an afternoon field trip to a historical preservation project or historic site. In 1962 Lawrence became the association's first president.

It is impossible to overstate the value of the support of Dr. Steen. He provided more than encouragement and interest; he supplied working space and the tangible support of his own money. As long as he lived

Dr. C.K. Chamberlain, co-founder of the East Texas Historical Association, served as the first editor of its publication, the East Texas Historical Journal.

he remained the association's most significant benefactor and served as president and as a director until his death on January 30, 1980. In 1978 the board of directors established the Ralph W. Steen Service Award to honor him and others who followed his example.

The *East Texas Historical Journal,* which Dr. Chamberlain edited until his retirement, is the only magazine of its kind in the state. It features articles that deal with its namesake region and sometimes with other aspects of Texas history. It contains reviews of books on Texas and the South and a column of news and book notes. In 1975 the association established the C.K. Chamberlain Award for the best article to appear in each volume of the *Journal.* The current editor, Archie P. McDonald, succeeded Dr. Chamberlain in 1972.

The association also annually presents the Ottis Lock Endowment Awards for excellence in teaching in secondary schools, junior colleges, and four-year institutions; for the best book on East Texas; a scholar-

ship is provided for an East Texan to attend the college or university of his or her choice; and small research grants are awarded to encourage the study and publication of East Texas history. This award honors a distinguished East Texas business and civic leader, and was established through the efforts of former East Texas Historical Association president Bob

Dr. Ralph W. Steen, co-founder and past president of the East Texas Historical Association.

Bowman of Lufkin, Texas. The Lucille Terry Historical Preservation Award honors an individual or community for distinguished work in this field.

The East Texas Historical Association has approximately 500 members and is still growing. It continues to receive outstanding support from Stephen F. Austin State University and from its president, Dr. William R. Johnson. Its endowment, though small in comparison to statewide organizations, is also growing, and its program is constantly expanding. Much of this progress is due to the healthy blend of lay and professional historians who meet to discuss their favorite historical topics and to learn more about their region.

HARRIS COUNTY HERITAGE SOCIETY

When a Houston landmark home was threatened with destruction in 1954, a group of concerned citizens formed the Harris County Heritage Society in order to preserve it. From modest beginnings the society has grown to include a historic church and five historic house museums with a sixth in prospect. All are located in Sam Houston Park in downtown Houston.

Over 100,000 people annually visit the park, where 200 trained volunteers conduct regularly scheduled tours and interpret the meticulously restored and furnished buildings. An old-fashioned Fourth of July picnic and candlelight tours of the park at Christmastime are among the seasonal public attractions offered by the society to residents of Houston and the Gulf Coast area.

In 1972 the complex became Houston's first museum to be accredited by the American Society of Museums. Its educational function is not limited to tours of the historic structures. Several programs are directed specifically to public schoolchildren, who are allowed to see, touch, and hear the stories of objects connected with the early development of Hous-

The collections of the Harris County Heritage Society include artifacts, documents, and audiovisual materials. Included are nationally regarded collections of toys and fire equipment as well as important regional collections of costumes, photographs, decorative art, radio and television materials, and commercial and business artifacts.

ton or to experience the exciting re-enactment by trained volunteers of a dramatic event in Texas history.

Not content with these accomplishments, the society has been determined for more than ten years to widen its educational horizons by constructing a world-class museum, The Texas Museum of History and Technology. To that end, it has assembled a first-rate professional staff and has acquired significant collections of Texas documents, early Houston photographs, over 22,000 artifacts, manuscript and printed materials, and historic art.

The 200,000-square-foot museum building, to be located in the park, will utilize these and future collections as well as traveling exhibits from the Smithsonian Institution and other museums to interpret our colorful heritage. Scientific and technological history will be interwoven

with political and social history to provide a clear understanding of the past and its impact on the future.

When completed, the facility will be a mecca for students and an exciting learning experience for visitors of all ages. In cooperation with the Houston Independent School District, Rice University, and the University of Houston, the new museum may also serve as a model with national implications for the teaching of history through the use of sight, sound, and touch. No comparable educational institution exists in Texas today.

Dedicated to the proposition that only through knowledge and appreciation of the past can a people adequately direct their future, the Harris County Heritage Society's 3,000 members, volunteers, and professional staff confidently anticipate the challenge of building the finest museum of its kind in the South— Houston's Museum of Texas History.

In 1954 twelve Houstonians assembled to save the Kellum-Noble House from destruction and, in so doing, set in motion the many projects of the Harris County Heritage Society. Built in 1847, the Kellum-Noble House is distinguished as an example of domestic Deep South architecture, as the home of one of the first building contractors in Houston, as the location of one of the city's earliest schools, and as the center of the first public park in Houston.

AHLFINGER WATER COMPANY

Max Ahlfinger and Jack J. Ahlfinger, first and second generation.

In the late 1880s German immigrant Max Ahlfinger traveled the Dallas countryside in a mule-driven wagon, dispensing nickel-a-bucket artesian well water to parched city and farm families. A century later that water route has evolved into a family-owned business that has grown with Dallas' need for water in a variety of ways: from bottled water for drinking to the development of new processes to use water in high-tech industry.

One of only five Dallas businesses that were founded before 1900 and are still owned by the families of the original owners, the Ahlfinger Water Company today is primarily concerned with supplying water to high-tech firms and developing and installing ultra-modern filtration systems. The company sold its bottled water division to McKesson in 1983.

But the Ahlfinger Water Company—which is managed by brothers Jack D. and Rocky Ahlfinger (third generation)—still operates on the same principle Max and Jack J. Ahlfinger founded on their wagon water route: hard work. "Water, not blood, runs through our veins," says Rocky Ahlfinger. "We're proud of our history."

That history started with Max Ahlfinger, whose water was so popular that customers would leave empty buckets on their front porches for Ahlfinger to fill before sunrise. By 1908 Ahlfinger was able to purchase a larger wagon. By 1915 he traveled his route in a motor car. His water, however, was still the same mineral-stocked artesian well water; free of algae and bacteria, it was water that Ahlfinger proudly touted on the sides of his wagons and cars as "The Purest Water in the World." Jack J. Ahlfinger (the second generation) progressed at a moderate, steady rate until the hard drought of 1956. Water became an almost sacred commodity. Four or five other well water firms sprouted in Dallas to help bring water into the city. Bottled water became the rage, and Ahlfinger stocked some local 7-Eleven stores with as much as 100 bottles of water a day.

After the drought subsided, most of the upstart water firms folded. But not Ahlfinger. The company was ready with bottled water when another crisis occurred in 1957: the great flood. "After the flood, people bought bottled water not because they had to, but because they wanted to," recalls Jack D. Ahlfinger. "A niche for bottled water had been created."

The Ahlfinger Water Company was responsible for introducing some revolutionary items into the bottling business. In 1956 the firm introduced the first five-gallon throw-away bottle. Later, Ahlfinger introduced the first throw-away gallon bottle. Both of these developments were quickly adopted by other bottling firms. In 1955 Jack J. Ahlfinger and John B. Atwood developed the first hand pump for five-gallon bottles.

In the early 1960s the Ahlfinger Water Company began purifying and selling water for industries. A major area of the firm's present focus is in the purification of water for use in rinsing computer chips in the microcomputer industry.

The company no longer sells bottled water to individuals as Max and Jack J. Ahlfinger did, but is still concerned with bringing quality water to the Dallas area. Presently, Ahlfinger is developing water purification units that fit under the sink and will be capable of producing water comparable to bottled water from the city tap.

Although the Ahlfingers are setting standards in the water revolution of the 1980s, the company still runs on the standard set by Jack J. Ahlfinger in the late 1960s: bringing quality water and service to the community.

In the early 1800s Max Ahlfinger traveled the Dallas countryside, bringing quality artesian well water to parched city and farm families.

CORNY DOG COMPANY, INC.

Johnnie Ferrantello and his wife, Thelma, during the World War II era and before the founding of Corny Dog Company, Inc.

The birth of the Corny Dog Company was inspired by the love of a specialty food item: the corny dog.

In 1956 Dallas food entrepreneur Johnnie Ferrantello was talking to Neil Fletcher, whose batter-covered hot dog on a stick had become the rage of the Texas State Fair. Fletcher's business was booming, but he didn't have the time to reap the benefits of what he envisioned was a gigantic wholesale market for the taste treat he and his brother had invented.

"He told Johnnie that if somebody would put corny dogs on the wholesale market, they'd make a million dollars," remembers Ferrantello's widow, Thelma Ferrantello, now chairman of the board of the Corny Dog Company, Inc.

Johnnie Ferrantello purchased some of Neil Fletcher's cooking equipment and the rights to sell corny dogs everywhere except at the Texas State Fair. Ferrantello, who was also in the soft drink, pecan-shelling, and pizza business at the time, then used one of his other business ventures to revolutionize corny dog production. He tailored the machinery used for dressing

chickens at his brother's poultry plant to mass-produce corny dogs. Using a system of conveyor belts that passed through hot grease, two corny dogs could be dipped at one time.

In 1962 the Corny Dog Company's product—called Woody's Corny Dogs—became the first such product on the wholesale market. Outside of Texas, however, the general public was still unaware of this new taste treat. Today corny dogs are sold throughout the United States. But the Corny Dog Company, which produces 150,000 corny dogs a day at its Harrison Street plant near downtown Dallas, claims distinction in terms of quality and experience.

After Johnnie Ferrantello's death in 1965, Thelma Ferrantello took over the operation of the firm, which recorded its first million dollars in gross sales in 1969.

Today the company's gross sales average five million dollars annually. Its corny dogs are purchased by groceries, food distributors, schools, theaters, sporting arenas, and restaurants across the United States. The Corny Dog Company's plant—complete with a 40-degree packing area—

is constantly being automated, from placing the all-beef, beef and pork, or turkey hot dogs on sticks to quick-freezing the product for packaging in bright red boxes, shrink-wrap film, or institutional containers.

The Corny Dog Company's trademark—a little wooden elf named Woody—has become well known since its creation in 1956. Recently the Ferrantello family took a box of their corny dogs to Aruba and caused quite a bit of excitement over the unusual novelty food. Those who tasted the Corny Dog Company's product seemed to agree with the firm's motto: "Try Woody's; They're Goodies!"

In 1975 Courtney Ferrantello, thirty-two, who grew up eating Woody's Corny Dogs, joined the firm as a partner with his mother, Thelma. Courtney busied himself with designing new packaging and helping in the responsibilities of the growing firm. He is presently the company's president.

For Thelma and Courtney Ferrantello, the future is in franchising. "We're planning, at this time, to franchise and to have stands in the Dallas area and, later, across the United States," Courtney Ferrantello explains. "We've even talked about the European market. We're also planning on finishing the automation we started. We're working on new conveyors and special freezers."

The Corny Dog Company is also at work developing new and exciting flavorings for its product, including chili, cheese, and jalapeño.

"Twenty years from now I hope my son, Jason Ferrantello, will be involved in the business," says Courtney Ferrantello. "By then the business will be completely automated. Our sales will be larger than ever. And our product will be just as good as it is today. We'll add different flavorings, but the basic corny dog will be the same. There's no reason to change a great product."

Thelma Ferrantello took over the firm on the death of her husband. Now chairman of the board, Mrs. Ferrantello has passed on the day-to-day operation of the business to son Courtney (left).

JET FLEET CORPORATION

Since its inception in 1969, Jet Fleet Corporation has become a standard by which other aviation charter companies are measured.

The company presently operates more types of jet aircraft from more cities than any other charter operator. Offering services in aircraft charter, maintenance, and management, Jet Fleet's motto is "We keep the blue chips flying"—a reference to its dedication to the corporate sector's growing need for private aircraft services.

It is an area of aviation that Jet Fleet knows well, for it was founded as a segment of a corporation. In 1969 LTV Corporation founded LTV Jet Fleet Corporation as a charter operation for a fleet of corporate aircraft the industry giant already owned.

From this foundation, the fledgling enterprise quickly set some industry precedents. Jet Fleet was the first air charter company to be certified under the 135.2 certificate (air charter) issued by the FAA. Shortly after its founding, Jet Fleet moved from its headquarters near LTV to its present location at the northeast corner of Love Field.

In 1982 Jet Fleet received the Commercial Business Flying Safety Award from the National Business Aircraft Association for flying more than thirty-five million safe miles. It leads the aircraft charter industry in miles safely flown by more than ten million miles. The firm's airplanes—which include Fan Jet Falcons, Lear Jets, King Airs, Cessna Citations, BAC 1-11s, and Gulfstreams I and II—service cities in the United States, Canada, Mexico, Europe, and Africa. Jet Fleet bases aircraft in Dallas, Houston, Midland, New York, Washington, D.C., and San Antonio, but the corporate headquarters is its terminal at Love Field in Dallas.

Jet Fleet's corporate headquarters is at Love Field in Dallas but the firm also bases aircraft in Houston, Midland, New York, Washington, D.C., and San Antonio. Jet Fleet services cities in the United States, Canada, Mexico, Europe, and Africa.

"Jet Fleet's ongoing goal is to provide the best customer service of any company in the world," says president Les Space. Charter sales and flight scheduling personnel are in the firm's headquarters twenty-four hours each day, and its planes are continuously ready for charter. Jet Fleet arranges all aspects of the charter and provides a host of other services, including ground transportation, hotel accommodations, catering, and any other special requirements.

Aircraft are maintained in Jet Fleet's Love Field facility, and the company is an approved service center for most jet-powered business aircraft. Its maintenance facilities include major engine and airframe work, a complete parts department, and one of the best-rated avionics shops in the country. To further accommodate its clients, Jet Fleet operates an "owner-assist" program, a management contract that allows the aircraft to be chartered, thereby reducing the owner's cost of operation.

L.H. LACY COMPANY

The highways, subdivisions, airports, bridges, and commercial buildings of Texas owe quite a debt to the L.H. Lacy Company of Dallas.

As the contractor for many of the state's major projects, the firm has amassed a list of completed projects that reads like a road map and guidebook to the state. From Austin's historic Driskill Hotel to Dallas' Love Field to the Interstate 35 link between Dallas and San Antonio, Lacy's presence in Texas cannot be ignored.

But while completing these projects, Lacy was also breaking revolutionary ground in the construction industry. The firm was one of the first contractors to pave concrete highways in Texas. Lacy was also among the first to use automatic equipment to place steel in the concrete of interstate projects. The procedure was so successful that in 1971 Lacy set the single-day concrete production record for a Texas highway. The company introduced modern paving methods to Dallas subdivisions and was among the first to use automatic subgraders and slipform pavers which improved the quality of streets and highways. And when the Federal Aid to Highways Act was passed in Congress in 1956, Lacy was one of two firms awarded the first interstate highway contract in Texas—I-45 on the present interstate system in Navarro County.

The company was founded in 1919 by the late L.H. Lacy, who had begun his construction career earlier with the St. Louis Southwestern Railway Company, serving as engineer in charge of construction work in the states of Texas, Louisiana, Arkansas, and Missouri. Lacy moved to Dallas in 1919 to establish a home-building firm. Four years later he ventured into commercial building projects, and by 1930 his business was undertaking engineering construction.

With "high ethical principles and improved technical quality" as the company's precept, Lacy guided his firm to set some impressive standards. Quality work at a reasonable

The L.H. Lacy Company was one of the first contractors to pave concrete highways in Texas.

pace, instead of just high volume, was Lacy's goal. Since his death in 1978, L.H. Lacy's ideals have been carried on by his son, chairman of the board Jerry Lacy, and his grandsons, executive vice-president Michael Lacy and vice-president Glyn Lacy. The company president is Jes McIver, who has been with the L.H. Lacy Company since 1958.

To handle its heavy project loads, the firm has devised organizational programs to promote efficiency. In paving, for instance, equipment is "leapfrogged" from one part of a job to another by separate teams, so that the crew can switch from one machine to another as paving progresses down the road. To maintain employee enthusiasm and morale, Lacy pays its workers above the going market rate and gives promotions on a merit basis.

With the same dedication to quality work that has guided it during the past sixty years, the L.H. Lacy Company continues to build Texas in the 1980s.

The firm continues to build Texas in the 1980s.

ALFORD REFRIGERATED WAREHOUSES, INC.

The sub-zero headquarters of Alford Refrigerated Warehouses—which sprawls across 1.5 million square feet in downtown Dallas—is the largest above-ground refrigerated warehouse in the world.

With an excess of 2.2 million square feet in its three Dallas locations, and with other warehouse operations in Houston and Corpus Christi, Alford is a major distributor for perishable and nonperishable foods throughout the Southwest.

The Alford family first entered the distribution business in the revolutionary days of the Republic of Texas. General George Alford was commissary general of the Republic of Texas, which meant he was "warehouse man" in charge of supplies for General Sam Houston.

Today Alford's side-by-side warehouse structures arc the Dallas skyline—defying a historical legacy and more humble beginnings. For the beginnings of the modern-day Alford's took place not on the battlefields of Texas, but in the accounting offices of Fred Alford, Sr., in 1936.

Alford was a senior accountant with the firm of Ernst and Ernst. He was dispatched by the out-of-state owner of Dallas' Merchants Cold Storage Company to probe the business' troubled books. Alford's comprehensive audit revealed that the firm was sound, but funds were being dissipated for personal luxuries by the local operators. Alford suggested a series of remedies, and advised the owner of his conclusions.

"The owner took my dad to dinner, and they began chatting about the business," recalls Fred F. Alford, Jr., now president of Alford Refrigerated Warehouses. "Finally the owner said, 'Well, if you're so smart, young man, why don't *you* run it?' Dad was thirty-seven, and the thought hadn't really occurred to him until this point."

Fred Alford, Sr., leased the Merchants Cold Storage Company's building from its owner for $1,000 a month, borrowing money from relatives and the First National Bank. A

Today the main plant of Alford Refrigerated Warehouses, Inc., located in Dallas, impressively arcs the city skyline.

blessing of three months' free rent from the firm's owner also helped. Alford then recruited many of his former colleagues and founded the Fred F. Alford and Company accounting firm located on the premises of the newly acquired cold storage company.

During World War II Alford began adding annexes onto the warehouses, and with war's end came a tremendous increase in need for refrigerated food warehousing. This was due in part to Clarence Birdseye who had convinced the country of the importance and convenience of frozen foods. In the late 1940s, with an increased business, Reconstruction Finance, and the cooperation of the Rock Island Railroad, Fred Alford expanded the company by building a curved warehouse structure along the railroad tracks in the shadow of downtown Dallas. As the popularity of frozen food grew, so did Alford's business. The company quickly became the "distributor for distributors," shipping frozen foods to wholesalers and grocery chains.

Fred F. Alford, Jr., first worked in his father's warehouses as a youngster, accomplishing a variety of tasks after school, on weekends and holidays, and during the summer months. When the Korean War was over the younger Alford was discharged from

the Armed Forces as a second lieutenant and returned to join the firm on a full-time basis. In the early years he worked in virtually all areas of the company, assuming an increasing agenda of responsibilities. The father-son combination was extremely effective, and the company expanded with substantial speed—far exceeding industry trends.

In the late 1950s the younger Alford oversaw the opening of a company plant in Corpus Christi and subsequently was responsible for its successful operation. In 1964 Alford returned to Dallas when his father became ill. Fred F. Alford, Jr., assumed the presidency of the business upon the death of his father.

Today the family-owned firm, under the direction of Fred Alford, Jr., and his daughter, B.W. Alford, vice-president/marketing, ships more than

one billion dollars in frozen food from its warehouses annually.

Alford Refrigerated Warehouses, Inc., is also committed to the efficient use of energy in all aspects of its operation. Fred Alford, Jr., was recently awarded the prestigious four-state regional Energy Award by the American Society of Heating, Refrigerating and Air Conditioning Engineers (ASHRAE). The award was in recognition of energy techniques instituted at Alford's Goodwill Square Warehouse in Dallas.

Alford Refrigerated Warehouses celebrated its golden jubilee in 1986—a celebration that coincided with the Texas Sesquicentennial. With a proud heritage based on a tradition of service and customer satisfaction, Alford looks forward to future challenges and opportunities as it embarks on the new horizons that lie ahead.

Alford-Houston, located near the Port of Houston, one of the largest and most active ports in the world, provides important import-export facilities.

HALL FINANCIAL GROUP

Hall Financial Group is an industry phenomenon. It was founded in 1968 by then-eighteen-year-old, college-bound, energetic Craig Hall, who invested $4,000 in a rooming house in his hometown of Ann Arbor, Michigan. Hall eventually sold the property at a profit and quickly invested his money in other projects. Thus began a remarkable career in real estate syndication, in which investors' capital is pooled to purchase attractive properties, specifically apartment complexes and office buildings. Hall's first syndication was in 1969, and by the end of the year his budding company owned and managed fifteen small properties.

Today the Dallas-based real estate investment firm owns more than $3 billion worth of property in eighteen states and represents over 7,000 investors in real estate limited partnerships. In 1984 Hall Financial Group purchased nearly $800 million dollars worth of real estate and raised approximately $275 million in investor equity. The company is the nation's seventh-largest owner/manager of apartment complexes, with more than 60,000 units, and is one of the largest private real estate syndication companies in the United States.

In the late 1970s, after a period of dramatic growth in acquiring apartment complexes, the Hall Financial Group began marketing its syndication service and its properties on a national level. In 1981 Craig Hall came to Dallas to open a regional branch. The branch succeeded so well that Hall began making repeated visits and quickly fell in love with the city and its exuberant business spirit. In 1983 he moved his firm's headquarters from Southfield, Michigan, to Dallas, the center of the Sunbelt's booming real estate market.

"Although we're a relative newcomer to Texas and the Dallas community, a lot of our business philosophy makes us more comfortable and compatible here than anywhere else," says Hall. "Our company believes in opportunity and a situation in which

The Woodway Tower, in Houston, is owned by the Hall Financial Group.

someone can excel, not because of where they came from but because of the quality of work they do."

Much of the firm's dramatic success can be attributed to the Hall Financial Group's philosophy and business strategy, which is explained in Hall's popular volume, *Craig Hall's Book of Real Estate Investing.* Essentially, the strategy involves purchasing under-performing properties in a buyer's market. The firm finances the properties in ways that will provide significant tax benefits to its inves-

Hall Financial Group has invested in the growing condominium market with purchases such as the Westlakes Villa in San Antonio.

tors and offer them future capital gains.

Philosophically, the Hall Financial Group has always based its business dealings on integrity and service, shunning short-term, quick-profit transactions. Hall also believes in closing acquisitions with its own funds, instead of buying properties subject to raising money from private investors. This practice often results in better prices and terms for the investor.

The Hall Financial Group has proven its ability to raise funds and soundly invest them. By January 1984 the company's general partners had a combined net worth well in excess of $150 million and liquid assets of more than $50 million. The previous year saw the acquisition of 16,626 apartment units and 875,000 square feet of office space. The firm's fund-raising arm, Hall Securities Corporation, also proved its ability to raise money, with $236 million in equity capital secured in 1983 alone.

Presently, the Hall Financial Group continues its expansion into the financial end of real estate investing, moving into pension fund partnerships and operating two savings and loan associations, Resource Savings Association and Hall Savings Association. Hall is also active in venture capital, funding small, growing companies in Texas and in other states.

To increase in-house productivity, the Hall Financial Group offers its employees unique cooperative programs. At the higher levels of management, members of Hall's team are involved in profit sharing. The company does not operate on a commission basis. Instead, members of the Hall team become part of a shared bonus plan. This way, "everyone's working toward the same goal," says Hall.

In 1984 the Hall Financial Group embarked on a $400-million office building investment program, purchasing two major downtown Dallas office towers and the American Motors headquarters complex in Southfield, Michigan. Also in 1984 Craig Hall made another significant personal investment: He became part owner of the Dallas Cowboys football team.

The Ivorytree Apartments are part of the firm's residential property investments in Arlington.

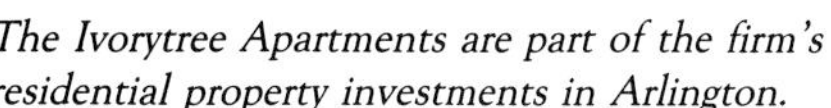

PIER 1 INC.

The eight-member buying team for the nation's leading direct-import specialty retailer, Pier 1 Inc., journeys to over sixty countries in search of handcrafted, unusual items for over 300 Pier 1 Imports stores in the United States and Canada.

While the firm has port-city warehouses in each quadrant of the United States—Houston; Anaheim, California; Chicago; and Savannah, Georgia; and now in Baltimore, Maryland—search-and-shop voyages begin at the 23-year-old company's international headquarters in Fort Worth, Pier 1 Inc.'s gateway to the world.

"This is a great place to run a nationwide business," Clark A. Johnson, president and chief executive officer, says. "We are equidistant from both coasts. We do all our buying overseas; there's no particular advantage in our being on either coast."

Fort Worth has been the hub of Pier 1's business since 1962, when the Tandy Corporation first ventured into the direct-import retail business.

"Tandy in the early 1960s was looking for new worlds to conquer," said Luther Henderson, the company founder, who was then vice-president

From sixteen stores in 1965, Pier 1 Imports has grown to a chain of over 300 nationwide. This Tampa facility began a successful expansion program, with thirty-one new store openings in 1984.

For twenty-two years Pier 1 buyers have shunned assembly-line factories, preferring the work of skilled craftsmen.

and treasurer of that organization. "We more or less accidentally stumbled onto the import store, which was a fairly new and different industry."

In a joint venture Tandy and Cost Plus Imports of San Francisco opened their first store the day after Thanksgiving, 1962, in San Mateo, California. Two additional stores were opened that same fall, offering curios from around the world that customers had never seen before. Not only were the items unique, they were also inexpensive.

Tandy ended its agreement with Cost Plus in 1965; Cost Plus had been assisting Tandy in buying merchandise for the stores. "We set out to do our own buying," Henderson explained. "But first we had to change the store name. We thought long and hard to come up with Pier 1. We liked the word Pier, and decided, 'Let's just be the first and the best.'"

By 1965 Pier 1 had sixteen stores in California and Texas. At that time the Tandy Corporation was also nurturing its recently acquired Radio Shack division. In 1966 Tandy decided to focus on Radio Shack's growth and divest itself of Pier 1. Henderson headed the group of Pier 1 employees

who purchased the division from Tandy and was named president of the newly independent enterprise.

The consumer reaction to the Pier 1 Imports store fueled one thought in the minds of company owners and directors—expansion. Pier 1 set into place the mechanisms of a modern retail chain operation.

He also knew that significant expansion could only take place under one condition. "It was my intention from the start that we go public, if we were ever going to expand," he related.

In 1969 Pier 1 offered its stock for public sale; it operated forty-two stores. The company obtained a listing on the American Stock Exchange in September 1970, and in November 1972 was listed on the New York Stock Exchange.

"The company expanded modestly at that time because it was privately held," Johnson says. "We expanded very rapidly after we went public. We were over 250 stores in 1972." Expansion included opening stores overseas in England, France, Ger-

many, the Netherlands, Belgium, and Australia.

Pier 1's heady expansion slowed, however, when the mid-1970s threw a number of stumbling blocks in the way of American business. "Our whole company was adversely affected by the oil embargo and the devaluation of the dollar in the 1970s. "We had a rough six years," Henderson explained. "Our foreign operations were the most severely affected. In 1975 we got out of Europe and Australia, and decided to concentrate on the United States and Canada."

In 1979 the dollar began strengthening against foreign currencies, and a key player soon returned to the firm's operations. Bob Camp had joined Pier 1 Imports as a trainee in a store stockroom in 1967. He became a store manager and was later promoted to regional manager. Camp was anxious, however, to establish his own business, "to be an entrepreneur." In 1971 he and a good friend moved to Montreal where they began Canada's first direct-import retail chain operation, which grew to eighteen stores. The partners sold their enterprise, Import Bazaar, to Pier 1 Imports in 1979. Camp returned to Pier 1 in 1980 to work as general manager of the U.S. import store di-

From its home office in Fort Worth, Pier 1 sends buyers to remote villages and cities in sixty countries in search of handcrafted furniture, decorative accents, and classic kitchenware.

To obtain hand-thrown pottery from Shipibo-Coni Indians, Pier 1 sends buyers to Peru. Motifs and techniques predate the era of Pizarro's conquistadores.

---

vision, responsible for 275 stores.

"From the mid-1970s on, the company's momentum had slowed somewhat," Camp says. "A number of ideas had been tried and had not been successful. Instinctively, I felt the basic concept was just as exciting as it had been in 1962. If we could just bring back the original excitement, bring back the romance of the business, we could win."

Bringing back the romance meant changing the look of the stores. Straight-shelf aisles were relaxed, white walls were painted, floors were painted brick-red, the lighting was softened, and the air was filled with spice candles and eucalyptus. The elements of "surprise and change" were reemphasized in the stores.

In addition to changing the stores' interiors, the corporation strengthened its buying team, closed unprofitable stores, implemented new incentive programs, and modernized the distribution system. Camp's instincts and gifted merchandising ability have proven to be the additions that the company's financially sound structure needed.

In 1981 customer counts began picking up, and year-end sales were record-breaking. This performance was repeated in 1982, 1983, and 1984, with customer counts and sales exceeding previous years.

The company plans on doubling the size of its operations by 1990, raising its store count to 500 units.

Future hopes rest on the consumer-driven nature of the company, the store managers, entrepreneurship, Pier 1's buying expertise in complex and

diverse world markets, the merchandise offered, 90 percent of which is all handmade, and the strength that emanates from the desire to be successful.

Interior decorators shop at Pier 1 for furnishings with natural warmth and modern styling. Their clients appreciate learning that "elegant" doesn't mean expensive.

AVIATION OFFICE OF AMERICA, INC.

Aviation Office of America flies with extremely varied company: from actor John Travolta to the Confederate Air Force. As an insurance management firm specializing in aviation, AOA participates in insuring 150 major airlines around the world. One of the largest insurance groups of its kind in the nation, with 175 employees worldwide and a headquarters as big as an airport terminal at Dallas' Love Field, AOA insures airplanes, airports, and assorted aeronautical enterprises.

The company's roots were planted in Beaumont, Texas, in the office of Jack G. Folmar, a former pilot and all-around aviation buff. "I liked insurance and I liked aviation," recalls Folmar. "But I didn't like structured insurance, like automobiles or houses." In 1957 Folmar combined his love for both aviation and insurance by founding Gulf Aviation Underwriters.

In addition to Folmar the company had one accountant, two office helpers, and clients in Louisiana, Arkansas, Texas, New Mexico, and the Republic of Mexico.

The aviation insurance business he entered, however, involved some hefty stakes: Scheduled airlines are insured for $500 million limits of liability. Because of the tremendous risks involved in insuring airlines and other large aviation enterprises, fire and casualty companies turn to insurance-management companies to handle their aviation insurance. In response to this need, Folmar founded AOA on October 1, 1962.

In 1965, eight years to the day after founding Gulf Aviation Underwriters, Folmar significantly expanded the AOA organization with the acquisition of the outstanding business of American Mercury Insurance Company and the General Aviation Underwriting Corporation. By 1970

Jack G. Folmar, who founded the firm in 1957, is the chairman of the board and chief executive officer.

Folmar landed his first large account—handling the aviation insurance coverage for Trans-Texas Airways (later Texas International and, presently, Continental Airlines).

At that point Folmar became convinced of the need for larger accommodations and decided to move his company from the port city of Beaumont to a more central location. Aviation insurance is mostly an international business, traditionally

centered in London. Folmar, however, chose Dallas as his headquarters. In 1975 he moved his company into a quarter-million-square-foot terminal building vacated by Braniff International, which had moved into the newly built D/FW Airport. For a year AOA was the only tenant at deserted Love Field, which recently has experienced a great, bustling rebirth.

The New York-based insurance holding company, Crum and Forster, purchased AOA in 1977, and the growth of the business continues. The AOA organization includes five offices in the United States, offices in London, and a variety of companies and subsidiaries.

The future of the company is as limitless as man's involvement with the skies. "We went from private aircraft into airlines," says AOA senior vice-president Charles Tarpley, a former Air Force and Pan Am pilot. "Now we're into satellites, which is an exciting new dimension. Eventually, I guess, every large corporation will have its own satellite facility, which will be insured just like cars or buildings."

After Braniff International Airways moved from this facility in the Love Field Terminal Building, it became the headquarters of Aviation Office of America, Inc.

OLMSTED-KIRK PAPER COMPANY

Robert M. Olmsted, Jr., and Robert M. Olmsted, Sr., stand next to a portrait of Harry Olmsted.

For three generations the Olmsted family has been selling paper products in Texas.

Harry Olmsted and Myron Kirk had worked together at Butler Paper Company before deciding to strike out on their own in 1922. They purchased the seventeen-year-old West Cullum Paper Company of Dallas, located on Marilla Street, and changed the name of their enterprise to Olmsted-Kirk Paper Company in 1923.

During a trip to his ancestral home that same year, Harry Olmsted had the idea of using the shield from his family crest in the company logo. He altered the English crest by removing the stag's head, which rested above the shield, and inserting the first letters of each partner's surname—O-K. Below the letters, written across the shield, is the word "Paper." Harry Olmsted's son, Robert M. Olmsted, Sr., recalls how thrilled his father was when it occurred to him to use what are perhaps the two most significant and frequently used letters in the English language, O-K, in his firm's logo. "You'd have thought that he found a million dollars under the bed," the corporate chairman notes.

When the giant, four-block-long Santa Fe building was completed a year or so after the name Olmsted-Kirk was implemented, the wholesale paper distributor moved into the fifth floor of the structure's fourth unit at 1033 Young Street.

Following Kirk's death in 1930, Harry Olmsted became sole proprietor. That same year his son and James S. Wagnon joined him and Fred Neary, who had been recruited in 1929. In 1932 Harry Olmsted accepted a position as vice-president and head of the trust department of First National Bank; however, he continued to advise his son and two associates and remained the company president until his death in 1941. The founder left his firm in loyal and dedicated hands: His son, James Wagnon, and Fred Neary worked together for fifty-two years.

In 1965 Robert M. Olmsted, Jr., joined the organization as a trainee; in June 1981 he was named president. His associate of twenty years and current executive vice-president, Charles "Corky" Clark, Jr., became a member of the firm in 1963.

Also in 1965 Olmsted-Kirk moved to its present headquarters at 2420 Butler Street, a 150,000-square-foot office and warehouse complex designed by the company. The corporation also has four additional offices and warehouses in Fort Worth, Houston, Waco, and Austin. From these facilities a sales staff of fifty, and approximately 150 additional employees, services customer needs relating to four divisions: fine papers, encompassing all printing papers; specialty papers, such as adding machine rolls, control tapes, and other rolled papers; industrial papers, which include toilet tissue, wrapping paper, and towels; and O-K Paper Centers, the name of six retail stores— opened in Dallas, Fort Worth, Austin, Houston, and San Antonio since 1980— that are designed to serve the needs of printers and consumers who want small amounts of paper immediately.

Robert Olmsted, Sr., explains that the corporation adheres to the high business standards his father believed in. Both he and his son are convinced that by continuing to provide excellent service and products, and by encouraging strong lines of communication within the organization, Olmsted-Kirk will maintain a steady growth into the future.

The Dallas office of the Olmsted-Kirk Paper Company.

DAUGHTERS OF CHARITY HOSPITALS

Texas in the late nineteenth century was a tremendously unhealthy place. Not only did its brawling cow towns and railheads have a deserved reputation for violence, but there was also a critical lack of medical facilities to treat those who fell victim to it, as well as to the many communicable diseases that preyed on pioneer families of the day.

It was into this atmosphere in the 1890s that a dedicated order of Catholic Sisters ventured to open some of the state's earliest private hospitals, and quietly began to alter the history of health care across the length and breadth of the Lone Star State.

For almost a century since then, the Texas hospitals operated by the Daughters of Charity of St. Vincent

The first Daughters of Charity hospital to be established in Texas, El Paso's Hotel Dieu Hospital opened in this towered structure on January 24, 1894, two years after its founding.

that began on the frontier. In their combined programs, Hotel Dieu Medical Center of El Paso, St. Paul Medical Center of Dallas, Seton Medical Center and Holy Cross Hospital of Austin, and Providence Hospital of Waco have extended life-giving benefits to countless thousands of Texans, past and present. As they continue to build and grow, future generations can be assured of the same historic commitment to health and healing that the hospitals have shown since the beginning.

That beginning took place in the

The old St. Paul Hospital, on Bryan Street in Dallas, was a landmark for generations before it was razed in 1968.

Austin's Seton Medical Center has grown from this original red-brick building to become the Capital City's largest hospital.

de Paul have been saving the lives and safeguarding the health of generations of Texans. During that incredible period of challenge and change, their record of dynamic growth, tireless effort, and a firm commitment to excellence has closely paralleled that of the state they serve.

Today the Daughters of Charity hospitals—now numbering five institutions in four Texas cities—continue to write new chapters in the story of devoted service and quality care

dusty, booming "Tent Town" that was El Paso some ninety-six years ago. The Sisters came to El Paso at the request of the Reverend Charles M. Ferrari, a priest who often tended the Tent Town sick, and other interested citizens. They started the hospital with some $1,680 in local contributions and furniture, bedding, food, and other supplies collected by the women of El Paso.

Hotel Dieu Hospital was chartered on June 28, 1892, and the following month the site for a permanent facility was purchased at the corner of Rio Grande and Stanton streets, which remains the site of Hotel Dieu Medi-

cal Center today. The towered edifice that housed the first hospital was completed on January 24, 1894, at a cost of $75,000.

In addition to being the first hospital in El Paso, Hotel Dieu has scored many firsts throughout the years. In 1898 it became the home of the first nursing school in the Southwest. The first cesarean section birth in the Southwest was performed there in 1908, and in 1972 the first renal dialysis center in the Southwest opened at Hotel Dieu.

Today it is one of the most mod-

Waco's Providence Hospital, which opened in 1904, is shown here as it appeared in the 1920s.

ern and sophisticated medical facilities in Texas. In addition to serving as a major center for the treatment of hemodialysis patients, Hotel Dieu is also a full acute care facility with complete medical and surgical services and advanced operating room and endoscopy techniques. In 1984 the medical center became a regional leader in innovative laser treatment.

The founding of Texas' second Daughters of Charity hospital—today's St. Paul Medical Center in Dallas—took place in 1896 in a strikingly similar fashion. Early that summer three Sisters arrived in Dallas from the order's Maryland headquarters and set about the task of establishing the city's first private hospital on a donated tract of land at Bryan and Hall streets.

St. Paul Sanitarium was chartered by the state on July 16, 1896, and nearly two years later, on July 15, 1898, the 110-bed hospital opened in a stately five-story, red-brick structure that was considered ultramodern for its time.

In 1900 the Daughters of Charity established the first school of nursing in Dallas, and it graduated its first three students in 1903. By 1915 the first of many expansions for the hospital had become necessary, and an annex was built to increase its total capacity to 300 beds. In 1922 a separate school of nursing was opened.

The St. Paul Clinic, which began offering free outpatient care to needy persons in 1906, has served untold thousands since its founding.

In December 1963 St. Paul Medical Center moved to a new home in a modern, 489-bed facility at Harry Hines Boulevard and Inwood Road. The addition of the Haggar Patient Tower in 1982 brought the number of beds to 600. Today the institution is an established leader in medical research and health education, is a major referral center, and is recognized as an outstanding teaching facility for residents and fellows in many fields of medicine.

This unique, modernistic building houses Austin's Holy Cross Hospital, the newest addition to the Daughters of Charity health care system.

In the spring of 1900 the Daughters of Charity expanded their hospital-building activity to Austin, fulfilling a dream dating back to 1887, when the idea for a new institution had been proposed by the women of St. Mary's Catholic Church. Ground was broken for Seton Infirmary in November 1900, and the hospital opened on May 28, 1902, with forty beds. Additions were built in 1912 and 1918, at a time when Seton became well known for aiding victims of flu and smallpox epidemics.

In 1975, after seven years of fund

raising and construction, the hospital moved from its original location at Tobin Park to a new facility on West Thirty-eighth Street and was renamed Seton Medical Center. A regional neonatal center opened in 1979, followed by the Central Texas Heart Institute in 1984. The Seton Good Health School, established in 1981, is a nationally recognized program of public health education. Today Seton Medical Center, Austin's largest hospital, is also a major referral center for all of Central Texas.

The Sisters opened Providence Hospital in Waco as a charity facility in a wide-open town often referred to as "Six-Shooter Junction." Public prejudice kept most patients away at first, except for the indigent poor, who were treated at a cost to the city of just seventy-five cents per day. But the hospital and its Sisters proved their worth to the community during outbreaks of flu, smallpox, and meningitis between 1911 and 1918, and the facility began to grow.

In 1950 the Waco Heart Clinic opened at Providence, followed by a coronary care unit in 1970. The first open-heart surgery was performed there in 1973 and the first angioplasty in 1982. It is now a leading cardiac care facility for Central Texas and is recognized for its outstanding rehabilitation program.

In 1982 the Daughters of Charity assumed sponsorship of Austin's Holy Cross Hospital, and it became their fifth major medical facility in Texas. As the site of the first oncology unit in Central Texas, established in 1969, Holy Cross is rapidly developing as a center for cancer treatment. It was fully integrated into the Daughters of Charity system in 1984, and a $16-million expansion program was initiated.

PEARLE HEALTH SERVICES, INC.

Dallas-based Pearle Health Services, Inc., operates primarily under the names Pearle Vision Center and Texas State Optical (TSO). According to its 1983 annual report—the firm went public on September 16, 1983—"Pearle Health Services, Inc., is the largest retailer of eye-care products and services in the United States and the world."

Don Phillips, president and chief executive officer since 1976, says that Pearle is larger than its nearest four competitors combined: Systemwide sales in 1984 were $357 million. Currently there are 1,256 vision offices in the United States, Mexico, Puerto Rico, the Netherlands, the United Kingdom, Belgium, and Canada.

"We think that we can build a billion-dollar optical business in five to seven years," says Phillips, "and by the end of the decade we can have a market share of 8 to 9 percent. We believe we can reach this goal with slightly over 2,000 stores. The long-term goal is a 20-percent share of the market, which would require 4,000 stores."

The annual U.S. market for optical services is estimated at $6.6 billion, and is growing by 8 to 9 percent. Industry reports show that nearly 47 percent of the people between the ages of thirteen and twenty-four, 61 percent of the people between the ages of twenty-five and forty-five, and 90 percent of the people over the age of forty-five require vision correction.

Pearle's marketing department research shows that consumers want a high-quality product at competitive prices, and a large selection of merchandise offered in convenient locations at convenient hours. Of course they also desire the best in professional medical care. Optometrists are located either in or near every Pearle Vision Center and TSO store.

In 1957 optometrist Stanley Pearle signed an agreement with Gordon's Jewelers to lease space within several of its Georgia stores. International Optical of Dallas, a major center for mail-order optical laboratories at the

time, completed the lab work for Dr. Pearle's small chain. Four years later Dr. Pearle merged his retail business with International Optical to form Opticks, Inc.; in May 1971 Opticks, Inc., opened its first store in Savannah, Georgia. The first-month sales goal of $5,000 was met in the first week.

In 1962 Zales Jewelry and Dr. Pearle signed lease operations in twenty-six stores located in eleven states. When the venture proved successful, Dr. Pearle decided to open several independent Pearle Optical offices. By December 1963 there were ten autonomous Pearle Optical stores, and Opticks' total sales were close to four million dollars.

Thirteen additional Pearle Opticals opened in Nebraska and Iowa in 1964. With the acquisition of Opticas Franklin of Mexico in 1965, Opticks, Inc., entered the international market.

Construction of corporate offices, laboratory, and warehouse facilities at 2534 Royal Lane in Dallas, were completed in 1966.

Will Ross, a hospital products manufacturer, bought Opticks, Inc., for twenty-eight million dollars in 1969. The company name was retained.

Pearle Optical stores were renamed Pearle Vision Centers in 1970, and the organization began to phase out lease departments in jewelry stores. Also during 1970, and in 1971, the firm purchased two established, well-respected East Coast optical chains: Rogers Optical, consisting of eight stores in Pennsylvania and Delaware, and Hillman/Kohan Opticals, with eleven stores in New York and New Jersey. Their names were retained until 1979, when they became Pearle Vision Centers.

In 1971 Opticks, Inc., purchased Spex Laboratories, an optical laboratory in Saddlebrook, New Jersey, to help meet the increasing demands made upon International Optical to fill prescriptions. Don Phillips joined the operation in 1971 as vice-president of planning and development, a position he held until he was named ex-

Donald J. Phillips, president and chief executive officer.

ecutive vice-president in 1974.

Pharmaceutical giant G.D. Searle purchased Opticks for $176.1 million in 1975, at which time it was renamed the Searle Optical Group as a division of G.D. Searle. With annual growth of 100 percent for several years, that division is now the world's largest retail dispenser of optical products.

The corporation expanded aggressively. In 1979 it acquired two eye-care chains, including TSO's chain of sixty-five stores and two laboratories. These acquisitions, combined with the newly opened Pearle Vision Centers, raised Searle's optical-division store count to 651 worldwide. Total 1979 sales exceeded $130 million.

A franchise program for Pearle Vision Centers was launched in December 1980. "With franchising," Phillips states, "we can meet our expansion goals, increase our market share, and create capital for reinvestment." He believes that franchising allows the company and the franchisee to do what each does best. The company provides real estate, marketing, purchasing, and merchandising expertise to its partners—certified ophthalmologists, optometrists, and opticians who purchase a Pearle Vision Center. The eye-care specialists, in turn, provide professional patient care and service, knowledge of the local market, and a knowledgeable and well-trained staff.

The store owners are highly motivated; the success of Pearle Vision Centers is their success. Pearle is committed to increasing the percentage of franchise stores, currently over 50 percent, to around 70 percent, approximately two-thirds of all stores, by mid-1986. In addition to opening new franchise stores, Pearle is converting company-operated stores to franchised stores. By the end of 1984 some 447 company-run stores were converted, moves that proved to be worthwhile; product sales increased more than 20 percent in these stores in their first full year of franchise operation.

By 1982 Searle Optical was operating 1,007 stores, and system-wide sales were over $257 million. G.D. Searle sold the majority of its holdings of the optical group through publicly traded stock in 1983. This move gave the newly formed Pearle Health Services, Inc., greater marketing freedom. By year's end Pearle Health Services operated 1,087 stores around the world, and sales were recorded at $304.5 million.

Pearle has led what Debra Tippett, director of marketing, calls "a shift in the industry." Before the existence of retail chains, which in 1983 had captured a 20-percent share of the market, as compared with 7 percent in 1974, the optical industry was inefficient, expensive, and little was known about its consumer. Pearle committed itself to changing that. The results are apparent in the Pearle Vision Center stores, where a customer can have an eye examination, choose

from the largest selection of frames and contact lenses available, and usually walk away only hours later with the proper prescription that is guaranteed for one year.

"Our biggest marketing challenge is to get people who have never been into an optical chain to come to Pearle," Phillips says. "Their thinking is, 'Well, if the optometrist were a good doctor he wouldn't be there.' But the facts show that the opposite is true."

A recent Federal Trade Commission study stated that "commercial optometrists fit cosmetic contact lenses at least as well as (if not better than) other fitters" and that prices charged by commercial firms are approximately 30-percent lower than sole practitioners.

Pearle Health believes that it can apply its retailing skills to other areas of health care. The firm is concentrating its investments and research in the dental industry and the immediate-care medical field. It began investing in the dental industry, which generates nineteen billion dol-

lars annually, in 1981 after acquiring a number of dental clinics in Florida.

Three years later Pearle entered the immediate-care field. Through a joint venture the organization now operates twelve Primacare Emergency Centers, which offer medical care and treatment of minor emergencies in a convenient location offering longer hours than a typical doctor's office and lower costs than a hospital emergency department.

In February 1984 Pearle opened its first optical "superstore" in Dallas, and plans to open a few more of these optical department stores, called Visionary, in Dallas in 1985.

Phillips states that the confidence with which Pearle Health Services strides into new ventures, and into the future, comes from the approximately 4,000 employees (7,000 if the franchisees are included).

"We have outstanding people," he explains. "We try to give them an environment where they can try new things. People who have ability, creativity, and good judgment are compensated."

REPUBLICBANK CORPORATION

"There is no finer place in the world to be in banking than in Texas," says Gerald W. Fronterhouse, the new chief executive officer and chairman designate of RepublicBank Corporation, the country's eighteenth-largest, and Texas' largest bank holding company.

RepublicBank Corporation was founded in 1974 and grew from a tradition of working together with businesses and individuals for the economic health and vitality of its customers and market areas. It has developed a wide range of expertise and products to serve the financial needs of its customers, with special emphasis on middle-market and emerging growth businesses, commercial real estate development, and established independent oil and gas producers.

RepublicBank Corporation's history is a continuation of the 64-year story of RepublicBank Dallas, which Charles Pistor, chief executive officer of the Dallas bank, calls the "flagship" of RepublicBank Corporation.

Oilman Tom M. Dees and attorney Colonel Eugene DeBogory opened Guaranty Bank and Trust Co. on February 14, 1920. The new bank had 659 accounts and $804,525.45 in deposits by the end of that first day. Two months after opening with an initial capitalization of $100,000, Guaranty Bank had one million dollars in capital and $100,000 surplus. In order to accommodate the average working person, Guaranty offered extended banking hours—9 a.m. to 8 p.m. on weekdays and 9 a.m. to 10 p.m. Saturdays—and became known as "the day-and-night bank."

James W. Aston, former RepublicBank Corporation chairman and current chairman of the executive committee, says, "This bank was very unpopular when the founders broke the rules. Other banks pulled the teller's curtain down promptly at one o'clock; the ball game was over. People thought we were mavericks and that the bank wouldn't last very long."

To ensure cohesion and breadth of outlook in its LOB strategy adopted in 1982, RepublicBank Corporation also established an office of the chairman. OOC members at the corporation's 1984 annual shareholders' meeting at RepublicBank Houston are (left to right) Joseph R. Musolino, James D. Berry, Charles Pistor, and Gerald W. Fronterhouse.

The innovative bank attracted innovative bankers. William O. Connor joined Guaranty as president in April 1920, after a 42-year career with the Sanger Brothers Department Store. Dees then became chairman of the board. And in May young Fred Florence joined the Dallas bank. He would serve the institution—and Dallas—for forty years until his death in 1960 and would become the first Dallas banker ever to head the prestigious American Bankers Association.

Connor and Florence broke more unwritten banking rules when they solicited business. "In those days banks didn't advertise," Aston says. "It was contrary to the ethics standards to ask for business. Mr. Connor's philosophy was different. He'd stand out on the street, introduce himself, ask where people did their banking business, and tell them that he'd like them to do their business with the Guaranty Bank. His idea was to first get them in the store, and if they bought a shirt, sell them a tie."

The bank acquired a national charter on April 29, 1922, and its name was changed to Republic National Bank. By 1925 its capital stock had increased to two million dollars—a 2,000-percent increase in five years—and Republic had outgrown its original home. The following year the bank moved into a new twenty-story "skyscraper," the Davis Building.

In the next three years two mergers significantly increased the size of the institution. On June 26, 1928, the bank absorbed Republic Trust and Savings Bank, and subsequently changed its name to Republic National Bank and Trust Co. In October 1929 North Texas National Bank was absorbed, and the name Republic National Bank of Dallas was adopted on January 12, 1937.

Florence succeeded Connor as bank president on January 8, 1929. The first years of Florence's presidency, years of desperation for many Americans, would test not only his banking ability, but also the very strength of his character. In an effort to ensure that "everyone" would do business at Republic, Florence sent his officers out to call on prospective customers, something unheard of in the banking industry at that time.

Republic National Bank's leadership recognized early that many banks failed during the Depression because of overconcentration in certain geographic areas and business practices. Republic, in the post-Depression years, looked for customers and appropriate business beyond its traditional base. It was among the first banks to lend money against oil at a time when oil had fallen to ten cents a barrel, and its future popularity as an energy source seemed hard to predict.

Karl Hoblitzelle, a well-known Dallas theater owner, whom Aston refers to as "one of the greatest philanthropists that ever lived," became a direc-

When it was completed in 1954 the 36-story RepublicBank building, topped by a 150-foot spire, was the tallest building west of the Mississippi.

tor of the bank in 1928 and later served as chairman for twenty years and then chairman emeritus. Hoblitzelle committed himself and the bank to serving the community and inspired generations of Republic leaders to devote interest, time, and money to Dallas.

Becoming an established force under Hoblitzelle and Florence, Republic developed into a strong yet flexible institution. Equal to the tribulations of the Depression and the similarly demanding challenge of anticipating change, the institution became one of the country's leading banks. It built a reputation for stability—its chain of annual dividends never broke. A growing physical presence in Dallas also emerged; in 1931 a twenty-story structure was added to the Davis Building, making it the largest office building in Texas— enough space to last until 1954 when a 36-story, aluminum-and-glass tower topped by a 150-foot spire was erected. A RepublicBank star shone on each panel that sheathed the building.

The physical growth of Republic reinforced two basic beliefs of the bank's founders. Dedication to serving its customers is essential, and growth in the Southwest is crucial to the general well-being of the country. Those beliefs, coupled with the bank's increase in shareholders' equity, meant that local corporations would more likely have their lending needs met at home, in Dallas, rather than having to turn to money centers on the East and West coasts.

Florence relinquished the presidency of the bank in 1957 to Aston, who began his career with Republic in 1945 after returning from Air Force duty. In 1945 Republic had 300 employees; it would have 3,500 when Aston retired.

In an effort to secure a logo for the bank, Republic adopted the silver star, which adorned the building's outdoor facade and dominated a great deal of the inside decor. The new logo gave rise to the term "Silver Star Service." More silver stars went up in 1964, when the bank opened

Fred Florence steers a crane to begin excavation on RepublicBank's new motor bank in downtown Dallas on February 2, 1960, with the guidance of Karl Hoblitzelle (left) and James Aston. Cumulatively, these three men led Republic as either president or chairman of the board for more than sixty-eight years.

its fifty-story tower adjacent to the original building.

The philanthropic spirits of Hoblitzelle and Florence greatly influenced Aston, who established his own reputation for leadership and humanitarian efforts. In March 1985 his service was acknowledged with the National Society of Fund-Raising Executives Award as Outstanding Volunteer Fund Raiser of 1984.

In 1965 Aston succeeded Hoblitzelle as chairman of the board of Republic, and James W. Keay was named the bank's president. Under their leadership, Republic opened its first international branch in London in 1970, expanding overseas to better serve its rapidly growing international customer base. Today Republic is the leading Texas bank internationally with branches and offices in Nassau, Singapore, Seoul, Mexico City, Sãu Paulo, Taipei, and Tokyo. Eleven percent of RepublicBank Corporation's loan portfolio is devoted to international business.

By 1974 the holding company movement was well under way, and RepublicBank's management and stockholders voted to reorganize the institution under a multibank holding company. On May 9, 1974, Republic of Texas Corporation was created as a registered holding company and acquired all of the capital stock of Republic National Bank. The next ten years would represent a decade of historic achievement for the corporation. Aston became the newly formed holding company's board chairman, and James Berry became its president.

In 1975 Houston National Company and its principal subsidiary, Houston National Bank, merged into RepublicBank Corporation. With Houston National Bank and Republic National Bank, the new holding company controlled two of the state's largest and strongest banks in Texas' top markets. In 1976 the holding company's stock was listed on the New York Stock Exchange under the ticker symbol "RPT." Since becoming a bank holding company, RPT's total market stock has increased over five times, net income four times, and assets and equity base five times.

When Aston retired in 1977, Berry succeeded him as chairman and chief executive officer of the holding company. In 1980 Charles Pistor moved from president to chairman of RepublicBank Dallas with Joseph R. Musolino as the new president of the company's lead bank.

In the period from 1977 to year-end 1984, with Berry as RepublicBank Corporation's chairman and chief executive officer, the holding company grew from eleven member banks to thirty-eight, with a major presence across the state. The 1983 acquisition of First National Bank of Midland, the largest independent bank in Texas, gave RepublicBank Corporation a strong standing in the Permian Basin and all of West Texas.

On April 16, 1985, James Berry, in anticipation of his imminent retirement, relinquished his title of chief executive officer to Gerald W. Fronterhouse, president and chief operating officer. Berry continued as chairman until his retirement in July 1986.

In order to best organize the corporation to anticipate change and compete most effectively, the bank adopted a unique organizational structure in 1982, which organizes the thirty-eight affiliate banks of RepublicBank Corporation into eight lines of business "LOBs": five banking groups (General, Corporate, Energy, Real Estate, and Houston), Trust, and two important internal LOBs (Funds Management and Operations).

RepublicBank's Real Estate Banking Group is the fourth-largest entity of its kind among U.S. banks for construction and development loans with a loan portfolio well diversified by product and geographic area. RepublicBank also provides leadership in numerous other types of loans and banking services. For example, the bank played the key financing role in the acquisition of the Dallas Cowboys football team by a consortium of businessmen led by H.R. "Bum" Bright, a well-known Dallas figure and RepublicBank board member.

Banking has changed since the days of Dee's and DeBogory's "day-and-night bank." Technology has created a modern version of the bank Republic's founders had in mind; automatic teller machines called TELLER 24 provide customer services any time, day or night.

The future promises even greater changes, and Republic bankers see the deregulation of the banking industry as their future. They look to the day when complete deregulation will free banks from the restrictions that currently affect where they do business, the product they offer, and that product's price. The corporation's leaders look forward to the day when RepublicBank can cross invisible state lines, open banks, and compete with nonbank financial institutions in the delivery of convenient services to the public.

"Silver Star Service means a customer-oriented way of doing business without geographical boundaries," Fronterhouse says. "Customers also have the assurance that RepublicBank will maintain a strong capital base and liquidity position to meet their needs regardless of the times. That is part of Silver Star Service."

DR PEPPER

In October 1985 Dr Pepper was in the midst of its celebration of 100 years of originality and indescribably good taste, when bottlers from all over the world met in Dallas and toasted the "world's most original soft drink."

The International Bottlers' Meeting convened only 100 miles from the birthplace of the nation's third-largest-selling soft drink—Waco, Texas.

Morrison's Old Corner Drug Store, owned by pharmacist W.B. Morrison, and originally located at the corner of Fourth and Austin streets in the heart of Waco, advertised itself as "The Biggest and Best in Texas." In the late 1880s it was the town's meeting place; the soda fountain was one of the store's main attractions, widely known for the original creations of the "soda jerks."

One of Morrison's young employees was Charles C. Alderton, a medical school graduate and transplanted New Yorker. Alderton worked at Morrison's Old Corner Drug Store as a pharmacist and often as a soda dispenser. He concocted "original" sodas by mixing a variety of fruit flavors. He had observed that when customers entered the store they were captivated by the combined scent from the cherry, raspberry, lemon, vanilla, and other flavor extracts. Any one of these served singly didn't measure up to the wonderful aroma of the combined fruits. Alderton continually experimented by mixing various combinations into one soda until 1885, when he happened upon a drink that became an overnight sensation.

As the popularity of Alderton's drink spread, more and more Wacoans began to call for it. The only problem was that it didn't have a name. As it happened a romantic memory from Morrison's youth was the inspiration for the new drink's name.

As a young man Morrison had lived in Rural Retreat, Virginia, where he had been employed at a drugstore owned by a prominent

Morrison's Old Corner Drug Store, at the corner of Fourth and Austin in Waco, was the birthplace of Dr Pepper in 1885. It was where Wacoans came to try "Doc" Alderton's new soft drink and get caught up on the latest news.

local physician named Pepper. Morrison had been infatuated with Pepper's attractive daughter, but the doctor had discouraged the romance. Morrison never forgot the episode and talked about it frequently. As his soda fountain patrons searched for an appropriate name for their favorite refreshment, someone suggested "Dr. Pepper."

The name immediately stuck, and it has remained the same with one minor alteration. In 1950 the period was deleted from the abbreviation "Dr.," as a graphics consideration when the style of the lettering used in the trademark was changed.

The drink itself is also much the same as Alderton's original concoction, but the formula was refined as the result of research conducted by R.S. Lazenby, a Waco beverage chemist and the owner of the bottling plant where Dr Pepper was first produced as a commercially bottled beverage. By 1886 the Artesian Manufacturing & Bottling Works, owned jointly by Lazenby and Morrison, was mass producing Dr Pepper for thirsty Wacoans. And by 1890 Dr Pepper was bottled at numerous locations in Texas.

It wasn't until 1922, when Dr Pepper moved its headquarters and operations to Dallas, that the soft drink's fame spread beyond the boundaries

Dr Pepper, like many up and coming products of the early 1900s, featured Gibson Girl models in its advertising. These attractive posters today are valuable collectibles as objets d'art from early Americana.

of Texas and the Southwest. By 1930 annual net sales exceeded $1.5 million; ten years later sales of nearly $3.4 million were recorded.

Dr Pepper's growth has been constant throughout its 100-year history. In 1980, with annual sales of $333 million, Dr Pepper became the third-largest-selling soft drink in the United States. Currently Dr Pepper has approximately 500 franchise bottlers in the United States and is now being sold in fifteen markets in the United Kingdom, Scandinavia, Western Europe, West Africa, the Middle East, Japan, and the Asia subcontinent. It has been on sale in Canada since 1961.

WILLIAMSON PRINTING CORPORATION

For Williamson Printing Corporation, one of Texas' largest commercial printers, the events of 1983 and 1984 will be easy to find in the company's annals; they will be in bold-face type.

In February 1983 the corporation's plant doubled in size. The Dallas-based concern, which offers full-service advertising, commercial, corporate, legal and financial printing, moved from its 100,000 square feet of floor space located in several buildings on Valdina Street, where operations had been since 1969, to a new building on 7.6 acres at 6700 Denton Drive, adjacent to Love Field Airport.

The following September Williamson Printing lost its leader, Bowen Williamson, who had purchased the printing company in 1968. At that time the firm employed forty-five people and had annual sales of approximately $600,000. Today there are some 400 employees and annual sales exceed thirty million dollars.

Bowen Williamson, along with his sons, Jerry and Jesse, was chiefly responsible for the company's dramatic growth and its garnering of national recognition. In 1983 the Printing Industries of America (PIA), in its National Awards Competition, gave the second-highest number of awards to Williamson Printing. Again, in 1984, the firm received forty-four awards in PIA's National Awards Competition, thereby tying for second place among all printing firms.

Jerry Williamson, current president of the corporation, believes his father left a lasting impression, not only as a business leader but also as a man of integrity. "He was a very compassionate person toward employees, customers, and suppliers," young Williamson says of his father. "He was honest in all his dealings and expected the same of others. He was reared to respect work in the old-fashioned work ethic."

The history of the company extends back 100 years. In 1884 the Dorsey brothers, James A. and Henry, formed a partnership and opened a printing company and office supply store. James, a gregarious, talented, and tireless promoter and entrepreneur, handled sales. Henry was quieter than his older brother, but no less talented in his own right. A highly skilled pressman, he ran the print shop on Elm Street.

The Dorsey Company was an immediate success, though it had more than its share of trouble in its early years. The plant was completely destroyed by fire twice between 1884 and 1900.

When the Elm Street building was gutted, the brothers moved a short distance to Main Street, but within a few years the calamity repeated itself. At the time of the second fire, The Dorsey Company was the largest firm of its kind in the region and one of Dallas' major businesses. Its ever-expanding territory, which included much of the Southwest, attested to sixteen years of growth.

Disaster, however, did not daunt the Dorsey brothers. They rebuilt with even greater confidence and created their own line of stationery with the phoenix bird as the watermark, symbolic of their rising from the ashes of the fires. In 1902 downtown Dallas

The original site of The Dorsey Company after the fire on May 27, 1898.

saw a six-story red brick factory and office building erected. The Dorsey Building, the second-tallest and one of the city's largest commercial structures in downtown Dallas, was located on the half-block bounded by Commerce, Jackson, and Poydras streets. For sixty-seven years this building remained the firm's headquarters.

During the first two decades of the twentieth century, The Dorsey Company established itself as "The Business Man's Department Store," one of the nation's premiere printing and office supply operations. Branch offices opened in Houston, Texas, and Muskogee, Oklahoma, while salesmen traveled the entire country, including the Territory of Arizona and the Indian Territory of Oklahoma, selling everything from ledgers to bank vaults. Henry Dorsey led the company's print shop in pioneering the lithography process and in introducing new engraving techniques. Under his direction, The Dorsey Company was among the first in the Southwest to engrave using steel and copper plates.

A Dorsey catalog from November 1912 explained to its customers why the firm had become larger than all its Dallas competitors combined. "The central location of The Dorsey Company, with its mammoth stores, warehouses, and factories at Dallas, Houston, and Muskogee; the exceptional railroad facilities of these cities with direct water-route connections with eastern markets, where raw ma-

This was the home of The Dorsey Company from 1902 to 1969.

terials are produced, enable the company to serve its patrons quicker and better than other concerns.

"Equipped with the latest improved machinery, the greatest time- and labor-saving methods and systems, and the highest class of workmanship known to the art of printing and kindred craft, the company is turning out a class of work that is equaled by the product of but few and surpassed for quality by that of none."

When James Dorsey died in 1913, Henry Dorsey bought his brother's one-half interest and became the sole proprietor. As a charter member of the Dallas Chamber of Commerce, Henry Dorsey was active in the "150,000 Club." This group was dedicated to building the city's popula-

From 1969 to 1983 Williamson Printing Corporation was located at 2263 Valdina, Dallas.

tion to that magic number before the 1920 federal census. Dallas went over the top with 8,000 to spare.

Happy days were fewer in number for the firm in the late 1920s. Henry Dorsey died in 1928. Henry Dorsey, Jr., took over the business, and the following year the stock market crashed. During the Great Depression businesses were forced to do without practically everything The Dorsey Company provided. Even the Dorsey-pioneered direct-mail advertising suffered. In order to help keep the concern operating, Henry Dorsey, Jr., cut his salary in half.

The Dorsey Company survived, but it never regained its earlier momentum. Then, in 1940, Bowen Williamson, a Vanderbilt University and

SMU alumnus, was hired as a salesman. Having been trained in the printing business by his uncle, W.R. Boyd, owner of the Boyd Printing Company of Dallas, Bowen was a new lifeblood to the foundering organization. He quickly moved up through the ranks, becoming sales manager, vice-president, and, later, a member of the board.

After Henry Dorsey, Jr., died in 1963, the business was placed in a trust administered by First National Bank of Dallas. The Dorsey Company was divided into an office supply company and a printing company. In 1964, Bowen Williamson became sole proprietor of the printing company when he leased it from the trust.

Then, in 1968, the trust sold the company to a third party. Bowen Williamson bought the printing division from the new owner, and in 1970 changed its name to Williamson Printing Corporation.

In 1969 the company moved to a new 35,000-square-foot facility in the industrial district near the market center. New personnel and improved equipment were added. The plant size doubled in 1972 to make room for additional equipment and a new Legal and Financial Printing Division.

Williamson Printing was the first in the region to have a half-size, heat-set web press in 1975. A full-size, heat-set web press was added in 1978, and a Houston sales office opened in 1979. A color-separations business, Classic Color Corporation, was created in 1980 to provide high-quality color separations to the industry.

In 1977 Williamson Printing became affiliated with the Ticor Printing Group, with offices in New York, Chicago, Los Angeles, and Houston, and with affiliates in London, Montreal, and Toronto. This group specialized in legal and financial

This has been the home of Williamson Printing Corporation since 1983.

printing. Two years later Williamson Printing purchased the Legal and Financial Printing Division of Lehigh/ Steck Warlick, the Southwest's pioneer in legal and financial printing. While legal and financial printing constitutes approximately 25 percent of the company's business, it is one of the most important segments; and it is aggressively pursuing continued growth in this area.

In celebration of the firm's 100 years of operation, the Williamson family, including Mrs. Bowen Williamson, a member of the board; Jesse Williamson, executive vice-president; Becky Williamson, salesperson; and sisters Speight Anderson and Elaine Antone; along with the employees of the corporation, decided to make a contribution to the City of Dallas, Old City Park, and its print shop.

"Instead of having a big party in celebration, we decided to show our thanks for the good things that have happened to us over the past century," Jerry Williamson explains. "We commissioned an artist to do two posters depicting Old City Park. We printed and donated them to the park, and they are being sold to help raise money for the park. We are also establishing a trust fund that will finance a person to run the print shop at Old City Park. The print shop had been one of the park's most popular attractions, especially with young schoolchildren, but lack of funds forced the park to close the operation. This fund will allow the park to hire a printer and make it become operational again."

As Williamson Printing Corporation begins its second century of service, its name is indelibly imprinted on both the past and the future.

FRYMIRE ENGINEERING COMPANY, INC.

Take the very best qualities of the American free enterprise system—pride, dedication, hard work, and old-fashioned caring—blend in a real-life version of the American Dream, add common sense, patriotism, and a down-to-earth approach, and you have today's Frymire Engineering Company, Inc. These timeless ingredients, coupled with the leadership of the company's founder, Thomas R. "Bob" Frymire, and its president, Miguel Zarazaga, have built Frymire Engineering into one of the Dallas area's most dramatic business success stories.

When Bob Frymire started the business in 1950, it consisted of himself and two employees and it operated out of a cramped 500-square-foot facility at the corner of Cedar Springs and Oak Lawn, across from the Melrose Hotel. Today the corporate offices and main manufacturing-warehouse complex of Frymire Engineering encompass some 80,000 square feet on a five-acre tract at 11120 Indian Trail in North Dallas.

Besides its Dallas headquarters, the firm has branches in Austin, Baytown, Houston, and San Benito, Texas, plus newly opened facilities in Oklahoma City and Tulsa, Oklahoma. All told, more than 800 employees serve Frymire Engineering and its customers in these seven locations. And it is these diverse and highly skilled individuals—engineers, mechanics, secretaries, draftsmen, truck drivers, machinists, and others—who are the real strength of the company and a primary factor in its success.

"Every employee is part of the Frymire family," says Zarazaga, "and an important member of our team. We do everything we can to let our employees know how valuable they are and how important their contribution is to the firm's overall success. Our best investment is our people, and we want to take care of them."

The pride and team spirit among Frymire employees—many of whom have been with the company for ten, fifteen, twenty, and even twenty-five

Bob Frymire, founder and chairman of the board.

years—is reflected in the high degree of customer satisfaction enjoyed by the business. At the completion of every job performed by Frymire service personnel, the customer is invited to comment on the quality and promptness of the service and the courtesy and expertise of those providing it. "We get very few unhappy customers," says Zarazaga, "but when we do, we want to know about it so that we can do something to correct it."

Over the past thirty-five years Frymire Engineering has used this genuine concern for the consumer to build an enviable reputation across Texas for exceptional quality and outstanding performance on every job. The firm is widely recognized for its ability to meet the needs of each individual customer in the areas of heating, air conditioning, plumbing, and electrical work for all types of commercial, residential, and industrial applications.

Part of its uniqueness lies in Frymire's painstaking procedure of counting and measuring all the products it manufactures, then placing them in kits to be sent to job sites

for installation. This practice not only increases efficiency and quality, but also enables the company to cut costs for its customers.

Frymire Engineering's deep concern for quality, employee morale, and customer satisfaction can be traced to the character of the remarkable man who started it all. Bob Frymire, who continues to serve the business he founded as chairman of the board, has set an example of leadership and commitment for everyone around him to follow. The strong entrepreneurial drive that led him to start the firm and keep building it steadily over the years has been balanced by his insistence on careful, sensible planning for each new stage of growth and expansion.

Bob Frymire is living proof of what faith in the free enterprise system can accomplish. One of the greatest demonstrations of his faith in that system took place more than a quarter-century ago, when he made the decision to hire a young Spanish immigrant who had just arrived in Texas, who spoke no English, and who had no experience in Frymire's type of business.

During the years that followed, that young man, Miguel Zarazaga, learned every phase of the business

The corporate offices and main manufacturing-warehouse complex of Frymire Engineering Company are on a five-acre tract at 11120 Indian Trail in North Dallas.

Miguel Zarazaga, president.

Twelve-Man Scholarship, vice-chairman of the Free Enterprise Committee, co-chairman of the Target Year 2000 Committee, and member of the Athletic Liaison Committee. In 1978 Frymire was presented the Jimmy Williams Distinguished Service Award by the Dallas A&M Club in recognition of his many services to the university.

Zarazaga, a native of Zaragoza, Spain, is proud of his rich heritage, but also shares Bob Frymire's devout sense of patriotism for his adopted homeland. "America is the greatest country on earth," he says. "I think that all Americans should realize how fortunate we are to be able to share the rewards of independence and free enterprise."

Patriotism and love of country are frequent themes in Frymire Engineering's advertising. In 1984 the company's patriotic ads—especially one that appeared in both Dallas newspapers on July 4, 1983, wishing "Happy Birthday" to the nation—were honored with the top annual award for advertising excellence by the Freedoms Foundation at Valley Forge.

More growth, progress, expansion, and precedent setting are ahead for Frymire Engineering as it reaches out toward new horizons, new goals, and new challenges. But at the same time, this amazing concern will continue to hold fast to the time-honored precepts, traditions, and standards that have made it—and America—what they are today.

Bob Frymire and Miguel Zarazaga believe that the formula for success is not much different today than it was when this country was founded more than two centuries ago. Zarazaga puts it simply when he says: "Take care of your employees and your customers, and you're going to be in good shape."

Of such stuff is the American system, and the American Dream, still made.

under Bob Frymire's careful tutelage. Today Zarazaga, too, is an example of what free enterprise can do. When he succeeded Frymire as president of the company in 1977, it was not only a reaffirmation of Frymire's original

judgment in hiring him, but a fulfillment of the classic American Dream.

Between them, these two men from different parts of the world and highly divergent backgrounds have used the tried-and-true principles of good business, along with fresh ideas and innovative concepts, to build one of the leading companies in a highly specialized field.

Even during the period of the firm's most rapid growth, Bob Frymire has found time and energy to invest in service to his community. A loyal alumnus of Texas A&M University, he has personally funded two permanent scholarships there and donated substantially to the A&M School of Engineering. He has served as president of the Aggie Club, is a founding member of the Diamond Century Club and the

WATSON ELECTRIC SUPPLY COMPANY

On March 31, 1947, thirteen weeks after Houston and Austin Watson had given notice of resignation to Westinghouse Electric Supply, the brothers set out to chart their own course. One month later, on May 1, the two opened their business, Watson Electric Supply Company, with two borrowed trucks and $7,000 in total assets.

The Watson brothers began their business with the idea of providing a new kind of personal service to the local electrical industry, and were confident that their combined experience qualified them to serve industrial and contracting businesses. When Houston resigned he was district sales manager responsible for three states and had established many contacts and friendships over the years with large electrical contractors, utility companies, and industries. Austin resigned as a purchasing agent; he brought to the fledgling enterprise inventory experience that, when combined with his brother's sales skills, would ensure Watson Electric's success.

The firm's inventory was nearly washed away or destroyed several months after business began. Dallas experienced what Houston remembers as the heaviest rainfall the city had ever had, "fourteen inches in fifteen hours." When Austin arrived at work that morning, everything was floating in a foot of water. He feared they were ruined. But many of the manufacturers replaced their stocked items without charge to Watson Electric. Despite its early misfortunes, Watson Electric had 800 loyal customers by the end of its first year of operation.

The company moved to its current Dallas location at 320 South Walton Street in 1949. Over the years Watson Electric has acquired additional buildings in the area and today it occupies four buildings totaling more than 100,000 square feet of office and warehouse space.

In 1950 Watson Electric opened its first branch in Tyler, Texas. Additional branch operations have since

Houston Watson, co-founder. Photo by Gittings

been located in Waco, Sherman, Palestine, Paris, Lufkin, Longview, Irving, Temple, Garland, Denison, Carrollton, Round Rock, Denton, Corsicana, and Gainesville.

The desire to better serve its customers by providing them with a local inventory led Watson Electric to expand, and the moves have proven to be to the company's advantage. The firm's four basic customer groups—industrial, utility, contractors, and commercial accounts—have all stated that local inventory is a prime consideration and reason for their support of Watson Electric.

A total of 260 people, forty of whom are salespeople, service customers from Watson Electric's seventeen locations. Both brothers regard their employees, many of whom have been with the company for over twenty years, as one of the key reasons for its uninterrupted growth.

Austin, who is chairman of the executive committee, also believes that the diversified inventory is a key to the firm's success. Today Watson Electric services 8,000 regular customers, 100 times the number of customers the company had in 1947. The April 1984 issue of *Electrical Wholesaling,* an electric industry magazine,

ranked Watson Electric twenty-second on its list of the 250 largest wholesale electric distributors among the 7,000 in the United States.

As the company has grown, it has

Austin Watson, co-founder. Photo by Gittings

truly become a family organization. Austin's son, Tony, and Houston's sons, Malcolm, Billy, and John, are all longtime, active employees. Malcolm has been president since 1974.

The world has changed since the day Austin and Houston received their first orders in the mail, and the changes justify the brothers' unshakable belief that Watson Electric's future will be brighter than ever: Today's world is an electronic world. Evidence of this is the fact that electronic motors and motor control equipment make up the largest single product line Watson Electric sells.

"I can remember the first electric iron, electric percolator, electric refrigerator," Houston, seventy-eight, says. "We used to go by the funeral home to get fans in order to cool us off. We have a greater future than when we started due to the fact that there is more of a demand. Individuals now require electric appliances more than they ever did earlier."

DAL-MAC CONSTRUCTION/DEVELOPMENT

Of all that Dal-Mac Construction/ Development has built in nearly thirty years of business, there is one thing that stands out to company president and chief executive officer Herbert H. McJunkin, Jr.—Dal-Mac's reputation as a quality builder, a reputation built over time with hard work, honesty, and a commitment to selling a quality product.

Indeed, the firm's steady growth is due to customer satisfaction. In the beginning, Dal-Mac's customers were home owners. Tired of the vagaries of the oil industry, young Herb McJunkin, with degrees in petroleum geology and engineering, left his job with a Houston oil company in the spring of 1958. He moved back to his native Dallas, borrowed $10,000 from a bank, bought five lots in suburban Mesquite, and applied for VA/FHA loan commitments to finance houses on these lots.

While waiting for issuance of the loan commitments, McJunkin, who had already obtained a real estate license and had begun selling houses on weekends while living in Houston, went to work for a home-building company in order to learn everything he could about construction. McJunkin was a quick study. Before the end of the year the five houses had been built, sold, and the bank loan repaid. With the sales profit, McJunkin purchased twenty lots in the Lake Highlands area of Dallas and built higher-priced custom homes.

During this early period McJunkin worked out of a small room attached to the rear of his Dallas home. He enlisted subcontractors to do most of the construction work, though he and his wife, Katherine, did some of the work themselves.

After four years of consistent growth, McJunkin's company was incorporated on July 6, 1962, as Dal-Mac Construction Company. By then McJunkin had decided to diversify his business to include commercial

Centre Phase IV, a high-rise office building erected by Dal-Mac Construction Company, at the crossroads of I-635 and Midway Road in Dallas.

construction to help sustain activity during slow periods in residential construction. Dal-Mac's first commercial job was erecting a prefabricated building for St. Paul's Lutheran Church in Farmers Branch.

Commercial projects gradually became the focus of Dal-Mac's energy. In 1967 the firm diversified further and began developing. "When you think of Dal-Mac Development, you think of a planned garden office complex or business park development that includes an abundance of beautiful landscaping," McJunkin says of his company, one of the first in the Dallas area to develop such business environments. Naturally, Dal-Mac developed and built the atrium garden office complex located on Spring Valley Road in Richardson, where the corporate headquarters has been since 1983.

Dal-Mac was also among the first developers in the area to design and build commercial projects, bringing together the expertise and capabilities of the two halves of the Dal-Mac whole—development and construction. Equipped with his engineering background, McJunkin led his business in tackling structural design work. He also believed strongly in the three-person design team of own-

er, builder, and architect long before the idea was popular.

Dal-Mac has grown in capabilities since 1958. Today the company can be called on to select a raw site and transform it; Dal-Mac will plan, finance, construct, finish-out, lease, and manage the completed project. All Dal-Mac services are available as part of a comprehensive package, or individually.

Increasingly, Dal-Mac is developing and constructing high-rise buildings, symbols of its growth and development over three decades. Consequently McJunkin is very "up" about Dal-Mac's future.

A "true versatile builder," Dal-Mac builds everything from warehouses to high rises on time, within budget, and to the customer's satisfaction.

Greenway, Dal-Mac's 88-acre office park, located in Richardson.

SMITH INDUSTRIES, INC.

Like many successful men, Nowery J. Smith had a knack for making the right decision at the right time. While still in his teens he made two of the most astute choices of his life: One was to marry his childhood sweetheart, Mildred Shields; the other, to leave Parkersburg, West Virginia, for Texas.

In the two decades after the Lucas gusher blew in at Spindletop, Houston had turned its attention from cotton to petroleum and, thanks to legendary oil pioneers like Nowery's uncle, Thomas P. Lee, was rapidly becoming a headquarters for all phases of the oil industry—production, refining, transportation, and supply. The eager young newlyweds found the future prospects of Houston irresistible.

After a brief apprenticeship in his uncle's Republic Production Company, Nowery moved into the supply side

Nowery J. Smith, founder of Smith Industries, is shown in his office in this late 1920s photograph.

of the industry and as vice-president of Petroleum Supply Company learned firsthand the needs of oil drillers and producers. Armed with this knowledge, Mildred and Nowery Smith made another significant decision in 1927—to form their own company. It was a joint enterprise since Mildred continued to take an active interest in the operation and development of the business. With five employees and a small building at 3610 McKinney, the Nowery J. Smith Company began buying and selling storage tanks for oil, gas, and water wells, oil separators, and related equipment.

By 1938 the firm had outgrown its McKinney Street location and acreage was purchased on the Hempstead Highway near the important railroad junction at Eureka, then on the outskirts of town. Again, the timing was faultless. The new plant was essentially a metalworking facility with fourteen employees. The United States was on the brink of World War II, and soon the shop was turning out parts for United States Navy vessels and earning the company a Navy "E" Award for its service.

Meanwhile, another Smith joined the organization. Charles Tyson Smith II, born in Houston in 1921, had grown up with the business, attended The University of Texas, and worked briefly for his father's firm before taking time out to serve in the Army Air Corps from 1942 to 1945.

After the war ended, the business—and Houston—began to develop rapidly. In the three years from 1946 to 1949, the Rogers Galvanizing Company was acquired, the Tyson Smith Company was organized to handle the manufacture and supply of oil field equipment, and the Nowery J. Smith Bolt Company was formed. With the expansion of the chemical industry and its need for

The Nowery J. Smith Company at 3610 McKinney Street distributed Lincoln Tank Company products when this photograph was taken in the early 1930s. Smith is seen standing at the right.

specialized coatings for equipment and storage containers, the firm moved into that field as well. In 1961 the individual companies united as Smith Industries, Inc.

Twenty-five years later Smith Industries is one of the largest privately owned petrochemical supply and service organizations in the Southwest. The industrial plant is still located on an enlarged tract at 8300 Hempstead Highway, as is the corporate headquarters, and storage and supply warehouses are scattered throughout the Gulf Coast region with a major installation near Columbus, Texas.

Tyson Smith II, who guided Smith Industries since its formation in 1961, still serves as chairman of the board, while his son, Charles Tyson Smith III, is a director and has been president since 1983. Other directors include Ray Bartula, William J. Berchey, Jr., Jimmy L. Manuel, W.R. Smith, Hadley Graham, Nowery Smith, and Ross McAlpine.

Putting together an organization of experienced people dedicated to the delivery of the ultimate in products and service to its customers has been the goal of the Smith family since 1927. The measure of their success can be found in the accomplishments of the firm's four operating divisions. The Galvanizing Division has the largest galvanizing kettles in the Southwest. An automatic shot-blasting process in the Special Coatings Division has made possible the application of paint and special protective coatings to large, already-fabricated tanks and assemblies. Engineers in the Oil and Gas Division design and fabricate state-of-the-art equipment for the production and processing of oil and gas and have made noteworthy contributions in the areas of glycol dehydration and water-pollution control within the oil industry.

Building Smith Industries has al-

most become a way of life for the family, but each member has found time to develop other interests as well. Nowery was a founder of River Oaks Baptist Church and the Pin Oaks Charity Horse Show. His son, Tyson, has been a lifelong lover of animals and has demonstrated that interest in his activities as president of the Houston Zoological Society and as vice-president of the Houston Livestock Show and Rodeo and the Houston Farm and Ranch Club. From 1957 until his mandatory retirement in 1971, Tyson was a member of the prestigious Young Presidents Organization. Even now his two sons, Tyson Smith III and Nowery Smith, are maintaining the family tradition.

Welch Brothers, tank erectors, was under contract to Nowery J. Smith in the early years of his career. The crew shown in this 1920s photograph includes (from left to right) Robert Welch, John Liddell, and George Welch.

Nowery J. Smith (left) and his father, Charles Tyson Smith, of Parkersburg, West Virginia, inspect the Nowery J. Smith Company's first manufacturing site on Hempstead Highway.

ELECTRONIC DATA SYSTEMS

The story of Electronic Data Systems and its founder, Ross Perot, is the stuff of which true-life entrepreneurial adventure stories are made.

The plot begins with a 32-year-old former Navy officer named Ross Perot. He became a star salesman at IBM, then founded a mushrooming computer services firm to design, install, and operate corporate data-processing systems for a fee. The new business was such a success that in EDS' first decade its worth climbed to the half-billion-dollar mark, and the company was on its way to becoming a legend in the international high-tech frontier.

On October 18, 1984, Perot's EDS was purchased for $2.5 billion by General Motors, of which EDS is a wholly owned subsidiary. The merger represents the largest acquisition in GM history. The year before, the nation had been riveted to the gripping exploits of Ross Perot's orchestration of the 1979 release of two EDS employees from an Iranian jail, chronicled in Ken Follet's best-selling novel, *Wings of Eagles*.

Throughout this varied saga, however, the company kept an even keel by offering its customers the same quality service that established EDS

Ross Perot, founder and chairman.

as a leader in its field.

EDS was founded in 1962. But its development began on June 27, 1930, with the birth of Perot. The son of a Texarkana, Texas, cotton broker and horse trader, young Perot was a typical small-town Texan. His drive, however, was nonetheless astonishing. He broke wild horses for one dollar per pony and peddled Christmas cards, seeds, and saddles. Because he delivered the newspaper in a poor section of town, he arranged to receive 70 percent of his subscription price as commission, instead of the normal 30.

After attending Texarkana Junior College for two years, Perot won admission to the U.S. Naval Academy. Later, serving on an aircraft carrier, he met a person who would change his life forever: an IBM executive who asked him to interview with the company once his tour of duty was over. Perot knew nothing about computers, but soon established himself as one of IBM's top salesmen. He was such a successful salesman that the firm put a cap on his salary, giving him plenty of time to think about furthering his career.

Perot was quick to learn the computer business. He soon realized that although customers were buying hardware, they needed someone to develop customized software and operate the systems once they were installed. To this end Electronic Data

Systems was born. Its first years were somewhat lean, with Perot using $1,000 from his savings to buy unused time on a computer owned by Southwestern Life Insurance Company of Dallas, then traveling to find companies to sell the time to at retail rates.

The firm's first big break came in 1963, when EDS sold a $5,128-a-month, five-year computer service contract with Frito Lay. In 1982 EDS landed a $656-million contract to manage the U.S. Army's data-processing system.

Today the company is a team of 35,000. It offers its services internationally and had 1984 revenues of $947 million. In 1979 Perot became EDS' chairman of the board and named Mort Meyerson president. Meyerson had joined EDS in 1966 as a trainee and built its health care division into the company's largest division.

With its merger with GM in 1984, EDS will become involved in every phase of its parent company's business—from robotics to invoicing to further computerization of GM plant operations. And though the merger with GM will offer EDS enormous opportunities in manufacturing and other fields, it is determined to keep the original EDS spirit of quality service alive.

Electronic Data Systems headquarters at 7171 Forest Lane in Dallas.

GOLEMON & ROLFE ASSOCIATES, INC.

At the close of World War II, Houston and Texas stood on the threshold of a period of phenomenal growth. The architectural firm of Golemon & Rolfe Associates, Inc., has played a distinguished and vital role in that growth process.

Organized in 1946 as a partnership with offices in Houston and Beaumont, the firm was incorporated in 1963. As a Texas business corporation it has developed into an award-winning architectural design enterprise whose diversified practice falls into five major areas: commercial structures; health care facilities; educational buildings; government, aviation, and convention center projects; and interior architectural and space-planning assignments.

The principals and associates at Golemon & Rolfe regard the business and art of architecture as a service profession oriented to the design and delivery of the highest-quality projects in conjunction with conscientious adherence to budgets and completion schedules. To attain these objectives the firm has assembled teams of creative, technically skilled, and highly motivated architects and support personnel.

With the acquisition of CADD Resources, Houston, in 1983, Golemon & Rolfe is now on the cutting edge of a technological revolution in the architectural field. By utilizing the computer-aided drafting and facilities management capabilities of CADD, Golemon & Rolfe continues to increase its diversity, efficiency, and cost-effective service to its clients.

While well-designed facilities, environments, and urban centers are of primary interest to Golemon & Rolfe, the management has long recognized an obligation to the general public as well as to clients. Devoting between 30 and 40 percent of his talent and energy to public service, Harry A. Golemon, president and chairman of the board, serves on the board of directors of the Houston Chamber of Commerce, the Harris County Heritage Society, and the Municipal Arts Commission. He is also president of the Houston Festival Foundation, Inc., and chairman of the Texas Historical Commission.

From offices in Houston and Austin the firm has provided a variety of architectural services throughout the United States, including Alaska and Hawaii, as well as Guam and Germany. Among recent projects with which the Golemon & Rolfe name has been associated are the Microelectronics and Computer Technology Corporation (MCC) headquarters building in The University of Texas' Balcones Research Center (Austin), Houston Intercontinental Airport terminals A, B, and C, Westin Hotel O'Hare (Chicago), The University of Texas System Cancer Research Facility (Houston), FBI Academy (Quantico, Virginia), and the George R. Brown Convention Center in Houston.

Since its establishment forty years ago, the firm of Golemon & Rolfe has more than exceeded the expectations of its founders. A second generation of architects is even now preparing a third generation of talented professionals within the organization to assume future leadership of this premier architectural firm in the Sun Belt.

TEXAS INSTRUMENTS INCORPORATED

The founders of Texas Instruments, left to right: Dr. Bates Peacock, Eugene McDermott, Cecil Green, and J. Erik Jonsson.

People in Texas and around the world know that the letters TI stand for the Dallas-based electronics giant, Texas Instruments. The more than 80,000 Texas Instruments employees, working in forty-seven plants in seventeen countries and in worldwide geophysical operations, know that the letters TI stand for the key to the company's success: technical innovation.

Technical innovation comes from new and creative ideas. Texas Instruments evolved from such an idea, one that was first voiced in the summer of 1917 by a young physicist, J. Clarence "Doc" Karcher.

That idea was a method for mapping structures far below the earth's surface by the use of seismic waves. The method was the basis for the development of the reflection seismograph, an instrument the oil industry would one day use for exploration. The reflection seismograph was also the cornerstone for Geographical Service Inc., which would later become Texas Instruments.

World War I delayed the development of Karcher's idea, and it was not until 1925, when Everett L. DeGolyer invited Karcher to join in forming Geophysical Research Corporation, that Karcher was given a chance to prove his seismic reflection theory. Five years later—as the nation was enveloped in the Great Depression and oil was virtually worthless—Karcher did what must have seemed at the time either very foolhardy or very brave: He left his job, went into partnership with another young scientist, Eugene McDermott, and started a new company, Geophysical Service Inc. Operating out of a headquarters office and shop in Dallas and a laboratory in Newark, New Jersey, GSI set out to search for oil using Karcher's reflection seismograph.

Early in its first year of operation, the company hired two other young men whose names, along with McDermott's, would become synonymous with TI. Cecil H. Green, a graduate of Massachusetts Institute of Technology, was named supervisor of seismograph field operations, and J. Erik Jonsson, a graduate of Rensselaer Polytechnic Institute, was recruited to supervise construction of instruments and equipment out of the Newark laboratory. In 1934 the laboratory and Jonsson moved to Dallas, where Jonsson would become an architect and builder of TI as its first president and board chairman, and an architect of the modern city of Dallas as its mayor for three two-year terms.

Within its first decade of business, GSI listed most of the major oil companies as clients for its seismic explorations. Crews fanned out into Mexico, Canada, South America, Saudi Arabia, Java, Sumatra, New Guinea, and India.

In addition, the occasionally idle crews located oil for GSI. This led to the formation of a separate production company, the Coronado Corporation, with GSI as a wholly owned

The Dallas headquarters of Texas Instruments Incorporated.

subsidiary. The resultant conflict of interest led Coronado's owners to sell out to a major petroleum producer. GSI was not included in the transaction; instead, it was purchased by a group consisting of Jonsson, Green, McDermott, and geophysicist Dr. Bates Peacock. The four signed the papers to purchase GSI on December 6, 1941—the eve of the bombing of Pearl Harbor.

For a time, as the geophysical exploration business was cut back by the war, it appeared that the foursome had bought a disaster. But GSI's people had a will to succeed and a technology in their hands that could easily be converted into military use. Jonsson appeared frequently in Washington, convinced the military that GSI's geophysical exploration methods could be applied to

In 1954 the firm became the first commercial producer of silicon transistors and the first to develop the commercial transistor radio.

submarine hunting, and sold more than one million dollars' worth of his company's instruments for defense between 1941 and 1945.

Jonsson's Washington sales trips also resulted in what he would later refer to as his greatest contribution to the company. Shortly after V-J Day Jonsson recruited 31-year-old Navy Lieutenant Patrick Eugene Haggerty, who had been in charge of all airborne electronic equipment production and procurement for the Navy's Bureau of Aeronautics, to come to work for GSI. Jonsson and Haggerty agreed that GSI should continue to manufacture electronic equipment. The two men also agreed upon another goal: to build not only a big company, but to build the best company in their areas of electronic capabilities.

In 1951 the company was renamed Texas Instruments Incorporated, with Erik Jonsson as its first president and Haggerty as executive vice-president.

Haggerty is often described as a visionary, and it was his vision that got TI into the semiconductor business. In the spring of 1952 TI obtained a license from Western Electric Company to manufacture transistors, which had been invented in 1948 in Western Bell's Telephone Laboratories. TI sales in 1952 were just over twenty million dollars, a figure that included the sale of ten transistors.

The first project engineer on the semiconductor program was a recent graduate of Southern Methodist University named Mark Shepherd, Jr. Shepherd managed TI's semiconductor operations until 1961, when he became executive vice-president of the company. He later went on to become president, and now serves as chairman of TI.

Through the development of high-frequency germanium transistors, TI opened a mass market for these devices. The new transistors were used in the first pocket-size radio, the Regency, designed by TI engineers and produced and sold by I.D.E.A. Corporation of Indianapolis, Indiana.

TI scored another technological breakthrough when it announced the first commercial production of silicon transistors in 1954—several years ahead of its competitors. The silicon transistor, which would operate at higher temperatures than germanium, opened the market for military applications of solid-state electronics.

In the late 1950s another TI inventor, Jack S. Kirby, conceived what was recognized as the next step beyond the transistor and the most important invention in the development of technology since the vacuum tube: the integrated circuit. The integrated circuit combined the functions of many transistors and other components on one tiny piece of material, and laid the foundation for today's "electronics revolution."

By 1960, with sales of $233 million and almost 17,000 employees, TI had surpassed Haggerty's goal of becoming a "good, big company," which he had defined ten years earlier as $200 million in annual sales.

Technological innovation at TI flourished in the 1970s with the company's introduction of the "miracle chip"—a chip that contained all the

logic circuits and memory cells of a computer on a single piece of silicon one-quarter of an inch square. TI developed a variety of consumer electronic products, including the Datamath* hand-held calculator, introduced in 1972, and a family of "talking" learning aids for children, beginning with the Speak & Spell*, that represented the first commercial use of synthetic speech.

Today's TI is the world's largest supplier of integrated circuits, and has built upon this technology base

The invention of the integrated circuit, which provides the basis for virtually all modern developments in electronics, was announced in 1958.

to become a world leader in radar, night vision, and missile-guidance systems; portable data terminals; electrical controls; three-dimensional seismic data collection and processing; industrial control systems; and other commercial, military, and industrial technologies. The newest area of TI's technology leadership is artificial intelligence, the science of making computers solve problems that have traditionally required human intelligence.

TI was founded on a commitment to encourage and promote new ideas. That commitment will lead the "good, big company" to greater growth and profitability in the future, through the creation of new products and new markets based on a continuing stream of technological innovation.
*Trademark of Texas Instruments Incorporated

BRIGHT MORTGAGE COMPANY

"Service is our only business," says Frank R. "Bob" Garrott, chairman of Dallas-based Bright Mortgage Company.

And at Bright Mortgage, service is big business. First-quarter 1985 showed a total loan portfolio of $3.3 billion, with 95,000 loans serviced, figures that position the firm among the largest privately held mortgage companies in the country.

Bright Mortgage, a residential and commercial mortgage company, has garnered such distinction with hard work and strategic acquisitions during its 61-year history.

Its beginning came in 1924, when former Mobil Oil Company employee Aubrey M. Costa and former Tennessee banker F.M. Love combined forces and formed the Southern Trust and Mortgage Company. Its first office was located in the Linz Building on Dallas' Main Street.

The Great Depression was rough on the fledgling enterprise. Costa and Love did everything from making a loan here and there to contracting home remodeling work in order to stay in business.

With the introduction of the Federal Housing Administration, which insured loans in the post-Depression 1930s, Southern Trust and Mortgage regained its footing and began to grow. "They started making some of the very first FHA loans made in Dallas," Garrott says.

In 1935 the firm began its ongoing association with insurance companies. The Business Men's Assurance Co. of Kansas City and California Western States Life Insurance were among the first to have a correspondent agreement with Southern Trust and Mortgage. However, the Robinson Act, a Texas law that required life insurance companies to invest part of their premiums in Texas, squelched insurance investments; the faith of many insurance companies in Texas' future was flimsy.

After World War II the Veteran's Administration began guaranteeing home loans, and the Robinson Act was rescinded. Southern Trust and

Mortgage began growing rapidly.

Love retired as company chairman in 1957 and sold his interest to Costa, who was president. Costa continued to run Southern Trust and Mortgage until the latter part of 1962, when he sold the firm to Bright & Schiff, an oil company headed by H.R. "Bum" Bright. Bright and his partner Schiff had decided to diversify their investments.

Costa remained with the mortgage company for eight years as its chairman of the board. When Costa retired, Bright assumed his position.

Other changes that occurred in the late 1950s and early 1960s would fos-

ter the company's growth. Up until the late 1950s mortgage firms considered savings and loan companies "deadly enemies," as Garrott says. Then they discovered that the two could work together. Savings and loans could invest excess funds that they couldn't invest in their local markets with mortgage companies. Savings and loans began buying loans from mortgage companies as investments.

In 1963 Southern Trust and Mortgage made an internal change that would be the cornerstone of all future expansion: The company began computerizing operations. Imagine

Bright Mortgage Company is headquartered in the Bright Banc building at 2355 Stemmons Freeway, Dallas.

handling the 95,000 monthly loan payments, each with varying principal, interest, and tax rates, without a computer. Five years later the firm moved to its current location, a high-rise building that Bright constructed at 2355 Stemmons Freeway now known as Bright Banc.

Southern Trust and Mortgage expanded tremendously throughout the 1970s. In the decade's first year a Houston office was opened, followed two years later by the opening of branches in Oklahoma City, Oklahoma; Albuquerque, New Mexico; and Denver, Colorado. The company's total loan servicing volume in January 1974 was $600 million. Then, in August 1974, Southern Trust and Mortgage kicked off a string of mergers with its acquisition of Texas-based Maxson-Mahoney-Turner Mortgage Company. By 1975 Southern Trust and Mortgage's loan servicing volume had jumped to just below one billion dollars.

Marshall Mortgage of Phoenix, Arizona, was acquired in 1977. In May 1978 Buckeye Mortgage of Columbus, Ohio, was purchased by the Texas mortgage company whose presence was expanding all over the Southwest. With this merger, Southern Trust and Mortgage entered the Midwest. The move into the Midwest forced the firm to drop the word "Trust" from its name: Laws there prohibit mortgage companies from having trust powers. The name was then changed to STM Mortgage Company.

In February 1979 STM moved farther west with its purchase of City and Suburban Mortgage of Los Alamitos, California, with offices also in Upland, California. A year later Schiff sold his interest in Bright & Schiff to Bright. In 1983 Garrott was named president of STM, only the fifth person to hold that office. Garrott had been associated with the mortgage company since 1958.

Bright continued expanding STM, whose 1983 total loan-servicing volume was $2.3 billion. On the last day of 1984 Bright bought Texas Federal Savings and Loan, established in 1925. The mortgage operation of the savings and loan was merged into STM, and on January 17, 1985, the name Texas Federal was changed to Bright Banc, and the name STM was changed to Bright Mortgage Company.

The once-stable industry that offered a small selection of long-term, fixed loans has become a volatile, complicated business that offers many sophisticated loan products—changes brought about by inflation and high interest rates. These changes require that a highly trained and knowledgeable corps of mortgage officers will provide professional service in order to meet customer loan needs. Service, then, is in the spotlight; excellent service is tantamount to success. Garrott says that Bright Mortgage will continue to concentrate on the service it offers. He says, "We really want to move up the ladder as far as size is concerned, as well as set a standard in the industry."

LONE STAR DONUTS

The ability to deliver fresh doughnuts each day to nearly 3,000 customers—restaurants, convenience stores, and other institutions—before they serve their first cup of coffee is part of the key to Dallas' Lone Star Donuts company's 35-year success story.

The firm's version of the doughnut invented during the Great Depression, quickly became America's breakfast staple—a nickel would buy two as well as a cup of coffee. It has been a Texas favorite since its earliest days of operation.

Trucks roll out of the 40,000-square-foot Beckley Avenue plant, which is capable of producing 4,000 dozen doughnuts an hour, headed for Dallas, Fort Worth, Temple, Austin, and San Antonio. The sale of fresh doughnuts accounts for 60 percent of the organization's business.

"Everything is timed. We work in minutes, not hours," states C.E. Burdine, board chairman and sole owner of Lone Star Donuts, whose corporate name is Burdine Industries. "We have a route-distribution system. All of our drivers operate independently. They run the service end of our business like their own compa-

S.M. Burdine, founder.

ny, which it is. It has been that way since inception."

In 1950 S.M. Burdine, J.L. Ward, and their wives, Lela Burdine and Orpha Ward, opened Oak Cliff's first doughnut shop. Together they and one employee, hired to cut the pastries, produced and delivered 300 dozen daily. The wives operated the 600-square-foot shop on Bishop Avenue where, in the beginning, they also sold baked goods. Eventually the sale of the baked goods was discontinued and the number of doughnut routes increased. The enterprise grew.

"It was a good doughnut, and the service was good," says C.E. Burdine, who joined his father's business in 1955.

S.M. Burdine acquired his partner's share of the company in 1957, a year that also marked the beginning of the automation of the plant. "We were the first in our area to automate," the present owner notes. "Up until that time, all dough was rolled out by hand and all doughnuts were cut by hand."

Father and son moved their growing operation to its current location in 1963. The founder died in 1969, leaving the business to his wife and two sons. Two years later C.E. Burdine purchased his mother's and brother's shares of the firm and became its sole owner. He remembers his father's business style with respect and a tinge of awe.

"My dad wasn't of the dynamic style that people associate with business today, but he probably accomplished more than most business people do. He was very soft-spoken. He'd be listening while you were talking. I attribute our laid-back atmosphere to him. He believed that in order to be in business, you didn't have to create a lot of undue pressure."

Burdine adds that his mother was "a driving force in the success of the family business." "We wouldn't be here today if they hadn't worked together," he emphasizes.

Early beginnings.

The company introduced frozen doughnuts and frozen hush puppies in 1972. Today, through fifty-five "food brokers," Lone Star Food Service Products—the frozen-food division—sells its products in forty-eight states. These sales account for approximately 40 percent of the organization's business. "We freeze our product with liquid nitrogen," Burdine explains. "It costs more than other methods, but we achieve a much better-quality frozen product because it takes only a minute and a half to freeze. For example, the doughnuts come off the line still warm, then they enter the nitrogen belt and freeze immediately—allowing no time for air to dry out the product."

Up until a few years ago Dallas residents saw the name "Lone Star Donuts" on thirty-two such specialty shops in the area. In 1968 the firm began a franchise operation, allowing the store owners to use its name and mix. Ten years later the company developed a new outlet—supermarkets. It sold fresh doughnuts on a daily basis to supermarket chains. A conflict became apparent. In 1980 the corporation decided to cease its franchise operation, although it continues to supply its mix to many retail stores.

While Lone Star's mainstay remains constant, the company looks to improve and expand as the doughnut market itself has grown steadily over the past twenty years. According to Burdine that market today is a billion-dollar one.

"Essentially, our doughnut is the same since 1950," he relates. "There have been changes in technology, health codes, and federal Food and Drug Administration laws, but the end product is still very close to the hand-cut product of 1950—only better. It's not as greasy, and it has a longer shelf life."

In 1984 Lone Star's research and

Present facilities.

development department perfected, and subsequently the firm introduced, baked Danish and cinnamon rolls that became part of its product line.

Burdine says that the influx of northerners to the South forced the company to consider new product offerings. "Traditionally," he notes, "there has been a difference in southerners' and northerners' taste in baked goods. Northern pastries are denser, heavier, than the lighter-than-air type donuts of the South." Pointing out that the two styles are now melding, he adds, "Today's southern doughnut is now a little heavier."

Future changes in the corporation will occur not only in products, but in operations as well. In 1986 Lone Star introduced to the Dallas retail market its new frozen hush puppy, one that Burdine feels is head and shoulders above those now on the market. The firm is also testing bakery goods for distribution to coffee-shop type stores. In addition, a new logo and new packaging are being approved as the organization prepares to enter retail markets.

A day in the life of a Lone Star Donut.

LOMAS & NETTLETON FINANCIAL CORPORATION

Among the nation's mortgage banking firms, Lomas & Nettleton Financial Corporation is the first in size and status; indeed, Dallas-based Lomas & Nettleton is the premier organization in its class.

The Lomas & Nettleton Financial Group offers comprehensive financial services to the real estate industry, primarily through mortgage banking, asset management, fiduciary services, short-term real estate lending, land development, and data services to other real estate lenders through three major operating divisions: The Lomas & Nettleton Company, which generates approximately 66 percent of annual gross revenue through mortgage banking services, L&N Management, Inc., the short-term lending division, and L&N Land Corp.

In his address to the general staff meeting, held October 1985, Jess T. Hay, L&N's chairman and chief executive officer since 1965, said, "Beyond any doubt ours is an organization which has produced results unequaled in the history of our industry."

Fiscal year 1985 marked the eleventh year of uninterrupted growth for Lomas & Nettleton. The firm's mortgage servicing portfolio grew from $4.8 billion at the end of fiscal 1975

Jess T. Hay, a native of Forney, Texas, has been chairman and chief executive officer of Lomas & Nettleton Financial Corporation since 1965.

to $20.2 billion at the end of fiscal 1985.

Currently more than 678,000 mortgage loans are serviced, involving 860 institutional investors; single-family loan production and servicing in all fifty states is the principal operation of L&N mortgage banking. More than 3,000 L&N employees work in the 150 offices currently maintained in forty-two states. Revenues for fiscal 1985 totaled $273 million, up $33 million from 1984, and nearly five times greater than in 1975.

In that same speech given at the 1985 staff meeting, Hay gave his viewpoint of L&N: "... L&N is the best, the most efficient, the most effective, and the most professional

and customer-centered organization in the mortgage banking industry today... throughout the past fifteen to twenty years one thing has not changed, and that is the character of our company. We remain today as we have been, at least since 1965, committed to the proposition that our central mission is to achieve profit with honor while producing steadily increasing profits for our stockholders. . . ."

The name Lomas & Nettleton Financial Corporation came about in 1965. The business was first organized and incorporated in Dallas in March 1960, under the name Wallace Properties, Inc. E.E. Wallace, Jr., one of the company's founders, served as its first chief executive officer from

John E. Lomas (left) and Edward L. Nettleton, shown at their desks in the early 1900s and in the insets at the top of photo.

The L&N ServiceCenter, opened in 1984, is home for Lomas & Nettleton's national loan administration division, which is responsible for servicing more than 678,000 loans.

March 1960 to October 1963. Capital included twenty-eight properties and $285,000. To supplement this, the company publicly offered its securities.

The firm's initial intention was to operate its original properties, and develop real estate for residential use in Texas, California, Georgia, and Florida. By 1961 that initial direction shifted, resulting in the sale of the original properties and the entering into the mortgage banking business through the acquisition in early 1961 of Institutional Mortgage Corporation, a Los Angeles-based firm with a mortgage servicing portfolio of $300 million.

This new direction proved fortuitous. In July 1963 Wallace acquired The Lomas & Nettleton Company of Connecticut, whose mortgage servicing portfolio totaled $350 million in unamortized principal amounts.

On September 27, 1965, Jess Hay was elected chief executive officer of L&N. That same year the corporate name, Lomas & Nettleton Financial Corporation, was adopted. Three years later Lomas & Nettleton became the nation's largest mortgage banker with its acquisition of the T.J. Bettes Companies of Texas and California. The Bettes mortgage servicing portfolio added $1.4 billion to Lomas & Nettleton's already bulging $850-million portfolio.

The following decade was one of further acquisition; by 1972 L&N was a national entity. United Mortgagee Servicing Corp., acquired in 1970, was the first purchase of the decade. The following year Northwest Mortgage was acquired, followed by the mortgage banking operations of Kardon Investment Company in 1972. Seven years later National Homes Acceptance Corp. was added. And in 1982 Advance Mortgage Company Ltd. of Southfield, Michi-

gan, an affiliate of Oppenheimer & Co., Inc., entered into a joint venture for the eventual merger of Advance's mortgage banking operations with those of L&N.

Today Lomas & Nettleton is committed to continued consistent growth, believing fervently that its size can only enhance customer ser-

Lomas & Nettleton today maintains a network of offices covering forty-two states and staffed by 3,082 experienced men and women trained to meet the needs of people throughout the nation.

vice. To ensure the best and most efficient mortgage servicing for its customers, L&N has built a state-of-the-art service center in Dallas, adjacent to the firm's data-processing center. The corporation's eight-story national headquarters for loan administration will, Hay says, "carry L&N, as the leader of its industry, through the balance of the twentieth century."

In keeping with the dreamers and builders of the companies that now

belong to the heritage of Lomas & Nettleton Financial Corporation, particularly John E. Lomas and T.J. Bettes, Hay is convinced that L&N has barely scratched the surface of the abundant opportunities available. If its employees, often referred to as the backbone of the corporation, will embrace the ideals of integrity and

character, professionalism and creativity, awareness and pride, loyalty and mutual dependence on one another, they can, Hay believes, achieve the dream of a company in the near future twice as large as today's Lomas & Nettleton.

INDUSTRIAL CATERING

In feeding the business and industry crews of Dallas/Fort Worth for thirty years, Industrial Catering is a company whose growth has both paralleled and propelled the growth of the area it serves.

The firm's 400 silver-sided catering trucks are a break-time tradition for hundreds of businesses, construction sites, and industries. Headquartered strategically in Grand Prairie between Dallas and Fort Worth, Industrial Catering services 15,000 businesses in Dallas/Fort Worth and Houston, and is the largest mobile industrial caterer in the country. The company's daily sales are $140,000, and retail sales are thirty-five million dollars a year. Its trucks serve 50,000 units of seventy different types of sandwiches, along with an array of candies, sundries, soft drinks, hot coffee, hot meals, and quick breakfasts, to 150,000 people each day and approximately fifty million people a year.

While feeding the masses, however, Industrial Catering has not lost sight of the ideals upon which it was

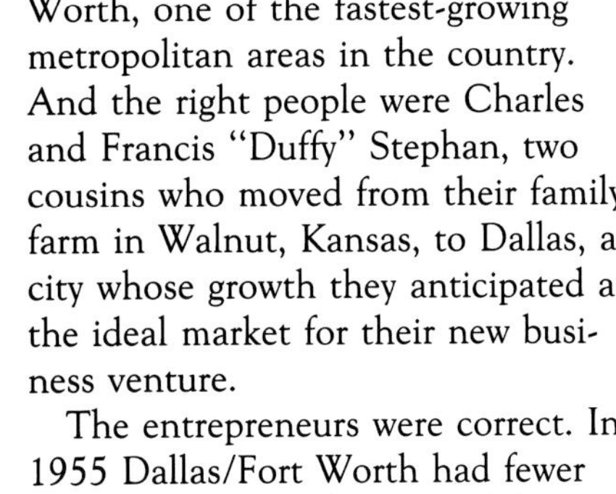

Joe Stephan (left), president of Industrial Catering, talks quality with C.E. "Gene" Burdine, owner of Lone Star Donuts of Dallas.

founded: quality food and service, loyalty to the hard work of its employees, and a fierce dedication to the area it serves. "Ours is a right time, right idea, right place, and right people story," says operations manager Gerald "Sarge" Griesinger.

The right time was the company's founding in 1955. The right idea was the creation of an industrial catering service to feed the area's booming development and construction crews. The right place was Dallas/Fort

Worth, one of the fastest-growing metropolitan areas in the country. And the right people were Charles and Francis "Duffy" Stephan, two cousins who moved from their family farm in Walnut, Kansas, to Dallas, a city whose growth they anticipated as the ideal market for their new business venture.

The entrepreneurs were correct. In 1955 Dallas/Fort Worth had fewer than 200,000 people. In 1984 the area had a population of approximately three million.

The Stephans began their business with a single catering van, with its sides cut out, offering sandwiches heated in a charcoal oven and cold soft drinks. By the end of their first year the Stephans had built seven routes with eight employees in Grand Prairie, and began a steady period of tremendous growth. Today Industrial Catering has seven computer-linked catering plants in the Dallas/Fort Worth area, and one each in Houston and Pasadena. Between fifty and sixty catering trucks are located at

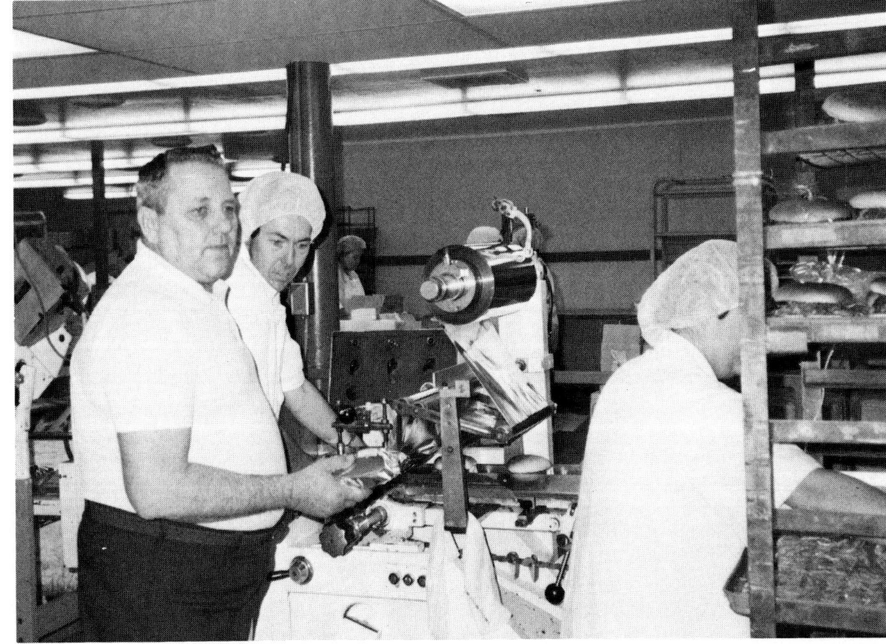

Francis "Duffy" Stephan (left), vice-president and co-owner, checks on quality and wrap as Junior Davis, kitchen manager, looks on. This kitchen produces more than 50,000 food units per day.

Mrs. Gene Skillman (left) has been with Industrial Catering for thirty years. Here she checks route lists with sales manager Jerald Beck, Cindy Wenk, and Joan Bush.

each plant.

"The business was started on a shoestring," says office manager Mrs. Gene Skillman. "It grew because of hard work. The Stephans put in long, hard hours and ran the routes themselves. They took very little money for themselves, working unselfishly. They had, and still have, a wonderful vision of what this company needs and should be."

The firm's two owners are indeed Industrial Catering's shining beacons. Joe Stephan came to the business after the death of his brother, founder Charles Stephan, in 1958. Both Joe and Francis are businessmen highly respected by their employees and lease (caterer) operators.

Indeed, one of the chief reasons for the company's success is the dedication of its people. Many of Industrial Catering's officers celebrated their twentieth or thirtieth anniversary, as the firm celebrated its thirtieth in 1985. Mrs. Gene Skillman has been with the Stephans since the company's founding thirty years ago. Fleet manager Don Westhoff has served for twenty-six years, Gerald Griesinger for twenty, sales manager Jerald Beck for fourteen, Houston manager Jon Griesinger for sixteen, and production manager Junior Davis for ten (including his years with Western Catering). Additionally, many plant managers have been with the firm for ten to fifteen years.

Tenure of service is a great asset at Industrial Catering, which promotes its employees from within and starts each person at a bottom level. All employees, however, share in the corporate philosophy that hard work deserves great rewards. "Our company works on a 'no-work, no pay' phi-

Fleet manager Don Westhoff (right) checks on the production of a new catering box with Reggie Combs. Building its own boxes gives the firm quality control.

losophy," says Gerald Griesinger.

Those who work for the firm enjoy Industrial Catering's self-funded major medical insurance plan, profit-sharing and stock option plans, regular bonuses, an in-house training center, and an excellent safety program with regular rewards for safety. Caterers receive $60 for each accident-free year, $125 for two years, and $1,000 for five years.

The GM trucks that the caterers drive are also treated with great care, in the firm's in-house truck shop. Industrial Catering builds its own catering boxes and coffee pots, and handles its own maintenance. "We never send a catering truck out that doesn't have everything needed for appearance and for safety," says Griesinger. "We take great pride in our fleet. We've been awarded several times for having the number one catering fleet in the United States. This is due largely to the work of Don Westhoff, our fleet manager."

A major ingredient in the company's fierce corporate pride is that the driver of each Industrial Catering truck is an independent operator, earning his own living. This fact pushes incentive and stokes efficiency. Representatives regularly call on prospective businesses, convincing them that fresh food from one of Industrial Catering's daily routes is far better for employees than a room full of vending machines.

Working together, however, is only part of the Industrial Catering story. The firm also plays together, at its sparkling I-Care Center, one of the largest company-owned physical fitness facilities in the United States. The center stands on fifteen acres across the street from the firm's corporate offices. It features a jogging track, softball field, short golf course, a full-size gym, and weight room, wet and dry sauna, whirlpool, and swimming pool. "In 1981 we began to realize that physical fitness was a goal to attain for good health and higher production among our people," explains Griesinger.

The I-Care Center is a great symbol of Industrial Catering's pride and devotion. Each employee and caterer receives regular physicals. No smokers are hired. Smokers already working for the company are encouraged to quit. The dedication to physical fitness has paid off in more than just soaring sales figures. It has contributed to better health of the caterers and employees.

It is this attitude of being fit to win that has guided Industrial Catering through its first thirty years, and the ingredients that founded the business will power its growth in the future.

Chuck Suitor (left) and James Swadley (third from left) have been with Industrial Catering for thirty years. Both Herman Hogan (second from left) and Doug Leverett (right) are twenty-year caterers.

Cindy Wenk (on bench) and Joan Bush (standing) take advantage of the I-Care Center, a health and fitness facility used to promote good health and unity among employees, caterers, and the community.

W.W. CANNON COMPANY, INC.

W.W. "Bill" Cannon

Since 1938 W.W. Cannon Company, Inc., of Dallas has been serving its customers' materials-handling and storage-planning needs.

W.W. "Bill" Cannon opened his enterprise on South St. Paul Street with a small stack of steel shelves and lockers. Although the little business was adversely affected when World War II interrupted the production of steel items for civilian use, it began to flourish after the war when manufacturers resumed production of steel shelves and storage products. Important factors in this growth were the innovative and quality products that Cannon continually added to his line.

In 1945 the founder's brother, L.H. "Jack" Cannon, joined the growing company as salesman for the automotive division. The two brothers were insistent on providing expert advice and quality products to their customers. They established business relationships that continue today with L.H. Cannon's son, Jack W. Cannon, who became a member of the firm after his graduation from college in 1967. The company's president since 1977, he attributes the growth of W.W. Cannon to the legacy of his uncle and father—belief in good service and a quality product. Jack Cannon died in 1973; Bill Cannon died in 1981.

Repeatedly, the organization was the first in the area to offer a new product to its customers. In the 1950s the "nut and bolt" type steel shelves were replaced with Borroughs-brand shelves, which are on brackets that

L.H. "Jack" Cannon

allow the customer to adjust them quickly and without tools. W.W. Cannon continues to represent Borroughs: For the past ten years it has been the manufacturer's number one dealer.

Also in the 1950s W.W. Cannon began selling a completely adjustable type of pallet racks. In the beginning the Cannon sales staff had to explain the product's use to customers. Today it is a rare large-storage facility that does not use a pallet rack for storing items that rest on wooden pallets. Forklifts can easily retrieve the loaded pallets from the racks.

In 1952 the company purchased land at 9739 Denton Drive and erected an 8,000-square-foot office and warehouse. An addition, constructed in 1976, brought the total square footage to 27,400.

The firm was incorporated in August 1953, and in June 1959 the W.W. Cannon Company of Houston was established. Sales offices in Oklahoma City, Fort Worth, Albuquerque, San Antonio, Austin, and Tulsa have subsequently been opened.

Jack W. Cannon's future plans include ensuring that each of the organization's eight sales offices grows to dominate its market—a goal well within reach. In addition to a complete selection of storage products that represent over 100 manufacturers, the corporation offers one of the largest inventories available in the Southwest.

The Cannon sales staff has decades of experience in saving the com-

Jack W. Cannon

pany's 2,500 to 3,000 customers space, time, and money by selecting the best products to solve their storage problems. The success of the sales force is proven by the fact that well over 50 percent of the organization's business is repeat business.

"We care about our customers," Jack W. Cannon relates. "We want to sell to them today, tomorrow, next year, and ten years from now."

THE ADOLPHUS

The Adolphus is Dallas' oldest and newest tradition. Since it underwent a dramatic $40-million renovation in 1981, other impressive changes have transformed the grand dame of Dallas hotels into an even more stunning and impressive showcase for quality and grandeur.

"If you have seen the TV show 'Hotel,' which is about an old hotel with fresh, young faces—that's us," says general manager, Ed deVries. "Not the old stuffy atmosphere."

The chief ingredient in this resurgence of The Adolphus is the input of the hotel's owner, Pat Colee of Westgroup, Inc., of Los Angeles. When the group first remodeled the hotel, it left an outside management group to take over day-to-day operations. Now, however, Colee and Westgroup are personally involved in the 21-story, 435-room hotel.

"They [the owners] were so committed to the artwork, interior decorating, and overall quality of the hotel, they felt they had to do it themselves," says deVries. "This commitment shows that they want to do everything first class. It's very different when a hotel is run by a corporation. The owners went through each room and personally redecorated. What we are trying to do is keep the old-style, famous hotel with an up-to-date atmosphere."

In keeping with that philosophy, The Adolphus is a combination of elegant antiques and fresh, bright attitudes. The hotel's collection of antiques and artwork is believed to be the finest of any American hotel. It numbers more than 200 rare pieces, and includes Flemish tapestries, an early nineteenth-century painting of Napoleon Bonaparte in ermine coro

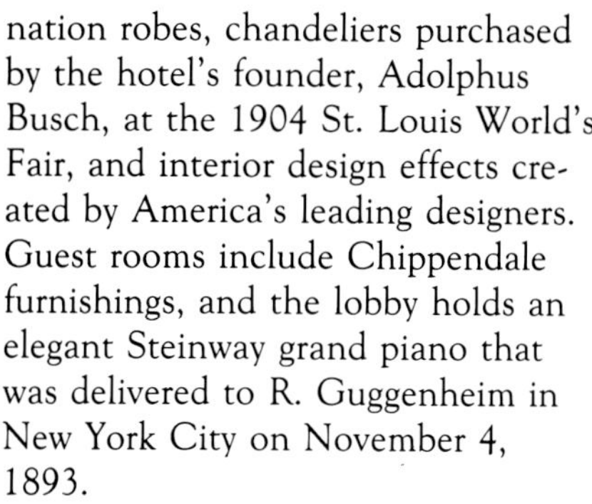

Rare paintings provide a rich background for The Adolphus' lobby, where high tea is served.

nation robes, chandeliers purchased by the hotel's founder, Adolphus Busch, at the 1904 St. Louis World's Fair, and interior design effects created by America's leading designers. Guest rooms include Chippendale furnishings, and the lobby holds an elegant Steinway grand piano that was delivered to R. Guggenheim in New York City on November 4, 1893.

The hotel's past, however, is one of the most dazzling features of The Adolphus, and its story is perhaps one of the richest in Texas hotel history. It was built in 1912 by St. Louis beer baron Adolphus Busch as a token of esteem for the city Busch considered his second home. Since then, the hotel has been the base around which the city of Dallas grew. Throughout the 1900s The Adolphus has ushered in the city's rites of passage: from the grand balls of the 1920s to the Texas-OU football celebration that rages through downtown Dallas each October.

Since its renovation, The Adolphus has brought many new "traditions" to the city: the institution of the lobby high tea, now a centerpiece of many fine hotel afternoons, and three stellar in-house restaurants, crowned by the critically acclaimed French Room.

The French Room restaurant features what is regarded as among the finest French cuisine in the country. It is guided by one of the world's most noted chefs, Jean Banchet, whose Le Francais outside Chicago continually receives critical praise. The French Room itself has grown to be quite a celebrity as well, winning a score of awards, including the coveted 1984 *Travel/Holiday* magazine award for dining distinction, which cited the French Room as "one of the outstanding restaurants of the world." The restaurant's surroundings are as exciting as the food, with large, colorful chandeliers, hand blown in Italy, casting a wonderful glow over

Patrons can enjoy cocktails in the elegant surroundings of the French Room bar.

columns in faux marble, bas-reliefs, and a handmade carpet in fifty-nine colors.

The hotel is located in the heart of Dallas' business district and is convenient to all that the vibrant city offers. To help in steering visitors through the city, The Adolphus' concierge is ready with a stock of information, tips, guides, and contacts. Recently the hotel was the recipient of the American Automobile Association's Five Diamond Award, bestowed only to establishments that provide the finest guest facilities, services, and atmosphere, and are therefore regarded as the best hotels in America.

Indeed, inside The Adolphus' palatial confines, two wonderful worlds meet, one of elegance and tradition, the other of contemporary expertise and comfort.

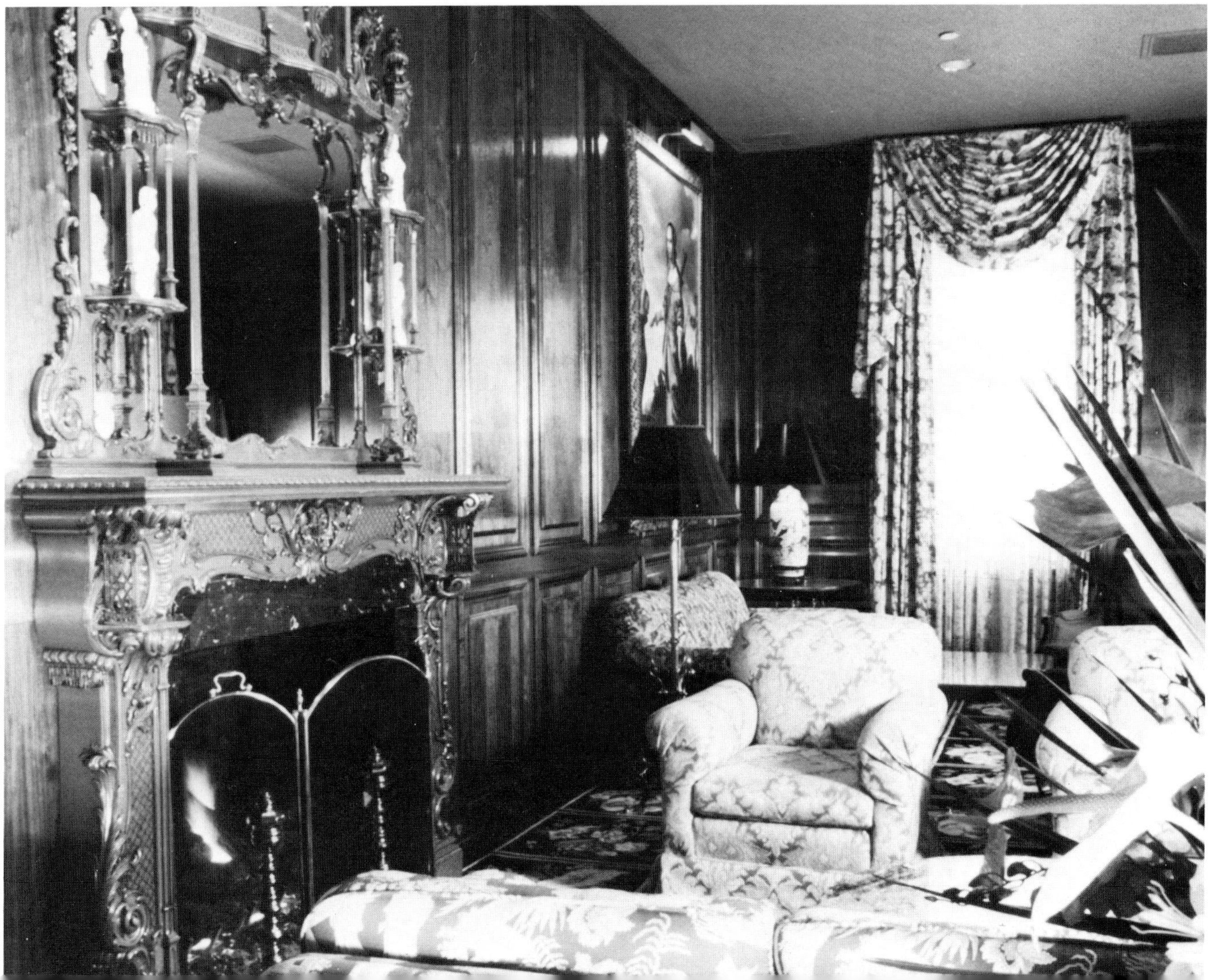

HALL-MARK ELECTRONICS CORPORATION

Hall-Mark Electronics Corporation may be the quietest big business in Dallas. The company, which distributes electronic systems and individual components supplied by major manufacturers, is the fifth-largest dollar-volume industrial electronics distribution firm in the country. The 25-year-old business had year-end 1984 revenues of $357 million and serves its nationwide customer base through thirty-two distribution centers.

Nestled in a North Dallas industrial complex, Hall-Mark works quietly, but carries big clout. The firm is truly one of Dallas' finest success stories. Hall-Mark's founder and chairman Jack Turpin states, "Though the general public might not know us, we are well known in the electronics industry."

In 1981 the Dallas-born company was sold to the Tyler Corporation. Today it remains Tyler's largest wholly owned subsidiary.

"In the late 1950s two significant developments took place: the beginning of the computer age and the beginning of the space program," says Turpin. "Technologies demanded by those two began the high-technology component business as we know it today."

However, industrial distribution centers at that time were located where the majority of the burgeoning electronics activity was located, in Southern California—and surely not in dry-docked Texas. Hall-Mark was born to serve the space program, particularly the NASA Crescent, which started in St. Louis, ran down to Dallas and Houston, and curved over to Florida. The government-oriented space program, which required high-technology materials to grow, became Hall-Mark's first customer.

The boom in the high-technology field, however, increased the electronic component needs of many businesses. Hall-Mark Electronics became the first, and remains the only, top-ten electronics distributor to be headquartered in the Southwest.

The company was founded in 1962

Hall-Mark Electronics Corporation opened for business at 4520 North Central Expressway in Dallas in January 1962.

by Jack Turpin, a former U.S. Navy officer who had held marketing positions with Westinghouse Electric Corporation for eight years. "There was a void in electronics distribution in the Southwest, and that's why we founded the company," he says. "The void was in the marketing of electrical components of a high-technology nature to the original equipment manufacturer, which was Hall-Mark's customer base. Our purpose was to serve that marketplace. You had fast-moving technology coming in as a result of the semiconductor phenomenon that then required totally new concepts in serving the customer. Our goal was to assist our customer in applying the high-tech products of the component manufacturer to meet the needs of our customer."

Turpin's concept of simply serving his customers resulted in the firm's slogan, "Hall-Mark Cares, Hall-Mark Serves." The corporation has done well in carrying out this slogan.

Turpin opened his doors with a staff of four on Dallas' bustling North Central Expressway. Early cus-

tomers included Collins Radio, Texas Instruments, and General Dynamics. In its first year Hall-Mark had sales of $222,000. Second-year sales were $1,060,000. Third-year figures reached $2.5 million. Today the company employs more than 1,350 people.

Hall-Mark distributes electronic components and systems products such as board-level products, capacitors, connectors, computer disk drives, high-speed printers, fans, modems, motors, relays, semiconductors, and switch products. Altogether, the firm stocks more than 70,000 different items in its mission of serving as the link between the manufacturer and the end customer.

Hall-Mark's mission has proven enormously successful. "We've far exceeded the growth of the industry, by continually achieving greater market penetration in all of our geographic locations, while expanding

Jack A. Turpin, founder, chairman of the board, and chief executive officer of Hall-Mark Electronics Corporation.

from Dallas to the entire United States," says Turpin.

The turning point in becoming a true national giant came in 1981, when Hall-Mark was acquired by Tyler Corporation. Before 1981 Hall-Mark served less than 40 percent of the available U.S. market. Today it serves approximately 95 percent of the available market on a nationwide basis. Hall-Mark's customer base exceeds 50,000 firms.

"The commitment and talents of our people are what makes this kind of growth possible," says Turpin. "The key to the business is anticipating our customers' needs, caring about the customer enough to meet those needs, and then meeting them. That's why Hall-Mark Electronics is here, and that's why, the Lord willing, we'll be here another twenty-five years from now."

Hall-Mark's corporate headquarters is located at 11333 Pagemill Road in Dallas.

HALLIBURTON COMPANY

Since 1919, when Erle P. Halliburton first rode a horse-drawn wagon into the Texas and Oklahoma oil fields, armed with his "new and improved" method for cementing oil wells, the Halliburton Company has continually sought improvements in petroleum production technology.

Today Halliburton is one of the world's largest and most diversified oil field services companies as well as one of the nation's largest industrial and marine engineering and construction firms. The corporate headquarters is located in Dallas, and general offices and plants of the major operating groups are in Duncan, Oklahoma; Dallas; and Houston.

Like many of the giants in Texas industry, Halliburton sprang from little more than the imagination and the drive of its founder.

Erle P. Halliburton had his first contact with the oil industry in 1916, when he went to work for the Perkins Oil Well Cementing Company. "The two best things that ever happened to me in business," he later said, "were being hired and then fired by the Perkins Company." Halliburton was discharged because he had suggested too many new ideas.

In 1919 he took his better ways to the oil boom at Burkburnett, Texas. A borrowed pump, wagon and team, and a hastily built mixing box of two-by-twelve boards became his Better Method Oil Well Cementing Company.

In those early fields every new gusher brought in a host of speculators. For them cementing the steel pipe in a well to improve control and to keep oil out of the water table was just a silly conservation technique; it had no value for lifting oil. For the fledgling company business was lean. Only with the backing

Erle P. Halliburton, founder.

from a foursome of roughneck friends did it survive at all.

But in 1920 oil was discovered near Ardmore, Oklahoma. To find more work Halliburton moved his small company across the Red River to Wilson, Oklahoma, and changed its name to the Halliburton Oil Well Cementing Company.

It was in those early days that one of Halliburton's major contributions to oil field cementing technology— the jet mixer—was developed. This device ended the laborious chore of mixing by hand the 250 sacks of cement used each day to cement a shallow well. Today's jet mixer can pump thousands of sacks of scientifically blended mixture into the world's deepest wells in less than two hours.

As the mid-continent fields spread, the business grew. In 1921 the headquarters was moved to Duncan, and a supply base and a machine shop were added.

Today Duncan is the headquarters of the company's Halliburton Ser-

This was Halliburton's first cementing unit, consisting of little more than a horse-drawn wagon, a pump, and a mixing box, at a well site in southern Oklahoma in 1920. Erle Halliburton is operating the high-pressure hose at the mixing box.

vices Division. In addition to major manufacturing and administrative facilities, Halliburton Services boasts the oil field service industry's foremost research center, where some 4,000 different projects are under way at any given time in thirty-five separate laboratories. Also located at Duncan is the Halliburton Energy Institute, which serves as a training center for both employees and customers. The firm's extensive training programs have resulted in its having the best-trained personnel in the oil field service industry.

Not far from where Erle Halliburton started his business, Herman Brown and his brother-in-law, Dan Root, were also active in 1919, forming a partnership to build roads in Central Texas. In recalling that beginning, Brown would laugh and explain, "Eighteen mules and a mustache put me into business."

That association, known as Brown & Root, ultimately became one of the nation's largest industrial and marine engineering and construction firms. Halliburton Company acquired Brown & Root in 1962.

Along the way Halliburton Company has acquired a number of other business ventures, beginning in 1957 with Welex Jet Services Inc. of Fort Worth. The company, which became Halliburton's Welex Division, is now headquartered in Houston. Otis Engineering Corporation of Dallas was acquired two years later, Highlands Insurance Company of Houston was purchased in 1963, and Dallas-based Life Insurance Company of the Southwest was added in 1965. IMCO Services of Houston, which originally was jointly owned with another company, was acquired outright in 1971; NUS Corporation, a Gaithersburg, Maryland, engineering and environmental services consultant, was purchased in 1978.

A milestone was reached in 1948, when Halliburton Oil Well Cementing Company's common stock was listed for trading on the New York Stock Exchange. The corporation changed its name to Halliburton Company in July 1960 and moved its headquarters to Dallas in 1961. At its incorporation in 1924, Halliburton had fifty-six people on its payroll. Today over 65,000 men and women work for the company around the world.

Erle Halliburton based his success on a simple philosophy. He explained, "Strength in an individual or a company or a country is not in being something, but rather in producing something . . . something that goes in the right direction."

Wherever Halliburton Company has gone, it has carried this philosophy. The firm has enjoyed exemplary international relations since its first fleet of pumping units rolled into Canada in 1929.

Today the transnational corporation operates or sells products in more than eighty-five nations. Much of the equipment, tools, technology, and engineering comes from bases in the United States. Yet operations in many countries are staffed entirely by well-trained citizens of those nations. Outside the United States 90 percent of Halliburton employees are non-U.S. citizens.

"It is not my idea just to make money out of a country," Erle Halliburton said in the early 1930s, "but to develop it and to raise the economic standards of its people."

In 1984 the firm, through a subsidiary in the United Kingdom, helped to advance petroleum marine technology by constructing and setting the hull section of Conoco U.K. Ltd.'s revolutionary new tension-leg platform. This structure, shown here leaving a yard in Scotland, will make possible the recovery of oil and gas from water depths in excess of 2,000 feet.

DIAMOND SHAMROCK CORPORATION

"Diamond Alkali got together with Shamrock Oil and Gas in 1967, and you might say that they're now living happily ever after."

That is how William H. Bricker, chairman and chief executive officer of Diamond Shamrock Corporation, describes the merger that gave birth to this billion-dollar company.

Indeed, the 1967 "marriage" of Shamrock Oil and Gas, of Amarillo, to Diamond Alkali, a Cleveland chemical company, resulted in a dynamic oil and gas company. Today's Dallas-based Diamond Shamrock Corporation, whose businesses are oil and gas, coal, and chemicals, ranks among the top 100 on *Fortune* magazine's list of the 500 largest U.S. industrial firms.

The two fiercely independent, and seemingly unrelated, companies seemed unlikely candidates for a partnership. In the 1960s both were strong, intermediate-size enterprises. Shamrock Oil and Gas did not have the muscle, however, to diversify and buy a chemical company, which was the trend in the oil industry in the 1950s and 1960s.

But Shamrock was definitely a candidate for acquisition. Many major oil companies came courting, but Shamrock was unwilling to bow to someone else's command.

"We'd have been rich, [had we accepted the offers[," said C.A. Cash, former chairman of the board. "But we would have lost our birthright to drill our own wells, to eat our own mistakes, to hit our own producers."

Meanwhile, Diamond Alkali was a large, successful chemical company, but it wasn't in the same league as Dow, Du Pont, Union Carbide, and Monsanto. But like Shamrock, it was a hot acquisition property, and oil companies courted Diamond Alkali just as they courted Shamrock Oil and Gas.

Raymond R. Evans was running the Diamond Alkali organization as president during this period. The grandson of the two founders, Evans could see, as Cash pointed out, "that in the age of plastics, a petrochem-

ical combine was the wave of the future, but he didn't want to be gobbled up by a big oil company anymore than Shamrock did."

Then came the unorthodox approach: Why couldn't a chemical company buy into an oil company? The oil company could tend its own business, and the chemical company could enjoy the benefits of the additional cash flow. The combination would also assure Diamond Alkali that it would get the petrochemical raw materials it required for its products.

Corporate leaders thought that the idea was a great one, and in 1967 Diamond Shamrock was formed. Years later a new logo was designed: three green diamonds that form a stylized shamrock.

Then, in 1969, William H. Bricker joined Diamond Shamrock. The son of a Michigan farmer, Bricker had graduated from Michigan State University and began an extremely successful career in agricultural chemicals.

Bricker, who was elected chief executive officer in 1976 and chairman in 1979, was the guiding force in the complete integration of the two industries—chemical and oil and gas.

"In the first half of the 1970s we vastly expanded our oil and gas exploration efforts," Bricker explains. Under his guidance, Diamond Shamrock management continued to look beyond the present for opportunities that would mean profitable growth and would enable the firm to prosper over the long term. More and more the future pointed toward energy businesses.

Consequently, the company began dramatically increasing its inventory

---

Shamrock Oil and Gas had grown from one station in 1932 to 200 by the mid-1940s. The Amarillo-based company was a forerunner to Diamond Shamrock Corporation, which today markets more than 2,000 independent and company-owned outlets.

of undeveloped leasehold acreage and launched an aggressive offshore drilling program. Reserves and production rose rapidly. Diamond Shamrock's transformation into a domestic integrated oil and gas company had begun.

Today the firm operates as five separate companies.

The Exploration Company's drilling rights extend over 3.7 million acres in the United States and Canada. Natural gas accounts for 75 percent of the company's production and reserves, though the focus is steadily shifting toward oil. The firm has committed its fortunes and future to the oil and gas industries. In 1984 nearly two-thirds of total capital spending went to exploration and production of oil and gas. Diamond Shamrock drilled approximately 300 net oil and gas wells in 1984, more than twice the previous year's drilling.

The International Petroleum Company's exploration and production activities extend from the Mediterranean to the China Sea. The newest of the five ventures, International Petroleum is responsible for oil and gas exploration, development, and production beyond the North American shores. At the core of this enterprise is the property acquired with Natomas Company in 1983. Natomas' oil production off Indonesia boosted Diamond Shamrock's oil reserves by 300 percent and production by 600 percent; Japan is the chief market for the Indonesian oil.

The Refining and Marketing Company believes that low-cost production at its strategically located refineries, and high-powered marketing in twelve states, is at the heart of the operating company's success. In 1983 Diamond Shamrock purchased the refining and marketing assets of Sigmor Corporation, a pioneer in the concept of combining self-service fuel outlets with convenience stores. From one gasoline outlet in 1932 to 200 stations in 1946, Diamond Shamrock now has 2,000 independent and company-owned outlets in the South-

west.

The Diamond Shamrock Coal Company began with the acquisition of Falcon Seaboard, Inc., in 1979, a Kentucky-based producer of high-quality sub-bituminous coal. Other acquisitions followed. In 1981 Diamond Shamrock's coal reserves were increased 70 percent with the purchase of Amherst Coal Company of West Virginia. Diamond Shamrock also has reserves in Pennsylvania, Illinois, Montana, and Alaska, bringing the firm's reserve total to more than 1.3 billion tons. Currently Diamond Shamrock is beginning the development of a one-billion-ton Alaskan coal resource that could prove to be the Pacific Rim's cheapest energy source.

Efficiency is the 75-year-old company's marketing edge. While no longer a soda ash producer, Diamond Shamrock Chemicals Company produces and markets hundreds of chemicals. These chemicals constitute its three divisions: chlor-alkali, soda products, and process chemicals. Commitment to the customer is what sets the division, which operates internationally, apart from the competition. Diamond Shamrock Chemicals Company could stand alone on the list of *Fortune* 500 industrial corporations.

Diamond Shamrock Corporation's strengths have been tested repeatedly during the first half of the 1980s. The surplus worldwide capacity to produce oil, natural gas, coal, and refined products has created a fiercely competitive energy market that pushes prices downward despite increased demand. In the face of this current difficult situation, the five companies that operate as Diamond Shamrock reported a combined record 1984 revenue of $4.5 billion. Looking ahead, corporate chairman Bricker attributes Diamond Shamrock Corporation's operating efficiency and flexibility, financial strength, and the "first-rate performance of dedicated employees," as reasons why the firm's 12,000 employees should be optimistic about their future.

ROCKWELL INTERNATIONAL

The presence of two large Rockwell International facilities in Richardson, Texas, has contributed significantly to the emergence of the Dallas/Fort Worth metroplex as one of the most important high-technology centers in the nation.

In the 1950s, Rockwell's Collins divisions were in the vanguard of the movement that led to the growth of today's high-tech corridor through North Dallas and the suburbs of Richardson and Plano.

The company's 6,500 local employees position Rockwell as Richardson's largest employer. Its annual payroll is approximately $170 million.

The firm's facility at Alma and Arapaho roads is headquarters for Rockwell's Commercial Electronics Operations, which includes three major businesses: Telecommunications, headquartered at the same site; Avionics, with headquarters in Cedar Rapids, Iowa; and Semiconductor Products, located in Newport Beach, California. These businesses employ some 15,000 people.

Also located at the Alma Road site is the Collins Transmission Systems Division, the largest of the Telecommunications businesses and one of the principal suppliers of lightwave (or fiber-optics) systems to the telephone industry. This division had its beginnings in Richardson in the 1950s, when it began pioneering the application of microwave communications. Since that time the company has been a leader in microwave technology, and today is the largest independent supplier of microwave communications systems.

Another large facility, located at Shiloh and Renner roads, is operated by Collins Defense Communications (CDC), a part of Rockwell's Defense Electronics Operations. This facility is headquarters for CDC's High Frequency Communications Division, and is one of the world's leading suppliers of command/control/communications/intelligence (C³I) systems. CDC has a role in every major element of the nation's strategic

communications network, known as the Minimum Essential Emergency Communications Network. Transportable and data communication systems and products manufactured at the Shiloh facility are key elements also in many tactical C³I networks.

Rockwell's involvement in Dallas began with an investment in Collins Radio Company in 1971. The two companies merged in 1973.

Originally headquartered in Cedar Rapids, Collins had started the Richardson facility in the 1950s, and later moved its corporate headquarters there.

Rockwell's role today in telecommunications is a natural outgrowth of Collins' beginning. Arthur A. Collins founded his company in 1931 (incorporated in 1933) and immediately started establishing a heritage of technological leadership and product quality.

Rockwell's Collins Transmission Systems Division is one of the nation's leading suppliers of lightwave communications systems and the largest independent supplier of microwave systems.

In 1933 CBS purchased the Collins transmitters that permitted Admiral Richard E. Byrd to make his historic public broadcasts from Antarctica.

During World War II the company was a leading supplier of communications systems to the Armed Forces, and later was cited as being a major factor in winning the war in the Pacific.

Over the years divisions at the Richardson facility have been involved in a long series of high-technology programs. For example, the firm participated in the first transmission of a photograph via a man-made satellite (a photo of President Eisenhower was transmitted from Cedar Rapids, bounced off the

Collins (now Rockwell) built a worldwide network of space tracking and communications antennae for the Apollo program.

From a single building constructed in the late 1950s, the Collins facility (now Rockwell) had grown into this complex by the late 1960s.

orbiting Echo balloon, and received in Richardson); designed, constructed, and installed a world-circling network of fifteen earth stations that enabled NASA to track and communicate with Apollo spacecraft during their voyages, including those to the lunar surface; conducted the first satellite transmission of a stereophonic program; installed advanced communications systems on Air Force One, the Presidential aircraft; installed communications systems on the TACAMO aircraft, which relay messages from the National Command Authority to the Ballistic Missile submarine fleet; provided Saudi Arabia with the largest microwave network ever conceived for implementation at one time; integrated advanced high-frequency communications systems at major Strategic Air Command (SAC) locations in the United States and at SAC bases overseas; became one of the pioneers in lightwave transmission, the communications technology of the future; and provided high-technology communications systems on thousands of other government aircraft, ranging from helicopters to wide-bodied jet transports.

The company supports more than 160 civic, educational, and community organizations in the Dallas area. In addition, it has taken a leadership position in area business, playing a major role in the effort to increase and enhance higher education

By the 1980s the Alma Road complex had attracted many other businesses.

opportunities in the Dallas/Fort Worth metroplex.

Rockwell International is a multi-industry company applying advanced technology to a wide range of products in its aerospace, electronics, automotive, and general industries.

AVIALL

Aviall's Fixed Based Operation is located at Love Field in Dallas.

The name Aviall is relatively new in the aviation industry, but the company it represents has a history of more than fifty years of service to the industry.

In 1981 two venerable institutions—Cooper Airmotive, Dallas, Texas, and Aviation Power Supply, Burbank, California—combined to form Aviall, a company involved in all segments of the aviation support industry. With 2,500 employees— 1,900 of whom are located in Dallas— Aviall is a $400-million international wholly owned operating division of Ryder System, Inc., and the largest independent turbine engine repair and overhaul agency in the world.

Aviall overhauls and services engines of regional and national commercial carriers, including Southwest, Braniff, Continental, Piedmont, Ozark, Air California, and USAir, in addition to corporate aircraft and helicopter engines.

But engine overhauling—which can run up to $500,000 per airliner engine—is only one facet of this diverse organization. Aviall can not only overhaul an airplane engine, it can supply an aircraft with new parts, fuel it, or house the plane in its hangars in Dallas.

The firm has five major activities: complete engine service for corporate aircraft; complete engine service programs for airlines; complete service for industrial turbines; an aircraft parts distribution system covering five continents; and operation of one of the world's largest private aircraft terminals.

Aviall's distribution of aircraft engine parts and components now has annual sales of approximately $160 million and has grown to over fifty branch outlets worldwide, linked predominantly by a computer network to determine where any part is in the system. This enables Aviall to get parts where and when they are needed.

In Dallas, Aviall's most visible activity is its Aircraft Services Division at Love Field, Red Bird, and Addison airports. Aviall's Love Field operation has 480,000 square feet of hangar space, a terminal that services 100 planes a day and pumps seven million gallons of fuel a year. Aviall's

Aviall provides airline turbine engine maintenance and management programs.

Turbine engine repair and overhaul for industrial applications is only one facet of this diverse organization.

Aviall overhauls and services both corporate aircraft and the engines of regional and national commercial carriers.

Love Field terminal is among the best-known and most popular business aviation terminals in the country. In an annual survey conducted among professional pilots, Aviall is consistently ranked among the best in the country.

In addition to aviation the company's industrial sector overhauls turbine engines used in the oil and gas industry for power generation, pipeline transmission, and gas collection.

All of these services are performed under a motto that represents the firm's pride and longtime reputation for quality service: "People, Skills, and Experience You Can Depend On." In fifty years the companies that formed Aviall have attained some impressive accomplishments: winning maintenance contracts for critical components on the aircraft that carried President Franklin Roosevelt during World War II; winning the first Air Force jet engine maintenance contract ever let to an independent company and the first jet shop certification granted by the FAA; winning the first certification given by United Technologies' Turbo Power and Marine Systems to perform shop overhaul on aeroderivative industrial gas turbines.

Aviall's tradition of quality began in 1932, in the aircraft mechanical shop of Edward F. Booth at Love Field in Dallas. Booth's shop evolved into Southwest Airmotive in 1940, and became a leader after World War II in jet overhaul, parts distribution, and terminal facilities for corporate and private aircraft. Meanwhile, in 1933 at Roosevelt Field on Long Island, Standard Aircraft Equipment Company was maintaining U.S. Presidential aircraft and expanding its aircraft parts distribution.

Aviall's modern future began taking shape in 1970, when Cooper Industries, Inc., of Houston bought Dallas Airmotive, then added South

west Airmotive and several other aircraft service firms as subsidiaries. Subsequently, in 1981, Cooper Airmotive and Aviation Power Supply—a major factor in West Coast aircraft repair, overhaul, and support—combined to form Aviall, and on November 12, 1985, Aviall merged with Ryder System, Inc., of Miami, Florida.

Today Aviall's future is bright, no matter what the economy is in air

craft sales. Whether it's an up or a down market in new aircraft sales, Aviall's business stays much the same. If people aren't buying new airplanes, they're operating their old ones. And when it comes to servicing their aircraft Aviall can handle the job.

Another facet of Aviall's business is its worldwide aircraft and wholesale parts distribution system.

TEXAS REFINERY CORPORATION

Since its founding on September 9, 1922, the Texas Refinery Corporation has suffered only growing pains. A.M. Pate's and Carl Wollner's Panther Oil & Grease Mfg. Co., the forerunner of Texas Refinery, began manufacturing axle grease, and later auto oils, in a small tin barn located in Fort Worth. The former salesman for a Dallas oil company, Pate, and his keen business-minded partner, Wollner, comprised the entire work force in 1922.

Today Texas Refinery has two plants in Canada, one in Mexico, and another in Luxembourg, in addition to its ever-expanding home office and manufacturing facilities at One Refinery Place in Fort Worth. A worldwide sales force of 5,000 sells TRC's products directly to customers in all fifty U.S. states, and in more than 100 countries.

The steady 63-year growth of the privately held, multimillion-dollar manufacturer of industrial lubricants and protective coatings is attributable to many factors. But A.M. Pate, Jr., TRC's chairman and chief executive officer, who has been with TRC for forty-seven years, believes that the success of his family's company is due mainly to the business policy set forth by his father and Wollner: TRC's founders believed in doing business by the Golden Rule—to treat others as you would have them treat you. Found on the inside of the back cover of every sales manual is TRC's creed. It states, "It is our sincere belief that the Golden Rule is undeniably appropriate for any business operation—to the benefit of everybody associated with the business, either as an employee or as a customer. And it is our unceasing determination to adhere strictly to that policy always."

Panther's modest tin barn housed office and manufacturing operations until 1928, when Pate and Wollner moved to TRC's current location. At that time TRC's thirty salesmen were canvassing thirty-five states.

During the Great Depression TRC was *the* exceptional company; it did not discharge one employee because of the difficult times. In fact, sales grew, though the word "growth" took on a new meaning in the post-Depression period when sales records were set, only to be topped by volume performances.

Growing product demands resulted in the firm outgrowing its facilities. In 1936 that problem was relieved with the completion of a three-story brick building, which became the central administrative office. TRC's executive headquarters remains in this facility.

During the 1930s TRC made more than external changes. In 1934 management developed a new product line to add to the established line of industrial specialty oils and greases: TRC began manufacturing protective coatings used in roofing and related building maintenance items.

Today the lubricant division offers more than 200 products, many of which are lubricating machines that didn't exist in 1922, while the protective coating product line comprises more than fifty products. TRC buys base stocks from other companies and refines them into 250-plus products.

TRC products were first sold outside of the United States in 1939. The export department shipped orders first to North and Central American neighbors. Then orders came from South America, Europe, and beyond. To accommodate worldwide expansion, TRC established a sister corporation in 1948, Texas Refinery Corporation of Canada Ltd., in Toronto. A.M. Pate, Jr., was named the newly formed venture's president. Yet another Canadian plant was built in Moose Jaw, Saskatchewan, in 1953.

In 1960 Texas Refinery Corpora-

Texas Refinery Corporation, an international firm doing business in all fifty U.S. states and more than 100 countries, had its humble beginnings in this tin barn in Fort Worth in 1922.

A.M. Pate, Sr. (left), and Carl Wollner, founders.

tion of Mexico, S.A., was formed, with offices and factory in Mexico City. Foreign plant expansion didn't halt there. In 1962 Texas Refinery Corporation Inter-Continental, S.A., was incorporated, with offices and plant located in Echternach, Luxembourg.

Three years later A.M. Pate, Jr., was elected president of TRC and all international affiliates. Pate relinquished this position to Jerry Hopkins in February 1985. Hopkins began his TRC career in 1958 as an addressograph machine operator. Pate is currently chairman of the board and chief executive officer.

Today the Texas Refinery industrial group boasts eighteen affiliated companies, including Panther Chemical Co., which manufactures industrial cleaners, and National Photographers Album Co., whose photo albums are sold door to door.

In May 1985 a new TRC subsidiary, United States Single-Ply Corp., became fully operational. The wholly owned corporation manufactures only one product, a single-ply roofing membrane. These membranes are self-contained, complete roofing and waterproofing systems in rolls, designed to apply over existing roof systems, or to be used in new construction.

This single-ply roofing, which

TRC formerly purchased from another company, generates half of its coating division sales. The new 21,500-square-foot manufacturing plant is located near TRC's main plant on the corner of Northeast Seventh and North Commerce. United States Single-Ply Corp. is capable of producing 1,200 rolls of the roofing membrane daily.

Wesley Sears, chairman of the executive committee, has been with TRC for fifty-one years. Sears' career spans most of the history of Texas Refinery. Sears says that its sales staff, which is trained by direct mail, is at the core of TRC's success. Sears believes strongly that during economically difficult times, only a strong sales staff will ensure continued corporate growth.

"We have always had a very strong

The firm was still known as Panther Oil & Grease Mfg. Co. when this 1934 photo of the entire staff was taken.

sales incentive," Sears says. "We have developed a philosophy of inspiring our salesmen rather than driving them. We are unique in that we hire salesmen past the age that most people do. A great many are past retirement age. We give them an opportunity, and we think we're lucky because we get all their years of experience."

TRC has also had the good fortune of receiving many years of dedication from its employees. In addition to Pate and Sears, fifteen officers, out of a total of thirty, have worked for TRC for twenty-five years or more. Eight of those fifteen have been with the company thirty years or more.

"We have a high retention of employees. We recognize our people's accomplishments. We have a lot of people who feel comfortable here. We're kind of like a family."

Sears continues, "We're very bullish about the future. We can weather any storm. We have in the past. We're strong financially and that gives us a good feeling. We're just naturally optimistic. We feel that we can make things happen. Our past record and good solid leadership support that belief."

One Refinery Place, the international headquarters of Texas Refinery Corporation in Fort Worth.

UTL CORPORATION

If a brilliant young electrical engineer had not managed to escape from Shanghai, China, on the last plane to leave before the Communists marched in in 1949, the United States might have been denied a major contribution to its sophisticated electronic defenses in the 1980s.

Fortunately, though, Dr. C.C. Lee, a recent engineering graduate of Shanghai's University of Utopia, was able to reach freedom in America and continue his education at The University of Texas in Austin, where he received his Ph.D. in electrical engineering in 1953. Dr. Lee came to the Dallas area and began a promising business career at Atlantic Refining Company and later at Temco Aircraft Corporation, a forerunner of today's E-Systems, Inc.

Today Dr. Lee is president and chief executive officer of the UTL Corporation of Dallas, which he founded after leaving E-Systems in 1968 as director of its Electronic Warfare Department. His company is recognized around the world for the development and production of high-performance, high-reliability Electronic Support Measure Systems—or ESM, as known in the E.W. defense industry. Dr. Lee himself is known throughout the U.S. intelligence community as one of the most innovative architects of modern automated intelligence gathering and processing systems.

Dr. Lee's own personal expertise in his field, plus the outstanding capabilities of his technical staff at UTL Corporation, can be credited for the firm's phenomenal growth and the exemplary reputation it has built as a U.S. Defense Department contractor over the years.

"In addition to himself, Dr. Lee assembled a small nucleus of highly skilled people when he established the company," says UTL vice-president Bernie Bernard, himself a member of that original team. "That first year, we had only twenty employees altogether, but we were able to succeed in a tough field against huge competitors because of our high

C.C. Lee, Ph.D., president and chief executive officer, established UTL Corporation in 1968.

degree of technical know-how."

Incorporated in 1968 as United Technology Laboratories, Inc., the firm was originally located at 4121 Forest Lane in Garland, Texas, and then moved to its own small building at 410 Kirby Street. In October 1974 UTL moved to a larger manufacturing complex and changed its name to UTL Corporation. Today the firm is located in a new facility at 1500 West Mockingbird Lane, Dallas.

From those twenty original employees, the company's total staff has

UTL Corporation of Dallas' new facility. The firm is recognized around the world for the development and production of its Electronic Support Measure Systems, or ESM, as known in the E.W. industry.

grown to 325 persons, most of them highly skilled technical experts. And the annual revenues have soared from just $1.3 million in fiscal 1969 to more than $26.1 million in 1985. By January 1985 UTL had a backlog of more than $60 million in defense contracts.

But these are not the only measures of the firm's important contributions to America's defense establishment. UTL has been entrusted with some of the most exacting assignments related to national defense. It has developed a type of miniaturized ESM

system that is completely integrated and "platform independent," meaning that it can be used in any ground-based, airborne, or shipboard application.

Being a relatively high-tech company, it has been able to take on the giants of the industry and win because of its expertise and capabilities.

AMERICAN PRODUCE AND VEGETABLE COMPANY

James LaBarba's children and grandchildren have inherited the riches of James' lifetime of hard work—American Produce and Vegetable Company, a Dallas food and wine distribution empire. They have also inherited the responsibilities that accompany such a bequest: to continually give American Produce new life in order to ensure its future growth.

LaBarba would, no doubt, be proud to witness the growth his wholesale food and wine operations have experienced in the hands of his descendants. In the past five years the firm that supplies the highest-quality food, food products, and wine to Dallas-area hotels, restaurants, institutions, airlines, grocers, and cafeterias has grown considerably.

LaBarba first came to the United States from Sicily. He began working in the Pennsylvania coal mines, where he might have stayed had it not been for an explosion that almost took his life.

In 1906 LaBarba married Katie Piccola, whom he had known since his childhood in Sicily. Three years later the couple moved to Dallas and opened a grocery store at 2610 Elm Street. They later moved their establishment to the corner of Nussbaumer and Oak streets.

LaBarba saw a need in Dallas for a new and updated produce house; in 1917 he established one at Pearl and Cadiz streets. In 1925 he constructed a building at Cadiz and Preston. It was a filling station, garage, and weigh station.

In 1936 a beer and wine distributing and importing business was added at Cadiz and Harwood. The beer distribution was later dropped. However, today American Wine and Importing Company is one of the largest wine distributors in the state of Texas, representing California wineries, as well as major European wine makers. The wine division operates branches in Houston, San Antonio, Corpus Christi, Midland, and Amarillo.

Also in the 1930s LaBarba established American Trucking Co. to transport his fresh produce from California. Today American trucks travel between California and Texas and the fleet has grown with many permits.

In 1947 "Mr. Jimmy," as he was fondly known to many Dallasites, retired. That same year he handed over the responsibilities of running the business to his five sons, who had been working with him since childhood.

American Produce and Vegetable Company was later restructured into separate divisions, with each son managing a division: Joseph "JoJo" LaBarba, American Produce and Vegetable Company, which currently handles over 3,500 food items; Anthony "Tony" LaBarba, American Wine and Importing Co.; Ernest LaBarba, American Pre-Packaging Co., established in 1953; and Carl LaBarba, American Trucking Co. and Southwest Juice Tree, established in 1979 to supply grocery stores with fresh juice machines and dried fruits and nuts. The fifth son, Sherman LaBarba, died in 1984.

The LaBarbas also own and operate LaBarba Realty Company, which manages properties leased by the other firms within the American organization.

In 1975 James' five sons handed to their six sons a major share of the responsibility for running the business.

The LaBarba family tradition has continued with Ernest and his son, James Ernest, working together in the Pre-Pac Division; Tony and his son, James Anthony, work in wine distribution.

The Food Service Division continues with JoJo and his sons, James Frank and Joseph, and his nephews, Lucian and Roger LaBarba. American Trucking is operated by Carl Michael with the assistance of his father, Carlo.

James "Mr. Jimmy" LaBarba, founder of American Produce and Vegetable Company, proudly poses for this 1947 photo, on the eve of his retirement, with his five sons (from left): Joseph, Anthony, Ernest, Carl, and Sherman.

DSC COMMUNICATIONS CORPORATION

DSC Communications Corporation was created as Digital Switch Corporation in 1976 with the goal of developing and marketing a central office switching system for local telephone companies. But as of early 1981 it was still without product or orders.

Fortunately a window of opportunity was opening. Conditions were changing dramatically in the telecommunications market, and technological advances were making significant advances possible in products and services for this market. DSC found itself in an advantageous position, with more than six million dollars in cash, a state-of-the-art product under development, and available personnel with outstanding management, marketing, and technical expertise.

Actually, the stage was set for changes in the telecommunications market in the 1960s, when Tom

Carter of Dallas obtained a U.S. Supreme Court ruling permitting his "Carterphone" to be used in connection with AT&T's telephone system. This opened the door for competition within the industry.

In 1976 two young engineers joined forces with two stockbrokers from the Washington, D.C., area and established Digital Switch Corporation. They foresaw tremendous demand for a telephone switching system utilizing state-of-the-art digital technology to process and bill telephone calls for local telephone companies. The new enterprise set up operations in Virginia and began work on just such a system.

Meanwhile, other important developments in the telecommunications field were taking place in the Dallas area, which was to become a major spawning ground for the industry. In 1968 James M. Nolan, with others, had founded Danray, Inc., and during the mid-1970s had hired James L. (Jim) Donald to be president of the company, partly on the strength of his eighteen years of experience with Texas Instruments, one of the early giants of the high-tech industry.

During this time a switching system developed by Danray caught the attention of another young firm, MCI Communications Corporation, which was interested in competing for long-distance telephone business. Subsequently, in 1978, Danray was acquired by Northern Telecom Limited; Donald stayed with Northern Telecom and Nolan began looking for new opportunities. One of the opportunities Nolan investigated was Digital Switch. Although it was a struggling venture, he and Donald, who had become disenchanted with Northern, found its potential interesting and saw it as a vehicle to take advantage of a vast opportunity that might not remain open for long.

Thus, in March 1981, armed with

a strong market perception, several years of telecommunications experience, and a conservative-but-aggressive management style, Jim Donald joined DSC in Virginia as chief operating officer. With him he brought two highly qualified engineers, Gunnar Korpinen and Leo Putchinski, who aided him in redirecting DSC's product strategy to focus on the long-distance telephone market.

By June, Donald was chief executive officer of the firm and had convinced Nolan to join it as board chairman. He had also moved DSC to the Dallas area, where the high-technology atmosphere, plentiful engineering talent, positive business attitude, and growth-oriented environment were to be important factors in the firm's success.

From the tiny nucleus of six employees who moved to Dallas in 1981, the company had grown to more than 2,600 employees by mid-1985. This phenomenal growth is symbolic of the high-tech explosion that has hit the Dallas area. "Dallas is becoming a real telecommunications center," says Jim Donald. "Businesses have begun to spawn new businesses. DSC has helped put the North Dallas/Richardson/Plano/Garland area in the country's top five telecommunications manufacturing centers."

By 1984 DSC's revenues had reached $320 million with net earnings of $44 million, ranking it as one of the largest public companies in the Dallas/Fort Worth metroplex in revenue and earnings. It was cited as one of America's top 500 growth companies for 1984, and had captured about 70 percent of the independent long-distance telephone switching market. By this time DSC had also expanded its customer and product base into other areas of the worldwide telecommunications market.

None of this success came accidentally, but as the result of a carefully structured, well-timed plan. In 1981 DSC concentrated all its efforts on completing the development of its first switching system. In 1982 management was beefed up and organiza-

James M. Nolan (left), chairman of the board of directors, and James L. Donald, president and chief executive officer, DSC Communications Corporation. © 1985, Bob Mader

tions were created to manufacture its products, serve its customers, and finance its growth. By the end of that year the firm had achieved a solid financial base through its earnings and both private and public financing transactions. In 1983 new products were introduced, product development programs were expanded, management was again strengthened, and DSC's financial condition was further improved by earnings of $27 million and $110 million in public financing.

In 1984 the company hit full stride, introducing new products as its customer base continued to expand. Development began on the DEX 5, an advanced switching system for local telephone companies. In June DSC acquired Granger Associates, an important step in its long-range plan to expand marketing opportunities by offering a wider variety of telecommunications systems.

In April 1985 the organization changed its name to DSC Communications Corporation to better reflect its long-term goal of becoming a leading worldwide supplier of telecommunications systems.

Later that year it was awarded a contract for digital switching systems in Japan, becoming the first U.S. switch manufacturer to gain entry to the Japanese market. December 1985 marked the successful sale and acceptance of the company's DEX 5 central office switching system.

Today the company is positioned for continued growth, relying on the same basic strengths that have carried it to its present position. DSC is built on a foundation of people—people whose full attention is focused on providing its customers with superior service and products—and on the quality products and financial strength that enable it to serve its customers both well and profitably. That foundation will be expanded in the same orderly fashion in which it has been built from the beginning.

Jim Donald insists that DSC people think of themselves as partners with their customers, in helping them attain their current and future goals. This essential long-term commitment, coupled with a realistic evaluation of future market conditions, gives DSC an excellent opportunity to be a leading international company. In 1986 Donald's goal is to continue building the team of people necessary to take advantage of this opportunity.

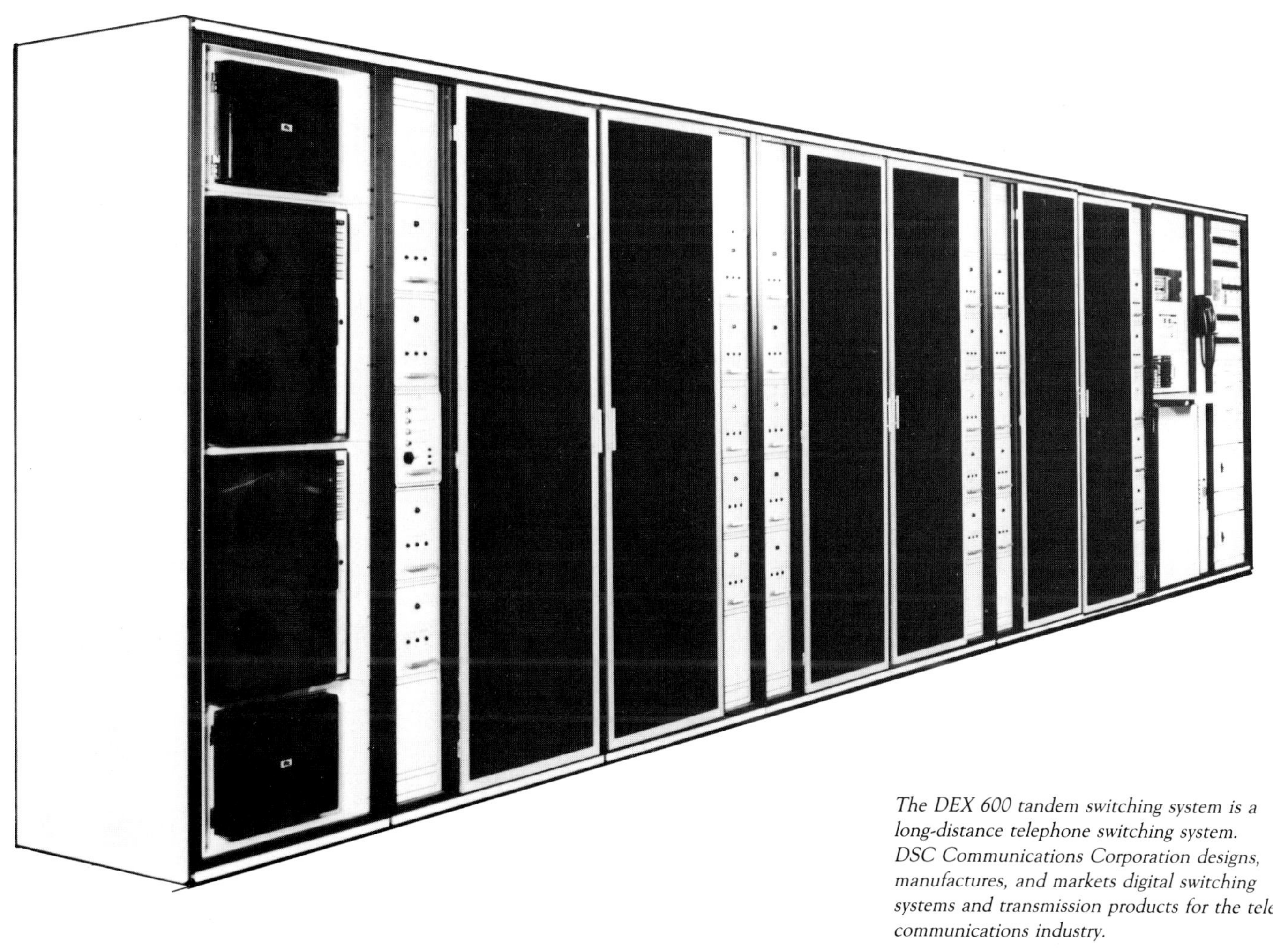

The DEX 600 tandem switching system is a long-distance telephone switching system. DSC Communications Corporation designs, manufactures, and markets digital switching systems and transmission products for the telecommunications industry.

NEC AMERICA, INC.

The international flavor of Texas business in the 1980s is graphically illustrated by the growing presence and contribution of a company that began halfway around the globe in Japan at a time when the Lone Star State was still primarily a land of cattle and cowboys.

Today NEC Corporation is one of the giants of the worldwide information technology industry, and the Texas operations of its U.S. subsidiary, NEC America, Inc., play a vital role in its overall leadership in this exciting, futuristic field.

NEC was founded in Tokyo in 1899 and has developed into one of the largest industrial concerns in the world, with sales of more than eight billion dollars in 1984 and some 78,000 employees in more than ninety plants and other facilities in Japan and a dozen other countries. NEC is engaged in research and development, production and servicing of more than 15,000 diversified products marketed in over 140 nations. It is one of the leading global suppliers of advanced communications systems—from computers to industrial electronic systems, and from electron devices to home electronics products.

Established in 1963 and headquartered in Melville, New York, NEC America maintains major facilities in Dallas, Chicago, Los Angeles, San Francisco, Washington, and Portland. Its Dallas plant was the firm's first production facility when it opened in 1978 on a seventeen-acre site in the Las Colinas area of Irving. Using the latest in advanced technology, it produces some of the most sophisticated telecommunications equipment in the world.

The Las Colinas complex includes two production facilities and an office building and serves as headquarters for NEC America's Switching Group and as an operations site for several corporate divisions. More than 700 people are employed at the complex in a variety of manufacturing, marketing, sales, service, training, and support functions, helping NEC continue to strengthen its U.S. marketing organization and production base.

As the first company in the world to introduce an all-transistorized computer in 1959, NEC is a recognized pacesetter in computer technology and telecommunications. It has built more than half of the world's satellite communications earth stations, installed the world's first commercial optical fiber communications systems, and supplied a wide range of the most advanced electronic switching systems all over the world.

The leadership of NEC believes that the awesome power of the computer and the far-flung reach of communications know no limitations. Together they form the infrastructure of a coming civilization in which information will be as indispensable to mankind as food, energy, and sunlight.

NEC's pioneering efforts in integrating these two great components into a mighty force for human good began more than two decades ago, when NEC chairman and chief executive officer Koji Kobayashi coined the term "C&C"—computers and communications—and charted a new course for the company.

Since then NEC has committed its best efforts toward integrating computers with communications technology and has seen "C&C" become the framework on which the world's information-related "new age" is being constructed.

Clearly, both Texas and NEC have come a long way in the past eighty-seven years. And just as clearly, a long, productive, and mutually rewarding partnership lies ahead for them in the future.

NEC America's first production facility in the United States is located on this seventeen-acre site in the Las Colinas area of Irving, along with headquarters for Switching Systems Division and regional offices for Facsimile, NEC Telephones, Inc., and Data Communications.

TESORO PETROLEUM CORPORATION

Recently, in an effort to promote better relationships between Texas and the People's Republic of China, Dr. Robert V. West, Jr. (left), chairman and chief executive officer of Tesoro Petroleum Corporation, hosted Ambassador Ling Qing, China's Ambassador to the United Nations. The Ambassador was in San Antonio at Dr. West's invitation.

The history of Tesoro Petroleum Corporation centers around substantial growth in a relatively short period of time. Tesoro was founded on December 16, 1964. Since that time it has grown from a small refinery and marginally productive groups of oil fields in the Southwest to a corporation with worldwide interests and annual revenues of nearly three billion dollars. The word *tesoro* means "treasure" in Spanish.

Although Tesoro officially began in 1964, the corporation was the dream of founder Dr. Robert V. West, Jr., several years before. Dr. West, Tesoro's chairman of the board and chief executive officer, received his Ph.D. in chemical and petroleum engineering from The University of Texas in 1949. Then he was hired by a San Antonio-based independent oil company controlled by a wealthy family group with oil and gas prop-

erties in West Texas.

At the time of receiving his degree Dr. West had various offers from large major oil companies but instead chose the small concern where he would have the opportunity to learn every part of the oil business. Dr. West enjoyed the "hands-on" approach, such as working in the oil fields with drilling crews and deciding whether or not to continue drilling at a particular site if oil or gas were encountered in the well, or if drilling problems developed.

Dr. West's spare time was used learning the intricacies of finance, a practice that was to serve him well in later years. Even at an early date he was preparing himself for the founding of his own corporate enterprise in the future. Just prior to forming Tesoro, he was president of Texstar Company, a subsidiary of Texstar Petroleum Corporation that was controlled by the family group.

Even though Dr. West had little actual capital, he managed to arrange for Tesoro to purchase the stock of Texstar Petroleum Company and to combine the two. As he states, "Tesoro was capitalized the only way I could do it—with debt. It was almost 100 percent. It had one of the worst capital structures of any company that's ever been formed."

Despite a shaky start, Tesoro survived and began to grow. A three-way merger with Sioux Oil Company and Intex Oil Company in 1968 was

a real boost for Tesoro. Says Dr. West, "We emerged from that transaction with a viable capital structure, public ownership, and a listing on the American Stock Exchange."

In 1969 Tesoro began reaching beyond Texas and formed a joint venture with the government of Trinidad and Tobago. That same year a new Tesoro refinery was constructed from the "grassroots" on the Kenai Peninsula of Alaska. Today Tesoro, with some 3,000 employees, has oil and gas activities in many states in the United States, as well as Bolivia, Indonesia, Trinidad, and Turkey.

Among its subsidiaries are Tesoro Alaska Petroleum Company, which operates the refinery at Kenai, Alaska, and eighty-four service stations in Alaska; Tesoro Crude Oil Company, which is a gatherer, purchaser, and reseller of crude oil, condensate, and natural gas liquids within the United States and in international markets; Tesoro Petroleum Distributing Company, which sells specialty petroleum products to drilling contractors in the United States; Tesoro Drilling Company, which operates eight drilling rigs in four states; and Land and Marine Rental, which supplies various kinds of equipment to the drilling industry throughout the United States. In addition, Tesoro has eighteen other subsidiaries and affiliates with interests in the United States and various foreign countries.

Petroleum energy will continue to play a vital role in the progress, welfare, and security of the United States, and Tesoro Petroleum Corporation is proud to be a part of the petroleum industry and will attempt to continue to expand its role in that industry to meet the energy challenges of America's future.

The headquarters of Tesoro Petroleum Corporation is located in San Antonio.

LA MANSIÓN HOTELS

The beauty of a Spanish hacienda with twentieth-century comfort aptly describes the three hotels bearing the name La Mansión.

The firm that built these three outstanding hotels is barely twenty years old. The River Hotel Company was established in 1966 to construct a hotel by 1968 for the opening of HemisFair, the pocket-size World's Fair in San Antonio. The site chosen, on the banks of the San Antonio River in the city's downtown, already had a four-story structure that was built in 1852 to house St. Mary's Institute, the first private boys' school in San Antonio. The school was founded by four French Brothers of the Society of Mary.

At that time San Antonio de Bexar was a dusty little village of about 3,000 inhabitants. Its history could be traced back some 130 years. Although San Antonio had been the northernmost regional capital of the Spanish and Mexican governments, its greatest claim to fame, at least in the minds of its inhabitants, was the inspirational role the Battle of the Alamo played in Texas history.

But the Brothers had come not to fight but to build a school, and build it they did. The strong, durable building was later incorporated into part of La Mansión del Rio fronting on College Street. A plaque is affixed to that portion of the hotel proclaiming the former school a Texas Historic Site.

As a school St. Mary's had no trouble drawing students, but paying tuition was another matter, and it was only after the Civil War had ended that the school began to flourish. The original two-story structure became a four-story building, but still it was not enough to accommodate the onrush of students.

The beautiful La Mansión del Rio, part of which was once St. Mary's Institute and is now a Texas Historic Site, is on the banks of the San Antonio River in the city's thriving downtown. Barges carry passengers on sightseeing trips down the river.

In October 1927 the San Antonio Bar Association began using the building for the San Antonio Law School, while other classes were being moved to the west side campus on land purchased several years earlier by the Society of Mary. In 1966 the St. Mary's University School of Law, now known as one of the finest law schools in the Southwest, also moved to the St. Mary's campus on Cincinnati Street. It was soon time for the old school building to begin welcoming travelers and visitors to the Alamo City as the Society of Mary presented the building to La Mansión investors.

Major renovation and internal reconstruction were necessary to create a floor plan suitable for the hotel. The Brothers' gymnasium of the upper level was converted into the upstairs ballroom and boardroom area. But most of the building remained as near as possible to the original layout constructed more than a century earlier.

The elegance of hacienda living is evident in each of the La Mansión hotels. The patios, the colorful Mexican tile, the water fountains, and the large rooms with antique brick walls and ceilings accented by hand-hewn timbers all give the feeling of the Spanish influence in south Texas. Traditional continental furniture is used throughout against a backdrop of warm, contemporary colors.

Ten years after the La Mansión del Rio was opened a second hotel was added. La Mansión del Norte, with 306 rooms, was completed at Loop 410 and McCullough in the burgeoning north side of the city. It carried out the gracious hacienda theme established at the first hotel. Its San Angel restaurant is a multi-winner of *Travel/Holiday* magazine's Fine Dining Award.

Early in 1979 the company grew again, with a multimillion-dollar project at the downtown hotel. Las

Swimmers enjoy the pool at La Mansión del Rio surrounded by Old World charm.

Canarias Restaurant, featuring fine Continental cuisine; 173 rooms; and the million-dollar Iberian Ballroom all were added at the same time, further enhancing La Mansión del Rio's position as a member of the prestigious Preferred Hotels Association, an exclusive international association of independently owned luxury hotels.

In April 1984 River Hotel Company, for the first time, opened a La Mansión Hotel outside San Antonio. La Mansión Austin exhibits the same uncommon attention to detail as the two existing properties. Designer Michael Stelea of Barry Design Associates, Los Angeles, traveled to Mexico exploring centuries-old haciendas, photographing ancient stone fountains to recreate in the hotel's courtyard, and buying antiques and pottery. His discoveries are thoroughly integrated into the hotel's color, textures, and appointments, so that La Mansión Austin is a twentieth-century interpretation of a stately Spanish Colonial home.

Three outstandingly successful hotels have led the River Hotel Company to continue its search in the Southwest for opportunities to build additional La Mansión hotels. Growth is expected to continue, but only on the measured course that emphasizes gracious service and exceptional accommodations at each location.

La Mansión del Norte, at Loop 410 and McCullough, carries on the Spanish hacienda tradition.

AUSTIN INDUSTRIES, INC.

Austin Industries, Inc., a firm recognized across the nation as a builder on a true Texas scale, represents—very literally—a bridge between the proud past of the Lone Star State and the limitless future stretching out ahead.

Known today for such huge projects as Texas' longest bridge and Dallas' tallest building, Austin Industries traces its history back nearly a century to a three-span, stone-and-steel bridge across the Brazos River near Seymour, Texas. That first bridge, constructed in 1889 by George Austin for the George E. King Bridge Company of Des Moines, Iowa, was the first of countless similar jobs in Texas for the firm.

Initially operating as an agent for the Iowa company, and then as an independent contractor, the firm was known by various names as it evolved over the next three decades. George Austin moved to Georgia in 1896, while his brother, Frank, remained in Texas, but they continued in business together in a partnership called Austin Brothers. George set up shop in Atlanta, and Frank supervised the company's Texas operations from Dallas.

In November 1900 Frank Austin hired young Charles R. Moore of Waco, first as a stenographer, then as "Traveling Agent, Contracting Agent, and Chief Engineer" for the firm. It was the beginning of an association between the company the Austins started and Moore and his descendants that has now spanned more than eighty-five years.

In 1908 the Austins severed connections with George E. King Bridge Company and struck out on their own. Two years later they bought a site on Coombs Street in Dallas, where they built a small steel-fabricating plant. As the company grew, Moore, a man of many talents, became a driving force within it.

When Austin Brothers, Contractors, was incorporated in 1914, Moore was named secretary of the firm and a member of its board. Just four years later, in 1918, he bought the

This triple underpass was built by Austin Bridge Company in downtown Dallas in the 1930s.

contracting portion of the business from the Austins and set up another new corporation with himself as president, Frank Austin as secretary, and George Austin as a stockholder. It was called Austin Brothers Bridge Company.

The new venture grew rapidly after World War I, but the event that really propelled it on its way was Moore's successful bid on a new causeway at Corpus Christi to replace one destroyed in a 1919 hurricane. At about that same time the firm did its first industrial construction, building foundations for the new oil derricks that were beginning to dot the Texas landscape.

Confusion over the similarity of the names of Austin Brothers, Contractors, and Austin Brothers Bridge Company caused the name of the latter to be shortened to "Austin Bridge Company" in 1923. And despite its other endeavors, the firm principally produced bridges—all kinds of them. Throughout the period between the world wars, its bridges became landmarks all across Texas, as well as in other states. Notable among those still standing today as monuments to the company's workmanship and skills are the Commerce Street Viaduct and the

The Gibbons Creek Steam Electric Station, near Carlos, Texas, was built for Texas Municipal Power Authority by Austin Power, Inc.

famed Triple Underpass at Commerce and Main streets in Dallas.

The post-World War II era saw Austin Bridge excel in the field of highway construction as Texas expanded its roads and began its first freeways. In 1945 the firm moved from Clarence Street in Dallas to a new 20,000-square-foot home on Singleton Boulevard. With the move came increasing diversification. Servis Equipment Company and Austin Road Company had already been organized as subsidiaries during the 1930s, and this trend accelerated as the postwar boom blossomed.

When Charles Moore died in January 1955, he was succeeded as board chairman of Austin Bridge by M.B. Solomon, his son-in-law and a successful attorney who had joined the business on a full-time basis in 1950. Today M.B. Solomon continues to serve the firm in an emeritus capacity, but its day-to-day operation has

This building, on Coombs Street in Dallas, housed the Austin Brothers Steel Company in 1912. The steel company was forerunner to Austin Brothers Bridge Company.

been directed since 1970 by his son, William T. Solomon, as president and chief executive officer. Another son, Charles Solomon, serves as vice-chairman.

In 1973 Austin Bridge changed its name to Austin Industries, Inc., and now ranks as the third-largest merit-shop contractor in America. It is a genuinely unique organization, not only because of its great growth and the diversity of its activities, but because it has remained in the hands of the same family management for nearly seven decades.

In 1986 Austin Industries expects total revenues to exceed $500 million. Its many-faceted operations are channelled mainly through three major operating groups: the Heavy Construction Group, which handles road and bridge building; the Industrial Construction Group, which builds power plants, petrochemical plants, and other large industrial facilities; and the Commercial Construction Group, which has emerged in the past ten years as one of the Southwest's principal office builders.

"We see our future as being very balanced among these three areas," says Bill Solomon. "We're on a path we want to stay on."

Since the firm pioneered merit-shop commercial construction with its first high-rise project in 1976, it has become the number-one builder of office towers in Dallas. The 72-story InterFirst Plaza, tallest structure in the famous Dallas skyline, provides perhaps the most impressive evidence of the firm's impact on commercial construction in the city. Other Dallas landmarks built by the company include Williams Square at Las Colinas, the Olympia & York Tower, 2200 Ross Avenue, and the Loews Anatole Hotel.

"The opening of D/FW Airport in the early 1970s came at a time when we were looking for new markets to enter," Solomon explains. "We felt it would have dramatic impact on the growth of commercial building in Dallas, and we saw that field as an outstanding opportunity."

InterFirst Plaza, the tallest building in downtown Dallas, was completed by Austin Commercial, Inc., in 1985.

Meanwhile, though, the company is also busier than ever in other fields. It has helped build more than eighty power plants and since 1975 has specialized in the construction of complete plants, not merely portions of plants. Since its first big industrial job—building the Lone Star Steel plant at Daingerfield—the firm has also built numerous petrochemical and other industrial installations.

And in road and bridge building, where it all began, Austin Industries continues as a national leader. Among its modern transportation marvels is the Queen Isabella Causeway, Texas' longest bridge, connecting South Padre Island with the mainland. The largest builder of residential concrete streets in the United States, it produces 2.5 million square yards annually in this operation.

From its headquarters on Stemmons Freeway in Dallas, where it moved in 1974, Austin Industries and its 6,000 employees have built an infinite variety of structures in forty states over the past decade, setting record after record in all areas of construction.

And whatever the future brings in Texas, it is safe to say that Austin Industries will be helping to build it.

TTI, INC.

Fifteen years ago Paul E. Andrews' future seemed bleak, indeed. After studying at The University of Texas, Andrews worked for several large defense-related industries, usually in the purchasing departments. Born and reared in Fort Worth, he intended to stay in the area, but found himself at the mercy of fluctuating military budgets, moving to three jobs in six years. Then, in 1971, disaster struck. Andrews was laid off from his current employer, General Dynamics, with no guarantee as to when he would be called back to work. Consequently, with economic survival as his primary goal, he decided to begin a small business of his own.

And survive he did. The first few years, however, were difficult. Since Andrews knew about purchasing for industrial electronics, he initially began brokering components to industry, operating by telephone from his home. Having no franchises, he took orders for anything he could obtain, finding and delivering the parts himself. After a few months he moved to a small office in the Ridglea Bank Building, but for two years the business remained a one-man operation. In 1973 TTI (initially named Tex-

In 1980 TTI moved to its present site at 4033 East Belknap.

Tronics, but quickly shortened to TTI) relocated to Guilford Road on Fort Worth's west side and hired its first employee. The firm was incorporated one year later. Together the two men worked long hours to modernize the little office, measuring, hammering, and sawing. But the labor paid off. Only one year later the business moved again, this time across town to East Lancaster Street. At this base TTI obtained its first franchise and increased business to over one million dollars.

In 1977 Andrews faced another major decision—to remain static, with only a few employees, or to expand and challenge the industry giants. Of course, he chose to compete. Andrews decided to concentrate on one segment of the electronics industry—resistors and capacitors, the "nuts and bolts" of electronics. These "passives" are the least expensive part of the industry and comprise about 15 percent of the electronic component market. But to win his share of contracts, Andrews would have to deliver more efficiently and rapidly than his competitors.

In order to expedite this change, he totally computerized the entire operation so that a customer would know immediately if a part was available. This innovation was such a success that within three years TTI moved to its present site on East Belknap and continued massive expansion.

By 1985 TTI employed over 250 employees in total, with approximately 150 workers in its Fort Worth facility (the largest of nine scattered from coast to coast). The company had twenty-five franchises, over fifty million dollars in sales, and was placing computer terminals in its clients' offices—clients such as Boeing, Texas Instruments, and General Dynamics. In just a little over a decade TTI, Inc., had become the largest resistor/capacitor distributor specialist in the United States.

In 1974 TTI relocated from Guilford Road on Fort Worth's west side to this facility across town on East Lancaster.

BAKER MANAGEMENT COMPANY

In 1966 C. Don Baker, now chairman of Baker Management Company and its subsidiaries, published the first issue of *Living* magazine in Seattle, Washington, and started what has become one of the largest and most successful networks of housing information publications in the nation—Baker Publications, Inc.

By the early 1970s Baker and his two brothers, Ray and Dick, had brought the *Living* magazine concept to Texas. Following the strategy of locating in high-growth markets across the booming Sunbelt, the Baker brothers first launched *Living* magazines in Dallas/Fort Worth and Houston. Although Baker Publications no longer publishes *Puget Sound Living,* the original *Living* concept, which was designed to aid transferees, newcomers, and local residents in their home-buying decisions, has now reached eight markets—Dallas/Fort Worth, Houston, San Antonio, and Austin, Texas; Tampa/St. Petersburg and Miami/Fort Lauderdale/Palm Beach, Florida; Denver, Colorado; and Phoenix, Arizona. The combined annual circulation of the Baker network of housing guides and magazines now exceeds 3.5 million readers.

With similar foresight, the Bakers formed Commerce Publishing Corporation in 1976 to inaugurate *Texas Business,* a statewide, monthly business magazine aimed at filling the gap between the local media and national business publications on issues that directly affect business people in Texas. From its inception, *Texas Business* has grown substantially in its outreach, influence, and editorial excellence, and currently has more than 160,000 regular readers across Texas, as well as nationwide and abroad.

Continuing to broaden Baker's magazine network, Commerce Publishing launched the *Texas Business/Office Guide* in 1981 based on the same concept as *Living* magazine, but with a focus on available commercial office space in a metropolitan area. The *Dallas/Fort Worth Office Guide* was successfully introduced in mid-1981 and has since expanded to a three-times-yearly publication. An office guide for the Austin/San Antonio real estate market made its debut in 1986, and similar publications are currently being considered for other cities.

Today Baker Management Company is a privately held, Dallas-based firm whose principal operating companies include Baker Publications and Commerce Publishing Corporation. Together they provide a wide range of publications to the real estate and business communities in eight growing metropolitan areas.

The senior management of Baker Management Company and its subsidiaries includes C. Don Baker, chairman of Baker Management and both subsidiaries; Ray L. Baker, chief executive officer of all three companies; E.J. Martin, president of Commerce Publishing Corporation and publisher of *Texas Business* magazine; and James P. Goodnight, president of Baker Publications, Inc. Dick B. Baker is senior vice-president of Baker Publications and publisher of *Denver Living.*

Photo by Tom Shanahan of The Idaho Statesman, *Boise*

PRESBYTERIAN HOSPITAL

Presbyterian Hospital of Dallas officially opened to receive its first patients on May 1, 1966, but the idea for what was to become one of Texas' largest and best-known health care facilities was actually conceived more than a decade earlier. The real start of Presbyterian Hospital can be traced to an after-church conversation in the spring of 1955 between Dr. William M. Elliott, Jr., then pastor of Highland Park Presbyterian Church, and Dr. Frank H. Kidd, Jr., a prominent Dallas physician and a member of the church.

"Dallas needs a new hospital, Dr. Elliott," said Dr. Kidd that Sunday morning. "And it ought to be connected with our church."

Coincidentally, Dr. Elliott had been thinking in the same vein. He heartily agreed, and within a few days the idea was broached to Dallas oilman and philanthropist Toddie Lee Wynne, Sr., who would become instrumental in a fund-raising effort that collected more than $4.6 million to build the hospital. Soon the first contacts were made with Roderic M. Bell, the dedicated hospital administrator who would become the guiding professional force behind Presbyterian. Slowly a dream began to take shape, to reach out for form and substance for a new hospital.

These four individuals, with the help of countless others and outstanding support from the community in general, made Presbyterian Hospital of Dallas a reality. Dr. Kidd became the hospital's first board chairman. Wynne and his family used their influence and support to make the hospital's construction a matter of pride and conscience in Dallas. And Bell became Presbyterian's first administrator in 1960 and served in that capacity until he assumed the presidency of the newly formed Presbyterian Medical Center in 1979. Bell retired in 1983.

In the fulfillment of their dream, these founders of Presbyterian Hospital gave their city an incalculable medical asset, one that has won widespread recognition for the highest-quality, most modern health care in such fields as maternity, urology, sleep-related disorders, and cardiovascular treatment, among others.

Today Presbyterian Hospital of Dallas has grown from its original 300 beds to an 838-bed facility that mirrors the phenomenal expansion of the fast-growing North Dallas area it serves. The hospital, located on 105 acres in North Dallas, includes Presbyterian Main, Presbyterian West

The 105-acre campus of Presbyterian Medical Center stretches along Walnut Hill Lane between Greenville Avenue and North Central Expressway in the heart of North Dallas.

(opened in 1977), the Margot Perot Women's and Children's Hospital and the Finley Ewing Cardiovascular and Fitness Center (both opened in 1983), and three professional buildings. Also located on the campus are a branch of Texas Woman's University Institute of Health Sciences and the national headquarters of the American Heart Association.

Since its founding in 1976, Presbyterian Medical Center has continued to grow and serve as an "umbrella" for a growing family of a number of enterprises, of which Presbyterian Hospital of Dallas is the largest. It also operates the 93-bed Presbyterian Hospital of Kaufman, the 50-bed Presbyterian Hospital of Winnsboro, and Presbyterian Village North, a 63-acre North Dallas retirement community with more than 400 residents.

Douglas D. Hawthorne was elected president in 1983. He had been a member of the administrative staff since 1970. R. Reed Fraley was named executive director of Presbyterian Hospital of Dallas in December 1983.

TEAGUE INDUSTRIES

The story of Teague Industries and the family who built it is also the story of the electrification of Texas over a period of more than sixty years, from the stringing of the state's first cross-country power lines in the 1920s to the high-tech era of fiber optics in the 1980s.

The founder of the company, Clifton C. Teague, first went to work for Texas Power & Light in 1923, and spent thirteen years with that firm as a lineman, bringing electric power to the inhabitants of towns all across North, East, and Central Texas—many of whom had never had household electricity before. At the time, a lineman's job was one of the world's most dangerous ways of earning a living. And, in fact, Teague's twin brother, Clinton, also a lineman, was electrocuted while working at Temple in 1934.

But Clifton Teague introduced his son, Gene, to his line of work when he was just a toddler. "He pulled me up to the top of my first pole when I was two years old," recalls Gene, now chairman of Teague Industries. "I grew up in the business, and by the time I was eighteen I was the youngest first-class lineman in the United States."

After serving with the Navy during World War II—as an electrician, of course—Gene became a partner with his father in a new enterprise, C.C. Teague and Son Construction Company, established in 1949. During the postwar building boom, the firm became one of the state's major contractors for the installation of power lines for large utility companies, municipalities, and the REA.

The Teagues soon branched out into other fields, too. In 1957 they bought a small saw company, renamed it Texoma Incorporated, and used it to produce a new type of all-hydraulic drilling machine for installing overhead electric utilities. Although the subsidiary venture was sold in 1967, the "Texoma drill" became famous in the utility industry and has helped revolutionize the way underground lines are installed.

"We've always been innovators," says Gene. "We were among the first companies in Texas to put electric lines underground, and we've become specialists in digging through the various types of rock in Texas."

In 1960 Teague Industries was formed as the parent company of C.C. Teague and Son and a new sub-

Clifton C. Teague

Clifton E. Teague

sidiary, Utility Construction Company, was established exclusively for underground work. Headquartered in Sherman for three decades, the main office moved to Plano in 1978, and in 1984 Teague Industries occupied a new 18,000-square-foot building on a prime eight-acre site in Richardson.

Clifton C. Teague died in an auto

Mike Teague

accident in 1979 while still actively running the company, but his son, Gene, and his grandsons, Mike and Pat, have continued to build the business in the tradition of its founder. Today Mike is president of Teague Industries and Pat is executive vice-president. The organization has grown from three employees to more than 200 and now operates four subsidiaries—C.C. Teague and Son, Utility Construction Company, Teague Land Company, and Teague Cable and Communications Company. The latter was formed in 1982 to specialize in the new field of fiber optics.

While installing countless thousands of miles of utility lines that benefit millions of Texans, the Teagues have also compiled an outstanding record of community service. Gene is an immediate past president of the 72-county East Texas Chamber of Commerce and has held many other voluntary civic posts. "We believe in being humanistic," says Gene. "That's a big part of our success."

And an electrifying success it has been, if there ever was one.

Pat Teague

RAY ELLISON INDUSTRIES

About 40 percent of the housing market in San Antonio is supplied by Ray Ellison Industries. From construction of a single home in 1949, the company has expanded and built more than 40,000 homes for San Antonians. There is no other builder in the nation who commands a similar market share in a major metropolitan area.

The impact of Ellison's activities on the city is awesome. Purchasing most products and services locally, the Ellison operation builds more homes than the next ten San Antonio builders combined, annually infusing the local economy with approximately a quarter-billion dollars in sales and some 10,000 jobs. Ray Ellison Homes is the largest individually owned home-building firm in the nation.

Today Ray Ellison Industries is a collection of businesses. Ray Ellison Homes remains the centerpiece, with the primary purpose of providing homes for city and area residents.

Ray Ellison Developments is responsible for management of the commercial properties of the parent company. This includes long-range planning for commercial land acquisition and usage, and for the development and lease or sale of office parks and industrial parks, commercial buildings, shopping centers, and apartments. Another function of Ray Ellison Developments is to negotiate joint ventures with other major developers and users in San Antonio. The firm also manages raw land not yet under development.

The component manufacturing plant uses state-of-the-art equipment to produce standardized roof trusses and wall units ready to assemble at the job site. The uses of new methods in the construction process led to the ultimate goal—a higher-quality home.

The Richmond Lumber Company, a member of the Ellison family since 1955, obtains and furnishes building materials used by Ray Ellison Homes.

World Wide Realty, organized in 1970, has grown to be one of the largest general real estate brokerage firms in the Alamo City. Organized in 1967, San Antonio Title Company closes the loan on a new Ellison home. Texas Homestead Mortgage Company has served as the loan-processing division of Ray Ellison Industries, and it is now among the major mortgage companies in the area.

The San Antonio Relocation Center is an important tool for those wishing to live in San Antonio by aiding newcomers in finding a home. Another function of the center is its readily available information on economic development, which is used by various agencies to stimulate interest in San Antonio as an area for industrial relocation.

The Lackland City Water Company, the largest privately owned utility in Texas, furnishes water and sewer services to Ellison neighborhoods.

Ray Ellison Industries, reflecting its founder's optimism, has continued to flourish despite periodic national recessions. Working with city planners and developers, helping to guide an orderly, continuous growth through proper zoning laws while still making every effort to retain the quality of life in San Antonio, Ray Ellison and his staff have been instrumental in keeping San Antonio the unique city it is.

In order to continue as the leading home-building force in the San Antonio market, Ellison uses sophisticated market forecasts made a year in advance to project, with incredible accuracy, the number and types of homes that will be needed, where they are to be built, and their price range. Each week, updates are available to compare results with projections, and adjustments are made accordingly. Ellison has gone beyond the short-range thinking that has characterized his industry, minimizing the risks of home building and allowing for growth over the long term.

Ellison's efforts have not gone un-

Ray Ellison received peer recognition in 1980 when he was named Professional Builder of the Year by Professional Builder *magazine. Roy Diez (right), the magazine's editor-in-chief, presented the award.*

Sunset illuminates a Ray Ellison model home complex. Now one of the largest privately held home builders in the nation, the firm got its start building one house at a time. © 1985, Harvey Smith

Ray Ellison's Signature Collection represents the spacious living and mastery of craftsmanship demanded by discriminating buyers of the 1980s.

noticed. Through the years he has received hundreds of honors in the form of plaques and scrolls which are displayed in the lobby of the firm's headquarters. In 1981 he was chosen Builder of the Year by *Professional Builder* magazine. That award is made annually in special recognition of the single most outstanding builder in the United States who has exhibited exceptional leadership and professionalism in the housing and light construction industries.

In 1983 Ellison was inducted into the prestigious Housing Hall of Fame. Of that honor, Jack Willome, president of Ray Ellison Homes, said, "We are proud of the fact that Ray Ellison is one of the nation's leading regional home builders. His impact on the city is evidenced by the fact that one in every ten San Antonians lives in a Ray Ellison home."

In 1984 Ellison, along with real estate giant Trammel Crow, was presented the 1984 Dealmaker Award. That award is given to outstanding individuals in the Texas real estate industry to honor and promote excellence in real estate transactions and developments.

With all of these accolades from building and real estate associations it would seem that Ellison might relax and bask in its glory, but such is not the case. The firm is constantly searching for more cost-effective ways to build even better homes. Through questionnaires, seminars, and focus groups, Ellison listens to the needs and wants of home buyers. He is aware of what kinds of homes and neighborhoods they are looking for, and his company plans accordingly. "Seventy-five percent of our buyers are first-time home buyers," he states. "We're experts at getting renters into home ownership."

The future demand for single- and multi-family housing, shopping centers, and office buildings in the San Antonio area is bright indeed. And, as new needs arise, the firm will be there to meet the challenges of tomorrow. As it has done in the past, Ray Ellison Industries will provide impetus and professional momentum to the growth and development of San Antonio.

KDF, INC.

From the brink of bankruptcy to the zenith of going for Olympic gold: Such has been the history of KDF, Inc.

Company president and owner Phil Koehne fulfilled a burning desire when the rifle he designed was used in the 1984 Olympic competition in Los Angeles.

The sign on the unimposing one-story concrete building just outside the town of Seguin proclaims the firm as home of "The World's Most Accurate Hunting Rifle." The sign, which had hung there since 1970, was nearly a matter of history when Koehne, a third-generation rancher from Cotulla, happened on the scene. An avid hunter, Koehne had come to buy a rifle at Kleinguenther Distinctive Firearms. Just as he arrived at the plant, Small Business Administration officials were changing the locks and posting foreclosure notices. Bankers were milling about, employees were taking inventory, and customers were surging in and out the doors. In short, all was mass confusion.

"I was one of the customers," explains Koehne. "I came in and bought a Kleinguenther K-14 rifle. I figured if I was ever going to get one of those rifles I had better get it now." After he made his purchase and looked over this fine rifle he decided that it would really be a shame if it disappeared from the U.S. market, since Kleinguenther was the only distributor. So, in 1978, just when it appeared the company might go under, Koehne bought 51 percent of the stock from Dooley Gilchrist, a nationally known safari hunter who had made a considerable investment in the enterprise. Suddenly Koehne, whose main interests had been land development, ranching, and investments, found himself in the gun business.

Everything went fairly well until the recession caught up with Texas in 1983. People in Texas (where more than half the KDF sales were made) practically stopped buying rifles. Undaunted, Koehne and his staff began

Phil Koehne, president of KDF, Inc., with the new XK-22 Olympic rifle. This is the only American-made rifle designed specifically for the Olympics.

a search for something that would bring fame to the company and eventually more sales. From this search was born the idea of producing an American rifle to use in the Olympics, something that had not been done for many years.

KDF, already the distributor for the world's most accurate hunting rifle, produced by the Voere Company of Voerenbach, West Germany, was a step ahead of any competition. The K-15 is guaranteed to place three shots within a half-inch group at one hundred yards. That accuracy would hold up well in Olympic competition but designing a world-class Olympic rifle required the collaboration of an Olympic champion.

Lanny Bassham, an Olympic shooter who had won the gold medal in Montreal in 1976, lives on a ranch outside Seguin where he runs an Olympic Shooting School, the only one of its kind in the United States. Six world champions have been developed at the school.

Koehne contacted Bassham, and they got together and immediately began sketching out a design for a superior Olympic competition rifle. KDF gunsmiths began putting in long hours building the prototype. The unique action designed by Koehne and Bassham places the loading port one full inch closer to the shooter so that reloading can be accomplished without getting out of the shooting position. The rifle was completed just minutes before they were scheduled to leave for the Olympic trials in April 1984.

Among the rifles distributed by KDF, Inc., are (top to bottom) the K-15 Featherweight, the VOERE Titan with optional double-set trigger, the K-15 with engraved action and custom Monte Carlo stock, the K-22 Standard, and the K-22 Deluxe.

The rifle, called the XK-22, was so impressive at the trials that two competitors who had trained for years on another rifle switched to the XK-22. Eun Chul Lee of South Korea and Soma Dutta of India liked the prototype so well that both moved to Bassham's ranch to practice with it on a day-to-day basis. Once the competition rifles were built, the two shooters began rigorous training for the summer competition only a scant few months away. The KDF gunsmiths threw themselves into the task of finishing not only the competition rifles but backup rifles as well.

While no gold medals were garnered by the two contestants, they did quite well. Interest in the rifle was intense. Within the next few years even greater refinements will be in-corporated in the XK-22, and one day it may well strike gold in the Olympics. After Malcolm Cooper won the gold medal in Los Angeles, he took an XK-22 home to England for evaluation, and a Norwegian rifle coach, Jens Nygaard, took one home to test in extreme cold. A biathlon (skiing and shooting) rifle for the Winter Olympics is under develop-ment by KDF in collaboration with Nygaard, who recently won the Nor-wegian National Senior Men's Championship with the XK-22.

Further developments at KDF in-clude a SWAT team rifle that is lighter, more powerful, and more ac-curate than those presently used. It incorporates their new "Recoil Arres-tor," a device that screws onto the end of the barrel and reduces a rifle's kick by 50 to 80 percent (depending on the caliber). This revolutionary Recoil Arrestor has paved the way for further development of new, harder-hitting cartridges. The first will be the .411 KDF, a .41 caliber rifle for large and dangerous game with possi-bilities for long-range military sniper use. It is so powerful that it can cut through one-half-inch steel plate at 100 yards.

For a little company nearly stran-gled by the cold hand of bankruptcy, KDF has come a long way.

FRIEDRICH AIR CONDITIONING & REFRIGERATION CO.

How to squeeze the maximum amount of chilling energy from a block of ice was a major goal of Ed Friedrich when he set out to design a better icebox in 1883. Until that time spoilage in perishables was quite high, resulting in a number of serious health problems.

The new Friedrich icebox was far superior to any other icebox design. The case, made of top-quality materials, had tight-fitting joints. Perishables were kept fresh much longer through the use of salt brine freezer cases. The doors closed tightly. Certainly some of the cabinet's artistry could be credited to the time Friedrich spent as a cabinetmaker working for his father.

Soon the company began to grow, and Friedrich's sons, Richard and George, joined him in the business. The building on Cherry Street, used for the manufacturing of refrigeration equipment, was soon expanded to 35,000 square feet.

It appeared the firm was on its way when disaster struck. In 1924 the Cherry Street plant burned to the ground. Even such a terrible setback did not deter Friedrich. At the age of sixty-two, when a lesser man might have simply walked away and retired, Friedrich rolled up his sleeves and began rebuilding. He met with local bankers, secured the funds, and the plant became a reality again.

Steady growth led to the construction of a new facility, covering the 1100 block of East Commerce. Although the firm had greatly accelerated its sales and production of refrigeration equipment, Friedrich insisted that uncompromising quality continue in every piece of equipment that bore his name. That same philosophy continues today at Friedrich Air Conditioning & Refrigeration Co.

A concept eventually put into practical use by George Friedrich changed the displays of fresh meats, dairy products, and produce in supermarkets. Open-type refrigerated cases replaced the old reach-in cases that contained doors that fogged

The forerunner of today's Friedrich Air Conditioning & Refrigeration Co. was founded by Ed Friedrich, shown here with unidentified employees in front of the original plant around the turn of the century.

over and caused leakage problems when seals came loose and the doors stood open, making refrigeration units work harder and waste energy.

The open cases were made possible by the "floating-air" principle in which a thermal barrier is created as cold air is pumped across the top of perishables and then drawn back into the case and recycled. In most cases the need for cooler doors was eliminated, product displays were greatly enhanced, restocking of units was far simpler, and, perhaps most important, customers could see and reach products much easier, thus creating better sales. By 1950 Friedrich had become one of the largest commercial refrigeration manufacturers in the world.

The company's next major move was to design and build a line of room air conditioners. Production began in 1952, and the air conditioner, boasting Friedrich quality and dependability, was an immediate success. The firm's reputation soon spread worldwide, and international distributors began selling the products. Today licensees on four continents manufacture the firm's products using Friedrich components and technical expertise. All units are, of course, built to Friedrich's high standards.

The corporation has always taken

great pride in being on the leading edge of technological advancements. Given the fact that energy cost to a typical supermarket is second only to labor and that 50 percent of that cost is attributed to refrigeration, Friedrich recognized the need for energy efficiency. The firm has responded to that need by assigning a high priority to the research and development of refrigeration systems and display cases built to operate efficiently while still maintaining performance.

The end result is the Friedrich F.A.C.T. I™ microprocessor-controlled, Uneven Parallel Refrigeration System. This complete minicomputer is instantly responsive to any immediate temperature changes, and it adjusts the system's load without inefficient, excessive compressor cycling. Friedrich refrigeration systems with F.A.C.T. I™ can cut store refrigeration costs by 40 percent or more. The F.A.C.T. I™ system coupled with heavily insulated display cases makes Friedrich the undisputed leader in the commercial refrigeration industry.

The Friedrich line of refrigerated cases is the hallmark of the refrigeration industry. Among the refrigerated cases offered are produce merchandisers, meat merchandisers, ice cream/frozen food merchandisers, dairy merchandisers, reach-in merchandisers, and walk-in coolers and freezers. The firm recently purchased Custom Commercial Coolers, Inc., a manufacturer of walk-in coolers and freezers. The acquisition becomes a part of the expanding Friedrich Commercial Refrigeration Division. Manufacturing will remain in Fort Worth, home of Custom Commercial Coolers, Inc.

A line of salad bar merchandisers has been introduced by the company's Commercial Refrigeration Division. This line includes new hexagonal and octagonal salad bar merchandisers and a free-standing cheese merchandiser. Also included is a hot food merchandiser. There are island salad bars, wall salad bars, and a custom-built side car complete with storage compartments.

Although the current systems and display cases are considered

The present Friedrich Air Conditioning & Refrigeration Co. is at 4200 North Pan Am Expressway in San Antonio.

Ed Friedrich's early attempts to build a better icebox are in marked contrast to Friedrich's products today. Here room air conditioners roll off the assembly line.

to be state of the art in energy efficiency and performance, Friedrich is constantly looking toward new technologies. A strong commitment to its customers will keep the firm in its present position as the quality leader in refrigeration systems.

For more than 100 years Friedrich Air Conditioning & Refrigeration Co. has set the highest standards for quality in all that it produces. What steps will be taken to ensure that these standards are maintained? President J.L. McMaken explains, "As a company, all of our people are dedicated to maintaining the highest-quality product offerings that can be obtained at a reasonable price in the markets in which we compete. It is this quality leadership and dedicated day-to-day building of a product, on time, with state-of-the art features and performance, that people will buy on a continuing basis."

For many years Friedrich has been known as a "people company." Man-agement is interested in the workers who turn out the product. As McMaken explains, "Any company should recognize that its very image and character is a combination of the people who work for that firm. As an example, most companies are better known by their telephone operator than probably any other person. I sometimes think that some businesses don't take the time to talk to their telephone operators to let them know that they are the true impression of the company."

Uppermost in the minds of all Friedrich employees, from management to plant workers, is turning out the best product on the market. It is the one way the firm can maintain its leadership position as the builder of the best and most efficient products. It is also the way Friedrich can successfully compete against the giants of the refrigeration and air conditioning industries. The customer who chooses Friedrich does so be-cause he or she wants the best. Knowing this, the firm keeps pushing toward its goal of even better products in the future.

Since the room air conditioning business has basically matured in the United States, Friedrich Air Conditioning & Refrigeration Co. has gone in search of other markets in which to expand sales. A Friedrich licensee in Saudi Arabia has grown to be as large as the parent company. Because economic conditions demand it, Friedrich seeks out those who will build room air conditioners that meet company standards. It is just not economically feasible to completely assemble a unit in San Antonio and then ship it thousands of miles to a foreign market. The ideal situation is to ship the parts from the U.S. factory and assemble the room air conditioners abroad.

Friedrich is currently looking into a number of foreign markets including South Africa, India, and various countries in South America. To select a market that will be both profitable and that also has the emerging market characteristics favorable to form joint ventures is something the firm is now investigating.

Friedrich has also cast an eye to the Orient. "China is an emerging market that is going to be much, much larger than the Saudi Arabian Middle East market that has emerged over the past twenty years," explains McMaken. "The Chinese are looking for technical aid and enhancement in joint ventures, a program whereby the government owns a piece of the business and Friedrich has a share."

Just over a century has passed since Ed Friedrich designed a better icebox to conserve a natural resource. Now and in the future Friedrich Air Conditioning & Refrigeration Co. is pledged to continue to conserve energy by building products worthy of the name Friedrich.

JAMES AVERY CRAFTSMAN, INC.

Kerrville craftsman James Avery strives to build a trusting, lasting relationship with people through his symbolic jewelry designs. "All of us are looking for meaning and purpose in life," the craftsman says. "I like to know what other people are looking for in life—not just something superficial but rather something deeper and more meaningful."

Avery's personal philosophy of giving encouragement and contributing to the growth of people who are searching for a deeper meaning in their lives permeates his company and his designs.

From his office, with its panoramic view of the picturesque but rugged Texas hill country, Avery says, "The thing I enjoy most is working with people, encouraging people to excel, to try to do everything better today than we did it yesterday. That is the challenge I relish."

When Avery was coming out of his agnostic period, he was an industrial design instructor at the University of Colorado. He crafted a cross for himself to herald the change in his values. Friends of his soon wanted a cross, too.

Avery came back strongly to the church in 1953—a fact that is evident in his early jewelry designs. The Prima Vera Cross, an eighteen-year-old design, remains one of his favorites because of its joyful and childlike spirit. "That piece is pretty much me," Avery explains.

Adaptations of traditional Ethiopian crosses are the focus of his latest humanitarian effort—to help in some way to feed the hungry in that country. "The Ethiopian people have a tradition of art and craftsmanship, particularly their crosses, that dates back hundreds of years," Avery says. Twenty-five percent of the proceeds from the sales of the Avery interpretation of Ethiopian crosses will be sent to Church World Service for Ethiopian hunger relief.

Still thought of as a religious jewelry designer, Avery's inspiration now comes from all of God's creation and includes sea shells, snowflakes, doves,

James Avery at the entrance to the firm's Kerrville headquarters.

One of James Avery's early creations and still a favorite is the Prima Vera Cross, shown here.

butterflies, flowers, eagles, and hummingbirds as well as armadillos, horned toads, and boots from the hill country region of Texas.

It has taken the craftsman only thirty-two years to become a Texas institution. In 1954 he made the decision to leave the academic world and return to Texas, where he had been stationed in 1943 as an Army Air Corps trainee, and create well-designed, well-made items that others might find meaningful and useful.

Avery built a simple workbench in the two-car garage adjacent to his Kerrville home and purchased a number of hand tools with his initial capital outlay of less than $250.

In the beginning he crafted accessories and furnishings for homes and churches as well as church altar pieces, but it was his sterling silver jewelry that captured the widespread attention of Texans and other customers across the southern half of the United States.

From that humble beginning, Avery now employs 420 people working in the Kerrville corporate headquarters built in 1968; production facilities in Kerrville, Fredericksburg, and Comfort; and twenty-three company-owned retail stores in four states. Avery's future opportunity lies in the retail business, which he calls "our best niche."

James Avery Craftsman is one of the official jewelers for the Texas Sesquicentennial observance.

ELLEN TERRY, REALTORS

Ellen Terry, founder of the real estate firm that bears her name, was awarded the Easterwood Cup by the Greater Dallas Board of Realtors as the 1984 Realtor of the Year for her outstanding contribution to the industry.

The difference between Ellen Terry, the tireless, courageous, and phenomenally successful founder of the four-year-old company, Ellen Terry, Realtors, and most other people is that she deals in goals, not in wishes. This small bundle of energy was just awarded the coveted Easterwood Cup by the Greater Dallas Board of Realtors, as the 1984 Realtor of the Year for her outstanding contribution to the real estate industry and the community, which is an unheard-of occurrence in such a short period of time.

"I believe there's a lot of difference between a wish and a goal," says this super saleslady, who has become a legend in Dallas real estate circles in the space of a few short years. "A wish is something you might want, but expect never to get. A goal is something you strive for and systematically plan out. We need to set specific goals to establish purpose in our lives."

In 1976 the sheltered, privileged life that Ellen Terry had always enjoyed came to an abrupt, shattering end. As a result of business reversals, she lost her fashionable home in the posh Dallas suburb of Highland Park, her Mercedes automobile, and ultimately her marriage as well. Ellen Terry assumes her share of responsibility for not being aware of the family finances and regrets that she was not a more supportive helpmate. She feels she should have become involved in and knowledgeable of the family's personal finances.

Suddenly, she was left with a lot to wish for. In her own words, the pretty, pint-sized (four-foot, ten-inch) mother of two was "at the bottom of the pit." She was faced with the urgent necessity of earning a living for herself and her children, and her only preparation for her new role as family breadwinner was a physical education degree from Southern Methodist University and her brief three-year experience as a gym teacher at one of Dallas' most prestigious schools, The Hockaday School.

"I knew I didn't want to go back to teaching, and I didn't have any secretarial skills," she recalls. "I started out in the travel business, but the income wasn't enough to survive on. My brother suggested I go into residential real estate, but I knew I couldn't wait to collect commissions, because I didn't even have enough money to pay my rent."

But when she found a company that would agree to pay her a small draw against future commissions, Ellen Terry did go into the real estate business, with incredible results. She didn't waste her time wishing, but immediately began setting—and achieving—goals for herself. The day after she passed her real estate exam, she made her first successful sales contact. And within her first forty-five days on the job, she had sold $600,000 worth of homes and made more money than she would have made in two years as a teacher or a secretary. She will always be grateful to the company that took a risk and hired her.

She had realized her initial goal, which was, in her words, "to be able to provide for my two children and keep us together in a comfortable environment." She had also uncovered a rare talent for selling expensive houses, found a permanent niche in a highly competitive field, and started moving toward other goals that might have seemed impossible at the time, even to the most wishful of wishful thinkers.

By the end of her first year as a residential real estate agent, she was not only the top Texas producer for the firm of Coldwell Banker, but was also the number two salesperson for the company on a nationwide basis. From Coldwell Banker she moved into an entrepreneurial partnership, forming a real estate firm with two brokers and specializing in quality homes in prestigious areas throughout Dallas.

In March 1981, after a prosperous two years in the partnership, she moved on to found her solely owned company, Ellen Terry, Realtors, and by the time the new venture was a year old, it had firmly established itself as the fastest-growing and most highly visible firm of its kind in the marketplace. Today the company she totally owns and heads as president employs more than forty sales associates, who are among the top earners in their field, and is recognized as the "Cadillac" of Dallas real estate brokerage firms.

During the 1984-1985 fiscal year, Ellen Terry, Realtors, sold and closed more than $153 million in residential real estate, which brought the four-year total sales volume to over $400 million. In addition to this phenomenal growth in the first four years, the company has established itself as a leader in the marketing of Dallas' finest properties by selling forty-seven estates valued at over one million dollars.

Ms. Terry, who was recently honored by her alma mater as a Distinguished Alumnus of Southern Methodist University, is a firm believer in sharing her success with others. Nearly two-thirds of her sales associates, for example, earned commissions on closed sales of six million to twelve million dollars individually during fiscal 1984-1985. Rather than singling out an individual as the top producer, each year the company's top sales personnel are honored by induction into its "Circles of Excellence."

"Our company's philosophy is to build a team of superstars who produce more each year as individuals because of team support and team spirit," she explains. "We believe that if you help other people achieve and get what they want in life, it will come back to you in abundance."

Ellen Terry herself has personally sold more than seventy million dollars worth of real estate during her career as a sales associate in the business, but now she manages and motivates her associates to be all they can be and, in so doing, her company is considered to be on the top plateau among residential real estate brokerage firms in Texas, while operating out of a single office at 5401 North Central Expressway. But in a larger sense, the 45-year-old native of Paris, Texas, has accomplished a great deal more than merely selling a lot of houses.

Today she uses the dramatic story of her personal and business success as the focal point of an inspirational message to others, and is becoming increasingly sought after as a motivational speaker for women's clubs, business and professional organizations, and civic groups. "I'm very frank and open about what happened to me," she says, "about the financial problems, the emotional reversals, the nightmares, the fears, because I hope that my story can help and encourage other people, especially when they feel devastated by circumstances that seem at the time insurmountable. If you believe in yourself and your God-given creative

Ellen Terry, recently honored as Distinguished Alumnus of her alma mater, Southern Methodist University, is a shining example of her own philosophy: "Anything the mind can conceive and believe, it can achieve."

abilities, there is definitely light at the end of the tunnel."

In her talks, Ms. Terry sets forth a simple but powerful philosophy: "Anything the mind can conceive and believe, it can achieve." Her goal is equally simple and equally dramatic. "I want to give courage and hope to other people who feel there is no hope," she says. "I want to inspire them to reach deep down inside and uncork that God-given potential to strive for and attain tremendous goals that many think are beyond their grasp."

It is impossible to estimate how many lives she may have changed for the better or how many she may change in the future, but as one associate points out: "She can motivate like a Zig Zigler, inspire like a Billy Graham, and lead like a Ronald Reagan."

Ellen Terry, despite all her success, still has goals, both in business and in life in general. "Our primary goal as a company," she says, "is commitment to excellence. There is no perfection in life, but there is excellence. I want this company to do the very best job in every area whether it be selling, listing, marketing, or providing guidance to our clients, and I want every staff member and associate to strive for excellence in every area of their lives whether it be professional, personal, spiritual, or physical."

Her personal creed is this: "Through adversity comes strength and what may often seem like a loss is truly a gain unrecognized. That problems can be turned into challenges that lead to opportunities if our focus is on the positives rather than the negatives in life. Success in life is based much more on attitude than aptitude, and true success comes from within when you make a positive difference in someone's life who may be hurting." Continuing to prove the truth of that creed is, for Ellen Terry, the most important goal of all.

TETCO

Tom E. Turner, president.

The American Dream has always been the rise of the hero from a relatively poor financial background to millionaire status through hard work and ingenuity. Tom E. Turner had just completed the eighth grade, when he left school to go to work in 1932. Those were hard times, and Turner found work in grocery stores so, at least, he had food. That dream must have seemed faraway for Turner when he packed his wife, Mary, and all their earthly possessions into his old Ford car and left Fort Worth for San Antonio.

By 1937 the Depression had a firm grip on the country, and Turner decided San Antonio might present more opportunities than his hometown. In the Alamo City he got a "break"—a night attendant's job at a service station. He received all of ten dollars for working an 84-hour week.

In December 1943 Turner's boss, Sigfried "Sig" Moore, decided to sell the company and retire. Somehow Turner managed to borrow the $350 necessary to lease a location and, once it was his, named it Sigmor in honor of his old employer. If anything, Turner was now putting in even longer days and nights. For a full day he ran the station, and, when he closed, he hopped aboard his small truck and delivered gasoline until late at night. Those sixteen-hour days were to continue for many years.

In the early 1940s Turner leased a second location and hired his brother as an operator. A short time later he leased a third station, and this time his wife, Mary, ran it. By 1950 there were twenty Sigmor stations in San Antonio. Turner's teenage sons became employees, and it was readily apparent that they had acquired

Fred A. Turner, senior vice-president.

their father's appetite for hard work. Later Tom Turner, Jr., and Fred Turner were to become integral members in Tetco (an acronym for Tom E. Turner Company).

Turner, never one to follow the book, startled a lot of oil companies and service station operators by his methods of running his business. Upon building new locations, he would emphasize and provide just a few select customer services. He built service stations on less expensive land in the middle of the block. The outlets were easily accessible to the motorist because there was no fight to get through traffic and red lights as often happened at the competitor on the corner.

Although the Turners stayed with full-service stations through the 1960s and early 1970s, they sensed that a big change was coming, and, when the time was right, converted to the shopping station concept with self-service gasoline. The transition was smooth and barely caused a ripple in the steady growth of Sigmor.

Beginning in 1971 Sigmor began a rapid expansion. The firm acquired Gensco, a national supplier of pipe. In 1974 Turner began construction on a 50,000-plus-barrel-a-day refinery at Three Rivers, Texas. In August 1977 he built a 240,000-barrel bulk-storage terminal at Corpus Christi, and two months later Gensco crews laid a seventy-mile pipeline to carry finished petroleum products from the refinery to the storage terminal. This was a daring adventure indeed for a man who had borrowed $350 for a service station. This time he made bank loans of several million dollars to complete the project, but, as it

Tom E. Turner, Jr., executive vice-president.

turned out, it was well worth the money and the effort.

The Sigmor Corporation continued to grow. Now there were 575 outlets in eighteen states, plus interests in other businesses such as broadcasting, security services, and various manufacturing and supply companies. Eventually, in 1983, Turner sold them to the Diamond Shamrock Corporation.

Today Tetco is a diversified enterprise. According to Tom Turner, Jr., "We plan to work on three phases of our business: trucking, which we bought back from Diamond Shamrock; real estate development; and the financial phase, which includes Bexar Savings and three local banks. As for real estate development, we're into shopping centers and a large community development known as Sonterra."

Sonterra (Portuguese for "land of dreams"), a luxury home and golf course development in north San Antonio, has five partners with Tetco as the majority stockholder and managing partner. Some 715 acres are being developed with 1,800 homes to be built. A 36-hole golf course, with all the amenities that go with a top-flight country club, is also being constructed at the site.

Tetco became involved in real estate development quite naturally. Before the sale of the service stations, plans had already been formulated to buy property, build a Sigmor station on part of the land, and develop the other part commercially.

One of Tetco's major projects is now nearing completion. The Bexar Savings Office Tower is under construction on land purchased when the company bought the savings association. The sixteen-story, 290,000-square-foot office tower overlooks Loop 410 near Harry Wurzbach. It is scheduled for completion during the sesquicentennial year. The Office Tower will house the Tetco corporate offices in the top three floors, and Bexar Savings will occupy the first three floors.

Even though the service stations have all been sold, Tetco still has a big stake in petroleum and other transportation businesses. More than 500 of its trucks travel the Texas highways, carrying everything from chemicals to steel and building materials.

"We think that if there is a secret to our success, it would be our ability to attract and keep the best people.

We have a management staff that we meet with periodically to go over opportunities and make recommendations," Turner explains. "We've reached the size now where our management team in each company makes the day-to-day decisions that affect their divisions."

Tom Jr. and Fred hope that their children will show an interest in Tetco to continue the family's participation in its growth. Tom Turner, Jr., continues, "My brother has five children and we have three. If they show any interest in working with Tetco, we would certainly give them encouragement, but we won't push it. The main thing that concerns us is that they be happy and enjoy whatever they decide to do with their lives."

Tetco's future plans include further land development, office complexes, and financial acquisitions. Led by a man who has "slowed down" to an eleven-hour day, six days a week, Tetco will continue to fulfill the American Dream.

The clubhouse at Sonterra, a luxury home and golf course development in northeast San Antonio.

CUSHMAN & WAKEFIELD

Cushman & Wakefield of Texas joined the Texas family of businesses in the early 1970s. Since that time, the company has been a pivotal force in the development and expansion of business in the state.

Texas was basking in the Sunbelt phenomenon. Major corporations outside the state were searching for a favorable, progressive economic climate; business within the state was booming, and developers, anticipating the surge of commercial growth, were raising impressive structures on the Texas skyline.

At the same time, Cushman & Wakefield, whose major operations were in New York and on the East and West coasts, was expanding nationwide to meet the market demands of its national and local clientele. Texas was a key target market.

The timing was right. Developers of Dresser Tower, a major new office building on the Houston skyline, were looking for a national real estate firm to serve as agent for the structure. Cushman & Wakefield accepted the assignment and in 1970 opened its first Texas office in Houston.

From its one office in Houston, the company has expanded to offices in five Texas cities: Austin, Dallas, Fort Worth, Houston, and San Antonio. Along the way, Cushman & Wakefield of Texas has aggressively served the major corporations in the nation seeking business bases in Texas. The firm offers a complete line of real estate services and has attracted top professionals in the field.

"Cushman & Wakefield is known for its expertise in most types of real estate transactions. What the company did in Texas is blend that national expertise with local talent to produce a strong Texas company," says Jay Dee Allen, Jr., one of the pioneer brokers to work for Cushman & Wakefield in Texas. Allen, a native Texan, joined the firm in 1976, and is now executive vice-president in charge of the Central Region, which includes all of Texas.

The Houston office market was formidable and complex in the 1970s. Dresser Tower was a major flagstone project in an unpredictable market. Cushman & Wakefield of Texas was the "new kid on the block" with a shiny red bike.

The company accepted the challenge to gain professional recogni-

The InterFirst Two Building in Dallas presented unique opportunities to Cushman & Wakefield as the real estate management firm expanded into its second Texas city in 1974.

tion and has become a respected force in the Houston real estate community. From serving that one building and client in 1970, the Houston office expanded to managing more than three million square feet by the end of 1985. It ranked fifth among fifty Cushman & Wakefield offices nationally in production and profitability, meeting the unique and cyclical demands of the Houston economy and becoming a partner with the Houston business community.

An equal challenge awaited Cushman & Wakefield in 1974 when it entered the Dallas market—again with a single project: the First International Building. Now known as InterFirst Two, the First International Building was the tallest structure in Dallas at that time. Most of the 56-story structure's 1.85 million square feet were unoccupied.

"Dallas was far from the booming office market it was to become a few years later," explains Robert T. Edge, now a Cushman & Wakefield executive vice-president. He and Allen teamed up not only to lease Inter-

Representative of the long-term leasing and management relationship between Cushman & Wakefield and its clients is the Corporate Square in San Antonio, one of many projects of the Hartford Companies that the firm manages across the nation.

First Two but also to establish Cushman & Wakefield in the Dallas market. The company steadfastly stood by its commitment, negotiating an eleven-floor lease with Mobil Oil Corporation that had a catalytic effect on completing occupancy of the Dallas landmark.

The Dallas office was established. In the 1970s and 1980s it gained momentum as it represented major corporations, such as American Airlines, Caltex Petroleum, and Celanese Chemical Corporation in relocations to Dallas.

The pattern set in Texas is not unlike that of the first Cushman & Wakefield offices in New York, where the firm's professionals provided aggressive leadership during an era of tremendous growth.

Founded in 1917 by J. Clydesdale Cushman and Barney Wakefield, the company was primarily involved in the managing and leasing of office buildings in New York City. By the time the building boom began in the 1940s, the firm was a predominant force on the Manhattan real estate scene. By the end of 1959 Cushman & Wakefield served as agent for 23 percent—nearly one-quarter—of all new office buildings in Manhattan. It represented numerous blue chip companies, many of whom remain clients on a national basis today.

Cushman & Wakefield of Texas is endowed with this legacy of leadership. The Houston and Dallas offices were soon followed by an office in Dallas' sister city, Fort Worth.

The relocation of the Western Company of North America to its world headquarters in Fort Worth in 1976 was the impetus for opening the third Texas office. The Western Company selected Cushman & Wakefield as leasing agent for its new structure.

Continuing aggressive growth in Dallas and Houston, the firm saw further expansion opportunities in the 1980s along the Austin-San Antonio corridor. The San Antonio office opened in 1982, followed by Austin in late 1984. In addition to these offices, Cushman & Wakefield performed a variety of real estate services in most major Texas cities.

Just as the New York City offices established a list of blue chip clientele, Cushman & Wakefield of Texas now serves an impressive number of national and Texas companies, offering a wide selection of real estate service lines: commercial brokerage, industrial/technical brokerage, retail brokerage, property management, financial services, and appraisal services.

Recognizing that Texas commerce and industry has a national and international impact, Cushman & Wakefield of Texas continues in partnership with Texas to explore growth opportunities. In 1970 the firm brought its national real estate network to Texas; today Cushman & Wakefield of Texas represents Texas business nationwide.

The 1010 Lamar Building in Houston is one of many office high-rise facilities leased and managed by Cushman & Wakefield.

EL PASO ELECTRIC COMPANY

Located at the corner of Oregon and Mills streets in downtown El Paso, El Paso Electric Company is known locally as "The Electric Company." The firm is housed in the Anson Mills Building, one of the older historic structures in the city. The building, completed in 1912, has been designated a Texas Historic Landmark as it was one of the earliest multistory, steel-and-concrete edifices to be built in the United States. The decision to place its offices in the Anson Mills Building symbolizes the corporation's long-standing historic ties to the city, as well as its view toward the future and its continuing commitment to provide El Pasoans with dependable, safe, and economical electric power.

A view of San Jacinto Plaza (circa 1930) from the Mills Building, the current home of El Paso Electric Company. The Hotel Hussman, now the Cortez, can be seen across the plaza.

In the 1920s vehicles such as this one provided service to El Paso Electric customers.

The Electric Company had its origins in 1901 as the El Paso Electric Railway Company and provided electric streetcars for the town's citizens. That same year the new venture bought the Brush Electric Light Company, a small plant founded in 1886, which provided direct current to the El Paso area. The success of the new enterprise was such that in 1902 an elaborate ceremony was held in which "Mandy," one of the mules that had long pulled the streetcars, was given a ride on an electric-powered car between El Paso and Juarez, Mexico, to signify the end of the old era and the beginning of the new.

From its earliest days El Paso Electric Company has sought to anticipate future needs and plan its expansion to meet the demands. In 1905 the firm purchased one of its major competitors, the International Light and Power Company, and nine years later took over the electrical operations of El Paso Gas Company.

By the early 1920s generating capacity of El Paso Electric turbines totaled 18,000 kilowatts, and service extended to some 15,000 customers. The economic boom of the 1920s witnessed the further expansion of the corporation westward into southeastern New Mexico and eastward to serve the farming and ranching communities of far West Texas.

The years during and following World War II brought unprecedented growth to the greater El Paso region, and The Electric Company was there to share in that growth and provide the power to fuel it. New generating units were constructed at existing power plants, and a new electric power complex was built near Farmington, New Mexico, to serve the growing needs of that state. At present, The Electric Company provides power to a population base of approximately 550,000 persons who live in a 10,000-square-mile area that stretches from the Caballo Dam in New Mexico, 110 miles northwest of El Paso, to Van Horn, Texas, 120 miles to the southeast.

In 1973 the firm took the bold step of committing itself to the future with its decision to participate in the Arizona Nuclear Power Project to be located at the Palo Verde Nuclear Generating Station, fifty miles west of Phoenix. Currently two of the three proposed generating units are operational, with the last one due to be completed by late 1987. At that time the three units will have a total generating capacity of 3,810 megawatts and will form the largest nuclear power generating facility in the United States.

The Electric Company also has explored the possibility of alternative sources of power to serve its customers' needs. In cooperation with New

El Paso Electric Company, begun in 1901 as the El Paso Electric Railway Company, provided electric streetcars for the town's citizens.

444

El Paso Electric Company is housed in the Anson Mills Building. Built in 1912, it has been designated a Texas Historic Landmark.

Mexico State University, the firm has conducted extensive experiments into solar power and wind generation of electric current. Although none has proven to be satisfactorily cost effective, El Paso Electric maintains its dedication to research as the most reliable way to prepare for the future.

In addition to providing for its customers' electric power needs, The Electric Company has sought to take the lead in improving the quality of life in El Paso.

Through its wholly owned subsidiary, Franklin Land & Resources, Inc. (FLR), El Paso Electric has used the Economic Recovery Tax Act of 1981 to retain tax dollars previously sent to Washington. In turn, FLR has aided the downtown El Paso community through the revitalization of two landmark structures, the Cortez and the Hotel Paso del Norte.

Each year during the Christmas season, the company provides for a large star to shine down on the city from atop nearby Mount Franklin to remind El Pasoans of the deeper meaning of that special time.

The newly formed El Paso Renaissance 400 project, enthusiastically supported by El Paso Electric Company and other leaders in business and industry, has worked to improve the economic and cultural development of the city. Focusing on such areas as education, recreation, arts and culture, housing, utilities, government, and international relations, the participants in Renaissance 400 are working and planning so that the

A streetcar line splits South El Paso Street. The mule-drawn cart on the right seems out of place alongside the early-model autos that chugged along this and other streets in the first quarter of the century.

city of El Paso will remain one of the more desirable living areas in the nation. El Paso Electric Company is proud of the role it has played in the success of Renaissance 400, the latest example of a commitment to El Paso that stretches back to the earliest years of the twentieth century.

The firm currently participates in the Arizona Nuclear Power Project, located at the Palo Verde Nuclear Generating Station fifty miles west of Phoenix. In 1987, when all three generating units are operational, they will have a total generating capacity of 3,810 megawatts and will form the largest nuclear power generating facility in the United States.

W.L. BATES CO., INC.

Much of modern-day Corpus Christi—the Sparkling City by the Bay on the bustling South Texas Gulf Coast—is built on real estate assembled and sold by W.L. Bates and the business he founded nearly four decades ago.

Today the W.L. Bates Company, which Bates heads as president and chairman, ranks as one of the largest and most successful real estate organizations in all of South Texas. And it is helping Corpus Christi to take advantage of its position as the gateway to offshore industries in the Gulf of Mexico, and as a natural site for the explosive high-tech development now occurring across the state.

During the 1980s the firm has closed an impressive series of land transactions that have not only established it as a regional leader in commercial and industrial real estate, but also have had lasting impact on the economy of Corpus Christi and the surrounding area.

Bates and his company were honored for these achievements in 1983, when he was one of three top figures in Texas real estate development named as recipients of the statewide Dealmaker Award. The prestigious award is presented annually by SHWC, Inc., of Dallas, a leading Texas architectural, engineering, and planning firm.

In receiving this honor, the W.L. Bates Company was specifically singled out for its role in the assemblage and sale of 3,000 acres adjacent to the Corpus Christi Ship Channel. Baker Marine Corporation is developing a large offshore service center on the site. Baker Marine is making land available for development in conjunction with the U.S. Navy home port, which is located in the center of the property.

As a Dealmaker honoree, Bates is part of a very small, very select group of distinguished Texans, including legendary builder Trammel Crow, billionaire computer magnate H. Ross Perot, and others. The Dealmaker Award signifies excellence in the creation of "deals" for the development of land and buildings in Texas. Recipients are first nominated by a statewide committee of business and community leaders, then selected by a panel of nine jurors from the real estate development industry. Following his selection for the award in

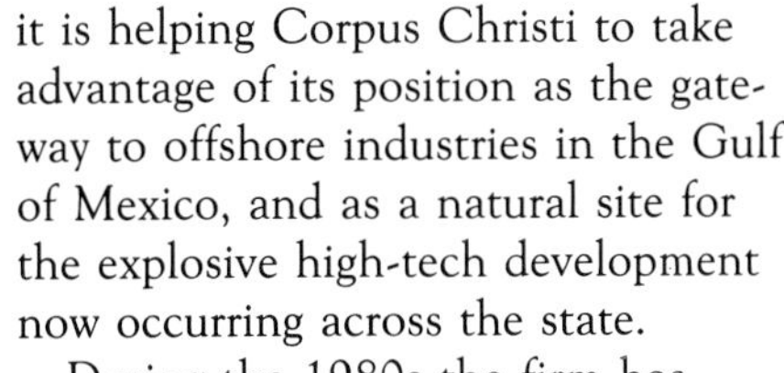

W.L. Bates, president and chairman of W.L. Bates Co., Inc., one of the largest and most successful real estate organizations in all of South Texas. © Portrait by Gold

1983, Bates was further honored by being named to serve on the selection jury to pick winners for 1984 and 1985.

The Dealmaker Award was among the most recent of many tributes paid to Bates during his forty years in real estate sales, and the Baker Marine transaction was one of a seemingly endless series of "deals" closed by Bates and his company since its beginning.

A native and lifelong resident of Corpus Christi, Bates was born there on August 8, 1923. His parents, the late W.L. Bates, Sr., and Agnes McAllister Bates, had moved to the city in 1911, when it was a small fishing port. Their son has seen it emerge into a major resort and industrial center of nearly 250,000 people, and, in more ways than one, he has been instrumental in that emergence.

Bates' early interest in real estate was motivated by F.M. Thomason, Real Estate. "I just naturally wanted to be a real estate salesman," he recalls. And in 1946, he realized that ambition by going to work as a broker for Thomason's firm.

Two years later, in 1948, Bates opened his own real estate agency in a small frame building in the 4600 block of Leopard Street, which he shared with real estate investor D.W. Grant. The firm's sales grew steadily over the years that followed, and Bates became an expert at the painstaking process of assembling large parcels of land for commercial uses and negotiating with dozens of property owners in order to finalize a single deal.

Beginning in about 1980, when an unparalleled boom in industrial and business growth started in Corpus Christi, Bates' expertise in land assemblage began paying greater dividends than ever before. During 1981 and 1982 the W.L. Bates Company recorded nearly $200 million in sales, including about twenty transactions of one million dollars or more. And this was only a sample of things to come.

"I don't sell any better than any-body else, I guess," Bates says in explaining his company's phenomenal sales record. "But I might work harder at it—and the harder you work, the luckier you get."

Experienced observers of the Corpus Christi market, however, credit Bates' ability, hard work, and intimate knowledge of the market—not mere luck—for his firm's success and rapid growth during the 1980s. The company's ten-member sales force has won both statewide and national recognition among developers interested in the Corpus Christi area. It handles numerous inquiries from outside the area about the availability of certain types of property.

Besides the Baker Marine deal, other prime property transactions during the past few years have included the assemblage of 3,000 acres on North Corpus Christi Bay from National Steel Corporation with a price tag of $42 million, the acquisition of property for the $30-million Sunrise Mall Shopping Center on South Padre Island Drive, and 1,600 acres of shoreline property from El Paso Natural Gas.

The list of major deals also includes a hotel site on Emerald Cove, an industrial park on North Padre Island Drive, the old Sears property on Leopard Street, now being developed as the new City Hall location, and other large development and redevelopment tracts. While commercial and industrial deals have been in the spotlight recently, the W.L. Bates Company also continues to be a major broker for South Texas ranch properties.

Bates has long been interested in industrial development and has served his community in a number of capacities relating to industry. In 1963 he drew up the first major industrial potential study for the Corpus Christi metropolitan area, and he is a past chairman of the Corpus Christi Industrial Commission.

The Bates agency has assisted in development or plant expansion projects for such firms as American Smelting and Refining, Berry En-gineering, Exxon, Coastal States Petroleum Company, Tenneco, Southwestern Refining, Champlin Petroleum, and others.

Although the firm is no longer involved in residential development, Bates previously developed such well-known Corpus Christi residential areas as Tropic Isles, Donna Park, Hudson Acres, Kingswood, Oak Ridge, and Jackson Heights. The company was associated in the development of the Pernitas Point subdivision at Lake Corpus Christi.

Bates is a past president of the Corpus Christi Board of Realtors, and was honored as the city's Realtor of the Year in 1966. He served as a member of the Nueces County Park Board from 1968 to 1976 and on the board of the Corpus Christi Better Business Bureau for nine years. He has also been active on a number of chamber of commerce committees.

He has been involved in state and federal studies and site acquisitions for the Padre Island National Seashore and Mustang Island State Park, has aided in land acquisitions for the Falcon Dam, an international project of the U.S. and Mexican governments, and has served as a consultant on the development of the McAllen Foreign Trade Zone.

An active real estate investor himself, Bates owns several farm and ranch properties, and owns an interest in The 600 Building, one of the largest skyscrapers in downtown Corpus Christi. His hobbies include growing prize-winning orchids and breeding and raising cattle. He and his wife established the Mr. and Mrs. W.L. Bates Ministerial Educational Fund at Brite Divinity School of Texas Christian University in Fort Worth. He is a member of many civic, professional, and fraternal organizations.

"Corpus Christi has finally reached the point where you can do more things than you once could," he says, "and things are happening faster these days."

Which is just the way W.L. Bates likes it.

THE CABALLERO MOTEL

Located a short five minutes from the sprawling El Paso International Airport, The Caballero Motel, member of the Best Western chain, prides itself on its long association with the city. Motel personnel know El Paso intimately and are anxious to share with visitors the marvelous hospitality of the city and its delightful variety of people.

One of the older urban centers in the state, El Paso has a most distinguished past that forms a vital part of the history of the greater Southwest. The influences of the Spanish, the Mexicans, the Indians, and the various other nationalities and ethnic groups that form America have all blended to form a cosmopolitan mixture that offers a little of everything to guests of the city.

Established in 1945, The Caballero Motel has helped make El Paso the modern city that it is today and prides itself on being able to offer its guests every convenience to ensure a comfortable, rewarding stay. The motel began as seventy-five well-

Visitors can enjoy the hospitality of The Caballero Motel and spend time exploring the beauty and magnificence of the American Southwest from its ideal location near the El Paso International Airport.

appointed rooms grouped around a central courtyard, much in the style of traditional Spanish architecture. Twenty-five additional rooms have been added since its founding, but owner Louis Maldanado and his staff have preserved the flavor of the original design. The central courtyard, shaded by large, well-manicured trees and accented by low shrubbery, forms the backdrop for a large swimming pool and other recreational facilities.

In addition to the aesthetically pleasing surroundings, guests also enjoy the benefits of a convenient location. Situated on Montana Street (the city extensions of U.S. highways 62 and 180), The Caballero Motel is easily located by visitors unfamiliar with the city, is close to downtown shopping, and can offer a variety of amusements to suit the most discrim-

inating traveler. Within the motel itself, a large restaurant, staffed by skilled chefs and attentive waiters, offers an impressive variety of international cuisine that focuses around the hearty, zesty fare of the Southwest. The motel lounge enables the weary traveler to relax quietly at the end of a hectic day's activities.

For those who wish to experience all that the area has to offer, The Caballero Motel can arrange for guided tours to El Paso's sister city, Juarez, Mexico. There motel guests will be treated with all the grace and charm that have come to signify life south of the border. They may also take advantage of the many opportunities to shop in the bustling marketplaces of Juarez and dine in any of the exquisite restaurants that cater to international guests.

The Caballero Motel extends to everyone an invitation to come to El Paso, accept its hospitality, and spend some time exploring and enjoying the beauty and magnificence of the American Southwest.

WHATABURGER, INC.

Whataburger, Inc., is one of the oldest and most successful quality fast-food restaurant chains in the entire United States today. "The great big taste you're hungry for—Whataburger" is a phrase familiar to all Texans and dominates the corporation's advertising from coast to coast and throughout the rapidly developing Sunbelt marketplace.

As it always has been, the chain's primary product is the Whataburger®—a quarter-pound, 100-percent pure beef burger served on a five-inch bun. At each of the company's restaurants, the customer may have his Whataburger "built to order," prepared with his choice of fresh lettuce, tomatoes, pickles, onions, salad dressing, ketchup, or mustard.

All Whataburger restaurants adhere to strictly controlled standards of high quality, cleanliness, and service, with special commitment and dedication to maintaining quality products. Indeed, the quality of the products and concern for individual customer preferences have been the driving force behind the success of Whataburger, and continue to be the cornerstones of its corporate philosophy.

The corporation was founded by Harmon A. Dobson in 1950 in Corpus Christi. Harmon, a true entrepreneur and a staunch believer in the free-enterprise system, made his dream a reality: "Provide the public with the ultimate burger—the

Whataburger, Inc., was founded by Harmon A. Dobson in 1950.

Grace W. Dobson, wife of the founder, is chairwoman of the board.

Whataburger."

The original Whataburger buildings were small, portable structures designed to be moved to new sites if and when traffic and population changes occurred. The first franchise was granted in 1953, and success was immediate. Soon, volumes began to exceed the potential of the original restaurant, and in 1961 the company designed a new, permanent A-frame structure featuring the now-familiar orange and white striped roof.

Volumes continued to grow steadily, and in 1966 an enclosed dining room was added to all A-frame restaurants. In 1974 new prototype-designed buildings were introduced, featuring dining rooms and drive-through facilities with the flexibility to accommodate various types of locations and to serve communities with varied populations.

In 1967 the firm suffered a major setback when Harmon Dobson, its founder and board chairman, died in an airplane accident. But Harmon's wife, Grace W. Dobson, immediately assumed responsibility and kept the corporation moving forward. Under

Mrs. Dobson's leadership, a new management team was formed, with Jim L. Peterson joining Whataburger, Inc., as president and chief executive officer.

Peterson, a nationally known figure in the restaurant industry, set forth a master plan that has made Whataburger a true leader in the food-service industry from coast to coast. Peterson and his management team have been frequently recognized for their outstanding contributions in such areas as governmental affairs, marketing, advertising, building design, quality control, research and development, training, and community involvement. As chairwoman of the board, Mrs. Dobson continues to embody the founding spirit and original goals of the company.

Because of the efforts, expertise, and dedication of its management and employees, today's Whataburger is truly what a burger should be!

Jim L. Peterson, president and chief executive officer.

The now-familiar A-frame structure with the orange and white striped roof was adopted in 1961.

BILLY PUGH COMPANY, INC.

Those who knew young Billy Pugh, back in the lean Depression years when he was doing odd jobs on and around the fishing and excursion boats piloted by his father, were pretty sure that Billy would follow the sea when he grew up. But few, if any, of them ever imagined that Billy Pugh would also become one of the unsung heroes of America's space program.

Along with the firm that bears his name, and the ingenious safety net he invented more than thirty years ago, Pugh holds a unique spot in the annals of the Space Age. Although he, his company, and his net had nothing directly to do with getting

Billy Pugh, founder.

the crews of sixteen U.S. Apollo missions *into* space, they played an indispensable role in getting them safely back to Earth again.

Today the walls of the corporate offices of the Billy Pugh Company, Inc., a few blocks from the Corpus Christi waterfront where Billy spent his boyhood, are adorned with mementoes of a vital contribution to space exploration. Among them are letters from lunar astronaut Neil Armstrong and other space pioneers, expressing their personal appreciation to Pugh and his company. And one of his celebrated nets—the one that lifted the Apollo 11 lunar landing team from the ocean on their return from the moon—hangs in a special place of honor in the Smithsonian Institution in Washington, D.C.

Long before orbiting capsules and men on the moon captured the nation's headlines, however, the "Billy Pugh net" had become a household term among people who earn their living on boats or in the vast offshore drilling industry. For many years the net was protected by two federal patents, and although the patents have now expired, there are surprisingly few imitations of its successful design. It remains the cornerstone of the Billy Pugh Company, a manufacturing firm that also produces many different types of marine and offshore safety equipment.

As Pugh himself says, "We really have no competition where nets are

concerned. We've sold thousands and thousands of them, to the U.S. armed services, to foreign governments, to police and fire departments, and, of course, to the offshore drilling industry, which is our biggest customer. The nets are the backbone of our business."

Countless lives had already been saved by Pugh's net by the time its wide acceptance and success led him to offer a modified rescue basket or net, suitable for one-man rescue operations, to the U.S. military in 1967. He thought the net could be used to rescue stranded GIs in the jungle combat zones of Vietnam. He also saw a capability for plucking astronauts from the sea after their space

capsules had splashed down. As it turned out, Pugh was right on target on both counts.

In 1968 the U.S. Navy signed a contract with Pugh. The Army and Marine Corps soon followed, and so did NASA. "Actually, they (NASA) contacted me," Pugh says, "after we started building nets for the Navy. We demonstrated the net for them at Houston and at Cape Canaveral, and they liked it."

At the same time the net was making history on NASA missions, it was also saving the lives of thousands of American servicemen in Vietnam, where the Billy Pugh net became as familiar a part of jungle warfare as the Army's "Huey" helicopter, on which it was standard air-lift rescue equipment.

In many respects, the inventor of the net is as unique as the net itself. Billy Pugh was, and is, a seafaring man. He was just sixteen when World War II came along in 1941, but Billy enlisted in the Coast Guard, and within two years became one of the youngest chief boatswain's mates in that service's proud history. After the war Pugh returned to his hometown and became harbormaster for the City of Corpus Christi.

"The job didn't pay real well," he recalls, "so I started a supply boat service on the side, and after a while it was doing well enough that I decided to devote full time to it." That was the beginning of the Billy Pugh Company, which, at its peak as a service business, operated a fleet of sixteen supply boats.

Among his customers and acquaintances at that time were Corpus Christi oilman C.G. "Gus" Glasscock and his son-in-law, Jimmy Storm, who were intrigued by the untried idea of drilling for oil beneath the unpredictable waters of the Gulf of Mexico. Glasscock and Storm designed and built the world's first offshore drilling rig and platform, and christened it "Mr. Gus." It brought about a new era in petroleum exploration when it became the first mobile rig to drill in waters more than

100 feet deep.

But there were problems—problems that were instantly apparent to a veteran seaman like Billy Pugh. "In the early 1950s, when the first offshore drilling started, there was just no safe way of getting people from boats onto the drilling platforms and back again. The rig top was sometimes 100 feet or more above the surface of the choppy waters, and getting there was dangerous work at best. They'd dangle a two-inch pipe with a net hung on it over the side, and the men would just hang on like monkeys until they could be pulled up and aboard."

In 1954 an offshore accident during such a haphazard transfer claimed two lives and left a third man seriously injured. But the tragedy gave Pugh an idea for a way to keep the same thing from happening in the future—a rope basket that could safely and easily transport personnel back and forth between boats and rigs. "I took some rope and built the first one in a fish house at Freeport," Pugh recalls. "Basically, we still use the very same design today, although there have been some improvements in materials and the type of flotation. Other than that, there've been very few changes."

The prototype of the Billy Pugh net was a 120-pound apparatus that resembled a seagoing elevator. Attached to a crane atop the rig deck, it could safely transport up to six men at one time. After its initial success aboard "Mr. Gus," word soon got out among other drillers and orders for more personnel carrier nets began to pour in. Suddenly, Billy Pugh, the seaman, found himself doubling as Billy Pugh, the manufacturer.

Meanwhile, the other part of his company was also growing. In 1959 Pugh established a yacht and boat repair service center, but the demand for nets and other safety equipment finally caused him to sell the yacht-service portion of the business in 1977. At that time, the Billy Pugh Company relocated its manufacturing facilities to 1415 North Water Street in Corpus Christi, where it currently employs about ninety persons.

In addition to all his other roles, Pugh is also an incurable adventurer. In 1985 he and a co-pilot planned to make the first known round-trip, transatlantic helicopter flight. Unfortunately, the copter was demolished in a crash caused by a "white-out" in the snows of Labrador. Pugh, however, was undaunted. "I average flying between 400 and 500 hours a year," he says, "and I plan to try it again. This time, I bet I make it."

Besides his manufacturing facility, Pugh operates a major offshore supply base with James E. Talley at Ingleside-on-the-Bay, near Corpus Christi. The base and its 50 employees serve the offshore drilling industry as Pugh himself has done for the past thirty years. But the versatile Pugh will be remembered best and longest as the man who brought a new dimension of safety to seagoing and airborne conveyances and their occupants—and an entire new meaning to the term "net profit."

THE T.O. STANLEY BOOT COMPANY

"This country didn't have to lose its (markets) for its cars, its radios, and its cameras—but it did. The foundation of a good product rests in its quality. If you recreate a pride in what you make and integrity in the way you do business, you'll survive. It's not magic—it's just the way it works."

These few sentences, both a pointed criticism as well as an implied challenge to business leaders, say a great deal about the blighted condition of some segments of American industry in the 1980s. They also reveal a generous insight into the personality and character of the man who uttered them. T.O. "Terry" Stanley, founder and chief executive officer of The T.O. Stanley Boot Company in El Paso, measures his words carefully and speaks from a conviction borne of close observation coupled with a sound, practical business sense.

Stanley has watched American manufacturing lose much of its competitive edge in the world's markets as better-quality foreign-made products have replaced American goods. And in a time-honored tradition that stretches back to the earliest days of this nation's history, he had embarked on a course that, if copied by others, will reverse the recent trend. Stanley doesn't presume to have answers to all the world's problems. He does, however, have much to say regarding the ways modern business can direct its efforts to attracting and keeping a loyal, satisfied clientele.

The T.O. Stanley Boot Company is a mirror reflection of the man who created it, and, in order to appreciate the firm's uniqueness in a world of conformity, one must attempt to understand the personal drives and motivations of Terry Stanley. Born some forty-three years ago in Big Spring, Texas, Stanley grew up working cattle with other cowboys and, in the process, absorbed those qualities of integrity, dependability, fairness, and respect for hard work that West Texans believe represent the very noblest traditions of their region.

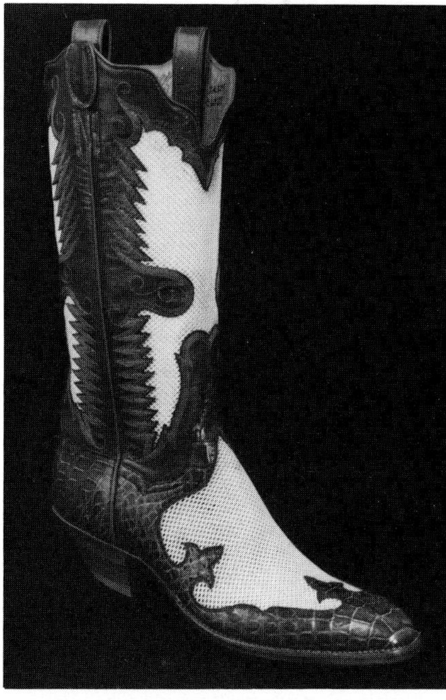

Upon reaching maturity, Stanley left to earn a bachelor's degree in art and to serve a hitch in the military before returning to West Texas to begin his career. In 1963 he began working for a small boot manufacturer and has been in the business ever since.

Stanley was involved in boot making during the late 1960s and the early 1980s that witnessed the arrival of the "Urban Cowboy" and ushered in a period of tremendous growth for the entire western wear industry. The new fad brought an increased demand for western clothing of all types, and manufacturers geared up their plants to increase production to meet the expanded markets. Boots, western shirts, and jeans began to appear on people in all walks of life. Bankers, actors, performers, businessmen, students, doctors, and lawyers in all sections of this country as well as overseas were sporting the latest fashions in western wear.

But, as T.O. Stanley observed, many manufacturers abandoned their commitment to quality as they scrambled to take advantage of demands for their products. The emphasis changed from one in which a sincere effort was made to give the customer his money's worth, to one in which the customer was given any-

thing for his money. The changes that accompanied the growth surge in the western wear industry led Stanley to make a fateful decision—he would start his own company and bring back to the industry that dedication to quality and customer satisfaction that he had seen when he

T.O. Stanley, founder and chief executive officer.

started in the business.

Acting on his belief that he could be successful, and with the encouragement and support of some close friends, Stanley opened the doors of The T.O. Stanley Boot Company in the recession-plagued year of 1979. The nationwide business downturn continued for several more years, but the firm prospered beyond anything its founder had dared to hope. He had staked his future on the conviction that there were people who still preferred quality over all other considerations in the boots they wanted.

Today, a scant seven years after its establishment, The T.O. Stanley Boot Company employs over 130 skilled craftsmen, all of whom demonstrate a deep and abiding commitment to make only the highest-quality western footwear.

This boot was made for Governor Mark White of Texas. It features the seal of the State of Texas inlaid with gold and silver..

As one enters the front door of the T.O. Stanley plant, one senses immediately that there is something refreshingly different about this company. The surroundings are relatively sparse, but comfortable. The people one encounters are uniformly friendly and seek to make the visitor feel genuinely welcome. Everyone says, "Hello," offers a cup of coffee, and stops to chat for a few minutes. While one may suspect, at first, that such gestures of friendship are not completely genuine, after a few minutes it becomes obvious that these are people who are sincere.

In the plant's main offices, one notices photographs of the many famous personalities who have bought Stanley boots, been pleased with them, and sent notes expressing their appreciation and satisfaction. Sammy Davis, Jr., Glen Campbell, Tennessee Ernie Ford, Eric Clapton, Gene Autry, Roy Rogers, the Bellamy Brothers, George Lucas, the Gatlin Brothers, Sam Peckinpah, and the Oak Ridge Boys are only a few of the individuals who, although they have the means to acquire boots from anywhere in the world, choose to wear those with the T.O. Stanley label.

Stanley explains that his is a custom boot operation on a larger-than-usual scale. It seeks to maintain the finer traditions of custom manufacture, but at a level at which greater numbers of people can be served. His craftsmen benefit from the use of modern technology and equipment if a better product will result. In other words, if a man using a machine can do the job better than a man working alone, the machine will be incorporated into the work place, provided, of course, that there is no sacrifice in quality.

A pair of boots from The T.O. Stanley Boot Company begin to take form when an order is received; none are made in advance for later sale.

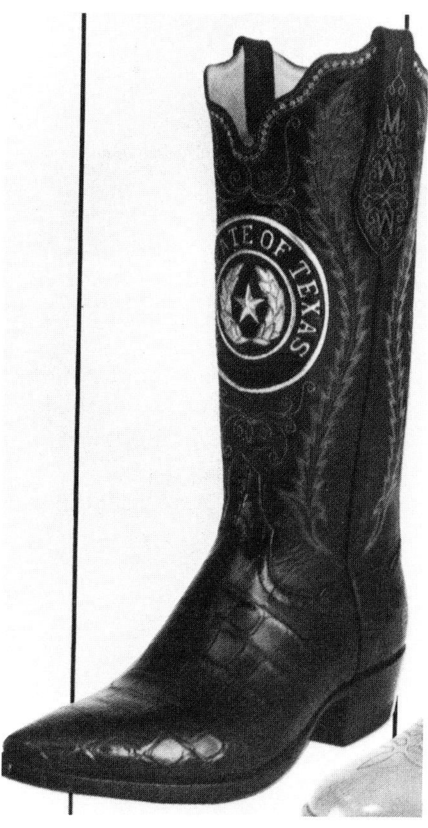

The customer makes a selection as to style, kind of leather preferred, heel and toe type, and so forth, and the craftsmen begin selecting the highest-quality materials for use. Over 300 separate procedures are required to make a Stanley boot, and throughout the process considerations of precision workmanship and attention to detail are uppermost in the minds of the employees.

If desired, T.O. Stanley personnel will assist in designing a boot that best meets the individual customer's needs. A good illustration of this can be seen in the boot style known as the Binion. Bennie Binion, a well-known Las Vegas casino owner, came to Stanley with a request for a boot that could be worn comfortably in the hot desert environment of southern Nevada. Stanley designers considered a number of possibilities and came up with a boot of alligator and kangaroo leathers inlaid with nylon mesh that would permit the free flow of air to the foot and lower leg. The finished boot exemplifies the keen craftsmanship and sensitivity to design traditions that have come to

characterize T.O. Stanley products.

As Stanley talks about his business, he does so in a voice that expresses both confidence as well as humility and gratitude. He knows he has done well and attributes much of that success to the people who work for him. He considers his employees to be the best available at what they do, and they all share Stanley's intense dedication to the pursuit of quality and excellence.

Stanley is pleased that his boots have been well received by his many customers whom he considers to be his friends. He is most gratified, however, by the enthusiastic reception given his products by professional cowboys, those who have worn boots all their lives and know almost intuitively how a boot should look, feel, and wear.

Stanley does not give boots away for promotional purposes, and yet many of the biggest names in the modern-day American West, including prominent ranchers, cattlemen, and rodeo stars, wear Stanley boots. He is proud of the fact that every year during the rodeo season in El Paso, the cowboys and other personnel that put on the show go around the area and receive free boots. They then go to The T.O. Stanley Boot Company and have Stanley design what they need and are happy to pay for them.

On those relatively rare occasions when Stanley can pause from his busy schedule and think of his company's future, his thoughts turn to things other than the material aspects of success. His yearning goes much deeper than simply greater financial rewards. As he puts it, "Money is only the barometer, how you keep score and measure your efforts against those of your competitors." What is truly important and worth any sacrifice is "what you leave behind after you're gone." He wants to bequeath to his children a certain legacy, that of a man who made a commitment to excellence and devoted all of his efforts and energies to attaining it.

RALPH WILSON PLASTICS COMPANY

Ralph Wilson Plastics Company, a manufacturer of decorative plastic laminates used for a wide variety of home and commercial applications, stands as a proud testament to the validity of the free enterprise system. The driving force that catapulted the venture from the smallest of eighteen competing businesses in 1955, its initial year, to its present rank as the leading laminate producer in the country came from the founding Wilson family. Ralph Wilson, Sr., was a businessman who had gotten his start in 1920 at age nineteen with his share of the proceeds from a corn crop of the family farm in Indiana.

Thirty-five years later, having sold his successful laminate-manufacturing company in California, he and his son, educated as a dentist and now known to employees as "Dr. Ralph," organized the new enterprise in Temple, Texas, with two groups of local businessmen: A.P. Brashear, A.P. Brashear, Jr., and W.A. Prewitt, Jr., in one group, and Angus G. Wynne, Jr., E.H. Holland, and Z.L. Majors in the other.

Although the senior Wilson boasted when he launched the business that he'd get to go fishing four days a week, Ralph Wilson Plastics Company turned a profit within a phenomenally short four-month period; the next year sales increased by 200 percent. Growth has been the by-word ever since, and the beauty of Wilsonart-brand decorative laminate can be found everywhere from a high-tech New York bar top to the surface of a New Orleans hospital nurses' station or a kitchen counter in Nevada.

Beginning with a team of forty employees in a brick and cement-block building by the tracks of the Santa Fe, Ralph Wilson Plastics now has over 2,000 employees nationwide with fourteen warehouses and a sales force from coast to coast. Two manufacturing plants produce more than 100,000 varieties of decorative laminate sold primarily to "post-forming" customers (an example of post-forming is the curved backsplash of a counter top) and to the manufacturers of school and office furniture, as well as to the manufacturers of cabinetry and tables for laboratories, restaurants, store fixtures, and a variety of other uses.

Dr. Ralph Wilson, Jr., who took the firm's helm when his father died in 1972, attributes success to several factors, not least of which is the mastery—and ongoing development—of a complex chemical-manufacturing process. From the outset the company has continually explored new frontiers in technology to produce the nation's leading line of ultramodern surfaces. In the early 1970s,

Ralph Wilson, Sr., founder.

for example, it developed two pioneering products for laboratory surfaces in twelve colors that were dramatically different from the conventional work surfaces. This breakthrough prompted a favorite expression from Dr. Ralph: "When Braniff ended the plain plane, we ended the drab lab."

Because employees share directly in the profits, they feel a strong incentive to improve the company. As Dr. Ralph explains, "My folks hustle. They're in business for themselves." Producing high-quality products, however, has been only a part of the team's strategy. Providing fast, error-free, efficient service to customers also has been a top priority from the beginning, and not an easy task, in view of the complexity of the busi-

Colored and patterned laminates from Wilsonart provide for many unique design opportunities for the kitchen, bath, and beyond.

ness, which involves over 100,000 different items and thus, numerous opportunities for mistakes.

Consequently, in 1960, Ralph Wilson Plastics initiated a plan, unprecedented in the industry, to design a synchronized scheduling system, all the way from customer order processing through manufacturing to delivery. In addition, the then-fledgling organization turned away from the seemingly sensible method of transporting goods that prevailed at the time among the giants in the industry: Those companies contracted for delivery services with common carriers upon whose schedules both the customers and manufacturers had to depend. Ralph Wilson Plastics decided to lease and operate its own trucks. Today, in contrast to the several weeks it takes competitors to deliver their products, Wilsonart, with

Ralph Wilson Plastics' Temple, Texas, plant has grown from 40,000 square feet to 350,000 square feet under one roof.

its fleet of ninety-nine red and white trucks, can guarantee arrival within "ten days anywhere in the United States!"

In 1964, less than ten years after its creation, the Wilson family purchased all the company stock and made it a publicly held corporation. Ralph Wilson Plastics then merged with Rexall Drug and Chemical Company in 1966. Rexall changed its name in 1969 to Dart Industries, Inc., which includes among its many holdings, Tupperware. Dart Industries let the founding ideals of the successful firm continue, with its own

The firm is also located in Fletcher, North Carolina, in this 350,000-square-foot facility.

management intact. In 1980 Dart Industries merged with Kraft Foods, and Ralph Wilson Plastics experienced a record earnings year.

The company has shown a commitment to the quality of community life even as it has spread its name throughout the United States. Ralph Wilson Plastics provides a large part of the local United Way budget and also helps support the Azalee Marshall Cultural Activities Center of Temple. In addition, it finances the Ralph Wilson Youth Club in Temple, "possibly one of Temple's most stabilizing forces," says Dr. Wilson. In 1966 employees started a scholarship fund with a $500 contribution, matched by $1,500 from the Wilson family. The fund is now a half-million dollars and keeps about twenty-five employees' children in college each year. Ralph Wilson Plastics also sponsors an annual free enterprise essay contest, with $1,500 prizes awarded to fifteen young winners.

The Wilsonart philosophy that people are the greatest resource of any enterprise has thus come through in all its endeavors: in the value it places on its employees, in its emphasis on serving its customers, and in its involvement with community affairs.

Part of Wilsonart's private truck fleet was recently awarded top safety honors by the National Private Fleet Conference based on the low accident frequency enjoyed by the company.

TEXAS MILITARY INSTITUTE

Since 1912 Texas Military Institute has been housed in this facility in Alamo Heights.

In 1951 General Douglas MacArthur made a return visit to his alma mater. Pictured, from left: W.W. Bondurant, chairman of the board; General MacArthur; and J.D. Miller, superintendent.

The alma mater begins:
> *On the city's border,*
> *reared against the sky*
> *Stands our alma mater,*
> *dear old TMI*
> *We swear allegiance,*
> *orange and black held high*
> *Hail to the colors, TMI*

And thousands have "hailed to the colors" and "sworn their allegiance" since the school's founding as West Texas Military Academy in 1893 by the Right Reverend J.S. Johnston, bishop of the Diocese of West Texas of the Protestant Episcopal Church. Among its distinguished graduates are General Douglas MacArthur; General Ralph E. Haines, Jr.; Dan Blocker, star of the long-running television series "Bonanza;" David R. Scott, astronaut, co-pilot, and orbital spacewalker for the Gemini 8 and Apollo 9 missions; and Henry E. Catto, Jr., director of public relations for the U.S. Department of Defense. Hundreds of others are leaders today in all walks of life throughout America.

The school was first located on Government Hill near Fort Sam Houston a short distance from downtown San Antonio. In 1912 it relocated to its present site in Alamo Heights, a residential suburb of the Alamo City. In the summer of 1987 it will move again to a sixty-acre campus near Loop 1604 and Interstate 10 in northwest San Antonio.

In 1972 young women were admitted to TMI. In 1987, for the first time, dormitories will be available on the new campus for male and female students. At present the enrollment stands at 320, with a teaching faculty of 35, which makes for a student/ teacher ratio of less than 10 to one. That ratio makes for a very healthy academic environment.

In trying to help each student realize his/her potential TMI has set forth these objectives: to provide a course of study that will foster an

Texas Military Institute's ROTC marching unit.

awareness of our cultural heritage; to provide a strong college preparatory program; to enable students to think logically and to be able to express their thoughts clearly in speech and writing; to help students develop effective study habits; to foster Christian growth through courses in religion, worship services, and assembly programs; to create an atmosphere that will encourage development of social sensitivity, responsibility, and self discipline; to encourage students to engage in community services—within and without the school; to encourage the development of an aesthetic sense by providing courses in literature, art, music, and drama; to provide a good health and physical education program; and to attempt to enroll students of different backgrounds in order that all may benefit.

These objectives have been taken seriously by the student bodies over the years. More than 98 percent of TMI graduates have gone on to institutions of higher learning such as Harvard, Princeton, Randolph Macon Women's College, Southern Methodist University, Texas A&M, The University of Texas, and Yale. Among academic awards presented TMI graduates have been the National Merit Scholar Award, National Achievement Scholarship, and the Legion of Valor Bronze Cross for Achievement.

Enrollment at TMI continues to grow but the reasons for sending a child to this private school have changed over the years, according to its president, the Reverend Canon A. Nelson Daunt. "In the early days through the 1960s there was a healthy respect for militarism and the disciplined life of a military school," states

Even though TMI was founded primarily as a military-oriented school, it has evolved into a well-rounded institution. Pictured, from left: Steven K. Howell; John K. Walters, executive chairman; and the Reverend Canon A. Nelson Daunt.

Canon Daunt. "Today parents are looking for boarding schools for the order that is absent in many homes, the discipline of study hall in the evening. Parents find they [the students] can't avoid all of the distractions that happen in an ordinary family. So they are beginning to recognize boarding schools for the order of the day more than just the discipline of the military school."

Although campus life has been good considering the limited space, the new TMI campus will offer the opportunity for many activities not possible at the old facility. The school week is presently five days with the campus closed on weekends. However, in the fall of 1987, when the new campus is opened, weekend activities will be developed. Drama, intramural athletics, and more social activities will be among those weekend projects.

Even though the school is relocating, its present main building, set high on a hill and looking somewhat like a medieval castle, will not be destroyed. It has historic significance in that it was the first precast, tilt-up concrete building in the United States when it was constructed in 1912. Several groups are interested in the nine-acre site along with the main building and the Douglas MacArthur Memorial Library. These groups want to turn the nine-acre campus into a retirement home.

Even though TMI was founded primarily as a military-oriented school it has evolved into a more well-rounded institution. "We have a very fine cadet corps unit," states Daunt. "It maintains the rank of an honor unit with distinction, something few schools can boast.

"But," he continues, "TMI today is a coeducational school with middle and upper grades, and, with our blend of church and military, we have a very strong unified sense of belonging and purpose to contribute the best we can so that our students will become the leaders of tomorrow."

TMI will continue to search for qualified students who will benefit from its educational philosophy and program. Who will be the next student with feet firmly planted on the ground and stars on his shoulders like General MacArthur? Who will be the next student who will walk among the stars as did astronaut David Scott? Who will be the next student to work among the stars in Hollywood as Dan Blocker did? Only time will tell, but it is certain that with the high standards maintained by Texas Military Institute there will always be leaders developed at the school.

As a member of that first class of 1893 so aptly put it on his final visit to TMI in June 1951, "This is where I started and I thank a merciful God that I am able to come back to the school again." Thus spoke the tall man, with the corncob pipe, dressed in his familiar khakis and Army cap—General Douglas MacArthur.

SOUTHWESTERN PUBLIC SERVICE COMPANY

On April 15, 1985, Texas Governor Mark White presented a plaque to the winner of the Ed C. Burris Award designating the "Business of the Year" in Texas. In describing the award recipient, Governor White noted, "This company provides us with positive proof that quality electric service doesn't have to mean skyrocketing electric rates. It has shown it can be done through effective cost-control measures. The company has continually worked hard to keep down all fuel costs, recently having renegotiated its coal-hauling contracts to save consumers millions of dollars in fuel costs." The business to which the governor referred was the Southwestern Public Service Company, a leader in innovative electric power generation for over eighty years.

With its corporate headquarters located in Amarillo, SPS has long been recognized as a leader in its field. In 1978 the firm was named the outstanding electric utility of that year by the editors of *Electric Light & Power,* the news magazine of the electric utility management and technology industry. The approximately one million people served by SPS have every reason to feel very pleased that their electric utility has received such distinguished recognition.

The Southwestern Public Service Company of today can trace its origins back to the beginning of the twentieth century and has evolved from the combined efforts of farsighted individuals in both Texas and New Mexico.

One of the earliest components of SPS was the Eddy Light and Ice Company, formed in 1894 in Eddy (now Carlsbad), New Mexico, which used the impounded water from a small dam to generate hydroelectric power to serve local citizens. In 1904 the city fathers in Roswell, to the north of Carlsbad, authorized the establishment of the Roswell Electric Light Company, to serve approximately 2,000 customers in that community.

Electricity in Roswell was generated initially by large diesel engines that were phased out in 1915 with the installation of a 500-kilowatt General Electric steam-driven turbogenerator. By that time the Roswell firm had joined forces with the local gas supplier and had become the Roswell Gas and Electric Company.

Concurrently with the developments in New Mexico, the town of Amarillo, Texas, to the east, was reaching a size that required greater sources of local electric power. The first successful electric power franchise in Amarillo was granted by that town's city council to E.L. Dohoney and John Porter, who began service in 1903.

The utility endured for nine years, at which time it was bought out by the Cities Service Company which had begun operations as the City Light and Water Company. In 1925 Southwestern Public Service Company, part of an eastern utilities holding company that had earlier begun operating the electric utilities in Roswell, Artesia, and Carlsbad, New Mexico, moved into Texas with the acquisition of the City Light and Water Company of Amarillo. The foundation of the modern-day firm had been completed.

The pattern and method of expansion of SPS through the years was similar to that of other utilities of the time. Characteristically, a number of small, rural towns in a particular region would establish generating facilities that were only large enough to meet local needs. Generally no thought or consideration was given to the idea of planning for expansion or future growth to meet increasing demands.

When the need for increased amounts of power did become apparent, the small, isolated firms found themselves without the necessary capital or expertise to handle expansion. They quickly saw an advantage to merging with a larger utility that could handle growth as well as guarantee more dependable power delivery to the areas already served.

Over the years SPS expanded out of Amarillo and into neighboring towns in the northwest Texas area, absorbing other utilities in the process. The Texas-New Mexico Utilities Company, the Panhandle Power & Light Company, and the Cimarron Utilities Company all became part of the SPS power network in the years prior to World War II. In early September 1942 the directors of the firm, meeting to discuss future areas for expansion, decided to focus their efforts on building the most efficient electric generating system possible in the territory they already served, instead of moving into other areas that could not be easily integrated, either geographically or economically, into the existing system.

In the years since that wartime meeting, Southwestern Public Service Company has become one of the premier power suppliers in the nation. It presently provides service to an area that extends from southwestern Kansas, across the Oklahoma panhandle, through the panhandle and south plains regions of northwest Texas, and on into the Pecos River Valley in eastern and southeastern New Mexico. Within that 52,000 square miles can be found a tremendous variety and diversity of resources and economic assets, including substantial acreage of irrigated farmland; vast oil and natural gas reserves; major facilities for the mining and production of potash, carbon black, and helium; as well as great herds of cattle for the nation's beef consumers.

The firm operates ten power plants that can generate a total of 4.3 million kilowatts of electricity for distribution over the 5,000 miles of transmission lines. The company also is interconnected with other utilities in New Mexico, Texas, and Oklahoma, thus improving the SPS system's reliability and holding down the per-unit cost of electricity to its customers. The approximately 2,400 SPS employees earn a total annual payroll in excess of seventy million dollars, which forms an important source of

Southwestern Public Service Company serves major wholesale customers through this substation at the first direct-current intertie designed by the firm. The electric utility also serves a population of more than one million in a 52,000-square-mile area covering parts of Texas, New Mexico, Oklahoma, and Kansas.

capital for the many communities in which they live.

Much of the impressive success of SPS derives directly from the management philosophy that permeates the entire organization. The company recognized very early that the electric utility business was unlike that of any of its corporate colleagues. It could not pick up its generating facilities and transmission lines and move them to an area that seemed more financially promising. It had to pin all its hopes and plans on the expansion of its service area and on providing better, more reliable, and more cost-efficient electric power to its customers.

For these reasons, SPS employees place a high premium on finding ways to cut costs. They also participate actively in civic affairs and give generously to the annual United Way and other campaigns in the towns and cities of their service territory. In the words of one of the corporation's recent publications, "The electric company as a public utility has a public responsibility to serve every person in the area efficiently, courteously, and economically. The electric company has a franchise that gives it the privilege of doing business and outlines the terms under which it will conduct its business, and, at the same time, imposes the responsibility of serving the area for the life of the franchise—good times or bad." The people at Southwestern Public Service Company obviously take this as a very solemn pledge.

SOUTHWESTERN BAPTIST THEOLOGICAL SEMINARY

In the spring of 1905 Benajah Harvey "B.H." Carroll, former pastor of the First Baptist Church of Waco, conceived the idea to which he would dedicate the remainder of his life—establishing a Baptist seminary in the Southwest. While riding a train across the barren Texas Panhandle to Amarillo, he envisioned God commanding him to build such an institution. At first he mentally balked at the mandate, feeling ill equipped to take on the responsibility because of deafness and infirm health. But after thinking about it and praying for guidance, he yielded to the irresistible order, and, upon returning to Waco, energetically pursued his goal.

Great change characterized the first five years of the seminary's existence. By August 1905 Carroll had secured donations and pledges totaling $22,000, enough to finance the school's operation for three years. He then received permission from the Baylor University trustees to transform the Theology Department into a separate and complete School of Divinity, granting bachelor's, master's, and doctoral degrees. Almost miraculously, within a week the newly created Baylor Theological Seminary

began classes, with Carroll serving as dean of the 150 students and five faculty members.

Despite this promising beginning, in 1907 Carroll requested that the Baptist General Convention of Texas, the denomination's governing body in the state, remove the seminary from Baylor, and grant a separate charter, name, and board of directors. (Baylor, of course, still maintained a theology department.) The general convention's members accepted the proposal the following year, calling the new institution Southwestern Baptist Theological Seminary. Reasoning that Waco could not support both schools, Southwestern directors approved an attractive bid from Fort Worth ($100,000 and 250 acres), and in 1910 Southwestern moved to its present location southwest of the city, with Carroll as president.

During the early years after the move Southwestern encountered many difficulties—enough to test its founder's faith. Certainly the most constant and pressing of these was securing continued funding. By that time Carroll was practically bedridden and had to carry on fund-raising

activities by correspondence. Board members operated on a year-to-year basis, with only their faith in God and the school's remarkable founder to sustain them. Furthermore, the campus was little more than a barren field; and as the students attempted to grow vegetables to supplement their diet, they found the plowed ground yielded more Johnson grass than garden crops.

And if these hardships were not enough, living conditions were particularly primitive. Only one building, Fort Worth Hall (now a men's dormitory), had been built, and all classes, as well as housing and the library, were crowded into that one structure. To make matters worse, the unfinished building boasted neither sewage facilities nor heat, thus making living especially uncomfortable. So onerous were these conditions that before improvement encouraged a gradual increase, enrollment dropped by 25 percent.

Since its founding the primary purpose of Southwestern Baptist Theological Seminary has remained

Looking down on the Southwestern Baptist Theological Seminary, Fort Worth.

The B.H. Carroll Memorial Building, the main facility on campus, was constructed in 1950.

the same—to provide quality training for ministers. Over the years, however, the institution has refined various methods to meet the changing needs of society. In 1910 the Women's Missionary Training School became part of the seminary; in 1915, one year after Carroll's death, the board of trustees added degrees in both church music and religious education. More recently, Southwestern has responded to modern social demands by offering advanced degrees in communications skills, church recreation, gerontology, psychology, counseling, and social work, as well as the traditional theological areas.

Originally designed to prepare Baptists for a frontier-type ministry, Southwestern Baptist Theological Seminary now has students from each of the fifty United States and over forty-one foreign countries, with 93 percent of these being Baptist and the remainder representing forty other denominations. Furthermore, the institution operates centers in Houston, San Antonio, and Shawnee, Oklahoma.

B.H. Carroll would be both astonished and proud of the modern-day Southwestern. It is the largest of the six Southern Baptist seminaries and educates almost 40 percent of the denomination's seminary students. The beautifully landscaped grounds now house fourteen major structures. In

Completed in 1983, the A. Webb Roberts Library houses one of the largest theological collections in the United States.

October 1982 church leaders and educators dedicated the $6-million A. Webb Roberts Library, which houses one of the largest theological collections in the United States. Furthermore, enrollment has steadily increased, and in the 1984-1985 term reached 5,086. With 101 full-time and 83 part-time faculty and 200 staff members, Southwestern Baptist Theological Seminary has more than fulfilled its founder's dream.

Fort Worth Hall was the first building constructed on campus, in 1910.

AMERICAN SOLAR KING CORPORATION

American Solar King Corporation is a product of the energy crisis of the early 1970s. It emerged prior to the Arab oil embargo with the philosophy that solar energy would take a leading role as an alternative fuel source. However, the company's founders believed that all forms of renewable and alternative energies would have a place in conserving fossil fuels for the applications to which they are uniquely suited.

In assessing the potential of solar energy, founder and entrepreneur Brian Pardo noted that if solar was to provide even one percent of the United States annual energy consumption, there would be a large market for the hardware necessary to capture and convert solar to consumable energy.

Bringing together elements of finance, research, and marketing, Pardo recapitalized the former Nevada company in 1976 as a Texas corporation headquartered in Waco. Having begun with six or seven employees in a 12,000-square-foot building, by 1985 American Solar King had grown to employ almost 500 people working out of a 140,000-square-foot facility that is the administrative, manufacturing, and research headquarters for this nationwide firm.

The mainstay of American Solar King has been a carefully engineered, flat-plate solar collector which, until 1981, was marketed through as many as 600 independent dealers. In revamping its marketing approach, the firm evolved a triad approach involving direct sales to residential and industrial markets with a strong reliance on highly technical research aimed at bringing marketable products on-line in a short period of time.

In 1982 the company began a test project of "SFI" (sell, furnish, and install) with Sears in the Boston area. The success of this pilot program led to its expansion to ten branches operating in the Sears solar program. Simultaneously, a direct-sales program in the Tennessee Valley Authority solar program netted American Solar King more than 80 percent of that market, operating from three branch locations.

The commercial aspect of the triad spawned a new concept in providing heated water or fluids for industrial applications. American Solar King's Solar Utility Program™ lets industries use solar hardware to produce needed heated fluids without the capital expense of buying a solar system themselves. American Solar King designs, builds, and maintains the custom system; a third party purchases the system and sells the product to the industry for a rate guaranteed to be

American Solar King Corporation's headquarters building in Waco encompasses over 140,000 square feet including manufacturing space, administrative offices, and research facilities. This is the growing company's third building in the first ten years of its active history.

20 percent less than its cost in meeting its needs through conventional energy means.

The firm acquired Daystar Corporation and Solar Thermal Systems, a subsidiary and a division of Exxon Enterprises, respectively, in 1981. It also gained rights to Exxon's research with desiccants, a vital link in the development of efficient solar space heating and cooling systems. These acquisitions, combined with American Solar King's own three-year effort, has brought about the development of a new heating and air conditioning product with the ability to purify stale indoor air with a potential energy cost savings of 50 to 70 percent.

Innovation in research and development, as well as marketing strategy and finance, has been the hallmark of American Solar King Corporation as it moves with the country through a period of conservation and growing emphasis on alternative, renewable energy resources—such as solar energy.

TEXAS BANKERS ASSOCIATION

Organized on July 23, 1885, the Texas Bankers Association is the oldest such state organization in the United States. As the voice of the banking fraternity, TBA immediately set about to provide direction and stability to a system that had inherited distrust from the Andrew Jackson/Sam Houston era. Through TBA, Texas bankers influenced the legislature and public opinion to obtain approval of a constitutional amendment in 1904 authorizing the chartering and regulation of state banks. National banks had been chartered by the federal government since 1864. After 1904 banking in Texas changed from a system of unregulated, unincorporated private banks and national banks to a dual banking system of privately owned but government-regulated state banks and national banks.

In 1911 TBA established the *Texas Bankers Record*, one of the foremost banking journals from that time to the present. In its history the publication has had only four editors and has never missed a month of publication. In 1986, the year of the Texas sesquicentennial celebration, the seventy-fifth anniversary of the magazine was celebrated by changing its name to *Texas Banking*.

During periods of challenge, TBA has provided leadership for banking and the state. In the 1890s the association successfully led efforts to control the spread of the boll weevil, following its devastating invasion of the cotton-growing states. In 1909 the legislature adopted a state deposit insurance scheme that required state banks to post a surety bond or pay mutual assessments into a depositors' "guaranty fund" to insure deposits in all state banks. This led to a period of promotion and expansion, and numerous persons without banking experience obtained state charters and opened banks. In 1913, with the passage of the Federal Reserve Act, TBA members exerted their influence through Colonel E.M. House of Austin, an advisor to President Woodrow Wilson, to secure location of one of

The headquarters of the Texas Bankers Association is located at 203 West Tenth Street, Austin.

the twelve Federal Reserve banks in the nation for Dallas. In 1917, when America entered World War I, TBA member banks led the state's Liberty Loan war bonds drive, and Texas oversubscribed its quota.

Between 1921 and 1925 eighty-three state banks failed, resulting in heavy assessments to keep the guaranty fund afloat; this began to affect the solvency of well-managed banks. TBA sought and obtained repeal of the guaranty fund law; at the same time chartering of state banks was made more restrictive. This experience was a prelude to the Great Depression, and after the bank holiday in March 1933, only twenty-six Texas banks failed to reopen. In light of the failure of the guaranty fund deposit insurance experiment, many Texas bankers initially were skeptical about the establishment of the Federal Deposit Insurance Corporation (FDIC) in June 1933.

From 1933 until 1980 banks were heavily regulated as to types of accounts that could be offered, interest that could be paid for deposits, and

interest that could be charged on loans. After World War II, when TBA member banks again gave all-out support to the war effort, banking entered a period of uniformity with minimum change. TBA's first professional executive, William A. Philpott, Jr. (1915-1963), retired and was succeeded by Sam O. Kimberlin, Jr. (1964-   ), and the association built permanent headquarters in Austin in 1977. In 1980 a major change in the banking environment was heralded by the passage by Congress of the Depository Institutions Deregulation and Monetary Control Act, which authorized banks to pay interest for deposits at market rates. Thus, near the end of TBA's first century, banking again entered an era of new challenges.

In addressing TBA's centennial convention in Austin in 1985, William M. Isaac, chairman of the Federal Deposit Insurance Corporation, said: "I've got to commend the Texas banks . . . your banking system is stronger than most states' and certainly stronger than the national average. . . . So, I am proud of you! You are good bankers, and you certainly have been very supportive of me and the FDIC over the years, and for that, I thank you."

GEOSOURCE INC.

Because nature favored Texas with a healthy share of the earth's petroleum supply, Texans had the opportunity to become leaders in developing geophysical methods and equipment for locating oil and gas both at home and around the world. Geosource Inc. represents a combination of the experience and products of many of the industry's pioneers.

Incorporated in 1972, Geosource entered the market in 1973 following the acquisition of Mandrel Industries—a subsidiary of the Ampex Corporation—and the Petty Geophysical Engineering Corporation. Mandrel was itself the product of numerous mergers, but the Petty organization had remained intact since 1925, when O. Scott Petty and his brother, Dabney, formed the corporation in San Antonio to field test seismic equipment of their own design.

Scott Petty would later recall the early days when he, Dabney, and their shooter, Conrad "Pop" Reichert, made up the firm's seismograph crew, and a Model-T Ford loaded with dynamite boxes and cumbersome seismic apparatus was the company's only equipment. He remembered, too, the bone-chilling rain of Texas winters and the muggy, mosquito-infested air of the Louisiana bayou country where the crews fought off cottonmouths, alligators, and snapping turtles while awaiting the precious predawn quiet to shoot leases for oil prospectors.

By the time Petty joined Geosource, it had become one of the major geophysical exploration companies, with crews operating worldwide, but reminders of those early days are preserved in the Petty Geophysical Museum, located in the Robert H. Ray Building which serves as the headquarters for the Petty-Ray Geophysical Division and Exploration Products Group of Geosource in Houston.

The Robert H. Ray Company's Texas heritage was no less distinguished than Petty's. As Coastal Oil Finding Company, Robert H. Ray

and Jack C. Pollard pioneered in the gravity method of detecting oil-bearing formations, offering torsion-balance surveys to the oil industry from 1929 until 1933, when Ray and Pollard parted company temporarily to take positions with major oil firms. In 1939 Ray formed the Robert H. Ray Company to provide gravimetric and magnetic surveys, and Pollard rejoined him two years later. Sam D. Rogers became a partner in 1942, forming the Rogers-Ray Company, which expanded its services to include seismic surveys. Ten years later R.S. Duty, Jr., and Norman P. Teague joined the Houston-based partnership and restored the Robert H. Ray Company name.

In 1959 the Robert H. Ray Company, together with the McCollum Exploration Company, formed McCollum-Ray International to offer weight-drop seismic exploration in foreign areas. Dr. Burton McCollum, another true pioneer in the field, had organized McCollum Exploration in 1923 and held master patents on many exploration devices including the weight-drop "Thumper" method that eliminated the dangerous explosive characteristics of seismic work. Later that year Robert H. Ray Com-

pany, Inc., was formed to acquire the outstanding stock of McCollum Exploration.

When Mandrel Industries acquired the Robert H. Ray Company in 1962, followed closely by Seismic Exploration, Inc., General Geophysical Company, Apache, and Frontier, it became one of the largest geophysical service organizations in the world, since it already included the manufacturing, development, research, and electronic capabilities implied by its name.

An interesting note is that most of the above-named acquisitions were founded by Texans—and primarily,

An early recording truck.

Houstonians. The men responsible for forming Seismic Exploration, Inc., were F. Fisher Reynolds, A.A. Hunzicker, and John D. Marr; for General Geophysical, Earl Johnson, Chester Sappington, and Tom O. Hall; for Apache, A. Ladner. Frontier was a Canadian company, and its founder, Ted Rozsa, was from Calgary.

Unlike most of the other organizations with which it became associated, Mandrel had its inception outside Texas. Formed as the Electric Sorting

Machine Company in Michigan in 1931, Mandrel acquired its new name following a merger in 1956 that included Electro-Technical Labs (ETL) of Houston. Since 1942 ETL had specialized in the manufacture of geophysical instruments, principally geophones.

With the acquisition of North American Geophysical Company in 1957 and the assets of the Texas Division of Clevite Corporation in 1959, the product line was supplemented by land and underwater gravity meters, magnetic recording systems, a new hydrophone, and other seismic devices. These operations, including Sensore, the major European manufacturer of geophones, which was acquired by Geosource in 1981, have evolved into the Exploration Products Group of Geosource, a modern pacesetter in the design, manufacture, and sale of sophisticated geophysical products.

In 1982 Geosource became a wholly owned subsidiary of Aetna Life and Casualty Company. Since July 1984, however, Geosource has been a subsidiary of Gearhart Industries, Inc., of Fort Worth, although its principal offices are located in Houston.

Presently, Geosource offers products and service in all major areas of geophysical exploration. It operates full-scale land seismic crews in environments ranging from mountain to marsh, from jungle to desert, as well as fully equipped modern seismic vessels and major processing centers around the world. Through the years its components have built up a staggering reservoir of experience and have developed innovative technology through applied research under the most difficult conditions.

Geosource has made many significant contributions to the geophysical industry including miniaturized digital grade geophones, advances in the McCollum "Thumper" method with sophisticated analog and digital technology, development of the "Common Depth Point" technique now universally used in seismic acquisition, the industry's first digital field summing system, first digital field correlator and vibrator control electronics, minicomputer-based processing systems and laser plotters, advanced receiver and source arrays such as Geo-Max™ and Varisource™, as well as the industry's most advanced digital seismic recording systems such as the MDS-10 followed by the MDS-16, the industry's first land-based, 1,016-channel telemetry system, utilizing fiber-optic technology and offering multiline recording capabilities.

Although the Geosource name is of fairly recent origin, its Texas roots are deep. With a record of over sixty years in the geophysical industry and the financial stability to develop and perfect technology while preserving organizational strength through fluctuating business cycles, Geosource Inc. looks forward to a future of continued service to the oil industry and to Texas.

This modern-day recording truck, when compared with its early-day counterpart, shows how equipment used by the geophysical industry has changed.

THE HORNE COMPANY

In 1836 Houston's first real estate agents, the Allen brothers, thought their new town on Buffalo Bayou would one day become a great city. Ninety years later another young real estate man shared that same thought, and he spent the rest of his life helping to make it happen. His name was William A. Horne.

When Horne moved from Corpus Christi to Houston in the early 1920s, the town was already growing in all directions and was on its way to becoming the largest city in Texas. All those new families needed homes, and developers were busily plotting subdivisions and selling lots to builders. The San Jacinto Trust Company alone had forty-two salesmen working in twenty-four subdivisions during the 1920s when Horne joined its sales force. He soon became manager of the real estate department.

The Depression halted Houston's frenzied growth and forced banks and trust companies to rethink their investment strategies. It forced Horne to think about his own future and the future of Houston. Sensing a reservoir of strength in the flexible, diversified economy, he formed the W.A. Horne Company and hired five agents to help handle real estate sales, leases, loans, and appraisals.

During the 1930s the company specialized in commercial brokerage in downtown Houston. "Main Street properties were the ones in most demand in those days," Horne told a *Houston Post* reporter in 1979. "Everything revolved around the downtown business district. There were only a few shopping centers in outlying areas. Most people lived close in. And transportation was partly by streetcar."

Today The Horne Company is the largest real estate brokerage firm in Texas and is ranked twenty-sixth in the nation. It employs some 300 people, owns and occupies its headquarters building at Main and Jefferson, and maintains offices in Austin, Corpus Christi, San Antonio, Midland, and Oklahoma City. The firm has expanded over the years to include

extensive research departments furnishing information to a number of specialized divisions: office building, land brokerage, industrial sales and leasing, property management, equity investment, farm and ranch, real estate securities (including Horne Securities Corporation and Horne Financial Corporation), and Horne Strategies.

While the recent tendency within the industry has been to grow through mergers, The Horne Company has chosen another path—The Office Network. Formed in 1977 to meet the needs of Houston clients in other cities, the Network is comprised of twenty-one firms in thirty-seven U.S. markets from New York to Los Angeles, in Canada, and Europe. Each has been identified as a firm whose objectives and methods are similar to those of The Horne Company. In this way, clients can always be assured of receiving good, in-

William A. Horne, founder of The Horne Company.

formed service in the real estate field.

Although W.A. Horne died in 1979, his sons were already experienced in the business. Howard W. Horne is now chairman of the board. Other officers include Sidney V. Smith, vice-chairman of the board; Ronald J. Hoelscher, president and chief operating officer; and David L. Cook, executive vice-president and manager of the Land and Industrial Brokerage Division, the largest in the city.

During the past sixty years Houston has grown to become not only the largest city in Texas, but also the fourth largest in the nation. Spectacular deals in Houston real estate have become legends throughout the world. Many of those transactions were the work of W.A. Horne and the company he founded.

COLLIN STREET BAKERY

When an itinerant German baker hopped a freight train in Chicago one day in 1894, he had no way of knowing that he and the secret recipe he carried in his head for a special kind of cake had a rendezvous with destiny in a small Texas town.

Railroad police caught up with young August Weidman when the train reached Corsicana, a bustling cotton and rail center southeast of Dallas that would soon become the site of the first producing oil well in the United States outside Pennsylvania and the scene of Texas' first oil boom. With his free ride in a boxcar abruptly ended, the penniless immigrant from Weisbaden, Germany, found a job in a local restaurant, doing the only thing he knew how to do—baking bread and pastries.

His culinary skills quickly caught the attention of Tom McElwee, a wealthy cotton buyer and local bon vivant with an interest in the Corsicana Opera House and show business in general. "Gus," McElwee told Weidman, "you really ought to open your own bakery."

When Weidman replied that he had no money, McElwee agreed to finance him in his own business, and in 1896 the Collin Street Bakery was born in a small, nondescript building in downtown Corsicana, with Weidman as its proprietor and sole employee. The bakery was an instant popular success, but Weidman was not nearly as good a businessman as he was a baker, and he soon turned the business end of the operation over to McElwee.

Today the Collin Street Bakery oc-

cupies an ultramodern 105,000-square-foot facility just two blocks from that original site, and is one of Corsicana's largest businesses, with seventy full-time and 600 seasonal employees. But even more important, the bakery and the special recipe that Weidman brought from Europe ninety-odd years ago are now world famous. Each year the Collin Street Bakery ships approximately four million pounds of its celebrated Deluxe Fruit Cake for some 300,000 mail-order buyers to all fifty states and nearly 200 foreign countries. "Many of our orders from faraway places are addressed simply to 'Fruit Cake, Texas,' but they always get here and we always fill them," says Bill McNutt, Jr., the bakery's president. "We're the world's largest maker of quality fruitcake."

The only change Weidman made in his recipe was the substitution of pecans, which were readily available in Texas, for the hazelnuts used in the European version. Today's cakes, in fact, are 27 percent pecans by weight.

The fame of Weidman's cakes was spread over the United States by ce-

lebrities brought to Corsicana by McElwee, many of whom stayed in the elegant hotel he opened in 1906 in the same building with an expanded bakery. These included opera star Enrico Caruso, boxer Jim Corbett, comedian Will Rogers, and baseball manager John McGraw. The first mail-order sales began in 1915, with circus mogul John Ringling North as one of the earliest customers.

The McNutt family became principal owners of the bakery in 1946, when McNutt's father, L.W. McNutt, Sr.; his uncle, R.F. Rutherford; Harry Cook; and H.M. Montgomery bought the business from McElwee's widow. Gus Weidman died the following year, but the reputation of his special cakes has lived on and multiplied.

McNutt credits the bakery's current management team of Norman Shaw, John Crawford, Maurice Pollock, Jerry Grimmett, Kenneth Power, and McNutt's two sons, Bob McNutt and Bill McNutt III, with the bakery's growth and success in recent years.

"We all take pride that out of little Corsicana (population 21,000) goes a superb product that helps brighten the holiday season for people around the world," McNutt says.

THE RICHARD GILL COMPANIES

One Gill Plaza, at 9601 McAllister Freeway in San Antonio, is one of many Gill Savings subsidiaries in the real estate limited partnership ventures.

The organization known today as Gill Savings is recognized as one of the financial institutions that made possible San Antonio's early skyline. In 1923 its founder, Richard Gill, took the first steps toward assembling the components that would make the company an integral part of the then-booming metropolis of 200,000 people.

At that time San Antonio was larger than Dallas or Houston and had a busy downtown area conspicuous for its buildings, which soared to fifteen stories and more. Most notable at the time was the Milam Building, which was twenty-one stories of air-conditioned comfort, the first structure in the United States equipped with that amenity.

During this period the city moved on wheels. The clatter of various-colored streetcars and the roar of automobiles reverberated to the top of its towers of concrete and steel. Buildings and doorways downtown glowed at night from newly installed neon signs. And the city discovered radio as an entertainment medium.

Richard Gill knew that San Antonio needed low-cost mortgage money to keep successfully moving forward. He used his business acumen to help the burgeoning city by signing a mortgage agreement with Massachusetts Mutual Life Company.

By 1925 Richard Gill's outstanding success attracted the attention of Howard Wheeler, president of his own growing mortgage company in Wichita, Kansas. Wheeler purchased 50 percent of the San Antonio firm, and it was renamed the Wheeler-Gill Company.

The 1920s continued to be a boom time for San Antonio. The Wheeler-Gill Company enjoyed rapid growth, along with the city, by financing most of the major buildings in the downtown area.

A decade later the country was pummelled by the disastrous years of the Depression. As a result, the company faced taking over many of San Antonio's commercial buildings for the lenders. It became a source of pride to Richard Gill, and his descendants, that the thirteen commercial buildings he managed (accounting for most of the major structures downtown at the time) were turned back to their original developers, rather than being confiscated for debts or taxes.

Wheeler-Gill underwent a change in corporate structure during the 1930s, when co-manager Winston Wheeler was involved in a near-fatal auto accident. He returned to Wichita to recuperate from his injuries. During his lengthy recovery, Winston and his father were tendered an offer by Richard Gill to buy back their half-interest in the company. They accepted, and the firm was renamed The Richard Gill Company.

This same period saw the organization add residential lending to its already-successful commercial loan program. In addition, it expanded into insurance and commercial real estate management of some of San

Gill Companies, a subsidiary of Gill Savings, is a limited partner in the Westlakes 1,000-acre, mixed-use development in the prime Sunbelt growth center of San Antonio.

Antonio's major buildings, including the Gunter Hotel, the Nix Professional Building, and the Blue Bonnet Hotel.

Events moved along smoothly until December 7, 1941. With the attack on Pearl Harbor, the United States launched into World War II, and personal interests were put aside for all-out support of the war effort. The Allied victory in 1945 placed San Antonio in an unprecedented position for growth and economic expansion.

The Richard Gill Company kept pace by offering new services, including consumer financing, residential construction loans, installment loans, real estate development loans, and GI loans. In the 1950s and 1960s the Irving Trust Company of New York provided banking facilities needed by The Richard Gill Company to develop a consumer loan department. Home improvement and auto loans became basic parts of the business.

As the 1970s began The Richard Gill Company again experienced a growth spurt. It needed to expand

Christopher Gill is chairman and chief executive officer of Gill Savings. Gill was named director in 1970 and president in 1976. He assumed the title of chief executive officer in 1979 and chairman of the board in 1983.

into the areas of commercial business and residential lending. In order to achieve this, however, it would require its own source of capital. This decision marked the firm's shift from functioning as an agent of other companies' funds to accumulating deposits.

This change in direction was achieved in 1974, when The Richard Gill Company purchased 96 percent of a nearby rural savings association. "We merged our companies in 1975," explains Christopher Gill, Gill Savings president and son of Richard Gill. "The modern history of our firm starts in 1975."

"Today," he continues, "we have assets of $1.4 billion. Thirteen branches of Gill Savings are open in San Antonio, Dallas, Houston, and Hondo. The future for Gill Savings Association is bright. We'll grow at a slower pace than in the past, because we feel that we're now large enough to handle the financial transactions

that interest us. We expect to continue to finance homes and commercial properties in the cities where we currently are active.

"As far as international finance is concerned," Gill remarks, "I think San Antonio can be a very important center of international commerce depending on how we handle our opportunities. I hope there would be a role there that would be consistent with our primary duty, which is to take care of our depositors' money."

He adds, "We view our business as a way of life. We have deep roots in our city and industry. Our family members have been bankers almost 100 years. We attribute our success to three things. First, we are a private company, and that gives us the opportunity to chart new paths in contravention to traditional thinking. Second, we are professionally managed. Finally, we have a strategic plan of management whereby we ask ourselves where we are going, why we want to go there, and how we should go about getting there. Our management team follows this plan in our daily management decisions. We are excited about what we have accomplished, and we are looking forward to an equally exciting future."

The Richard Gill Company during the 1950s, when it was on East Houston Street.

469

THE CONGREGATION OF THE SISTERS OF CHARITY OF THE INCARNATE WORD

Few other areas of our society have experienced more sweeping changes during the past 150 years than the health care field. The Congregation of the Sisters of Charity of the Incarnate Word has been a vital instrument in effecting those changes.

When the congregation was founded in 1866 to build and staff a hospital in Galveston, the sick and injured were generally treated at home—if they had a home. Who would care for the homeless, the sick poor, and the aged was a question of grave concern to Claude Mary Dubuis, second Roman Catholic Bishop of Galveston, whose diocese at that time included all of Texas.

From his native France Bishop Dubuis found his answer. Three nursing Sisters from a city hospital called l'Antiquaille volunteered for the mission to Texas. Although they were to be allied with the Order of the Incarnate Word and Blessed Sacrament, a cloistered educational community, theirs was to be a new religious family devoted to the care of the sick and the destitute.

After a brief period of preparation, the Sisters accompanied Bishop Dubuis to Galveston. In less than six months the small, frame Charity Hospital—later known as St. Mary's Infirmary—was opened on April 1, 1867. It was not a moment too soon. From July to October the Texas Gulf Coast was ravaged by a yellow fever epidemic that took the lives of 1,150 in Galveston alone.

During the remainder of the nineteenth century the Sisters continued their work in Galveston at St. Mary's Infirmary and at St. Mary's Orphanage, which had developed in part as an aftermath of the fever epidemic of 1867. The Sisters also reached out to other communities whenever the need arose.

In 1869 Sisters of Charity were sent to San Antonio to staff Santa Rosa Hospital, and a new and separate congregation was formed. That same year others left Galveston in answer to an urgent plea from Father Joseph Querat of St. Vincent's Church in Houston. There they staffed a school until 1873, when members of the older Order of the Incarnate Word and Blessed Sacrament became available to take over the teaching duties.

At the request of Father Thomas Hennessy of the Annunciation Church, the Sisters returned to Houston in 1887 to open St. Joseph's Infirmary in the same two-story building on the northwest corner of Franklin and Caroline where they had taught fourteen years before. During a severe smallpox epidemic that broke out in 1890, the Sisters earned the city's gratitude and respect by tending the sick not only at St. Joseph's but also those confined

The 1912 graduating class of St. Joseph's School of Nursing is shown gathered around the Lourdes Grotto on the grounds of St. Joseph's Infirmary on Crawford Street in Houston.

The Villa de Matel is the motherhouse of the Sisters of Charity of the Incarnate Word in Houston.

Sister Shawn comforts a young patient.

in the pesthouse on the banks of Buffalo Bayou west of the city.

By 1894 a new hospital building had been completed opposite the original location, and the Sisters were caring for county as well as private patients when fire swept through the buildings. Although the patients were saved, the hospital was destroyed, and a Sister and a postulant were killed. With the help of the citizens of Houston, the Sisters were able to reopen St. Joseph's in a larger brick building on Crawford, the beginning of the present St. Joseph's Hospital complex.

As the nineteenth century drew to a close, Sisters of Charity were staffing the Santa Fe Hospital in Temple, and were operating Hotel Dieu in Beaumont and St. Anthony's Home for the Aged in Houston. In Galveston the gracious mansard-roofed masonry buildings of St. Mary's Infirmary had become familiar landmarks in Galveston's "East End," while down the island at the old Green Place near West Beach, ten Sisters watched over ninety-four children at St. Mary's Orphanage.

During the weekend of September 8, 1900, Galveston was visited by the worst disaster ever to strike the North American continent—a tropical hurricane that severely damaged the brick infirmary, demolished the convent and chapel, and wiped away St. Mary's Orphanage, killing all ten

Sisters and ninety-one of the children. Only three boys escaped to tell the story of that fearful night, when over 6,000 Galvestonians lost their lives. Rebuilding was painful, but the twenty-three novices who were removed temporarily to St. Anthony's Home in Houston attested to the faith and future strength of the community.

If the last century had been marred by sorrow and the frustrations associated with any pioneer enterprise, the next was to be a time of accomplishment and growth. A revised constitution for the community created the office of superior general. When the constitution was approved by Pope Saint Pius X in 1912, the congregation became a pontifical institution.

During the early 1920s a decision was made to remove the motherhouse to Houston. Named in honor of Mother Jeanne Chezard de Matel, foundress of the Order of the Incarnate Word and Blessed Sacrament, the Villa de Matel was completed in 1928 on a 72-acre site facing Lawndale.

Today the serenely beautiful convent buildings, the exquisite Lombard-Romanesque chapel, and the modern corporate office facility have become not only the home of a religious community but also the headquarters of an ever-expanding health care organization that operates fifteen health care centers in Texas, Louisiana, Arkansas, California, and Utah, and sends Sisters of Charity to missions in Ireland, El Salvador, Guatemala, and Kenya. In addition, the congre-

gation operates schools, staffs clinics, carries on pastoral and prayer ministries, administers its congregational affairs, offers management services in health-related areas, and plans to provide subsidized housing to qualified residents in Long Beach, California.

The congregation accomplishes these works through three parent and a number of subsidiary corporations representing its major areas of activity. A $15-million systems department serves as the "hub" for the design and transmission of patient care programs used throughout the SCH Health Care System and generates financial and statistical data for each of the centers and for the corporate headquarters in Houston.

As its continuing and future goals, the congregation is determined to provide the finest and most advanced facilities and cost-effective care to patients while remaining ever-mindful of the growing health needs of the entire communities it serves.

For 120 years the Sisters of Charity of the Incarnate Word have devoted their skills and energies to the state of Texas and its residents. The monetary value of their presence has never been measured, but the inspiration of their lives is a priceless legacy to us all. Sister Mary Loyola Hegarty, present superior general, expressed it simply: "Serving with gladness."

Rehabilitation is a specialty at St. Anthony's Center, located at 6301 Almeda Road in Houston.

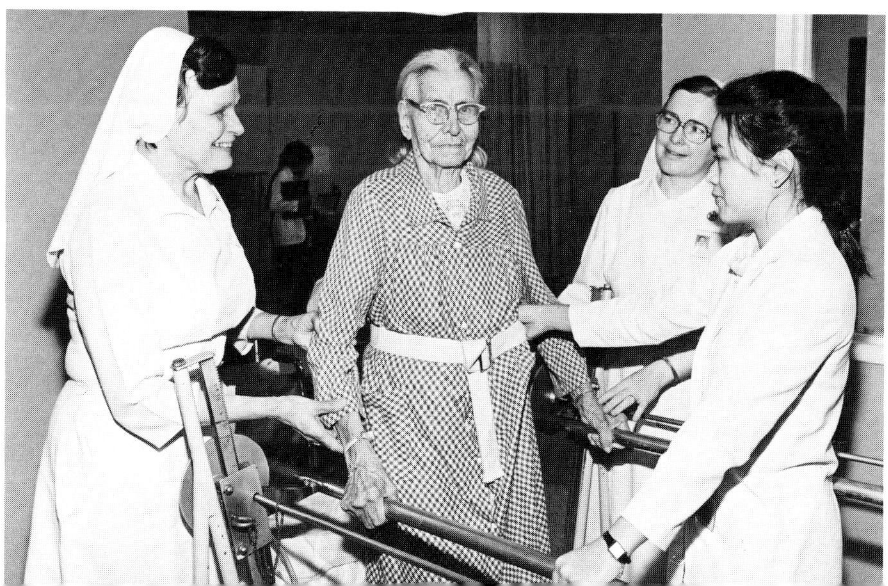

THE TRAILWAYS CORPORATION

"Go Big Red, Go Trailways," was the slogan adopted by The Trailways Corporation in 1979 after James L. Kerrigan, former chairman of Greyhound Lines and current chairman and chief executive officer of The Trailways Corporation, led a group of investors to purchase the Dallas-based company from the Holiday Inn Corporation. The slogan, which reads like any good high school or college football cheer designed to spur a team to victory, reflects the sustained enthusiasm of this firm, whose buses have been on the road since 1945.

The Trailways Corporation does more, however, than own and operate buses: Its subsidiaries manufacture buses, offer domestic and overseas charter and tour services, provide package express services, operate park-and-ride commuter services in metropolitan hubs, and operate fast-food franchises, one-person snack bars, and catering services in many markets around America.

The world's largest privately held intercity motorcoach carrier, Trailways Lines, Inc., is the core of The Trailways Corporation, and the place where it all began.

In 1945 two independent intercity bus companies banded together and formed Continental Bus System, Inc., the forerunner to Trailways Lines, Inc. R.C. Bowen had been operating his firm, Bowen Motor Coach Company, since 1927 when it began as two separate concerns, Lone Star Bus Lines and Old Spanish Trail Bus Lines. Their names suggest the routes they covered—Texas and New Mexico. Bowen bought small Texas bus lines until the owner of Tri-State Transit Company, and its subsidiary, Southern Bus Lines, M.E. Moore, bought the Bowen Motor Coach Company in 1943. The bus lines of the two companies were unconnected until 1945, when they merged under the name of Continental Bus System,

James L. Kerrigan, chairman and chief executive officer of The Trailways Corporation.

Inc.

Today Trailways Lines, Inc., provides regularly scheduled passenger and express package service to more than 12,000 cities, towns, and communities in forty-two states. Trailways routes cover 63,000 miles.

Trailways Lines, Inc., is the largest member of the National Trailways Bus System, an association of independent carriers who operate under the Trailways name. The NTBS was established in 1936 to give small carriers competitive leverage by giving their passengers access to the other NTBS members' destinations. Under Kerrigan's leadership, NTBS has grown from eleven members to over seventy.

"In order to survive in the bus industry, and to participate in its growth, you need national identification," Kerrigan explains. "Only Trailways can give the independent operator that I.D."

In 1979, when Kerrigan got behind The Trailways Corporation's wheel, his first priority was to ensure that his passengers would be comfortable while traveling. He set out to upgrade buses and all company facilities, with impressive results. Today the Trailways fleet is modern and efficient and the Washington, D.C., Trailways terminal, opened in 1984 and heralded as the most efficient

and beautiful bus terminal in the country, exemplifies the firm's commitment to improving its facilities.

The axiom that imitation is the sincerest form of flattery could be applied to one of Trailways' most recent innovations—ticket prices that are determined by uniform mileage tariffs. In 1984 the majority of the other bus carriers adopted this system.

Since the deregulation of the travel industry in 1982, Trailways has not lost a moment in developing the group charter and tour market where Trailways sees great future potential.

In December 1982 the firm's char-

Dallas was the first municipality to utilize the services of Trailways Commuter Transit, Inc., for its park-and-ride needs.

The Eagle Model 10 bus is the flagship of Trailways' national fleet.

ter and tour departments began to offer complete tour services (including arrangements for air, sea, and land transportation, food, lodging, and sightseeing), to charter customers. Trailways was the first in the industry to teach travel agents how to package customized tours for their clients through a series of tour seminars and the first to offer joint air and bus tickets.

In order to make these services readily available to the public, Trailways has equipped its charter and tour telemarketing center in Dallas with the latest in communication and data-processing systems. During one toll-free phone call, potential clients can have itineraries planned and the prices quoted.

The Trailways Corporation's Transportation Group is particularly optimistic about one market whose horizons seem without boundaries—the public sector. In 1984, for the first time, a public transit authority, namely the Dallas Area Rapid Transit (DART), awarded a full transit contract to a member of the private sector, Trailways Commuter Transit, Inc. Trailways currently provides DART with sixty-seven of its top-of-the-line buses and ninety-five employees. Together they manage and ensure the on-schedule running of over ten routes that link the far-reaching suburbs to the intracity bus system.

Part of Kerrigan's newly purchased Trailways package in 1979 was a small interest in Eagle International, Inc., a bus-manufacturing plant in the Rio Grande Valley. In 1979 Eagle

Trailways was one of the first companies to be recognized by President Ronald Reagan with a C Flag for community service. Trailways received the flag for its Operation: Home Free program, which provides runaway youths with a free ride home.

produced just 209 buses, of which forty-nine were sold to other companies. In 1981 management exercised an option to purchase Eagle, and quickly began expanding the plant's manufacturing capabilities and modernizing the Eagle motor coach. The Eagle International staff quickly responded to the needs of the industry by incorporating the product ideas of its buyers into new buses. Members of the National Tour Association said they wanted a bus with a plush interior, similar to that of a first-class airplane cabin. The Eagle Model 10-LT, introduced in 1983, fits the bill, with enclosed parcel racks, individual air and reading light controls, and plush seats.

With the opening of a second bus-manufacturing plant in Harlingen, Texas, in 1983, the Trailways Manufacturing Group has an annual pro-

duction capacity of over 1,000 buses. Product improvements and plant expansions were justified. Of the total intercity bus equipment sales to the public sector in 1984, Eagle amassed an impressive 80 percent share.

Consistent, hardy growth in the sales of its subsidiaries, the development of new markets, and the unceasing improvement of the bus fleet and facilities cannot help but foster feelings of pride at "Big Red."

But there is one ongoing concern of The Trailways Corporation, one that has nothing to do with the bottom line, one that evokes great feelings of pride throughout the firm's ranks—Trailways' Operation: Home Free program. Established by Trailways in cooperation with the International Association of Chiefs of Police, Operation: Home Free provides a free ride home to runaway youths. In the first eighteen months of the program, Trailways carried home over 7,000 young people; an average of fifteen runaways per day now take advantage of the program.

"Now that we have Operation: Home Free, we have a valuable tool to offer these kids," Norman Darwick, executive director of the IACP, says. "They can go home free, on their own, and without any strings attached."

"We do not view Operation: Home Free as a special and limited offer," Kerrigan explains. "It is our company's way of responding to President Reagan's request for private-sector initiatives in filling public needs. We're in the transportation business and these kids need transportation."

President Ronald Reagan awarded one of the country's first C Flags to Trailways Corporation for its Operation: Home Free program on December 10, 1984, when he unveiled the first major White House awards program to recognize outstanding contributions made by businesses and associations to their communities.

THE SOUTHLAND CORPORATION

From its 1927 founding as a Dallas ice company to its present strength as a 7,500-plus-convenience-store network, The Southland Corporation epitomizes one of the most phenomenal success sagas in American retail history.

With its 7-Eleven stores, Southland pioneered the convenience store concept of today. 7-Elevens are located in forty-three American states and throughout the world. The establishments serve nearly eight million customers each day, providing a convenient mix of food staples, beer, soft drinks, fast-food items, and gasoline.

Southland's growth into a conglomerate with total 1984 revenues of $12.1 billion and 61,800 employees owes much to America's growing dependence on quickly accessible, drive-in food and gasoline. It is a dependence that Southland helped foster and one that it presently serves well; 95 percent of all 7-Elevens are open twenty-four hours a day, and their list of products and services is constantly expanding.

But Southland extends further than convenience stores. The diversified company also directs more than 350 Chief Auto Parts units, 50 Gristede's and Charles & Co. food stores and sandwich shops in New York, and 40 Super 7 gasoline outlets. It additionally operates 7-Eleven stores in Sweden and Mexico, and licensees manage 7-Elevens in Japan, Australia, Taiwan, Hong Kong, Singapore, Malaysia, the Philippines, and the United Kingdom. All combined, the firm operates more than 11,600 various stores worldwide.

On August 31, 1983, Southland acquired Citgo Petroleum Corporation from Occidental Petroleum Corporation; the acquisition includes a refinery complex in Lake Charles, Louisiana, a 65-percent interest in the Cit-Con lubricants refinery, and total or partial ownership in approximately 16,000 miles of crude oil and refined products pipelines. Citgo presently supplies conveniently purchased gasoline to 3,173 7-Eleven stores—another successful innovation that quickly captivated the 7-Eleven customer base.

Size, however, is only part of the

This small frame building in Oak Cliff was the first 7-Eleven store (formerly "Tote'm") and the first open-front, drive-in food and beverage store anywhere. Previously a retail ice station operated by The Southland Corporation, Store No. 1 launched a unique idea in food retailing when it began selling milk, bread, and eggs in mid-1927 for the convenience of its customers.

Southland story. Another involves ingenuity and anticipating the desires of the customer. Southland's 7-Eleven stores were the first convenience stores to install video games, self-serve soft drinks, and fast food that customers heat in on-site microwaves. Another innovation is the installation of automatic bank teller machines, through which customers can conveniently obtain cash.

Southland has always been an active participant in community activities. It was a corporate sponsor of the 1984 Olympic Games in Los Angeles, for which the firm constructed a stadium, the 7-Eleven Velodrome, for the cycling events. As a sponsor of the annual Labor Day Jerry Lewis Telethon, Southland and its employees have raised more than forty-two million dollars in ten years for the Muscular Dystrophy Association. Southland Dairies was the first corporate sponsor of the March of Dimes and has sponsored the annual Mothers' March for Birth Defects since 1978.

The formation of Southland began in 1924, not with mergers or acquisitions but with a good idea: selling Texas' first ice-cold watermelons off the docks of Dallas' Consumers Ice Company. The idea belonged to Joe C. Thompson—a young and ambitious former groomsman, stable cleaner, ice loader, and bookkeeper—who had joined Consumers Ice Company immediately after his graduation from The University of Texas' business school. The watermelon idea was a grand sales success. The company quickly expanded its ice plants to five and its retail ice docks to sixteen.

In 1926 Joe Thompson was named secretary/treasurer of Consumers Ice Company. A year later he learned that Claude S. Dawley was seeking to locate a group of ice companies to consolidate into one large firm. Intrigued with the possibilities, and with the blessing of Consumers behind him, Thompson purchased 2,500 shares in the new Southland Ice Company—which included the Consumers Ice Company as its largest and most profitable operation.

From these beginnings both Thompson and Southland embarked on a remarkable path of growth. Within its first year the enterprise began testing the sales of groceries at its ice docks. Because the groceries were such a hit, the firm began calling its stores "Tote'm," referring to the customers toting their purchases home. The Tote'm name was changed to 7-Eleven in 1946, to reflect the shops' operating hours. By Southland's twenty-fifth anniversary in 1952, there were 100 7-Eleven stores nationwide. By 1966, five years after Joe Thompson's death, his son, John, was running a corporation that included 2,000 7-Eleven units. Two years later Southland went public with 750,000 shares of common stock; in 1971 it grossed one billion dollars in annual sales. The Thompson family is still deeply involved in the management of the company. John Thompson serves as chairman of the board; Jere W. Thompson is president; and Joe C. Thompson, Jr., is senior executive vice-president.

In 1987 the firm will expand further still—when it christens Cityplace, a high-rise development near downtown Dallas, which will become The Southland Corporation's new headquarters.

However, the company never strays from the ingredient it was founded on—a commitment to convenience and service—no matter how rapidly the Southland world continues to expand.

Today The Southland Corporation is a 7,500-plus-convenience-store network.

A San Angelo cafe proprietor poses in 1930 with his staff. Gone is the saloon look of a Western cafe. Instead, art deco decor shows that the frontier has been civilized. Courtesy, Alexandria Greer

PATRONS

The following individuals, companies, and organizations have made a valuable commitment to the quality of this publication. Windsor Publications, Inc., the East Texas Historical Association, and the Harris County Heritage Society gratefully acknowledge their participation in *In Celebration of Texas.*

The Adolphus*
Ahlfinger Water Company*
Alford Refrigerated Warehouses, Inc.*
American Produce and Vegetable
  Company*
American Solar King Corporation*
Austin Industries, Inc.*
James Avery Craftsman, Inc.*
Aviall*
Aviation Office of America, Inc.*
Baker Management Company*
W.L. Bates Co., Inc.*
Bright Mortgage Company*
Homer L. Brinson
The Caballero Motel*
W.W. Cannon Company, Inc.*
Collin Street Bakery*
The Congregation of the Sisters of
  Charity of the Incarnate Word*
Corny Dog Company, Inc.*
Cushman & Wakefield*
Dal-Mac Construction/Development*
Daniel Drug
Daughters of Charity Hospitals*
Diamond Shamrock Corporation*
Dr Pepper*
DSC Communications Corporation*
Electronic Data Systems*
Ray Ellison Industries*
El Paso Electric Company*
Thomas C. Ferguson
Friedrich Air Conditioning &
  Refrigeration Co.*
Frymire Engineering Company, Inc.*
Geosource Inc.*
The Richard Gill Companies*
Golemon & Rolfe Associates, Inc.*
Hall Financial Group*
Halliburton Company*
Hall-Mark Electronics Corporation*
The Horne Company*
Industrial Catering*
Ingleside Historical Society

Jet Fleet Corporation*
KDF, Inc.*
L.H. Lacy Company*
Mr. and Mrs. Max S. Lale
  Marshall and Fort Worth, Texas
La Mansión Hotels*
Lomas & Nettleton Financial
  Corporation*
Lone Star Donuts*
McFinCon Incorporated
NEC America, Inc.*
Olmsted-Kirk Paper Company*
Pearle Health Services, Inc.*
Pier 1 Inc.*
Presbyterian Hospital*
Billy Pugh Company, Inc.*
RepublicBank Corporation*
J. Murray Riddell, M.D.
Rockwell International*
Smith Industries, Inc.*
The Southland Corporation*
Southwestern Baptist Theological
  Seminary*
Southwestern Public Service Company*
The T.O. Stanley Boot Company*
Teague Industries*
Ellen Terry, Realtors*
Tesoro Petroleum Corporation*
Tetco*
Texas Bankers Association*
Texas Instruments Incorporated*
Texas Military Institute*
Texas Refinery Corporation*
The Trailways Corporation*
TTI, Inc.*
UTL Corporation*
Ralph R. Wallace, III
Watson Electric Supply Company*
Whataburger, Inc.*
Williamson Printing Corporation*
Ralph Wilson Plastics Company*
Jeanette Winfree

*Partners in Progress of *In Celebration of Texas.* The histories of these companies and organizations appear in Chapter 13, beginning on page 353.

BIBLIOGRAPHY

The literature of Texas must begin with the original sources, the diaries, letters, reminiscences, and artifacts of the past. Several excellent depositories are available in Texas. Among the most used are the Eugene C. Barker Center and the archives at The University of Texas at Austin, and the State Archives, a division of the Texas State Library, located in the same city. The Texas Institute of Cultures and Library of the Daughters of the Republic of Texas, both at San Antonio, the Dallas Historical Society's archives located in the Hall of State on the Fair Grounds at Dallas, the San Jacinto Museum, and the Star of the Republic Museum at Washington-on-the-Brazos are excellent research centers. Nearly every university in Texas supports an archives in its library, usually concentrating on the history of its service region.

Specialized bibliographies and periodicals include:

Carroll, H. Bailey, and Gursh, Milton R. *Texas History Theses: A Checklist of Theses and Dissertations Relating to Texas History Accepted at The University of Texas, 1893-1951.* Austin: Texas State Historical Association, 1955.

Connor, Seymour V. *Texas: A History.* New York: 1971.

Fehrenback, T.R. *Lone Star: A History of Texas and Texans.* New York: 1968.

Friend, Llerena. *Checklist of Texas Imprints, 1861-1876.* Austin: Texas State Historical Association, 1963.

Jenkins, John H. *Basic Texas Books; an Annotated Bibliography of Selected Works for a Research Library.* Austin: The Jenkins Company, 1983.

Raines, C.W. *Bibliography of Texas.* Austin: privately printed, 1896. Reprint. Austin: Gammell, 1934, and Houston: Frontier, 1955.

Richardson, Rupert N. *Texas: The Lone Star State.* Revised by Ernest Wallace and Adrian Anderson. New York: 1943.

Streeter, Thomas W. *Bibliography of Texas, 1795-1845.* 5 Vols. Cambridge: Harvard University Press, 1960.

Webb, Carroll and Walter P., eds. *Handbook of Texas.* 2 Vols. Austin: Texas State Historical Association, 1952.

Winkler, Ernest W. *Checklist of Texas Imprints, 1846-1860.* Austin: Texas State Historical Association, 1949.

The following works, listed alphabetically, are recommended for future reading on the fascinating subject of Texas history.

Abernathy, Francis E. *Tales From the Big Thicket.* Austin: University of Texas Press, 1966.

Atwood, Elmer Bagby. *The Regional Vocabulary of Texas.* Austin: University of Texas Press, 1962.

Bainbridge, John. *The Super Americans.* Garden City: Doubleday Publishing Co., 1961.

Bancroft, Hubert Howe. *History of the North Mexican States and Texas, 1531-1889.* San Francisco: A.L. Bancroft and Company, 1883, and the History Company, 1889.

Barker, Eugene C., ed. *The Austin Papers.* Washington: U.S. Government Printing Office, 1924-1928. Austin: University of Texas, 1927.

Barker, Eugene Campbell. *Mexico and Texas, 1821-1835: University of Texas Research Lectures on the Causes of the Texas Revolution.* Dallas: P.L. Turner Company, Publishers.

Barr, Alwyn. *Black Texans; a History of Negroes in Texas, 1528-1971.* Austin: Jenkins Publishing Company, 1973.

Bendichek, Roy. *Adventures With a Texas Naturalist.* Garden City: Doubleday & Co., Inc., 1947.

Biesele, Rudolph Leopold. *The History of the German Settlements in Texas, 1831-1861.* Austin: Press of Von Boeckmann-Jones Co., 1930.

Binkley, William Campbell. *The Expansionist Movement in Texas, 1836-1850.* Berkeley: University of California Press, 1925.

Bollaert, William. *William Bollaert's Texas.* Norman: University of Oklahoma Press, 1956.

Bolton, Herbert Eugene. *Spanish Exploration in the Southwest, 1542-1706.* New York: Charles Scribner's Sons, 1916.

__________. *Texas in the Middle Eighteenth Century: Studies in Spanish Colonial History and Administration.* Berkeley: University of California Press, 1915.

Brown, John Henry. *History of Texas, From 1685 to 1892.* 2 Vols. St. Louis: L.E. Daniell, 1892-1893.

Castañeda, Carlos Eduardo. *Our Catholic Heritage in Texas, 1519-1936.* Austin: Von Boeckmann-Jones Company, 1936-1958.

Clark, James Anthony and Halbouty, Michel. *Spindletop.* New York: Random House, 1952.

De la Peña, José Enrique. *With Santa Anna in Texas: A Personal Narrative of the Revolution.* College Station: Texas A&M University Press, 1975.

Dixon, Sam Houston and Kemp, Louis Wiltz. *The Heroes of San Jacinto.* Houston: The Anson Jones Press, 1932.

Dobie, J. Frank. *Coronado's Children; Tales of Lost Mines and Buried Treasures of the Southwest.* Dallas: The Southwest Press, 1930.

Ehrenberg, Hermann. *With Milam and Fannin; Adventures of a German Boy in Texas' Revolution.* Dallas: Tardy Publishing Company, Inc., 1935.

Frantz, Joe Bertram. *Gail Borden, Dairyman to a Nation.* Norman: University of Oklahoma Press, 1951.

Friend, Llerena Beaumont. *Sam Houston: The Great Designer.* Austin: University of Texas Press, 1954.

Gambrell, Herbert Pickens. *Anson Jones: The Last President of Texas.* Garden City: Doubleday & Company, Inc., 1948.

Gard, Wayne. *The Chisholm Trail.* Norman: University of Oklahoma Press, 1954.

Garrett, Julia Kathryn. *Green Flag Over Texas: A Story of the Last Years of Spain in Texas*. Austin & New York: Jenkins Publishing Co., 1969.

Garrison, George Pierce. *Diplomatic Correspondence of the Republic of Texas*. 3 Vols. Washington: Government Printing Office, 1908, 1911.

Gould, Lewis Ludlow. *Progressives and Prohibitionists: Texas Democrats in the Wilson Era*. Austin & London: University of Texas Press, 1973.

Gray, William Fairfax. *From Virginia to Texas, 1835: Diary of Col. Wm. F. Gray, Giving Details of His Journey to Texas & Return in 1835-1836*. Houston: Gray, Dillaye & Co. 1909.

Gulick, Charles A. et al., eds. *The Papers of Mirabeau Buonaparte Lamar*. 6 Vols. Austin: A.C. Baldwin & Sons, vols. I-II; Von Boeckmann-Jones, Inc. vols. III-VI, 1921-1927.

Haley, James Evetts. *Charles Goodnight, Cowman & Plainsman*. Norman: University of Oklahoma Press, 1979.

Hogan, William Ransom. *The Texas Republic: A Social and Economic History*. Norman: University of Oklahoma Press, 1969.

Horgan, Paul. *Great River: the Rio Grande in North American History*. New York & Toronto: Rinehart & Company, Inc., 1954.

James, Marquis. *The Raven: A Biography of Sam Houston*. Indianapolis: The Bobs-Merrill Company, 1929.

Jenkins, John Holland. *Recollections of Early Texas: the Memoirs of John Holland Jenkins*. Austin: University of Texas Press, 1958.

Jenkins, John Holmes III. *The Papers of the Texas Revolution, 1835-1836*. 10 Vols. Austin: Presidial Press, 1973.

Kemp, Louis Wiltz. *The Signers of the Texas Declaration of Independence*. Houston: The Anson Jones Press, 1944.

Kingston, Michael T., ed. *The Texas Almanac and State Industrial Guide*. Dallas: A.H. Belo Co., 1983.

Lea, Tom. *The King Ranch*. Boston & Toronto: Little, Brown and Co., 1957.

Lubbock, Francis R. *Six Decades in Texas; or, Memoirs of Francis Richard Lubbock, Governor of Texas in War Time, 1861-1863. A Personal Experience in Business, War and Politics*. Austin: B.C. Jones & Co., 1900.

Martin, Roscoe Coleman. *The People's Party in Texas: A Study in Third Party Politics*. Austin: The University of Texas, 1933.

Matthews, Sallie Reynolds. *Interwoven, a Pioneer Chronicle*. College Station: Texas A&M University Press, 1982.

McDonald, Archie P. *Hurrah For Texas. The Diary of Adolphus Sterne*. Waco: Texian Press, 1969.

McLean, Malcolm D. *Papers Concerning Robertson's Colony in Texas*. 9 Vols. Fort Worth: Texas Christian University Press, vol I-III; and Arlington: The UTA Press, 1974-1982.

Meinig, Donald William. *Imperial Texas: An Interpretive Essay in Cultural Geography*. Austin: University of Texas Press, 1969.

Miller, Thomas Lloyd. *Bounty and Donation Land Grants, 1835-1888*. Austin & London: University of Texas Press, 1967.

Morton, Ohland. *Teran and Texas. A Chapter in Texas-Mexican Relations*. Austin: The Texas State Historical Association, 1948.

Muir, Andrew Forest. *Texas in 1837: An Anonymous, Contemporary Narrative*. Austin: University of Texas Press, 1958.

Nance, Joseph Milton. *Attack and Counter-Attack: The Texas-Mexican Frontier, 1842*. Austin: University of Texas Press, 1964.

Newcomb, William Wilmon, Jr. *The Indians of Texas, From Prehistoric to Modern Times*. Austin: University of Texas Press, 1980.

Nixon, Patrick Ireland. *The Medical Story of Early Texas, 1528-1853*. Lancaster, Pa: The Mollie Bennett Lupe Memorial Fund, 1946.

Olmsted, Frederick Law. *A Journey Through Texas; or, a Saddle-Trip on the Southwestern Frontier; With a Statistical Appendix*. Austin: Von Boeckmann-Jones Press, 1962.

Proctor, Ben. *Not Without Honor: The Life of John H. Reagan*. Austin: University of Texas Press, 1962.

Ramsdell, Charles William, Sr. *Reconstruction in Texas*. New York: Columbia University, 1910.

Richardson, Willard and Richardson, David. *The Texas Almanac, 1857-1873: A Compendium of Texas History*. Waco: Texian Press, 1967.

Sibley, Marilyn McAdams. *Lone Stars and State Gazettes: Texas Newspapers Before the Civil War*. College Station: Texas A&M Press, 1983.

Smithwick, Noah. *The Evolution of a State; or, Recollections of Old Texas Days*. Reprint. Austin: University of Texas Press, 1983.

Spell, Lota Mae (Harrigan). *Music in Texas: a Survey of One Aspect of Cultural Progress*. Austin: 1936.

Spratt, John Stricklin. *The Road to Spindletop: Economic Change in Texas, 1875-1901*. Austin: University of Texas Press, 1970.

Warner, Charles Albert. *Texas Oil and Gas Since 1543*. Houston: Golf Publishing Company, 1939.

Webb, Walter Prescott. *The Texas Rangers: a Century of Frontier Defense*. Austin: University of Texas Press, 1965.

Weber, David Joseph. *The Mexican Frontier, 1821-1846: The American Southwest Under Mexico*. Albuquerque: University of New Mexico Press, 1982.

Williams, Amelia, and Barker, Euguene C., eds. *The Writings of Sam Houston, 1813-1863*. Austin & New York: Jenkins Publishing Co., 1970.

Yoakum, Henderson King. *History of Texas From Its First Settlement in 1685 to its Annexation to the United States in 1846*. New York: Redfield, 1855.

INDEX

Judge Roy Bean, the "law West of the Pecos," is shown here holding court in the town of Langtry, Texas, in 1900. This building served as both saloon and courthouse. Courtesy, National Archives